Natural Law
Volume I

The International Library of Essays in Law and Legal Theory

Schools

Natural Law, Vols I & II *John Finnis*
Justice *Thomas Morawetz*
Law and Economics, Vols I & II *Jules Coleman and Jeffrey Lange*
Critical Legal Studies *James Boyle*
Marxian Legal Theory *Csaba Varga*
Legal Reasoning, Vols I & II *Aulis Aarnio and Neil MacCormick*
Legal Positivism *Mario Jori*
American Legal Theory *Robert Summers*
Law and Language *Fred Schauer*
Sociological Theories of Law *Kahei Rokumoto*
Rights *Carlos Nino*
Law and Psychology *Martin Levine*
Feminist Legal Theory *Frances Olsen*

Areas

Criminal Law *Thomas Morawetz*
Tort Law *Ernest Weinrib*
Contract Law, Vols I & II *Larry Alexander*
Anti-Discrimination Law *Christopher McCrudden*
Consumer Law *Iain Ramsay*
International Law *Martti Koskenniemi*
Property Law *Elizabeth Mensch and Alan Freeman*
Constitutional Law *Mark Tushnet*
Procedure *Denis Galligan*
Evidence and Proof *William Twining and Alex Stein*
Administrative Law *Denis Galligan*
Child Law *Harry Krause*
Family Law, Vols I & II *Harry Krause*
Welfare Law *Peter Robson*
Medicine and the Law *Bernard Dickens*
Commercial Law *Ross Cranston*
Communications Law *David Goldberg*
Environmental Law *Michael Blumm*
Conflict of Laws *Richard Fentiman*
Law and Religion *Wojciech Sadurski*

Legal Cultures

Comparative Legal Cultures *Csaba Varga*
Law and Anthropology *Peter Sack*
Hindu Law and Legal Theory *Ved Nanda*
Islamic Law and Legal Theory *Ian Edge*
Chinese Law and Legal Theory *Michael Palmer*
Japanese Law and Legal Theory *Kiochiro Fujikura*
Law and Development *Anthony Carty*
Jewish Law and Legal Theory *Martin Golding*
Legal Education *Martin Levine*

Future Volumes

Human Rights Law, Socialist Law and Legal Theory, Sociology of Law, Labour Law, Common Law and Legal Theory, Civil Law and Legal Theory, Law and Society, African Law and Legal Theory, Soviet Law and Legal Theory and Cumulative index.

Natural Law
Volume I

Edited by

John Finnis

University of Oxford

NEW YORK UNIVERSITY PRESS
REFERENCE COLLECTION

Manufactured in Great Britain

First published in the U.S.A. in 1991 by
NEW YORK UNIVERSITY PRESS
Washington Square
New York NY 10003

Library of Congress Cataloging-in-Publication Data
Natural law / edited by John Finnis.
p. cm. – (The International library of essays in law and legal theory).
Essays originally published in various publications.
Includes bibliographical references and index.
ISBN 0-8147-2605-4 (cl-set) – ISBN 0-8147-2603-8 (cloth : v. 1) – ISBN 0-8147-2604-6 (cloth : v. 2) :
1. Natural law. I. Finnis, John. II. Series.
K428.N37 1991
171′.2–dc20 91-2045
CIP

Printed in Great Britain by Galliard (Printers) Ltd, Great Yarmouth

Contents

Acknowledgements *vii*
Series Preface *ix*
Introduction *xi*

PART I A MID-CENTURY DEBATE

1 Lon L. Fuller ([1956] 1958), 'Human Purpose and Natural Law', *Natural Law Forum* **3**, pp. 68–76. 3
2 Ernest Nagel (1958), 'On the Fusion of Fact and Value: A Reply to Professor Fuller', *Natural Law Forum*, **3**, pp. 77–82. 13
3 Lon L. Fuller (1958), 'A Rejoinder to Professor Nagel', *Natural Law Forum*, **3**, pp. 83–104. 19
4 Ernest Nagel (1959), 'Fact, Value, and Human Purpose', *Natural Law Forum*, **4**, pp. 26–43. 41

PART II NEO-SCHOLASTIC THEORY: FOR AND AGAINST

5 Thomas E. Davitt (1960), 'Law as Means to End – Thomas Aquinas', *Vanderbilt Law Review*, **14**, pp. 65–99. 61
6 Kai Nielsen (1959), 'An Examination of the Thomistic Theory of Natural Moral Law', *Natural Law Forum*, **4**, pp. 44–71. 97
7 Hans Kelsen ([1963] 1973), 'Foundation of the Natural Law Doctrine', *Anglo-American Law Review*, **2**, pp. 83–111. 125
8 Albert Broderick (1964), 'The Radical Middle: Natural Right of Property in Aquinas and the Popes', *Solicitor Quarterly*, **3**, pp. 127–59. 155

PART III THE NEW CLASSICAL THEORY

9 Germain Grisez (1965), 'The First Principle of Practical Reason: A Commentary on the *Summa Theologiae*, 1–2, Question 94, Article 2', *Natural Law Forum*, **10**, pp. 168–201. 191
10 Neil MacCormick (1981), 'Natural Law Reconsidered', *Oxford Journal of Legal Studies*, **1**, pp. 99–109. 225
11 Germain Grisez, Joseph Boyle, and John Finnis (1987), 'Practical Principles, Moral Truth, and Ultimate Ends', *American Journal of Jurisprudence*, **32**, pp. 99–151. 236

PART IV FOR AND AGAINST THE NEW CLASSICAL THEORY

12 Henry Veatch (1981), ''Natural Law and the 'Is'–'Ought' Question: Queries to Finnis and Grisez'', in *Swimming Against the Current in Contemporary Philosophy*, The Catholic University of America Press, pp. 293–311. 293
13 John Finnis (1981), ''Natural Law and the 'Is'–'Ought' Question: an Invitation to Professor Veatch'', *Catholic Lawyer*, **26**, pp. 266–77. 313

14	Ralph McInerny (1980), 'The Principles of Natural Law', *American Journal of Jurisprudence*, **25**, pp. 1–15	325
15	John Finnis and Germain Grisez (1981), 'The Basic Principles of Natural Law: a Reply to Ralph McInerny', *American Journal of Jurisprudence*, **26**, pp. 21–31.	341
16	Robert P. George (1988), 'Recent Criticism of Natural Law Theory', *University of Chicago Law Review*, **55**, pp. 1371–1429.	353

Name Index 413

Acknowledgements

The editor and publishers wish to thank the following for permission to use copyright material.

American Journal of Jurisprudence for articles: Germain Grisez, Joseph Boyle and John Finnis (1987), 'Practical Principles, Moral Truth and Ultimate Ends', *American Journal of Jurisprudence*, **32**, pp. 99–151, and John Finnis and Germain Grisez (1981), 'The Basic Principles of Natural Law: a Reply to Ralph McInerny', *American Journal of Jurisprudence*, **26**, pp. 21–31 and Ralph McInerny (1980), 'The Principles of Natural Law', *American Journal of Jurisprudence*, **25**, pp. 1–15, and Lon L. Fuller (1958), 'A Rejoinder to Professor Nagel', *Natural Law Forum*, **3**, pp. 83–104, and Germain Grisez (1965), 'The First Principle of Practical Reason: A Commentary on the Summa Theologiae, *Natural Law Forum*, **10**, 1–2 Question 94, Article 2, pp. 168–201, and Ernest Nagel (1958), 'On the Fusion of Fact and Value: A Reply to Professor Fuller', *Natural Law Forum*, **3**, pp. 77–82, and Ernest Nagel (1959), 'Fact, Value and Human Purpose', *Natural Law Forum*, **4**, pp. 26–43, and Kai Nielsen (1959), 'An Examination of the Thomistic Theory of Natural Moral Law', *Natural Law Forum*, **4**, pp. 44–71.

Catholic Lawyer for article: John Finnis (1981), "Natural Law and the 'Is' – 'Ought' Question: An Invitation to Professor Veatch", *Catholic Lawyer*, **26**, pp. 266–77.

The Catholic University of America Press for article: H. B. Veatch (1990), "Natural Law and 'Is'–'Ought' Question: Queries to Finnis and Grisez", in *Swimming Against the Current in Contemporary Philosophy*, The Catholic University of America Press. Reprinted by permission.

Journal of Philosophy for article: Lon L. Fuller (1956), 'Human Purpose and Natural Law', *Journal of Philosophy*, **58** pp. 697–705. Reprinted by permission from the Journal of Philosophy.

Oxford University Press for article: Neil MacCormick (1981), 'Natural Law Reconsidered', *Oxford Journal of Legal Studies*, **1**, pp. 99–109. Reprinted by permission of Oxford University Press.

Barry Rose Law Periodicals for article: H. Kelsen (1963)(1973), 'Foundation of the Natural Law Doctrine', *Anglo-American Law Review*, **2**, pp. 83–111.

Vanderbilt Law Review for article: T. E. Davitt (1960), *Vanderbilt Law Review*, **14**, pp. 65–99. Copyright © Vanderbilt Law Review.

The University of Chicago Law Review for article: Robert P. George (1988), 'Recent Criticism of Natural Law Theory'. *University of Chicago Law Review*, **55**, 1371–1429.

Every effort has been made to trace all the copyright holders, but if any have been inadvertently overlooked the publishers will be pleased to make the necessary arrangement at the first opportunity.

Series Preface

The International Library of Law and Legal Theory is designed to provide important research materials in an accessible form. Each volume contains essays of central theoretical importance in its subject area. The series as a whole makes available an extensive range of valuable material which will be of considerable interest to those involved in the research, teaching and study of law.

The series has been divided into three sections. The Schools section is intended to represent the main distinctive approaches and topics of special concern to groups of scholars. The Areas section takes in the main branches of law with an emphasis on essays which present analytical and theoretical insights of broad application. The section on Legal Cultures makes available the distinctive legal theories of different level traditions and takes up topics of general comparative and developmental concern.

I have been delighted and impressed by the way in which the editors of the individual volumes have set about the difficult task of selecting, ordering and presenting essays from the immense quantity of academic legal writing published in journals throughout the world. Editors were asked to pick out those essays from law, philosophy and social science journals which they consider to be fundamental for the understanding of law, as seen from the perspective of a particular approach or sphere of legal interest. This is not an easy task and many difficult decisions have had to be made in order to ensure that a representative sample of the best journal essays available takes account of the scope of each topic or school.

I should like to express my thanks to all the volume editors for their willing participation and scholarly judgement. The interest and enthusiasm which the project has generated is well illustrated by the fact that an original projection of 12 volumes drawn up in 1989 has now become a list of some 60 volumes. I must also acknowledge the vision, persistence and constant cheerfulness of John Irwin and the marvellous work done by Mrs Margaret O'Reilly and Mrs Sonia Bridgman.

TOM D. CAMPBELL
Series Editor
The Faculty of Law
The Australian National University

Introduction

In ethics and political theory – the disciplines fundamental to jurisprudence or legal theory – the term 'natural law' refers to the set of propositions picking out (1) basic human goods, (2) general requirements of right choosing, and (3) the specific moral norms deducible from those requirements as they bear on particular basic goods. A theory of natural law, or *natural law theory* is, therefore, a theory which argues that propositions of those three sorts can be *true*, and offers to identify at least some of these true propositions and their implications for theory and practice.

Opposition to any particular natural law theory can therefore come from two sources: (a) from other theories (including other natural law theories) which identify as true some different propositions about the good and the right; and (b) from sceptical theories arguing that such propositions cannot be *true* but can only represent the opinions of an individual or community.

If some natural law theory is at least fundamentally correct, we must reject as loose and misleading the common saying that natural law has a 'history which is a series of eclipses and revivals from the Greeks to the present time'.[1] All such statements confuse natural law with theories about it. Theories, opinions and doctrines have a history, marked indeed by periods of popularity and unpopularity, eclipse and revival. They have historically important effects, for good and ill, on human practice, being used sometimes to rationalize and sometimes to subvert great evils. The psychological and cultural origins and impact of such opinions can be usefully studied. And if the sceptical denial of natural law (the claim that *all* natural law theories are fundamentally misconceived) were correct, there would be no other sense in which natural law could usefully be studied. But every natural law theorist should firmly deny that natural law has any sort of history of eclipses and revivals, and should equally deny that the origins and impact of belief in natural law are matters of central importance to a natural law theory. For, if there are true principles and norms of natural law, they are true independently of any theories, opinions, doctrines, or traditions.[2]

Have I so defined 'natural law' that every cognitivist or objectivist ethics – every theory which holds that some moral propositions are really *true* – is a natural law theory? Ernest Nagel reasonably complained about such an expansive use of the term.[3] But my definition suffices to distinguish a distinct set of theories within the broader set of non-sceptical theories. By giving priority to the category of basic human goods, the definition distinguishes a natural law ethics from any ethics of the Kantian mould, and makes implicit reference to the related concepts of human flourishing and human nature. By referring to a plurality of principles, requirements and norms, it implicitly distinguishes a natural law ethics from any consistent utilitarian ethics.

Still, the definition I offered does not convey all that needs to be said about the tradition of natural law theories. That tradition has three main features:

1 Critique and rejection of ethical scepticism, moral dogmatism, and conventionalism;
2 Critique and rejection of fundamentally aggregative conceptions of the right and the just

(utilitarianism or, more generally, consequentialism or proportionalism or, more narrowly, wealth-maximization);

3 Clarification of the methods of the descriptive and explanatory social theories (political theory or political science, economics, jurisprudence or legal theory).

The essays in this first volume deal mainly with the first of these three concerns. Those in the companion volume are mainly concerned with the second and third concerns; they touch also on the tradition's more specifically jurisprudential concerns, which are:

1 to show how an understanding of law presupposes a practical understanding (that is, an understanding of the point, the good) of community, justice and rights, and authority – as reasons for choice and action;
2 to show how a definition (that is, a summary of one's understanding) of law can and should include a reference to the moral functions or point of law (especially, but not only, the procedural 'ideals' of the Rule of Law), without thereby excluding immoral laws from the lawyer's or legal theorist's perception or the study of jurisprudence;
3 to show how positive laws are derived from natural law (moral principles) in at least two radically different ways; and
4 to show how unjust laws, being laws, can sometimes create moral obligations, but always lack the moral authority (and thus a part of the character) which laws, by virtue of being lawfully made, characteristically have.

The issues discussed in the essays in this first volume might seem remote from the concerns of the lawyer or even the legal theorist, but they are fundamental. No secure conclusions can be reached on any legal or legal-theoretical issue save on foundations of principle such as are explored in these essays.

Most contemporary scepticisms about the basic human goods, and/or the requirements of practical reasonableness, are based on a logically illicit slide from 'is' propositions to 'ought' propositions. This particular form of invalid reasoning is, in fact, particularly common in the modern era, though also assiduously employed in the ancient manuals of scepticism[4] which were reintroduced into European discourse in the 16th century. A short list of well-known examples will suggest the link between ethical scepticism and ethical conventionalism and dogmatism:

- X is not universally/commonly regarded as good/obligatory; so X is not good/obligatory.[5]
- In modern thought (or: in contemporary society), X is widely regarded as not good/obligatory; so X is not good/obligatory.
- In modern thought (or: in contemporary society), X is widely regarded as good/obligatory; so X is good/obligatory.
- I have a sentiment of approval of X; so X is good (or worthwhile... or obligatory... or...), at least for me.
- I am committed to, have opted for, chosen, decided upon... the practical principle that X ought to be done; so X ought to be done, at least by me.

Explicit natural law theory was launched, by Plato and Aristotle, precisely as a critique of *non sequiturs* such as these. As Ernest Nagel acknowledges in his critique of a certain sort of natural law theory, the distinction between 'is' and 'ought' is clearly respected by Aristotle (and, one may add, his followers such as Thomas Aquinas).[6] It is, indeed a distinction much more carefully respected in Aristotle and Aquinas than in David Hume.[7]

The essays by Lon Fuller to which Nagel was replying[8] perhaps suggested to H.L.A. Hart a claim which, however, Hart casts in universal terms:

> Natural–law theory . . . in all its protean guises, attempts to . . . assert that human beings are equally devoted to and united in their conception of aims (the pursuit of knowledge, justice to their fellow men) other than that of survival . . .[9]

But who ever asserted this? Certainly the classical theorists of natural law all took for granted, and often bluntly asserted, that human beings are not all equally devoted to the pursuit of knowledge or justice, and are far from united in their conception of what constitutes worthwhile knowledge or a demand of justice. Hart objects against natural law theories because the conception of 'the human end or good for man' proposed by 'the classical exponents' of natural law was 'complex', 'debatable' and 'disputable'.[10] But those classical exponents would have replied that the question of what is truly good for humankind is indeed complex, debated and disputed, and that they had made rather extensive contributions to the debate. The fact that there is controversy is not an argument against one side in that controversy.

The claim of the classical and new-classical theorists is that any sane person who has enough experience of human possibilities to understand terms such as 'life', 'health', 'knowledge', 'skill', 'friendship', 'harmony' is capable of understanding that life and health, knowledge, skill in work and play, friendship, harmony of feelings with reason and of both with action, and perhaps a few other basic forms of human opportunity are indeed good, that is, give point and value to any human existence, are worth having, *leaving to one side* all particular predicaments and implications, all assessments of what commitments to forms and choices to make, all moral demands, all questions of how to pursue these goods. These theorists fully acknowledge the great diversity of opinion on all these further questions, questions whose exploration constitutes the bulk of their own work in ethics and political and legal theory. As Leo Strauss remarked with some justice: 'realization of the variety of notions of right is *the* incentive for the quest for natural right'.[11]

Ethical scepticism is touched on in several essays in Volume II.

Fallacious sceptical reliance on variability of opinions about human good and ill, right and wrong, is central to Max Weber's theory of law and society, a theory which profoundly influenced mid-20th century opponents of natural law theories of law (for example, Hart): see Finnis (1985) (II) at 84–5.

Ronald Dworkin, in Dworkin (1982) (II) at 173–8, touches on the 'threat of scepticism'. He distinguishes between 'internal' and 'external' scepticism. What I am calling scepticism corresponds to his term 'external scepticism'; Finnis (1987) (II) at 370–6 argues, in effect, that a sound theory of natural law *supports* an 'internal' scepticism about Dworkin's claims about right answers in legal 'hard cases'. But on the important foundational issue of 'external' scepticism which condemns as illusory the whole practice of affirming moral propositions as true, Dworkin (1982) (II) at 173 remarks that the best of the sceptical arguments is the 'demonstrability hypothesis', which claims, in effect, that there are no true *indemonstrable*, self-evident propositions. As Dworkin observes, the claim is self-refuting.

A significant element in the new classical theory of natural law is its demonstration that sceptical denials of at least one basic human good – the good of truth and knowledge – are self-refuting. Natural law theory is, indeed, a theory which tries to account for the fact that doing it (or questioning it) is worthwhile. Theories which make no room for the fact of their existence (for example, Hume's clever theory of mind which omits to account for cleverness), or for the worth of their own pursuit, are self-refuting.[12]

The strategy of arguments from self-refutation should not be misunderstood. They do not demonstrate the proposition the denial of which they refute. Rather, they defend that proposition by showing that to argue against it is irrational (ultimately, self-contradictory). They work by drawing attention to facts, insights and judgements so immediately involved in the sceptic's own conduct as to be (self-)evident and undeniable. They seek, in effect, to get the sceptic to attend to his or her own questioning, understanding, arguing, and judging from, so to speak, the inside – to attend to the relevant considerations not as facts about people's opinions, but rather *as those considerations have their relevance in one's (his or her) own thinking*. Then the sceptic may come to understand that his or her own concern for the comfortless conclusion that ethics is an illusion is itself a concern for a true good, the good of truth, and for the moral rightness of fidelity to it.

And then, just as one comes to grasp the practical truth that truth (and knowledge of it) is a good 'in its own right', intrinsically, not merely as a means to some further end – a basic human good – so one may come to grasp other basic goods. If these other basic goods and practical principles cannot be defended directly by an argument from self-refutation, still the argument from self-refutation demonstrates that the general, 'external' arguments of the radical sceptic undercut themselves, 'prove too much' and therefore prove nothing. The collapse of those general arguments leaves the field clear for a careful reflection on what really are the goods which give intrinsic point and worth to whatever one can intelligently do. That is the reflection for which Grisez (1965) cleared the ground and whose results are briefly summarized in Grisez, Boyle and Finnis (1987) at 105–20.

It is worth noting, even at this point, that the strategy of this critique of scepticism and *internal* reflection on practical understanding is closely paralleled by the main strategy of a contemporary jurisprudence such as Hart's: attention not merely to the externals of structure, practices or even feelings, but rather to the characteristic reasons people have for acting in the ways which go to constitute distinctive social phenomena (such as law). Contemporary jurisprudence rightly focuses on types of justification for decisions.[13] In this, it is continuous (whether it wishes to be or not) with the fundamental course of reflection which issues in a natural law ethics and political theory.

Part I A Mid-20th Century Debate

I have already touched on this debate between Fuller and Nagel, and will return to it in the Introduction to Volume II. For present purposes its main importance is as an illustration of the confusion and inconclusiveness of a discussion which, on both sides, fails to consider the intrinsic ends of human life, the basic human goods, 'from the inside' that is, *as they are understood in practical reasoning itself.*

Nagel (1958) at 79–80 can readily grant that in assessing the efficacy of means to ends (of using a stick to open a clam) one is judging both fact and value. The question of the relation between 'facts' and 'values' becomes of importance only when considering what it is reasonable to say (that is, to think) about ends whose value is not as means to further ends, that is, about *basic* ends or *intrinsic* goods. Fuller ([1956] 1958) at 71 gets close to identifying a basic end (corresponding to the inclination of curiosity), the intrinsic good of finding out the truth (about clams and about stars and...). But at the crucial point he slides away from identifying it, and speaks instead *externally*: 'I understand what the boy is doing... because of our shared human nature'. That statement, though its key phrase 'because of' remains intolerably vague, is doubtless true. But it adds nothing to the understanding of what the boy is doing, and amounts to changing the subject just as the intrinsic good of truth and knowledge was coming into focus. Indeed, the full sense of 'our shared human nature' could not emerge unless we understood – as we do, by an underived practical insight – that knowledge is a good for any of us, that is, that an ignorant and confused human being is, to that extent, a being in bad shape.

Similarly, Fuller, at 73, prefers to speak *about* the articulation of shared purposes, instead of articulating some purpose or purposes which his readers could then respond to with understanding and an affirmative interest. He leaves inextricably confused the question whether purposes *are* in fact shared and the question whether there are ultimate purposes which it is truly foolish not to share.

Nagel (1958), for his part, is content to leave entirely unexplained the sense in which 'analysis' could yield 'principles for assessing legal rules' (77), or in which 'moral theory' might 'provide' standards for 'adjusting' conflicts between human ends or the human pursuit of ends (81). He does not seem to notice how his own talk of 'human needs' involves the very 'fuzzing [of] the distinction between fact and value' about which he is complaining (82). Nor does he observe that he himself is treating 'liv[ing] amicably together' (81–82; see also 78) as an intrinsic good. In speaking of co-operation between human persons 'for the attainment of their diverse ends' (82), he does not attend to the difference between a self-centred and a truly friendly co-operation – between a co-operation in which I co-operate *only* for the attainment of my own ends (the attainment by others of their ends being for me of no intrinsic interest), and a co-operation in which the attaining by others of their ends is for me (part of) the very point of my co-operation. He does not ask whether law and, in general, life in political (let alone familial or other smaller) communities makes full practical sense other than as a co-operation of the second sort, in which friendship and fairness are values as ends in themselves, not merely means to ends which I happen to have adopted for myself.

Fuller's response fails to clarify the issue decisively. His key phrase, 'a satisfactory life in common' (84), leaves intact the ambiguity to which I have just referred. Thus the 'collaborative quest' (85) remains deeply ambiguous, and the claim that society has 'proper ends' (85) remains completely question-begging.[14] His appeal to 'some community of purpose and some common human nature' (95), like his reference to 'a process of living and deciding' (101), leaves in shadow the very purposes (ends, goods) *which appeal to practical intelligence and reasonableness* and are thus (so to speak) entitled to be common. That appeal to reason, that desirability or worth, can be made apparent only by *attending to the ranges of human opportunity* with a view to grasping what is intrinsically worthwhile, and what deficiencies and obstructions are to be avoided. Talking about 'insight and understanding' is no substitute for summoning up insight and reflective practical understanding by *displaying* (recalling) the relevant human possibilities and *thereby* inviting readers to recollect their understanding that such-and-such goods do indeed give point to certain opportunities for human choice and action, for any human being – and *thus* are 'common purposes'.

Nagel (1959) offers, finally, a fundamental ethical and political principle: 'conflicts are to be decided [by] principles whose use has been discovered to yield greater human dissatisfactions or lesser dissatisfactions or both' (42). Leaving aside the issue of aggregation (see Grisez (1978) (II), and Introduction to Volume II), we may notice the even more fundamental issue: Is this 'are to be' an 'actual end-in-view men entertain' (42)? How could that fact be the source of its claim on us? Or is that principle, 'conflicts are to be resolved', rather an end whose claim on our conflict-resolving opportunities, and on our choices to increase, tolerate, or resolve conflicts, is a claim *in reason* because harmony between human persons is an intrinsic good? And if the latter, is that intelligible good the only such good, or rather one amongst others?[15]

Part II Neo-scholastic Theory: For and Against

By 'neo-scholastic theory' I intend to refer to a body of writings which offered to convey to 19th- and 20th-century readers the thought of Thomas Aquinas, the 13th-century philosophical theologian, and some of his successors in the later-medieval and renaissance schools of theology. These writings intended to participate in philosophical discourse, but tended to commingle properly philosophical inquiry with two other intentions: to expound the thought of Aquinas, considered as an unsurpassed *authority*, and to accept what support might be given to certain premises and conclusions by the authority of theology (or, more precisely, of the Catholic faith).

This commingling of diverse intentions tended to impair not only the philosophical arguments of the neo-scholastics, but also the accuracy of their expositions of Aquinas, whose work came to be seen through the spectacles of one or another *school* or tradition of philosophical doctrine. The two representative essays here selected illustrate these weaknesses rather vividly. One may judge from them how well-deserved was the disrepute into which natural law theory had fallen by the mid-20th century, given that (until the *de facto* collapse and relative disappearance of neo-scholasticism after about 1965) natural law theory was being proposed far more widely in neo-scholastic than in other forms.

The neo-scholastic theory proposed by Davitt (1960) and Broderick (1964) and attacked by Nielsen (1959) is not the only neo-scholastic theory of the fundamental principles of natural law. Indeed, it is not the neo-scholastic theory which Grisez (1965) makes it his principal concern to criticize and replace. But it is representative enough, and is founded on ideas of a well-known recent Thomistic philosopher, Jacques Maritain.

Maritain admits that the expression 'knowledge through inclination' is not used in Aquinas's discussions of natural law.[16] But he thinks that such non-conceptual, 'obscure, unsystematic, vital knowledge by connaturality or affinity' is what Aquinas *must* have in mind when he says that 'reason naturally understands as good all the objects of man's inclinations'.[17] Grisez (1965) at 172, n.11 and 196, n.75 indicates briefly but accurately that this is a thoroughgoing misunderstanding of Aquinas. When Aquinas speaks of understanding something as good, he is referring to a quite ordinary, unmysterious, *conceptual* understanding.[18] Nor is there anything esoteric about the way one's intelligence can grasp that the anticipated or actual states of affairs which are the *objects* of sub-rational inclinations are *instances* of intelligible goods, whose sheer intelligibility as (basic human) goods needs no demonstration, no reference to other goods or sources of intelligibility or of attractiveness to that rational inclination which we call *will*.[19]

Despite their intent to follow Maritain, neither Davitt nor Broderick in fact adhere to his suspect and textually unwarranted appeal to a non-conceptual 'knowledge by inclination'. Where Maritain says that the 'connatural knowledge' of first principles of natural law is 'obscure', Davitt thinks it '*clear* and connatural',[20] and fully conceptual: 'It is the knowledge that we have which results from our judging, without any reasoning process,[21] that what is in agreement with our basic inclinations or drives is good and that what is in disagreement with them is bad.'[22] The relevant concept is the conceptually complex concept of a certain property of a possible object of choice: the property of *being in agreement (or disagreement) with one of my basic inclinations*. The proposition alleged by Davitt to be self-evident (known without reasoning) is: whatever has that property is good. It must simply be said that that proposition is (a) not at all self-evident, and (b) is nowhere said by Aquinas to be either a principle of practical reasoning (that is, of natural law) or the basis of any principle of practical reasoning. The link which Davitt again and again asserts between *in agreement with my drives*, *good for me* and *necessary end of (my) human action* remains opaque and question-begging. From '*is* in agreement with my drives' one cannot, without additional premises, infer 'is good for me' or '*ought* to be pursued by me'.[23] Thus Davitt's repeated reference to the 'demands' or 'directives' of one's drives remains an empty metaphor.[24] Worse, it presents the human person as a sort of puppet pulled hither and thither by inclinations which reason and rationally shaped choice merely *serve*, as means serve ends. Indeed one must observe, in passing, that such a representation of the foundations of the moral life is offensive to human dignity.[25]

The same must be said of Broderick's claims: that the content of natural law is 'identified *by* our most fundamental natural inclinations';[26] that the 'primary natural law precepts are known and acted on... *as prerational*'[27]; that practical reason knows not man's intrinsic ends but only 'which means to take and moves to make' to achieve them.[28] Equally remote from Aquinas is Broderick's invention of a basic principle that one must not 'reverse one's natural inclinations'.[29] Nor does Aquinas's theory of natural law anywhere argue: nature is purposeful, therefore the 'is' of one's natural inclinations, under reason, is the moral 'ought'.[30]

Both Davitt and Broderick overlook and in effect defy one of the most fundamental and all-pervasive axioms of Aquinas's philosophy: that one comes to understand the nature of an active reality (for example, human persons) by understanding its capacities and inclinations, and one comes to understand *them* by understanding the corresponding activities, and one understands these activities by understanding their objects.[31] The objects of willed human activity are intelligible goods. So practical reason's primary, underived understanding of basic human goods *precedes* our theoretical understanding of inclinations, capacities and human nature. Equally, our understanding of human goods *adds* to, *transcends*, all our inclinations as experienced; our experience of inclinations is only *data for* our understanding of the goods which could be realized in the states of affairs to which those inclinations incline us.

Kai Neilsen, then, can scarcely be severely blamed for presenting as Aquinas's a theory which in fact is quite foreign to Aquinas: 'Aquinas believed that the good is somehow the normal. It is found by observation... by studying man's inclinations and reflecting on them... by apprehending what life really is.'[32] None of those statements could be defended; it would be truer to say that, for Aquinas, one comes to apprehend what life really is by coming to understand what are the intrinsic goods, the basic components of human flourishing. Each of the other statements would be truer if similarly reversed. Each of the four objections Neilsen advances tells against Davitt and Broderick; none of them tells against Aquinas's theory as expounded and then developed in Grisez (1965) and Grisez, Boyle and Finnis (1987).

As for Neilsen's own view of ethics, it falls foul, as Grisez (1965) at 195, n. 74 observes, of the truth that an 'ought' cannot be derived only from an 'is', not even the 'is' of 'I have decided'.[33] Nor can any sense be made of the idea that 'we as moral agents must decide what is good and evil' (Nielsen (1965) at 70). So far from being a necessity, this is not even a possibility; truths, even practical truths about human goods and the reasonableness of our pursuing them, cannot be constituted simply by our willing ('deciding') them to be true.

Kelsen ([1963] 1973) displays some of the consequences of a rigorous adherence to the contention that normativity can be no more than the content (meaning) of an act of *will* (85–87, 110).[34]

A first consequence (very fundamental, but usually overlooked) is that, in this contention, 'will' itself is understood in a way radically different from its meaning in Aquinas and in 'new classical' theorists such as Grisez. In the latter, will is essentially response to the rational desirability of some good judged by the acting person to be intelligible, worthwhile either for its own sake or for the sake of some intrinsically worthwhile good. Will is not every inclination that can move a human being to act, but precisely the inclination and capacity to respond to what *intelligence or reason* proposes. The notion that will, so understood, could have authority over reason, or be the source of normativity, is simply incoherent – an absurd attempt is get an *ought* from an *is*. One can of course will, that is, take an intelligent interest in and indeed make a free choice to pursue and realize, some option which one knows or believes to be less than fully reasonable; but even here, there is no choice, no act of *will*, unless the option chosen seems to one to be reasonable *in some respects*, that is, seems to offer some *intelligible good* which is somehow not included in the fully reasonable option or options.[35]

A second consequence of defining a norm (practical principle, standard of choice) as the content of an act of will is that the notion of good becomes derivative: 'In as much as a norm establishes that certain conduct ought to be performed, it creates a value'.[36] This in turn has drastic and pervasive implications. The idea of good with which Aristotle, Aquinas, and the new classical theorists work is the idea of fullness of being, of perfection or flourishing, of realization of potentialities and openness to more abundant realization of them. Such a concept obviously entails that a being (or community of beings, or state of affairs, or action) will characteristically be *more* or *less* good, in respect of one or other intelligible form of good, and more or less richly endowed in relation to the various intelligible forms of good which it can instantiate.[37] It follows that goodness and all such related concepts as reasonable, natural, virtuous are, in Aristotle (and Aquinas and the new classical theorists), not all-or-nothing but matters of measure or degree. Thus Aristotle and Aquinas can happily say *both* that a tyrant aims at the well-being of his people (that is, at their being in good shape for him to exploit, to be adulated by, to use to overcome his external enemies, etc.) *and* that a tyrant ignores the well-being of his people (that is, the well-being for its own sake, and for the sake of each of his subjects) in favour of his own well-being. Similarly, they can say that tyranny is both natural (as giving effect to inborn feelings of self-preference) and unnatural (as flouting reason's demand that goods be distributed in the community according to a rational, fair order, not according to feelings of self-preference). And so on. Thus there simply dissolves that whole series of contradictions which Kelsen thinks he sees in Aristotle, and by his belief in which Kelsen is driven to the desperate expedient of questioning the authenticity of passages quite central to Aristotle's thought. These are not contradictions, but sober recognition of the distinctions between levels and aspects of goodness, of rationality, of virtue, of community, of friendship, of constitutionality, etc.[38] There is no significant contradiction in Aristotle on these matters, any more than there is contradiction in saying: 'This sort of inhuman behaviour is all too human'.

A third consequence of Kelsen's 'will'-conception of normativity is that it is this conception, not any faithful attention to the tradition, that obliges him to argue that natural law, if not sheer nonsense, must be a matter of *divine will*. Hence his laboured but none too careful attempt (83, 109–11) to explain away the views of those theorists who have contended that natural moral law would be intelligible as rationally directive and binding even if (*per impossibile*) there were no divine creator: 'the true meaning of what [they] said', Kelsen claims, 'is [just] that the validity of natural law cannot be *revoked*, not even by the will of God' (109). (Kelsen, like every radical voluntarist, does not and could not explain why a normativity wholly dependent on will cannot be freely revoked by the same will.) A quick way of suggesting how far Kelsen is misrepresenting the tradition is to observe that, for Aquinas, the first principles of natural law *are*, while the existence of God *is not*, self-evident to the human mind. There is nothing incoherent in the classic position that (a) both the idea of moral obligation and the content of a reasonable morality can be understood and rationally adhered to without benefit of the premise that there is a God, or that God cares about human choices, *and* (b) the existence and nature of God can be shown to be such that moral principles and norms and conduct have a *further* intelligibility and force.[39]

One may add that Kelsen's appeal to the 'authority' of Victor Cathrein SJ is in vain. It is clear enough, even from the short passage quoted by Kelsen (110–11), that Cathrein's theory of natural law belongs to the type which Grisez (1965) shows is quite distinctly different from Aquinas's conception of law in general and of natural law in particular.[40]

Part III The New Classical Theory

This body of theory has been expounded principally in books.[41] The essays collected in this part set out only a fragment, though it is the more fundamental part, of the theory's conception of the principles of natural moral law. They give no exposition of the specifically *moral* principles which shape moral and legal norms and judgements. For a brief account of how those principles are conceived in the theory, one may look to George (1988) at 1394–1400 and George (1989) (II) at 1472–3.

Grisez (1965) is not the easiest of these essays. But one will be amply repaid for one's effort of following both its interpretation of the most important single passage in the entire history of natural law theory, and its critique of the neo-scholastic misinterpretations of that passage – misinterpretations from which flow all the other weaknesses in neo-scholastic theories of natural law.

MacCormick (1981) is a sketch and critique of the new classical theory by a sympathetic jurisprudential opponent of natural law theories. The sketch is a broadly accurate overview of some main aspects of the theory and of its extension into the properly legal and jurisprudential. The critique comes down to 'the argument from queerness' (107): Can we believe in some order of objective human goods, good independently of anyone's acts of valuation or attitudes of appreciation, without postulating an ontology (an account of the real state of the universe) too queer to be believed?[42]

To say 'Too queer' is to appeal to some standard of ordinariness (non-queerness). If one takes as one's standard of ordinary entities, qualities and relationships those entities, qualities and relations which are the subject-matter of physical, chemical and biochemical theories, then one will have to judge that intentions, meanings and truth (for example, Mackie's or MacCormick's own *intention* to assert a *meaningful* proposition picking out the *truth* about the limits of ontology) are utterly queer. But it would be self-refuting to banish intentions, meanings and truth from 'the universe'. I have already indicated that it is self-refuting to argue for banishing intelligible goods. The entire appeal to 'queerness' does no more than propose an entirely *a priori* (unargued) sentence of banishment on a considerable part of our human intellectual life – the life of understanding certain possibilities as opportunities, as possible instantiations of human good(s).

The new classical theory has attracted a good deal of criticism, especially from some neo-scholastics who consider it unfaithful to Aquinas and/or Aristotle. Samples of the latter criticism are McInerny (1980) and Veatch (1981) and the second of the two books reviewed in George (1988). The long but rather terse and complex essay, Grisez, Boyle and Finnis (1987), restates the foundations of the theory (but not its account of specifically moral principles, nor its analysis of human action, nor any of its moral and political implications) in a way which seeks to respond to the misunderstandings which have provided most of the fuel for the critics' *auto-da-fe*. An annotated bibliography (148–51) provides further orientation. In that bibliographical note, notice the annotation to Finnis and Grisez (1981): these authors do not concede that they have misrepresented Aquinas, or that the neo-scholastic interpretation is more faithful to him, but they do not think that the adequacy of any theory (including their own) should be judged by its correspondence with the views of *any* previous philosopher or theologian.[43]

Part IV For and Against the New Classical Theory

This part comprises two fairly short and self-contained debates to which I have already alluded, together with Robert George's helpful overview.[44] It is supplemented by George (1989) (II) at 1457–64.

Notes

1 Davitt (1960), p. 98. References in this form (using original page folios) are to essays included in this volume. Where an essay is in the companion volume on *Natural Law*, its date is followed by (II).
2 See Finnis, John (1980), *Natural Law and Natural Rights*, Oxford University Press, pp. 23–25, 50.
3 Nagel (1958), at p. 77.
4 See especially Sextus Empiricus, *Pyrrhonean Hypotyposes* III, xxiv, pp. 198–238.
5 See the 'second standard criticism' mentioned (supported?) by Nielsen (1959), p. 57.
6 Nagel (1959), pp. 40, 41.
7 See Grisez (1965), p. 195 n. 74; for documentation see Finnis, *Natural Law and Natural Rights* pp. 33–8, 47–8, 53–5. It was certainly not Hume who 'made us realize [that] ... "Man ought not to steal" is quite different from... "Man does steal"', as Neilsen (1959), p. 59 quite groundlessly claims.
8 Fuller [1956] (1958) p. 73 (the 'school of natural law has kept alive faith in [the] process... that may be called the collaborative articulation of shared purposes') and Fuller (1958) pp. 84–5.
9 Hart, H.L.A. (1958), 'Positivism and the Separation of Law and Morals', *Harvard Law Review*, **71**, 593, p. 623 (this is the essay to which Fuller (1958) (II) is a reply).
10 See Hart, H.L.A. (1961), *The Concept of Law*, Oxford University Press, p. 187.
11 Strauss, Leo (1953), *Natural Rights and History*, Chicago University Press, p. 10. See further Finnis, note 2 above, pp. 29–33, 50–2.
12 The argument is most fully deployed in Finnis (1977), 'Scepticism, Self-refutation and the Good of Truth', in Hacker and Raz (eds), (1977), *Law, Morality and Society: Essays in Honour of H.L.A. Hart*, Oxford University Press, pp. 250–4, 258–66; also in Finnis, note 2 above, pp. 73–5, 79–80; Finnis, *Fundamentals of Ethics*, Oxford University Press & Georgetown University Press 1983 pp. 4–6.
13 See Finnis (1987), (II) pp. 357–9.
14 The persisting ambiguities and mistakes in Fuller's notion of vicarious participation in a process of evaluation (88) can be identified if one reflects on the discussion of Kronman's argument in Finnis (1985), (II) pp. 87–9.
15 For example, amongst the set of goods identified in Grisez, Boyle and Finnis (1987), pp. 107–8.
16 Maritain, J. (1954), *Man and the State*, Hollis and Carter, London, p. 82, n.2.
17 Maritain, loc. cit., quoting the passage from Aquinas, *Summa theologiae* I–II q. 94 a. 2 which is translated in Grisez (1965), pp. 170–1 and discussed in Grisez, pp. 180–1.
18 Aquinas's talk (which is in other parts of his work) of 'knowledge by connaturality' refers only to the way in which a person with the right emotions and dispositions will be able to *judge* rightly in moral matters; there is no suggestion that the *content* of this judgement is non-conceptual. See John E. Naus, (1959), *The Nature of the Practical Intellect according to Saint Thomas Aquinas*, Gregorian University Press, Rome, pp. 146–7.
19 See Grisez (1965), p. 180; Grisez, Boyle and Finnis (1987), pp. 104–9; Finnis, note 2 above, pp. 60–4.
20 Davitt (1960), p. 76.
21 'Without any reasoning' is in no way equivalent to 'without any concepts'. One knows that the whole is greater than any of its parts without reasoning, but only by having the concepts of whole and part.
22 Davitt (1960), p. 77, n.91.
23 Again, it is not 'my drives [that] indicate certain elementary actions that are good and necessary for my self-development' (Davitt (1960), 81); rather it is my intelligence that indicates that certain possibilities to which I am in fact inclined are also truly instances of goods (opportunities) which are intrinsic to the development and flourishing of any human being and therefore of me too. Davitt, pp. 86–8 shows an uneasy awareness that there are texts in Aquinas which do not fit his (Davitt's) inclination-centred theory of natural law; but he fails to see the solution, which is simple: if one re-reads the texts which Davitt cites p. 75 nn. 79–82, it is clear that not one of them gives any

support to his thesis that the inclination/tendencies/drives themselves are the directive principles of natural law.

24 To say this is not to impugn the suggestive value of Davitt's survey of the anthropological, psychological, and philosophical literature on universal human drives/inclinations: Davitt (1968), 'The Basic Values in Law: A Study of the Ethicolegal Implications of Psychology and Anthropology', *Transactions of the American Philosophical Society* (NS) **58**, part 5. A proper use of such work is suggested in Finnis, note 2 above, pp. 81–5.

25 No doubt, one 'cannot act on account of that toward which [one] has no basis for affinity in [one's] inclinations' (Grisez (1965), p. 180), but to say that is by no means to say that *the point of* one's choices and actions is to give effect to, or to follow, or to act in accordance with, those inclinations. Human choice and responsibility have dignity because human acting is acting for a *reason* which one *chooses* to pursue.

26 Broderick (1964), p. 148 (emphasis added).

27 Ibid. (emphasis added); this bluntly contradicts Aquinas's view that the primary principles of natural law are the first principles *of practical reason*.

28 Ibid.

29 Broderick (1964), pp. 149, n. 99 and 152, n. 106. The Latin passage quoted and heavily relied upon in the former footnote says no more than that there are some features of reality (including, no doubt, human realities) which are not ruled and measured by human reason because they are not themselves a matter of human choice, for example, one's digestive processes. It in no way proposes a principle *of choice and action* ('If you have the option of reversing your inclinations, do not choose it') over and above the naturally known practical principles which guide all human choice.

30 Broderick (1964), pp. 148, 153.

31 'per obiecta cognosc[i]mus actus, et per actus potentias, et per potentias essentiam': *in II de Anima* lect 6 (n.308); 'obiecta sunt priora operationibus in via definiendi' (ibid. n. 305); 'obiecta praecognoscuntur actibus et actus potentiis': *Summa Theologiae* I qu.87 a.3c; see also, for example, I q.77 a.3c; I–II q.18 a.5; 72 1c; *in IX Meta*. lect. 7. See also Finnis, note 12 above, pp. 20–21, 25.

32 Neilsen (1959), p. 47.

33 See the reliance on decision, especially in the quotation from A.J. Ayer, in Nielsen (1959), p. 66.

34 This essay appears in a translation which is not fully reliable and contains many typographical or similar mistakes. But its drift is clear enough. Amongst the errors: 'Nichomachean' should be 'Nicomachean'; the quotation marks at the end of the first paragraph on 91 should go after 'virtue' in the previous line, and the quotation marks at the end of the next paragraph should go at the end of the preceding sentence; 'Summa contro gentiles' should read 'Summa contra Gentiles'; 'art and end' on 104 should read 'act and end', and 'ratio speculative' should read 'ratio speculativa'; the citation to Aquinas in the footnote on 106 is fictitious; the quotation from Cathrein at the bottom of 110 should be closed by quotation marks at the end of the sentence in line 5 of 111. For another critique, see Kelsen (1949), 'Natural Law Doctrine before the Tribunal of Science', *Western Political Quarterly*, **2**, pp. 481–513.

35 See Grisez, Boyle and Finnis (1987), pp. 122–5, especially the section 'How to make immoral choices'.

36 Kelsen (1973), p. 85. The sentence later on the page, 'it is the validity of a value that bestows validity on a norm' introduces a particularly gross example of the fallacy of deducing an ought from an is; the passage following the quoted sentence makes it clear that, in Kelsen's view, a value has the validity it has (and which it then lends to a norm or norms) *by being accepted or desired*.

37 Thus, for example, a scholar can only be more or less learned; a clever crook is both rational and unreasonable; a scholar can be both flourishing (in knowledge) and not flourishing (in friendship and/or fairness and/or health).

38 For a fuller exploration of this, see Finnis, note 2 above, pp. 9–11, 20, 366.

39 See further Grisez (1965), pp. 200–1; Grisez, Boyle and Finnis (1987), pp. 141–7; Finnis, note 2 above, pp. 48–9, 371–413; Finnis (1989), 'On Creation and Ethics', *Anthropotes*, **2**, pp. 199–206.

40 On the relation between obligation and divine will, see further Grisez, (1983), *Christian Moral Principles*, Chicago, pp. 101–2: the normative force of God's commands cannot follow from the mere fact that he commands, any more than from the fact that we choose; God's will ought to be followed, but for a *reason*: that he is leading and guiding us towards our true good; by wisdom and free choice God makes us what we are and thus settles the true requirements for our fulfilment, but God makes no additional choice to make those requirements *obligatory*; their being requirements of integral human fulfilment is what makes them obligatory. See also Finnis, note 2 above, pp. 403–5.

41 Notably, Boyle and Grisez, (1979), *Life and Death with Liberty and Justice*, U Notre Dame P; Finnis, see note 2 above; Finnis, see note 12 above; Grisez, (1984), *Christian Moral Principle*, Franciscan Herald P, Chicago; Finnis, Boyle and Grisez (1987), *Nuclear Deterrence, Morality and Realism*, Oxford University Press.

42 For the roots of this argument in David Hume (it is fundamental to his grand argument that 'moral distinctions are not derived from reason') and, more recently, John Mackie, and a reply, see Finnis, note 12 above, pp. 57–60.

43 See also Finnis and Grisez (1981), pp. 30–1.

44 George concludes that Hittinger's *A Critique of the New Natural Law Theory* is interpretatively mistaken and philosophically misguided and question-begging. For an ample selection of Hittinger's mistakes in expounding the theory he offers to criticize, see Grisez (1988), 'A Critique of Russell Hittinger's Book, *A Critique of the New Natural Law Theory*', *The New Scholasticism*, **62**, 438–65. Many other instances could be added to those assembled by Grisez. In short, the work scarcely engages with any of the views of the theorists whom it offers to criticize.

Part I
A Mid-Century Debate

[1]

HUMAN PURPOSE AND NATURAL LAW*

Lon L. Fuller

It is difficult to achieve effective communication in any discussion of a term that bears as many meanings as does "natural law." An adequate semantic analysis of this term would not only have to discriminate among such distinct meanings as can be discerned, but would also have to undertake something much more difficult, that is, to trace the complicated overlappings among these meanings that make them appear to have some sort of family resemblance. Such an analysis would not advance the purposes of this paper, for the problem I wish to present relates to a fundamental insight of ontology of the sort that may indeed be presupposed in the process of definition, but can scarcely be advanced by it.

It may help to avoid misunderstanding if I state briefly what I am not attempting to do in this paper. I am not, in any usual sense, advancing a "theory of natural law." I do not bring with me any code of nature. I do not hold myself open to deal with problems of casuistry, to say how "my concept of natural law" would solve this or that case. My concern is primarily to present a problem, and only incidentally and imperfectly to suggest a solution for it. The problem to which I address myself is one with which most theories of natural law attempt to deal, however clumsily. It is a problem that positivism commonly treats as simply nonexistent.

The problem I have in mind is that which arises when we attempt to reconcile the now generally accepted dichotomy of fact and value with a purposive interpretation of human behavior. For it is my thesis that when we accept the full consequences that flow from a view which treats human action as goal-directed, the relation between fact and value assumes an aspect entirely different from that implied in the alleged "truism" that from *what is* nothing whatever follows as to *what ought to be.* Let me illustrate.

I see at a distance a boy who holds in his hand a small, gray, roundish object. He seems to be contemplating this object intently. After a period of hesitation, he places the object carefully between his palms and repeatedly presses on it. He then relaxes his grip, holds the object loosely in his left hand, and begins to look about him on the ground. He apparently finds

* Professor Fuller's article originally appeared at 53 Journal of Philosophy 697 (1956). It is reprinted here by permission of the editors.

what he wants, for he bends over and picks up a stick. This he uses for a while to prod or push against the object. He then throws the stick away and bends to strike the object several times against a rock. Shortly he gives up this activity and walks about as if undecided what to do next. Suddenly he begins to gather sticks together, arranges them on the ground in a pile, lights a match to them, places the object in the fire, and then stands off in an attitude of expectancy.

Now it is obvious that something happens to this account, a sudden accretion of meaning occurs, when we learn that the boy was throughout trying to open a clam. Without this clue I could not interpret what I observed, retain accurately in memory the shape of the events that occurred, or give to another a really coherent account of what happened.

A former age would have said quite simply that this clue of purpose was necessary to "understand" what was happening. Let us, however, define "understanding" in terms consonant with modern conceptions of scientific method; that is, let us consider that we have "understanding" when we are able to *control* and *predict* events. It is obvious that any chance I might have of redirecting the boy's actions, by diverting him into a new line of activity, would depend in large measure on my knowing what he was trying to do. In a similar manner, if at any stage I was able to predict what he would do next — for example, if I had guessed correctly what he would do after he had gathered the sticks together — it would be because I had discerned, in general terms at least, the purpose he was pursuing.

Now it can be demonstrated, I believe, that in any interpretation of events which treats what is observed as purposive, fact and value merge. In such a case the view that value is something foreign to a purely factual account — something projected by the observer on the thing observed — simply will not stand scrutiny. If I can predict that the boy's attempt to open the clam by pressing it between his hands will soon be given up, it is because I know that this is not a "good" way to open clams; judged in the light of the boy's purpose it lacks "value." Here the structure of the events as they unroll — the reality of what happens through time — contains an element of value, so that we can say: "This is bad, it will not last," or "This is good, we may expect it to continue."

It will be objected at this point, I am sure, that this whole demonstration rests on the most transparent of fallacies. It will be said that a "value" element is no more intrinsic to the facts I have recounted than it would be, let us say, if I were to observe a five-foot ladder leaning against a fifteen-foot wall. Certainly this state of affairs, as related, suggests nothing like a value judgment, yet I can say of it, "This is bad," *if* I assume that someone of normal stature plans to use the ladder to scale the wall, and *if* I provisionally accept his purpose as a valid one. The only difference between this case and my previous illustration, it will be said, is that as we watch the boy with the clam, the observation of the physical events, the perception of the boy's purpose, and our provisional acceptance of that purpose as a standard for valuing what occurs, all proceed contemporaneously, so that what is in principle distinct is here blended, thus creating an illusion that fact and value have somehow merged. That they remain distinct even when we are observing the results of purposive action is made clear by the illustration of the ladder and the wall.

This argument ignores the fact that when we are dealing with purposive action projected through time, the structure that we observe, recall, and report lies, not in any instantaneous state of affairs, but in a course of happening, which can be understood only if we participate in a process of evaluation by which the bad is rejected and the good retained. If I look over the shoulder of a mathematician working on a problem beyond my comprehension, I cannot predict or control what he will do, nor will I be able to give more than a trivial account of what I have observed. In such a case, as in that of the boy and the clam, the "fact" of the event can be understood only by one sufficiently capable of evaluation to know what is happening when a good thing is embraced or a bad one rejected. If any of my illustrations produces an "illusion" it is that of the ladder leaning against the wall, where an interruption in purposive action leaves a deposit in the form of a temporary collocation of physical objects we can talk about without importing into it any greater purposive element than is intrinsic to all language.

At this point it will be argued, I am sure, that my observations confuse the question of ultimate value with that of selecting the most effective means for realizing an immediate purpose. It may be true, it will be said, that to understand and describe purposive action we have to participate vicariously in an act of valuation, but any such valuation is necessarily relative to what Dewey called the "end-in-view." That there are good and bad ways of opening clams leaves untouched the question whether opening clams is itself an activity entitled to be called good.

But is it true that a course of purposive action can be understood simply by perceiving at any given moment of time whatever immediate purpose is then being pursued? Shall we treat the shift from one purpose to another as a kind of miracle, neither requiring nor permitting any participation by the observer in the evaluation that produced the shift?

In my now sadly overworked molluscoidal illustration I described a case where a series of apparently discrete acts were directed toward what I called a single purpose. Actually it would have been better, even in that simple case, to speak, not of a purpose, but of a congeries of related purposes. "Opening a clam" by pressing on it is obviously something different from the "opening" that might result from prying. But suppose a still greater shift in the direction of the boy's activities. He is told, for example, that there is an aquarium nearby where he can observe clams feeding and digging in the sand as they would in their native habitat. He drops his clam and runs to look at the aquarium. Shall we say that there has now been a complete break in the continuity of his actions, or shall we say that he has merely hit on a better means of satisfying what was his true purpose throughout? Other shifts in the boy's activities might be imagined, such as putting down the clam and turning to an encyclopedia, where before reaching the C's he becomes entranced with an article on astronomy. The essential point I am trying to convey is that to understand a course of action of any complexity a single "purpose" does not suffice. If I understand what the boy is doing it is because of our shared human nature, a nature that in both of us is at all times incomplete and in process of development.

Any single human purpose — whether expressed in actions or words — is an incomplete thing when severed from the total system of which it forms a part. The meaning of any given purpose is always controlled by latent purposes in interaction with it. This is beautifully illustrated in an example of Wittgenstein's:

> Someone says to me: "Show the children a game." I teach them gaming with dice, and the other says, "I didn't mean that sort of game." Must the exclusion of the game with dice have come before his mind when he gave me the order?[1]

Those who claim large powers to ascribe to words or human actions a meaning innocent of evaluation will do well to ponder this example.

The dilemma we confront when we attempt to apply the fact-value dichotomy to human purpose may be restated in terms of the means-end relation. To anyone who reflects on moral issues two lines of thought will open up with respect to means and ends, each carrying with it the quality of self-evidence. On the one hand, it seems clear that the selection of an apt means for the realization of a given end is an activity engaging man's reasoning faculties and his capacity for accurate analysis and observation. The

1. Philosophical Investigations 33 (1953).

other line of thought leads, with equal persuasiveness, to the conclusion that this activity must have a terminal point and that the end ultimately pursued cannot be determined by analysis or observation, but must in some manner or other be projected upon events. These two lines of thought can coexist peacefully so long as they are not applied to any process of decision. When that happens the distinction that holds them apart disappears and their latent conflict becomes manifest. For when we are confronted with the necessity of making an actual decision about a course of action, means and ends no longer arrange themselves in tandem fashion, but move in circles of interaction.

We are thus faced with a dilemma like that presented by the wave and corpuscular theories of light in physics — two views, each of which seems valid when taken in isolation, prove impossible to combine. In ethics, unfortunately, this conflict manifests itself precisely at the only point where theory makes any difference in human affairs.

I do not pretend to be able to remove the difficulties presented by this problem. I suggest that part of the trouble lies with language. The forms of language, particularly those operating with subject, verb, and predicate, are well suited to describe action unilaterally projected, but are an awkward instrument for dealing with interaction. The words we use to describe mental activity may also confuse the issue. The term "reasoning" seems apt when applied to the process of selecting the most effective means for realizing an accepted end, but inappropriate for describing the process by which, through reflection and contemplation, we make up our minds "what we really want," though in practice the two processes go forward in interaction and both engage the higher nervous centers.

No doubt the true source of the difficulty lies deeper. The means-end problem is simply an outcropping of the deeper mystery of life itself. Living matter is distinguished by the fact that it combines two qualities that do not appear together in inanimate matter: directiveness and adaptability. In the obscure interaction of these two qualities lies the source of our difficulties with the means-end problem. Perhaps the mystery that attaches to the formation of ends is only a particular expression of that which surrounds all biological phenomena which seem to project themselves from within the organism. We see no cause for wonder when an animal takes cover to escape the cold, but feel we have witnessed a near-miracle when another animal responds to the same stimulus by growing longer hair — though we would be hard put to it to explain why the one phenomenon seems so commonplace, the other so mysterious. Perhaps in the case of the animal that grows a thicker coat to meet the winter our difficulty arises from the fact that the familiar means-end relationship seems lacking, so that an end appears to realize itself directly. Our minds feel comfortable, in other words, when we are dealing with the means-end relation, but become uneasy when we attempt to understand the members of this relationship in isolation from one another.

If these meager suggestions have any value at all it will be in helping to identify the problem, not in providing a solution for it. Indeed, I believe the issue we now confront is not that of solving the problems, but of deciding how we should comport ourselves in the absence of a solution.

One answer to this predicament is by now thoroughly familiar. In its most extreme form it runs somewhat as follows: The validity of human ends and "values" is not a matter for reasoned demonstration. While the selection of an apt means has the quality of an intellectual undertaking, a means without an end is a monstrosity. Until we have selected an end by some fiat of the will, any discussion of means is therefore futile. Every means-end problem is unique. If it were not, this would imply that the formation of ends is itself a lawful process, subject to rational cognition, which, it is assumed, cannot be the case.

From the same human predicament, an opposing school of thought extracts the opposite conclusion. Since in the process of decision means and ends interact, it is impossible to assign in advance precise limits to the role of reason. Let us therefore push our understanding as far as it will take us into the obscure area where means and ends interact; let us seek collectively to discover as much agreement in this area as the nature of the case permits.

This view asserts the reality of a process that may be called the collaborative articulation of shared purposes. Through the centuries it has been — in spite of all of its extravagances and dogmatisms — the school of natural law that has kept alive faith in that process. Is the faith justified?

I believe we have much evidence that it is. In the affairs of daily life, we all know from personal experience that in moments of crisis consultation with a friend will often help us to understand what we really want. It does not make much difference whether our adviser tells us, in effect, "Look carefully to your means," or "Consider carefully your end." The effect of the advice is in either case to initiate a process of reflection and consultation that may change our whole understanding of ourselves. The rapport needed to make such a consultation profitable is obviously difficult to achieve, and it may seem, therefore, that collaboration on such a personal level is without relevance to the larger issues of law and ethics.

Yet I think that in the history of the common law we have an example which teaches how a social institution may derive its integrity and vitality from the same spirit of consultation as that which animates the discussion of two friends sharing a problem together. The common law is not the work of any one judge, but of many, collaborating through time. In the course of its history the implementation of its rules has been improved and refined. At the same time, the rules themselves have often been revised to make possible an effective implementation of them. Though the common law is said to be built on precedent, there is no controlling verbal formulation of the meaning of any particular precedent. What the court said in a former case is always subject to reinterpretation as new situations arise. The scope of the precedent is determined not only in the light of the end-in-view pursued by the court that decided it, but in the light of ends then out of view because not stirred into active consciousness by the facts of the case being decided. The problem posed by Wittgenstein's example of the children's game is so familiar to the common law as hardly to seem novel at all. And, except for occasional lapses into literalism, its response has always been, "No, he did not mean that kind of game."

What I have called the collaborative articulation of shared purposes is also illustrated, I believe, on a much homelier plane, familiar to everyone. I refer to the problem of giving an adequate definition for everyday words. In modern discussions of semantics it is a commonplace to assert that the lexicographer is merely an observer and recorder of usage. This is nonsense. We all know that developing a good definition for a familiar word is hard intellectual labor. If one will take a common word like "stove" or "money" and compare his own offhand definition with that given in a good dictionary, he may learn, to be sure, that usages exist which he overlooked or which were unfamiliar to him. But what he will chiefly discover is how miserably his own definition failed to articulate clearly the purposive core of the word, which he "knew" as well as anyone, but was unable on short notice to bring to adequate formulation. A good lexicographer not only knows more about usage than you and I, but his skill in analysis may enable him to predict, more successfully than we could, how we ourselves use the word in contexts we have not yet confronted.

The modern rejection of any notion that men may by pooling their intellectual resources come to understand better what their true purposes are is revealed in the scorn that generally greets essays carrying such titles as, "What is Art?" Of course much that is pretentious and empty appears under such titles, but the modern rejection does not rest on the quality of the offerings, being grounded rather on principle. It is said that any such title invites a confusion of fact and value and serves generally as a cover for a fraudulent intent to pass off the subjective opinion of the author about what art ought to be for a description of what it is in fact — as if it were possible to describe a major area of human striving without participation in that striving and as if that participation could be otherwise than creative! If the objection is more radically phrased so that it could not be removed by changing the title to read, "What I Think Art Ought to Be," then what is really being rejected is the reality of what I have called the collaborative articulation of shared purposes.

That rejection makes itself most tragically felt today, I believe, in our failure to carry on the work of former generations in analyzing and discussing what may be called the forms of social order. I use that term broadly to include rules, procedures, and institutions — all the ways, in short, in which the relations of human beings to one another are subjected to a formal ordering, whether by consent, habit, or command. As I use the term it cuts across law, politics, economics, sociology and ethics, and even includes systems of play. Thus, contract, adjudication, the majority principle, and the three-strike, four-ball rule are all forms of social order.

These forms are generally viewed only in their most obvious aspect, that is, as means to the realization of human ends. But they are also themselves ends, in two closely related senses. They are ends in the sense that, although we make them, they help to make us what we are, man's dependence on society being what it is. Any particular economic system not only serves to satisfy antecedent wants, but also generates its own peculiar pattern of human wants. Secondly, any form of social order contains, as it were, its own internal morality. Thus, we may judge football by an external standard and say, "Football is a good game," but we may also judge it by standards drawn from its own internal requirements and say, "Football will become impossible if this sort of thing is allowed to go on." We may appraise adjudication as a means of settling disputes and compare it with alternative methods of accomplishing the same object. We may also analyze its intrinsic demands and recognize that any attempt to combine the functions of judge and mediator represents a dangerous undertaking. Finally, we may agree with Proverbs that, "The lot causeth contentions to cease, and parteth between the mighty," though we may regret that the wisdom of Solomon was not applied to define more precisely for us the kinds of contentions that are most suited for disposition by a casting of lots. At the same time, deliberate resort to chance as a form of social order makes its own technical demands if it is to be in fact what it purports to be.

These remarks may be taken to indicate an interest in practical problems of economics, law, and politics, rather than any concern for ethical theory. I believe, however, that the forms of social order cast their shadows across ethical discussions which contain no explicit reference to them. Thus we find the ideal of voluntary settlement (contract), or the informed judgment of a disinterested third party (adjudication), or the majority principle serving as tacit premises in discussions that seem remote from anything like the technical problems of social organization.

The issues I have tried to suggest in these concluding remarks range from the most trivial to the most crucial that human beings can face. These issues were once in active discussion and dispute. We are still living with the resolutions former generations found for them. It is difficult to see how the interrupted work of these generations can be resumed until we have reacquired some measure of sympathy for the essential aims of the school of natural law.

[2]

ON THE FUSION OF FACT AND VALUE: A REPLY TO PROFESSOR FULLER

Ernest Nagel

ALTHOUGH THE DOCTRINE of natural law is obviously not uncongenial to himself, Professor Fuller explicitly disclaims that in his contribution to this symposium he is arguing for any version of natural law theory. But unless I completely misunderstand him, his paper does make a vigorous plea for developing standards for evaluating the practices and the rules of the law, with the view to determining and clarifying the import of the legal order for human life. On the question of the paramount importance of such a double task, nothing divides me from him. No social institution, and certainly not the law, is exempt from moral criticism. And in my opinion it is one of the major, though not exclusive, tasks of an adequate philosophy of law to analyze proposed principles for assessing legal rules; to develop, in the light of such analysis, responsibly grounded criteria for evaluating the law; and to construct thereby the intellectual tools with the help of which we may form objective estimates of the worth of existing as well as of projected bodies of law.

It is a notorious fact, however, that on the basic issue as to the source and nature of standards of evaluation, philosophies of law are widely at variance, the variety of proposed standards and of their attempted validation being at least as great as the variety of moral theories in the history of thought. It is well to note, therefore, that the doctrine of natural law, either in its ancient or in its medieval formulations, is just *one* of many theories that have been advanced concerning the nature of the standards to be used. I must emphasize this obvious point, because in much recent literature the label "natural law doctrine" is often attached to almost any view which proposes objective standards for the moral evaluation of the law. In my opinion, this rather indiscriminate extension of the label debases the intellectual coinage, and produces little but confusion. But in any event, though I agree that the law is subject to moral criticism, and though I believe that the formal standards involved in such criticism may have an indefinitely large (if not universal) range of application, I wish explicitly to disavow any commitment, as a consequence of this belief, to what I take to be the distinctive tenets of natural law theory. And since my function in this symposium is simply that of a commentator, I can only register my conviction that natural law doctrine supplies neither a tenable nor a useful basis for evaluating existing law.

But despite my agreement with what I understand to be the aim of Professor Fuller's paper, I am frankly puzzled by the considerations he introduces to support his views; and I am not at all confident that I have grasped either his intent or his argument. I shall nevertheless try to show that 1) insofar as I do understand it, the contention upon which he places greatest weight is thoroughly unsound; 2) his implicit conception of purposive behavior and of human history is at least dubious; and 3) his premises are not obviously relevant for grounding his conclusions.

1) Professor Fuller begins his discussion by challenging what he calls the "truism" that "from *what is* nothing follows as to *what ought to be*." He bases his dissent on the claim that "in any interpretation of events which treats what is observed as purposive, fact and value merge," so that value judgments cannot be regarded as "something foreign to a purely factual account." (p. 69) Is this challenge of the dictum that what ought to be does not follow from what exists well taken?

a) The dictum may be, and indeed has been, interpreted to assert that statements of what is the case are always irrelevant to the determination of what ought to be. And if Professor Fuller finds the dictum so construed to be dubious, I must again admit my agreement with him. If, however, he is merely challenging the dictum when read this way, he has misunderstood many writers whom he has criticized for subscribing to the dictum, since they espouse the dictum with a different interpretation of it. There certainly have been thinkers in recent years, even among the group of so-called legal "realists" and "positivists," who, though they profess the truism Professor Fuller is questioning, also maintain that responsible claims as to what ought to be must be supported by empirical study of the physical, biological, and social requirements of human life, and of the import of various institutions and regulations. Within the framework of such a moral theory, judgments as to what ought to be done do not follow logically from judgments as to what is actual; nevertheless, judgments asserting what ought to be are conceived as hypotheses about ways of resolving conflicting needs and interests. Accordingly, though on this view there is a sharp distinction between what is and what ought to be, value judgments are not thereby regarded as foreign intrusions into the study of human behavior.

b) It seems unlikely, however, that Professor Fuller is claiming no more than that judgments of fact are *relevant* to the determination of the adequacy of judgments of value. For as he explicitly says, he believes that in the examination of purposive behavior the notions of fact and value merge, so that a sharp distinction between judgments of fact and judgments of value cannot be made. But I do not find this contention plausible. On the contrary, Professor Fuller's own example seems to me to reinforce the distinction he thinks he is undermining; and his discussion, insofar as I understand it, appears to me to establish what is at best a tautology.

i) I shall first try to show that Professor Fuller's illustration presupposes the distinction between fact and value. According to him, when we once grasp the purpose which actuates a boy's manipulation of a clam, we discover in the structure of events as they unroll "an element of value"; and we can anticipate whether a certain action will be continued or not, because the action is recognized as good or as bad as a means for achieving the boy's objective. But just how does the example show that fact and value *merge?* In characterizing one of the boy's actions as "bad," it is surely pertinent to ask *what* it is we are so characterizing; and the answer must inevitably be descriptive of a fact. Indeed, unless a careful factual account can be given, one which is not colored by a surreptitious value imputation, we cannot judge competently whether the act does have the value attributed to it. When a physician prescribes penicillin as good for the cure of pneumonia, his value judgment, if it is competently grounded, is predicated on the assumption that he knows the condition of the patient as well as the effects of the drug on the human body; and though the physician may tacitly assume the correctness of the factual data, and may be uninterested in the descriptive facts except insofar as they bear upon his aim to effect a cure, it is imperative to distinguish clearly between what the facts are and an evaluation of them with respect to a certain end. Similarly, when in a court of law an individual is on trial for a crime, it is imperative to establish with utmost care just what the person did do, before a judgment is rendered on the goodness or badness of his acts in relation to the crime with which he is charged. It is undoubtedly true that many people do not distinguish their value imputations from the facts they are judging; but this is surely regrettable, and does not mean that the distinction cannot be made. In short, I do not find that Professor Fuller has given us any reasons for holding that in discussing purposive behavior the distinction between judgments of fact and of value breaks down, or that in such contexts fact and value merge.

ii) I next want to argue that in claiming an element of "intrinsic" value to be present in situations involving purposive behavior, Professor Fuller is asserting what is at best a tautology. When we are dealing with such behavior, we are *by hypothesis* concerned with ascertaining among other things whether, and if so with what degree of effectiveness, a given set of actions contributes to the realization of some assumed goal. It would therefore be self-contradictory to maintain, on the one hand, that we are seeking to determine just what an act achieves in bringing about a certain end, and to deny, on the other hand, that in such an inquiry value judgments do occur because they are irrelevant. Indeed, whenever we are analyzing the operations of a system which is assumed to be a teleological or "goal-directed" one, *whether the system is a purely physical one or involves the presence of human agents,* value judgments necessarily occur with respect to the roles played by the component "parts" of the system in maintaining or progressively realizing specified "goals." All this, however, seems to me logically truistic, for it simply explicates what it is we are doing when we are studying purposive or other forms of teleological behavior. But although Professor Fuller maintains that in such inquiries the merging of fact and value can be demonstrated, I hope to have said enough to show that on this point he is mistaken. Moreover, while he explicitly notes the objection to his view that the actions he is considering are not "intrinsically" valuable, but possess a value only insofar as they are functional or dysfunctional in relation to specified ends, I have unfortunately not succeeded in ascertaining how he thinks he has turned the force of this objection.

2) There is, however, another thesis for which Professor Fuller also breaks a lance, but which is far from being a truistic one. He reminds us that the structure of purposive action is not constituted by a set of discrete happenings. He notes that even in the case of the working out of what is ostensibly an "immediate" or "single" purpose (as in the example of the boy manipulating a clam), a "congeries of related purposes" is in general operative, and that in consequence we cannot hope to understand the course of purposive action "simply by perceiving at any given moment whatever immediate purpose is then being pursued." (p. 70) So far these observations seem to me sound. But is the only alternative to an atomistic conception of human purposes and goals one which assumes that all immediate purposes, whether individual or social, are elements in a temporally developing but organically integrated system of ends? While I am not confident that I have understood the positive import of Professor Fuller's rejection of the atomistic conception, it is some such view as this which is suggested by much that he says.

[He declares, for example, that "any single human purpose . . . is an incomplete thing when severed from the total system of which it forms a part," (p. 71) and he also says that the meaning of any single purpose is always controlled by the "latent" purposes in interaction with it. Again, he asserts that in what he regards as the somewhat "mysterious" process wherein we determine "what we really want," we frequently consult with friends and so engage in a process of the "collaborative articulation of shared purposes"; (p. 73) and he cites the history of the common law as an example which teaches "how a social institution may derive its integrity and vitality from the same spirit of consultation as that which animates the discussion of two friends sharing a problem together." (p. 74)]

Such a view, in any case, I find incredible, for it is incompatible with the identifiable facts of contemporary human experience, as well as with the known character of human history. There is much evidence to show that individuals and groups sometimes engage in a collaborative process in which common goals are established and articulated. There is no evidence that the total life of a human individual or of the human race is a process in which a shared common purpose is gradually though imperfectly created and unfolded. (Indeed, I cannot make clear sense of the supposition that what is loosely called "human history" *is* a single *process.*) I cannot even see in the history of the common law the operation of such a process; and I find it gratuitous to assume that the manner in which legal precedents were used in courts of common law in the nineteenth century for settling historically novel issues, would have been regarded by seventeenth century common law judges as implementations of a common end-in-view, where that end-in-view was "then out of view because not stirred into active consciousness by the facts of the case being decided." (p. 74) An end-in-view that is nevertheless not explicitly present in active consciousness seems to me just a myth, the product of the same type of dubious reasoning which assumes that the outcome of a complex series of changes can be explained only by postulating the outcome as already "implicitly present" in the initial terms of the series.

I can on this occasion only assert dogmatically what seems to me obvious — that in actuality there are competing and even incompatible human objectives, both individual and social, and that the task of moral theory is to provide standards with the help of which such conflicts may in some measure be adjusted. Accordingly, the mere existence of purposes and goals does not settle the question as to what ought to be done when a moral problem arises. It is chiefly for this reason that the distinction between what is actual fact and what ought to be is both unavoidable and useful when moral deliberation is initiated. I should like to add, however, that though the assumption of a universally shared if tacit common human purpose is dubious, it does *not* follow that men with different "ultimate" objectives cannot live amicably together and cooperate effectively for the attainment of their diverse ends. The assumption that it *does* follow is just a mistake in analysis.

3) This brings me to my final difficulty with Professor Fuller's essay. I am entirely unclear how his claim concerning the fusion of fact and value, even if the claim were sound, is relevant to his belief in the possibility of an objective moral evaluation of the law, or what light that alleged fusion throws on the nature and authority of the principles to be employed in such evaluation. The norms for a responsible assessment of legal rules, so I am supposing, must codify the more enduring and general objectives of the institution of the law, on the basis of available though corrigible knowledge about individual and social needs. Such norms therefore provide a measure for judging the adequacy of existing legal arrangements and practices, and they supply general directives for estimating the worth of particular legal rules as well as for introducing needed changes in the law. These norms may not be invariant for all societies and for all times without thereby losing their authority for a given social order; and a philosophy of law sensitive to innovations in that order and to fresh knowledge about human needs and capacities will suitably modify its principles of evaluation. But implicit in this conception of the office of standards of criticism is the distinction between fact and value; and I do not see how, by denying that distinction, one can hope either to establish the need for such standards or to clarify their nature and function. A *fully embodied* ideal ceases to be an *ideal*; and an action is purposive only as long as the ends sought by that action have not already been achieved. It is only by a prolepsis that the qualities which may characterize the possible outcome of purposive behavior can be predicated as intrinsic features of that behavior. Accordingly, I find little but confusion in fuzzing the distinction between fact and value. By refusing to make that distinction we not only contribute nothing to the problem concerning the nature and role of principles of moral criticism. My fear is that by refusing to make it, or even by softening its edges, we are well on our way to ignoring that there is such a problem at all.

[3]

A REJOINDER TO PROFESSOR NAGEL

Lon L. Fuller

WHEN I HEARD that Professor Nagel would comment on my paper at the 1956 meeting of the Eastern Division of the American Philosophical Association I looked forward with real anticipation to learning his views on the central problem of my essay. I have never been content either with my own way of presenting that problem or with my somewhat groping attempts to answer it. Phrases like "a merger of fact and value" are unsatisfactory and serve not so much to extend knowledge as to acknowledge and chart its limits. I had hoped that a logician of Professor Nagel's acumen would either sharpen my phrasing of the problem or identify some fault in my analysis responsible for creating the appearance of a problem where none in fact existed.

So far as I can see, neither of these things happened; and by the time I reached the end of Professor Nagel's comments every hope I had entertained for a profitable exchange had been shattered. To be sure, Professor Nagel begins on a tentative note and with an expression of apologetic doubt whether he has truly understood my meaning. But as he proceeds, these uncertainties disappear; and before he is through, I am presented as someone intent on "fuzzing" the most obvious truths, presumably in the interest of some unclean social doctrine. Indeed, I am made to "break a lance" for the most extraordinary views: that the whole of human history is a single process which may be described as the unfolding of one purpose shared by all mankind; that if the judges of former centuries could revisit the earth they would recognize that our courts are merely bringing to more successful articulation what they had been trying to say centuries before, etc. When one is confronted by misinterpretations of this magnitude, it is hard to know where to begin in trying to re-establish effective communication. I shall, however, do my best.

The Meaning of "Natural Law"

In the first paragraph of my essay I recognized the difficulties which arise from the fact that the term "natural law" has many meanings. My object was to concentrate on one crucial issue which seems generally to be implicated whenever men speak of the opposition of the schools of "natural law" and "positivism." I considered it unwise to complicate that issue by attempting to pass judgment en route on the views of the differing schools of thought which may be brought under the common rubric of "natural law."

This invitation to narrow the scope of the inquiry was declined by Professor Nagel. He assumes that there is some single body of beliefs called "the natural law doctrine" which may safely be left undefined, and that he is in a position to assert that this undefined doctrine "supplies neither a tenable nor a useful basis for evaluating existing law." He also feels justified in asserting that this "doctrine" is one that I do not find "uncongenial."

To avoid further misunderstanding I should like to record here that I do not accept any "doctrine of natural law" which asserts one or more of the following propositions: 1) the notion that the demands of natural law can be the subject of an authoritative pronouncement; 2) the notion that there is something called "*the* natural law" capable of concrete application like a written code; 3) the notion that there is a "higher law" transcending the concerns of this life against which human enactments must be measured and declared invalid in case of conflict. I do not know whether Professor Nagel regards as a perversion of language any theory that calls itself "natural law" and at the same time makes the exclusions I have just outlined. If he does, I can only plead in defense that this particular perversion is at least as ancient as Aristotle, in whom I find no trace of the elements I reject.

On the affirmative side, I discern, and share, one central aim common to all the schools of natural law, that of discovering those principles of social order which will enable men to attain a satisfactory life in common. It is an acceptance of the possibility of "discovery" in the moral realm that seems to me to distinguish all the theories of natural law from opposing views. In varying measure, it is assumed in all theories of natural law that the process of moral discovery is a social one, and that there is something akin to a "collaborative articulation of shared purposes" by which men come to understand better their own ends and to discern more clearly the means for achieving them.

Apparently this notion of a "collaborative articulation of shared purposes" is to Professor Nagel the sheerest nonsense, with the qualification that "individuals and groups" do at times "engage in a collaborative process by which common goals are established and articulated." The meaning of this concession, and the reason it is restricted as it is, are unclear to me. The explanation nearest at hand is that Professor Nagel believes that collaboration of the type I have envisaged is possible only within a group where some uniformity of moral values has already been impressed on its members by a common social environment. If this is the meaning intended, it remains puzzling why collaborative discussion could clarify or improve a culturally conditioned uniformity; a man scarcely turns to his fellows for assistance in discerning what the forces of his environment compel him to do; one hardly needs help in responding to inevitability. I am inclined to believe that even with respect to the small group Professor Nagel means something different by his articulation of common goals than I do when I speak of an articulation of shared purposes. He apparently believes that even within the small group it is absurd to think that a pooling of insight and experience could assist the members of the group to understand more truly their own ends. This interpretation seems to be supported by the fact that Professor Nagel couples the "articulation" of common goals with their "establishment." Apparently he has in mind that "common goals," that is, goals already understood and shared, may be "articulated" by being brought unchanged to adequate verbal expression, and may then be "established," that is, given some formal sanction as a part of the rules governing the activities of the group. Beyond this he seems unwilling to concede any function to collective intellectual effort.

At this point I encounter what is to me the most puzzling aspect of the philosophy implied in Professor Nagel's comments. On the one hand, he seems to reject as intellectual folly any collaborative quest for a better understanding of the proper ends of a society. At the same time, he castigates "the doctrine of natural law" for pretending to be the only theory that attempts to formulate "objective standards for the moral evaluation of the law." This claim he counters by asserting that the natural law doctrine is only one of many ethical theories professing to offer "objective standards" of moral evaluation. One wishes at this point he had identified at least one of these rival theories and had explained how it is that a standard can be "objective" and yet not be capable of improvement by common intellectual effort.

One can understand the reluctance of a scholar to force within the compass of a short article a discussion of subtle and complex theories. On this ground one may excuse Professor Nagel's failure to specify and describe any ethical theory that does not profess "the natural law doctrine" and yet yields "objective standards for the moral evaluation of the law." This excuse could have been claimed with better grace, however, had the same scholarly restraint been applied to the discussion of natural law, where Professor Nagel seems quite content to deal and judge in terms of verbal slogans.

Perhaps it is unfair to suggest that Professor Nagel has applied a double standard of scholarly restraint in dealing with his friends and his foes. He obviously considers that my article demanded a counterattack and he may therefore rightly claim the license accorded the polemicist. If this be conceded, it still remains true that his failure to take a clear position with respect to any ethical theory other than that of natural law makes it difficult to discern the vantage point from which he dispatches his critical shafts. In a concluding section of this reply I shall indicate the sort of ethical theory that seems to be implied in Professor Nagel's statement of his position. Meanwhile, it is first necessary to clarify the crucial issue that separates us.

Toward a Delimitation of the Issues

One argument made by Professor Nagel seems to me to be quite unresponsive to any issue raised by my article. This is his declaration that what I am asserting "is at best a tautology," and amounts to saying that there is an element of evaluation in any inquiry which seeks to determine how effectively a purposive system (such as a machine or a human being) is accomplishing its objective. I must say that however groping and unsatisfactory my discussion may be, I do not think I was foolish enough to advance as an important truth the proposition that evaluation equals evaluation.

I have never denied that there are two postures of the mind toward reality that can be called "descriptive" and "evaluative." The question I proposed for discussion was whether an attempt at description can succeed in eliminating evaluative elements when it is addressed toward the functioning of a purposive system. It was precisely because I wished to raise this question without running the risk of falling into a tautology that I chose my illustration of the boy with the clam, where descriptive and evaluative efforts cannot at the outset be considered as being carried on simultaneously because we do not at first know what the boy is trying to do.

Another false issue seems to me to be raised by those passages in Professor Nagel's article in which he appears to say that I am, in effect, counselling snap judgments, that if my views were taken seriously the physician would feel free to prescribe remedies without diagnosing his patient's condition, the judge to sentence the accused without hearing the evidence, etc. I see nothing in my position suggesting any disparagement of careful observation, painstaking analysis, patient reflection, or the fair treatment of defendants. Professor Nagel's assumption to the contrary simply reflects his belief that none of these desiderata will be achieved unless we are prepared to accept his views concerning the nature of the evaluative process. This simply brings us back to the central issue of the whole debate.

Still another general point is made which, it seems to me, in no way advances our discussion. This consists in asserting that my "premises are not obviously relevant for grounding my conclusions." By this I take it Professor Nagel means to suggest that even if I were correct in what I have to say about the relation of "is" and "ought," I would still have established nothing "obviously relevant" to the assertions made, and the questions raised, in the latter part of my article. Certainly I can understand why Professor Nagel is unable to discern any clear line of thought connecting the various portions of my article. Essentially he seems to regard the questions I raise concerning the relation of "is" and "ought" as nonsensical. If I myself were to encounter an ethical theory which took as its starting point the question whether all garks are savigrous I, like Professor Nagel, would have difficulty in seeing what either an affirmative or negative answer to that question would entail.

It is Professor Nagel's deep conviction that the question I am raising is nonsensical which is responsible, I believe, for the truly colossal failure of communication which has taken place between us. The fact that he approaches my whole article with that conviction has made it impossible for him to approach sympathetically the notions I was trying to expound in the last part of my article, though I regret to say it has not prevented him from passing some sweeping negative judgments about views which he seems obviously not to have understood. If there is any hope for understanding, it must lie in a clarification of the basic issue raised by my article.

A Restatement of the Issues Raised in my Article

As I see it, two closely related issues are raised by the exchange between Professor Nagel and myself:

(1) Is it always possible to give an adequate non-evaluative account of any object that is itself the subject of an evaluation?

(2) If so, does evaluation become legitimate (or "competent") only when its object is first identified by such a non-evaluative account?

If I understand him correctly Professor Nagel gives an affirmative answer to both of these questions. While the assumption that an affirmative answer is the proper one runs through his whole article, so far as I can see Professor Nagel devotes only five sentences to what seems to be an argument for his position. These five sentences are as follows:

> I shall first try to show that Professor Fuller's illustration presupposes

> the distinction between fact and value. According to him, when we once grasp the purpose which actuates a boy's manipulation of a clam, we discover in the structure of events as they unroll "an element of value"; and we can anticipate whether a certain action will be continued or not, because the action is regarded as good or as bad as a means for achieving the boy's objective. But just how does the example show that fact and value *merge?* In characterizing one of the boy's actions as "bad," it is surely pertinent to ask *what* it is we are so characterizing; and the answer must inevitably be descriptive of a fact. Indeed, unless a careful factual account can be given, one that is not colored by surreptitious value imputation, we cannot judge competently whether the act does have the value attributed to it.[1]

If there is any "tautology" in our exchange, I submit it lies in these sentences. If it were true, as Professor Nagel assumes, that we can always give two distinct accounts of any course of purposive action, each adequate within its own realm, the one descriptive, the other evaluative, then it would certainly follow that the evaluative account would constitute a judgment or a series of judgments about the object of the descriptive account. The question is whether this separation of the two kinds of accounts is always possible or profitable, and whether accuracy of description is always promoted by eliminating evaluative judgments.

In my illustration of the boy and the clam I had supposed that even if we were interested in the "pure fact" of the occurrences there related — say, in the directions and dimensions of the boy's physical movements — we could envisage that "pure fact" more accurately if we knew what the boy was trying to do. The effect of a disclosure of the boy's purpose in bringing about a sudden enlargement of perspective was to be explained in part, I had assumed, because we were now in a position to participate vicariously in a process of evaluation; that is, we could now understand (and thus describe more accurately even in purely physical terms) what happened when the boy moved from one activity to another. These suppositions still seem to me to be completely justified, and I find no reason advanced by Professor Nagel for abandoning them.

In understanding the point of my illustration it should be noted that it does not relate to a single action, but to a course of conduct extending through time, in which transitions from one act to another are determined by judgments as to what is apt and what is not for the accomplishment of the boy's purpose. In this connection I should like to recall a passage in my

1. *Supra*, 79.

article, the thought of which seems to me to be largely ignored in Professor Nagel's criticism:

> [W]hen we are dealing with purposive action projected through time, the structure that we observe, recall, and report lies, not in any instantaneous state of affairs, but in a course of happening, which can be understood only if we participate in a process of evaluation by which the bad is rejected and the good retained.[2]

The insistence that there must always be something that can be described in non-evaluative terms before evaluation itself can be justified reminds one of the controversy about empirical verification that arose out of the movement called logical positivism. Logical positivism started with the proposition that it is only those sentences which can be "empirically verified" that are meaningful, that is, proper subjects for intelligent discussion and argument. As it gradually became clear what complexities inhere in the notion of empirical verification, particularly as applied to "a sentence," the adherents of logical positivism found it necessary to retreat from their original position. A convenient cover for this retreat was found in the notion of verification "in principle." It having been discovered that it was impossible in practice to give a meaningful account of what would be involved in actually verifying a sentence empirically, the original proposition was modified to read: "Only those sentences are meaningful that are *in principle* subject to empirical verification." So in a similar manner we now find it being asserted that "in principle" evaluation never becomes justified until we have described accurately in non-evaluative terms the thing we are evaluating.

How far this insistence can be carried is illustrated in the comments of another critic. In a book discussed by this writer I had remarked that if we were confronted by a dubious assemblage of mechanical parts and were to ask of it, "Is it a steam engine?" and, "Is it a good steam engine?" these two questions would "overlap mightily."[3] My critic responded that this is not necessarily so at all and indicated that the whole difficulty could be removed by a little definitional ingenuity. He suggested that by stipulation we might define a steam engine in non-evaluative terms, as requiring certain parts, arranged in a certain relationship to one another.[4] Of course, an attempt at such a definition might be made, but what earthly purpose could

2. *Supra*, 70.
3. THE LAW IN QUEST OF ITSELF 11-12 (1940).
4. Samuel Mermin, *The Study of Jurisprudence—A Letter to a Hostile Student*, 49 MICHIGAN LAW REVIEW 39, 65 (1950).

it serve unless it be to support "in principle" a philosophic position taken in advance and now confronted by an embarrassing example? Parenthetically, it can be confidently predicted that the attempt at a "non-evaluative" definition of a steam engine would inevitably miss its mark; ambiguities would always be latent in the definition which would have to be resolved in favor of that meaning most apt in describing a machine fit to serve the general purpose of a steam engine. Professor Nagel's position seems to be essentially that of the critic just discussed. He too supports the rigid separation "in principle" of "is" and "ought," though he cautiously refrains from informing us how he himself would describe in non-evaluative terms those physical actions which he would categorize as "good" or "bad" attempts to open a clam.

In seeking to keep the discussion of the relation of "fact" and "value" on a level where misunderstanding is least likely, I have emphasized in my writings situations involving physical movements and artifacts like chairs and steam engines. This is the arena of discussion most uncongenial to the tentative conclusions I have attempted to convey, for here what I have to say runs counter to the tacit assumptions of language itself. It is on this elementary level that unreflective common sense is most inclined to embrace the fallacies of what may be called the pointer theory of meaning.

If we move the discussion to the realm of legal and moral ideas, the whole controversy assumes a different aspect. Here the picture of a kind of evaluative finger pointing itself toward "things" loses even the specious appeal it has in more elementary contexts. During the oral discussion of my paper I attempted unsuccessfully to induce Professor Nagel to state how he would deal with problems of the following sort: Let us suppose a rule of the common law. Though this rule is treated by lawyers, judges, and legal scholars as if it were a single, existent thing, it never receives quite the same verbal formulation in any two statements of it. In such a situation evaluation may be comparatively easy. To those who have given serious thought to the problems involved, it may be possible to range the various formulations of "the rule" roughly on a scale of adequacy; in any event it is easy to recognize gross ineptitudes. But what shall we say of "existence"? What "is" the thing, or what "are" the things, lawyers have in mind when they agree in saying, "*This* is a poor formulation of *the* rule"? In neither case can the "thing" be mere words on paper, for the same words will provoke different responses in different readers. A perceptive reader may pass over almost unnoticed an inadequacy in formulation, since his mind seizes at once the thought toward which the author was groping unsuccessfully. The mind of a less perceptive reader may waver in indecision among various obscure and unsatisfactory meanings. The same uncertainty of response even more obviously makes impossible a definition of "the rule" in terms of patterns of human behavior. I have asked, and I ask again: In this sort of context how do we apply the dogma that before we can evaluate we must first define clearly in non-evaluative terms the thing it is we are evaluating?

The fundamental article of the positivist faith is that "law" either exists or does not and that no evaluation is involved in reaching a judgment about its existence. I have tried to show the difficulty in maintaining this belief when we apply it to "law" in the sense of a "rule of law." But suppose the question to be, not that of the existence of a particular rule of law, but of a legal order. Here again the view of positivism is that a legal system can be thoroughly "bad" from top to bottom by any number of standards and yet be a regime of law. But by what process of judgment do we decide whether something "is" a legal order?

I suppose that no one would discern a "legal order" in any of the following imaginary situations: 1) verbal directives called laws are issued by something that calls itself a government, but there is no discernible correspondence whatever between the acts of those who purport to enforce the law and the rules they purport to enforce; 2) verbal directives called laws are issued, but they are all kept secret or are published in a cipher known only to the legislator; 3) verbal directives called laws are issued, but they are all retrospective in effect and no prospective laws are ever enacted. In all of these situations there is so gross a departure from the ideal of a legal order, even of an order devoted to evil ends, that nothing exists in any of them we would be tempted to call "law." Yet the ideal of a legal order is never attained perfectly. In all legal systems there is some discrepancy between formal rules and governmental actions taken pursuant to them. Everywhere we encounter the problem of poorly drafted rules and rules that are conveyed inadequately to those who are affected by them. Probably all governments have from time to time undertaken to cure past irregularities by retroactive statutes.

If what I have just said is correct, it follows that the "existence" of a legal order is always a matter of degree and cannot be measured in "non-evaluative" terms. How, then, in determining whether a legal order "exists" do we distinguish between the "existent thing" and its "value"? Or is the doctrine of a strict separation of "is" and "ought" to be rescued once more "in principle"? Will the answer be that there must always exist in a given society some particular complex of words, attitudes, and actions before I can say of it, "This falls short of the ideal of a legal order"? What utility is there in this insistence if in fact the only significant thing I can say about this social complex is that it *does* fall short of the ideal of a legal order? Surely it would be absurd to assert that I must colligate in "neutral" terms every existent thing embraced by such a judgment before the judgment itself can be "competent." To do so would be like saying that unless we can trace the precise trajectory of a marksman's bullet we have no right to assert that it missed the target. Surely we can say that a legal system is missing its target without having to report the precise angle of divergence of every human action that contributes to that missing. We can also say of something that calls itself a legal order that it is missing that target so woefully that it cannot in any meaningful sense be termed a system of law. It has, if you will, so little "value" that it has ceased to "exist."

Until Professor Nagel, or someone sharing his views and possessing his logical acumen, is prepared to take a position with reference to questions of the sort I have just posed, there seems no escape from the conclusion that for the time being professional philosophers of his school of thought are more concerned with supporting a theory taken in abstraction from the law than they are with lending a hand in solving the problems of legal philosophy.

Fact and Value in the Administration of the Law

In his brief reference to courts of law, Professor Nagel appears to assume that the administration of the law presents no special difficulties for his view. Indeed he seems to believe that it is especially obvious in the law that evaluation cannot be competent unless it is directed toward an object first identified in non-evaluative terms. I believe, on the contrary, that an open-minded examination of legal problems will reveal how impossible it is to maintain in any actual process of human decision a rigid separation of fact and value of the kind recommended by Professor Nagel.

The great advantage of the study of legal materials lies in the fact that the law cannot be content to maintain a distinction "in principle"; if it accepts a distinction as sound, it is compelled to find some way of giving effective expression to it in the actual decision of controversies. If it is believed that a witness must report what he saw in completely non-evaluative terms, then the judge must decide what questions may properly be addressed to him and what forms his responses may take. Let me illustrate the difference between problems as they arise in the administration of the law and as they are likely to be conceived in philosophic discourse.

Two philosophers are debating about "value" and "fact." One of them says, "It is not true that evaluation only becomes possible if its object can be identified in non-evaluative terms. For example, I can say of a dancer, 'He is trying to tango, but is not succeeding.' I can say this even though it would be impossible for me to describe what he is in fact doing." His opponent, quite undisturbed by this example, may reply, "Ah, but there must always exist some pattern of motions to which your value judgment that his attempt to tango is unsuccessful can apply; otherwise it would be meaningless. The more accurately this pattern is described, the more competent will be the value judgment passed on it." There the matter has to rest.

Suppose, however, that a dancing couple is employed by a night club on the basis of an assurance that they can do all the standard ballroom steps. On their first appearance a tango is played, and they are discharged for being unable to tango. They bring suit for improper discharge. In support of its case the company operating the night club wishes to put on the stand various patrons who were present during the disputed dance. The judge must now decide what form their testimony may take. Will they be required to describe the dance performed in terms of physical motions, leaving it to the jury to determine whether the dance so described is an adequate tango? Or will they be permitted (subject to cross examination on their competence) to say something like, "Whatever they were doing, it was not a tango"?

The philosopher may be inclined to distrust the alleged lessons of legal experience. He may consider that the judicial process is surrounded by an air of exigence not conducive to clarity of analysis, or that the law to get its job done has to make compromises that would not be tolerated in philosophic discussion. I do not think the possible contribution of the law to philosophic theory can be dismissed so casually. After all, the most relevant peculiarity of the law lies in its responsibility to reach and explain decisions. It seems to me that modern epistemology is coming more and more to recognize that there is an element of responsible decision in all intellectual activities, including those of science.[5] One philosopher suggests that the present "age of analysis" is giving way to an "age of decision."[6] Surely if this is true the decisional science called law should offer something of interest to the epistemologist.

I have already tried to show that in legal reasoning generally no such distinction as that insisted on by Professor Nagel is or can be made. Consider, for example, the rules which state under what circumstances the various

5. Michael Polanyi, The Logic of Liberty (1951).
6. Morton Gabriel White, Toward Reunion in Philosophy (1956).

forms of legal responsibility arise. Most of these rules will turn on fault or negligence. A enters into an oral agreement with B: he thinks he said one thing; B interpreted him to mean something else. In general the principle is that there is no contract if both were at fault in the misunderstanding or if both were without blame. If, however, one was negligent while the other was not, the court will enforce the contract in accordance with the understanding of the prudent party. The term "negligence" is plainly a term of evaluation, but there is generally in the law no "non-evaluative" colligation of the things or instances to which this term should be applied. The ways of missing the target are countless and unpredictable; they can only be given a meaningful classification under the rubric "misses."

Again, though it is said to be the function of a jury to determine "facts," when a jury is asked to bring in a special verdict, the question addressed to it will almost invariably be one soliciting what in philosophic discussions would be regarded as an evaluation: "Was the defendant proceeding with due care?" "Was the apartment in suitable condition for occupancy?"

Generally speaking it is only with respect to the testimony of witnesses that it becomes possible even to consider maintaining a distinction between evaluating and identifying the object of the evaluation in "neutral" or "factual" terms. There is in this field an interesting experiment directed toward giving effective legal sanction to the desideratum urged so strongly by Professor Nagel. This is the Opinion Rule as developed in this country, though not followed in England or on the Continent. In general terms this rule states that an ordinary witness who has observed some event may testify only to what he heard and saw; he may not give "opinions."

Under this rule a witness who observed an accident when an automobile skidded on glare ice may not tell the jury that the defendant was going "too fast"; he must instead attempt to estimate the speed of the car in miles per hour and leave it to the jury to say whether operating a car at that speed under the conditions then obtaining was an act of negligence. Again, a witness may not describe a fence along a railroad right of way as being "not in a fit condition to turn cattle," but must attempt some more "factual" account of its condition, from which the jury may decide whether a fence so described was "fit" to turn cattle.

There have always been exceptions to this rule. Curiously, one of the most firmly established is that relating to testimony concerning economic value. Under this exception a plaintiff is permitted to testify, for example, to the value of services rendered as a part-time housekeeper or to the value of a used desk lost in shipment. Other exceptions permit the witness to say that a person "looked angry," or "acted insane," or "seemed to be sick." Perhaps statements of the last-mentioned variety might be dismissed from the present discussion on the ground that, although they may be called "opinions," they are not evaluative. I suggest, however, that the difficulty in knowing just what kinds of testimony should be regarded as "evaluative" is something that should be pondered before Professor Nagel's view is accepted as a general guide in the actual solution of legal problems of proof.

With all its exceptions and qualifications, the Opinion Rule has been condemned, I believe, by every careful student of the law of evidence.[7] The reason for this condemnation does not lie in the notion that the jury ought to have the benefit of the witness's opinion or "value judgment." It is rather that in many situations it is simply impossible for the witness to communicate to the jury the fact of what he saw in non-evaluative terms; he can feel more assured of his own honesty if he says "the car was going too fast when it skidded," than if he is compelled to give an estimate of its speed in miles per hour. Of course, the conclusion that a statement of value, "too fast," may be the most effective way of communicating a situation of fact to the jury presupposes some community of purpose and some common human nature shared by the witness and the jury. Some may regard this as a fatal objection to it. But those concerned with the actual administration of the law have to accept this supposition if it seems to have reality in the discourse of man with man.

Ends Out of View and the Collaborative Articulation of Shared Purposes

We now reach that portion of my article where, in Professor Nagel's opinion, absurdity reaches its acme and where he confesses he finds my views "incredible."

With respect to the "end out of view," Professor Nagel's demonstration of the absurdity of my remarks is somewhat facilitated by a misquotation in which I am made to speak of the "end-in-view" being "out of view." While I certainly said nothing like that, the idea I attempted to convey was that in

7. 7 WIGMORE ON EVIDENCE §§1917-1929 (3d ed., 1940). MCCORMICK, EVIDENCE 19-28 (1954); AMERICAN LAW INSTITUTE, MODEL CODE OF EVIDENCE, Rule 401 (1942). The virtual abolition of the rule as it existed in the American common law in Rule 401 of the CODE is thus explained, p. 201: "Where a witness is attempting to communicate the impressions made upon his senses by what he has perceived, any attempt to distinguish between so-called fact and opinion is likely to result in profitless quibbling. Analytically no such distinction is possible."

disposing of controversies and issuing directives we may operate within a framework of purposes which conditions our decisions even though only certain of these purposes are called into consciousness by the facts of the case at hand. Although I had thought of this as being an almost obvious truth of psychology, it is for Professor Nagel a "myth."

All I can assert in response is that I am unable to attribute any clear meaning to Professor Nagel's discussion of this point. What he *seems* to say — which I in turn find "incredible"— is that our actions and words can never be directed or conditioned by any end or assumption not actively present in consciousness. If this were so, I could not go into the library and come back absorbed in reading a book unless I had formed the conscious purpose of returning to my office. I am puzzled by Professor Nagel's failure to touch even tangentially on the illustration I borrowed from Wittgenstein. I say to another person, "Show these children a game." The possibility that this might be taken to mean they should be taught to throw dice does not enter my mind. Had the addressee of my remarks been a notorious gambler, I might well have added, "but not your kind of game." In the actual context of my remark, however, there was as little reason to give conscious attention to that possibility as there is for me to ask myself as I get out of bed in the morning whether the floor will be still there to receive me. In his illustration Wittgenstein asks whether I can truthfully say, "I did not mean that kind of game," only if I had consciously considered the throwing of dice and had consciously excluded it. I can see no justification for Professor Nagel's casual dismissal of this problem with such epithets as "myth" and "product of dubious reasoning."

Closely associated with the notion of "the end out of view" was my discussion of the "collaborative articulation of shared purposes." Here again Professor Nagel seems to me to say nothing to which I can respond except by trying to convey more adequately the point I attempted to make in the first place.

Let me this time give an illustration in the form of a series of imaginary judicial decisions. Of necessity, my presentation will be schematic, and I shall have to leave it to the reader familiar with the growth of the common law to say whether I have truthfully portrayed any aspect of the judicial process. The cases that follow are given in the order of their assumed chronology. The parties in each case are different persons, but to facilitate comparisons the symbols used to designate the parties will be the same throughout and will indicate the role played by the particular party; thus in all five cases *O* will designate the original owner of the horse which came by theft or fraud into the hands of *T*.

Case No. 1. *T* steals *O's* horse and sells it to *G*, who pays full value for it and had no reason to know it had been stolen from *O*. *O* brings suit against *G* to recover the horse. *Held*, for *O*. One of the deterrents to thievery is the difficulty of disposing of stolen goods. If a purchaser like *G* were able to take free of the claim of the true owner, a market for stolen goods would be created and, thus, an incentive to theft. In any event, it was impossible for *T*, a thief who had no rightful title to the horse, to pass any title to *G*; he who has nothing can give nothing.

Case No. 2. *T* buys a horse from *O* giving as payment a forged note purporting to be that of *X*. *T* knew that the note was forged. After delivering the horse to *T*, *O* discovers that he has been defrauded. He brings suit against *T* to recover the horse. It is argued on behalf of *T* that *O* delivered the horse to him with the intent to confer title; the horse is now *T's*, and *O's* only remedy is to sue for the price. *Held*, for *O*. The passage of title was vitiated by the fraud of *T*; title throughout remained in *O*.

Case No. 3. The case is similar to *Case No. 2*, except that after receiving possession of the horse, *T* sold it to *G*, who knew that *T* had bought it from *O*, but had no reason to know that *T* had worked any fraud on *O*. *O* brings suit against *G* to recover the horse. It is argued on behalf of *O* that title remained in him in accordance with the principle laid down in *Case No. 2*. Since *T* had no title, he could pass none to *G*. *Held*, for *G*. It would be an intolerable burden on commerce if purchasers of property were compelled to scrutinize the details of a transaction by which the former owner voluntarily delivered it into the hands of the person now offering it for sale. Fraud takes many and subtle forms; if the victim could not recognize it, it is unreasonable to ask of a stranger to the transaction that he ascertain whether it was present. With respect to *Case No. 2*, all that was said there was with reference to the legal relations between the owner and the defrauder; the court's mind was not directed toward the possibility that a subsequent purchaser, like *G*, might intervene. The principle we are here applying is that if the horse is in the hands of *T*, or of someone who knew of his fraud, it may be recovered by *O*. In the hands of an innocent purchaser like *G*, the horse may not be recovered by *O*, for reasons we have already indicated.

Case No. 4. The case is like *Case No. 3*, except that after buying the horse from *T*, *G* sold it to *K*, who, before he bought the horse from *G*, had been informed of the fraud worked by *T* on *O*. *O* sues *K* to recover the horse. It is argued on behalf of *O* that *K* was not an innocent purchaser, since he knew of *T's* fraud when he bought the horse. In accordance with the principle laid down in *Case No. 3*, *O* became entitled to the horse when it came into the hands of *K*. *Held*, for *K*. If the argument made by *O* were accepted, it would be possible for a person in the position of *O* to destroy the value of the title acquired by *G* simply by giving general publicity to the fact that *T* had induced the sale by fraud. Thus the objective of protecting the bona fide purchaser *G* would be defeated, for his property would become unsaleable. When the court in *Case No. 3* said that *O* could recover the horse from anyone who knew of the fraud of *T*, it did not have in mind the possibility that the horse might have passed previously through the hands of a bona fide purchaser like *G*. When the horse was bought from *T* by *G*, title to it was perfected and was no longer vulnerable to attack by *O*. *G* was then free to sell it to anyone he saw fit.

At this point I urge the reader to stop and consider whether we are now at the end of this development, and whether there is any new situation likely to arise which will require a reformulation of the principles laid down in *Case No. 4*. When he has assured himself on that point, he may proceed to

Case No. 5. This case is like *Case No. 4*, except that *K* not only knew of *T's* fraud, but had participated in it by forging *X's* name on the note used by *T* to pay *O* for the horse. *O* sues *K* to recover the horse. *K* rests his defense on the reasoning of *Case No. 4*; *G* had title to the horse and was free to sell it to anyone he saw fit. If *K* was guilty of any misconduct, that is a question for the criminal law; it ought not to affect his property rights. *Held?* . . . Perhaps the point of my illustration will be most effectively conveyed if at this point I leave to the reader, not only the burden of decision, but the more onerous burden of explanation.

To me it does not seem absurd to claim that the series of cases I have reported reveals something that might be called "the collaborative articulation of shared purposes." If this expression seems too pretentious, I would be content to say that these cases show that communication among men, and a consideration by them of different situations of fact, can enable them to see more truly what they were all trying to do from the beginning. In answer to Professor Nagel's contention that nothing like this can happen except in a tightly knit group, I suggest that, without losing their point at all, the five cases I have reported might each be separated by a half century from its predecessor, and that the courts which decided them might be those of five different nations. To be sure, the legal development I have suggested would be unintelligible to a human being who knew nothing of property, or of sale, or of contract. But what is the use of a search through time and space for this creature, unless it be to discredit any attempt to discover and articulate those principles which will promote a satisfactory life in common for the human beings we know and understand, and by whom we can in turn be understood?

I hope it will be clear to the reader, as apparently it was not to Professor Nagel, that I am not foolish enough to suppose that the whole essence of legal history is compacted in the phrase, "the collaborative articulation of shared purposes." The history of the common law reveals many things, including instances of wooden literalness and even of corruption. All I am asserting is that the development indicated in my series of imaginary cases is one important aspect of legal history. How important it will be in the future depends upon whether it is Professor Nagel's philosophy of adjudication that is accepted or that which I have attempted to express here.

Before leaving the question of the efficacy of collective endeavor in defining moral and legal ends, I should like to raise for brief consideration the problem of the utility of hypothetical or imaginary cases. Throughout the centuries it has been thought that such cases may be useful in legal and moral discussions. It has been believed that sounder decisions will be reached when a wide range of such cases has been taken into account. I should like to ask how such cases fit into Professor Nagel's views of the decisional process. To be sure, we can expect him to say that they are admissible whenever their facts can be defined in non-evaluative terms. But the question is not whether they are admissible, but *why* are they useful? Am I again falling into an absurdity if I suggest they are useful because they facilitate a process I have called the collaborative articulation of shared purposes?

What is at Stake?

I have already indicated the difficulties that confront me in responding to Professor Nagel's contention that even if my premises were correct they would not justify my conclusions. Since from nonsense nothing follows — not even more nonsense — it is a little hard to know what one can say at this point in self-defense.

I can only affirm my conviction that the differences between him and me are of fundamental importance. At the present time the prevailing philosophy of ethics seems to me to have descended to a level of triviality that is truly appalling. It is my belief that this decline has been due to a general acceptance of the thesis espoused by Professor Nagel.

Perhaps I can best convey my view of the present state of ethical theory by saying it calls to mind a picture something like this. A human being, *A*, is engaged in doing some act, such as giving money to a beggar, or paying a gambling debt, or dragging the unconscious victim of an automobile accident to the side of the road. An observer, *O*, points to *A's* action and is heard to say, "This is good." At this signal ethical theoreticians begin swarming in from all sides. Their first act is to relieve the scene of the encumbrance of *A*, who is ousted without ceremony. This done, all gather round *O* and embark on a lively disputation in which everyone talks at once. How shall we characterize that sentence *O* just uttered, "This is good"? What is its "semiotic status"? Is it a mere ejaculation equally meaningful and equally meaningless, whether emitted in private or in public? Is it, in other words, like the "um-um" of a man enjoying a pot roast? Or is it perhaps a kind of news report to others about *O's* inner state? Is it such a report coupled with an invitation to others that they join in this inner state? Or instead of being viewed as a mere invitation, shall *O's* remark be interpreted as demanding or claiming that others should or must share his approving glow? Is *O* announcing an invitation or a directive that others do what *A* was just observed to do? At this point someone is heard to shout, "You are wrong, *O*. What *A* did was bad, not good." *O* starts to defend himself, but before he can complete a sentence the theorists swarm round him again and begin debating the kinds of demonstrations or assertions that *O* may properly employ in supporting his position. Can he only say, "Well, I feel that way"? Or can he adduce something that can be called "proof," "validation," "justification," or "explanation" for his position? What is the quintessential difference between proving a fact and demonstrating that a value judgment is right?

So the debate moves in endless circles. If the reader thinks there is exaggeration in my figurative account, I suggest that he consult the literal, sober, and useful report made in the 1957 issue of the FORUM by Professor Nakhnikian.[8] If ethical theory is ever to escape from the wordy muddle in which it is now bogged down, I suggest that the first step will have to be to bring *A* back on the scene. If we consult with him we shall learn that his act was not an isolated event, but a response to a problem or an opportunity, and that this response was that of a whole man, or of a man trying, feebly or forcefully, to become or to remain whole. Before we can pass judgment on *A's* response we shall have to inquire whether *A* had adequately defined the situation — that is, the problem or the opportunity — that presented itself to him. We shall have to inquire whether there were other responses available to *A* that would have been more apt. We shall have also to ask

8. George Nakhnikian, *Contemporary Ethical Theories and Jurisprudence,* 2 NATURAL LAW FORUM 4 (1957).

whether *A* gave enough thought to defining the situation and to selecting his own response, or whether, perhaps, he wasted his time in giving more thought to these problems than the situation properly demanded. As we ask these questions it will become increasingly apparent that we are no longer concerned with an isolated action, but with a process of living and deciding. If in this transition we lose the existent datum toward which *O* pointed an approving finger, we shall in compensation regain contact with questions that are real in the lives of human beings.

The poverty of the results produced by so many empirical studies of human attitudes and preferences seems also to be traceable to a methodology deriving essentially from the position taken by Professor Nagel. No one would deny, I suppose, that human attitudes and preferences characteristically change with time. It is also clear, I believe, that if the organization and proper orientation of the attitudes and preferences under study is a problem, not only for the individuals being studied, but also for the observer, the observer will be unable to predict the future course of these attitudes and preferences. One who knows the answer to a puzzle can often predict roughly the steps another will follow in solving it; if the observer is ignorant of the answer, he can only participate vicariously in the process of solution. In this participation the "clear" distinction between what is observed and its appraisal disappears. Where human attitudes and preferences are of real interest they generally relate to problems of life that are problems equally for the observer and for the observed. The consequence is that if the social scientist studying attitudes and preferences is to secure anything that can be called a reportable "datum," he must take toward his subject a point of view that effects a cross section through time, producing a kind of instantaneous snapshot arresting all motion and development. This operation does violence to the nature of the thing under observation, so that its essential reality is lost. When an attempt is made to restore at least a part of that reality, it consists in taking a series of snapshots, spaced through time and revealing a "trend." If this "trend" conveys any significant meaning, it is generally because in interpreting it we surreptitiously reintroduce the process of vicarious evaluation that was ruled out by Professor Nagel's maxim at the outset. The result is that after a study conducted by the method I have described, our understanding of the subject matter often seems to have been impoverished rather than enriched.

No one would dream of following any such self-defeating procedure if the inquiry fell within the area, say, of technology. Suppose, for example, we wanted to ascertain the "preferences" of construction engineers in solving some problems of their specialty. It would be apparent at once that we would have to take into account knowledge, experience, and insight. Plainly a statement of preference coming from a wise and experienced engineer is not only more valuable than, but something different in fact from, that of a younger and less experienced one. The older man might very well state more accurately than the younger what the latter's preference would actually be if he were forced to deal with the problem in question. The younger man may report his own preference inaccurately because he is unable to discern the demands of the situation until it becomes something he must face in real life; the older man's insight and understanding can dispense with this crutch of direct confrontation.

So soon, however, as we touch on anything that seems to smack of "values," all of this common sense falls into the discard, and the quest for the elusive "neutral" datum is resumed with almost religious fervor. Yet is it not plain that insight and understanding can play a role in ethical judgments as well as in those of engineering? When we encounter differences of opinion among lawyers about what are in fact the ethical standards of their profession, do not these differences often reflect variations in insight and experience, rather than different opinions as to what actually "exists"? It is true of course that before we can weigh insight and experience into the balance we must ourselves participate in the process of judgment going on in the minds of our respondents. When this happens some fuzz may develop around the distinction between fact and value, but I do not think this too high a price to pay for recovering meaningful contact with reality.

These are brief and inadequate observations about what seem to me to be the things at stake in the debate between Professor Nagel and myself. I should like to make it clear that my fundamental objection to his position is that it is intellectually untenable. I do believe that a general and literal acceptance of the theory would entail disastrous consequences for law and morality. But these consequences would result from the falsity of the theory, not from the fact that it was consciously aimed at producing them.

Is the Purpose of Law and Morality the Resolution of Social Conflict?

As one studies his remarks it is not easy to discern clearly Professor Nagel's own legal and moral philosophy; the negations of his article so outweigh the affirmations, both in number and explicitness, that it takes some searching to find any of the latter at all. I believe, however, that there are two passages which reveal a positive theory of morality, and presumably also of law. Essentially this is the theory that the basic and perhaps exclusive object of morality is to resolve human conflicts. On page 78, "judgments asserting what ought to be are conceived [by Professor Nagel] as hypotheses about ways of resolving conflicting needs and interests." Again, on page 81, he asserts that "there are competing and even incompatible human objectives, both individual and social, and that the task of moral theory is to provide standards with the help of which such conflicts may in some measure be adjusted."

As applied to the law this is a conception closely associated with the position of legal positivism. There are traces of it in most writers belonging to that school, though as usual it is Kelsen who brings the view to most explicit statement:

> Justice is an irrational ideal. . . . Regarded from the point of view of rational cognition, there are only interests, and hence conflicts of interests. They can be solved by an order that either satisfies one interest at the expense of the other, or seeks to establish a compromise between the two.[9]

The notion that the purpose of law is simply to settle disputes is almost a cliché of legal thinking, though I think a dangerous one. When one extends the same view to morality, as Professor Nagel apparently does, it certainly loses any platitudinous quality it might previously have had, and becomes a novel and even startling conception of the role played by moral rules in human life.

It is not difficult, I think, to show the inadequacy of any theory which treats law and morals as being exclusively concerned with the resolution of conflict. In the first place, any such theory must default before the question, What conflicts *require* resolution? Some conflicts between individuals and groups are beneficial, some are harmful.[10] How shall we discriminate between the two? The second major default of the suggested theory is in answering the question, *How* shall we resolve particular conflicts? If the resolution of conflicts is to be a rational process it must in time develop principles, and those principles will inevitably enter into and shape the lives of men for good or ill. How then are we to articulate those principles by

9. *The Pure Theory of Law and Analytical Jurisprudence,* 55 HARVARD LAW REVIEW 44, 48-49 (1941).

10. Sociology, which in recent years has tended to take absence of conflict as its only criterion of social health, is becoming concerned with the possible values of conflict. See LEWIS COSER, THE FUNCTIONS OF SOCIAL CONFLICT (1956).

which conflicts and disputes are to be decided? If the answer is that we should choose those principles which give the greatest assurance that conflict will not recur, we are simply brought back full circle to the theory's first default.

If the theory is as unacceptable as I have just indicated, why is it even suggested that the purpose of law and morality is exhausted in the resolution of conflict? An easy answer would be to say that this view is required if the principle of a sharp distinction between fact and value is to preserve even a minimum plausibility; the recognition that law and morality have more affirmative tasks would make it clear as daylight that the "existence" of both of them consists in a striving which we can understand only in terms of ends that are never fully attained.

I believe, however, it would be unfair to suggest that Professor Nagel adopts the theory of law and morality he does only because this theory enables him to maintain his principal position. Rather I think the explanation lies in a moral conviction of the value of diversity and variety in human life and in the directions of human striving. This is a view I ardently share. I have attempted elsewhere to show, however, that though the moral goals of legal positivism are worthy, it serves these goals badly and indeed endangers the very ideals it so properly holds to be precious.[11] I refer the reader to that discussion as a supplement to what I have been able to say here. I believe it will be found to offer a sympathetic account of the essential aims of positivism — or at least as sympathetic an account as is possible when it is assumed that one's opponents in argument do not truly understand their own motivation. But in conclusion I want to repeat that my objection to Professor Nagel's view does not rest on any conjectural motivation that may lie behind it, but on the ground that it seems to me to falsify the relation between human beings and the reality by which they are compelled to orient their lives.*

11. *Positivism and Fidelity to Law—A Reply to Professor Hart's Essay,* 71 HARVARD LAW REVIEW 630, 669-672 (1958).

* Professor Nagel has indicated his intention to continue this discussion in the 1959 number of the FORUM. He plans to consider also Professor Witherspoon's comment, "The Relation of Philosophy to Jurisprudence," which appears in the "Notes" section of this number at 105-134.—Ed.

[4]

FACT, VALUE, AND HUMAN PURPOSE

Ernest Nagel

There is, in general, little intellectual nourishment to be found in rebuttals to rejoinders to replies. Nevertheless, even if rational debate accomplishes nothing else, it often succeeds in locating sources of misunderstanding; and it is with this minimal objective in mind that I am continuing my exchange with Professor Fuller.[1] In offering the following comments on his *Rejoinder* to my *Reply* I am impelled by the hope, not indeed of convincing him that his views on the issues under discussion are mistaken, but of persuading him that if, as he repeatedly complains, I have not grasped his thought, at least part of the reason for this may be unclarities in his own presentation and defense of his doctrines.

By way of preface, let me assure him that if I really have misrepresented him in my *Reply*, as he claims, I have done so unwittingly, and that if I have misunderstood him it has not been for lack of trying to comprehend his contentions. In preparing my *Reply*, I not only devoted much careful thought to his paper, but in the attempt to understand it I made myself familiar with his previous publications on the issues raised by him.[2] Moreover, I discov-

1. Lon L. Fuller, *Human Purpose and Natural Law;* Ernest Nagel, *On the Fusion of Fact and Value: A Reply to Professor Fuller;* Lon L. Fuller, *A Rejoinder to Professor Nagel* — all in 3 Natural Law Forum (1958). All page references in the text are to this source.

In the same volume of Natural Law Forum, Professor Joseph P. Witherspoon contributes an extended comment on the exchange between Professor Fuller and myself, under the title, *The Relation of Philosophy to Jurisprudence.* Professor Witherspoon's essay is in considerable measure a sermon addressed to me on how to read a text, and in particular Professor Fuller's texts, since according to him I have failed to grasp the plain meaning of Professor Fuller's words. How reliable an interpreter of those words Professor Witherspoon is, I will not venture to say. However, the substance of his position, insofar as it is relevant to my discussion with Professor Fuller, is contained in his remark: "What law *is* cannot be separated from what it is *for,* and what it is *for* cannot be separated from what it *ought to be.*" (p. 108) Now in my *Reply* I made unmistakably clear that I believed the law is subject to moral evaluation, so that on my view also existing law is not to be *separated* from considerations of what the law ought to be. On the other hand, I argued that an evaluation of the law is not intelligible, unless we *distinguish* what the law *is* and what it *ought to be.* But in the light of my brief quotation from him, Professor Witherspoon accepts this distinction, and therefore appears to agree with me and to disagree with Professor Fuller, who does not countenance the distinction. I must therefore leave Professor Witherspoon's contribution to "the cause of intellectual community" for assessment by Professor Fuller himself.

2. For the sake of the record, I add the following information. My *Reply* was my contribution, as an invited ten-minute commentator on Professor Fuller's paper in a symposium on natural law, held at the 1956 annual meeting of the American Philosophical Association,

ered that other students of the subject, whose competence to deal with the questions under discussion I regard as indisputable, found difficulties analogous to those I encountered in Professor Fuller's views. It seems to me not unreasonable to suggest, therefore, that it is not entirely the fault of his critics if, as he maintains, they have failed to understand him.

I

Professor Fuller's central thesis, as formulated in his first paper, is that "in any interpretation of events which treats what is observed as purposive, fact and value merge." (p. 69) Although he rejects as "quite unresponsive" (p. 86) my argument that in making this claim he is at best asserting a tautology, to my regret he does not come to grips with my difficulty, and I have found nothing in his *Rejoinder* which requires me to retract my criticism as pointless. I have nevertheless profited from the restatement of his major thesis, and in consequence I believe I am able to present more clearly my continuing difficulties with his central claim. There are in fact three sorts of defects I find in his arguments for it: a confounding of several disparate senses of the word "evaluation" (and, correspondingly, of the word "value"); a failure to distinguish between a term as *evaluative* and a term as *vague;* and a confusion of the question whether or not men actually use a term without explicitly recognizing the distinction between fact and value, with the quite different question whether or not it is possible and important in such cases to make that distinction. It will not be convenient, however, to discuss each of these defects separately.

1. Professor Fuller fully agrees that the mind may have a "descriptive" as distinct from an "evaluative posture" toward reality, although in his view these postures merge when we are dealing with purposive events. He reformulates the issue as stated in his original essay in two related questions: "(1) Is it always possible to give an adequate non-evaluative account of any object that is itself the subject of an evaluation? (2) If so, does evaluation become legitimate (or 'competent') only when its object is first identified in such a non-evaluative account?" (p. 87) He maintains that the answer in each case is negative, basing his conclusion on a number of illustrative examples. However, the first question seems to me unclear as it stands, and requires some discussion of what is to be understood by "adequate" and "evaluation."

Eastern Division. Professor Fuller was one of the two main speakers in this symposium. My mandate was to comment on his paper, not to write an independent essay expounding my own views. Professor Fuller's repeated complaint that my *Reply* contains no affirmations of my own moral and legal philosophy therefore seems to me unreasonable.

a) Professor Fuller nowhere explains what is the force of the adjective "adequate." It is manifestly a value term, and involves at least tacit reference to some purpose or objective for the sake of which an account is undertaken. Thus, when a physicist offers a non-evaluative account of a given system of pulleys (i.e., when he assumes a "descriptive posture" toward his subject matter), if his aim is simply to discover what is the mechanical advantage of the system, his account is *not* inadequate because he fails to note the weight of the pulleys, the length and tensile strength of the cord, or the purchase price of the machine. On the other hand, a builder assessing the physical and economic suitability of the pulley system for lifting construction materials used in his business, *would* be giving an inadequate account were he to ignore these items. In brief, *every* account of things and processes, whether it is descriptive or evaluative, is instituted for the sake of some objective; and the adequacy of an account can be judged only by reference to the purpose for which it has been instituted. But although this point is obvious, it is also important. For it calls attention to the circumstance that an account may be entirely adequate (relative to a given purpose), even when the account is an admittedly non-evaluative one, despite the fact that it does not provide an "exhaustively" detailed and "absolutely" precise description of the subjects under discussion.

Nevertheless, Professor Fuller appears to ignore this obvious point when, in reverting to his original molluscoidal example, he claims that even if our concern in giving an account of the boy's behavior with the clam were "in the 'pure fact' of the occurrences there related — say, in the directions and dimensions of the boy's physical movements — we could envisage that 'pure fact' more accurately if we knew what the boy was trying to do." (p. 88) If our intent is to characterize the boy's behavior with a view to relating his activities to his purpose (assuming that he has one), we will undoubtedly attend to different things in his total behavior than if our intent were something else; and even if our interest is to evaluate the boy's behavior as a means for achieving his aims, we will doubtless note varyingly different features in his actions should we modify our conceptions (or hypotheses) concerning the boy's objective. Professor Fuller is very perceptive when he calls attention to "the effect of a disclosure of the boy's purpose in bringing about a sudden enlargement of perspective." But I can find no warrant for his assertion that when we realize what the boy is trying to do, we are able to give a more accurate account of the boy's physical movements. For the accuracy of an account, like its adequacy, can be judged only in reference to the purpose for which the account is instituted. However, since an account undertaken for assessing the boy's behavior as a means for realizing his ostensible objective has a different purpose than an account undertaken for describing the directions and the dimensions of his physical movements (perhaps for the sake of determining whether the boy has recovered from a crippling illness), the adequacy or the accuracy of the latter account follows from the former one neither in strict logic nor in normal fact. This is not the only example in which Professor Fuller has apparently forgotten that the adequacy of an account is relative to the purpose controlling that account. I shall try to show that his claim concerning the merging of fact and value is in part the consequence of his not remembering this point.

b) The primary, though I think not exclusive, sense in which Professor Fuller employs the term "evaluation" is for judgments in which the worth of some action, process, or object is assessed as a means for achieving some end, however tacitly or vaguely the end may be entertained, and whether or not the judgment is explicitly formulated. At any rate, this seems to be the sense required in his discussion of the original molluscoidal example, as well as of several others he advances in his *Rejoinder* in support of his central thesis. Some of these latter examples are especially helpful to me in stating my difficulties; and since I would be repeating myself were I to comment on each of Professor Fuller's illustrations, I will examine only two of them in the present context.

i) Professor Fuller raises the question whether the "existence" of a "legal order" in some society can be decided without evaluations being involved in the process. However, he declares that "the *ideal* of a legal order is never attained perfectly," so that "the 'existence' of a legal order is always a matter of degree and cannot be measured in 'non-evaluative' terms." How, then, he asks, "in determining whether a legal order 'exists' do we distinguish between the 'existent thing' and its 'value'?" (p. 91, my italics) Moreover, he suggests it would be absurd to maintain that we must first describe in neutral, non-evaluative terms "every existent thing embraced by such a judgment [i.e., a judgment as to whether a legal order exists] before the judgment itself can be 'competent.'" (p. 92)

I have several comments to make on this example of an alleged merging of fact and value. Professor Fuller is perhaps calling our attention to the familiar difficulty of formulating a "suitable" general definition of "legal order" (although I am sure he intends more than this) precise enough to enable us to decide in a uniform manner whether a given social system (e.g., Hitler's Germany) is an instance belonging to the extension of that term. But in any event the term "legal order," like many other terms in common use, has no precise definition, certainly not one that is acceptable to all who employ it. Although there may be a considerable measure of uniformity in the way men apply it in many instances, it is also clear that many individuals differ in the criteria they associate with the term for its correct application. Accordingly, two individuals who disagree on whether a given society possesses a legal order, may disagree not because they base their predications on different descriptive (or non-evaluative) accounts of the society, but simply because they operate with different standards for the correct application of the label. In an analogous way, a bat may be characterized as a bird by one person and denied that characterization by another, because the connotations of the term "bird" are for them not the same, even though they agree in all other respects in their accounts of the object both have observed.

Now although Professor Fuller is not proposing a fully developed definition of "legal order," he does suggest what for him must be a component in any acceptable definition of the term. If I do not misread him, he is saying that no system of politically enforced regulations can properly be called a "legal order," unless the system approximates to an "ideal" order, and so embodies patterns of human behavior which both conforms to certain minimal moral standards and contributes to the realization of a progressively unfolding series of moral ends. Accordingly, so I understand him to maintain, it is not possible to decide whether, for example, a legal order did exist in Nazi Germany without characterizing the operations of Hitler's society in evaluative terms. I will not dispute here the suitability of a definition of "legal order" along the lines Professor Fuller suggests (despite my doubts about the desirability of a definition of the term which would require us to refuse this title to a "thoroughly bad" system of politically instituted and enforced regulations), since the precise form which a definition of the term ought to take is not pertinent to the issue under discussion. I gladly admit that if the term is to have any connotation, there must be *some* minimal conditions for its correct application; and I also freely grant that a definition such as the one Professor Fuller appears to have in mind is entirely possible. Nor do I deny that on his and similar conceptions of what is a legal order, any decision as to whether or not a legal order exists in a given society involves the use of evaluative terms. For if such conceptions are adopted, it is trivially or tautologically true that evaluative terms must be employed. What does puzzle me, however, and leads me to wonder whether I do understand him, is why Professor Fuller thinks he is not asserting the tautology to which I tried to call his attention in my *Reply*.

It is barely possible that Professor Fuller finds my criticism "unresponsive," because I have not made sufficiently clear that when anything is characterized in what I propose to call "functional" terms, the use of such terms *necessarily* requires evaluative judgments. Let me therefore try to make my point with a biological example. A certain organ in the human body can be identified as a kidney by way of its gross anatomy, so that in the anatomical sense of the word we can give an account of some particular kidney (or of kidneys in general) in what are commonly regarded as non-evaluative terms. However, we have discovered that one of the normal functions of kidneys so identified is to maintain the blood in a certain chemical state. We may in consequence (and indeed frequently do) include this capacity of the organ in our conception of what it is to be a kidney. We may in fact make it part of our notion that to be a kidney an organ must maintain the blood in an "ideal" chemical balance, even if we should discover that actual organs vary in their capacity to do so; and we may in consequence come to regard it "a matter of degree" whether a given organ is really a kidney. On either of these two suppositions, however, the term "kidney" in its functional sense is an evaluative term, since we can determine whether a given organ is a kidney only by assessing its performance as a means for achieving a certain end.[3]

Similarly, in the sense associated with it by Professor Fuller, the functional term "legal order" is *necessarily* an evaluative one, because in that sense no system of human activities is a legal order if it is not conducive to the maintenance and the realization of certain moral objectives. Accordingly, though we may all agree in all our non-evaluative accounts of the Hitler regime, if there is room for doubt whether the decrees and enactments issued under the Nazis, together with the mechanisms of enforcement, were means for attaining those objectives, there is ground for doubt whether a legal order existed under Hitler. But if my statement of Professor Fuller's view is reasonably accurate, is he not after all asserting a tautology when he claims that this example illustrates a merging of fact and value?

But in any event, he heaps scorn on the notion that for an evaluative account to be legitimate, its object must first be identified in non-evaluative terms. He declares that to urge this notion is

> like saying that unless we can trace the precise trajectory of a marksman's bullet we have no right to assert that it missed the target. Surely we can say that a legal system is missing its target without having to report the precise angle of divergence of every human action that contributes to that missing. We can also say of something that calls itself a legal order that it is missing that target so woefully that it cannot in any meaningful sense

3. To avoid misunderstanding, I want to emphasize that on my view it is a *discovery* that kidneys identified by way of anatomical features do in general have this capacity, and not the result of any decision concerning the connotation to be assigned to the word "kidney." However, if in the light of that discovery we decide to modify the initial sense of the word, it is a consequence of this *decision* that to be a kidney (in the new, functional connotation of the word) necessarily implies the possession of the indicated capacity.

> be termed a system of law. It has, if you will, so little "value" that it has ceased to "exist." (p. 92)

Ridicule and exaggeration, however, though they doubtless have their use, do not really turn the point of an argument. Professor Fuller is battling with straw men if he supposes those whom he calls "positivists" to maintain that a necessary condition for a competent evaluation is an absurdly minute and photographically precise non-evaluative description of the object evaluated. It has apparently not occurred to him that the sole alternative to an evaluative account is not an impossibly detailed non-evaluative one. And he seems to have forgotten in this instance, as he did in the example I discussed earlier, that every account is unavoidably selective, and that the adequacy of a non-evaluative account has to be measured, not against an ideal of "absolute" precision, but in relation to the particular purpose that instituted it. Accordingly, since a non-evaluative account that is not exhaustive of its subject may nevertheless be adequate to the purpose of the account, and since the judgment that an account is adequate involves an evaluation, I can explain Professor Fuller's tacit assumption that a non-exhaustive but adequate account of its subject must somehow be evaluative, only on the hypothesis that he mistakenly thinks the evaluative character of a *judgment of adequacy* of an account entails that the account is itself evaluative.

However this may be, I do not understand how anyone is able to evaluate anything responsibly, unless he can identify that thing in non-evaluative terms. If he is unable to do so, even though in a relatively sketchy and imprecise way only, I find it a puzzle to know *what* is being evaluated. I am, of course, *not* maintaining that such non-evaluative descriptions are in all instances explicitly formulated, and are invariably distinguished from evaluative judgments. Thus, the builder in my example above may not formally assert such statements as "The cord in this pulley is 200 feet long" and "This pulley is capable of doing the kind of jobs I need done in my business more effectively and economically than any other machine now on the market." Nor may the builder be aware in making such judgments (whether or not he states them explicitly) that one of them is descriptive while the other is evaluative. I *am* maintaining that the builder can be evaluating something only if he identifies that thing (perhaps only by way of unformulated perceptions) in non-evaluative terms. Moreover, I believe that when some evaluation of ours (such as my builder's) is challenged, we can meet the challenge responsibly only if we first articulate our descriptive characterizations, distinguish as carefully as we can our tacit evaluations from our factual claims, and perhaps (in order to make our evaluations more reliable) increase the detail and the precision of our descriptive accounts. Professor Fuller questions the utility of such descriptive accounts, at any rate in his discussion of the "existence" of a legal order, on the ground that "the only significant thing [we] can say about [a] social complex is that it *does* fall short of the ideal of a legal order." (p. 92) But their utility seems to me obvious, if we are at all concerned with diagnosing a social complex, with the objective of changing what is actual in the direction of a better approximation to some ideal. Does Professor Fuller have a better alternative to the general policy of determining what is the actual state of affairs (with a degree of precision depending on the problem), as a condition for competent prognosis and therapy?

ii) Consider next Professor Fuller's example of the dancing couple who bring suit for improper discharge from employment, where the point at issue is whether or not the couple really did perform a tango. He notes that in such cases the judge must decide what form the testimony of witnesses may take; and he suggests that witnesses might not be required to describe the dance they saw performed "in terms of physical motions," and would be permitted to testify somewhat in the fashion: "Whatever they were doing, it was not a tango." (p. 93) Professor Fuller therefore concludes that an adequate account of the action in dispute in this case would not be presented in non-evaluative terms, so that in this instance, at any rate, ostensibly factual description and evaluation coalesce.

My comments on this example will be brief. I have already argued that it is a blunder to suppose that the sole way of characterizing anything in non-evaluative terms (in this instance a dance) is to describe it "in terms of physical motions" — where such a description will count as an adequate one only if it states every detail in the pattern of motions embodied in the performance. Moreover, were this standard for a non-evaluative description adopted, most, if not all, of the accounts of things we are accustomed to regard as non-evaluative would then have to be rebaptized as evaluative ones. Accordingly, by doing violence to the accepted distinction between judgments of fact and judgments of value (i.e., to the sense of the distinction in terms of which the issue raised by Professor Fuller is formulated), the question under discussion would be settled in Professor Fuller's favor — but only by redefining the terms used in stating the issue, and so reducing the latter to triviality. Thus, when we characterize a certain occurrence as the flight of a barn swallow, few of us are capable of rendering in explicit language the detailed patterns of the bird's shape, coloring, or motion. Nevertheless, most of us would probably deny that in describing that occurrence in the stated manner we are engaged in an evaluation. Whatever it is that we are doing when we declare that a certain occurrence is the flight of a swallow (or that a certain performance is not a tango), we are *not* making an evaluation in the sense of assessing the worth of a thing as a means for realizing some objective.

But what is it that we are doing in such cases? It will be helpful to note that the terms ordinarily employed in identifying and describing things connote more or less extensive (and more or less precisely delimited) classes of attributes. Accordingly, no term is correctly predicated of a given object, unless the latter does in fact possess all the connoted attributes. On the other hand, we rarely make sure (sometimes because we are not in the position to do so) when we predicate some term of an object that the latter actually possesses each of the connoted attributes; and in consequence, the available observational evidence on the basis of which a term is applied to an object is usually (if not invariably) logically insufficient to guarantee with demonstrable certainty the correctness of the predication. For example, the connotation of the term "oak tree" includes the attributes of having leaves with a characteristic shape, a bark with a distinctive texture and color, a trunk and limbs with a certain grain and degree of hardness, a capacity for producing acorns, and so on. But when judging a tree to be an oak we do not normally first establish that the object really does have all these traits, and we base our judgment on noting the presence of a relatively small number of them.

Nevertheless, though in cases of this sort the observational evidence for a predicative judgment may be logically incomplete, the incompleteness may vary. In some instances the evidence may be so extensive that the judgment is accepted as beyond reasonable doubt. In other cases the evidence is far less compelling, and the judgment is felt to be only probable in some degree. In short, predicative judgments are commonly asserted on the basis of incomplete evidence, which must be "estimated." This estimation is sometimes a conscious and deliberate weighing of the evidence. At other times, especially in routine situations of life, there may be no explicit consideration of the observational data; in such cases a deliberative estimation is replaced by habit, so that predicative judgments are asserted — with varying degrees of confidence on the basis of the observed data — almost automatically. But to estimate the weight of evidence, in whatever way such an estimate may be made, is to engage in an activity that is not improperly characterized as an "evaluation" — though in a sense of the word distinct from the senses thus far discussed. Certainly the witnesses in the dancing couple example, who testify whether or not the couple were performing a tango, are *not* offering an evaluative account of the performance, in the sense that they are assessing an action as a means for realizing some purpose. They *are* offering an evaluative account, in the sense that their predicative judgments are ostensibly based on estimates of the evidential weight of their observed data. Accordingly, I concur entirely in Professor Fuller's view that "there is an element of responsible decision in all intellectual activities" (p. 93), if this means that the decision in question involves an evaluation in the sense just indicated. However, unless different meanings of "evaluation" are confounded, the occurrence in the dancing couple example of evaluations in the present sense does not support his claim that the example illustrates the merging of fact and value.

2. Professor Fuller thinks that the administration of the law presents special difficulties for the view that "in any actual process of human decision [there is] a rigid separation of fact and value." (p. 92) I have already discussed the case of the dancing couple, one of the several examples he employs in this connection to support his thesis. I want to examine another example in this group, in order to exhibit another facet in my difficulties.

Professor Fuller cites the rule that if one party to an oral contract was negligent in interpreting the terms of the agreement while the other party was not, the court will enforce the contract in accordance with the understanding of the prudent party. He appends the comment that "the term 'negligence' is plainly a term of evaluation, but there is generally in the law no 'non-evaluative' colligation of the things or instances to which this term should be applied." (p. 94) I need hardly say that on questions of law I am happy to be Professor Fuller's pupil. However, when he declares that "negligence" is "plainly a term of evaluation," he does not seem to me to be making a judgment simply in his capacity as a distinguished legal scholar. To be sure, the term "negligence" contains an evaluative component, as does the biological term "kidney"; for an action is characterized as negligent with reference to the likely consequences to which, in the light of our general experience, actions of that type are believed to lead. It is also undoubtedly the case that there is in general no descriptively characterized and precisely demarcated set of things to which the term is applied in the law. Nevertheless, as innumerable writers on legal subjects have noted (and I hope I do not appear to be presumptuous in venturing to remind Professor Fuller of this), the law of torts recognizes standards of nonnegligent action — even if those standards are determined in part by uncodified custom, are elastic, and are subject to alteration as society itself changes. Accordingly, the term "negligence" is not *merely* evaluative (any more than is the term "kidney"), so that in a large number of instances its application is controlled by rules referring to paradigmatic situations that are identifiable in non-evaluative language.

On the other hand, the term "negligence" is notoriously a highly vague one. It is vague in the sense that the term "bald" is also quite vague, while for all practical purposes the term "kidney" is not — in the sense, namely, that there is a large class of actions for which habits of usage are indeterminate as to whether or not the term applies to them. In consequence, when borderline cases become subjects of litigation, a decision must be made whether or not to include them in the extension of the term. Such decisions are frequently made in the light of evaluations of the conjectured consequences of those acts, and under the influence of the purposes (whether explicit or tacit) of those making the decisions. Nevertheless, the fact that evaluations and purposes enter into the formation of such decisions does not blur the distinction between "is" and "ought." On the contrary, that fact does not make nonsense of the question whether, prior to a decision to count a given action as an instance of negligence, the action *ought* to be included in the scope of some law dealing with behavior deemed to be negligent, or whether, subsequent to that decision, the action *ought* to have been so included. Unless an action, even though a borderline case for the application of the law, is presented to a court by way of an account which is at least partly non-evaluative, I confess my inability to understand what there is for the court to decide.

Accordingly, when individuals disagree in their judgments on whether or not a given action is marked by negligence, their disagreement may have various reasons: The individuals may agree in their conceptions or criteria of negligence, but may differ in their evaluations of the likely consequences of actions similar to the one under consideration; they may agree in their criteria, but they may be basing their judgments in this particular case on different non-evaluative accounts of the action being discussed; or they may disagree (just as men often disagree in classifying some person as bald) primarily because of the vagueness of the term "negligence" and because the given action is a borderline case. Professor Fuller's claim that the term "negligence" is "plainly a term of evaluation," and that its use illustrates the merging of fact and value, thus seems to me to be a consequence of his lumping together under the ambiguous rubric "evaluation" such quite distinct factors that may control men's judgments.

Professor Fuller's examples show beyond doubt how difficult it frequently is to make descriptive judgments not colored by tacit assumptions concerning human purposes and by implicit moral evaluations. But he is flaying an imaginary whipping boy when he castigates those who believe a distinction must be made between "is" and "ought," if he supposes them to maintain that the distinction is one that men invariably make or can make easily and without effort. He is not arguing to the point when he notes, in support of his major thesis, that the Opinion Rule is condemned by careful students of the law of evidence. For the issue, as I understand it, is not whether most witnesses are able to disentangle fact from opinion, or fact from value, especially when they are testifying on matters in which they may have received no serious training. The issue is whether the distinction between "is" and "ought" is not implicit in all moral deliberation, and whether, in the interest of making our evaluations more responsible, a persistent effort to make that distinction explicit in practice is not of highest moment.

II

I now turn to Professor Fuller's view that there is "a process that may be called the collaborative articulation of shared purposes," exhibited not only "in the affairs of daily life" (p. 73) but also in the history of the common law. (p. 74) In my *Reply* I stated my agreement with his rejection of an atomistic conception of human purposes and goals. But I also expressed my disagreement with what seemed to me to be a "holistic" interpretation of individual and social purposive action which he adopted, an interpretation according to which, as I understood it, there is an implicit collaborative pursuit of valid "forms of social order" by men, even when this end-in-view is not explicitly entertained by them. In his *Rejoinder* Professor Fuller charges me with misquoting him, when I criticized him for maintaining that men pursue such objectives even when they are "out of view." (p. 95) However, this is a gratuitous accusation, and he obviously did not consult his original essay from which the quotation (n.b., not *mis*quotation) was taken and to which page reference was given. But in any event, in his *Rejoinder* he repeats the substance (though not the phrase "out of view") of the position I had criticized, for he declares that "in disposing of controversies and issuing directives we may operate within a framework of purposes which conditions our decisions even though only certain of these purposes are called into consciousness by the facts of the case at hand." (p. 96) Since in my *Reply* I did say that "an end-in-view that is nevertheless not explicitly present in active consciousness seems to me just a myth" (p. 81), I am bound to explain why in my opinion Professor Fuller *is* accepting a myth as "an almost obvious truth of psychology." (p. 96)

Let me say at once that like Professor Fuller I accept as an obvious truth the familiar fact that many of our purposive actions, directed toward realizing some objective lying in the future which had been consciously envisaged by us as an end-in-view at some time or other, are performed by us through force of habit, so that the objective is not continuously in consciousness during the action. For example, it would never have occurred to me to question such facts as that I often leave a friend's home with the intent of returning to my own residence, and then walk, board a train, converse with companions, and do much else besides, without the thought of my objective crossing my mind during most of the process. Nor do I question that I may gather with neighbors with the aim of developing plans for getting better schools in our community, but that this objective does not remain in the foreground of anyone's attention at every moment of the discussion, and that none of us had any clear ideas at the start of the meeting as to what such plans involve. I do deny, however, that if, as a consequence of a set of actions which have been deliberately instituted for realizing a certain goal, a quite different outcome is obtained that was neither intended by anyone nor ever consciously entertained even as a possible end-result, this actual outcome is the "end-in-view" that controls and determines the various decisions which may have been made during the process. I readily admit that the ends-in-view we consciously pursue are often only vaguely conceived by us when we begin to deliberate about ways to realize them or when we initiate some action in order to realize those ends; and I also admit with equal alacrity that when such initially vague objectives become more definite, and are perhaps even realized in some precise but surprising form, we may judge the outcome of our deliberation or action as something that we had "really wanted" from the beginning. But I regard it as a myth to suppose, and at best as a perversion of language to say, that the *unintended* product of our actions is the "end-in-view" toward which those actions had been *directed* all along. Such a supposition seems to me no less a myth because it is professed by some contemporary schools of psychology, which maintain that unconscious *purposes,* though never actually entertained by an individual, are nevertheless the "objectives" and determinants of his behavior.

In point of fact, Professor Fuller does not make it easy for his readers to grasp what he understands by the "collaborative articulation of shared purposes." In his original essay he rejected the claim that it is futile in human affairs to debate means until ends are proposed; and he construed the history of the common law in particular as a process in which rules of law are improved, not only to achieve the explicit ends-in-view courts entertain in interpreting precedents when applying them to the concrete cases under litigation, but also "in the light of ends then out of view because not stirred into active consciousness by the facts of the case being decided." (p. 74) In my *Reply* I agreed that there is indeed a collaborative articulation of shared purposes, in the sense that at various times and among various groups of men there are collaborative attempts at establishing and articulating common goals.[4] But I took issue with what seemed to me the possible import of Professor Fuller's words that however much men may be separated in space and

4. Professor Fuller takes me to task for admitting the existence of a collaborative articulation of shared purposes only with the qualification stated in the text. He construes the

time, and however little they may be explicitly aware of any common objectives, mankind is a single community engaged in a collaborative search for "forms of social order," and that the history of the common law illustrates this collaborative articulation of shared purposes. And I rejected this view, though I expressed doubt whether Professor Fuller subscribed to it, on the ground that it is mythical (in the sense of the preceding paragraph) and that it is incredible history.

In his *Rejoinder* Professor Fuller dismisses my criticisms of this view as beside the point and as not pertinent to anything he said in his original essay. He now reformulates his thesis, and helpfully offers a temporally ordered series of five (imaginary but allegedly typical) judicial decisions to illustrate the collaborative articulation of shared purposes in the common law. Nevertheless, I still fail to understand what his thesis is, if it is not the one I found untenable in my *Reply*. He declares his examples "show that communication among men, and a consideration by them of different situations of fact, can enable them to see more truly what they were all trying to do from the beginning" (p. 98) — as if I had denied that communication between men often clarifies common purposes. The difficulty I find in the examples is that though they supposedly illustrate a collaborative articulation of shared purposes, Professor Fuller himself suggests that each judicial decision in the series can be assumed to be separated from its predecessor by a half century, and that courts deciding the five cases might well be those of five different nations. But what reason is there for supposing that the problem confronting the court in the fifth decision was envisaged by the first court, or that the actual purposes and ends-in-view of the first court were shared by the last one in the series? If there is no compelling evidence for such supposals, how does Professor Fuller differentiate his view from the one I criticized in my *Reply,* and why does he think he is not subscribing to the mythical notion of purposive human action which I had attributed to him?

Let me therefore cite some actual examples of judicial decisions rather than contrived ones. To the best of my knowledge, no one has shown that a common, shared purpose underlies the series of judicial decisions concerning

qualification to mean that according to me such processes take place "only within a group where some uniformity of social values has already been impressed on its members by a common social environment." He therefore asks with obvious irony "why collaborative discussion could clarify or improve a culturally conditioned uniformity." (p. 85) However, Professor Fuller has read my qualification in a sense I had not intended; and I certainly did not maintain, as he suggests I did, that it is absurd to suppose "a pooling of insight and experience could assist the members of the group to understand more truly their own ends." As I explain in the text above, my qualification was intended to express my rejection of the notion that a single "purpose," at best only occasionally at the focus of explicit attention of a relatively small number of men, underlies the development of such institutions as the common law.

the liability of manufacturers of "things by their nature dangerous," beginning with *Thomas v. Winchester* in 1852 and terminating in *MacPherson v. Buick Motor Co.* in 1916. I do not find it obvious that there is such a purpose; a reading of some of the leading decisions in this bit of legal history does not seem to me to support the claim that there is one; and in any event the hypothesis that there is one does not, as far as I can make out, help to explain why the notion of inherently dangerous things has undergone the transformations that it did. Similarly, it is far from evident that the purposes of the U. S. Supreme Court in *Plessy v. Ferguson* in 1896 were shared by the Court in 1954 when the latter reversed the "separate but equal" rule laid down by the former. At any rate, I can find little but an expression of a blind act of faith in the view that the history of common law is the history of an implicit search for "those principles which will promote a satisfactory life in common for the human beings we know and understand." (p. 99) It is a conception of history dominated by the tendency, so rightly censured by Professor Butterfield, of seeing in the outcome of a series of historical changes "a purpose that has been attained, when very often it is a purpose that has been marred." [5]

Perhaps because I have failed to understand Professor Fuller's thesis concerning the collaborative articulation of shared purposes, I have also failed to find in his *Rejoinder* a resolution of my difficulty in seeing any connection between that thesis and his central thesis on the merging of fact and value. To be sure, he may believe that the truth of his views on the moral purposes underlying the development of the common law entails the truth of some form of natural law doctrine, so that the principles which promote a satisfactory human life are eternally valid and are gradually discovered through the collaborative articulation of common purposes. In consequence, if there were such an entailment, that doctrine would be a necessary presupposition of the interpretation of the development of the common law which Professor Fuller appears to hold. However, the conception of the nature of moral principles and moral values implicit in that doctrine has been historically associated with a firm *distinction* between the "is" and the "ought," and certainly does not imply the denial of this distinction. Accordingly, even if this doctrine as well as Professor Fuller's perspective on the history of the common law were accepted as sound, his views on that history would nevertheless not constitute relevant evidence for his central claim that fact and value merge. I am therefore compelled to render the Scotch verdict that a connection between these views and this central claim has not been proven.

5. Herbert Butterfield, The Whig Interpretation of History 40 (London, 1931).

III

I would like, finally, to comment briefly on two subsidiary issues Professor Fuller raises in his *Rejoinder*.

1. Professor Fuller asserts that the general acceptance of the thesis espoused by me (he does not explicitly say which thesis, but the context suggests that it is the one which maintains the "is" and the "ought" to be distinct) is responsible for the triviality of prevailing ethical philosophy. (p. 99) Although I believe neither his description of current ethical philosophy nor his wholesale condemnation of it is well informed, this does not seem to me to be the occasion for citing chapter and verse in disproof of his contentions. But I cannot bypass this opportunity to express my astonished wonder over the novel claim that to maintain a sharp distinction between "is" and "ought" is to court triviality. It is a distinction to which Aristotle, Spinoza, Kant, Mill, and more recently Santayana, M. R. Cohen, and Dewey subscribed, to name but a few thinkers who helped me to realize its importance. And I must add, for whatever it may be worth, that until Professor Fuller raised the issue, it had never occurred to me that the ethical philosophies of these men are trivial. I must also confess, furthermore, that until he expressed an ostensible doubt whether there is "any ethical theory that does not profess 'the natural law doctrine' and yet yields 'objective standards for the moral evaluation of the law'" (p. 85), I had always assumed that Mill and Dewey, among others, did propound ethical theories which propose objective standards of moral evaluation.

2. Professor Fuller comments adversely on the notion, stated briefly and only in passing in my *Reply,* that judgments of value are hypotheses about ways of resolving conflicting needs and interests. For he maintains that no theory of law is acceptable which holds the purpose of the law and of morality to be exhausted in the resolution of conflicts. (p. 103)

I would be seriously lacking in appreciation of the complex problems any ethical theory must solve, were I to attempt at the tail end of what is essentially a polemical article an adequate statement and defense of the conception of value judgments which I professed in my *Reply.* I can do no more on this occasion than indicate briefly why Professor Fuller's strictures on that conception seem to me without force. In the first place, he observes quite rightly that not all conflicts are harmful, and not all require legal intervention. He therefore rejects as inadequate the conception that value judgments are hypotheses for resolving conflicts, on the ground that this conception does not state how beneficial conflicts are to be distinguished from harmful ones. However, my brief formulation of that conception was not advanced as a full-scale analysis, but only as an indication of a necessary condition for the institution of value judgments, not the sufficient conditions for their introduction. The formulation was intended to suggest why value judgments cannot rightly be regarded as self-certifying, and why questions concerning their validity can be settled only by reference both to the actual ends-in-view men entertain in given situations as well as to non-evaluatively described matters of fact (including the satisfactions and dissatisfactions men obtain, or are likely to obtain, from pursuing those ends). But in any event, I agree with Professor Fuller (if that is indeed the point of his criticism) that the distinction between beneficial and harmful conflicts cannot be made exclusively in terms of the notion of conflict. For without reference to the kinds and varieties of satisfactions and dissatisfactions men obtain from their activities, the distinction makes no sense to me. However, no proponent of the conception of value judgments under discussion has to my knowledge ever assumed anything to the contrary. The first part of his criticism therefore seems to me to be directed against a nonexistent target.

But Professor Fuller also maintains, in the second place, that if the resolution of conflicts is to be effected through a rational process, principles must in time be developed that enter into and shape the lives of men for good and evil. He therefore rejects the view of value judgments under consideration, because it allegedly fails to state how those principles are to be articulated by which conflicts and disputes are to be decided. However, though to be sure my *Reply* did not discuss these questions, the standard and readily available literature on the subject certainly does, so that the allegation seems to me baseless. In brief, the answer to Professor Fuller's censure is as follows. Certain types of conflict generate consequences that are discovered to be injurious to the well-being not only of those who may engage in them, but in various ways and degrees of other members of a community. These conflicts are also discovered to be capable of regulation, where some forms of regulation turn out to acerbate the undesirable consequences of conflicts, while other forms are found either to diminish the harm those conflicts produce or to divert the springs of human action into channels so as to generate consequences which augment human satisfactions. Accordingly, the principles by which conflicts are to be decided are principles whose use has been discovered to yield greater human satisfactions or lesser dissatisfactions or both, and in general to increase the happiness and well-being of the communities of men in which those principles are employed. This answer certainly offers no solution to any concrete problems in which conflicts require to be adjudicated. It suffices to show, however, that Professor Fuller's criticism is far from fatal.

Professor Fuller's animus against those he calls "positivists" — a category which appears to include everyone who maintains a firm distinction between "is" and "ought" — seems to me to have its source in the curious belief that anyone who accepts this distinction is barred in principle from evaluating the law in terms of objective moral standards. But such a belief is not only incompatible with the historical record concerning the role of "positivistic" philosophy as a critique of social institutions. The belief is also based on a false conception of how the study of fact can be related to the study of value. I find it difficult to escape the impression that those who hold the belief accept it on grounds of a fallacious argument — an argument entirely analogous to one which would conclude that a biologist, seeking to ascertain the various characteristics of microorganisms, whatever may be the import of such organisms for human life, is thereby precluded from distinguishing bacteria harmful to the human body from bacteria beneficial to man.

Part II
Neo-Scholastic Theory: For and Against

[5]

LAW AS MEANS TO END—THOMAS AQUINAS

THOMAS E. DAVITT, S. J.*

The importance of a man can be judged by his influence on the thinking of other men. Periodically during the course of the centuries men have appeared who exercised this power to a commanding degree. The presence of "great" names in all fields of human endeavor attests to this.

These are the adventurous spirits whom men of lesser mettle choose to follow as their leaders. They are the men of stature whom others recognize as masters and by whom they allow their minds to be formed and their thinking influenced. Not that these pioneers are to be followed slavishly to the last detail and no independent thinking done after them. That would be the death of any future progress. But it is from these men of exceptional insight, imagination and vision that others take their first inspiration and general direction of thought.

Such a man was Thomas Aquinas. He was a trail blazer in many regards, one of them being especially his work on law. His was the first systematically organized treatise on law and its philosophical roots, and over the years it has been recognized as a masterful accomplishment. Consequently, during succeeding generations this work has been a powerful factor in shaping the minds of countless men on the nature and significance of law.[1]

By way of an overview of this article, it may be said that its purpose is to present Aquinas' philosophy of law to the average lawman, who is not necessarily trained in this type of legal thinking. This entails an obvious difficulty for which there is no ready solution. All that can be done, it seems, is to set out Aquinas' thinking on this subject and let him speak for himself.

A comprehensive treatment of law includes an inquiry into its nature and promulgation, its end, content and source, and its sanction and the reason why it obliges. Aquinas examines these characteristics of law first in regard to man-made law, for man-made law is easily observable, and second in regard to God-made law. The interrelation between the two is then indicated. His treatise on legal philosophy is not without grounds for observations and comments which, consequently, will be made. Finally, because the practical value of principles can best be seen in their application to fact situations, the

* Professor of Jurisprudence, Marquette University School of Law. Author, *Elements of Law* (1959).

1. On the life (1225-1274) and works of Aquinas see MARITAIN, ST. THOMAS AQUINAS (1948); CHESTERTON, ST. THOMAS AQUINAS (1933); CHENU, INTRODUCTION A L'ÉTUDE DE SAINT THOMAS D'AQUIN (1954).

impact of Aquinas' thinking on certain contemporary legal problems will be pointed out.

Although Aquinas wrote as a theologian and his principle work is a "Summa of Theology," nevertheless within this framework he addressed himself to problems that were philosophical in nature and were solvable according to observable data and reasoning thereon.[2] On this basis rests his philosophy of law as such, even though at times he applies it to matters known from theology.

Man-Made Law

Before any of the other aspects of law can be profitably investigated, what law is in itself must be examined. Aquinas ascertains this by examining man-made law. Law is seen to be a rule or measure of human actions, since by it men are either induced to act or are restrained from acting in a certain way.[3] A speed law, for instance (and to use a modern example), is such a rule. Embodied in this rule is a means-end relationship: a certain maximum speed limit is needed to ensure safe driving conditions. This relation of speed to safety can be almost scientifically determined by tests conducted by traffic engineers. The basis of the means-end relationship of law is, then, an objective fact situation and Aquinas' entire concept of law is anchored in this relationship.

Nature

But is a law merely the words by which it is made known, or is it something much more important that is expressed through the words? Because words or symbols are but a medium of communicating ideas in the mind of the speaker or writer, the words of a law are only the expression of something of much greater significance in the minds

2. Aquinas, Summa Theologiae I, Q. 1, art. 3. (1267-1273). See the English translation, Summa Theologica of St. Thomas Aquinas (Benziger ed. Dominican transl. 1947). All reference to Aquinas, unless otherwise specified, will be to this major and most readily available work. Hereinafter it will be cited as ST.

The basic distinction between theology and philosophy should be recalled. Theological convictions are based on the authority of divine revelation and faith therein. Faith is an assent of the mind to a proposition, not because of evidence, but because of the trustworthiness of the one speaking—whether he be human or divine. Philosophical conviction, on the other hand, is based on observable phenomena and reasoning thereon. This may be about the order found in nature and about its cause, God. Although God is not a directly observable datum, as far as the working of the human mind is concerned, he is the one intelligible explanation of this phenomenon of order which is observable.

Those who would rigorously exclude all other ways of acquiring knowledge except the scientific method, which is indispensable in certain types of inquiry, should critically examine the inevitable non-scientific assumptions and commitments in the scientific method itself. See especially Polanyi, Personal Knowledge (1958); and his The Study of Man (1959).

3. 1-2 ST 90, 1.

of lawmakers. The words of a law communicate the directive judgment of the lawmakers (or a majority of them) that a certain means is in some degree factually necessary for obtaining a desired end—that a speed limit of 65 miles per hour, for instance, is necessary for safe driving conditions. Essentially, then, law is an act of lawmakers' reason and not of their will. For it is the function of men's reason and not of their will to order means to an end.[4]

True, the will of lawmakers plays an important part in the desire to enact a law, which in turn inspires the drafting, introduction and passage of new laws. But the core of law is not what lawmakers desire. It is rather the resulting directive judgment of their reason which embodies the perceived necessity of certain means for the common welfare. This directive judgment may be called a "command," provided law is taken in this sense of a directive judgment of reason,[5] and not merely as an expression of the sovereign will to be carried out by force.[6] This kind of law Aquinas calls *human* law.[7]

Promulgation

Promulgation of a law is necessary if the law is to have its intended effect, the guidance of the people. They cannot be directed by a rule of which they have no knowledge.[8] Promulgation, being the application of the directive judgment of lawmakers to the people,[9] cannot be designated as part of the law itself. What is applied must already be constituted before it can be applied to something else.[10] This distinction between law and its promulgation will be of capital importance when we examine "natural law."

End

The end or purpose of law is the common good of the people.[11] The common or public good consists principally of peace (the condition of unity among the people brought about by order) and security (the condition of assurance engendered by a sufficiency of the necessities of life and of safety resulting from adequate protection of the country).[12] Certain institutions which contribute to peace and security also pertain to the common good, such as legislation and its sanctions, good

4. *Ibid.*
5. 1-2 ST 17, 1.
6. See AUSTIN, LECTURES ON JURISPRUDENCE OR THE PHILOSOPHY OF POSITIVE LAW, 12-13 (Campbell ed. 1875).
7. 1-2 ST 91, 3; 1-2 ST 95-97.
8. 1-2 ST 90, 4.
9. *Ibid.*
10. 1-2 ST 16, 1; 1-2 ST 17, 3. See also 2 LOTTIN, PRINCIPES DE MORALE 97 (1947).
11. 1-2 ST 90, 2; 1-2 ST 95, 4; 1-2 ST 96, 1; 1-2 ST 96, 3.
12. AQUINAS, DE REGIMINE PRINCIPIUM 1, 15 (1267). See the English translation, ON KINGSHIP 63-67 (Eschmann ed. Phelan transl. 1949).

appointments and elections,[13] and just adjudication.[14]

Peace and security in turn possess their value because they are, in the last analysis, ends related to men's last end. They are the conditions necessary for men to live responsible, knowingly decided lives through which they can develop and perfect themselves.[15] Looked at from this comprehensive viewpoint, the purpose of law can be said to be to bring about right living among men, that is, to make men good.[16] Not that a law by itself can make men do what is right and at the same time make them desire to do it. But it can at least induce men to refrain from doing what is wrong because of the fear they have of incurring punishment.[17]

The whole concept of the common good refers to that type of good which is communicable to all the people,[18] in contradistinction to a proper or private good, say food, which is communicable only to single individuals.[19] As far as political life is concerned, the public good is pre-eminent to proper or private good.[20] For, it is only within the matrix of the common good that the proper good is attainable.[21]

The common good is obviously, then, not a sum total reached by adding together the proper, say consumer, goods of individuals. It is a good of a completely different nature. Neither is the common good a collective good, such as would be the meal a group is about to consume. This would have to be divided if each is to receive a share. If the number of participants increases, the amount of food available for each decreases. This is not the case with the common good of peace, security and the like. These are not decreased by the number of those who share and the number of participants does not result in each one having less.

In this view, law is a helpful, protective guide. Its necessarily restrictive aspect is only for the purpose of accomplishing a good in which the people can participate. The sole reason for air lane and altitude restrictions on aircraft is that safer flying conditions may be enjoyed by all and that all may thereby more certainly reach their destination.

Content

The content of law for Aquinas is, in general, justice or that which is just.[22] This may be commutative or exchange justice which should

13. *Ibid.*
14. 2-2 ST 60, 6.
15. Aquinas, De Regimine Principium 1, 15 (1267).
16. 1-2 ST 99, 1; 1-2 ST 92, 1.
17. 1-2 ST 96, 3, 2; 1-2 ST 107, 1, 2.
18. 1-2 ST 28, 4, 2.
19. 2-2 ST 58, 7.
20. 2-2 ST 58, 6, 3.
21. 2-2 ST 47, 10, 2.
22. 1-2 ST 95, 3; 1-2 ST 96, 4.

obtain between individual and individual but which has an indirect relation to the common good, for instance, the matter of today's tort or contract law.[23] Or it may be contributive or legal justice which ought to prevail between individuals as members of a community regarding those things which are directly promotive of the common welfare, for example, the provisions of criminal law.[24] Or it may be distributive justice which should exist between those who govern and the governed concerning the administration of the common good; for instance, benefits such as social security or burdens such as taxes.[25]

Only matters of moment, and not the inconsequential or trivial, should be considered as fit content of a law.[26] Implicit in the concept of a just law, then, is its necessity for the common welfare and its possibility of fulfillment by the people.[27] Hence, for the content of a law to be just it must be related to the common good, be proportioned to the needs of the people, and be enacted by those with lawmaking authority.[28]

A prime over-all requisite for a law from the viewpoint of Aquinas' philosophy of law, then, is that it be just. If it is not just, if it lacks this essential element, it is no law at all. It is rather perversity, corruption, violence and tyranny.[29] To most lawmen, it may seem unintelligible to say that an unjust law is no law. For, from the lawyer's standpoint a statute or judicial decision is "law" until it is respectively repealed or overruled, regardless of any other consideration as to its justness.

There are two possible explanations of the lawman's difficulty with the proposition that "an unjust law is no law." First, his philosophy of law may be positivistic and he may hold that "is" and "ought" in law coincide. By the very fact that a law exists, it is just. Or, second, while his philosophy of law may not be positivistic and may be similar to that of Aquinas, as a lawyer he may feel that a law cannot be said to be "no law" until it is superseded by another legal rule. If such be the case, it would profit him to advert to what is occurring here. Two different approaches to law are resulting in two different evaluations of law. What is taken to be a legally valid law by lawmen may be considered to be a morally bad law by philosophers. The philosophers of law presuppose that beyond man-made law there are other norms or rules according to which law can be evalu-

23. 2-2 ST 61, 1 & 2.
24. 1-2 ST 96, 3; 2-2 ST 58, 5 & 6.
25. 2-2 ST 61, 1 & 2.
26. 1-2 ST 96, 2.
27. 1-2 ST 95, 3.
28. 1-2 ST 96, 4.
29. 1-2 ST 92, 1, 4; 1-2 ST 93, 3, 2; 1-2 ST 95, 4; 1-2 ST 96, 4; 2-2 ST 60, 5, 1.

ated and judged just or unjust and that these other norms should be brought to bear on the question of a "just" law. For in this view the "is" is not necessarily identical with what "ought to be" in law.[30] This will be discussed later under *Obligation*.

The determination of what the content of law will be is law in the making. This determination involves the stages of deliberation, evaluation and decision. It has to do with ascertaining what means will contribute most to the common welfare. For instance, there may be a question of determining the best means of preventing smog from enveloping a city, again to use a modern example. Various techniques and devices for controlling fumes from automobile exhausts and industrial stacks will have to be examined and evaluated. Finally, a decision will have to be made and a directive issued to the people. This directive judgment, as we saw above, is the law. The process of deliberation, evaluation and decision which led to it is prudence.[31] Hence, the directive judgment which is law is an act of political prudence.[32]

The important conclusion for modern lawmen is that lawmaking is prudence and therefore it is not science. Science is the knowledge we have of the necessary and constant. It can be substantiated by induction and deduction. Scientific conclusions are verifiable by checking with observable data. Prudence, on the other hand, is the judgment we make concerning the right use of means to an end in contingent and variable human situations. Prudential conclusions are corrected by conformity with right intention.[33]

Take the decision of the father on vacation with his family to take a train instead of some other means of transportation, because he judges it to be the safest mode of travel. A journal on one of the cars is cracked, the train is wrecked, and his family is killed. Was his decision a prudent one? Yes. He could not have had scientific knowledge regarding every piece of equipment on the railroad. His intention was to choose the means of transportation that, according to the best information available to him, was the safest. From the viewpoint of the fact situation, his decision was not a good one and his good intention does not protect him from incurring the physical consequences of his mistake. But from the standpoint of himself, his decision, the only one possible in his situation, was both a good decision and a prudent judgment. In law, the judge's determination regarding which facts in a case are to be admitted as material and

30. The reasoning of the court in the Nürnberg trials (irrespective of its jurisdiction) has, more than any other recent event, thrown into clear relief the issue of "is" and "ought" in law.
31. 1-2 ST 57, 4-6; 2-2 ST 47, 8.
32. 1-2 ST 17, 3, 1.
33. 1-2 ST 19, 3, 2; 1-2 ST 57, 5, 3; 1-2 ST 63, 2, 3; 1-2 ST 65, 2.

which excluded as immaterial is many times a prime example of prudence, not science, in action in daily lawmaking.

Source

The source of law for Aquinas is principally legislation, although decisions by judges and customs established by the people also play their part. For law is made mainly by the people or by their representatives who have been given public authority.[34] Only such persons are capable of directing actions which are related, immediately or mediately, to the common good.[35] For this reason those particularly charged with the care of the common welfare have the special duty of steadily desiring the common good.[36] Legislators should be ready to change laws when it will benefit the common good. Such changes, however, should not be made hastily but with caution, since laws derive much of their efficacy from their habitual observance by the people. Hence, the habits that the people have formed of obeying a certain law should not be broken except for reasons that clearly benefit the public welfare.[37]

The people also make law by establishing customs.[38] They have the basic authority to make law and their directive judgment regarding something as necessary for the common good is law providing it is clearly manifested. This manifestation is made through the repeated actions of custom. For external actions make known the internal acts of reason and will. The constantly repeated actions of the people then, constitute the promulgation of custom-law.[39] If the custom is established notwithstanding a statute to the contrary, the custom may render the statute nugatory or require a particular construction of it. In such a situation the toleration of the custom by the lawmaking representatives of the people is tacit approval and implicit adoption of the custom as law.[40] Hence, custom may make law, interpret it or

34. 1-2 ST 90, 3; 1-2 ST 91, 1; 1-2 ST 97, 3, 3.
35. 1-2 ST 96, 3.
36. 1-2 ST 19, 10; 1-2 ST 58, 5; 2-2 ST 47, 7.
37. 1-2 ST 97, 2.
38. 1-2 ST 97, 3, 2. There may be those who have difficulty in seeing custom as a source of law, especially if they have adopted Austin's view that law is a command of the sovereign to be enforced through power. If so, two facts should be recalled. First, custom is a source of law inasmuch as it determines the construction to be put upon certain parts of common and statute law. Mercantile law is an example. See Adams v. Pittsburgh Ins. Co., 95 Pa. 348, 355, 40 Am. Rep. 662 (1880). Second, custom taken as a body of governing regulations, such as it is especially among primitive peoples, has its own form of punishment which in effect is legal sanction. Such are the sanctions of ridicule, discrimination, ostracism and exile which can mean death, and the like. This striking fact, born out by anthropological and ethnological data, has caused a realization of the inadequacy of Austin's definition of law and the necessity of its abandonment. See GLUCKMAN, THE JUDICIAL PROCESS AMONGST THE BAROTSE OF NORTHERN RHODESIA xiii-xvii (1955).
39. 1-2 ST 97, 3.
40. 1-2 ST 97, 3, 3.

abolish it.[41]

Judges also, as mentioned, make law. Adjudication by someone with public authority is necessary for the settlement of disputes among litigants,[42] when they are not able to compose their differences among themselves.[43] The very title judge[44] implies the determination of what is just.[45] The judge is the interpreter of what is just; he is "living justice."[46] One of his main qualifications, therefore, is that he be capable of judging rightly.[47] His prudential decision regarding what is just, if it is not to be arbitrary, must be reached according to written laws, for these embody both natural and positive rights.[48] Such a procedure is the application of written law to a particular case and the judge's decision can be looked upon as a particular law concerning some particular fact.[49] And because it is public authority that is being exercised in both legislation and adjudication, the decision of the judge is to be obeyed and enforced in the same manner as the enactments of legislators.[50]

The construction that a judge will give to a piece of legislation should be guided by humane discretion, because the best of enactments can not possibly include all the imaginable cases that could arise under it. Hence, where a literal construction of a statute would work harsh injustice in individual cases, the judge's decision should not follow the letter of the law. It should rather be according to equity—the intention of the law.[51]

Legislation is superior to adjudication, according to Aquinas, for three reasons which make interesting reading during these days of large legislatures and judicial review. First, it is easier to find a few wise men who are capable of framing right laws than it is to find many men who would be required to judge rightly in individual cases. Second, legislators deliberate at length on what is to be the content of a law, whereas judges must make decisions regarding single facts in situations that arise suddenly. It is easier for men to see what is right from a consideration of the many facets of a problem than solely from some one fact. Third, legislators judge universally and about future events, whereas judges decide about the present regarding which they are affected by love or hate or the desire to promote their

41. 1-2 ST 97, 3.
42. 1-2 ST 104, 1, 1.
43. 2-2 ST 60, 1, 3.
44. Judex: jus dicens (literally, "declaring what is right").
45. 2-2 ST 60, 1.
46. 1-2 ST 95, 1, 2; 2-2 ST 67, 3.
47. 2-2 ST 60, 1, 1.
48. 2-2 ST 60, 5.
49. 2-2 ST 67, 1.
50. 2-2 ST 60, 6; 2-2 ST 67, 1.
51. 2-2 ST 60, 5, 2; 2-2 ST 120, 1 & 2.

own interests. Because the living justice which should be embodied in the judge is not to be found in many men and is flexible, legislation should determine how matters are to be judged in as many instances as can be and leave as few things as possible to the decision of judges.[52]

Sanction

The consequences or sanction of obeying and disobeying a law are the reward and punishment that ensue thereupon.[53] Our actions are good or bad according to whether or not they are ordered to a right end.[54] In law this is the common good. Men have the power of intelligent, voluntary free decision in their actions.[55] This decision can be affected by ignorance, violence, fear, passion and the like.[56] Inasmuch as men have freedom of decision they have dominion over their actions and are responsible for them. Hence, their actions are imputable to them as their authors. To impute the goodness or badness of actions is to praise or blame.[57]

Further, our actions affect society directly or indirectly, just as "he who hurts the hand, hurts the man."[58] If the actions are good, they benefit society. If they are evil, they injure society. And because of this relation between our actions and their effect on society, justice demands a return by way of reward to those who benefit society and by way of punishment to those that injure it. This is the merit or demerit that is due for good or bad actions.[59]

In this manner and to this extent there is a "reintegration of the equality of justice."[60] Those who observe the law are rewarded first and foremost by the common good that the law is intended to procure. Those who obey speed laws, let us say, are rewarded with safe driving conditions. Some laws also add specific rewards, such as bounties. Violators of speed laws are punished by the deprivation of safe driving conditions, the common good the law is designed to bring about. Further deprivations may be affixed by the law such as fine or imprisonment.

A balance is thus re-established between the violator's defiance of public authority and his eventual submission to it. He preferred his own desires, in his act of violating the law, to those of public authority. Now he is compelled to subject his desire to that of public authority insofar as he must undergo punishment, of one kind or

52. 1-2 ST 95, 1, 2.
53. 1 ST 22, 2, 5.
54. 1-2 ST 21, 1.
55. 1 ST 19, 10; 1-2 ST 1, 1.
56. 1-2 ST 6.
57. 1-2 ST 21, 2.
58. 1-2 ST 21, 3.
59. 1-2 ST 21, 3; 1-2 ST 114, 1.
60. 1-2 ST 87, 6.

another, against his desire.[61] Hence, punishment is the deprivation of a good, consequent upon the violation of a law, and against the will of the violator.[62] Such would be the deprivations, affixed by law, of property by fine, of liberty by imprisonment, of physical well-being by flogging, and of life itself by capital punishment.

In a word, a man's punishment for a violation such as we have exemplified would be twofold: first, he is deprived of the safe driving conditions that the law was designed to bring about (an intrinsic sanction) and, second, he is deprived of other goods as stipulated by law (extrinsic sanctions).[63] Punishment would not be necessary in human living, according to Aquinas, if it were not for the historical incident when the first man put himself beyond the law by disobeying it.[64]

Obligation

Obligation, for Aquinas, is based on the necessity of a means for an end.[65] If a man desire to cross the ocean and the only means of doing so is by ship (air or water), then it is necessary that he use a ship.[66] He is free not to use a ship, but if he does not, he will not get across the ocean. It is of the very nature of duty or what is due, therefore, that there be an order of exigency or necessity of a means to the end to which it is ordered.[67] In other words, obligation in Aquinas is based on the supposition of a desired end and can be defined as the moral necessity (not physical necessity) of choosing the means necessary for a desired end.[68]

At first glance this concept of obligation may appear to be purely relative and hypothetical—I am obliged to choose to take a ship *if* I wish to cross the ocean. As will be seen later regarding obligation, such is not the case. Obligation is ultimately absolute and categorical.

The manner in which a means may be necessary for an end varies. Some things are more necessary for good human living than others.[69] Without speed restrictions on automobile driving, safe driving conditions on streets and highways would be impossible. Without various

61. *Ibid.*
62. 1-2 ST 87, 2 & 6.
63. The simplistic confusing of all punishment with revenge or the *lex talionis* implies a failure to understand punishment in its relation to law's purpose, law's infraction and law's enforcement. This failure is largely the result of that segment of psychiatric thinking which interprets men as irresponsible beings who are not to be blamed, and therefore not to be punished, for what they do. See the *Durham* case, (Durham v. United States, 94 App. D.C. 228, 214 F.2d 862 [1954]) discussed under "Crimes" below. See also DAVITT, THE ELEMENTS OF LAW 195-216 (1959).
64. 1-2 ST 87, 7; 2-2 ST 163, 2.
65. 1-2 ST 99, 1.
66. 1 ST 82, 1.
67. 1 ST 21, 1, 3; 2-2 ST 58, 3, 2.
68. *Ibid.*
69. 2-2 ST 80.

other traffic rules, say double parking regulations, although conditions of safety would be more or less possible, they would not be so to the same degree.

God-Made Law

Laws made by human lawmakers presuppose another kind of law, that made by a divine lawmaker. The existence of the divine legislator can be known by reasoning from observable data.[70] The evident order that is observable in all things indicates that they are governed by a governor, for order wherever found bespeaks an intelligent orderer.[71] But what can be known by reasoning from evidence can also be revealed and known through faith.[72] Hence, since all men are not capable of such reasoning, the existence of the divine lawmaker has been explicitly revealed so that each and every man can know with certainty the end to which his life must be related if he is ultimately to attain happiness.[73]

Nature

The supreme plan in the mind of the eternal lawmaker regarding the government of the universe is a law,[74] for it is a directive of all things to their proper end or good.[75] The eternal lawmaker is in a position of authority; since all things are created by Him, all things are subject to His authority and direction.[76] And because whatever the mind of God conceives is eternal and not temporal, this supreme plan of direction for created things is fittingly called the *eternal* law.[77]

Promulgation

The promulgation of the eternal law occurs in two ways: *implicitly* in created natures and *explicitly* through revelation. Implicit in the dynamic nature of men, as in all living beings, are drives both for completion or perfection as well as for the means that will lead to this end.[78] Put another way, men have an urge to seek what is good in general for them and for certain elementary goods in particular that are necessary for them. These inclinations or tendencies constitute a directive principle of action intrinsic to the very nature of a thing.[79] They are a participation and reflection of the eternal law,[80]

---

70. 1 ST 2, 3.
71. 1 ST 103, 1. See Polanyi, The Logic of Liberty 154 (1951); and his Personal Knowledge 34 (1958).
72. 1 ST 1, 1. See Gilson, The Christian Philosophy of St. Thomas Aquinas 13-14 (Shook transl. 1956).
73. 1 ST 1, 1.
74. 1-2 ST 91, 1.
75. 1-2 ST 93, 1; 1 ST 103, 1.
76. 1 ST 103, 5.
77. 1-2 ST 91, 1.
78. 1-2 ST 91, 2.
79. 1-2 ST 93, 5, 1.
80. 1-2 ST 91, 2; 1-2 ST 93, 2.

and as such are in fact its promulgation.[81] This promulgation of the eternal law through the dynamic nature of created beings is designated by Aquinas as the *natural* law.[82]

Explicit promulgation of the eternal law is had in the revelation of the Old and New Testaments.[83] Such a special divine promulgation was necessary because men cannot know with absolute certainty by their natural capacities either what their end actually is or what they ought to do regarding all actions, even interior ones, in order to reach it.[84] This explicit promulgation of the eternal law, known only through faith in the One revealing, is called by Aquinas *divine* law.[85]

End

The common good which is the end of the eternal law has various aspects some of which are known through natures and others only through revelation. All beings manifest in their natures an inclination to act in a manner perfective of themselves, as we have just seen. The resultant order of the universe is a common good in which all participate.[86] This master drive is for what is good for men, that is, for that object or good which will completely satisfy their desires and thereby make them perfectly happy.[87] Men's nature being the same, this end must be common to them all. Hence, this ultimate end of men is a common good.[88] What it is specifically we shall see below.

Other drives of men indicate other ends that have the nature of a common good, but which eventually are limited ends, ends related to men's ultimate end. Men have a drive to preserve themselves and their kind in existence. The resultant continued existence of the human race is a common good.[89] Men also have basic drives to live together with other men in community and to do so rationally, that is, by using their powers of intellect and will. The consequence of this is a social condition in which at least an elemental sense of justice and order prevail. This is a common good in which all share.[90]

From their basic drives men have a clear and connatural knowledge that what is good for them and will make them happy is an end for which they should strive.[91] But any further knowledge about what

81. 1-2 ST 93, 5, 1.
82. 1-2 ST 91, 2. Whether natural law is right reason has been the subject of some controversy. On this point see "'*Law' as Knowledge of Law*" *infra;* see also 1-2 ST 74, 7.
83. 1-2 ST 91, 4.
84. *Ibid.*
85. 1-2 ST 91, 4, 1.
86. 1 ST 15, 2.
87. 1-2 ST 90, 2; 1-2 ST 94, 2; 1-2 ST 2, 8.
88. 1-2 ST 90, 2, 3.
89. 1-2 ST 91, 6, 3; 1-2 ST 94, 2.
90. 1-2 ST 57, 3; 1-2 ST 94, 2.
91. Connatural knowledge is "knowledge through inclination." 1 ST 1, 6, 3.

their end actually is or what the means of reaching it are must come through reasoning and revelation. Men can reason that eventually their drive for happiness can be completely satisfied only by something extramundane.[92] They can further reason that the attainment of the object or good that will bring this condition about must pertain to their highest powers—intellect and will.[93] But how this can actually take place, men can know with certainty only through the explicit divine promulgation of the eternal law.

It is through divine revelation that men learn with certainty what the object is that will satisfy their desire for happiness and how its possession is possible. For it is through revelation that men ascertain that this object is God, who is the perfect good itself, and that the possession of God is possible for men in a manner that completely exceeds all human power.[94] Final and perfect happiness is had by men only when they meet God face to face and come to know Him as He is in himself.[95] Although the manner in which the perfect good is possessed by the individual is the same as it would be if he were the only human being in existence,[96] nevertheless, because factually it is communicated to others, this supreme good has the aspect of a common good.[97] This common good is the final end and purpose of all the directives of the eternal law.[98]

Content

The content of the eternal law promulgated through nature is indicated by the demands of the basic inclinations.[99] These drives, to

---

It is the knowledge that we have which results from our judging, without any reasoning process, that what is in agreement with our basic inclinations or drives is good and that what is in disagreement with them is bad. 1-2 ST 58, 5; 1-2 ST 94, 2. Thus we connaturally judge, conscious of our basic drive for self-preservation, that preserving our lives is a good and not an evil. On this matter see Maritain, *On Knowledge Through Connaturality*, 4 REV. OF METAPHYSICS 473 (1951).

92. 1-2 ST 2, 8.
93. 1 ST 26, 2; 1-2 ST 3, 3, 5.
94. 1-2 ST 5, 5.
95. 1-2 ST 3, 8.
96. 1-2 ST 4, 8, 3.
97. 1 ST 60, 5, 5.
98. 1 ST 103, 2.
99. The *locus classicus* for the matter of this and the next paragraph is 1-2 ST 94, 2. Other citations will be added, however, where pertinent.

Anthropological and ethnological data abundantly attest to the existence and functioning of these drives. See, *e.g.*, GILLIN, THE WAYS OF MEN 227-29 (1948); LINTON, THE STUDY OF MAN 133-50 (1936). Paleontological-biological evidence also attests to the presence and working in men of these dynamic inclinations and to their relation to evolutionary processes. "In man, considered as a zoological group, everything is extended simultaneously—sexual attraction, with the laws of reproduction; the inclination to struggle for survival, with the competitions it involves; the need for nourishment, with the accompanying taste for seizing and devouring; curiosity to see, with its delight in investigation; the attraction of joining others to live in society. Each of these fibres traverses each one of us, coming up from far below and stretching

which we have just briefly alluded, are: first, the master drive for what is good or perfective, that is, for that object which once permanently possessed will cause complete happiness;[100] and second, the drives for the fundamental requisites for attaining this end. These are: to preserve self in existence, to continue the race by sexual propagation,[101] to live with other men in community and therein to distinguish elementarily between justice and injustice,[102] and to use the power of intellectual knowledge in discovering what is true (especially regarding the origin and purpose of life) and the power of free decision in choosing what is good and will lead to this end.[103]

How does a man know of these demands of his basic drives? Are they self-evident to him or does he have to reason to them? The immediate objects of the inclinations are known without a reasoning process.[104] They are known by connatural knowledge. Hence, happiness, self-preservation, sexual union, just communal living, knowledge and self-direction are known as good and not as evil by all men who are from the medical viewpoint normal human beings. How each of these objects is to be sought in individual instances, it should be noted, is a matter for reasoning, as is demanded by the drive for knowledge and self-direction.

The immediate objects of the basic inclination or drives that are known connaturally and with certainty may be said to pertain to the natural law absolutely, while other mediate objects that are known by means of a reasoning process and with the possibility of error, pertain to it relatively.[105] Hence, all men know at least that much of the eternal law with certainty and with their natural powers

---

beyond and above us. And each one of them has its story (no less true than any other) to tell of the whole course of evolution—evolution of love, evolution of war, evolution of research, evolution of the social sense." Teilhard de Chardin, The Phenomenon of Man 179 (Wall transl. 1959).

100. 1-2 ST 5, 8.

101. 1-2 ST 91, 6, 3; 1-2 ST 100, 11, 3.

102. 1-2 ST 94, 5, 3; 2-2 ST 57, 2.

103. 1-2 ST 94, 4, 3. These drives are an essential part of men's nature. They have to do with men's existence and with what is good and perfective of men. They are steady and definite in every man. To be carefully distinguished from these essential drives are accidental tendencies to evil. These vary with individuals and are not constant. The proclivity to steal or murder is not definite in every individual man, as is the drive for self-preservation, as even anthropological findings bear out.

The influence of Immanuel Kant has been greatly responsible for the attitude, prevalent during the last three hundred years, that the physical and biological drives of a living being were not to be considered as indications of what was good for that being. See Kant, Groundwork of the Metaphysics of Morals 57-58 (Paton ed. 1947). But this attempt to "purify" philosophy and law of everything empirical and to rule out actual means-ends relationships could not but result in the empty formalism that lawmen especially have found so ineffective in dealing with day to day fact situations.

104. 1-2 ST 94, 2; 1-2 ST 100, 1.

105. 1-2 ST 100, 1; 1-2 ST 100, 11. See also 1-2 ST 91, 4.

alone which is promulgated in the common principles of the natural law.[106]

But at this juncture a distinction of vital importance for the understanding of this matter must be made. Do all normal men connaturally recognize the demands of their basic drives as being also demands of the eternal law? Does an atheist or a primitive Ifugao, who are normal men from the medical viewpoint, recognize in their basic drives the natural promulgation of the eternal law of God? Obviously not. For in order to come to such an understanding they would first have to reach the conviction that God exists and that He is a creator-lawmaker. Their minds may change, of course, and they may eventually come to this realization. Failing this, they can only view the demands of their nature as normative directives which oblige because they express an ordering or means necessary for an end—what is good for them. The demands need not be viewed as formal demands of law in order that their obligatory force be recognized.[107]

When it is said, then, that the connatural knowledge every man has of the basic demands of his nature is actually a natural recognition of the demands of the eternal law, it must be remembered that such an insight implies the vantage point of a conviction already reached that the eternal lawmaker exists and that in every created nature, including that of the atheist and primitive, the promulgation of His eternal law is recognizable. Only a man who is convinced that God exists as creator and has philosophized however rudimentarily on this fact, can see in the basic drives the natural promulgation of the eternal law. The working of the eternal law in its dynamic promulgation in natures is always there, but it is not always identified as such by all men.

The content of the eternal law as promulgated through divine revelation is clear and explicit. It includes the decalogue and the added precepts. Thus, for example, to the commandment regarding the keeping of the sabbath day are added the ceremonial precepts. And to the commandment concerning theft are added the precepts concerning usury and fraud.[108] Knowledge of these directives is had solely through faith. Faith, be it recalled, is an assent of the mind to a proposition, not because of evidence, but because of credibility of the authority of the person presenting the proposition.[109]

106. 1-2 ST 93, 2.

107. But unless the demands are ultimately seen as related to the eternal law, the rational (men) would have to be considered as receiving direction from the irrational (natures). The rational is seen to be guided by the rational only when the ordered drives of natures are recognized as an expression of the divine mind's plan of creation.

108. 1-2 ST 100, 11.

109. 2-2 ST 1, 4. See note 2 *supra*.

Source

The source of the eternal law is, then, the divine lawmaker. It is God as governor of the universe.[110] As creator of natures with their dynamic inclinations He is the source of the eternal law naturally promulgated;[111] and as revealer in the Old and New Testaments He is the source of the eternal law divinely promulgated.[112]

Sanction

The sanction for observing or violating the eternal law is the gain or loss of its end. This reward or punishment, then, is intrinsic to the means-end relation of the law rather than extrinsic and affixed as further inducement to keep the law,[113] as may be the case in man-made law.

The sanction of the eternal law naturally promulgated is the gain or loss in varying degrees of the goods of self-preservation, the propagation of the race, community living with a prevailing sense of justice, and the acquisition of knowledge and the exercise of free decisions.[114] The reward for observing the eternal law divinely promulgated is all these goods and beside as a final reward the vision of God permanently possessed.[115] The punishment for violating this law is the loss of these goods in varying degrees and the ultimate loss of the possibility of union with God forever.[116]

Obligation

The obligation of the eternal law rests on a means-end basis. As promulgated through created natures, the eternal law expresses itself in the basic drives of all beings[117]—whether recognized as such by the individual or not as explained above. These inclinations, inasmuch as they are for means and ends perfective of beings, bespeak the necessity of these means for these ends.[118]

Such a necessity need not be promulgated in a grammatical proposition only. Symbols, for instance, also convey such an ordering. A large brilliantly illuminated arrow directing me to drive to the right at the beginning of a divided highway is as much an expression of a means necessary for an end as any grammatically expressed proposition, even if I do not know it represents lawmaking authority. It could conceivably have been put there by public minded neighbors who had seen too many accidents occur in front of their homes in

110. 1 ST 103, 5; 1-2 ST 90, 1; 1-2 ST 93, 1.
111. 1 ST 103, 8; 1-2 ST 91, 2.
112. 1-2 ST 98, 2; 1-2 ST 106, 1.
113. 1-2 ST 21, 3-4; 1-2 ST 114, 1-3; 1-2 ST 87, 1-8.
114. 1-2 ST 94, 2.
115. 2-2 ST 175, 3, 4.
116. 1-2 ST 87, 3-4.
117. 1-2 ST 91, 2.
118. *Ibid.*

the absence of proper action by a lax highway commission. But the assumption is that the arrow is an expression of law and pleading ignorance thereof would hardly constitute a defense if I am arrested for disobeying the directive and driving down the wrong side of the highway. So also do drives or inclinations express an ordering.

The necessity of means for an end, as we have seen, is the basis of natural obligation,[119] which in turn is the ground for the obligation of all man-made law.[120] For it is in the first connatural judgment the mind makes regarding action, namely that what is good for me is to be sought, that the necessity of means to end is first recognized by the human mind.[121]

Obligation, as noted above, may appear at first sight to be relative and hypothetical—I ought to choose to eat, *if* I desire to preserve my life. But obligation is not relative and hypothetical if it is anchored in an absolutely and categorically desired end. Obligation is, as we have seen, the moral necessity of choosing means necessary for a desired end. But the over-all end of my actions as determined by my master drive is desired absolutely and categorically.

My master drive determines that I cannot but desire and seek what is good for me. According to the way I am structured, whenever I act it must be under the aspect of being for this end. The good is that which is necessary for my self-development or happiness. Implicitly, then, I connaturally judge that I must do whatever is necessary for this end. And because this end is desired with physical necessity and with no choice on my part,[122] obligation which is based thereon is absolute and categorical.

But how do I know what is good for me, and how do I know what will lead to this end? My other basic drives indicate certain elementary actions that are good and necessary for my self-development. One of these is my drive for self-preservation. Since I connaturally judge that whatever I have a basic drive for is good and necessary for me, I recognize without reasoning that I should preserve my life. (Even when a man has brought himself to the point where he thinks that self-destruction is "good" for him, it is a matter of observation that the drive for self-preservation and a realization that it is a necessary good for him persistently assert themselves up until his act of self-destruction. This is why some degree of inward struggle always accompanies suicide in a medically normal person.) Hence, I am obliged absolutely and categorically to use the means necessary for the preservation of my life.

119. 1 ST 82, 1; 2-2 ST 58, 3, 2.
120. 1-2 ST 93, 3.
121. 1-2 ST 94, 2.
122. 1 ST 19, 10; 1-2 ST 10, 1.

Such likewise is the case regarding all the other possible actions of my life, for they inevitably are either good and necessary for me or they are not. In many instances I will have clear directives, whether these come from the basic drives themselves or from man-made statutes and decisions or from divine revelation. But in many situations I will have to rely on my own reasoning for an evaluation. I am obliged to use some kind of ship, if I desire to cross the ocean, to revert to the example mentioned above. But why should I desire to cross the ocean? Depending principally on the reason why I am making the journey, crossing the ocean could be for me an evil, a good but not necessary, or a necessary good. If, whatever be the reason, I judge that crossing the ocean is good and necessary for me, I am obliged to desire it and to employ means necessary for its accomplishment for I am structured to seek what is good for me and I judge this action to be necessarily related to this end. I am physically free to refuse to do what I recognize is necessary for this end, but I am not physically free to decide what this, my end, is.

The obligation of the eternal law divinely promulgated rests on the same means-end basis. The end is clearly known.[123] And the means of obtaining this end are also precisely known in the revelation of the Old and New Testaments. Because of this relation of what is commanded to men's end, the commands and precepts of revelation oblige.[124]

In sum, then, regarding obligation we can say that all men who are normal human beings judge connaturally the obligatory character of the order of means to end expressed in their basic drives, whether they relate this to the eternal law or not, as mentioned above. Some men, who ponder on the nature of men and the world and come to a conviction that an eternal lawmaker exists, may see the drives of nature as the promulgation of the eternal law. Finally, all men who believe in divine revelation can, without too much difficulty, attain this comprehensive view of natures as related to the divine plan of creation.

INTERRELATION

The relation of man-made law to God-made law promulgated in natural drives is one of complement and therefore implicit dependence. From the promulgation of the eternal law in natural drives men know of certain elementary and common principles of action, as we have seen. These principles, while furnishing an elementary guide for human activities, still must be applied to individual cases. This is done either by deducing conclusions from these principles

123. 1-2 ST 3, 8.
124. 1-2 ST 99, 1; 1-2 ST 107, 2 & 3. See also 1-2 ST 21, 1.

(from the principle that one man should not harm another, the conclusion can be drawn that one should not kill another) or by adapting them to particular situations (from the principle that the evil-doer should be punished, a more specific determination must be made regarding what kind of punishment should be administered in particular instances).[125] Because of the great difference in the needs of various peoples, the common principles cannot be applied to all men in the same way. Hence, there will be a great diversity of man-made law among various peoples.[126]

In view of the role played by man-made law in the application of the naturally known common principles of action, those principles become the very fabric of statutes and decisions, whether recognized as such or not. The concept of obligation itself in man-made law derives from the necessity of means to end expressed in the basic drives, as already noted.[127] All areas of man-made law have their roots in the demands of the basic drives. Legal enactments regarding health and safety, sex and domestic living, ownership and contract, to mention but three areas of law, take their meaning and value from the fact that the preservation of life, the use of sex, the distinguishing of "mine" from "thine" are naturally recognized as good and not as evil. No legislator or judge has ever found it necessary to establish the rightness of these actions in general by legal decree. Men connaturally judge, in law and otherwise, that these actions are not evil in themselves but rather are good.[128]

The relation of man-made law to the eternal law divinely promulgated is one of the relatively certain being clarified by the absolutely certain. Besides the eternal law naturally known and its complement in man-made law, a more clear and precise divine revelation of the eternal law was necessary for four reasons: first, the actual end of men cannot be known by natural powers and a higher directive is needed; second, human judgment regarding contingent and particular matters is uncertain and liable to error and absolute certainty is necessary in these matters; third, human directives can only cover the exterior actions of men and their interior actions as well must be directed; and fourth, human law cannot pretend to punish all evils for if it did so it would do away with many good things, and all evils must eventually be punished.[129]

The comprehensiveness of Aquinas' thinking on law becomes evident at this point. The primordiality of the eternal law naturally pro-

125. 1-2 ST 91, 3; 1-2 ST 95, 2.
126. 1-2 ST 95, 2, 3.
127. 1-2 ST 94, 2; 1-2 ST 99, 1.
128. 1-2 ST 94, 2.
129. 1-2 ST 91, 4.

mulgated in relation to man-made law, the necessity of providing man-made law to complement this naturally known eternal law, and the final insufficiency of both of these which is remedied through the divinely promulgated eternal law, all attest to the sweep of his thought in this most vital matter.

Observations and Comments

At this juncture certain remarks seem called for regarding Aquinas' treatment of law. Some of these will be by way of general observations, others in the nature of specific comments.

A cursory glance at the references given above in our précis of Aquinas' position will readily show that they have not been drawn exclusively from the relatively small section of his work entitled "On Laws."[130] This is the section that has been frequently reprinted and which most American lawmen read when they desire to know something of the thought of Aquinas on law. They do not realize that anything like a comprehensive understanding of this man's position on law can be achieved only by going far beyond this section to other parts of his entire work. This is understandable since his thinking on law is organically integrated, as it should be, with his thinking regarding the meaning of existence and of human nature.

The nature of the common good and of obligation, for example, is nowhere developed in specific treatments by Aquinas. There were good reasons for this. The common good was accepted in his time as a "dictum authenticum," that is, a valid concept that needed no verification. It was something like the notion "common welfare" is today. But unlike the broad and vague notion of "common welfare," the idea of the common good has a concise and technical meaning which could be and was stated by Aquinas. This was not done, however, in any one locus. Only by ranging over the entire works of Aquinas, where the common good is found discussed obiter in relation to other subjects, can anything resembling a rounded idea of the common good be obtained.

Similarly, there is no explicit treatment of obligation in the works of Aquinas and understandably so. Law for him entailed the relation of means necessary for an end. If an end was desired and a certain means was necessary to attain it, one would be obliged to choose this means in order to reach the end, as we saw. In such a view, obligation is no problem and, once again, Aquinas touched on it obiter when treating some related matter. Obligation becomes a problem only when the objective relation of means to end grounded on a fact situation is blocked off from functioning as a basis of obligation, and

130. 1-2 ST 90-96.

obligation is said to arise solely from the subjective will's "ought for ought's sake."[131] Hence, a knowledge of the meaning of obligation in Aquinas can be acquired only by going beyond the section entitled "On Laws."

More pointedly, however, certain comments need to be made. These will be only briefly mentioned here rather than being extensively developed, since the lengthy treatment which their complexity demands would be out of place in an article of this scope. These comments will have one thing in common: they will call attention to differing ways in which Aquinas uses the word "law."

"Law" as Directive Judgment

First, Aquinas' main division of law is into eternal law, natural law, human law, and divine law.[132] But, as we have already mentioned above and will note again below, he explains both natural law and divine law as promulgations of the eternal law. If this is the case, "law" is being used in his principal division in two different senses: one refers to human and eternal law, the other to the two ways in which the eternal law is promulgated, namely, natural law and divine law.

The use of the word "law" as a designation for both man-made and God-made law is the division of "law" that we have employed in this article. If law is an ordering or directive judgment of reason, the main distinction of law should be between those directive judgments that are formed in the minds of men and those that are formed in the mind of God; for the most fundamental division possible of existing things is that between created beings and uncreated being, which in this context implies the distinction between created minds and uncreated mind. On this basis, the first and controlling division of law is into man-made or human law and God-made or eternal law. In each of these instances, the word "law" is used to designate a *proportional* fact situation in which there is an actual similarity between the directive judgment in the mind of men and the directive judgment in the mind of God. There are, obviously, proportional differences also such as the differing sources of lawmaking authority and differing common goods.[133]

"Law" as Promulgation

Second, if natural law and divine law are called "law," in what sense is the word used? What Aquinas designates as "natural law" is, according to his own explanation, the natural promulgation of the

131. See KANT, *op. cit. supra* note 103, at 68.
132. 1-2 ST 91.
133. On the analogy of law see DAVITT, THE ELEMENTS OF LAW 150-52 (1959).

eternal law.[134] What he titles "divine law," again on his own accounting, is but the revelatory promulgation of the eternal law.[135] But can the promulgation of a law be termed "law"; and, if so, with what meaning?

When Aquinas gives his definition of law, he seems to include promulgation as part of it.[136] Promulgation, however, as he explains in this same article, is the "application" of a rule to individuals according to which they are to be guided. This application takes place when the rule is made known to them.[137] Promulgation, then, as explained by Aquinas and in spite of the fact that he seems to include it in the definition of law, is not part of the essence of law. What is applied must be already constituted what it is before it can be applied, as already noted. For instance, a cane is a cane before it is applied or used by an old man.[138] Promulgation, therefore, is but a prerequisite condition for a law to become an effective guide.[139]

Accordingly, if the natural promulgation of the eternal law is called "law" (natural law) and the revelatory promulgation of the eternal law is called "law" (divine law), the word "law" in these instances is not being used in a sense based on proportional facts as is the case concerning man-made (human law) and God-made law (eternal law). But because of the relation of promulgation to the directive judgments of lawmakers, as the necessary condition for their efficacy, promulgation does in a way partake of the effectiveness of law. For this reason "law" is *attributed* to promulgation as when we call the written statute "law." When "law" is used at all regarding promulgation, then it has to be understood as being attributed to it.

"Law" as Knowledge of Law

Third, besides saying that "natural law" refers to the inclination through which the eternal is naturally promulgated, as we saw above, Aquinas also says that "natural law" is the "light of natural reason" by which we discern what is good and evil.[140] This apparently inconsistent explanation of the nature of "natural law" presents a problem. To call our reason (by which we know the naturally promulgated eternal law) "law," is to extend the use of the word "law" beyond the directive judgment of the lawmaker, and beyond its promulgation, to the subject's knowledge of the law. But in what sense can the word "law" be used to denote the subject's knowledge

134. 1-2 ST 91, 2; 1-2 ST 93, 2; 1-2 ST 93, 5, 1; 1-2 ST 94, 2; 1-2 ST 94, 3.
135. 1-2 ST 91, 4; 1-2 ST 91, 4, 1; 1-2 ST 98, 3, 3.
136. 1-2 ST 90, 4.
137. *Ibid.*
138. 1-2 ST 16, 1; 1-2 ST 17, 3.
139. 1-2 ST 90, 4. See also 2 LOTTIN, PRINCIPES DE MORALE 97 (1947).
140. 1-2 ST 91, 2; 4 AQUINAS, COMMENTARY ON THE SENTENCES OF PETER LOMBARD 33, 1, 1 (1256).

of the law?

When I learn what the traffic law is from its promulgation through a roadside sign or symbol such as mentioned above, can the judgment I thereby make be termed "law"? It would seem not. My knowledge of the law is not the law. Hence, if the connatural knowledge I have of the eternal law expressed in the ordering of my basic drives is termed "law," it is in a sense that has no relation to the manner in which "law" is used in ordinary legal parlance. At this point, communication breaks down between those who use the word in this sense and the legal mind.

Why, it should be asked, did Aquinas say in one place that natural law is the light of reason and in another place that it is the basic inclinations? This seeming discrepancy has long since been noted.[141] Although these two meanings are interrelated, they are not the same. "Reason" refers to knowing and "inclination" pertains to seeking.[142]

An answer may be that it was merely a matter of emphasis for Aquinas. Men's inclinations are rational inclinations inasmuch as man is rational and his reason is what specifies him uniquely as a man. Reason is that part of man that is like his creator. The only way that men can act is according to what they judge is good for them and it is only through a judgment of reason (with or without a syllogistic process) that men recognize an action as good or bad. Without this judgment of reason, the relation of agreement or disagreement between the action and some norm would not be recognized.[143] In this sense reason, judging with good intention, is the norm of the goodness or badness of human action and can be said to "participate" in the divine reason's lawmaking.[144]

But if this relation between an action and its norm is not to be merely a subjective one originating solely within reason itself (as Kant said it was), it must be grounded on an objective basis, one which is outside reason and according to which reason judges. This is recognized by Aquinas. For when he explains how reason can be a rule for human actions, he says that its guide "is derived from the created things that man knows naturally" as well as from divine revelation.[145] And according to Aquinas himself, as we have seen,

141. See LECLERCQ, LA PHILOSOPHIE MORALE DE SAINT THOMAS DEVANT LA PENSÉE CONTEMPORAINE 391-392 (1955).

142. 1-2 ST 94, 2.

143. Moreover, the part that reason plays in men's lives needed stressing in Aquinas' time. There were those who felt that men's minds were either darkened by paganism or enlightened by revelation. The function of reason, especially as a prerequisite to faith in revelation, needed emphasis and Aquinas supplied this to no small degree.

144. 1-2 ST 90, 1, 1; 1-2 ST 91, 4, 1; 1-2 ST 93, 2.

145. 1-2 ST 74, 7.

these "created things" are men's basic drives or inclinations.

Men do participate in the divine reason's law-ordering, dynamically expressed in their nature, by connaturally recognizing it through their own reason and by directing their actions accordingly. But they do not participate in the divine reason's law-ordering in the sense that their own reason is a co-planner, co-creator of nature and drives, and co-lawmaker with the eternal reason. Man is not God.

"Law" as Reasoned Conclusions

Fourth, if the inclinations are not retained as the starting point of reasoning regarding the goodness and badness of human action, there will be a tendency to allow the "light" of reason to take their place. All judgments concerning the goodness and badness of human actions will be said to belong to the natural law inasmuch as these judgments depend on their relation to "reason" which is the "proper principle of human acts."[146] Thus, Aquinas explains, reason starts with naturally known principles and proceeds in various ways to judge in diverse matters.

Some judgments are reached immediately and with very little consideration, for instance, that parents should be honored and that no one should kill or steal. Other judgments are reached only after much consideration, for example, that the aged should be honored.[147] This is the basis for the traditional distinction between primary, secondary, and tertiary precepts of the natural law.[148] All of these judgments, not only those connaturally known through the inclinations but also those that are reached by way of reasoned conclusions from these primary judgments, "belong to the natural law."

But, as Aquinas recognizes, many of the judgments that need consideration may be in error. In fact, this is the precise reason why revelation is necessary.[149] If this is the case, in what sense can these reasoned conclusions be called "law"? They are not certain knowledge of the law as are the connatural judgments and even these cannot with accuracy be termed "law," as we have just seen. Further, it is an immemorial axiom that a law about which there is a doubt does not bind. The reason is that if there is doubt, the law has not been clearly and certainly promulgated. And if a law is not fully and undoubtedly promulgated to us, we cannot be expected to be obliged by it. But when error is possible in knowing what a law is, it has not been clearly promulgated.[150] Hence, it would seem better

146. 1-2 ST 100, 1.
147. *Ibid.*
148. On the inutility of continuing this distinction see LOTTIN, MORALE FUNDAMENTALE 120-125, 183-188 (1954).
149. 1-2 ST 91, 4; 1-2 ST 100, 11.
150. This is not the same as "ignorantia non excusat." The ignorance of the law which does not excuse presupposes that there exists a law that has

not to designate as "law," not only the connatural judgments by which we know the eternal law, but also the conclusions we reach by reasoning from these principles.

Rather, these reasoned conclusions should be termed what they actually are: attempts to determine what is good and bad regarding human actions, say using nuclear bombs, in the absence of clear and specific directives. These judgments should be in conformity with divinely revealed eternal law and with the statutes and decisions of human law. But in the absence of such specific directives or of a knowledge of them, all that men can do is reason, deductively and inductively, from the connaturally known elementary demands of their basic drives and conclude what seems best to them in particular situations. These judgments are obligatory on individuals, not because they represent certain knowledge of a law, but because they are the only norm of goodness or badness the individual has according to which he may guide himself. This norm he must follow since for him personally in many circumstances there is no other.

This is the situation whether the reasoning be done by private persons or by those with public authority. The conclusions that legislators and judges arrive at when reasoning from the basic demands of men's nature can be, upon occasion, no more certain and free from error than those of the people who elected them. For although the people can give their representatives the authority to govern them politically, they cannot give them what they do not have, namely, the insight always to reach reasoned conclusions that are free from error. The authority which the people have to direct their own actions, which is delegated in part to their representatives, does not derive from a certain knowledge of the minutest possible demands of their nature. Rather it comes from the necessity of determining, in the absence of other guides as we have just noted, what is best in a given situation.

It can therefore be said that the conclusions reached by legislators and judges take on the aspect of law because they are embodied in a prudential judgment which is a legal directive of the people concerning means necessary for their common good. For this purpose the people have delegated lawmaking authority and it is many times by this type of judgment alone that lawmakers can guide the people. Although as far as the lawmakers themselves are concerned their judgments are rectified by conformity with right intention, as we

been properly promulgated and concerning which this particular individual is ignorant. Although he may not be morally guilty of committing a crime, nevertheless on account of evidential expediency he cannot be held to be legally excused. On the other hand, the principle "lex dubia non obligat" calls in question the very existence of the law. If the law existed, it can be assumed to have been properly promulgated. Otherwise, it does not oblige.

saw above, nevertheless in reference to the fact situation at hand these judgments are quite often only relatively certain and may quite possibly be in error.

It should be noted that Aquinas does not attempt to show how judgments regarding killing, stealing, honoring parents and the aged, and the like, are deducible from the certainly known principles which he has already established as the point of departure for any reasoning concerning the goodness or badness of human activities.[151] It is conjecturable that if he had made this attempt, which would have meant keeping the demands of the drives in center focus, a more careful statement would have resulted regarding the status of conclusions reached by the reasoning of individuals as natural "law."

Aquinas, however, did not have the opportunity to revise this section of his work. He died a few short years after it was written. As has been remarked, "It is unfortunate for the clarity of his views toward natural law that Aquinas, who died at the age of forty-nine (or forty-seven), did not live longer so as to be able to elaborate the full implications of his philosophy of the natural law."[152]

Another result of keeping the inclinations fixedly in view would undoubtedly have been a more limited concept of natural law which, taken in its strict sense, would be confined to those judgments that are known connaturally from the basic drives. Such judgments are common to all men who are normal according to medical standards and therefore have universal validity. If, on the other hand, the accent is put on "reason," this can be wrongly interpreted and "natural law" can come to mean what is common among "reasonable" (or even civilized) people. Such an interpretation could be the explanation of why more candid and critical attempts have not been made to ascertain what the universal judgments of the natural law actually are.

It has been said that emphasis on "reason" has

> for two thousand years tempted thinkers away from the search for universal elements. The trouble is that therewith our own interpretation of what is reasonable decides the outcome of our research in advance. We are naturally always inclined to consider our own ideas about justice reasonable and those of others that conflict with ours, unreasonable. Whenever reasonableness is the issue, we cannot decide it in an intersubjectively plausible manner by referring to our own reason . . . . Therefore it is most important to stick to the identification of those elements in the sense of justice that are universal and invariant in *all* people, and not only in those whom we call reasonable.[153]

151. 1-2 ST 94, 2.
152. BROWN, THE NATURAL LAW READER 100 (1960).
153. BRECHT, POLITICAL THEORY 394-395 (1959). See also 386, 490, 492.

"Blue-Print" Theory

Further, it is only when the word "law" is restricted to its proportionately factual use regarding man-made and God-made law and to its attributive use concerning their promulgations, that the "blue-print" notion of natural law fostered by Locke and others can be avoided.[154] This is the idea that natural law is some sort of a formal code of specific ideal precepts, deducible with mathematical certainty, which human law must match and reflect if it is to be just.

Such a "natural law" is actually moral philosophy turned legal discipline. Instead of recognizing man-made law as the complement and development of relatively few certain moral principles, men began to look on the conclusions deduced from these principles as "original" law in conformity to which the provisions of man-made law were a duplication or a "copy." The view was that somewhere behind or above legal rights, which pertained to "law," there was an explicit code of natural rights, which was a matter of "morality." Such thinking could not but produce a sharp distinction between law and morality.

It must be admitted that sometimes the interpretation put on Aquinas' natural law can sound like that of Locke. Such is the case, for instance, when it is said that natural law is "a code levied on all men"[155] or that "by examining his nature with the light of reason man develops the natural law into a formal code of moral principles."[156] It may be true that Aquinas' use of the word "law" regarding reasoned conclusions has misled some into holding the "formal code" interpretation. But his express recognition of the possibility of error in these conclusions should be enough to alert the perceptive reader to be wary of adopting any such position.

In Aquinas' mind natural law, far from being a mechanical archetype of man-made law, is rather its organic *élan vital.* The implications of the natural demands of men's nature are "open" to a continuous evolving through the human legal process. Aquinas' position is, therefore, "far from an abstract rationalism which seeks to deduce by reason a solution for every specific concrete question. Thus there is plenty of scope in his construction for a sociological-realistic form of legal politics."[157]

In sum, as far as this "comment" goes, Aquinas uses the word "law" in reference to four different data: the directive judgment of lawmakers (human and eternal law), the promulgation of this judgment

154. See LOCKE, AN ESSAY CONCERNING HUMAN UNDERSTANDING, bk. 4, c. 3, n. 20 (Pringle-Pattison ed. 1934); GROTIUS, DE JURE BELLI AC PACIS, bk. 2, c. 20, 43, 1 (Whewell ed. 1853).

155. HIGGINS, MAN AS MAN 115 (1949).

156. FAGOTHEY, RIGHT AND REASON 187 (2d ed. 1959).

157. ROSS, ON LAW AND JUSTICE 245 (1959).

(natural law and divine law), the knowledge acquired without reasoning that we have of the eternal law naturally promulgated ("primary knowledge of the natural law"), and conclusions reached by us through reasoning from these primary principles ("secondary and tertiary knowledge of the natural law"). From our above examination, it is evident that the word "law" is used analogously and validly in the first two instances; proportionately so regarding man-made and God-made law, attributively so concerning the promulgation of law. Its use in the other two instances is such that, as far as the legal mind is concerned, no communication takes place.

Applications

One of the most important applications of Aquinas' philosophy of law relates to its main presupposition. This is his philosophy of human nature according to which men are essentially composed not only of matter but also of spirit with its two powers of intellect and will. This unique nature sets men apart from all else in creation. Each man is a distinct, separate entity with a dignity peculiar to him and to him alone.[158]

Individual and Society

When the question is raised, then, whether the individual man or society is the more important and whether man-made law should favor the one or the other, the basis for an exact answer is at hand. Inasmuch as men need and must work for the temporal, political common good of peace, security and the like, society is more important and individual men are subject to the laws that are designed to bring these ends about.[159] But insofar as by their very nature men have a destiny that transcends the temporal and the political, individuals are more important than society and should not be restrained by man-made law from pursuing those activities that pertain directly to this higher and ultimate end.[160]

This interpretation of the nature of men is the lode star that guides all thinking regarding life and law. Aquinas himself did not draw the implications of his philosophy of law regarding the various areas of law as we know them today, for this was not his purpose. But because it is fairly obvious what some of these applications would be at least in broad outline regarding certain controlling points in law, they will be briefly indicated.

Constitutional Law

Constitutional law, besides establishing the type of government

158. 1 ST 75-83; 1-2 ST 2, 8; 1-2 ST 3, 3.
159. 1-2 ST 21, 3, 2; 1-2 ST 90, 2; 1-2 ST 96, 4.
160. 1-2 ST 2, 8; 1-2 ST 3, 4; 1-2 ST 21, 4, 3.

we have and fixing the limits of its authority, is also concerned with the protection of the rights of individual citizens. The method by which this is accomplished is principally "due process." In its procedural aspect, due process presupposes the substantive claims of individuals. In its substantive aspect, it attempts to strike a balance between private claims and public needs. But what are the grounds on which rest the validity of the so-called "inalienable" rights of individuals?

According to the thought of Aquinas, the grounds for the "inalienable" rights of men can be found in the basic drives of their nature which demand certain elementary things as necessary for men's self-development and eventual perfection. In other words, the "inalienable" rights of men do not derive from a contract made by men when they supposedly transferred from a hypothetical "state of nature" to a state of political government.[161] They derive, rather, from the demands of men's political nature as it is now and always was. The demands of men's nature (and in this sense "natural law") naturally coexist with man-made law. They are not in unnatural competition with it. They are in fact its leitmotiv.

Nor do the "inalienable" rights derive from some sort of basic norm arrived at by international agreements which must be kept.[162] For the question can be immediately raised: why should agreements be kept? The answer must be either that they should be kept simply because they should be kept, which is no answer at all; or it must be that keeping agreements is necessary for the common good of men as demanded by their very nature.[163] It is only when an interpretation of human nature such as that of Aquinas is rejected, that men are driven to such strained and far-fetched notions concerning the origin of men's natural rights.

Criminal Law

In criminal law the thrust of Aquinas' philosophy of man and law can be seen most clearly. This is especially true in the light of certain contemporary trends such as those represented in the *Durham* decision.[164] The thinking of the court in this case works dead against the grain of Aquinas' entire thought. The underlying assumption of this decision is that, for all practical purposes, only the mentally defective or diseased commit crimes.[165] This assumption rests on the further one that the "modern science of psychology" has ruled out as

161. See HOBBES, LEVIATHAN, pt. I, c. 13 (Molesworth ed. 1839); LOCKE, TWO TREATISES ON GOVERNMENT, 2d Treatise, c. 2, 6 (Cook ed. 1947); ROUSSEAU, THE SOCIAL CONTRACT, bk. I, c. 6 (Watkins transl. 1953).

162. See KELSEN, GENERAL THEORY OF LAW AND STATE 369 (1945).

163. See *Contract Law* below.

164. Durham v. United States, 94 App. D.C. 228, 214 F.2d 862 (1954).

165. 214 F.2d at 875, 876.

passé the interpretation of men as beings who, although perfectly sane, can be led by the condition of their will and desires to choose knowingly and freely to go against what their reason judges to be the right thing to do.[166]

As we have already seen above in discussing the sanction of man-made law, Aquinas holds that men are responsible beings because they have the power of knowing and freely deciding. Actions that are knowingly and freely decided are caused by their doers, they belong to them, and are therefore imputable to them as good or bad. Sanity, like knowledge, is a prerequisite condition for a crime. A lack of it, insanity, is not a cause of crime but may rather be the reason why the accused is not guilty of committing a formal crime at all. Factors such as ignorance, violence, fear, anger, passion, compulsions, mental defect and the like may affect both knowledge and the freedom of decision. Insofar as they do, responsibility and imputability are lessened or completely nullified. Absolute freedom is not required and relative freedom can be sufficient.

But this does not mean that every time a crime is committed one of these factors must have been at work. When this is the case it has to be proved, not presumed. For instance, an accused may be mentally defective but this condition will have to be established on medical evidence. What the commission of every crime does signify, however, is that the condition of the accused's will was such that he chose to put himself above the law and egotistically preferred his desires to those of society as expressed in the law. Such would be the case if the judge himself who wrote the *Durham* decision chose to violate a speed law, which would be at least a misdemeanor if not a felony under some circumstances.

The presence of mental disease is an abnormal condition. The presence of a lawbreaking disposition in our will is not a disease nor is it abnormal. It is as normal as is a law-abiding state of will, though obviously of an entirely different value. To give the word "normal" a statistical meaning in this context and to label the nonconformist a "sociopath," is to betray a superficiality unworthy of reputable psychiatry.

Tort Law

In torts also the force of Aquinas' thought can be seen in relation to a contemporary tendency and again this is in reference to the root problem of responsibility. This is logically consistent since "the general principles of criminal and civil liability are the same . . . ."[167] Absolute or strict liability, where the ability to pay is often a relevant

166. 214 F.2d at 871.
167. Holmes, The Common Law 44 (1881).

factor in determining liability, plows head-on against the current of Aquinas' thinking. This theory assumes that in cases where there is no intended harm or negligence, liability cannot be related to any blameworthy act on the part of the tortfeasor. He has committed no fault, such as occurs when there is intended harm or negligence. In undertakings such as keeping dangerous animals, using high explosives or poisonous sprays, or bringing upon land dangerous quantities of substances not naturally there, liability is said to be "without fault" and must be related, not to the defendant's "fault" which does not exist, but to some extrinsic factor such as his ability to pay.

Again, as we have seen above, for Aquinas, responsibility originates in the doer's decision to perform the action. He is thus the cause of the act and of what follows as a result of the act. On this basis rests his responsibility and liability. There is an intrinsic relation between liability and the decision to act. Hence, the consistent explanation from this point of view is that, although there may be no fault in strict liability cases (if there were it would be morally wrong to engage in such enterprises), nevertheless there is assumed responsibility in them. On the decision to engage in these activities and thereby assume responsibility for them is grounded the tortfeasor's liability. This, it is now conceded, is the principle of law expressed in *Rylands v. Fletcher* and not ability to pay, which appears to have been born of a misinterpretation of this famous case.[168]

The importance of locating the grounds of responsibility in torts is the same as it is in crimes. Either it must be held that the basis of responsibility is ultimately some factor within the actor or that it is something outside him. Either it will be his knowing and free decision to do the act as explained above or it will be something like "ability to pay" in torts and "society's failure" in crimes. These alternatives represent two different philosophies of responsibility and law.

Property Law

In property law there is an assumption made in one half of the legal world that is totally rejected in the other half—that men have a natural right to private ownership especially of the means of production such as land, ore, coal, oil, gas, uranium and the like. Aquinas' position in this matter is cognate with the legal thinking prevalent in what is now termed "the free world."

First, in general it is natural for man to have dominion over things external to himself. This is why things were made. The imperfect

168. Rylands v. Fletcher, L.R. 3 H.L. 330 (1868). See PROSSER, SELECTED TOPICS ON THE LAW OF TORTS 179-80 (1953).

is for the sake of the perfect[169] and through his reason and will man can put them to his own use.[170] This he must do if he is to sustain his own life.[171] There is, then, a common aspect to things according to which all things are made for all men.

Second, in particular it is natural for men to own things as their own for several reasons. Men work more solicitously when expending their efforts on something that is their own. This causes affairs to be conducted in a more orderly fashion. As a consequence, each man being content with his own, a more peaceful condition is ensured. For it is when things are not possessed by men as their own that quarrels arise more frequently.[172]

It could be objected that according to nature all things are common to all men and that to possess things as one's own is contrary to this common ownership of goods. Aquinas explains that the natural law does not "dictate" that all things should be possessed in common and that nothing should be possessed as one's own. Rather, men recognize the practical necessity of possessing external things as their own for the reasons just mentioned and establish the institution of private ownership.[173]

Third, an important qualification is added by Aquinas. Although men may possess things as their own, they must never lose sight of the common aspect of things as noted first above, that is, that all things are created for all men. Hence, men must be prepared to share what they have with others in their need.[174] The Marshall Plan of giving economic aid to needy countries (apart from the political motives that to some degree inspired it and the manner in which it has at times been administered) could perhaps be pointed to as an example of this principle in action on the national level.

Contract Law

Contracts, or more specifically the part played by one type of consideration in contracts, is one final area of law in which the implications of Aquinas' thinking may be indicated here, although there are many more such areas which cannot be treated within the confines of this article. Contracts are promissory agreements. Contracts are said to oblige in Anglo-American law because of consideration. Consideration, in its most important form, is the price bargained and paid for a promise. Such bargain and exchange consideration is evidence of intention to enter upon a legal contract and as such is

169. 2-2 ST 64, 1.
170. 2-2 ST 66, 1.
171. 2-2 ST 66, 1, 1.
172. 2-2 ST 66, 2.
173. 2-2 ST 66, 2, 1. See also 2-2 ST 57, 4, 2. For a further developed rationale of property, see Davitt, Elements of Law 259-69 (1959).
174. 2-2 ST 66, 2.

designed to prevent fraud.

As is well known among lawmen, consideration is an Anglo-American contractual phenomenon. It is not part of the contract of non-English speaking countries. In these countries the doctrine of "cause," as evidence of intent to contract legally, is prevalent. The cause of a contract is taken to be the immediate end which the contractor has in view: the intent to exchange jural relations of title, claim and duty regarding some particular object. This intention obviously carries the implication of benefit to another party and, as such, is not too much different from consideration as has often been pointed out.[175]

For Aquinas a promise is the means by which one man binds himself to another. It entails an act of reason by which one man directs what he himself is to do for another.[176] This mental act is manifested by words, oral or written. Words are the natural, external signs of interior mental acts as we have already noted.[177]

The keeping of the promise that one man makes to another is a form of natural honesty and truthfulness.[178] If a man changes his mind and thereby redirects his actions towards the promisee otherwise than he had manifested by his words, he is guilty of a form of deception and lying. For it is unnatural for a man to signify by his words something other than what he has in his mind.[179] Men are social animals who owe one another whatever is necessary for the preservation of human society, and it would be impossible for men to live humanely in society unless they trusted each other as speaking the truth one to the other.[180] The keeping of promises is demanded, then, by the nature of men's power of speech and its relation to social needs. It is because the keeping of contractual promises is a means necessary for the common good, then, that contracts oblige.

In other words, if contractual obligation is said to derive from consideration, something outside the nature of the contractual promise itself is made the basis of the obligation. If, on the other hand, contractual obligation is seen to arise from the very nature of a promise itself, the ground of this duty is intrinsic to the nature of the contractual promise and its relation to the common good. True, evidence of the intention to contract and bind legally is necessary. Consideration can be evidence of this intent—as can cause, a writing or a seal. But taken in this evidentiary capacity, consideration is not

175. See SALMOND, JURISPRUDENCE 374 (8th ed. 1930).
176. 2-2 ST 88, 1; 2-2 ST 88, 4; 4 AQUINAS, COMMENTARY ON THE SENTENCES OF PETER LOMBARD 38, 1, 1, 1 (1256).
177. 2-2 ST 110, 3.
178. 2-2 ST 88, 3, 1.
179. 2-2 ST 110, 3, 5.
180. 2-2 ST 109, 3, 1.

the reason why contracts oblige. It is merely evidence of the intention to bind legally.

Conclusion

The work of Aquinas can furnish us with the firm guide lines in our thinking regarding law. As noted above, it is undoubtedly a masterful accomplishment. Nonetheless, being a pioneer endeavor it has, to use an expression of the French, the defects of its qualities. Its main outlines are solid and will stand foursquare as the test of the centuries has proved. On the other hand, clarifications of terminology are needed; adjustments are called for; details must be filled in. But the main inspiration and direction of Aquinas' thought are as right and valid today as they were the day he first put pen to paper and began to write "On Laws."

Undoubtedly one of the most important aspects of his contribution is natural law and its relation to eternal law. The vitality of natural law is shown by its history which is a series of eclipses and revivals from the Greeks to the present time.[181] And it is important to note in this regard that "the natural law which today dominates the greater part of legal philosophy is not a revival of the eighteenth century rationalist systems, but a thread of scholasticism that has been picked up again."[182]

But it must be remembered, in assessing the practical value of Aquinas, that his thought is an integral whole. It is a synthesis organically related to his philosophy of being and of man. This fact has sometimes been overlooked as when it is said, for instance, that "If we disregard the metaphysical and the dogmatic [in Aquinas], there are favorable opportunities for an understanding between this trend [Thomism] and a realistic study of law."[183] This is much like saying that if we only prescind from the economics and the dialectical materialism in Marxism there are great possibilities for accepting this ideology as a way of life.

No, the thinking of Aquinas, like that of any consistent man, must be taken in its entirety if it is to be comprehended at all. More discerning are the remarks that "what has really been revived is a strong sense of the need which gave rise to the doctrine of natural law in the past: the need for a standard of justice by which to evaluate the positive law, a standard firm and yet not subject to the criticism which destroyed the older natural-law doctrines" and that this is "a broad philosophical problem" to which only a tradi-

---

181. See Brecht, Political Theory 138-142 (1959).
182. Ross, On Law and Justice 255 (1959).
183. *Id.* at 245.

tion such as that of Aquinas "has a coherent metaphysical answer."[184] It is only when Aquinas is approached on this radical level that an insight is possible into the profound implications of his thought on law.

184. FRIEDRICH, THE PHILOSOPHY OF LAW IN HISTORICAL PERSPECTIVE 188 (1958).

[6]

AN EXAMINATION OF THE THOMISTIC THEORY OF NATURAL MORAL LAW*

Kai Nielsen

THEORIES OF NATURAL MORAL LAW have deep roots in our culture. They have emerged again and again in our western tradition, not, however, without important variations. They are less appealing in times of social and political stability than in times of social crisis. In times when man turns against man, voices are always raised to remind us that man by virtue of his very humanity has certain inalienable rights and certain absolute correlative obligations to his fellow man. Like Antigone, we appeal to moral laws that transcend an ethnocentric "closed morality" of social pressure. In our recent history, liberalism, both theoretically and practically, has faced dilemmas; liberalism has been subjected to penetrating and varied challenges. Saddled with this situation, some theologizing political scientists have hoped to find in the classical doctrine of the natural moral law a "new" and more secure moral foundation for democracy and a solution to the modern liberal predicament. As incisive a student of the changing human scene as Walter Lippmann, has in his *The Public Philosophy* attempted a modern adaptation of the classical natural moral law theory as the way to wisdom in our social life and politics. By return to a secure foundation in the classical tradition of natural moral law, we can underwrite democracy and escape the quandary of "the masterless man" searching—perhaps unconsciously—for his "soul" or for a point of view for which he can live and die. A social ethic, firmly grounded in the natural moral law, will supply a dynamic standard to enable us to root out the modern malaise that says, with James Joyce, "Ours is an age of exhausted whoredom, groping for its God."

I believe the philosophical and ethical theory operating in these classical natural moral law theories to be basically mistaken. Therefore, I do not believe they can serve as adequate theoretical justifications for democracy or for anything else. Rather than criticize Lippmann explicitly, I will turn here to Lippmann's mentors, that is to say, I shall turn to the well-articulated and thoroughly developed theory of natural moral law that we find in Aquinas and in some contemporary Thomists. In this con-

* I should like to thank Professor Warren C. Hamill of St. Anselm's College for his helpful criticism of an earlier draft of this essay, though I should not like to suggest that he would agree with my criticisms of Aquinas.

nection, I shall pay particular attention to the arguments of Jacques Maritain and F. C. Copleston.[1]

It is important to note that I am not contending it is unintelligible to speak in some vague and unanalyzed sense of a natural good or goods that men generally incline toward.[2] I am only contending here that the scholastic, philosophical theory about natural law is in some basic respects unsatisfactory and, in the last analysis, unintelligible. I neither assert nor deny there are some basic moral evaluations common to the human animal. I should think that there are some, but the problem is too amorphous to be settled as yet. We need first a detailed analysis of what is meant by the terms, 'common good,' 'pan-human good' or 'basic moral evaluations,' and we need a thorough comparative anthropological investigation of what moral appraisals are actually made in radically different cultures. To take a stand pro or con, prior to such investigations, is unreasonable. I shall try here to fairly state and criticize the Thomistic theory of natural moral law.

I shall do this in the following way. In I, I shall make some remarks about what has been taken by the Thomists to be the proper setting for an adequate statement of the natural moral law theory. Then in II and III, I shall turn to the epistemic side of Thomistic ethical theory. In II, I state and evaluate Maritain's conception of "knowledge through inclination" and in III, contrast Thomas' ethical theory with theological voluntarism and criticize the Thomistic concept of something being self-evident in itself. In IV, I shall elucidate what Aquinas means by 'natural moral law' and contrast it with his other conceptions of law. In V, I shall state and then critically comment on the primary and secondary precepts of the natural moral law. In VI, I shall first discuss two standard difficulties with the natural law theory and then turn to two less frequently voiced, but more radical criticisms, that — to my mind — take us to the heart of the matter. Finally, I shall turn in VII and VIII to some puzzles about morality and teleology that might, in the light of my arguments in VI, prove worrisome.

---

1. The basic texts involved are St. Thomas Aquinas, Summa Theologiae I-II, Qq. 90-108; and Summa Contra Gentiles, Book III; Copleston's major treatment occurs in F. C. Copleston, Aquinas, ch. V (Baltimore, 1955). For Jacques Maritain's most recent extended examination, see his Man and the State (Chicago, 1951); The Range of Reason (New York, 1951); and *Natural Law and Moral Law,* in Moral Principles of Action 62-76 (ed. by R. N. Anshem, New York, 1952). I have also drawn from some unpublished lectures given by Maritain at the University of Toronto in 1952. For a brief but excellent summation of Aquinas' view see Clifford G. Kossel, S. J., *The Moral View of Thomas Aquinas,* Encyclopedia of Morals 11-23 (ed. by V. Ferm, New York, 1956).
2. The Oxford moralist, P. H. Nowell-Smith, makes an analysis of natural good that seems to me a step in the right direction. P. H. Nowell-Smith, Ethics 171-82 (Baltimore, 1954). Note also my remarks at the end of my essay, *Reason and Morality,* 28 Journal of Higher Education 271-275 (1957).

I

Aquinas and contemporary Thomists like Maritain and Copleston give a large place to reason in their Christian ethical theory. They argue that if man doubts God's revealed Word, he can by the use of his reason come to know that God exists and that there are certain natural moral laws carrying obligations. By his reason alone, man can know certain natural goods. Aquinas' approach here bears the stamp of Aristotle's "commonsensical philosophy of ethics."

Though "metaphysical ethics" is now out of fashion in most quarters, Aquinas' theory has no plausibility at all apart from his conception of the nature of the universe.[3] In evaluating Aquinas' ethics we must keep constantly in mind his physics and cosmology. As Copleston remarks, Aquinas "sees the moral life in the general setting of the providential government of creatures" (p. 212), that is to say, Aquinas, like Aristotle, thinks the universe is purposive. It has a destiny and a rationale. The universe is not just some vast machine or conglomeration of atoms swirling in the void. The end of all activities in nature, says Aquinas, is God. In medieval physics, it is believed that all natural motions are just so many attempts to reach the changeless. Sublunar substances seek re-establishment in their proper places. Celestial motions cannot falter; they return upon themselves in perfect circles. Nevertheless, they are still motions. Only God is absolutely motionless and changeless. All motions and all things try to attain God, the motionless or changeless Being. We know that knowledge of and union with God is man's highest good; all other goods are finally instrumental to that good. But as Sisyphus sticks to his job with his stone, we ineluctably quest for that highest good. We know God exists, but we contingent, changing creatures never obtain God or knowledge of His essence in this life. But, unlike Sisyphus, we mortals have a surcease from striving, for after death there is a complete apprehension of God in His very essence.

Maritain emphasizes that conceptions of the natural moral law cannot be secularized, as in Grotius or Paine, without cutting out their very heart. The natural moral law theory only makes sense in terms of an acceptance of medieval physics and cosmology. If we give up the view that the universe is purposive and that all motions are just so many attempts to reach the changeless, we must give up natural moral law theories. One might say, as a criticism of the Thomistic doctrine of natural moral law, that since medie-

3. Kossel remarks: "The moral science of Aquinas is deeply rooted in metaphysics and theology." Kossell, *op. cit. supra,* note 1 at 12.

val physics is false then it follows that natural moral law theory must be false. While agreeing with this criticism, I think it is too short and too easy a way out to carry complete conviction. Contemporary Thomists would like to say that somehow the medieval view of cosmology or metaphysics is distinct from physics, and though the physics is false, the cosmology is still true. This seems to me just an evasion. If the word 'cosmology' means anything at all, it seems only to denote bad armchair physics. The so-called disciplines of cosmology and metaphysics have made no progress in discovering the categorial features of the world. This is so partly because of the very unsettled and indefinite signification of the words 'cosmology' and 'metaphysics.' In such a situation, it seems to me quite unrealistic to think we can use such disciplines as a basis for anything very substantial.[4] In this connection, it might be noted, incidentally, that Copleston, in his recent book, *Contemporary Philosophy,* is extremely cautious in his claims for metaphysics.[5] He rightly criticizes many things in contemporary and analytic philosophy, but in the process, he seems to have been bitten by the empiricists' bug! I shall not, however, rest my argument on this general blast against speculative philosophy though I should like to remark that my contention does not turn on a logical positivist rejection of metaphysics as nonsense. There may be, as Peirce suggests, both good and bad metaphysics and metaphysical methods.

II

Leaving aside all talk about the adequacy or inadequacy of metaphysics, let us look directly at Aquinas' moral philosophy. Aquinas believed that the good is somehow the normal. It is found by observation; that is to say, it is to be discovered by studying man's inclinations and reflecting on them. It is to be seen by apprehending what life really is. It is important to note, however, that this is an odd kind of "seeing" or "apprehending." As Maritain makes perfectly clear, it is a direct, immediate, nonconceptual "knowing through inclination" or "knowledge through connaturality."[6] And it is important to remember here that Maritain is not just trying to urge a view of his own but is also trying to elucidate what Aquinas really meant when he said we have knowledge of the natural moral law.

---

4. Sidney Hook's critique of Thomism on this point seems to me essentially correct. See Sidney Hook, *Scientific Knowledge and Philosophical Knowledge,* 24 PARTISAN REVIEW 215-34 (1957).
5. See particularly ch. V and XII.
6. See JACQUES MARITAIN, THE RANGE OF REASON, ch. III (New York, 1952). See also his contribution, *Natural Law and Moral Law,* in MORAL PRINCIPLES OF ACTION (ed. by R. N. Anshem, New York, 1952).

Let us look a bit more carefully at this doctrine, for it is, according to Maritain, central to the Thomistic theory of natural moral law. Unfortunately, as Maritain also emphasizes, it is an extremely obscure doctrine. This so-called "knowledge through inclination" seems unlike what we ordinarily call "knowledge." It seems more like a feeling or an attitude. I am at a loss here to find an intelligible use for "knowledge," and I am far from sure that we can see clearly from Maritain's account exactly what it is that he wishes to say. (Here he could use a few lessons from G. E. Moore.) So in setting forth this aspect of Maritain's doctrine, I will be forced to use quotations liberally.

We discover first that knowledge through inclination is entirely nonrational and nonconceptual, even though produced in the intellect.[7] It is important, according to Maritain, for two reasons: 1) it "obliges us to realize in a deeper manner the analogous character of the concept of knowledge" and 2) it is important because of the role it plays in our knowledge of human existence.[8] It is obviously not a deductive kind of knowledge, and it is not knowledge through sense experience or speculative knowledge through "intellectual intuition." [9] Maritain remarks: "the intellect is at play not alone, but together with affective inclinations and the dispositions of the will, *and is guided and directed by them.*" [10] It is knowledge expressing the inner propensities of our being. It may be "incapable of giving account of itself, or of being translated into words." [11] We find it occurring in mystical experience and in "poetic knowledge," but the best paradigm for it is in moral knowledge. For Aquinas, our philosophically unmediated moral experience is the prime example of knowledge through inclination. In a very puzzling passage, Maritain remarks of Aquinas:

> It is through connaturality that moral consciousness attains a kind of knowing — *inexpressible in words and notions* — of the deepest dispositions — longings, fears, hopes or despairs, primeval loves and options — involved in the night of the subjectivity.[12]

Maritain does not deny that the facts are relevant to moral appraisal, but he adds that the moral agent must take into account "secret elements of evaluation which depend on what *he* is, and which are known to him through

---

7. MARITAIN, THE RANGE OF REASON 22 (New York, 1952).
8. *Ibid.*
9. *Id.* at 29.
10. *Id.* at 23 (italics mine).
11. *Ibid.*
12. *Id.* at 26 (italics mine).

inclination, through his own actual propensities. . . ."[13] Moral judgments which express the natural moral law are not known through any "conceptual, discursive, rational exercise of reason."[14] Instead, through inclination we grasp that what is in line with pervasive human desires and wants is good, and what conflicts with that is bad. Moral philosophy does not discover the moral law, though (in some unspecified sense) it critically analyzes and elucidates moral standards.[15] Objective moral standards (ultimately the natural moral law) are known immediately through inclination.

In this murky doctrine of "knowledge through inclination" there is (so far as I can understand it) a good bit that is true as well as a good bit that is false. I shall first remark on what seems to me true in the theory and then I shall turn to what I take to be wrong with Maritain's theory.

First, Maritain is right in claiming that the concept of knowledge has an analogous character, that is to say, the word "knowledge" gets used in several different but not unrelated ways for several different purposes. My only question here is whether Maritain has either elucidated one of its many common uses or clearly stipulated a new use. Secondly, Maritain is also right (following Aristotle) in regarding moral knowledge as a kind of practical knowledge and in claiming that moral philosophy cannot by itself supply standards of moral appraisal. Surely, if a man had never experienced pain, remorse, deprivation, desire and the like, moral distinctions could have no meaning for him. A completely unmoved spectator of the actual would and could make no moral judgments or reflective moral appraisals. Furthermore, moral appraisals are practical in the sense that they are to guide action and alter behavior and not just to describe a state of affairs. But this claim has been clearly explicated from within an essentially empiricist point of view without any of Maritain's obscure constructions.[16]

Let us now consider difficulties in Maritain's conception of "knowledge through inclination." First, the work of philosophical analysts like Ryle and Wittgenstein makes it questionable whether one can sensibly speak of a kind of knowing "inexpressible in words and notions." To call something that cannot be conceptualized or expressed "knowledge" seems like an early retreat into a kind of obscurity that makes philosophical appraisal impossible. How can we, if we doubt there is really such a kind of knowing, rationally resolve this doubt? Or, even more basically, what is it that Maritain is claim-

13. *Ibid.*
14. *Id.* at 23.
15. *Id.* at 28.
16. Philip Blair Rice has recently developed a renovated ethical naturalism in which this is one of the cornerstones of his philosophy. See PHILIP B. RICE, ON THE KNOWLEDGE OF GOOD AND EVIL (New York, 1955); and P. H. NOWELL-SMITH, ETHICS (Baltimore, 1954).

ing? It is a truism to say that in philosophical *appraisal* we must necessarily deal with what is expressible.

My second critical point about his doctrine of knowledge through inclination is connected with the last part of my second positive point. In effect, Maritain sets forth a naturalistic theory at the foundation of natural moral law:[17] what man strives for is good and what man avoids is bad. But at the same time he claims that only a supernatural sanction will do for morality and will avoid the chaos of our time. Yet, on his doctrine of knowledge through inclination and on his natural moral law theory, the man in moral perplexity needs only to observe the desires and wishes of his fellow man and by seeing what they generally seek he will know what is good and what he ought to do. It is very difficult to see how this doctrine differs very much from that of Russell (in his *Human Society in Ethics and Politics*) and Hume where they claim that reason is and ought to be the slave of the passions and that the fundamental data for and basis of ethics are the emotions, passions, and impulses. The Thomistic label "knowledge through inclination" only serves to label the baby "legitimate" in the eyes of the supernaturalists. And to call attention to the distinction between *jus gentium* and *jus naturale* is not at all to the point here, for it is claimed that by noting the actual pervasive desires and wants of the human animal we can at least dimly come to know the natural moral law.

III

Maritain, however, would not wish to accept this reduction — there are other elements in his theory that run counter to that and may provide him with a way out. For Aquinas and for Maritain good is not simply what God wills, as the theological voluntarists claim. God's intellect is logically prior to His will, according to St. Thomas. He wills the good because it is good. Aquinas' medieval opponents, Scotus and Ockham, hold different views. Scotus claims that God's will is prior to His intellect. In understanding human good, we must look to what man wills or strives for. William of Ockham goes all the way with this theological voluntarism. Something is good simply because God wills it. Goodness is in the will and not in any order of being or reality. What is right or wrong morally is not subject to rational proof as in Aquinas. Many people feel that this voluntarist view leads logically to moral skepticism.[18] It can be argued plausibly that on the one hand volun-

17. See, for example, William Frankena, *Ethical Naturalism Renovated,* 10 The Review of Metaphysics 457-73 (1957).
18. See E. W. Hall, Modern Science and Human Values 289 (Princeton, 1956).

tarism leads to Luther, Kierkegaard, and Barth, and on the other, to Hume's and Russell's view that reason is and ought to be the slave of the passions, the basic difference being that the former are supernaturalists and the latter are not. But for Aquinas, as for the Stoics, good is somehow in the very nature of things. The highest goodness is an attribute of God's very essence. This essence we know only after death. But we know now *that* God is (as opposed to knowing *what* He is); and we apprehend the natural moral law as the part of the eternal law that God allows us to understand with our reason. Our knowledge of it is not precise, but we genuinely know the unchangeable and eternal good, though we must remember this is "knowledge through inclination." This natural knowledge of good and evil is far from clear, but we do have it; and it is well to remember that this practical knowledge is claimed to be certain though cognitively unclear knowledge. By this, Aquinas (as well as Maritain) means that the natural moral law is self-evident in itself though it may not be self-evident to us.

We must, however, look into this peculiar claim of self-evidence. The uses of this word are many and varied. It is tempting to take an empiricist and pragmatist line and argue that all talk of "self-evidence" is useless or absurd because "self-evident truths" are tautological and existential statements are all less than certain. I do not — at least not here — want to make that strong claim, but only to argue that talk of "self-evidence in itself," as an idea that corresponds to the idea of the Divine Craftsman, does not make for clarity. On such a theory, statements can be self-evident in themselves quite apart from any human knowledge of them. Maritain emphasizes that it is God's Reason, not man's reason, that is the source of the natural moral law. For its authority natural moral law depends solely on "Divine Subsisting Reason." The cardinal error of Grotius and the *philosophes* (old and new) is to take natural law to be a "law of human nature" as deciphered by human reason. To do so is to make the egregious error of substituting human authority for Divine Authority, human reason for Divine Reason, as the standard for moral good. Natural moral laws are indeed rationally self-evident, but they are self-evident to God and not necessarily to man. Even assuming we can make sense of all this talk, such a conception of self-evidence still does not help us out at all, for how do we know, as moral agents faced with practical problems, which of the many moral imperatives are the self-evident laws of God? The important thing is to have something self-evident *to us,* or at least some reliable knowledge of God's natural moral law. With a natural moral theory we can, supposedly, bypass the appeal to faith made by neo-orthodoxy and by Christian existentialism. In Thomistic ethics (old and new) we have held out to us the promise of a rational ethic and rational decision procedure for what we ought to do in particular situations; but in reality, since human reason is not adequate to decide what is a natural moral law or what is or is not self-evident in such a situation, we are no better off with such a theory than with the severest fideism.

"Natural moral laws are self-evident in themselves" and "Natural moral laws are known through inclination" are two exceedingly obscure statements that raise more problems than they solve. The doctrines they express hardly function as aids to a rational solution of the problems connected with our knowledge of good and evil.

IV

Now let us see a little more specifically what Aquinas and his contemporary followers mean by "natural moral law." Perhaps here we will at least discover how to start out. The natural moral law is distinct from the laws of nature in the scientific sense of "law of nature." A law of nature is a hypothesis. It functions predictively, though there is no need to say this is all the laws of nature do. But they must at least do this. If something is a law of nature we must be able to infer from it "If so and so is done, such and such will happen." Natural moral law, on the other hand, is normative and at the same time somehow part of the very structure of the universe. It not only says what is the case, but it says what ought to be the case.

Natural moral law, for Aquinas, is not merely what is on the books. This he calls positive law. But he argues that even positive law is genuinely law only when it does not conflict with natural moral law. Law, for Aquinas, is essentially a normative or a moral notion. He defines a law as "an ordinance of reason for the common good, promulgated, and emanating from him who has care of the community." Certain elements should be noted in his definition. 1) An ordinance is a precept, or a rule, saying so and so must or should be done. It is meant to guide conduct and not just tell us what has been done, is being done, and will be done; rather it tells us that something *ought* to be done. 2) It is a rational precept, not just a command. Yet it carries an obligatory or imperative force. 3) It is for the general good or happiness of the community. It is not just any command, and it is not just for some partial good. 4) It must come from a legitimate authority. 5) It must be publicly stated or proclaimed.

There are four basic kinds of law for Aquinas (natural moral law is, of course, one of these). First, there is the Eternal Law. The Eternal Law is God's law or blueprint for the universe. It is law governed by Divine Reason. It emanates from God as Sovereign and is promulgated by Him for the good of His Creation in several ways. The natural moral law is that part of the

Eternal Law that man can apprehend with his unaided reason. It is not a creation of man's reason, but emanates from God's reason. Man's reason is quite passive with respect to the natural law. Man does not alter it or change it. Man is not the measure of all things. Rather, God is the measure of all that is and of all that is good. Mankind can apprehend this good, but he does not create or alter it, even by his collective decisions. (It is crucial to recall, as I pointed out in II, the nature of this "apprehension." It consists in what Maritain called "knowledge through inclination.") This natural moral law is the second kind of law. Divine Law is that part of the Eternal Law which God makes known through Divine Revelation and the like. It is not grasped by man's reason but is given to man as an Eternal Truth of Divine Revelation. The fourth kind of law is the human law. The particular precepts for the common good devised or fashioned by human reason are called human laws. These laws are not just given to us but they are the expression of human reason and decision. Human law, however, while not derived from natural moral law must be compatible with it. If a human ordinance conflicts with the natural moral law, it is a perversion of the natural moral law. One of the natural laws states that man must seek to preserve his own being. If we had a particular rule that said "All students who flunk from college must commit suicide," it could not be a human law, for it is incompatible with the natural law that "We ought to preserve our lives." A human law (to use Maritain's example) that is compatible with the natural moral law is the law that "people must stop at red lights — go at green lights." This human law is completely conventional and relative. Yet it is important that we have such a convention and that it is compatible with the natural moral law.

We should not forget that all these laws are either moral laws or they are directives that must be in accordance with moral laws. They are, in their proper spheres of application, guides for conduct. The natural law, Divine Law, and Eternal Law are unalterable and eternal. They are basic moral truths that hold as truths irrespective of any feelings or emotions on our part. They are binding on our conscience and we have a duty to obey them whether we have favorable attitudes toward them or not. And the human animal can know with absolute certainty, according to the Thomists, that certain natural moral law precepts are true. Our "knowledge" here is not "discursive knowledge" but that strange, immediate, "nondiscursive knowledge" Maritain calls "knowledge through inclination."

When we read Aquinas himself, and do not reflect on the sense of "knowledge" relevant here, we are easily led to believe that a claim is being made that, in some plain sense of "knowledge," we have certain knowledge of some eternal moral truths. But, as I shall try to show in V and VI, if we take "knowledge" in any of its ordinary senses it becomes exceedingly doubtful if we have any such knowledge of eternal moral truths. Faced with these difficulties it is natural to try to construe "knowledge" in a different way, as "knowledge through inclination," but then, as I have indicated, we end up by using the mark (token, sign-vehicle) "knowledge" in a very different way from the way we normally use it, while still keeping all the honorific features of "knowledge." We have, in short, made a *persuasive definition.* And when we actually keep in mind what is counting as "knowing moral laws" here, have we really a more objective claim about the foundations of morality than we have in Hume or Russell? Indeed we have a claim that sounds more objective than Hume's or Russell's, but when we consider the special way we "know" these laws (and this is our sole evidence for them) is it really any more objective than these "subjective views" that Thomists so frequently deplore?

V

Let us now consider the actual precepts of the natural moral law. "Good is to be done and gone after, and evil is to be avoided" is the primary natural moral law from which all others are derived, and it is the first principle of practical reason.[19] Aquinas and his contemporary followers insist that all the other natural laws are based on this vacuous first principle of natural moral law. This, of course, is a very weak base indeed. For, unless we assign some denotation to the word "good," as used above, this first principle of the natural moral law would be completely compatible with the most extreme kind of relativism. But from the first principle of the natural moral law we cannot determine what the denotata or criteria of application of "good" will be. All we can conclude from this primary principle is that if something is good we have to seek it. It does not tell us what to seek.[20] (Is Aquinas' statement here really anything more than a bit of linguistic information, disguised because it is stated in the material mode? Is Aquinas, here, really saying anything more than "If we call something 'good' then we must also say that it is something that is to be sought, everything else being equal"? But this informs us about our linguistic behavior; it hardly gives us the foundation of an objective rational ethic that will save us from the "dark night of subjectivity.")

Our knowledge of the other natural moral laws is much less certain. We know them (as Maritain most emphatically argues) immediately and non-

19. Practical reason is reason that is concerned with what is to be done. See John Ladd, *Reason and Practice*, in THE RETURN TO REASON (ed. by John Wild, New York, 1951).
20. COPLESTON, AQUINAS 214-5 (Baltimore, 1955).

conceptually by natural inclination. They are the ends we necessarily seek in virtue of our very humanity. We might list the ones Aquinas mentions, stating them clearly as normatives, so as to bring out their moral force.

1. Life ought to be preserved.
2. Man ought to propagate his kind.
3. Children ought to be educated.
4. Men ought to know the truth about God.
5. Man ought to live in society.
6. Ignorance ought to be avoided.
7. Offense ought not to be given unnecessarily.

These are all supposedly based, in some manner, on man's natural inclinations. It is claimed they are based on human nature. However, according to Aquinas, not all our inclinations are natural inclinations, for some can be "corrupted by vicious habits," and again the natural knowledge of good in them (people with vicious habits) is "darkened by passions and habits of sin." Aquinas is contending that there are some cross-cultural or pan-human characteristics that we might use in constructing a definition of "human nature." Like Plato, Aquinas is claiming that man is distinguished from the other animals by his ability to reason. If man examines his natural inclinations, he will discover that there are certain unalterable pan-human natural moral laws. Copleston states Aquinas' argument here in the following manner: "For although man cannot read off, as it were, eternal law in God's Mind, he can discern the fundamental tendencies and needs of his nature, and by reflecting on them he can come to know the natural moral law." (p. 213) Copleston continues: "Every man possesses also the light of reason, whereby he can reflect on these fundamental inclinations of his nature and promulgate to himself the natural moral law. . . ." (p. 213) Purely natural man is not left in ignorance of the eternal law which is the ultimate rule of all conduct. The natural law part of the eternal law is not simply a Divine Fiat. Rather, we moral agents recognize its inherent rationally binding force. Though the first principle of natural law only tells us that good is to be done and evil is to be avoided, we give concrete content or non-zero denotation to our concept of good and evil "by examining the fundamental natural tendencies or inclinations of man." (p. 215) By examining man's nature and natural inclinations one can discern the good for man in the natural order.

Now, St. Thomas does distinguish between primary and secondary precepts of the natural moral law. The secondary precepts are not relative. But they do have only a limited contextual application, that is, they apply only to certain classes of acts. As Copleston remarks, what Aquinas means in saying that they can be changed is that such natural moral laws are altered when the circumstances of the act may be such that it no longer falls into the class of actions prohibited by the precept. Copleston uses the following example: "We can say in general that if someone entrusts his property to us for safekeeping and asks for it back, we ought to return it. No sensible man would say that if someone entrusts us with a knife or a revolver and asks for it back when he is in a state of homicidal mania, we are obliged to return it." (p. 219) Copleston then generalizes: "In its general form, however, the precept remains valid. We can say with truth that Aquinas believed in a set of unalterable moral precepts." (p. 219)

Maritain, though he makes a great show of wishing to square Aquinas' theory with the facts of moral relativity, does not seem to go beyond this above position in any significant manner. For Maritain there are certain fundamental "dynamic schemes" of natural moral law that are unalterable and are universal. In particular contexts they are subject to an "indeterminate expression." In fact, the same natural moral law can have different and distinct "indeterminate expressions," although they all must be compatible with the more general rule. The general rule is not changed. Unfortunately, the only examples Maritain gives us of culturally relative moral rules are rules of human law or positive law. However, no one questions their relativity or conventionality; what we want to know is what he would say about the actual and anthropologically confirmed exceptions to all seven of Aquinas' natural moral laws listed above. (Since this could conceivably be read as an admission on my part that we can derive an "ought" from an "is," it is more precise — though more cumbersome — to say: "Aquinas' claim that natural moral laws are expressions of the natural inclinations of all men conflicts with the anthropological claim that these are not always and everywhere expressions of natural inclinations.") No doubt he would say such inclinations, when they occur, are perverted or primitive. But this begs the question, for it is only by at least an implicit reference to a *moral standard* that we can determine which rules are "perverted," "primitive," or "corrupt." The natural moral law theorist, however, is supposedly building a normative ethic on man's actual natural inclinations, rather than on the inclinations of certain men called "good or non-perverted men." If the natural moral law theorist is to be consistent, he cannot simply proclaim a standard of moral appraisal and then say that all those who do not act in accordance with it are perverted or evil. Instead, the standard is supposed to come somehow from the very feelings and inclinations of all men.

VI

The above are only some of the puzzles engendered by the Thomistic theory. As clear as Aquinas' kind of theory may seem the first time around, it becomes far more difficult to comprehend after a closer look. Its taxonomic structure hides fundamental confusions, though on Aquinas' behalf it must be said that they were confusions which might naturally arise in his cultural context.

In pointing up these difficulties, I shall first turn to two standard difficulties that have been traditional stumbling blocks for students of natural moral law theories. I do not think these are the most basic difficulties, but I do think these standard difficulties are genuine and need looking into. I doubt that they can be answered satisfactorily from within the Thomistic position of natural moral law. I shall examine them first and then turn to what I regard to be the two more philosophically interesting and more basic difficulties in the natural moral law theory.

The first standard difficulty emerges when we compare the natural moral law theory with some of the things now being said in social psychology. It is frequently said that *from the point of view of science,* there is no such thing as an essential human nature which makes a man a man. The concept of human nature is a rather vague cultural concept; it is not a scientific one.[21] While I think this criticism is surely debatable, it does raise a problem for the natural moral law theory since it is clear that the statement, "there is an essential human nature," is not the obvious, self-evidently true statement Aquinas and his contemporary followers take it to be.

The second standard criticism is a stronger one. It appeals to the facts of cultural relativity. If we go to actual cultures and study them, we find that all of the natural moral laws listed above by Aquinas are broken somewhere by some people. If it is answered, "Well, most cultures obey the above rules," two replies can be made.

First, it can be said that the reply in itself assumes that what most people find natural and better, is natural and better. To assume this, however, is to presuppose the value of a naive kind of democracy; we determine what is good by counting noses or by a Gallup Poll. Moral issues become vote issues. Aquinas, of course, would not wish to say they are "vote issues." Moreover,

21. OTTO KLINBERG, SOCIAL PHILOSOPHY (New York, 1940). On the other hand, A. H. Maslow and Weston LaBarre, along with others, have spoken in a supposedly scientific sense of "a human nature." See A. H. MASLOW, MOTIVATION AND PERSONALITY (New York, 1954), and WESTON LABARRE, THE HUMAN ANIMAL (Chicago, 1954).

why must we accept this "democratic" standard as our ultimate standard? If we say that people simply do accept it, we not only make a statement that is anthropologically false, but we also go in a circle. We use our democratic standard to establish our democratic standard. Secondly, it is the case that for the natural moral laws which are fairly concrete, there is not this majority agreement. If we turn to the more general natural moral laws, we find that they are so vague that they hide all sorts of differences that both parties would regard as crucial. As anthropologists, like Ralph Linton, have pointed out, all cultures have a concept of murder. But if we try to give the concept of murder some specific content which would cover its use in all cultures, we run into difficulty. While all cultures agree that murder is wrong, this is completely compatible with the Eskimos' killing members of their family if they do not feel they can make it through the winter; or with infanticide in Polynesia and Greece; or with the old Scandinavian habit of clubbing one's older ancestors to death so that they may go to Valhalla. But for these people this killing is not murder which is by implicit definition wrong. Just what will count as murder in the given culture varies radically. To say that all cultures have a concept of murder tends to obscure basic radical moral differences. To suggest that these are just indeterminate expressions of the basic moral law blurs a crucial way in which our judgments of good and evil are relative.[22]

There are two more basic difficulties with Thomistic natural moral law theory that I would like to consider now. First, even if it is the case (contrary to what was said above) that there is basic cross-cultural universal acceptance of certain fundamental moral beliefs and/or attitudes, it would *not* follow that the Thomistic natural moral law ethic had been established. This agreement could be explained at least as adequately by a theological voluntarism, the kind of meta-ethic offered by Russell and Hume, or by a Deweyian kind of naturalism. Russell, for example, would not talk of an apprehension of natural moral law emanating from God. He could explain the same facts by saying that those common moral ideals are expressions of commonly held attitudes or commonly felt emotions. They express the common decisions we men make in virtue of our common interests and similar make-up. Recalling that Aquinas and Maritain must invoke the strange doctrine of "knowledge through inclination," it might well be argued that Russell's kind of theory is to be preferred because it is simpler. Applying Ockham's razor, we might naturally remark that Aquinas' "hypothesis" is one we can well dispense with.

22. This point has been made very forcibly both for morals and for art criticism by George Boas. See George Boas, *Cultural Relativism and Standards,* in VISION AND ACTION 112-132 (ed. by Sidney Ratner, Rutgers, 1953).

The same point can be put differently. Because we have (if we have) a common human nature and in accordance with it make certain common moral appraisals, it does not follow that there is a natural moral law in the Thomist's sense. Even if it is true "that all men share some very vague ideas about the good for man, precisely because they are men who possess certain natural tendencies and inclinations in common," this does not serve as a proof that these shared ethical ideals are *God-given* rather than man-made. It does not even serve to make such a belief plausible.[23] One can accept some pan-human agreement about what man's good is without being committed to Aquinas' moral philosophy. As a matter of fact, Erich Fromm makes a similar argument from a naturalistic and neo-Freudian point of view.[24]

It must be added that this form of "natural moral law" based on universally shared attitudes is not enough for Aquinas, for it does not establish that they are self-evident, unchanging moral laws. Thomists need a stronger basis than the unity of human nature to establish their natural moral law theory. If there is no unity or common human nature, the Thomists are clearly wrong; but if there is a unity or common nature to the human animal, it does not follow that the Thomists are right.

I suggest, finally, that the whole theory rests on the confusion between *what ought to be* and *what is.* As Hume made us realize, the statement, "Man ought not to steal," is quite different from the statement, "Man does steal."[25] Men steal when they ought not. Sentences with an "ought" in them belong to a different *logical type* than sentences with an "is" in them. From factual statements alone, including statements of fact about human nature, we cannot deduce or derive any "ought" statement whatsoever. Values and facts are distinct, and Aquinas and his followers are not clear about this distinction, precisely because they looked upon nature as purposive, as having some kind of moral end in itself. This conception of a purposive nature is not only false but it also serves to obfuscate the basic distinction between facts and values that is so essential if we are to understand the nature of moral argument and decision.[26]

23. See in this context A. I. Melden and W. K. Frankena's contributions to the symposium *The Concept of Universal Human Rights,* in *Science, Language and Human Rights,* 1 THE AMERICAN PHILOSOPHICAL ASSOCIATION 167-189 (1952).
24. ERICH FROMM, MAN FOR HIMSELF (New York, 1947).
25. Hume's celebrated passage occurs in Book III, Part I, Section 1 of his A TREATISE OF HUMAN NATURE.
26. In a brilliant and readable interpretation of the history of ideas, Professor E. W. Hall has indicated how value elements have been gradually taken out of science and how in moral reflection we have become progressively clearer about the distinction between "ought" statements and "is" statements. He also indicates how this raises philosophical problems about the validation of moral and evaluative statements. I might add that I am indebted to Professor Hall for a general kind of framework in which much of my argument develops. See E. W. HALL, MODERN SCIENCE AND HUMAN VALUES (Princeton, 1956).

VII

Now it may be felt that the last two sentences in VI are sweeping and wholly unjustified. Where have I established that nature is not purposive and where have I shown that there are no "moral facts" in a purposive nature? The basic issue, it may be felt, is simply passed over.

I do not believe this to be true; that is to say, I do not believe that my case against Aquinas' conception of the natural moral law depends on my rejection of Aquinas' metaphysics or cosmology. Indeed his and Aristotle's conception of a purposive nature seems to me at best false and at worst unintelligible, but my argument against the natural moral law theory does not turn on that belief.

It is possible, however, both to make strong arguments against this metaphysical view and to show that even if these Thomistic metaphysical claims were true, the essential puzzle about the "is" and the "ought" would remain. As Bréhier, Koyré, and others have pointed out, with the arrival of Newtonian physics and Cartesian philosophy there disappeared from the scientific outlook all consideration of purpose and value.[27] An experimental psychologist like Tolman or a biologist may speak of "purposive behavior," but in Aquinas or Aristotle "purposive" and "purpose" have a very different meaning. To ask "What is Jones' purpose?" is to ask about Jones' motives or intentions (or their behavioral correlations). Now it may be the case that the distinctively philosophical parts of Descartes are a great mistake, but it will hardly be claimed that Newtonian mechanics is a mistake, though even here we must in retrospect distinguish between Newton's physics and the quasi-theological and metaphysical conceptions he shares with Henry More and Raphson. "A new and fruitful scientific conception," Toulmin remarks, "is often hatched from an egg of a very different sort, and for some time fragments of its original shell may (so to say) adhere to its plumage."[28] Galileo may well have been a Platonist, but we can accept Galileo's contributions to physics without embracing his Platonism, just as we might accept Berkeley's theory of knowledge without assenting to his views about the value of tar water; Newton, in later editions of his *Principia,* urged certain orthodox theological views, but Newton's physical theory is logically independent of his metaphysical and theological beliefs. No physicist today would dream of arguing that Aristotelian dynamics ought to replace modern physical theory. Aristotelian physical theory, *qua* physical theory, is only of historical interest.

27. E. Bréhier, 2 Histoire de la Philosophie, fasc. 1, 95 (Paris, 1929) and A. Koyré, *Galileo and Plato,* 4 Journal of the History of Ideas 400 (1943).
28. Stephen Toulmin, 67 Philosophical Review 572 (1958).

And modern physical theory, as Hall has argued convincingly in his *Modern Science and Human Values,* does not treat nature as good or bad. Nature is not regarded as purposive, and values are not taken to be some very special and mysterious facts of nature.

I am perfectly well aware that Thomists would claim that such statements as "Nature is Purposive" and "There is a Necessary Being or an all-good God" are metaphysical statements and they are supported in a different way from scientific ones. But I do not believe (as I said in I) that this metaphysical position has been made intelligible, much less established as true. The basic difficulties about purpose or design in nature seem to me to go back at least to Hume and Kant; and I agree (and I believe most non-Scholastic philosophers would agree) with Broad's verdict: "I have seen nothing in the writings of those who have tried to rehabilitate the argument which effectively rebuts their [Hume's and Kant's] adverse verdict." [29] It is true that certain defensive moves have been made against Kant and Hume, though it seems to me that Hepburn, Anderson, O'Connor, Smart, Nagel, Watts, and Edwards have recently made decisive arguments against these Thomistic metaphysical claims.[30]

I can only briefly indicate one line of argument against claiming that there is (in the relevant sense) purpose in nature. Suppose we grant that in the parts of the universe we have observed there is truly a marvelous adaptation of means to ends. From the movements in our solar system to the return of the homing pigeon and the pollination mechanisms of plants, things proceed in an amazingly orderly way. But we cannot conclude from this that the universe has in the appropriate sense either a purpose or a Designer. (It could not, of course, fail to have some design in the sense of having some structure.)[31] Even *if* it is the case that all processes directed by intelligent creatures involve adaptation of means to ends, this does not entail that all adaptation of means to ends is the product of intelligence. What reason have we to believe that those marvelous adaptations, which are not independently known to be deliberately designed, have a design and designer or a purpose? How could we test whether the human eye, the solar system, or ants were so de-

29. C. D. Broad, Religion, Philosophy and Psychical Research 190 (New York, 1953).
30. Ronald Hepburn, Christianity and Paradox, ch. 9 and 10 (London, 1958); John Anderson, *Design,* 13 Australasian Journal of Philosophy 241-256 (1935); D. J. O-Connor, An Introduction to the Philosophy of Education 115-126 (New York, 1957); J. C. C. Smart, *The Existence of God,* in New Essays in Philosophical Theology 28-46 (ed. by A. Flew and A. Macintyre); Ernest Nagel, Sovereign Reason 17-35 (Glencoe, Illinois, 1954); G. S. Watts, *The Thomistic Proofs of Theism,* 35 Australasian Journal of Philosophy 30-46 (1957); Paul Edwards, *The Cosmological Argument,* in Rationalist Annual 63-77 (1959).
31. Leibniz, Discourse of Metaphysics.

signed? What would count as a failure here and what would count as a successful test? I do not believe there is or can be a test here. If someone claims he intuits it, others can and will, with equal legitimacy, claim they do not intuit it. The very meaning of "test" will then become otiose at this juncture.

To say we can legitimately use an analogical argument at this point also gives rise to insuperable difficulties. The human eye may be like a beautifully balanced machine or a work of art in certain respects, but it is like a vegetable or rock in others. Why should we pick one analogy rather than another? If we say because one more adequately illustrates one claim rather than another, then we can say: But what *independent* reason have you to believe that one claim — the design claim — is the correct claim? We must then leave analogy or make another analogy, to which the same objection could be made. And there seems to be no good reason why the design claim should be accepted as the correct claim. Furthermore, what does it mean to say, "The universe has a purpose," taking "the universe" either collectively or distributively? Presumably, if "the universe" is taken distributively, "the purpose of the universe" is equivalent to the sum of all the individual purposes. But how do we sum them? What does this look like? And even if we can sum them, do we not then supposedly have some overall purpose? What would it be like for the universe to fail to have a purpose? What would have to happen or not have to happen in order for us to recognize or fail to recognize that it is true or even in any degree probable that the universe has a purpose? If, in an attempt to avoid the above difficulties, "the universe" is taken collectively, then to discover purpose in the processes in the universe would not at all prove the universe as a whole has purpose. In either event, if "purpose" is being used analogously to "purpose" in "My purpose is to take the island" or in "Jet fighters have a purpose," then our uses of "purpose" must have a minimum of one distinctive property in common. But what is this property here? And if no common property is signified by "purpose," then "purpose" is surely being used equivocally.[32]

These arguments are not new and they are not at all exhaustive of all the moves that can be made by both sides. They are of necessity put with exceeding brevity; if I were to expand these arguments I would merely be going over what seem to me well-worn though decisive arguments that are essentially outgrowths of Hume's and Kant's arguments, though this is not to say that they have not been tailored to meet attempted rebuttals of Hume and Kant.

32. Paul C. Hayner, *Analogical Predication*, 55 THE JOURNAL OF PHILOSOPHY 855-62 (1958).

VIII

This short argument and "appeal to authority" will no doubt seem unconvincing to some, but to try to say why metaphysical explanations of this type are unintelligible would involve another essay, if I were to do justice to the question. But for the sake of this discussion I will grant what I believe to be contrary to fact, namely, that "Necessary Being" and "final cause" have an intelligible use. Let us also assume for the sake of the discussion that sentences like "Nature is purposive," "Man and nature have a final end," and "Men were created to worship God" are true. My crucial point is: *Even if these sentences really can be used to make genuine statements that are in fact true, no normative or moral statements can be derived from them.*

Philosophers who deny that we can logically derive or base a moral claim on a metaphysical position will say, as William Dennes does:

> A system of metaphysics, if it were known to be the truth or the probable truth about the order of entities that constitute the universe, would of course be superbly instructive. But there is one thing it could not enable us to do logically or intelligibly, and that is to determine from what really is what really ought to be: to derive from judgments of fact, judgments of value. It could only be by taking the symbol "good" to mean precisely what it meant by "real," and nothing more than is meant by "real," that we could say that metaphysics, as a theoretic discipline, determines or demonstrates the nature of value. But then our statement, "what is metaphysically real, and only that, is good," would mean precisely what is meant by either one or other of the empty truisms: "Whatever is metaphysically real, and only that, is metaphysically real," or "whatever is good, and only that, is good." [33]

---

33. William Dennes, *Knowledge and Values,* in SYMBOLS AND VALUES: AN INITIAL STUDY 606 (ed. by Lyman Bryson, New York, 1954). Father Gallagher has replied to Dennes on this point but I do not believe he obviates the basic difficulty advanced by Dennes about deriving a moral statement from a metaphysical statement. Gallagher says, with respect to the quotation from Dennes given in the text: ". . . a Scholastic would say that every actually existing thing (that which is real — *a res*) is good. Even the devil, insofar as he exists according to the creatural nature God gave him, is good." But the "is" in Gallagher's two sentences is not the "is" of identity but the "is" of predication. We can deny these two statements themselves without self-contradiction; and the last one is clearly a moral judgment, and the other would be if it were not a bit of indirect discourse. ("Every actually existing thing is good" is a moral utterance.) To say "Evil, as such, is a privation and that reality, as such, is good" is to make another moral judgment and not to indicate how we could set up a metaphysic as the basis or foundation of our moral norms, even if we can understand (as I do not) what "privation" as "a deflection from his [the Devil's] original reality, in the direction of nothingness" means. Gallagher is right in saying that *if* we accept his moral judgments quoted above as leading moral principles or as normative defining principles of natural moral law (functioning like the ground rules of chess) then " 'good' can mean precisely what is meant by 'real' "; but Dennes' point and my point is that in ordinary moral discourse there is no such rule of language and that to make one

Those who think they can discover what they ought to do from a discovery about "ultimate nature of reality" are tacitly assuming that what is metaphysically real or "ultimately real" ought to be done or ought to be. But it is not self-contradictory or even logically odd to say, "X is an ultimate reality whose nonexistence is inconceivable, but X ought not to be." What is ultimately real could be evil or it could be quite neutral. There is no rule of language which indicates an identity of meaning between what is real and what is good or obligatory. To make such a rule by linguistic fiat and to claim that such a linguistic fiat *ought* to be accepted because it gives us a clearer, more *adequate* foundation for morals is itself an expression of a value judgment; and if such a value judgment is made, we must for the sake of clarity give up the idea that we can derive a moral statement from purely metaphysical statements and/or metaphysical and empirical statements alone.

That many plain men infer "X is obligatory" from "God wills X," "X is in accord with our essential human nature," "X is of the true nature of Being" and the like, indicates they have tacitly, and perhaps even unconsciously (as in a Peirceian acritical inference) assumed "What God wills is obligatory," "What is in accord with our essential human nature is good," etc. But here these hidden premises are themselves moral judgments; the "is" in the above sentences is not the "is" of identity, and all these statements may be denied without self-contradiction.

Someone might still claim that I have not yet really met the Thomist or Aristotelian case. I have assumed a "metaphysical system" or a set of categories in which fact (including "metaphysical facts") and value are distinct, but, it might be urged, the Thomistic-Aristotelian system is denying just that, for some facts and values at least. When it is claimed that nature is purposive, there is just this conflation of fact and value. I find this claim obscure almost to the point of unintelligibility. It is the obfuscation I was complaining about at the end of VI. There seems to be no intelligible job for these words here. We cannot do the usual things with them and we do not know what new things to do except that in some exceedingly obscure way they indicate that some claim is being made about a more secure foundation for our morality.

But even *if* we can intelligibly indicate how the fact-value or evaluative-descriptive dichotomy does not apply to a statement like "Nature is purposive" and *even* if we can show that these "metaphysical realities" are at one and

is in itself to make a value judgment and not to derive moral statements from metaphysical statements about reality. See Eugene Gallagher, *Comments*, in SYMBOLS AND VALUES: AN INITIAL STUDY 615 (ed. Lyman Bryson *et al.*, New York, 1954).

the same time facts and values, I still do not see how we can derive ordinary moral or evaluative conclusions from them.

I must explain my meaning here. Moral questions are practical questions. They occur when questions arise about what is to be done or whether what was done in the past was the thing to have done. Most paradigmatically, moral statements are used to guide conduct.[34]

We have a clear case of moral reasoning in Thucydides, *The Peloponnesian War.* (1.68 ff.) Sparta's allies come to Sparta to discuss the difficulties with Athens over Potidaea and Corcyra and to decide whether to break up the Delian confederacy and fight Athens. The question is clearly a question about what to do. Their interest in what was the case was limited to discovering those facts which would help them decide how to *act.* The Corinthians advised the Spartans: ". . . choose the right course, and endeavor not to let Peloponnese under your supremacy degenerate from the prestige that it enjoyed under that of your ancestors." Some Athenians, who happened to have been in Sparta, countered by bidding the Spartans "not to dissolve the treaty, or break your oaths, but to have our differences settled by arbitration according to our agreement." In weighing the considerations the majority of Spartans were for war, but their old king, Archidamus, urged peace. He warned them of their inferiority in ships and of Athens' invulnerability and advised them to "have a care that we do not bring deep disgrace and deep perplexity upon Peloponnese." He finally urged the Spartans to prepare for war but not to initiate aggression. But the Ephor Sthenelaidas (a politically astute rabble-rousing moralist) countered this and exhorted the Spartans to "Vote . . . for war, as the honor of Sparta demands, and neither allow the further aggrandizement of Athens, nor betray our allies to ruin, but with the gods let us advance against the aggressors." The Spartans considered these contentions and finally with their allies decided on war. The point here is not to deny that reasoning went on and that factual considerations were involved but to point out that all of this was instrumental to arriving at a decision.

Moral problems are problems of choice, and moral reasoning is practical reasoning about how we should act. Even when *we* say "The Spartans were clearly wrong in declaring war" we do not make a purely theoretical statement. Rather we are saying (in effect) that the Spartans ought to have acted in a certain fashion and we imply that if we had been similarly placed we would have heeded Archidamus and not declared war. Moral questions are, necessarily, questions concerning what to do. This is the basic sense in which

34. P. H. Nowell-Smith, Ethics 11-22, 95-104 (Baltimore, 1954); Kai Nielsen, *The Functions of Moral Discourse,* 7 Philosophical Quarterly 236-248 (1957); and *Speaking of Morals,* 2 The Centennial Review 414-44 (1958).

a moral judgment is prescriptive, directive, or normative.[35] We are only interested in what is the case to the extent that knowing what is the case is instrumental in helping us decide what to do.

With these remarks in mind, it should not be hard to see that no moral or evaluative statements follow from these so-called "fact-value statements" or from "fact-value statements" together with some plain empirical statements. If I, as a moral agent, discover that, in some peculiar way, the "fact-value" "The Universe is purposive," is true and that I, as a being in the universe, have a purpose or an end, it still does not follow that I have *ipso facto* resolved any moral perplexity by noting how it is that I behave. The discovery that "teleological explanations" rather than "nonteleological explanations" best explain how I behave does not entail any moral conclusion.

Suppose my moral perplexity is to discover, in Kierkegaard's phrase, "How I am to live and die"; that is to say, to find out "the purpose of my existence." Now, by putting it as "What is the purpose of my existence?" I make it sound as if I were asking a question of the same logical type as "What is the purpose of my doorbell?" — a question that can admit of a clear factual answer. But though these questions have a grammatical similarity they have very different uses in human discourse. As Ayer has well said:

> . . . what is being sought by those who demand to know the meaning of life is not an explanation of the facts of their existence, but justification. Consequently a theory that informs them merely that the course of events is so arranged as to lead inevitably to a certain end does nothing to meet their need. For the end in question will not be one that they themselves have chosen.[36]

My teleological discoveries will not in and of themselves resolve my problem of choice. They tell me *how* (in what way) I am living but they do not tell me how *I am* to live and die. "X has such and such end" does not entail "Do X." When a perplexed person asks: "What is the meaning of life?" he is almost always asking a practical question. He is trying to decide what he is *to do,* and he is only interested in knowing what is the case to the degree that a certain understanding is essential for any action. It is an answer to this *practical* question that his "soul longs after, as the African desert thirsts for water." [37] But no general description of the world, no causal explanation — teleological or otherwise — entails an expression of a decision; and the

35. R. M. Hare, *Universalisability,* ARISTOTELIAN SOCIETY PROCEEDINGS 295-312 (1954-55).
36. A. J. Ayer, *The Claims of Philosophy,* 7 POLEMIC 24 (1947).
37. Soren Kierkegaard, in A KIERKEGAARD ANTHOLOGY 4-5 (ed. by Robert Bretall, Princeton, 1951).

language of purpose, as used in moral discourse (though not necessarily in philosophical interpretations or morality), is a bit of practical discourse in which the key expressions function to express decisions, intentions and the like. They describe as well, but shorn of this expressive or performatory use the utterances are without normative or prescriptive import.

This same general point can be made in another way. When "Life has a purpose" is taken as a physical or metaphysical explanation or description of human behavior and *not* as an expression of an attitude or of an intention to act in a deliberate, responsible, self-conscious manner, no moral decision or resolution to a practical problem is entailed by the discovery that I am "purposing" or moving to my natural end. If my behaving teleologically is *just* something that happens to me by virtue of my being a human being, then it cannot also function prescriptively. And this tautology has a point because it marks a distinction in the uses of language.

Since taking a moral position necessarily involves the making of a decision, I (as a moral agent) still will have to decide and resolve to seek this end that I notice human beings in fact seek. I must make, by a moral decision, this purpose or end (including my *purpose* or *end,* so metaphysically defined) *my* purpose or end. But this is something I must, as a mere matter of the logic of the situation, choose or decide to do. I cannot just infer it, observe it, or grasp it by some "intellectual intuition of being." I may see or notice purpose in the metaphysical sense; but until I have, by my own free resolution, decided I should act on this information, I have not arrived at any moral conclusions.

I cannot derive (1) "This is my purpose" or "This is my goal" taken as expressions of decisions from (2) "This is my purpose" or "This is my goal" taken as a metaphysical statement of some odd "value-fact." But since it is very easy to confuse the metaphysical statement (2) with the moral pronouncement (1), we tend to think that if (2) is true we have answered our practical question about what I am to do and how I am to live and die. Since the words "purpose" and "end" get redefined in (2) they can now be used so that purpose could exist even if no people were making decisions or resolutions and the like. On the metaphysical interpretation, "The purpose of my life is. . ." is treated very much like "My life expectancy is. . ." But in ordinary discourse "The purpose of my life is. . ." is used primarily not to state a fact but to announce a policy. To ask "What is the purpose of my existence?" is to ask "What ought I to do?" This is a practical question about what to do and does not involve us in any metaphysics at all.

When we think we can derive moral conclusions from the metaphysical statement that "Human life, and therefore my life, has a certain purpose," we transfer the ordinary moral meaning of "purpose" onto the metaphysical statement, making the metaphysical statement into (among other things) an expression of a decision. The metaphysical statement in effect redefines "purpose" but the redefinition is leaky; the old use sneaks back in and gives the analysis far greater plausibility than it *in fact* has.[38] But the metaphysical statement is not meant to be such a practical utterance, and "purpose" on the metaphysical use will not bear such a burden.

It may be replied, "But it really will, and metaphysical statements have their practical uses too. That is the small *grain* of truth in the contention that 'metaphysics is disguised poetry.'" But then it must also be admitted that, so used, the metaphysical statement (2) can no longer be understood as presupposing that it makes sense to speak of the purpose of human beings apart from what attitudes they adopt, what intentions they express, or what decisions they make. To say "Life has a purpose even though no one thinks so or cares about anything" will no longer make sense except as a moral expression of intention on the part of the user. But I should think a Thomist would want very much to argue that life does have a purpose even though no one thinks it does or makes any resolutions. The natural moral law, on a Thomistic interpretation, is not a summary expression of our most pervasive and basic decisions. If some super Communists or super Fascists did some very thorough super brainwashing, all of us might come to believe that life has no purpose, existence no end. We might all come to believe that we die and rot and do what we do because in some basically arbitrary way we have been so stimulated, but Thomists would argue that even in such a malebolge the natural moral law would still obtain. Even if the super Communists or super whatnots became trapped by their own propaganda and no one even dimly understood Life's purpose, life would, in such a view, still have a purpose. Such a *Brave New World* situation is conceivable; but even if it did obtain, the unwritten Laws of God would remain in force: human existence — the Thomists would say — would still have its original and distinctive purpose, for the natural moral law is something ordained by God, not something made by man. Maritain repeatedly warns us that man is not the measure of good and evil, and man is not the measure of "the purpose of men"; rather, man dimly apprehends the natural moral law and the purpose of his existence, and this purpose would exist even if no one thought it existed. But if what I said above is correct, such a view cannot be true.

38. See Ronald Hepburn on "leaky redefinitions" in Ronald W. Hepburn, *Literary and Logical Analysis,* 8 THE PHILOSOPHICAL QUARTERLY 342-57 (1958).

IX

I have tried to state and appraise the Thomistic theory of natural moral law. My central criticisms of the theory occur in VI; VII and VIII are primarily directed to those who may feel my last criticism in VI would not hold if the universe has purpose or design. I have contended there is no good reason to believe the universe has this purpose; and even if there were this purpose, we still could not derive moral conclusions from this true statement about our world or from observations of human behavior. But even if all this is rejected, my other three criticisms remain.

It is perhaps natural for someone to reply to my arguments in VIII: "Aren't you really ringing changes on what G. E. Moore called the 'naturalistic fallacy'; aren't you really just showing that evaluations are evaluations and descriptions are descriptions and that, as long as human discourse has the functions it has, we cannot reduce the one to the other, though we can point out that certain words and sentences can, and do, function both descriptively and evaluatively?" And the answer to this is "Yes."

But then an interlocutor might remark: "To be clear we must accept this, but isn't it also clear that if 'good' is to have any meaning at all — and surely it has — it must be connected with what human beings in their rational moments strive for, desire, or need? If good isn't what reasonable human beings really want when they understand their place in nature and the causes and consequences of their desires and their distinctively human qualities, pray tell what is it or what can it be? If we really come to understand 'what man is for,' will we not come to understand — all subtleties about the 'is' and the 'ought' aside — what is really good and what we really ought to do? Now isn't it the case that honest and reasonable men could claim the contrary only in their studies?"

And once again I would want to say "yes," but I would also want to block some very mistaken inferences from this that the Thomists make and to make some crucial and hardheaded qualifications to this. I attempted to do this in VI, but let me make it perfectly clear that I am not in the least suggesting that all is dross in Aquinas. It is abundantly clear that he is one of the great moral philosophers. Calling attention to the importance of understanding ourselves and our place in nature in determining what we ought to do is a permanent and useful insight of the Thomistic-Aristotelian tradition, though I think in connecting it with the rational commands of the Deity this insight has been badly blurred.

If we are to gain a firm understanding of the foundations of morality, it is necessary to explain and note the mistaken inferences and to make clear the necessary qualifications. Three of these might be re-emphasized here:

1) "What are people for?" — though linguistically similar to "What are chairs for?" or "What is the liver for?" — is very different from either of these quite different questions. I have contended that there is no good reason to believe there is a Designer. If there is no Designer, "What are people for?" would not have an answer like "What are chairs for?" There would be no room for the answer: "People were made for . . ." I have also argued that there is no clear evidence from the sciences of man, presently at least, that justifies our saying "What are people for?" has an answer like "What is the liver for?" From a scientific point of view it has been denied that we can speak meaningfully of "the nature of human nature."

2) Even if there is, as Sartre reminds us, human nature a posteriori but no "essence" of man, may not man, as Nietzsche said, be something to be surpassed; or may it not be the case, as D. H. Lawrence seems at times to suggest, that we ought to seek to destroy or at least submerge that which is distinctively human and firmly fix ourselves in our animal ancestry? I do not, of course, wish to urge either of these positions, but I do wish to point out that they are intelligible and that we cannot refute them by simply pointing to what people want or to what is normal, assuming (as we cannot in fact) that there are clear cross-cultural criteria for "normalcy." And it is just here that the importance of the features centering around the "naturalistic fallacy" becomes relevant; reflection on Moore's distinctions should make us realize that in morals, after we weigh up all the considerations for and against something, it still must be the case that we as moral agents must decide what is good and evil. (The force of "must" in both occurrences is logical.) The existentialists have dramatized this fact about the moral life in a very misleading way, but Ayer, Hare, and Nowell-Smith have recently made us see how this is a logical truth about the functions of normative discourse.

3) Even if there is an anthropologically confirmed "core" to the human animal and a notion that man has a distinct function, this would in no way serve to establish the Thomistic theory of the natural moral law. Such "natural good" would be quite explicable on a theory like Dewey's or Fromm's, and it is equally compatible with the kind of rational ethic articulated by Toulmin, Nowell-Smith, and Baier. It is even compatible with Russell's or Hume's theory. And some of these theories have the advantage of making far fewer assumptions than does the natural moral law theory. If there is no "core to the onion," the natural moral law theory is wrong; but if there is, it

does not at all follow that the natural moral law theory is right or even probable.

Finally, I want to make it clear that I see no good reason to say that if a theory like Aquinas' and Maritain's is unsound the foundations of morality totters, throwing us into the "night of subjectivity." Even if Hume, Russell, and Ayer in their analyses of morality are right, it still does not follow that there can be no rationality to the moral life.[39] There is no good reason at all to say, "If there is no God, then everything is permitted." This is in itself a moral judgment; it can be denied without self-contradiction, and there are those who in the name of morality would deny it. In a perfectly plain sense, some moral judgments can be justified and some objective moral appraisals can be made.[40] Rejection of the Thomistic ethical theory need not entail nihilism, cynicism, subjectivism, or relativism. And it does not even entail that there are no "natural moral goods." A recognition of the unsoundness of the Thomistic natural moral theory does not make the moral life or the life of reason impossible, but should, if correct, further it. And this should be a blessing for the man who, in W. D. Falk's phrase, is committed to the principle of nonevasive living.

39. I have tried to show how Russell's analysis does not involve these nihilistic and irrational implications in my forthcoming article, *Bertrand Russell's New Ethic*, METHODOS.

40. This has been ably argued by STEPHEN TOULMIN, AN EXAMINATION OF THE PLACE OF REASON IN ETHICS (Cambridge, England, 1951); and by KURT BAIER, THE MORAL POINT OF VIEW (Ithaca, 1958). I have tried to argue for this myself in my *Justification and Moral Reasoning*, 9 METHODOS 98-111 (1957); *The Functions of Moral Discourse*, 7 PHILOSOPHICAL QUARTERLY 236-248 (1957); *Good Reasons in Ethics*, 24 THEORIA 9-28 (1958); and in my forthcoming article, *The Good Reasons Approach and Ontological Justifications of Morality*, to be published in THE PHILOSOPHICAL QUARTERLY.

[7]

Foundation of the Natural Law Doctrine

Hans Kelsen
Translated by Carmen G. Mayer

This paper was delivered by Prof. Kelsen in 1963 at the Saltzburg Colloquium on the Natural Law in Political Theory, under the title "Die Grundlage der Naturrechtslehre" and published in the Osterreichische Zeitschrift für Offentliches Recht, vol. XIII, bk. 1-2, pp.1-37 (copyright: Springer-Verlag Wien 1963).

Introduction

Accepting your invitation to speak about natural law in this group of followers of the natural law doctrine, I did not have in mind to convert you to my opinion that the validity of natural law *cannot be accepted* from a *scientifically* rational standpoint. For I do not consider such a conversion possible and I will explain why this is true in a moment. The basis for the natural law doctrine is the answer to the following question: what is the sole premiss for the acceptance of the validity of an eternal, unalterable law which is immanent in nature? Whoever feels unable—as I do—to accept this premiss, is also unable to accept its consequence.

Such a premiss is—as I will attempt to explain—the *belief* in a just divinity whose will is not only transcendental but also immanent in nature which has been created by this divinity. Arguing about the truth of such a belief does not serve any useful purpose. Neither he who has this belief nor he who does not can be convinced of the contrary by rational arguments. While in my opinion this belief is the essential and unavoidable premiss for a true natural law doctrine, my position here is a rather strange one with respect to those who, in spite of this belief of theirs, are of the opinion that the validity of natural law is independent of the will of an all-mighty and all-good divinity. The role I play here is not that of an *advocatus diaboli* (although that is what you expect of me) but exactly the opposite, that of *advocatus dei*. I hope, anyhow, that this fact will soften any pointed remarks in the following discussion which otherwise might offend the feelings of one or the other faction.

I

"Law"—whether understood as positive law, created actually by people and different from moral law, or understood as a right, just, natural law corresponding to moral—is essentially a norm. It has a specific meaning, the linguistic expression of which is "ought". The meaning of a norm, or better, the meaning which *is* "norm" is: something ought to happen; particularly living beings and especially human beings ought to behave in a certain way under certain circumstances. We call this meaning prescription and distinguish it from description which is only a declarative statement. The meaning of a declarative statement —or better, the declarative statement is the meaning—is: something is, *i.e.* it exists or is somehow constituted; in particular, things, living beings and human beings actually do behave in a certain way under certain circumstances. A norm is not an account of facts; a prescription is not a description. The difference is obvious. The norm is the meaning of an act of will, an act of will directed towards the conduct of another person. The norm aims at the determination of will of another person while the descriptive statement aims at his thinking process, at his knowledge; the declarative statement informs the other person of something. Expressed in a figurative way: the norm proceeds from one person's volition to another person's volition; the declarative statement proceeds from the thinking process (knowledge) of one person to the thinking process (knowledge) of another person. Hence, a statement is true or false. A norm, however, is neither true nor false; rather it is valid or not valid. There is absolutely no parallel or analogy between the truth of a declarative statement and the validity of a norm. I emphasize this, being aware of its contrast to a generally accepted opinion which I too shared for a long time. If an analogy or parallel could exist between the truth of a declarative statement and the validity of a norm, then the contradiction exclusion rule that applies to two contradictory statements could also, after all, be used *per analogiam* for two norms in contradiction with each other. In the same way that only one statement out of two contradictory ones can be true, and the other statement must be false, so only one norm out of two contradictory ones would be valid while the other norm would have no validity. But this is not the case. If it were true that only one norm would be valid out of two, one of which ordered a certain conduct while the other ordered the avoidance of the same conduct, there would be no norm conflict whatsoever. If only one norm out of two is valid, there is in fact only one norm and no conflict takes place. For it is the validity of a norm that originates its specific, even if ideal, existence, its being; a norm which is not valid does not exist, it is not a norm. The existence of norm conflicts, which is a situation when two norms are both valid and one norm orders a certain conduct while the other commands the avoidance of the same conduct, cannot be denied. We frequently encounter norm conflicts, especially between norms belonging to a given positive legal order and norms belonging to a certain moral order. When a norm of a moral order commands never to kill a person, but a legal norm commands us to kill people in war or in execution of capital punishment, all we have is our choice as to which norm to abide by and which norm to violate. But we have no power to deprive of validity that norm we do not wish to abide by. This norm remains valid, otherwise we would be unable to violate it. To be sure, conflicts between norms belonging to the same normative order, especially conflicts within one and the same legal order are also possible and are not at all exceptional.

In as much as a norm establishes that certain conduct ought to be performed, it creates a value. If a thing is as it ought to be, it is "good", it is valuable. If a thing is not as it ought to be, it is "bad" and contrary to any value. A declarative statement refers to reality, *i.e.* it declares *that* a thing really exists or *how* it really is. Consequently, the difference between *ought*-norms and *is*-statements is based upon the contrast between *ought* and *is*, the contrast between value and reality. This contrast is given in the form of an unalterable dualism because of our rational thinking process that corresponds to the principle of logic. In a way, indeed, that *ought* and *is* cannot be deduced from each other and *vice versa*, nor does one concept derive from the other. From the fact that something exists does not follow that something ought to exist; from the fact that something ought to be does not follow that something is. No value can be deduced from the reality, no reality can be deduced from any value. Our statements concerning reality are true if they correspond to it. Their truthfulness does not depend on our will. If they are true, their truth is an objective truth. The statement, "if a metal is heated it stretches", is true whether we want it or not and this truth is evident to all thinking beings. On the other hand, since there is a value involved in connection with a norm—norm being the meaning of an act of will—many different, conflicting values can claim validity. It is the validity of a value that bestows validity on a norm, and for different people, at different times and in different places, many different norms are valid. The dualism of norm and declarative statement, of *ought* and *is*, of volition and cognition has the following unavoidable consequence: values are always merely subjective, never objective, *i.e.* there are no values the validity of which is as objective as the truth of statements dealing with reality. Now, if the essence of a value is subjective, this value is likewise only relative; relative with regard to the will, the meaning of which is the value-constituting norm, and relative to those persons for whom the norm was made and whose conduct it regulates. This means, however, that the validity of a value-constituting norm does not exclude the validity of a contrasting norm and thus it does not exclude any other value that is in contrast with the first value, in the same way as the objective truth of an *is*-statement does exclude the truth of a contrasting *is*-statement. This is especially also the case, when the word *value* is understood not only as the relation to a norm—set up by an act of will—but also the relation of an object to a wish, so that the judgment "something is *good*" means that such a thing is desired, and the judgment "something is *bad*" means that it is undesired.

The subjectivity and relativity of value is, however, a consequence that many people—not all—can hardly endure. First of all, our need for justification of our conduct is not fully satisfied by the acceptance of values that are merely subjective and relative. If the validity of a norm, to which we often respond only with an enormous effort for its contrariety to our own inclination, proves at the end to be arbitrary and therefore does not at all exclude the validity of a completely constrasting norm, in complying to such a norm we are not so sure about the value of our conduct as we are sure about the truth of a declarative statement. This happens, however, when—or it happens *just because*—we do not consider sufficiently the authority and the motivating force of a normative moral or legal order, if those who are subject to such orders consider the value constituted by the norms of these orders only as subjective and relative. Hence springs the attempt to prove the validity of norms that are not the purport of any human act of will, that need not be "established" or "positive" in order to be valid, norms that are binding directly by virtue of their contents, independent of any human will, norms that constitute values which are as objective as the truth of statements concerning reality. To attain this, however, the dualism of *is* and *ought*, of reality and value, of norm and declarative statement, of volition and cognition, forced upon us by our rational-logical thinking, must be set aside. This is possible only by departing from the sphere of our rational-logical thinking and thus from the sphere of our empirical reality and especially from the sphere of empirical acts of will and their purport, and by resorting to a transcendental, metaphysical sphere where the existence is possible of such a will that at the same time is thought, where a moral duty is possible that at the same time is existence, where norms are possible that are at the same time declarative statements, where law is possible that at the same time is justice as well as truth. It is the ascent from man to God, from science or philosophy to theology. And this is the passage from a legal or moral positivism to the doctrine of natural law.

II

What all the various definitions of natural law have in common—the essence of what is called "natural law"—is validity of norms which are not meaning or purport of any human acts of will; consequently, the values constituted by these norms are by no means arbitrary, subjective and relative. In order to answer the question, "What should be a person's conduct under certain circumstances?" one has not—according to the natural law doctrine—to inquire about the act of will of a person acting as legislator in matters of morality or law, or about any custom that originated from the norm in question. The norm results from the nature of things this particular norm refers to. These things are either the circumstances under which a man ought to behave in a certain manner or the man himself whose conduct is in question. The circumstances are a part of reality and are inseparably connected to the whole of reality.

Therefore, the nature of things is the nature in the meaning of the totality of reality or it is the nature of human beings. The latter are either the drives inherent in human beings or that which distinguishes human beings from animals—their reason. In the latter case, natural law appears as law of reason. In any case, the natural law doctrine is characterized by the acceptance of norms that are immanent in nature, and thus by the acceptance of the immanence of values constituted by such norms either in the reality of nature in general or in the nature of human beings in particular. It is the immanence of a moral duty in everything that exists. Nature in general or the nature of human beings (especially their reason) prescribes a certain conduct for human beings. Nature in general or human nature in particular becomes the norm-making authority.

At this point it can perhaps be admitted that norms do not necessarily have to be purports of human acts of will. But in no case can it be admitted that there are norms which are not purports of any act of will, even if there is not any *human* will involved. A nature with immanent norms must also have a will immanent and these norms are the expression of such will. But from where does a will come into a nature which is nothing else, from the standpoint of our empirical-rational knowledge, but an aggregate of facts of existence that are connected to one another as cause and effect? A will in nature is either an animistic superstition or it is the will of God in the nature he created, the immanence of divine value in the reality. If norms are immanent in the nature of man, especially in his reason, we cannot refer to his empirical-human reason which, from a purely psychological point of view, is only the ability to think and to learn. But the norm-setting reason must at the same time be capable of cognition and volition. Something like this cannot exist in the domain of empirical reality, provided such reality is described without any logical contradiction. Nevertheless, the principle of excluded contradiction (a principle of human logic) has no relevancy to a transcendental, superhuman sphere beyond any empirical reality, if we accept its existence. With regard to divine reason we can afford a statement that would be absurd with regard to human reason, namely, that such reason is a function of both cognition and volition. With regard to God we may say that cognition and volition are one in him. We read in *Genesis* (ii, 17 and iii, 5): "And the Lord God commanded the man . . . but of the tree of the knowledge of good and evil, thou shalt not eat of it. Neither A.V. nor R.V.—now corrected to A.V. version. . . . And the serpent said unto the woman . . . in the day ye eat thereof, then , , , ye shall be as gods, knowing good and evil." Knowing what is good and what is evil, God wishes that good be done and evil be avoided. His will is comprized in his knowledge. The contradiction in the assertion that God wills while he recognizes is no more relevant from a religious-theological viewpoint than the contradiction contained in the assumption that God, in his all-goodness, wishes only what is good, yet in his omnipotence creates what is evil. Human reason with volition and cognition, *i.e.* the practical reason of man, is actually the divine reason in man whom God created in his own image.

III

The theological-metaphysical character of the assumption of a value that is immanent in reality becomes evident when we analyse a philosophy which represents the principle of immanence of value in reality in a classical form: the Aristotelian doctrine of entelechy.

Entelechy means a movement that is inside all things and is directed towards a certain purpose. This purpose is to achieve perfection of that particular thing. This purpose is objective and exists by nature; it means that a thing has to be as it ought to be, which is "good". In *Metaphysics* I, 7, Aristotle contrasts it with Platonic doctrine by saying that Plato's idealistic doctrine claims this purpose to be a transcendental idea, *i.e.* the idea of good, while entelechy is the movement towards good, this movement being immanent in all things. The concept of entelechy is the expression of the teleological interpretation of nature that is essential to the Aristotelian philosophy. Such an interpretation, however, presupposes a theological basis conception, whether consciously or not, whether explicitly or implicitly. To the unavoidable question, "where does the purpose of nature come from?" there is no other answer but the assumption of a transcendental authority that gives to nature its purpose. In Aristotle's philosophy this is also the case, although it does not appear very clearly owing to certain characteristics of his metaphysics. For this reason this idea has not always been recognized by the traditional interpretation of Aristotle.

The central concept of his metaphysics is God as "unmoved mover". Since everything that is movable must be moved by something, there must be some moving force (*Physics*, VIII, 4, 5), something that moves without being moved itself (*Metaphysics*, XII, 7). This force is deity. It is a "living, eternal, best being". It is the absolute good, it is the highest, absolute purpose (*On the Heavens*, II, 12). Since every movement derives directly or indirectly from deity and every movement aims at good, which is the immanent purpose in nature, the movement towards good can be nothing else but the purpose that deity established for nature, and good in nature can only be the divine value that is immanent in reality. Since any value can only be established by a will, the good contained in nature must be the divine will in nature. In fact, Aristotle states explicitly: "But God and nature create nothing that has not its use" (*On the Heavens*, I, 4). In *Nichomachean Ethics* (VII, 1153 *b*) is stated: 'All things have by nature something divine in them" and in *Ethica Eudemia* (VIII, 2): "There is only one question: what is the beginning of movement in the soul? Obviously it is deity as in the whole universe. After all, everything is moved by deity." In his treatise, *On Generation and Corruption* (II, 10), we read:

> God perfected the entire being by giving substance to the process of becoming, having its purpose in itself . . . All natural creatures strive for

what is eternal and unalterable and demonstrate, as much as possible, their inner connection with the universal essence and substance by their repeated reproduction.

A consequent theological interpretation of the world is necessarily tied to the assumption that God must not only be transcendent to but also immanent in the world. It is the idea that Goethe expresses in poetic form as follows:

Was wär' ein Gott, der nur von aussen stiesse,
Im Kreis das All am Finger laufen liesse!
Ihm ziemt's, die Welt im Innern zu bewegen,
Natur in sich, sich in Natur zu hegen.
Sodass, was in ihm lebt und webt und ist,
Nie seine Kraft, nie seinen Gueist vermisst.[1]

The immanence of God in the world is by no means peculiar to pantheism. Nor can the Roman Catholic theology avoid the assumption of the immanence of God in the world. I quote a Roman Catholic theologian, the Jesuit, Walter Brugger: "The true immanence of the world in God and the immanence of God in the world is not abolished by his being transcendental." This idea of God's immanence in the world is obscured in Aristotle's metaphysics, for he describes God as pure thought, as sheer thinking reason. He tries to explain in his own affirmation about God being the prime cause of every movement as follows: "God is best and most desirable in itself; he moves as being loved" (*Metaphysics,* XII, 7). Finally Aristotle does admit that the purpose we find immanent in nature is a purpose that has been established for nature by God's will. He raises the question (*Metaphysics,* XII, 10): "In what way the nature of the universe contains the good and the supreme good?" This evidently means, in which way does nature get its purpose? And he answers this question by drawing a parallel between the relationship between God and nature and the relationship of a commander to the discipline of his army. "For the army's good is found both in its discipline and in the leader; for he does not depend on the discipline, but it depends on him." The discipline of the army is the commander's command and thus it is established by the commander's will. The discipline is good because the commander's will is good. In the same way the order of nature is established by the will of God. It is good because God's will is good. All that which is good in nature is the will of God, which is good. At the end of the chapter we read: "The world refuses to be governed badly." A quotation by Homer concludes the chapter: "The rule of many is not good, one ruler let there be." If all that exists is good, it is good because it is governed by God, because it obeys the command of the divine commander. The thinking reason of God reveals itself, in conclusion, as a reason that also wills because it commands.

[1] Approximately: There is no God whose finger outward pushing
Would like a carousel the world get rushing.
He gave the world an inward drive,
Nature in him and he in it contrive.
But beings living in him as their source
Will never lack his spirit and his force.

But also human reason is, according to Aristotle, not only a thinking and perceiving reason, it also manifests its will by commanding. The inner contradiction, inherent to the concept of a reason that thinks and wills at the same time, becomes evident at the moment when Aristotle splits the reason into a theoretical or speculative and a practical reason. This double concept is found in his work, *On the Soul* (XII, 10). He says that there are two causes of movement: drive and reason. Reason is considered the cause of movement in so far as it refers to human action and sets a certain action as man's goal. it is precisely this which makes it practical reason. The essential function of practical reason is to give precepts and orders. However, Aristotle says that it is the thinking reason that commands to pursue or to avoid an object (III, 9). But this is not possible psychologically. An order, a command can only be the purport of a will. In *Ethics* (I, 13), Aristotle makes a distinction between a rational part and an irrational part of soul, and further, within the irrational part, between a vegetative and an appetitive part. He says that the vegetative part has nothing in common with the reason, but that the appetitive part participates in it somehow, in so far as it listens to and obeys reason; so that "the irrational element is in some sense persuaded by a rational principle". Now, a reason that both commands and is obeyed in return can only be a reason that both thinks and wills, in a word the practical reason. Such a reason can only be a divine reason or the divine reason in man. It was not Aristotle himself who asserted this. It was his faithful pupil Thomas Aquinas who first drew such a consequence from the Aristotelian doctrine of reason.

IV

Though it seems unavoidable that Aristotelian metaphysics with its belief in entelechy—the belief in the immanence of value in reality—must lead to a doctrine of natural law, the general opinion that Aristotelian philosophy contains a natural law doctrine or even that Aristotle is the founder of such a doctrine, does not withstand critical testing.

Since natural law represents justice which results from nature, and justice represents a moral claim, Aristotle's attitude towards the natural law doctrine can be understood only in the context of his teachings concerning justice, and his teachings concerning justice can only be understood in the context of his ethics. In this connection we have to point out, however, that Aristotelian ethics is split. The subject of Aristotle's ethics is "the good . . . for which all strive" (1094*a*) and which is the purpose of human life. This good is bliss, "the chief good" (1097*b*). Aristotle identifies this bliss with virtue (1098*b*). As previously in his *Protreptikos*, in his *Nichomachean Ethics* Aristotle likewise considers sheer cognition —the contemplative activity of men—to be this supreme good. In book X he proclaims it to be "the highest virtue" (1177*a*). It implies renunciation of worldly affairs and turning towards eternal values. This contemplative activity is thus declared the supreme moral value. Hence,

Aristotle presents deity as pure thought. On the other hand, Aristotle recognizes also a political morality which refers to the conduct of citizens in the state and is, therefore, not compatible with the morality of pure cognition. This political morality is the main topic of the *Nichomachean Ethics*. From the standpoint of this political morality justice is "the complete" and "the entire" virtue (1129*b*, 1129/30*a*). But after having praised the contemplative activity, in book X as "the highest virtue" and "the noblest activity", Aristotle declares: "But in a secondary degree, the life in accordance with the other kind of virtue is blissful", (and with the expression "the other kind of virtue justice is designated in the first place (1178*a*)".

Aristotle tries to cover such a contradiction by stating, at the beginning of the second book, as follows: "Virtue is of two kinds, ethical and intellectual. Thus, the virtue of pure cognition is qualified as a non-ethical virtue. But a non-ethical virtue is a contradiction in itself as long as 'virtue' represents 'goodness' and hence a moral value."

Morality, the main topic of the *Nichomachean Ethics*, is a political morality, for Aristotle calls his ethics "political science". All that is just is indicated by him as belonging to "political science" (1094*a*). What Aristotle conceives of as good is not Plato's transcendental idea of good, but it is a "good for man" (1094*a*). It is a "good for man" in general, but in particular "good for the state", for Aristotle writes: "Even though it be the case that good is the same for the individual and for the state, nevertheless the good for the state is manifestly a greater and more perfect good, both to attain and to preserve. To secure the good for one person only is better than nothing, to secure the good for a nation or a state is a nobler and more divine achievement."

Since good is bliss and bliss is virtue, the following question arises for Aristotle: "What is virtue?" (1101*b*). His immediate answer is: "The true statesman seems to be one who has made a special study of virtue since his aim is to make the citizens virtuous and law-abiding men: we have an example in the lawgivers of Crete and Sparta." This means: virtue is something that the statesman in his function as legislator wants to realize by inducing citizens to abide by the laws of the state, *i.e.* the positive law. Justice is a virtuue, even the "complete" virtue and the "sum of all virtue". It is the virtue of citizens and, being such, it is constituted by their law-abiding conduct, in their conduct according to the positive law. In this way, from the very beginning in the first book of his *Nichomachean Ethics*, Aristotle excludes any justice that would be different from and constrasting with positive law.

As already mentioned, Aristotle distinguishes an "intellectual" virtue and an "ethical" virtue. Justice is ethical virtue. This virtue is described in the beginning of the second book:

> The ethical virtue is the product of habit and none of the ethical virtues is engendered in us by nature, for no natural property can be altered by habit. For instance, it is the nature of a stone to move downward; it cannot be trained to move upward though you should try to train it to do so by throwing it upward into the air a thousand times. Nor can fire be

trained to burn downward, nor can anything else that naturally behaves in one way be trained into a habit of behaving in another way. The virtues, therefore are engendered in us neither by nature nor in violation of nature. Nature gives us the capacity to receive them, and this capacity is brought to maturity by habit (1103*a*).

Since none of the ethical virtues is given us by nature, and yet justice is virtue, justice is not given to us by nature. Justice cannot be engendered in us by nature, for Aristotle refers to nature here as the necessary and unalterable flow of events. A stone moves downward by nature; by nature the fire burns upward. It is not nature that makes man just in the way that it makes the stone fall and the fire burn upward. Men can be either just or unjust. But the stone has no choice to fall or to climb, the fire has no choice to burn downward or upward. He is just who behaves as he ought to behave, but also he is able to behave in another way and be unjust. All that exists "by nature" exists in the way it necessarily has to be and cannot be different. Justice as virtue is "neither springing from nature nor is it directed against nature". Now, if justice is not engendered by nature there can be no natural law, for natural law means natural justice. One becomes virtuous in general and just in particular not by following nature but by following law. "What occurs within states" provides one piece of evidence for the statement that ethical virtues have not been constituted by nature. It is the lawgiver who makes the citizens virtuous by training them in the habit of right action; and this is the aim of all legislation, not only of the "true" statesman, as mentioned before. The legislator, not nature, makes citizens virtuous and in this way also just. He makes them virtuous and especially just by making them law-abiding. This is the goal of every legislator. To be just means, therefore, to obey all laws of the state. But at this point Aristotle observes: "If he [the legislator] fails to do this, he is a failure; this is what distinguishes a good constitution from a bad one." The reader of Aristotle is inclined to understand from his teachings that a good statesman renders his citizens virtuous only by subjecting them to good, *i.e.* just, laws. Yet such is not the meaning of the quoted passage. Its true meaning is that *every* legislator wants his citizens to become virtuous by inducing them to obey the laws he enacted. He does not always succeed. The lack of success does not depend upon the lack of justice in his laws but rather upon the fact that he does not use suitable means in order to get his laws obeyed by all citizens. Most likely Aristotle has in mind here the same idea that is expressed in the beginning of the third book of the *Nichomachean Ethics* (1109*b*, 16, 16 to 1110*a*, 15): he points to "rewards and punishments" imposed by the legislator as reaction to the obedience or lack of obedience to his laws. If Aristotle believed a statesman makes his citizens virtuous only by subjecting them to good, *i.e.* just, laws, he would have put the difference between good and bad laws, just and unjust laws, at the very top of his inquiry. The words: "this is what distinguishes" *i.e.* "this" understood as greater or lesser skill displayed by the legislator, "a good constitution from a bad one", cannot be interpreted as what distinguishes a legal order with good, *i.e.* just, laws, from another legal order with bad, *i.e.* unjust, laws. The constitution of a state is not identical with the laws enacted by its constitutional legislator.

In connection with this topic Aristotle stresses once again his idea that man is neither good nor bad by nature; hence he is neither just nor unjust by nature. He states: "You will become a good harpist from playing the harp well, a good builder by building well, and a bad one from building poorly." The capacities (good or bad) result from the corresponding activities. "Were this not so, there would be no need for teachers of the arts but everybody would be born a good or bad craftsman. The same then is true of the virtues." That means, since justice is a virtue, man is not by nature just or that which is just does not originate within the nature of man but from some other source. It has to be imparted to man somehow from the outside. According to what was said before, the source becomes evident: it is the law of the state. Aristotle, however, says here: there is need of a teacher; man must be taught by the political science of ethics which "enacts laws about what man has to pursue and what he has to avoid" as he stated before. By saying this, Aristotle confuses political science with politics, the latter being the activity of the statesman in his function as legislator. In fact, he declares right afterwards (1103*b*, 1 to 1103*b*, 27):

> Our present study has a practical aim unlike the other branches of philosophy, for we are not investigating the nature of virtue for the sake of knowing what it is, but in order to become virtuous, without which result our investigation would be of no avail. We have consequently to carry out an inquiry into the region of conduct and to ask how we are to act rightly.

Here there creeps into Aristotle's words a confusion that even in our times is quite common: precisely the confusion between sciences that describe norms, such as ethics and jurisprudence, with the object of these sciences, such as prescribing morality and prescribing law. Such confusion results from the Aristotelian concept of practical reason. For Aristotle continues:

> Now the formula to act in conformity with right principle is common ground, and may be assumed as the basis of our discussion. And after having characterized virtues as a mean state, Aristotle says: "They are within our control and are voluntary and, as such, prescribed by right reason. (1114*b*, 25).

Also in another connexion Aristotle refutes the idea of a natural justice. Stating that virtues are not capacities, he says,

> We are not pronounced good because we are capable of certain emotions; neither are we called bad for the same reason; nor are we praised or blamed because of such reasons. Further, we possess certain capacities or talents by nature; but we are not born good or bad by nature (1105*b* to 1106*a*),

and hence just or unjust. Here again there is no natural justice.

Book V of the *Nichomachean Ethics* is dedicated to the problem of justice. Aristotle differentiates various concepts of justice. He says,

> The law abiding man and he who observes equality will both be just. The *just*, therefore, means that which is lawful and that which is equal, and the unjust means that which is illegal or that which is unequal (1129*a*).

According to this statement, the principle of legality and the principle of equality appear as two different and separate forms of justice. But shortly after this we read:

> Again we see that the law-breaker is unjust and the law-abiding man just. It is, therefore, clear that all lawful things are just in a certain sense of the word, for what is lawful is decided by the legislator, and the decisions of the legislator we call rules of justice.

This justice is identical with lawfulness, whereby, under "law" we are to understand the positive law with any contents whatsoever. Aristotle does not make here any distinction between a just positive law and an unjust positive law. Every positive law is just, for "all that is lawful" *i.e.* actual law enacted by a legislature "is just".

> The actions that spring from virtue in general are, in the main, identical with the actions that are according to law, since the law enjoins conduct displaying the various particular virtues and forbids conduct displaying the various vices (1130*b*).

Since justice is virtue and the positive law enjoins conduct displaying the various particular virtues, positive law, *any* positive law must be just. In a later context we read further (1134*a*, 28),

> Justice can only exist between those whose mutual relations are regulated by law; and law exists among those between whom there is the possibility of injustice. For law [this is doubtless positive law] is the separation of what is just and what is unjust.

And in *Politics* (Book I, chapter 2, 1253*a*) Aristotle writes:

> But justice, which is the essence of all morality is a matter of state. The administration of justice is the principle of order in political society. It is also this administration of justice [*i.e.* positive law] to determine what is just.

These words signify no more nor less that positive law and justice converge.

Should the principle of equality be different and separate from the principle of legality, then a conflict between the principle of legality and that of equality would be possible. Any positive law violating the principle of equality would have to be considered unjust from the standpoint of the principle of equality. But this is not the case, according to Aristotle. He presents the concept of legality—the concept of positive rightfulness—as the extended principle of justice in which the principle of equality is included as principle of special or particular justice. Referring to this legality he states: "Justice in this sense is perfect virtue" (1029*b*, 14) and "Justice in this sense is not a part of virtue but the whole virtue. And its opposite injustice is not a part of vice but the whole of vice". And Aristotle continues,

> What we are investigating, however, is the justice as a special kind of virtue, since we hold that there is such a thing as justice in this sense; and similarly we are investigating injustice as a special kind of vice . . . Consequently, there is another sort of injustice, which is a part of injustice in the universal sense, and there is something unjust which is a part of the unjust in general in the sense of *illegal* (1130*a*, 5).

Hence, there must be a justice which is part of the whole justice in the sense of legality, that is, in the sense of positive rightfulness. The special justice, which is a part of justice in the universal sense and in the meaning of positive rightfulness is equality. Let us quote further:

> It is clear that there are more kinds of justice than one, and that the term has another meaning besides virtue as a whole. We have then to ascertain the nature and attributes of justice in this special sense (1130*a*, 27).

About the outcome of his investigation Aristotle informs us only that this "special justice" is equality, and that its relation to justice—virtue as a whole—is the same as the relation "of a part to the whole", for unequal is unlawful though not everything unlawful is unequal . . .For injustice in this sense is a part of the universal injustice, and similarly the justice we are now considering [this refers to the principle of equality] is a part of universal justice", which means legality, *i.e.*, positive rightfulness. Between justice in this sense and the justice of equality no conflict can ever arise, for the latter is comprised in the former. All rules of positive law are just but among these rules there are some which are just in a particular sense—those that apply the principle of equality.

Nevertheless, Aristotle cannot ignore the existence of positive legal orders that do not apply equality to all citizens in the like proportion. He says,

> The enacted laws . . . aim at the common well-being either of all or of the best or of those who hold power determined either by virtue or in some other similar way (1129*b*, 14).

Also such a positive order is justified that does not aim at general well-being of all citizens but exclusively at the advantage of a favoured group. Such preference, however, is considered rightful because the criterion for it is "virtue" or at least something "similar", *i.e.* some moral value. With such a preference Aristotle does not see any violation of what he calls "equality". In order to justify not only a democratic but also an aristocratic and monarchial legal order in accordance with the principle of equality, he develops his thesis of proportionality as equality. All positive legal orders, he says,

> . . . agree that justice in its distribution must be based on merit of some sort although not always the same sort of merit. Supporters of democracy identify it with freedom, supporters of oligarchy with wealth or with noble birth, and supporters of aristocracy with virtue. That which is just, then, is a species of the proportionate. For proportion is equality of relations . . . (1131*a*, 12). Justice is thus that equality in virtue of which a just man . . . operates proportionate equality . . . (1134*a*, 4).

Proportionate justice is distribution or assignment based upon a certain value, be it freedom, wealth, or virtue. But that means that it is based on something which is considered a value. In this way the concept of equality is replaced by the concept of a subjective and, therefore, relative value. Consequently, each legal order that assigns duties and rights according to any subjective and, therefore, relative value whatsoever—and every positive legal order does assign duties and rights according to such a value—may be justified as corresponding to the principle of equality.

Such an identification of positive law with justice is incompatible with a true natural law doctrine. A doctrine of natural law must allow the possibility of a contrast between both these doctrines—at least in principle—although it strives for reducing any such possibility to a minimum.

In his justification of positive law Aristotle does not go so far as to declare all positive orders equivalent. Law, it is said, enjoins all virtue and forbids all vice and, indeed, "rightly if the law has been rightly enacted, not so well if it has been hastily conceived" (1129*b*. 14). The value difference consists only in a greater or lesser degree of being rightly enacted. Such difference is not explained by the intention of a law but by the law technique, *i.e.* by the fact that one law has been drafted carefully, the other one carelessly.

From the assertions that "all that is legal is just" and that law enjoins "to live according to the various particular virtues" would follow that a good citizen, *i.e.* a man whose conduct corresponds to all norms of the positive law, must also be good and just from the point of view of morality. However, Aristotle states something that is not in harmony with his identification of positive law with justice: "I think that it is perhaps not exactly the same to be a good person and a good citizen in each of the various states." It appears that the author of *Nichomachean Ethics* was, after all, a little frightened of the consequences that the identification of justice with legality would lead to. At any rate, considering the text related to this topic, there can be no doubt that positive law is identified with justice.

Basically, this idea is only consequential to the assumption that reality with immanent value in itself must be, in principle, good. After all, positive law is established by a real action; it is a real, actually existing law and should therefore be regarded substantially as good, *i.e.* just. Here, the inner contradiction of a natural law doctrine that wishes to supply a value measure for positive law becomes evident. Norms can be deduced from nature, from human nature in particular, only if nature is good. Now, if it *is* good, there is no need for norms to prescribe how people ought to behave, since they would have to behave in the desired way just following their own nature. Only when human nature is not good there is need for norms. Law exists, says Thomas Aquinas, not because of the good ones but because of the wicked ones (*Summa Theologica*, I-II, 96, 5). But if man's nature is wicked, no natural law can be deduced from it. The Aristotelian doctrine of entelechy substantially presupposes a good reality and represents an optimistic interpretation of nature. It is, hence, nothing but consistent and consequential, when the Aristotelian ethics virtually aims at a justification of positive morality and of positive law, both representing the social order actually established by men.

The difference between *physikon dikaion* and *nomikon dikaion* is expressed in the sentence, "Political justice is of two kinds, one natural, the other conventional". With political justice (*politikon dikaion*) nothing else can be understood but the positive law of a community that is composed of free and equal citizens. For, earlier, we read,

> The object of our investigation is at once justice in the absolute sense and political justice. The latter means justice as practised between free and equal persons living a common life for the purpose of satisfying their needs (1134*a*).

With the concepts of natural and legal (or conventional) justice—*physikon* and *nomikon dikaion*—Aristotle distinguishes two kinds of positive governmental law. This is possible because the Greek word *dikaion* means both justice and positive law. The difference between *physikon* and *nomikon dikarion* is constituted by the fact that natural rule of justice "has the same validity everywhere and does not depend on our considering it law or not. A rule is conventional or legal when, in the first instance, it can be settled in one way or the other indifferently; having once been settled, however, it is no longer arbitrary". This means: that among rules of positive law, there are such that regulate matters in a certain way; these matters may be settled only in this particular way and in no other as, for instance norms forbidding murder and theft; and there are norms which regulate matters in a certain way but the same matters may be regulated also in a different way, so that these norms have an arbitrary character. For example, norms regulating traffic prescribe two approaching cars to give way to the right and not to the left. Since natural justice involves norms of positive law, Aristotle must have rejected the idea that natural justice be immutable.

> Some people think that all rules of justice are merely conventional because, whereas a law of nature is immutable and has the same validity everywhere, as fire burns both here and in Persia, the concepts are seen to vary. This is not absolutely true but only to a certain degree. Among the gods, indeed, it is perhaps not true at all; but in our world, although there is such a thing as natural justice, its rules are variable.

Variable, yes, but only to a certain extent! Also those rules of positive law that are not at all arbitrary—prohibition of murder, theft, etc.—are not everywhere completely the same. At various times, with various nations they are different. But their differences from one situation to another remain within certain limits. Between these norms of positive law that are considered just "by nature" and those norms of positive law indicated as just "by law", there is only one difference: the former are much less variable than the latter. Here, the first definition of "just by nature" in the sense of "what has the same validity everywhere" is considerably modified. For, if a rule is variable—even to a small degree—it cannot have the same validity everywhere. At any rate, these conditions preclude the assumption of a true natural law which is valid everywhere for all mankind and which maintains the same contents for ever[2]

---

[2] After the words: ". . . although there is such thing as natural justice, its rules are variable", we read: "Nevertheless there is a law which is law by nature and there is another law which is not law by nature. But what kind it is, what its character is, which of the variable norms are instilled by nature and which are not just by nature but by law or convention (even if both are variable)—these are obvious questions. If both kinds of justice are variable the decision what kind and character belong to the natural justice and which ones to the legal justice is absolutely not obvious. Moreover, the natural and the legal justices are here described as two kinds of justice within "what likewise can be different" while earlier that which can be so but can also be different is being

Since positive law—essentially positive law alone—is just, any possibility of conflict between *physikon* and *nomikon dikaion,* as essential for every true doctrine of natural law, cannot be taken into consideration at all. To say nothing of the fact that, in case of such a conflict, the invalidity of the positive law, *i.e.* of *nomikon dikaion* could be claimed.

---

distinguished, as legal justice, from that which has the same validity everywhere and which was called natural justice. And further, "This determination can be applied conveniently also to other things. For example, the right hand is stronger by nature; nevertheless there are persons capable of using both hands in the same way". If one has to understand that a natural rule can have exceptions then the meaning differs from the former assertion that not only that which is legally just but also that which is naturally just is variable. For, as far as variability of positive law is concerned, there are no exceptions to any rule involved. Also the following paragraph is not without objection from the standpoint of logic. "As far as those rules of law are concerned which are based upon convention and usefulness, a similar case is given as with measures and weights. Since neither the measures for wine and wheat are everywhere the same; larger in the place of buying, smaller in the place of selling." Conceived of literally, this is impossible, since purchase and sale are only two sides of the same transaction. If the quotation intends to express the idea that one buys a larger quantity for the same price in wholesale while the quantity of purchased goods is smaller when bought in retail, then it is incomprehensible that this parable has anything in common with that which is just by nature. The rules of law which are based upon convention and usefulness must be presupposed, here, as natural justice. For the following tex treads: "Likewise those rights which are not set by nature but by men are not the same everywhere, since the constitutions are not everywhere the same." Therefore, constitutions are not emanated by nature but are intended only as human law, *i.e.* norms of law established by men. However, in the ensuing quotation, constitutions of states are indicated as being established by nature. "Everywhere only one constitution is established by nature, that one which is best." But if everywhere only one constitution is natural, such natural law cannot be variable. There are some more statements in this chapter which are so manifestly questionable that they may hardly be attributed to such a great thinker as Aristotle. This is the case with the declaration that a man, who unites with a woman having the knowledge that she is married but without having thought over his action which is motivated by passion, and a man who has stolen something, both, act unjustly. However, they *are* not unjust. Above all, after that was considered just which establishes and preserves the happiness of the state-community, and the law of the state prescribes all virtues (thus also the virtue of justice), after this justice which is safeguarded by the law of state was declared the highest of all virtues, and after in the above-mentioned chapter (1134*a*, 20) was stated that Aristotle was searching for "justice in a state" (*politikon diaion*) he states later (1134*b*, 13): "Governmental norms are neither just nor unjust; they follow the law and they were established only by those who are capable of lawful actions by their nature." Earlier, however, justice has downrightly been identified with legality, *i.e.* with governmental justice; and later Aristotle denotes *politikon dikaion* as being just partly by nature and partly by law. This is a contradiction which cannot be eliminated by any interpretation.

It is hard not to believe that the statements in book V of the *Nichomachean Ethics,* which are considered crucial for the alleged natural law doctrine of Aristotle, have not been vitiated. If these statements allow us to deduce any position, assumed by Aristotle, in respect to a natural law doctrine at all, they certainly do not allow us to regard Aristotle as a representative of a natural law doctrine. In his "*Erläuterungen zu der Nikomachischen Ethik*" Clarifications to the *Nichomachean Ethics*) *Kirchmann* maintains, with regard to the mentioned portion of book V, where the distinction is made between *physikon* and *nomikon dikaion* (between natural and positive justice: "Either this chapter was written by Aristotle with great carelessness or this text has been corrupted later . . . Further, it is evident that book V is a compilation of a mediocre pupil or a preparatory work written by Aristotle himself in earlier days."

Yet such a conflict cannot come up at all, if we consider Aristotle's method of thinking about the difference between *physikon* and *nomikon dikaion* in his *Nichomachean Ethics*. For *physikon dikarion*, which is natural law, in fact is only a component of the *politikon dikaion, i.e.* of positive governmental law. These norms are the ones that more or less agree within all positive legal orders.

In *Magna Moralia* (1194*b*, 30*f*) we read: Do not suppose that, if things change owing to our use, there is not, therefore, a natural justice, because there is. For that which continues for the most part can plainly be seen to be naturally just."

Aristotle thought he was able to establish that all positive legal orders do not differ substantially in regulating certain circumstances. Norms that regulate these certain circumstances are called by him natural law. But if "natural law" does not define anything but those precepts that are common in all positive legal orders, then every positive law is natural law, and this so-called natural law is then unable to fulfil a function which is essential to a true natural law, *i.e.* to be a value meter for the positive law. Then we no longer are able to distinguish between a just and an unjust law with the appeal to natural law. At any rate, Aristotle takes over the distinction between "by nature" (*physei*) and "by law" (*nomos dikaion*), usual at his time, but the meaning given to it by Aristotle renders it completely irrelevant from the standpoint of a true natural law doctrine.[3] Aristotle himself uses the term of natural law only in view of justifying positive law. This appears clearly in his attitude towards slavery. Aristotle defends this institution with the justification that there are men who are slaves by nature.

If "the nature" of the alleged Aristotelian natural law is the nature which Aristotle mentions in his *Politics* I, 2 (1253*a*) with the words, "It is evident that the state is a creation of nature, and that man is by nature a political animal", then positive law must be regarded as natural law—

[3] Many recent law philosophers pervert not only Aristotle but the entire concept of natural law. Their arguments are as follows: Since man lives always and everywhere in society and hereby submits himself to a social order regulating his conduct in relation to his fellow men, the validity of such an order must suit human nature. In fact, all social orders are in agreement with one another as far as certain precepts are concerned, for example, the prohibition to kill members of the same community or certain members of the community. Given such fact, they draw the conclusion that there is a natural law ensuing from the nature of man. There are no grounds for such a conclusion. The fact that men live always and everywhere in a social order which regulates their conduct gives no evidence that such order results from their nature. This social order compels men to renounce the satisfaction of many of their drives, primarily of their so-called drive of aggression. Such aggression drives are natural in the same measure as drives aiming at mutual assistance. Social orders are in accord as well as in conflict with nature that actually conditions man. If we are unable to establish as natural law nothing but those provisions which are common to all legal orders, then it is correct what was said, in the text under examination, about the *physei dikaion;* it cannot perform the essential function of a true natural law which is different of possibly conflicting with positive law. And it can by no means perform this function, if one has to admit that such natural law is variable, as it is the case with the recent doctrine of a variable natural law.

in the sense of this doctrine. According to this doctrine, every state, not only the Greek *polis*, is a creation of nature. The natural existence of a state is based upon the fact that man is by nature a political animal, *i.e.* organizing himself in a state. This does man in general, not only the Greek. "He who by nature and not by mere accident is without a state is either above humanity or below it . . . He who is unable to live in society, or who has no need because he is sufficient for himself, must be either a beast or a god; he is no part of a state. A social instinct is implanted in *all men* by nature." And *each* state has a legal order "for law is nothing else but the reigning order existing in the political community [the concept used so far, which means: in each state]. Consequently, law which is an essential attribute of the state in the form of positive law must be creation of nature and, thus, natural law. And since it is law that decides what is just, as indicated in the previously quoted passage, every positive law must be *physei dikaion* even if Aristotle does not label it so in this connexion.

The belief that Aristotle speaks for a natural law doctrine gets some support by his distinction between good and bad constitutions, or right and "perverted" constitutions. But since, for Aristotle, not only the right constitutions (*i.e.*, monarchy, aristocracy, and polity) but also the degenerated constitutions (*i.e.* tyranny, oligarchy, and democracy) are constitutions of *states*, and these states as states are the creation of nature together with their necessary legal order, this nature cannot be the criterion for the value of a constitution and its good or bad, right or perverted quality. By evaluating a constitution as bad or perverted, Aristotle does not mean that such a constitution is contrary to "nature" as he refers to in his writings about state as creation of nature and about man as political animal by nature. With a law of "nature" in *this* sense of the word, his doctrine concerning perverted constitutions has no connexion.

Such an insight is rendered more difficult by the fact that Aristotle has in mind, in his doctrine of state, two different concepts of state, and —perhaps—two different concepts of nature, without emphasizing this explicitly. This is dependent upon the fact that he confuses the description of existing states (*i.e.* declarative statements of what a state in different countries and at different times really *is*) with a normative-evaluating image of what and how a state *ought to be*. After having characterized the state (and that means *all* states) in book I of *Politics* as a natural community in which men (that means *all* men) live out their nature of political animals, in book III Aristotle defines the state as "a body of citizens sufficing for the purpose of life" (1275*b*); a citizen is only "he who has the power to take part in the deliberative and judicial administration". Such a body, however, is not a state that exists everywhere and at all times, but a state as it ought to be according to Aristotle's opinion, and as it more or less materialized in some—not in all—Greek communities. Aristotle admits:

> Our definition of citizen is best adapted to the citizen of a democracy; but not necessarily to citizens of other constitutions—which however also constitute states (1275*a*).

But communities without "citizens" in the sense of the quoted definition (communities that are not democracies) are likewise "*states*" in the very sense of the Aristotelian concept expressed in book I of *Politics*; these communities do have conditions and laws to determine what is just. They, too, are creations of nature and with them their positive law, which is essential to their existence, are derived from nature. Later, Aristotle again defines the state as "a community of freemen" (1279*a*) which, however, means: the state ought to be a community of freemen but it is not always. For Aristotle distinguishes between constitutions "that aim at a common interest" and those "that aim exclusively at the interest of the ruling class" (1279*a*). The first forms, he says, "are true forms of government", and calls the other constitutions defective and "perversions" of the right ones; they are despotic in character for treating their subjects as slaves. Nevertheless, they are constitutions of states. Aristotle indicates explicitly the three perverted forms of government (tyranny, oligarchy, and democracy) as "constitutions" (1289*a*) that constitute states. "They too" [oligarchy and democracy] "have a kind of justice" (1280*a*). Referring to both of these perverted constitutions, he even states: "They "arise" (1301*b*) and hence they must exist by nature. But in book III (1287*b*) we read:

> Tyranny is not according to nature and neither are such the other perverted constitutions; they are rather contrary to nature.

This passage is not only in open contradiction to one of the principle theses of the Aristotelian doctrine of state which claims the existence of all states by nature, where people organize themselves owing to their political nature, but in strict contradiction also to the immediate preceding sentence:

> There are men who must be governed by a despot, others rather by a king, and yet others for whom polity is a just and advantageous form of government.

Well, the perverted constitutions are "despotical", and whenever they rule over people who by nature must be subjected to a despotical rule, they are natural. The passage in question contradicts, moreover, statements contained in book III (1286*b*), where Aristotle explains why and under what circumstances the perverted form of state (tyranny, oligarchy, and democracy) arise. Referring to democracy, he says that under specified circumstances "no other form of government appears to be any longer feasible to establish"; and hence it cannot be contrary to "nature", as the basical description of book I refers to. It is more than doubtful whether the sentence concerning the perverted constitutions is authentic, owing to the consideration that it contradicts everything Aristotle ever expressed with regard to the essence of state. If it is authentic, then Aristotle employs here a different concept of nature from that from which his doctrine of state originates; the new concept does not consider nature as it exists in reality but rather as an ideal nature, as it should exist from the standpoint of a certain value. This means, however, that the perverted constitutions are contrary to something that is a postulate presented as "nature". But a similar "nature" cannot be the nature of a natural law doctrine. That isolated passage, outside the spirit of the context of the entire Aristotelian doctrine of state, can certainly not be considered for an Aristotelian doctrine of natural law.

The idea of a natural law, different from and possibly contrasting the positive law, and equivalent to justice in the specific sense of the word, that Aristotle purposely avoids in his ethics, appears in full light in his *Rhetoric*. Here, natural law in the prerogative as "universal law" is confronted with positive law in its prerogative as "particular law". Particular law is that which each community lays down and applies to its own members; this is partly written and partly unwritten. Universal law is law of nature. For there really is, as everyone to some extent divines, a natural justice and injustice . . ." (I, 13). Earlier, however, Aristotle writes as follows: "Law is either particular or universal. By *particular law* I mean that written law which regulates the life of a particular community; by *universal law* all those unwritten principles which are supposed to be acknowledged everywhere" (I, 10). In this passage, "universal law" is not explicitly identified with natural law, and positive law is characterized as "written" rule, whereas in the other passage, where universal law is identified with natural law, positive law is mentioned "partly written and partly unwritten". Aristotle makes the following remark (I, 14): ". . . The written laws depend on force while the unwritten ones do not." Later (I, 15), natural law as unwritten law is again mentioned in opposition to positive law as written law. His attempts to bring all these contradicting formulations into harmony remain futile. The important thing is Aristotle's emphasis on the possibility of a conflict between the unwritten natural law and the written positive law. The purpose of such emphasis, however, is exclusively rhetorical, in order to show the advocate the argumentative advantages resulting from reference to one or the other concept. We read here (I, 15), "If the written law tells against our case, clearly we must appeal to the universal law, and insist on its greater equity and justice. We must argue that the juror's oath, I will give my verdict according to my honest opinion, means that one will not simply follow the letter of the written law. We must urge that the principles of equity are permanent and changeless and that the universal law does not change either, for it is the law of nature, whereas written laws often do change . . ." It is obvious that what Aristotle advises the advocate to emphasize before the court, is not any doctrine of natural law of his. The statement that natural law does not change is in direct opposition to what Aristotle maintains in his *Nichomachean Ethics*. The next quotation leaves no doubt that the mentioned work about the art of rhetoric does not contain any Aristotelian philosophy of law but only the forensic advice for the advocate to resort to the natural law doctrine, a practice which at that time was quite common whenever positive law was not favourable to the advocate's cause. Aristotle recommends that the orator present the opposite theory, if this helps his cause. "If, however, the written law supports our case, we must urge that the oath to give my verdict according to my honest opinion is not meant to make the judge give a verdict that is contrary to the law, but to save him for the guilt of perjury if they misunderstand what the law really means." The advocate is also advised to express in court the opinion that violation of the unwritten law is a more serious misdemeanour than violation of the written law. And Aristotle adds the following advice: "We shall turn the case about so that great injustice appears from action against the written positive law (*Rhetoric* I, 14).

To the question which one of the two mutually exclusive opinions concerning the relationship between natural and positive law, chosen by the teacher of rhetoric to fit this or that circumstance is considered true by the teacher of ethics, Aristotle gives no answer. But his silence is an answer too; an answer to the question whether Aristotle speaks for a true natural low doctrine. And this answer can only be negative.

V

It was not Aristotle himself but Thomas Aquinas who, on the basis of the Aristotelian philosophy, developed a natural law doctrine. The theological character of this doctrine is unequivocal.

The Aristotelian entelechy reappears unmistakably in the work *Summa contro Gentiles*. In book III,, 16, we read:

> Every being is ordered to this end (ordinatur in finem) . . . The end of everything is that in which its appetite (appetitus eius) terminates. The end of everything is a good . . . The end of each thing is its perfection perfectio) . . . Each thing is ordered to a good as an end.

But this good is God. We quote from chapter 17:

> Nothing tends toward a thing as an end, unless this thing is a good, or is therefore necessary that the good, as good (*bonum in quantum bonum est*), be its end. Consequently, that which is the highest good (*summum bonum*) is, from the highest point of view, the end of all things. But there is only one highest good, and this is God . . . So, all things are ordered to one good, as their end, and this is God.

Then in the next chapter there is written: "God is the end of things in a way that each thing attains him in its own way (obtinendum)." Perfection is the immanent end of all things. This is the Aristotelian entelechy. Perfection is God's action, for it is God who leads things to perfection. This is said in *Summa Theologica* (I, Questio 103, art. 1):

> It is not fitting that the supreme goodness of God should produce things without growing them to their perfection . . . It belongs to the divine goodness, as it brought things into existence, so to lead them to their end.

If nature moves towards an end, it is because God commands nature to aim at good as to its end, and nature complies with God's command. Therefore, the essence of existence is good, *i.e.* it is as it ought to be in compliance with God's commandment. Thomas Aquinas writes again (I, Questio 5, art. 1): "Goodness and being are really the same." And furthermore: (I, *Questio* 48, art. 1):

> Hence it cannot be that evil signifies being or any form of nature. Therefore it must be that the name of evil is signified as the absence of good.

> And this is what is meant by saying that evil is neither a being nor a good. For, since being, as such, is good, the absence of one implies the absence of the other.

Existence and norm converge.[4]

Such a denial of any dualism of existence and norm that rests essentially upon a metaphysical-theological basis is predominant in the thesis about the nature of man. Again, in *Summa Theologica* (I-II, 94, 2) we read that "Inclinations that are part of human nature belong to the precepts of natural law". The inclinations of human nature are precepts of natural law for and inasmuch as they are determined by the practical reason. Following in Aristotle's footsteps, Thomas Aquinas distinguishes between *ratio speculative* and *ratio practica* (*Summa Theologica*, I-11, 90, 1). Functions of the practical reason are: commanding, legislating, dictating norms as precepts for the good and right conduct (I-II, 17, 1; I-II, 90, 1). Law is the rule and the measure for what ought to be done and what ought to be avoided (I-II, 90, 1). But the human practical reason, of itself, is not this rule and this measure but the principles impressed on it by nature, are general rules and measures (I-II, 91, 3). Now, these principles, impressed on human reason "by nature" (naturaliter) originate, after all, from God who provided man with reason; and human reason is practical, norm dictating reason only in so far as divine reason dwells in it. Now, divine reason governs the world according to an eternal law. This eternal law is conceived of as being immanent in the divine reason. Man created by God is endowed with reason in so far as human reason partakes of a share of divine reason, whereby he has a natural inclination to his proper art and end in conformity with the eternal law; and this participation of the eternal law in the rational creature is called the natural law (I-II, 91, 1 and 2). Thomas Aquinas takes the concept of the eternal law and its immanence in the divine reason over from St. Augustine who defines God's eternal world plan as follows: "*Ratio divina vel voluntas Dei ordinem naturalem conservari jubens, perturbari vetans*" (Divine reason, being God's will, bids the order of nature be maintained and forbids its being disturbed—*Contra Faustum Manich*, 22, 27).

[4] F. C. Copleston points out in his work *Aquinas*, Pelican Book A. 349, Penguin Books Limited, Harmondworth, Middlesex, 1955, p.146: "According to Aquinas every being, considered as such, is good . . . Being and good (when the word is used in this ontological sense) have the same denotation . . ." St. Thomas hits upon the idea of identifying *to be* and *ought-to-be-so, i.e.* good, inasmuch he wishes to avoid the consequence that God, being good, has also created evil, to which faith in God's omnipotence leads in respect to evil. Since St. Thomas cannot simply deny the existence of evil—were there no evil, there would be no room for moral order—he interprets it as something that has negative value, as a deficiency. As such it does not appear to be "created". Copleston says: "If, therefore, every being is good there is no need to postulate an evil deity as creator of evil [as it is found in Manicheism]; for evil is not and cannot be the direct term of creative activity. Nor, indeed, could there be an evil deity, if by this we mean a sheerly evil being. For sheer evil is an impossibility."

With regard to natural law, St. Augustine says: "Who else than God has written the natural law into the hearts of men."[5] Divine reason, having the eternal law and hence the natural law immanent in itself, is endowed with will: "ratio *vel* voluntas." As a consequence, St. Thomas teaches: Just is what is in accordance with the rule of reason, and the first rule of reason is natural law (I-II, 95, 2). "Natural law is nothing else but a participation in rational creature of the eternal law" (I-II, 101, 2).[6]

[5] The view that natural law is written on the heart of men evidently traces back to St. Paul and his Letter to the Romans II, 14: "When Gentiles who have not the law do by nature what the law requires, they are a law to themselves, even though they do not have the law. (15) They show that what the law requires is written on their hearts while their conscience also bears witness and their conflicting thoughts accuse or perhaps excuse them on that day when, according to my gospel, God judges the secrets of men by Christ Jesus." Therefore, no doubt is left that it is God, according to St. Paul, who wrote the commandments of law on the hearts of all men, thus also on those of the Gentiles. This is how St. Augustine interprets St. Paul's doctrine (Augustine: De Serm. Dei in monte, II, c.9, n.32).

A. P. D'Entrèves who quotes this passage in his treatise *Natural Law, An Introduction to Legal Philosophy*, London, 1955, p.39, observes: "St. Thomas' theory of natural law is laid down as an interpretation of man's nature and his relation to God and to the universe. Natural law is unintelligible unless we realize its close link with the eternal divine order on which the whole creation ultimately rests."

In his work *A History of Philosophy*, Vol. II, Westminster, Maryland, 1955, Frederick Copleston stresses the metaphysical and theological foundation of St. Thomas' natural law doctrine. With regard to the *lex eterna* he states: "This eternal law, existing in God, is the origin and fount of the natural law, which is a participation in the eternal law" (pp.408-409). "It is very important to realize clearly that the foundation of the natural law, in the eternal law, the metaphysical foundation of the natural law, does not mean that the natural law is capricious or arbitrary, that it could be otherwise than it is; the eternal law does not depend primarily on the divine will but on the divine reason" (p.409). But the divine reason means also the divine will. Copleston's exposition takes this idea into account when he says: "We must not imagine that God is subject to the moral law as something apart from himself. God knows his divine essence itself and so cannot change; God will it certainly, but it does not depend on any arbitrary act of divine will . . . ultimately the moral law is what it is because God is what he is, since human nature, the law of whose being is expressed in the natural law itself depends on God" (p.409-410). In his work *Aquinas* Copleston says (p.214): "For Aquinas therefore it is human reason which is the proximate or immediate promulgator of the natural moral law." Nevertheless, he continues: "This law is not without a relation to something above itself, for it is, as we have seen, the reflection of or participation in the eternal law." Thus for Aquinas it is the human nature to be the proximate and immediate promulgator of the natural law. Natural law, however, is in an essential relationship to something that belongs to a higher order, since this is—as we have seen—a reflection of or participation in the eternal law. Eternal law originates from God. Hence comes the definition that natural law is nothing other than participation of the rational creature in the eternal law. Without the divine eternal law there can be no natural law.

Henry W. Jaffa (*Thomism and Aristotelianism*, The University of Chicago Press, 1952, p.187) finds that St. Thomas attributes to Aristotle still another principle which is asserted by Thomas himself: "Belief in a divinely implanted natural habit of the moral principles." This is, as Jaffa states, a principle of revealed theology. Here Jaffa admits that, according to Thomas, moral principles and, hence, natural law are "divinely implanted" in man, *i.e.* implanted by God. But such a concept cannot be found in Aristotle.

Eternal law is the rule of world by divine reason. Natural law emanates directly from human reason intended as practical reason, but only because and in so far as human reason partakes of a share of divine reason, because and in so far as natural law partakes of a share of eternal law. For it is the natural law where the eternal law of divine reason reveals itself. The authority of natural law is, after all, the authority of God. Returning to *Summa Theologica* (I-II, 97, 3) we read: "The divine and the natural law proceed according to God's will." No doubt is left about the theological-metaphysical foundations of Thomas Aquinas' doctrine of natural law. Nevertheless, it is a true natural law doctrine. This is shown also by the author's attitude towards the relationship between natural law and positive law. The binding power of positive law is given only in so far as it corresponds to the natural law. Should it conflict with natural law, it has no validity, it is no law. "Every human law has just so much of the nature of law, as it is derived from the law of nature. But if in any point it defects from the law of nature, it is no longer a law but a perversion of law" (I-II, 95, 2). Such is the consequence of the divine authority in the natural law.[7]

The divine reason, which through the eternal law governs the world as legislative reason, is identical with the will of God (I-II, 93, 4). Whence, also the practical reason of men is both cognitive and volitive in view of its legislative activity. Therefore, to be just means at the same time to be true, and justice means at the same time truth.

> Since the volition is rational appetite, when the rectitude of the reason which is called truth is imprinted on the wwill on account of its nearness to reason, this imprint retains the name of truth, and hence it is that justice sometimes goes by the name of truth" (II-II, 58, 4).

When Jesus said to Pilate: "For this I was born and for this I have come into the world to bear witness to the truth" he actually means justice.

VI

Also Kant admits, in his doctrine of practical reason as moral legislator, that the practical reason in man, which is at the same time cognitive, volitive, and legislative by setting norms of natural law in the form of rational law, is the divine reason in man. The autonomy of will consists in the fact that the moral law originates from human will as intelligence. Kant proclaims the autonomy of will as the supreme prin-

[7] Nevertheless, one has to bear in mind that, from an historical point of view, the character of the natural law doctrine is predominantly conservative. It aims at the justification of the existing positive law. Likewise this proves correct with respect to the scholastic natural law doctrine. This shows Prof. *August Knoll* in his work *Catholic Church and Scholastic Natural Law* (Vienna, 1962). The natural law doctrine, he says, in the way it developed as the "servant of theology", defended, as order willed by God and nature, first slavery, then serfdom, then colonial endentured labour in connexion with trade of human beings, and finally the feudal system as long as all this was positive law. He refers to the fact that Thomas Aquinas justifies slavery with the principle "to each his own" which he deemed natural law by presenting the slave as being assigned to his master (*Summa Theologica*, I, questio 21*a*, 1 and 3).

ciple of morality (*Foundations of the Metaphysics of Morals*, Akademie Ausgabe, vol. IV, p.440). In compliance with this autonomy principle, it is the practical reason in man which is his moral legislator. In this respect, Kant's practical reason seems to differ from the practical reason of Thomas Aquinas, who conceives of practical reason as of a share of the practical reason of God, who in the last instance is our moral legislator. But Kant is unable to uphold his priniciple of the moral autonomy of man, for he endeavours to *prove* God's existence as the supreme moral legislator with the help of this practical reason. In his *Critique of Judgment* (Akademie-Ausgabe, vol. V, p.444) he writes:

> Since it is only as a moral being that we recognize man as the purpose of creation, we have . . . as regards the reference (necessary for us by the constitution of our reason) of natural purposes to an intelligent world cause, we have one principle enabling us to think the nature and properties of this first cause as supreme ground in the kingdom of purposes . . . From this definite principle of the causality of the original being we must not think Him merely as intelligence and as legislative for nature, but also as legislating supremely in a moral kingdom of purposes.

Consequently, the source of our moral law is neither the intelligence of man as his will nor the will of man as his intelligence, but it is the intelligence of God or God's will as intelligence, where, in the last instance, our moral law originates. It is not man but God, the original Being, who is our moral legislator. In *Foundations of the Metaphysics of Morals* (IV, p.455) Kant writes:

> The moral *ought* is therefore man's own volition as a member of the intelligible world, and it is conceived by him as an ought only in so far as he regards himself at the same time as a member of the world of sense.

For man as an intelligible being there is no *ought* and, therefore, no imperatives are valid inasmuch as his will coincides with his *ought*. But such an intelligible being, whose will signifies an *ought* for the empirical being, can only be God. Kant confirms it (p.414): "Thus no imperatives hold for the divine will or, more generally, for the holy will. The *ought* is here out of place, for the volition in itself is necessarily in unison with the law" [this means with the *ought*]. According to the *Critique of Judgment*, we have to conceive of God, the original being, as "well-knowing", "all-mighty", and as both "all-good and just at the same time" (VI, p.444). If God is to be accepted as our supreme moral legislator, then our moral duties are not, or not sufficiently, characterized by the term precepts springing from man's own reason. They have to be considered, or at least *also* considered, to be commandments of God. True, Kant states in his *Metaphysics of Ethics* that ethics can, "as pure practical philosophy based on man's own inward legislation, treat singly of the relation existing between man and man, and this is for us the only comprehensive thing; but as for relations existing between God and man, these far transcend all our powers of knowledge, and are absolutely incomprehensible" (VI, p.491). But in *Religion within the limits of Reason alone* (VI, 6) Kant writes: "Morality thus leads ineluctably to religion, through which it extends itself to the idea of a powerful moral lawgiver outside of mankind", and on p.153, "Religion, subjectively regarded, is the recognition of all duties as divine commands." And in Kant's *Opus Posthumum* (presented and revised by Erich Adickes, *Kant-Studien*, n.50, 1920, p.802) we find the following sentence: "Our moral-practical reason contains the categorical imperative to consider all human duties as divine commandments."

Thus, Kant's ethics terminates at the very same point where Thomas Aquinas left it five hundred years before.

VII

It is easy to understand how the natural law doctrine, after its predominance in the seventeenth and eighteenth centuries and its relapse in the nineteenth century, has reappeared in the foreground of the social and legal philosophy in the ewentieth century, following two world wars, as reaction to Nazism, Fascism, and in particular to Communism. It was accompanied by religious-metaphysical speculation and its religious-metaphysical origin is beyond any doubt. It traces back to the philosophy of the Stoics, but already in the *Fragments* by Heraclitus we find some very similar ideas. For example in *Fragment 112*, "To obey nature in speech and action is the highest virtue and true wisdom". In *Fragment 114*, Heraclitus mentions a divine *logos* where all human laws must be nourished. But only the Stoic philosophy defines clearly the concept of natural law, wherein its divine origin is unambiguous. In a *Fragment* by Kleanthes, a leader of the Stoic school, it is said:

> Honoured be the eternally omnipotent Zeus, head of all immortal beings, cause of the creation, ruler of the universe according to law. Yes, every mortal shall pay homage to Thee for we are of Thy breed, resembling Thee in reason and language . . . Thou united good and evil in one in order that a reasonable eternal law might regulate all the universe . . . For men and gods there is no higher privilege than law, which is our and their common duty to praise. Another *Fragment* reads: "Both of you, Zeus and Fate, direct me to my place! I follow you without hesitation. Should I refuse, I would have to go the same path anyway moreover, as a wretch.

Sauter[8] observes rightly, that fate does not mean any other power separate from deity but deity itself which is immanent in the universe. The Stoic Chrysippos teaches: "No other origin, no other evolution of justice may be found than in Zeus and nature common to all men." Cicero, following the Stoic philosophy, teaches that God is founder, proclaimer and judge of the law of nature which in contrast to positive law is eternal and unalterable. (*De Republica*, XXII, 33). The Stoics and Cicero influence the Patristic natural law doctrine, primarily that of St. Augustine who, as already mentioned, borrows from the Stoics their concept of eternal law by saying, "Who else but God has written the natural law on the hearts of men?" (*De serm. Dei in monte*, II, c.9, n.32).

[8] Johann Sauter: Die philosophische Grundlagen des Naturrechts (Philosophical foundations of natural law), Vienna, 1932, p.45).

At any rate, the attempt was made within the natural doctrine itself to have it emancipated from the theological-metaphysical foundations. Grotius explains in the *Prolegomena* to his work *De lure Belli ao pacis* that natural law, as intended by him, would be valid even under the assumption there were no God, adding, of course, that such an assumption could not be done "without the utmost wickedness". But in his very next paragraph (12) he says: "Natural law—comprising that which relates to the social life of men as well as that of a larger sense, proceeding as it does from the essential traits implanted in man—can nevertheless rightly be attributed to God, because of his having willed that such traits exist in us." And his definition of natural law is: "Natural law is a precept of reason, which points out that an act, according to whether it is or is not in conformity with rational nature, has in it a quality of moral baseness or moral necessity and that, in consequence, such an act is either forbidden or commanded by the author of nature, God" (Liber I, cp.I, para. X, 1). Natural law is a precept of the reasonable nature; but nature is God's creation and, hence, precepts of the reasonable nature are precepts of God. Grotius is unable to uphold his attempt to render the validity of natural law independent from the faith in God's existence. For he was a faithful Christian, as all followers of the classical natural law doctrine were although, as it seems, some of them were aware that, without faith in a nature created by a just God, the assumption of a law which is just and immanent in nature is, consequently, not possible. The claim of the validity of natural law independently from faith in God's existence might have originated from the tendency to guarantee the validity of natural law against disbelief. Such a claim, however, must not be confused with the thesis that the validity of natural law is independent from the will of God. The true meaning of what was said above is such that the validity of natural law cannot be revoked, not even by the will of God. This is the consequence of the belief that God's will cannot comprise anything that is contrary to his essence and his nature and that, therefore, his power is limited by his own nature, and that his omnipotence cannot mean that the object of his will can be anything whatsoever. Since the natural law is justice, God cannot wish the annulment of its validity, since this would mean that God wants to be unjust. But since God, according to his nature, is just he would no longer be God if he wanted to be unjust. Anselm of Canterbury expresses the same idea in his *Cur Deus Homo* in the sentence: "The saying 'what God wills is right and what he wills not is not right' should not be understood in the sense that it still would be right, if God wished something that is incorrect only because it is God's will. If God wishes to lie, it does not follow that telling lies is right, but rather that in such circumstances he is no God." In another chapter Anselm maintains, God has no power to change his will "which he wanted, in advance, to be unchangeable". This would be "more impotence than power". Since God wished natural law to be unchangeable, he cannot wish to change or even to abolish it.

VIII

In order to show you the futility of the attempt to conceive of the validity of a true, eternal, and immutable natural law independently of the will of God, I would like to point to a Catholic author, in conclusion, whose authority is certainly not questioned by anybody in this assembly. In his *Moralphilosophie* (Moral philosophy), 5th ed., 1911, p.546, Victor Cathrein[9] defines natural law as "the sum of . . . binding norms that become valid for the whole of mankind by nature itself and not in consequence of any positive statute". Natural law, he says, can be summarized in the two precepts of right "give to each his own" and "you shall not do injustice to anybody". These are empty phrases for they do not define, somehow, any human conflict. They become meaningful only when norms, which are positive, *i.e.* established by acts of a will, determine what belongs to each and what is injustice. But we are not dealing with that subject. Cathrein believes that certain norms can be derived from these two precepts by deduction, "and this independently from any supernatural revelation, and also independently from any positive divine or human decree" so that such norms belong to "the natural law in the very sense of the word" (p.547). Such derived norms are, according to Cathrein, the following ones: "You shall not kill, you shall not commit adultery, you shall not steal, you shall not cheat, you shall not bear false witness, you shall obey your legitimate authorities and keep contracts entered into." Referring to these norms, he openly admits: "Those principles belong to the decalogue" (p.549), *i.e.* the norms involved have been established by the will of God, and by no means independently of any divine or human command. By objecting that Cathrein is of the opinion that these norms are valid not because they are regarded as the purport of divine acts of will but are independent of such acts, one attributes to Cathrein the opinion that the significance of the promulgation of the Ten Commandments—pronounced under lightning and thunder on Mount Sinai by God and written by God himself on two stone tablets—was declaratory alone and not constituent: that God, on Mount Sinai, only proclaimed the validity of norms that had always been valid independently of his will. Such is certainly not the interpretation of the report given by the Holy Scriptures of the mentioned event. But this is not of decisive importance. A norm—and natural law, according to Cathrein, is norm—can only be the purport of an act of will. This fact is admitted by Cathrein himself while discussing the question of whether natural law is rational law, as many assume. It is correct, no doubt, he says on p.548, that "the contents of natural law are practical and binding principles which are recognized by reason spontaneously. But it would be incorrect to think that the binding force of these commandments springs from reason alone. Legal obligation is a claim

[9] Viktor Cathrein, 1845-1931, (Jesuit) since 1863, since 1882 professor of moral philosophy in Holland. Eminent philosopher of morals and social ethics of German language. (Translators remark.)

directed by the will of the superior to the will of the subordinate. But man cannot be the subordinate of his own will. Our reason announces like a herald, so to speak, those claims that the reasoning will of the creator of nature directs to our will. Therefore it is perferable to use the term "law of nature" to "law of reason". Natural law, then, is those claims that the reasoning will of the creator of nature transmits to our will. If those norms are valid "by nature itself", it is true only because they are directed to our will by the reasoning will of the originator of nature.

Cathrein explains the grounds for the existence of natural law as the necessary basis for positive law. He asks the question (p.556), "What is the source from which human society or human authorities get the right to impose duties on us?" "The answer can only be as follows", Cathrein says, "Nature itself—or better—the originator of nature confers them this right." From the nature of man we learn that God wills the existence of human society, and that no society is possible without an authority establishing positive legal order. Hence, it is God who confers the right to promulgate laws on such an authority. "This right and the corresponding legal obligation are given by the natural moral law, and constitute the indispensable basis for every positive law. They are not rooted in the will of man, but in the will of God."

BIBLIOGRAPHY

In addition to the original works as indicated by Kelsen in his text, following works have been consulted. Quotations from the listed works were used but partly and only when they were corresponding to the meaning as interpreted by Kelsen.

The Basic Works of Aristotle, Richard McKeon Edition, Random House, New York, 1941.

The Works of Aristotle, W. D. Ross, Clarendon Press, Oxford, 1924, vols. 3, 9, 11.

Aristotle: The Nichomachean Ethics H. Backham, M.A., Harvard University Press, Cambridge, 1947.

On Man in the Universe, edited by Louise Ropes Loomis, D. van Nostrand Company, Inc., New York, 1943.

Aristotle: The Art of Rhetoric, John Henry Freese, G. P. Putnam's Sons, 1926.

Thomas Aquinas: Summa contro Gentiles, translated by Vernon J. Bourke, Hannover House, Garden City, New York, 1936.

Thomas Aquinas: Summa Theologica, translated by the Fathers of the English Dominican Province, Burns Oates & Washbourne Ltd., 1922.

The Holy Bible, revises standard version, Thomas Nelson & Sons, New York, 1952.

The Holy Bible, King James' version.

Immanuel Kant: Foundations of the Metaphysics of Morals, Lewis White Beck, R. P. Wolff, The Bobbs-Merill Company, Inc., Indianapolis, 1969.

Immanuel Kant: Critique of Judgment, J. A. Bernard, Hafner Publishing Company, New York, 1951.

Immanuel Kant: The Metaphysics of Ethics, J. V. Semples, 3rd edn., T. & T. Clark, Edinburgh, 1871.

Immanuel Kant: Religion within the limits of Reason alone, I. M. Greene and H. H. Hudson, The Open Court Publishing Company, Chicago, 1934.

Grotius: De Iure Belli ac Pacis, Francis W. Kelsey, Clarendon Press, London, 1925.

[8]

THE RADICAL MIDDLE: NATURAL RIGHT OF PROPERTY IN AQUINAS AND THE POPES

ALBERT BRODERICK, O.P.*

UNTIL very recently modern use of the term "radical" in a political-economic context was restricted to designating the left wing. In recent months in the United States "radical" has become familiar in a new pejorative sense, some extreme conservatives being dubbed the "radical right." In the original benign sense of "radical" as root, fundament, basis, the Aristotelian–Aquinas–Catholic view of property as a natural right might be called "the radical middle," ranging well within the extremes of "rugged individualism" on the one hand and utopian communism on the other. Similarly, the natural law thought in this same tradition, of which the natural property right is but an instance, may be considered "radical" in jurisprudence, and between the speculative formalism of the Law of Nature School of the not so recent past and the value agnosticism so prevalent today. The "radical middle" would seem entitled to scholarly consideration on two grounds at least: (1) as the most principled explanation of the development in the West in the past half century of combined systems of private and common ownership and management of property, and (2) as an illuminating exemplification of the most traditional and objective among theories of natural law.

A recent higher critic writes on two separate but, in his view, allied problems.[1] The first, which he correctly treats as a theological problem (although one suspects he deals with it as one of deductive logic): "Has it *consistently* (his emphasis) been the view of the Church . . . that private property is a natural right?" The second, which he deals with as a problem of jurisprudence and, one is permitted to feel, too succinctly: "What, if any, jurisprudential value is there in saying that a right is natural?" As to the first question he starts from the untraditional proposition that for Aquinas common ownership, and not private property, was a natural right. Reviewing a selection of Catholic authors, he then concludes that there have been "various changes in Catholic doctrine, which together make up a fundamental evolution from the time of Aquinas." In short, in the critic's view, the "doctrine" on the nature of rights of property has changed. With respect to the

* LL.B., S.J.D. (Harvard), Assistant Professor of Law, The Catholic University of America.

[1] Harding, "The Evolution of Roman Catholic Views of Private Property as a Natural Right," THE SOLICITOR QUARTERLY, April, 1963, pp. 124–37.

jurisprudential value of natural rights he simply calls upon the familiar "doctrine" of Professor Friedmann:[2] one's attitude to "natural law matters is a matter of personal predilection which cannot be shown to be right or wrong." But, he concludes, somewhat puzzlingly, "it can be shown to be good or bad, based upon weak or strong evidence."

There are three parts to his account with respect to private property; each part is either misleading or erroneous. Our higher critic begins with the half-truth that to St. Thomas the natural right is ownership in common, not in private. His second part deals with the period between Aquinas and the papacy of Leo XIII at the end of the last century. In this period, he tells us, the "Aquinas doctrine" of the primacy of common ownership was "discarded," and an absolutist doctrine of private property was sown. Finally, with Pope Leo XIII for the first time this absolutist version was clearly adopted; subsequent popes have denied any change, although in fact the doctrine has been softened by them a bit.

Since the alleged inconsistency in Catholic property doctrine stems from the assertion that Aquinas opted for common property, rejecting private as a natural right, we must first examine the analysis of St. Thomas on this point. Once the exposition of Aquinas on property is grasped as an admirable concrete instance of his natural law views, the other pieces fall into place. We shall then examine the treatment of property in the writings of Leo XIII, Pius XI, Pius XII and John XXIII which the author taunts as "changing" the doctrine while proclaiming its consistency. But since our higher critic's error is the result of a surprising, but not uncommon, misunderstanding of the traditional natural law doctrine, we shall attend to this at some length.

Although the papal teachings have a special theological significance to the believer, they are obviously designed on their face to carry weight with a wider audience. These papal authors have repeatedly cited Aquinas as their doctrinal antecedent here, so if our critic's assertion that they have abandoned St. Thomas' position is correct, the popes indeed have perpetrated a monumental hoax. It is, happily, quite a straightforward matter to give satisfaction, I believe to the critic himself, that they have not.

1. NATURAL RIGHT OF PROPERTY: AQUINAS AND THE POPES

Aquinas' Property Views

Full domain over "exterior goods" belongs only to God, says Aquinas, in the first of his two *Summa* articles on property. But, he adds, these goods are destined for the needs of men. The question then

[2] See Friedmann, *Legal Theory*, 4th ed., 1960. The property themes of this same article also parallel Friedmann's views (*ibid.*, pp. 52 and 316). Friedmann's two major works, *Legal Theory* and *Law in a Changing Society*, 1959, are two of the most learned recent jurisprudential works in English, but his analysis of these matters bears reconsideration.

remains. Under what form of property should men exercise their relative domain over these goods? Or, as Aquinas puts it, Is it "lawful for a man to possess a thing as his own?"[3]

In his answer, St. Thomas distinguishes between the "administration" (*potestas procurandi et dispensandi*) and the "enjoyment" (*usus*) of "exterior goods."[4] In the sense of "administration" or power of management of goods it is not only "lawful" that there be individual property, "it is necessary for human living." But "enjoyment" of goods is conceived as if the basic objective were common and social, rather than selfish and private. It consists ultimately in the needs of all men to exist and to develop physically, emotionally and intellectually, and this by using "exterior goods." This common goal, from which no man is excepted, constitutes a primary moral position. We recall the purpose of "exterior goods" that Aquinas had identified in Article 1.[5] The justification of individual property, or "administration," on the other hand, is primarily economic and political, instrumental towards achieving the general overriding goal. Only consequentially, then, is private property a "natural right."

[3] *Summa Theologiae*, Second part of the Second Part (*Secunda Secundae*) Question 66, Article 2 (II II, 66.2). The following treatments of our subject are particularly useful—

Deploige, "La théorie thomiste de la propriété," *Revue Neo-Scholastique*, Vol. 2, 1895, pp. 61–82, 163–175, 286–301.

Horvath, *Eigentumsrecht nach dem hl. Thomas von Aquin*, Graz, 1929.

Jarrett, *Social Theories of the Middle Ages*, London, 1926.

McDonald, *The Social Value of Property According to St. Thomas Aquinas*, Washington, 1939.

MacLaren, *Private Property and the Natural Law* (Aquinas Papers, No. 8), Oxford, 1948.

O'Rahilly, "St. Thomas' Theory of Property," 9 *Studies*, 1920, pp. 337–354.

Perez Garcia, *De Principiis Functionis Socialis Proprietatis Privatae apud div. Thomam Aquinatem*, Avila, 1924 (Cf. summary in *Bulletin Thomiste*, 1925, pp. 263–269).

Renard, "Propriété privée et propriété humaine," Appendix to *La théorie de l'Institution*, Paris, 1930.

Renard et Trotabas, *La fonction sociale de la propriété privée*,Paris, 1930.

Schwalm, "La propriété d'aprés la philosophie de S. Thomas," *Revue Thomlste*, 1895, pp. 93 f.

Spicq, *Les péchés d'injustice* (Translation with notes and appendices of *Summa*, II II, 63–66), Paris, 1934.

——, "La notion analogue de *dominium* et le droit de propriété", *Revue des Sciences Philosophiques et Theologiques*, 1931, p. 52 f.

——, *Potestas procurandi et dispensandi. Ibid.* 1934, p. 82 f.

——, *Dominium, possessio, proprietas* chez S. Thomas et chez les Juristes romains, *Ibid.*, 1929, 269 f.

Utz, *Freiheit und bindung des Eigentums*, Heidelberg, 1949.

See also discussion and bibliography in *Bulletin Thomiste*, 1932, pp. 603–6 concerning points of controversy on St. Thomas' property doctrine—such as: Is work the unique source and justification of property? and, Is private property a necessary consequence of original sin for St. Thomas? (*Yes*—Horvath, *No*—Schilling, Tonneau). We abstract almost completely from these aspects in this article, which can be viewed as a preliminary study dealing with central points on which agreement is general in the literature cited.

[4] We here treat St. Thomas' answer to Article 2. We return to Article 1 at pp. 141–3.

[5] i.e. II II, 66.1 (discussed *infra*, p. 46–47). ". . . the doctrine of St. Thomas on property is formally theological. 66.1 is only a rational elaboration of revealed truth." Spicq, *Les péchés d'injustice*, p. 281, n. 1.

Aquinas defined "natural right" in an earlier question (II II, 57.3), as "what is fitting and commensurate to man's very nature." He added there that this may come about in two different ways: "without deliberate adjustment, as male is adapted to female for generation," or simply by a judgement as to the consequences. To illustrate this last he says "Take ownership,[6] for example; in the abstract there is no reason why a field should belong to this man rather than to another; but if you consider its development and peaceful exploitation, then a piece of property may well be allocated to one rather than to another." The contention is that in the concrete situation natural rights may be dictated "from a judgement of the consequences." Does this not require the intervention of human legislation? And does not this negate the naturalness of the "right"? Not so, says St. Thomas, for the value of the ensuing regulations is "established by the evidence of their natural reasonableness."[7] There may be, on the other hand, a "right" that is determined not by the self-evident nature of things, not by its natural reasonableness, but by private agreement or by legislation alone. And this would be regarded as merely a "positive" right, as distinguished from "natural" right. (II II, 57.2).

We are now ready to return to the basic article on private property with which we began (II II, 66.2). Recall that Aquinas had stated that private property was not only "lawful," but "necessary for human living," and therefore a natural right "dictated from a judgement of these consequences." (Cf. II II, 57.3, cited *supra*). The three functional reasons enumerated by Aquinas have been much cited. The first:

> . . . because each man is more careful in looking after what is in his own charge than what is common to many or to all.[8]

St. Thomas was a member of a religious community which lived a rule of common property, so his experience may not be denied—

> Secondly, because human affairs are conducted in a more orderly fashion when each man is charged with taking care of some particular thing himself. . . .

The third reason deals with the peaceful effect in a regime of private ownership—

> . . . because a more peaceful state is preserved when each man is contented with what is his own.[9]

And here again St. Thomas turns to experience, for "we observe that quarrels arise more frequently among people who share in common and without division of goods."

All this is under the head of "administration"; it remains to consider

[6] *Proprietas possessionum.*
[7] *Ipsa naturalis ratio ea instituit.*
[8] Aquinas adds that "in the latter case each would shirk the work and leave to another that which concerns the community, as we see when there is a great number of servants." II II, 66.2.
[9] St. Thomas adds: "We know from experience that quarrels more frequently arise among those who own something in common and undivided." II II, 66.2.

"enjoyment." Here Aquinas suggests that man "ought to possess goods, not as his own, but as common." This phrase, it develops, signifies the responsibilities and social functions of "private ownership." From above property is limited by God's overriding dominion (II II, 66.1), from below by the claims of our fellows (and not only in their extreme need), to a share in the enjoyment of the property which it is our "natural right" to own, or "administer" (II II, 66.2).

But does this analysis of Aquinas' texts stand up when he answers an objection (that he himself poses): "that according to the natural law all things are held in common," and therefore that private appropriation is "unlawful." His answer is at first brush puzzling—

> . . . community of goods is attributed to the natural law not in the sense that natural law dictates that all possessions should be in common and that nothing should be possessed as one's own.[10]

The true sense of attribution of common ownership to the natural law, he adds, is that the division of possessions is not made by natural law but by human agreement, which belongs to positive law.[11] Hence, Aquinas concludes, "private ownership is not contrary to natural law, but is an addition to it devised by human reason." But does this not still leave common rather than private ownership as the "natural right"?

The answer to this question is an unqualified "No," on Aquinas' analysis. At primary (prerational, irreversible) natural law there is nothing but the generic right, common to all and absolutely primary, to the share in the goods of the earth. There is at this stage nothing at all by way of choice or preference of a particular, specific regime of property for achieving this end. This choice of regime of property is made by human reason, and ordinarily incorporated in human positive law. But this is no arbitrary choice by reason—the evident circumstances and consequences upon which reason reflects requires choice by positive law of a regime of ownership that is in some sense private. This is, as St. Thomas says, a typical secondary natural law or *ius gentium* situation.

Aquinas distinguishes between two kinds of natural law rights, or natural law. There is the "natural right" that comes about "without deliberate adjustment"; we have seen the example of the natural adaptation of the male to the female for generation. In this sense private property is not a "natural right." Historically community of goods may have come first. There is no doubt that the role of property is "to benefit the species."[12] But human reason reflecting upon human

[10] II, II, 66.1.3.

[11] It is true, of course, that the particular form of the regime of ownership is here recognised by Aquinas to be subject to the decision, or legislation, of the political community. The problem remains, Is private property in any sense a natural right? And in what sense? We take this up in the next paragraph.

[12] Spicq, *op. cit.*, p. 287.

experience sees that this general benefit would not be best achieved by a regime of common property to the exclusion of private administration. And when there is an evident reasonableness, as in this case of private property, even when enactment occurs the evident natural justice (of private regime of property), antecedes the positive legal enactment.[13] Private ownership is thus in this sense a "natural right."

Whether one agrees with Aquinas' views on private property or not, it has been rather well understood in the legal literature that this was his position. Thus Cairns in his still valuable book of a generation ago, *Law and the Social Sciences*,[14] points to Aquinas' as a functional approach to the notion of private property as a "natural right," as distinguished from the absolutist position.

Cairns discusses three chief legal theories of property. There is what he calls *the* "legal theory" of property, the joint authorship of which he ascribes to Hobbes, Montesquieu and Bentham. In Bentham's form this theory makes property the creation of law—

> Property and law are born, and must die together. Before the laws there was no property: take away the laws, all property ceases.[15]

A second legal theory of property, according to Cairns, is one developed by the American courts, "the natural or 'higher law' theory according to which property is a natural right, superior to all human laws, which in fact merely discover and declare it."[16]

Although he sees roots of this theory in the Greeks, the Romans and the middle ages, Cairns suggests that

> Its infiltration into Anglo-American law was partly due to its acceptance by Coke and Blackstone, but above all. . . to the writings of Locke who rationalised the doctrine by basing it upon the social compact and its handmaiden the State of Nature.[17]

More satisfactory to Cairns is "a conception of property based upon its social utility. This is the distinction between property for use and property for power, or, as it is now termed, the functional theory of property."[18]

Cairns explains this theory as making a distinction between "morally justifiable" property—"which involves the discharge of definite personal obligations"— and "morally unjustifiable" property— a mere passive claim "on wealth produced by another's labour."[19] But our interest in Cairns' contrast of the absolutist "natural rights" theory

[13] St. Thomas, *Commentary on Aristotle's Ethics*, Bk. V, 1. 12.
[14] New York, 1935, p. 72 f.
[15] Bentham, 1 *Works*, p. 308, cited, Cairns, *op. cit.*, p. 72. Cairns suggests that the theory implies so broad a meaning of law as to lack real significance.
[16] Cairns, *op. cit.*, p. 73.
[17] *Ibid.*
[18] *Ibid.*, p. 75.
[19] *Ibid.*, Cairns overstates the extent of Aquinas' even tacit commitment to the theory as Cairns has outlined it.

of property and the "functional" theory is his attribution of roots of the latter to Aristotle and Aquinas—

> From the standpoint of the functional theory, the justification of property rests in the fact that property, when widely used, is for society a necessary condition of its health and efficiency and of its continued existence. This was the argument of Aquinas.[20]

Cairns does not himself follow Aquinas' doctrine back to the text of Aristotle's *Politics*, but he accepts the Carlyles' assurance[21] that its foundation was in Aristotle. His contrast of Aquinas' doctrine with that of the Church Fathers is too sharp; and yet Cairns' comments here are worth repeating—

> The Fathers, particularly Basil and Ambrose, had, contrary to the Anglo-American theory, dogmatically contended that private property was opposed to natural law because all things had been given to men in common. Aquinas stated their arguments with characteristic fairness and neatness and refuted them by showing that the establishment of private property is due not to natural law but to positive law or human agreement and that it is not therefore contrary to natural law but is added to it by human reason. But Aquinas did not stop here. He wisely saw that merely because it was lawful to possess property it did not follow that property was necessary. His argument is the first complete justification of property and was adopted *in extenso* by those who followed him; and it was never improved upon. Property "is necessary to human life for three reasons," he wrote . . . .[22]

And then follow the three "functional reasons" which we considered earlier in this discussion.

The same absolutist flavour that discredited the Lockeian "natural rights" theory of property brought into discredit the general Locke-inspired theory of natural law and natural rights. But just as Cairns has taken care to absolve Aquinas of involvement in the casualty of the absolutist property theory, so interested scholars have taken care to distinguish the 18th century Law of Nature school, with its absolutist conceptualism, from the traditional natural law theory that took form in Aristotle and Aquinas.[23]

In the recent Catholic tradition, when Pope Leo XIII in the Encyclical *Rerum Novarum* in 1891 emphasised private property as a "natural right" he specifically rested his case, not upon the tradition of Locke, but upon the very arguments from Aquinas' *Summa Theologiae* that we have just elaborated.[24]

Since private property as a "natural right" rests upon a "judgement of the consequences" by human reason it may be asked why as circumstances change the notion of private property as a "natural right"

[20] *Ibid.*, p. 76.
[21] *Ibid.*, Cairns cites Carlyle, 5 *Medieval Political Theory in the West*, 1928, p. 18.
[22] *Ibid.*
[23] See, for example, Pound, *Introduction to the Philosophy of Law*, pp. 17–20, 44, and Rommen, *The Natural Law*, 1947, p. 75 f. For a fine contrast of the traditional natural law doctrine and the "legal theory" of property of 19th century American "liberty of contract" jurists see Wu, *The Fountain of Justice*, 1955.
[24] See *supra*, p. 130.

should not also change. The only philosophical answer to this suggestion is a practical one. Look at man, as he is today. Are the functional reasons suggested by Aquinas still persuasive? Even the followers of Marx with his millennial optimism with respect to man, have had to postpone the application of their doctrine of a propertyless society. But while the basic notion persists in man's reason, and in actual practice, that "private property" is "fitting and commensurate to man's nature," it is also true that the particular mode of private holding of property is not rigidly imposed, and indeed changes from milieu to milieu, from age to age; and we shall see that the development in the papal teaching from Leo, through Pius XI and Pius XII to John XXIII, merely reflects the diversity in unity of Aquinas' doctrine.

The Recent Papal Property Doctrine: Leo XIII

By training and by inclination Leo XIII was prepared for his major acknowledged role in the papacy, laying the cornerstone of the modern Catholic restatement of social doctrine. The great agitation of the day stemmed from the socialists: that a "right" of private property was a human invention, and a deluded one that cushioned the rich in their surplus amidst human poverty, ignoring the natural equality of men. In his first Encyclical, or teaching letter to his Church, *Quod Apostolici Muneris* (Dec. 28, 1878),[25] Leo defended "the right of property sanctioned by the natural law," and urged that "the right of property and of ownership, which springs from nature itself must not be touched and stands inviolate." Unlike the socialists, he wrote, the Church recognises "inequality in possession" as one of the many actual inequalities among men, but it "provides with special care for public and private tranquillity in its doctrines and teachings regarding the duty of government and the distribution of the goods which are necessary for life and use . . . . She is constantly pressing on the rich that most grave precept to give what remains to the poor."

There was here no fresh analysis of the property question, rather a stress upon elements of the traditional Catholic doctrine that were then under most heavy attack. This preliminary contact with the "social question" was a mere foreshadowing of the major work that was just ahead. On May 15, 1891, after several years of preparation, the Encyclical *Rerum Novarum* appeared. Since it is the admitted Magna

[25] The encyclicals of Leo XIII are printed in varied collections. The official Latin versions are found in *Acta Leonis* XIII, 26 vols. Rome, 1878–1903, *Acta Sanctae Sedis*, Vols. 11–25, Rome, 1878–1903. In English translation the encyclicals are usually found, rather soon after issuance, in the London *Tablet*, and many are published separately by the Catholic Truth Society of London. References in this article to Leo's encyclicals are made to the collection edited by Etienne Gilson, *The Social Teachings of Leo XIII*, Doubleday (Image Book), New York, 1954. *Quod Apostolici Muneris* appears at pp. 189 *et seq.* of that collection.

Carta of all that has come since in Catholic social doctrine it calls for careful examination. Was it a restatement in modern terms and an adaptation to contemporary conditions of the traditional doctrine? Or was it, as our higher critic suggests, a new twist, an inversion of the order of priority between private and common possessions that had been contained in the teaching of Aquinas?

In *Rerum Novarum* the focus of the discussion is again supplied by the contemporary socialist contentions "that individual possessions should become the common property of all, to be administered by the state or by municipal bodies."[26] Far from solving the social problem, urges Leo, this policy would deprive the working man of "the impelling reason and motive of his work . . . : to obtain property and thereafter to hold . . . as his very own . . . what is necessary for the satisfaction of his needs." This remuneration, and also the right to "disposal of such remuneration just as he pleases." The true solution is not less private property, but more.[27] And if the moral obligation of the rich to distribute their surplus is not effectuated, the state has a role here to ameliorate the maldistribution." (This, in 1891, was revolutionary.) But the absolutist socialist arguments for compulsory general state ownership must be rejected as "emphatically unjust, for they would rob the lawful possessor, distort the functions of the state, and create utter confusion in the community."[28]

The panoply of reforms suggested by *Rerum Novarum* is beyond our immediate concern; we confine ourselves here to the issue just noted, compulsory general state ownership. It must be rejected, says Leo, and on two grounds: its practical inadequacy, and its injustice. It is the latter contention, and the basis for it, "the inviolability of private property," that we turn to consider. Leo's argument is tightly drawn. His basic criteria are twofold: divine revelation and right reason. These complement each other and do not find themselves in conflict. We shall focus our discussion upon the rational argumentation. Some arguments develop from metaphysical starting points that are common postulates even to many who reject metaphysics; others accent practical utility; still others the common opinion and experience of mankind. The key sentence for our discussion is this: ". . . every man has by nature the right to possess property."[29] By grasping what Leo intends by "man," by "nature," by "right" and by "property" we shall have the key to his teaching.

[26] Gilson, ed., *op. cit.*, p. 207, n. 4.
[27] "Socialists, therefore, by endeavouring to transfer the possessions of individuals to the community at large, strike at the interests of every wage earner, since they would deprive him of the liberty of disposing of his wages, and thereby of all hope and possibility of increasing his resources and bettering his condition in life." Gilson, ed., p. 207, n. 5.
[28] *Ibid.*, n. 4.
[29] *Ibid.*, p. 208, n. 6.

Man

Leo here distinguishes man from "animal creation." They have much in common: basic instincts of self-preservation and "propagation of the species." But man has a power of intelligent choice."[30] He is "master of his own acts."[31] His needs and his plans are not only for the present, but for the future.[32]

Nature

"Nature" to Leo means most often "prior to the formation of any state."[33] Thus because of man's capacity to plan and his recurring needs "Nature . . . must have given to man a source that is stable and remaining always with him from which he might be able to draw continual supplies."[34] And this is "the earth and its fruits. There is no need to bring in the state. Man precedes the state and possesses, prior to the formation of any state, the right of providing for the sustenance of his body."[35]

Right

A "right" to Leo (and its correlative, "duty") is a claim (and correlative obligation) in justice. A "natural right," then, is such a claim in justice that exists, as we have just seen, "prior to the formation of any state." One instance he recounts is a "natural right" of association. To enter a private society, Leo teaches, "is the natural right of man; and the state has for its office to protect natural rights, not to destroy them."[36] The same argument is advanced for "natural rights" of the family: "inasmuch as the domestic household is antecedent, as well in idea as in fact, to the gathering of men into a community, the family must necessarily have rights and duties which are prior to those of the community, and founded more immediately in nature."[37] Chief of all the "natural rights" of man is that of self-preservation.[38] And this entails that "each one has a natural right to procure what is required in

[30] "It is the mind, or reason, which is the predominant element in us who are human creatures." Gilson, ed., *op. cit.*, p. 208, n. 6 (official paragraph no.).
[31] *Ibid.*, p. 209, n. 7.
[32] *Ibid.*
[33] *Ibid.* When talking in terms of revealed religion Leo interchanges "nature" with "the eternal law and the power of God, whose providence governs all things." *Ibid.*, p. 208.
[34] *Ibid.*, p. 209, n. 7.
[35] *Ibid.*
[36] Leo goes on to urge that if the state forbids that its citizens form associations "it contradicts the very principle of its own existence, for both they and it exist in virtue of the like principle, namely the natural tendency of man to dwell in society." *Ibid.*, p. 233 n. 51 The premise here, of course, is the Aristotelian premise that man is by nature, i.e. pre-rationally, a "political animal." *Pol.*, Bk. 1, Ch. 2. Aquinas also calls this "a social animal." *Comm. Pol.* Bk. 1, lect., 1. "Natural" here bespeaks "natural inclinations."
[37] *Ibid.*, p. 211, n. 15 Leo asserts only that "the family has at least equal rights with the state in the choice and pursuit of the things needful to its preservation and its just liberty."
[38] *Ibid.*, p. 229, n. 44.

order to live."[39] This points to another "natural right" antecedent to the state, and thus not subject to withdrawal at the whim of the state,[40] namely, the right to property.

Property

Does the conclusion that man possesses "prior to the formation of any state," the right of providing for the sustenance of his body"[41] entail *private* ownership? Does Leo's further contention that by his labour "man makes his own that portion of nature's field which he cultivates"[42] purport to establish more than the eminent suitability of private property? To Leo these arguments for private property are "strong and convincing."[43] But does his total position not come to this: (1) the earth is "for the use and enjoyment of the whole human race"; (2) this does not exclude private property;[44] (3) the choice of the method of providing man's subsistence by these goods of the earth is not to be left to the whim of the state; (4) reason, the "common opinion of mankind," "the practice of all ages," the confirmation of most civil laws, all concur in consecrating "the principle of private ownership, as being pre-eminently in conformity with human nature."[45] (6) The conclusion thus emerges—

> Private ownership . . . is the natural right of man, and to exercise that right, especially as members of society, is not only lawful but absolutely necessary.[46]

Leo cites here St. Thomas.[47] He also enumerates the three practical reasons advanced by Aquinas for the superiority of private ownership over a regime of common possession. And he adds two further key points of Aquinas' property doctrine: (*a*) "The limits of private possession have been left to be fixed by man's own industry, and by the laws of individual races."[48] (*b*) "Man should not consider his material possessions as his own, but as common to all to be shared with others in need."[49]

[39] Gilson, ed. *op. cit.*, p. 229, n. 4.

[40] The intervention of the state is not completely excluded from the areas of these "natural rights." Leo's call for state activism in an era of "*laissez faire*" was one of the scandals of the day. Thus "if within the precincts of the household there occur grave disturbance of natural rights, public authority should intervene . . . ." *Ibid.*, p. 212, n. 14. And again, "There are occasions, doubtless, when it is fitting that the law should intervene to prevent certain associations . . . ." *Ibid.*, p. 233, n. 52.

[41] *Ibid.*, p. 209, n. 7.

[42] *Ibid.*, n. 9. He argues that it is not "just that the fruit of a man's own sweat and labour should be possessed and enjoyed by any one else." *Ibid.*, n. 10.

[43] *Ibid.*, p. 210, n. 10.

[44] *Ibid.*, p. 209, n. 8.

[45] *Ibid.*, p. 210, n. 11.

[46] *Ibid.*, p. 217, n. 22. The fact that Leo has used the words "absolutely necessary" here, whereas Aquinas said merely "necessary" should be noted as a problem. However, not only does Leo immediately cite St. Thomas as his authority here, but the very passage in which Aquinas gave the practical reasons for what he called the "necessity" of private property, in II II, 66.2. Commentators do not divide Leo from Aquinas here.

[47] *Ibid.*

[48] *Ibid.*, p. 209, n. 8.

[49] *Ibid.*, p. 217, n. 22.

Leo comes back here to the starting point of Aquinas,[50] the ultimate objective of material goods, their availability for the subsistence and development of all. In cases of extreme need, it is an obligation in justice to help another out of one's surplus beyond his own family's needs. And self-help is lawful in cases of extreme necessity when the obligation of justice has not been fulfilled.[51] In cases of "less than extreme necessity it is still a duty" to give to the indigent out of what remains over when what one's own necessity demands has been supplied . . . ."[52] But beyond the extreme cases the duty is not one of justice, "but of Christian charity—a duty not enforced by human law."[53] To what extent may this duty become one binding in justice, and be brought within the ambit of human law? This is to be a chief area of development for Catholic social doctrine in the pontificates to come.

Pius XI (Quadragesimo Anno, May 15, 1931)

Forty years after *Rerum Novarum*, Pope Pius XI saluted Leo's pioneer effort as "the Magna Carta upon which all Christian activity in the social field ought to be based, as on a foundation.[54]" Introducing a milestone of his own making, the Encyclical *Quadragesimo Anno*, Pius promised to "recall" and "defend" Leo's social doctrine and to "develop it more fully on certain points."[55] His first major point for development is "ownership or the right of property." Purporting merely to reaffirm what Leo had said on property, Pius rephrases the traditional dichotomy between ownership and use[56] with a new precision in terms of "the twofold character of ownership, called usually individual or social as it regards either separate persons or the common good."[57] He stresses anew the two functions of private ownership itself: (1) "that individuals may be able to provide for themselves and their families";[58] and (2) "that the goods which the Creator destined for the entire family of mankind may through this institution [private ownership] truly serve this purpose through the maintainance of a certain and definite order."[59] He next underscores with new clarity the

[50] i.e. in II II, 66.1.

[51] This instance, elaborated by Aquinas in II II, 66.7, is not specifically referred to by Leo, but it has been constant Catholic doctrine. Cf. Denzinger, *Enchiridium Symbolorum*, n. 1938b: "*In extremis aliena auferre iustum est.*" For a different view see Harding, *loc. cit.*, p. 134. For authority here Denzinger cites *Rerum Novarum*, n. 22.

[52] Gilson, ed., *op. cit.*, p. 217, n. 22.

[53] *Ibid.*, (the official Latin text of which appears at *Acta Apostolicae Sedis* (AAS), Vol. 23, 1931, pp. 177–228).

[54] The Encyclical *Quadragesimo Anno* is as widely available in English as any modern papal letter. We are using the volume edited by Terence P. McLaughlin, C.S.B., entitled *The Church and the Reconstruction of the Modern World: The Social Encyclicals of Pius XI*, Doubleday (Image Book), New York, 1957, at p. 219 f. See p. 231, n. 39 for place cited.

[55] *Ibid.*, p. 223, n. 15.

[56] Cf. II II, 66.1–2.

[57] McLaughlin, ed., *op. cit.*, p. 234, n. 45.

[58] *Ibid.*

[59] *Ibid.*

instrumental function of private ownership, a means of establishing "limits on controversies . . . over ownership."[60] And yet the foundation of this teaching, he says, is "a principle established by Leo XIII: The right of property is distinct from its use."[61]

Pius next passes to the lively controversies of the years since Leo's letter that sought to give greater practical effect to what Leo had called the obligation in charity, and not justice itself, to provide for others out of surplus goods. Pius' two major conclusions here taken together constitute a fresh contribution to the doctrine:

(1) He firmly resists the efforts of some Catholic thinkers to bring the obligation of private owners to distribute their surplus into the category of strict justice.[62] He stands firmly by Leo's refusal to bring under commutative justice the obligation of owners "to use their property only in a right way," agreeing that there are involved here "other virtues obligations of which 'cannot be enforced by legal action.' " This last clause is Leo's, but note that the obligation is no longer restricted by Pius to "charity" alone. Pius is here launching a term fresh to the traditional doctrine, "social justice," which had been much discussed in Catholic social circles in the preceding two decades.[63] But Pius' main stand here is firmly with Leo: "They are in error who assert that ownership and its right use are limited by the same boundaries; and it is much farther still from the truth to hold that a right of property is destroyed or lost by reason of abuse or non-use."[64]

(2) His second major conclusion, however, marks a notable advance; it has two steps. In the first place, although Pius resists attempts that would "restrict the individual character of ownership to such a degree that in fact they destroy it," he does approve the efforts of those who would define the "limits whereby either the right of property itself or its use, that is, the exercise of ownership, is circumscribed by the necessities of social living."[65] This defining activity is to be no mere academic pursuit. For Pius builds here upon Leo's principle of state activism, no longer (in 1931) so revolutionary as it was: "To define these duties in detail when necessity requires and the natural law

[60] *Ibid.*, n. 47.
[61] *Ibid.*, p. 235, n. 47; the passage cited in *Rerum Novarum* is Gilson, ed., p. 216, n. 19.
[62] ". . . commutative justice commands sacred respect for the divisions of possessions and forbids invasion of others' rights through exceeding the limits of one's own property." McLaughlin, ed., *op. cit.*, p. 235, n. 47.
[63] Delos discusses the various terms used to designate the same reality in a note to Gillet's French translation of II II, 57–62, *La Justice*, Vol. 1, at p. 57, n. 1: "In calling this justice *general*, St. Thomas put the accent on its *function*, and not on its *object;* in calling it *legal* he accentuated its *formal* object, the common good; today in calling it *social* we emphasise its *end* which coincides with its *object* following the general law of coincidence between an end and a form, the end being in the order of action and the form being in the order of being." There is no general agreement with this interesting analysis.
[64] McLaughlin, ed., *op. cit.*, p. 235, n. 47.
[65] *Ibid.*, n. 48.

has not done so is the function of those in charge of the state." There is a role here, then, for the state and positive law—

> . . . public authority, always under the guiding light of the natural and divine law, can determine more accurately what is permitted and what is not permitted to owners in the use of their property.[66]

There is room for change in the institution of property: "history proves ownership, like other elements of social life, to be not absolutely unchanging." There is, however, this limit to the state's proper scope of action: "The natural right itself both of owning goods privately and of passing them on by inheritance . . . is a right that the state cannot take away." For both man and the family are prior to the state. The right, again, is natural, i.e. not given by the state; although the state may adjust it in light of the common good, it may not take it away in its root.

> For since the right of possessing goods privately has been conferred not by man's law, but by nature, public authority cannot abolish it, but can only control its exercise and bring it into conformity with the common weal.[67]

Again the twofold contention that we have seen in Aquinas and in Leo, that private property is a natural right, but largely instrumental, with the ultimate objective of property being to provide for "the common interests of all and in an orderly way." For "the division of goods which results from private ownership was established by nature itself in order that created things may serve the needs of mankind in fixed and stable order."[68] Pius offers a programme with respect to a just division of property—

> To each must be given his own share of goods, and the distribution of created goods must be effectively called back to, and brought into conformity with, the norms of the common good, that is, social justice.[69]

These concepts are general, it is true, but new guidelines had here emerged to which subsequent social thinkers would add substance.

Pius XII (*Pentecost Message, June 1, 1941*)

Perhaps the chief social document of Pope Pius XII was his Pentecost Message of 1941 which was delivered in the form of a radio broadcast. It reiterates that the right of private property is from the natural law. But it stresses with a special clearness that the right of every man to use material goods for his own sustenance is "prior to all other rights in economic life, and hence is prior even to the right of

[66] *Ibid.*, n. 49. Again indicating his continuity with Leo and Aquinas, Pius cites *Rerum Novarum* (Gilson, ed., *op. cit.*, p. 209, n. 8) *re* God's leaving "the limits of private possessions to be fixed by the industry of men and the laws of peoples."

[67] McLaughlin, ed., *op. cit.*, p. 236, n. 49. Pius here cites *Rerum Novarum* (Gilson, ed., p. 231, n. 35).

[68] McLaughlin, ed., p. 240, n. 56.

[69] *Ibid.*, n. 58.

private ownership."[70] It reiterates that the right to own private property should not be permitted to obstruct the flow of "material goods created by God to meet the needs of all men, to all equitably, as justice and charity require."[71] The focus on justice—social justice—in this regard followed up the lead that Pius XI had given beyond the original limitation of Leo to an obligation in charity.

John XXIII (*Mater et Magistra, May 15, 1961*)

The last major papal document dealing extensively with private property was *Mater et Magistra* of Pope John XXIII. This, like the other major papal papers we have discussed, served to commemorate *Rerum Novarum*. This time at the very outset coupled with the identification of private property as a natural right beyond the legitimate reach of the state, is the reminder that natural law also recognises "a social aspect to private property."[72]

John notes increased activity of public officials in stimulating output of goods and furthering "social progress for the benefit of all citizens."[73] He recognises primacy for individual activity as a protection against political excesses by the state, but in the absence of "appropriate activity of the state . . . there occurs exploitation of the weak by the unscrupulous strong."[74] The test offered by Pope Pius XI, the "principle of subsidiarity"[75] is given new prominence as a guide to restraining excessive state activism.

The stress going back to Aquinas upon the primary objective of economic activity in a society—the general interest, or common good—is renewed as John offers a new formula for the economic prosperity of any people. It is to be assessed—

> . . . not so much from the sum total of goods and wealth possessed as from the distribution of goods according to norms of justice, so that everyone in the community can develop and perfect himself. For this, after all, is the end toward which all economic activity of a community is by nature ordered.[76]

[70] This clause is from a paraphrase of Pius XII, *Pentecost Message*, 1941, in *Mater et Magistra* of John XXIII 9, see n. 72, *infra*. The property passages of the *Pentecost Message* are summarised *infra*, p. 150.

[71] Pius XII, *Pentecost Message*, June 1, 1941, reprinted *American Ecclesiastical Review*, Vol. 105, Oct. 1941, p. 281. The clause quoted appeared previously in Pius XII's Encyclical *Sertum Laetitiae*.

[72] John XXIII, *Mater et Magistra*, May 15, 1961, (Latin text in Vol. LIII of *Acta Apostolicae Sedis*, pp. 401–64): references are made to Paulist Press (New York) pamphlet edition; *Ibid.*, p. 14, n. 9. "He who uses his right in this regard must take into account not merely his own welfare but that of others as well."

[73] *Ibid.*, p. 23, n. 52.

[74] *Ibid.*, p. 25, n. 58.

[75] ". . . a fundamental principle of social philosophy, fixed and unchangeable, that one should not withdraw from individuals and commit to the community what they can accomplish by their own enterprise and industry. So, too, it is an injustice and at the same time a grave evil and a disturbance of right order, to transfer to the larger and higher collectivity functions which can be performed and provided for by lesser and subordinate bodies." (*Quadragesimo Anno*, McLaughlin, ed., *op. cit.*, p. 247, n. 79).

[76] *Ibid.*, p. 30, n. 74.

The same point is made again as John insists as "a strict demand of social justice" itself that "with the growth of the economy, there occur a corresponding social development. Thus, all classes of citizens will benefit equitably from an increase in national wealth."[77]

Perhaps more than any other papal letter *Mater et Magistra* emphasises the influence of changing conditions in society upon Christian social doctrine. For example, one of Aquinas' three functional arguments for private ownership has been affected by the widespread separation of ownership and control in large enterprises. This had already been noted by Pius XI. John also points out that tranquillity with respect to the future once sought in private accumulation of property was now fulfilled to a considerable extent by social insurance. But there is still, he insists, no foundation for doubting the "principle whereby it is established that men have from nature a right of privately owning goods including those of a productive kind"[78]: as a corollary of the "fruitfulness of labour," as a safeguard of "the dignity of the human person and the free exercise of responsibility in all fields of endeavour," and as strengthening "the stability and tranquillity of family life, thus contributing to the peace and prosperity of the commonwealth." These arguments are familiar. And so is the contention, basic to all the writings we have here considered, that the right of private property—

> . . . is rooted in the very nature of things, whereby we learn that individual men are prior to society, and hence, that civil society is to be directed toward man as its end.[79]

As with Aquinas and with his papal predecessors John invokes "experience and history." He adds a bit of current history not available to the earlier writers—

> . . . socio-political groups and associations which endeavour to reconcile freedom with justice within society, and which until recently did not uphold the right of private property in productive goods, have now, enlightened by the course of social events, modified their views and are disposed actually to approve this right.[80]

Comparison of Aquinas' and Papal Doctrine

We return to Aquinas to recapitulate his notion of property: for him property is a power over material things. The first problem is "the existence and extent of this power."[81] In the first of his two main *Summa* articles on the property question, "which is only a rational

[77] *Ibid.*, p. 29, n. 73.
[78] *Ibid.*, p. 38, n. 108.
[79] *Ibid.*, n. 109.
[80] *Ibid.*, n. 110.
[81] Deploige, "La théorie thomiste de la propriété," *op. cit.*, at p.61.

exploration of revealed truth,"[82] St. Thomas shows that only the Creator has supreme power and proprietorship over these goods; but in the providential scheme they are here to satisfy man's needs, and so man has natural domain over them with respect to reasonable use for his needs, his well-being and the development of his faculties."[83] Aristotle had concluded to man's natural dominion over material goods by his teleological insight that in the purposeful hierarchy of the universe the less perfect exists for the benefit of the more perfect,[84] an analysis St. Thomas accepted in his *Commentary on the Politics*. So much for the first article. Its treatment of the natural right of man to material goods was entirely independent of the kind of regime of property, whether it should be common, private or a combination.

When Aquinas turned to this in the second article he "resolved the problem of property in the same way as Aristotle . . . by balancing the advantages and disadvantages of only two regimes," the communism of Plato's *Republic* and private property.[85]

St. Thomas distinguishes between ownership and control on the one hand, and enjoyment of goods on the other. In the first category the private regime is preferable for the three practical reasons we have seen. But as to enjoyment the common end takes first place; there is always a social function, in the modern phrase, to private property.[86]

Both the *Summa* of Aquinas and the papal writings obviously purport to be theological documents. Each consists of combinations of scriptural revelation, patristic teaching and natural reason, usually rather closely interwoven. Thus with respect to property both Aquinas and the encyclicals cite and discuss in the scriptural and theological dimension passages of Genesis and the Psalms which deal with God's dominion over his creation, the passages of the Decalogue forbidding theft and coveting of property, the New Testament admonitions to be generous of one's possessions. Both quote frequently writings of the Church fathers, especially as to the social character of property. But, in addition, Aristotle's metaphysics, ethics and politics.[87] are drawn on extensively by Aquinas, who in effect reproduces Aristotle's doctrine on private property.

The popes draw from Aquinas specifically and directly, but make no reference to Aristotle. We shall not dwell here on their scriptural, patristic and other more properly theological passages. It would, however, seem profitable to discuss both the metaphysical (or natural

[82] Spicq, *Les péchés d'injustice*, *op. cit.*, p. 281.
[83] Hoc naturale dominium super ceteras creaturas competit homini secundum rationem in qua imago Dei consistit. II II, 66.1.
[84] *Politics*, Bk. 1, Ch. 5, 7.
[85] Cf. Deploige, *op. cit.*, p. 66: also Aristotle, *Politics*, Bk. 2, Ch. 1, 2, and St. Thomas's *Commentary* on these places.
[86] II II, 66.2.
[87] Especially as interwoven in *Politics*, Bk. 2.

law) and empirical phases of the property doctrine, what we might with deliberate inexactness term the philosophical dimension of these theological doctrines.

We need not argue here whether the ontological priority of man to society, that society is for man and not man for society is a Christian rather than Aristotelian position. It is shared as a postulate, at least, if not as a metaphysic, with political and economic liberal individualists. Thomistic doctrine does not partake of the absoluteness of these schools, however, and failure to grasp this point has resulted in confusion of the Thomistic with the absolutist doctrine on natural rights, and particularly, as we have seen, with the "natural right" of private property as advanced by John Locke and his followers. While the priority of the human person to the society, and to the state or other group to which he belongs, for Catholic doctrine underscores one aspect of its justification of private ownership, the arguments kept to the fore by Aristotle, Aquinas and Leo XIII are the functional considerations that the institution of private property, as a practical matter of human experience with selfish men living in social groups, offers the best method of administering property and thus for the development of man's faculties, the very object for which he joined the social group itself.

The first objective of society, then, is providing the opportunity for the development of the faculties of the individual person; for this end men naturally (i.e. as by a prerational instinct) congregate in social groups, although their reason does not hesitate to confirm this. Furthermore, man's living in social groups and needing goods and social transactions of some sort in order to survive and, further, to live fruitfully, has proven private ownership the most satisfactory means of handling these goods and transactions. This is a conclusion of man's reason, reflecting on his experience, a choice that has been made in practice, to some extent, by most human societies known to date. There have been exceptions, of course. But these have been limited for the most part to special segments of societies, such as religious groups living a life apart. When applied to a whole society rejection of private property has had its chief prominence in utopian literature such as Plato's *Republic* (not entirely here) and More's *Utopia*, or in theory as yet practically unexecuted, such as the communist doctrine of Marx.

But there is a primary affirmation of Aquinas—and he is following not only Aristotle here, but Revelation as interpreted by the fathers of the Church—that the basic function, in the world, of exterior goods is to satisfy the needs of individual men, not one here and there, but all of them to the extent possible. Such satisfaction we have already noted is the objective of any social group as to its members. This objective of fairly satisfying the needs of all would be possible without private ownership in a Paradisiacal society with a plenitude of goods. Hence it would be wrong to say that private property was "natural" to man in the same sense as the urge to survive, and to live socially; it was not a "natural," prerational given; it was devised by man in his peculiarly human capacity to reason upon his experience. It was not universally verifiable; it admitted of variation according to changing times. Reason itself could except it from applicability to special situations, e.g., religious communities. Individual theorists could reject it *in toto*. But it would remain applicable, and recognisable as such by most.

There remains, however, a sense in which the essential "commonness" of property remains relevant. The basic mechanics of ownership and control may remain "private," but this "privacy" is not an end in itself, but merely a means to achieve the overriding primary objective of the existence of exterior goods—the fair allocation for enjoyment by individual persons who make up society. This aspect has sometimes been referred to as "the social function of private property." While most difficult of application in the here and now, the proposition is proposed as of universal validity, an inevitable consequence of the primary natural law conception of man as a "social animal," as well as of his survival value. This means that the institutions and laws of a given society that do not give due recognition to this social factor in property are unjust. It also means that individual holders of "private property" that (1) fail to take care of needy members out of their surplus; or (2) that fail to make their resources socially productive are guilty of social injustice. This latter individual fault, or sin, may occur irrespective of the existence of enforcement procedures under the laws of society. But the popes' calling for legislative definition and sanction of the obligations of social justice calls to mind that for Aquinas the object of law and legal or general justice (his terms for social justice) was the same—the common good.

With respect to unjust laws or institutions in a society which flagrantly ignores the principles of distribution of social resources, a point may be reached where the normal moral obligation to obey the relevant positive laws is dispensed with, leaving them as sheer force. The point of applicability is, again, difficult to assess, but it can be found. And this is no less true because overriding considerations of public order and safety, scandal, and the like, enter into the moral equation. The difficult decisions of point of applicability of this doctrine of "social function" or "commonness of property" continually falls upon the legislature of a society. In some societies, such as the United States, it may in some instances devolve upon the courts. The relative role of legislature and courts with respect to this task depends upon the constitutional and the institutional framework of the particular society. But it should be too apparent that this is the area in which planning has played so large a recent role in this country,[88] and in which the Supreme Court of the United States has been concerned in recent years with the whole range of cases from sit-in strikes and public condemnation rights, to lunch-counter demonstrations and the like.[89] It is true that considerations of public order may ethically dictate acceptance of the judicial, or legislative decision in even the more disputed situations as final (till changed);[90] but neither court nor legislature is dispensed from weighing the objective factors of a natural social morality in order to achieve a "right" or "just" determination in their formulation of the applicable rule.

One graphic verification of the "commonness of property" has enjoyed consistent adherence from the time of Aquinas to present day Catholic teaching: in "extreme" necessity a person may take property of another without being guilty of theft.[91] This concept, frequently cited as a "horrible," sometimes referred to as no longer viable,[92] does not suggest that any subjective view by a property aspirant of his "needs" makes something his for the taking. The doctrine insists upon "extreme" necessity, and means that a man need not starve when society has failed to arrange its laws to satisfy his dire needs and when other men have not fulfilled their "social function" to him as property owners. Taking those bananas was not theft. And consequently a positive law, or judicial decision, punishing such an action as theft would not be true law, Aquinas would say, but sheer administration of social force. Aquinas would not, of course, deny that penalties were inflicted here by the Lower Slobovian legal system; he would deny that such a decision though formulated into a rule that was enforced deserved the name "law."[93]

To this point we have merely investigated Catholic social doctrine

[88] In this connection see, for example, Mellows, "Planning Legislation in Perspective," THE SOLICITOR QUARTERLY, Vol. 2, April, 1963, p. 109 f.

[89] See Cairns, *Law and the Social Sciences*, *op. cit.*, p. 79—"Long ago, when limitations upon property became necessary, legal thinking freed itself from the absolutism of natural rights, and the functional theory is not needed as a liberating agent. Property is constantly being confiscated without compensation on the ground that it promotes the health, safety, morals and general welfare of the people. The abolition of slavery, the enactment of the prohibition law, which deprived brewers and saloon-keepers of millions of dollars of property, prohibited 'uses' under zoning laws, the destruction of property infested with pests injurious to plants and fruits . . . the forbidding of employment of miners for more than eight hours a day, and the enactment of a law prohibiting a street car passenger to (*sic*) sell his transfer, are common examples." This catalogue of items from 1935 may seem somewhat trivial in the light of more recent experience.

[90] Calling the "principle of institutional settlement" "the central idea of law," Professors Hart and Sacks write, in their mimeographed course materials—"The principle of institutional settlement expresses the judgment that decisions which are the duly arrived at result of duly established procedures of this kind ought to be accepted as binding upon the whole society unless and until they are duly changed." (*The Legal Process: Basic Problems in the Making and Application of Law*, Cambridge, 1958.)

[91] II II, 66.7.

[92] The suggestion (Harding, *loc. cit.*, p. 134) that "the principle of Q. 66.7 is abandoned" in current Catholic doctrine "should be re-examined." Cf. Denzinger, *Enchiridium Symbolorum*, 1938b. See n. 51, *supra*.

[93] Much of the tiresome repetition of Aquinas' text that "an unjust law . . . is no law at all, but rather a species of violence" (I II, 93.3.2) might be dispensed with if we recognised

from the standpoint of the charge made against it of inconsistency. We now consider the framework of the doctrine, correctly identified by our higher critic as the natural law.

2. NATURAL LAW

Perhaps the most useful way to discuss Aquinas' doctrine of natural law in a juridical and philosophical, rather than in a theological and metaphysical dimension, is to start as did Aristotle and the Romans with the positive civil law itself. In the *Ethics* Aristotle divided the positive law (*δικαιον πολιτικον*),[94] into the purely civil law (that is just because enacted), the (*δικαιον νομικον*), and the natural civil law, (*δικαιον φυσικον*) (that is enacted because just). Ernest Barker reminds us that for the Greeks the word law (*δικε*) had about it an aura of "just," somewhat like the French *droit*.[95]

The Roman jurists, as Aquinas notes, started with the positive civil law of Rome (*ius civile*);[96] in the *praetor peregrinus* court handling the claims of non-citizens there grew up a body of law made up of the most commonly accepted principles of various national laws (*ius gentium*). From this some Roman jurists ascended to the notion of a natural law common to all mankind (*ius naturale*). It is interesting that in his commentary on the passage of the *Ethics* that we just considered, Aquinas classes the Romans' *ius gentium* with the *iustum naturale* (*dikaion fusikon*), rather than with the *iustum legale* (*dikaion nomikon*). It is positive law in the same sense that the "due process" clause of the United States constitution is positive law; but like "due process" it has a "natural" foundation. This ascent from positive law to natural law by the *via romana* is an empirical progression much like the contemporary search in national, European federal, and international law for "general principles of law."

---

that Aquinas does not deny that Lower Slobovian jurists and citizens alike probably say that their "law" is, for example, that "extreme necessity is no excuse for taking another's property." St. Thomas denies the ethical force of such a "law." He goes further —to an extent that a jurisdiction accepting Aquinas' definition of "law" would be proceeding justly and legally if it denied return of an escapee outrageously convicted in another jurisdiction. Yet in practice this result is reached, without philosophical justification being attempted, in many instances of refusals of extradition requests by governors of northern states for southern state convictions on racial grounds. Professor Corwin took a different view of this question: "The arguments of the analytical school against higher law notions must be conceded to this extent: it is better to confine the term 'law' to rules enforced by the state. But that fact does not prove that the term should be applied to all such rules. In urging that it should be, the analytical thinkers endeavour to steal something—they try to transfer to unworthy rules supported by the state the prestige attaching to the word 'law' conceived of as the enbodiment of justice. The trouble with the analysts, in other words, is not that they define 'law' too narrowly, but too broadly." (Corwin, "The 'Higher Law' Background of American Constitutional Law," (1928), 42 *Harvard L. Rev.* 149, 409, Cornell Univ. Press reprint (1955), p. 89.)

[94] Literally, "political justice." *Ethics*, Bk. V, Ch. 7, 1134b, 18 f.

[95] Barker, *The Politics of Aristotle* Introduction, p. lxix (1958, 1st Amer. ed.).

[96] There is an illuminating analysis of an "ascending" natural law in Renard, *Le droit, l'ordre et la raison*, Paris, 1927, pp. 60 f.

We can profitably refer here to St. Thomas's fresh approach. For Aquinas the content of natural law in its purest and universal sense is identified by our most fundamental natural inclinations. It is, then, as prerational that primary natural law precepts are known and acted on. Naturally, before conscious reasoning, a man is pointed to the human good that it is his earthly role to seek. For this reason all natural law can be reduced to the principle "do the human good, avoid evil." To some, this principle seems empty, but correctly understood it is rich. For it insists that man, like all creation, is taken by Aristotle and Aquinas to be purposeful; he is inclined to an objective that is knowable and achievable. This is the human good; it is identifiable to man by his basic inclinations—some shared with plants (to live), and animals (to sense), others proper to himself (to think, reason, choose, live socially and be free).

The characteristic part of man's natural equipment is his reason. This reason like man's other natural faculties and drives is at the outset, at least, naturally inclined towards its fulfilment. For reason means not merely a speculative faculty by which man can proceed deductively from principles to conclusions. It is also a practical faculty by which man knows which means to take and moves to make to achieve objectives, first the objectives of the whole man: to live (and hence to eat, drink and sleep), to propagate the species—these shared with plants and animals—his special roles to act reasonably and to live socially. Very little reflection tells man that other steps are absolutely necessary to achieve these natural objectives. We have seen that some form of property—some food and clothing at least—must be made his own by man to enable him to live. The primary propositions concerning man's natural inclinations, according to Aquinas, together with such others that they thus entail are the primary natural law. Because St. Thomas conceives nature as purposeful, for him the "is" of these inclinations, *under reason*, is the moral "ought." "Do the human good" in the sense of "fulfil reasonably these natural inclinations" becomes for Aquinas not a physical or psychological proposition, but a moral one, and the reduction of all the others.

It has always been a puzzle and a curiosity that Ulpian, one of the most cited among Roman jurists in the *Digest* of Justinian, had defined *ius naturale* as what "nature taught all animals."[97] And yet while recognising that human living required that man's inclinations be subjected to reason, man's special inclination to "the human good," Aquinas adopted Ulpian's words as phrasing primary natural law.[98]

[97] Sir Frederick Pollock referred to Ulpian's definition as "that unlucky phrase," cited, D'Entrèves, *Natural Law*, 1951, p. 27.

[98] See, for example, II II, 57.3; *Comm. on IV Sentences* (of Peter Lombard), d. 33, q. 1, a. 1.

These primary propositions alone (plus those they entail) are universal.[99] The other actions that man's experience and practical reason tell him are for the most part necessary to achieve his basic objectives are also called "natural law" precepts by St. Thomas. Reason tells man they are evidently, though not absolutely, necessary for success here ; they are not mere arbitrary choices, rather they are well tested, general in scope and for the most part accurate guides to conduct, "oughts" widely recognised; sometimes Aquinas calls these secondary precepts, or proper conclusions,[100] of natural law, sometimes he refers to them, in a special use of the old Roman term that became common in later scholastic use, the *ius gentium*.[101] A favourite example of Aquinas of this second grade "natural law" is private ownership of property.[102] The right to use of goods, absolutely necessary to men for them to live, is in general a common primary natural right of all the race in general—and in the concrete for any man in immediate dire need. The "*private* property" is secondary, true for the most part, the best known arrangement, *ius gentium*, no more.

The continuity of Aquinas doctrine in recent papal thought is exemplified in a most telling way by a passage of Pope Pius XII treating of the property doctrine itself that we have reserved until now.

There is, he said in the 1941 *Pentecost Message*, the primary natural right of every man to the use of material goods of the earth, for survival and development—

> Every man, as a living being gifted with reason, has in fact from nature the fundamental right to make use of the material goods of the earth . . .[103]

[99] Thus it does not belong even to reason to reverse what Aquinas calls man's natural inclinations, but only to order them. In a passage so crucial that the original Latin text is given here, St. Thomas writes: dicendum quod ratio humana secundum se non est regula rerum: sed principia ei naturaliter indita sunt quaedam regulae generales et mensurae omnium eorum quae sunt per hominem agenda, quorum ratio naturalis est regula et mensura, *licet non sit mensura eorum quae sunt a natura* (emphasis added). *Summa*, I II, 91.3.2. "It must be said that human reason is not of itself a rule of things: but principles naturally contained in it are so many general rules and measures of all those acts that must be done by man; natural reason is the rule and measure of these acts, although it is not the measure of those things that are from nature."

Some characteristic primary natural law principles of Aquinas (which he calls sometimes "common principles," "most general precepts," and "first general principles" among various expressions) include: "good is to be done and pursued, and evil avoided," conserve your being according to your nature, propagate the race, bring up and instruct your offspring until they shall be able to fend for themselves, act according to reason, act according to virtue, know the truth, love God, live in society, conserve the order of justice and give to each his own. The justification for calling lesser precepts "natural law," he tells us, is simply that "it is necessary that whatever follows from natural law in the nature of a conclusion is natural law; just as from the principle that no one may justly be harmed it follows that there must not be theft; which indeed pertains to the natural law." Aquinas, *Comm. on Ethics*, Bk. V, l. 12.

[100] I II, 94.4.

[101] II II, 57.3.

[102] *Ibid.*

[103] Pius XII, *Pentecost Message*, 1941, *op. cit.*, (n. 71, *supra*), at p. 281.

The precise form that this right of use, common to all men, should take is left undefined—

> . . . while it is left to the will of man and to the juridical statutes of nations to regulate in greater detail the actuation of this right.

The right implies a superiority over any particular existent forms of holding property—

> This individual right cannot in any way be suppressed, even by other clear and undisputed rights over material goods.

It becomes incontrovertibly clear that Pope Pius XII has been talking here about the "common" aspects, or "social function" of property (Article 1 of St. Thomas); he now turns to the private ownership of Article 2—

> Undoubtedly the natural order, deriving from God, demands also private property and the free reciprocal commerce of goods by interchange and gift, as well as the functioning of the State as a control over both these institutions.

And what is the order of importance between the right to use and the right of private ownership?

> But all this [private property and its incidents] remains subordinated to the natural scope of material goods and cannot emancipate itself from the first and fundamental right which concedes their use to all men . . . .

One would have thought that by now everyone, natural law apologists with the others, had renounced the idea that natural law could offer an immutable deductive code with precise answers to this problem and that logically produced. It is surprising to see a scholar couple with natural law in the tradition of Aristotle and Aquinas a Kantian-type subjective "natural law" doctrine—natural law with a variable content according to one's inner lights into which "you can dump what rubbish you like."[104] In a day that scorns empty concepts and overboard generalisations how scientific is a study that meets the precise and modest claims of Aquinas by ridicule, rejecting natural law as a "common denominator" so broad "that ill-fitted companions can shelter under its roof: Grotius and Selden, Locke and Hobbes, for example."

Whatever may have been the treatment of "natural law" in Kantian hands, in French Revolutionary doctrine, and in the ballooning absolutes of 19th century American "liberty of contract" jurists against whom Holmes fulminated effectively, no "traditional" natural law jurist would deny that a doctrine of natural law devoid of ascertainable objective content is fair game for the strictures of Kelsen, Holmes and Friedmann among so many. Kelsen's retreat to a logical formalism is an attempt to find a kind of certainty, but it is a "logical certainty"

[104] Harding, *loc. cit.*, p. 137. The succeeding quotations in this paragraph are from the same place.

consciously fleeing the maddening confusion of values. In truth, Kelsen's dry renouncement of the jurist's responsibility here merely shifts to other disciplines the task of finding objective criteria for the content of the law.

There is ground for difference of opinion whether particular unjust measures of an operating and not thoroughly horrendous system should be called "laws." But how can the jurist content himself with justifying the worst efforts made in the name of law, rather than striving for the best? Whether its answers be taken from a religious belief, from metaphysics, or from consciously accepted jural postulates or a prioris, in every system there must be an ultimate primacy—either the development and happiness of the individual persons who compose the society, or the furtherance of the collectivity itself. This basic choice, you may say, is a "given" to the legal system, as are the other major chosen purposes that it seeks to achieve. But, once chosen, they are a part of the system and preside over its success or failure. If the jurist identifies a legal system as a social means of achieving justice he is surely concerned with the choice of basic and prime purposes. If, like Kelsen, he is disinterested as a jurist in objectives of the law and content to establish a system of regular, predictable applications of rules he settles for less. Does the history of law from Greek and Roman times in the West up to the 19th century not show the law's bias towards a goal of individual justice? Does it not show also a concern with fixing a limit to law in terms of specific purposes, rather than merely in terms of identifying the supreme sovereign legislative authority? The advance of the past half century has been the recognition that law must play an affirmative, active role no longer restricted to the political dimension negatively resisting invasion of individual freedoms, but in the economic dimension affirmatively satisfying human needs.

The focus today, as Hauriou and Delos have pointed out,[105] is upon the content of law, the objective facts of the lives of men and societies: development, changing times, changing needs, changing availabilities for fulfilling them. Only by finding out all about man that we can, in his individual physiology and psychology—by all the means available to each age—and in his activities in social groups as well—are we in a position to provide positive law, and social institutions, with the accurate and "strong evidence" needed to fix and achieve the goals of any society by means of its legal system, considered not simply as a system of adjudication but of legislation and administration as well—a broader function for jurisprudence than Kelsen will admit. Certainly,

[105] Hauriou, *Principes de droit constitutionnel*, 2nd ed., 1929, Preface. Delos, "La théorie de l'institution," *Archives de Philosophie du Droit et de Sociologie Juridique*, 1931, pp. 97–153 at pp. 150–1: "an important change has been introduced into the study of the juridical rule. It is no longer studied independent of its social *matter*, and as if the juridical *form* were the whole of the juridical rule (*règle de droit*) and its very essence."

you say, even if we should know all that man is, physically and psychologically and in his social activities, this would give us no value, no "ought" to guide our formulation of "good." To the "a priori" of the ultimacy of the individual in society, St. Thomas adds another that is fundamental to his moral, social and legal thought: That the "is" in man is reason's guide to the "ought."[106] This is the basis of the objective system of natural law. From Aristotle to Aquinas to Maritain, Hauriou, Renard and Delos. The last three authors just named[107] have followed up the increasing activities of sociology by urging that the legal system is no mere hierarchy of rules, but a co-ordination of developing institutions. Man must be studied and known not only as an individual, and as a member of an organised national society, but as a member of the panoply of private social institutions that, no more than he, are at the mercy of the governing power in society.

Aquinas and the popes we have discussed consider natural law within a theological framework, that is, as known by man, a free, rational creature, an image of his providential Creator; his natural inclination is towards not only the "human good," but the divine "Good," as well. To a remarkable degree Plato in one respect, and Aristotle in another, anticipated in their metaphysics the Christian formulation. Within this framework Aquinas, borrowing from Stoics and Augustine more than from Aristotle, sees the moral aspect of the divine ordination of the universe as the "eternal law."[108] The natural law in this sense is seen as man's participation in this "eternal law," so to speak, as the "image" of the divine Creator reflecting his knowledge and his love. These theological considerations have been kept out of our previous discussion of natural law, but it is evident that they do not conflict in any way with what has been said. Though it may, perhaps, be less difficult for a believer to satisfy himself of its moral binding force.

[106] The perennial misunderstanding here is that this argument would make man, in the particular attitudes and dispositions in which he is found, in this society or that, the norm of what he should be. It is true that sociological investigation is designed to tell us what man and societies are actually doing, and the facts concerning their motivations to the extent that they can be gathered with dependability. The doctor must know current diseases. But there must also be knowledge of man as a member of a well-defined species, how he should function—both physically and psychologically and morally. The premise of natural law, according to the authors we have noted, is that man's basic natural inclinations furnish the objective guide for application of the moral "ought." The natural inclinations to continue living, to eat and drink, to live sexually and socially must be directed and moderated by reason; but reason is not free to reverse the natural function of these inclinations, or to dispense with anything absolutely necessary for carrying on these natural activities. So, withholding necessary food, for example, is always against natural law.

[107] See particularly Hauriou, "La théorie de l'institution et de la fondation," 4 *Cahiers de la Nouvelle Journée*, 1925, p. 10 f.; Renard, *La théorie de l'institution*, 1930; Delos, La Theorie de l'Institution, *op. cit.* A selection from these and other writings of the "French Institutionalists" will be published shortly by the Harvard University Press as a volume of the Twentieth Century Legal Philosophy Series. See, in this connection, Broderick, "Sur une nouvelle edition des institutionnalistes français," *Archives de Philosophie du Droit*, 1963, pp. 277–84.

[108] I II, 93.

The natural law may often be affirmed empirically when, in Aristotle's phrase, reason is not inflamed by emotion. In any event, an inductively arrived at conclusion that nature is purposeful may suffice to found a postulate, that species *homo*, when known as an *is*, furnishes the objective content of the moral *ought*. Such a postulate would seem, at any rate, to be less contrary to human experience than that of logical positivism and David Hume, and more reasonably realistic than the value agnosticism of the higher critic.

3. JURISPRUDENTIAL VALUE OF "NATURAL RIGHTS"

It is time to turn to the question of our higher critic, "What, if any, jurisprudential value is there in saying that a right is natural"?

The negative approach will do as a starter. What is the consequence of denying that it is useful to speak of a "natural right"? Does this denial merely assert that all "legal rights" require recognition by the organised power of society? Or does it not also imply that there is no objective standard by which that power may identify the claims it will recognise as legal? Does denial of "natural rights" not exclude our testing the content of law, and limit us to identifying, in one way or another, the authoritative source? In what way can we escape this reduction if we do not insist that there are some claims which demand recognition by a society, at least if it is to be just? The exact range of these claims is not always agreed upon, certainly it is to a considerable degree fluid rather than fixed, and often difficult to ascertain. But effort, risk and uncertainty are cheap compared with absolutism, even of the legislative variety.

We suggested at the outset that the problem of property was an admirable microcosm in which to study the traditional objective scheme of natural law. It is true that the property question claims a remarkably slender place in Aquinas' writings. Indeed Pope John XXIII in *Mater et Magistra* calls Catholic social doctrine a work developed largely in the years from Leo's *Rerum Novarum*. Yet Etienne Gilson, commenting on Leo's social encyclicals, makes this considered judgement—

> The whole doctrine of these encyclicals rests upon the notion of law as developed in the *Summa Theologiae* by Thomas Aquinas.[109]

In no field of the law has there been such a wholesale transference of a body of social and moral philosophy into positive law as in the fields of *droit social* and of the just-born-yesterday subject of labour law, in the various legal systems of the world. In France the influence of Catholic social thinking, particularly the Semaines Sociales, upon development of labour and social legislation is an accepted fact.[110]

[109] Gilson, ed., *op. cit.*, p. 336.
[110] Cf. Rivero and Savatier, *Droit du travail,* Paris, 1960, p. 41.

Its inspiration in the New Deal social legislation in the United States has been no secret. Today's spectacle of a major British political party packaging a programme of proposed social legislation that parallels in unblushing detail the teaching of the encyclicals also suggests that there is, perhaps, some jurisprudential value after all in the notion of developing natural rights that have their origin in the developing natural needs of man living in today's resource-full society.

What practical alternative is there to natural rights?

Is there no "natural right" invaded if a healthy and innocent man is deliberately hung, starved to death, prevented from marrying and raising children, giving divine worship in some reasonable social way, deprived of his physical freedom by official whim? Do the lived lives of people in any "civilised" country support the academic suggestion that a society which does not give "legal" recognition to such "natural rights" may still pose as civilised? But, our higher critic says, your claim is broader than this. Do not Aquinas and the social popes say that a positive law that denies a "natural right," say of "private property," is not "law" at all? To remove any basis for quibbling and make the answer clear, say that the "private property" infringement is a statute in a land of abundance and small property owners confiscating without compensation 100 per cent of all land and all personal property. Aquinas and the popes, would say that this clear violation of a "natural right" is not valid "law."[111] The doctrinaire positivist reminds us that this statute is enforced in Lower Slobovia. In this sense, if you like, it is Lower Slobovian "law." To one identifying "law" simply by identifying the accepted lawmaker, there is no problem. To one insisting upon an understanding of "valid law" that looks both to its author and to its content, this is not "law." There is no puzzle here.[112]

But whatever view be adopted as to the "unjust law," it remains that clearly identifiable natural rights are clear guides to enactment of just legislation (less clear rights furnish less clear guidance). Negatively, they warn off, or give pause, as to measures that impinge on primary human functions, such as statutes forbidding certain adult marriages, enforcing compulsory sterilisation, etc. Affirmatively they point towards legislation providing for more adequate satisfaction of basic human needs. The papal invitations to legislate implementing the social function of property are a case in point. This category differs from the previous one. The precise lines of the natural right are here defined by the action of positive law itself. But the inchoate obligation

[111] In so far as a human law "deviates from right reason it is called an unjust law; in such case it is no law at all, but rather a species of violence." I II, 93.3.2.
[112] See n. 93, *supra*.

of some to make productive social use of their idle surplus property did pre-exist the legislation as something already due (*droit objectif, debitum*); the legislation created the faculty in particular subjects (rights) to enforce the obligation; previous to the legislation the obligation existed in social justice and charity alone, undefined as to obligees and as to amount; after the legislation there existed a precise legal and "subjective" right (*droit subjectif*) with specified dimensions.

Fascinating problems remain to be solved. To what extent can private institutional structures and their internal law come to be recognised by a national society as producing the stuff of enforceable positive law?[113] Far more attention is due to the pioneer work of Hauriou, Renard and Delos in this institutional field than has yet been paid them in the common law countries.[114] Short of positive legislation, when does the *droit social* become *droit tout court*? This problem bothers the continental jurists no less than ourselves. Leon Duguit, better known in England than most French jurists because of his sponsorship here by Harold Laski, calls attention to this point—

> . . . to my knowledge there is no sociological philosopher who has tried to determine the exact moment when a social norm really becomes a juridical norm. Jurists should do this, and in France the only one who has really tried is . . . Geny.[115]

No one struggled longer with this problem than Duguit himself; and his motivation was to wrest law clear of the popular legislative voluntarism of the French Revolution and the state voluntarism of the 19th century German jurists, much as current common law jurisprudence struggles to free itself from the voluntaristic monism of Austin without surrendering to subjectivism, or to sociological positivism. Duguit, who boasted of his positivism and his hate for metaphysics, wrote 40 years ago—

> The older I grow the more I study and penetrate the depths of the problem of law, the more I am convinced that law is not a creation of the state; that it exists apart from the state; that the idea of law is entirely independent of the idea of the state; and that a rule of law is imposed upon the state as upon individuals . . . .[116]

It is not surprising that Duguit, struggling for a rational basis for the content of his "rule of law" found strength in Aquinas, despite Aquinas' insistence upon authority as an element of law—

> The analysis of the sentiment of justice has been made by St. Thomas Aquinas

[113] Of lively current interest to both continental jurisprudence and papal documents is the problem of enterprise. See Despax, *L'entreprise et le droit*, Paris, 1961, and John XXIII, *Mater et Magistra*, *op. cit.*, p. 32, n. 84 f. For an interesting discussion of the relation of the concept of "enterprise" to the papal teaching see Bigo, "L'entreprise, étapesd 'un progrès doctrinal," *Revue de l'Action Populaire*, June 1962, p. 44 f.

[114] See n. 107, *supra*.

[115] Duguit, "Objective Law," (1920) 20 *Columbia L. Rev.* 816; (1921) 21 *Columbia L. Rev.* 17, 126, 242, at p. 126.

[116] *Ibid.*, 21 *Columbia L. Rev.* 17, 21.

in terms which have never been surpassed and which it will not be out of place to repeat (then he quotes for 18 lines passages from *Summa*, II II, q. 58.8, 61.1, 2).[117]

The law to such men is no open book, but neither is it a logical juxtaposition of indifferent rules furnished by some outside source. Law has a mission of justice that they are not too proud to avow. And they have not renounced the possibility of ascertaining content in a rational, orderly way. Are they wrong? When we have identified, or postulated, the ultimate lawgiver, and the hierarchical descent and logical progression of legal rules from him as from a source, have we exhausted the role of the jurist? Is the content of the law merely "a matter of personal predilection which cannot be shown to be right or wrong?"[118] What "strong evidence" is there for this position? It is time for the higher critics to meet the actual claims of their real, live opponent, rather than setting up stale straw men of "natural law" systems long rejected, and with gay banter in Shavian fashion batting them down. Turning to the natural law side, the dialogue would be sharpened by clarification of some terminology, refinement of the interplay of revelation and magisterial authority with natural law in papal teaching, and continuation of efforts for greater precision between social and moral norms and juridical norms.

It is too late in intellectual history for us to cower helplessly in the shadow of Hume.[119] It is true, as Fuller indicated, that the great fear of the scholar is to be thought naive.[120] But a writer who considers it naive today to enter discourse beyond sense data and logic betrays not naiveté, but unawareness of 20th century thought. Such men as Bergson, Husserl, Heidegger, Jaspers, Marcel, Merleau-Ponty, Sartre and (late) Wittgenstein may not have been right, but they have certainly broken the naiveté barrier to metaphysical discussion.

Aristotle warned us long ago that "it is the mark of an educated man to look for precision in each class of things just so far as the nature of the subject permits."[121] His further caution here might be apropos of our discussion of natural law property doctrine—

> We must be content, then, in speaking of such subjects and with such premises to indicate the truth roughly and in outline, and in speaking about things which are only for the most part true and with premises of the same kind to reach conclusions that are no better.[122]

[117] *Ibid.*, p. 32, n. 12.
[118] Harding, *loc. cit.*, p. 137.
[119] But lest we be too hard on Hume, Professor H. L. A. Hart recently unearthed a sense of "natural law" he finds in Hume: Hart, *The Concept of Law*, 1962, p. 187.
[120] "Positivism was the only theory of law that could claim to be 'scientific' in an Age of Science. Dissenters from this view were characterised by positivists with that epithet modern man fears above all others: 'naive'." Fuller, "Positivism and Fidelity to Law—A Reply to Professor Hart" (1958), 71 *Harvard L. Rev.* 630, 659.
[121] Aristotle, *Ethics*, Bk. 1, Ch. 1, 1094b, 25.
[122] *Ibid.*, 1094b, 20–23.

This is the philosophical approach of Aquinas in moral and social matters, and of the Church which follows his philosophy here. But natural law conclusions in the theological context of papal teachings stand in a different focus for the believer, who relies on a "teaching power" of divine origin in the popes as well as on their "right reason," than for the extra-confessional reader. And yet, the lesson of recent development of social rights, and of property and labour law suggests that both Aquinas and the popes can be read agreeably in a philosophical and juridical dimension in particular natural law matters, without a general commitment to their authority or to their views on other subjects.

Towards Reunion in Jurisprudence?

There is little in this dialogue with our higher critic that would hold out much hope for establishing a jurisprudential bridge between the opposing positions. However, recent studies by a prominent jurist of the positivist persuasion not only considerably narrows another gap, but give interesting "empirical" support to the jurisprudential value of natural rights.

In a carefully measured rapprochment with natural law theory,[123] Professor H. L. A. Hart suggests a restricted sense in which natural law is acceptable to him: the tacit assumption that the proper end of human activity is survival. He does not talk in terms of a "natural inclination" to live, as Aquinas does in his formulation of his most primary index to the content of natural law. Hart will not take it, as does Aquinas, as a universal, unchanging truth of human nature that man naturally desires to continue his existence. But Hart does indicate that he, with Hume and Hobbes, sees "in the modest aim of survival the central indisputable element which gives empirical good sense to the terminology of Natural Law."[124] While Hart would take it as "a mere contingent fact which could be otherwise," yet "survival has still a special status in relation to human conduct and in our thought about it, which parallels the prominence and the necessity ascribed to it in the orthodox formulations of Natural Law."[125] From this notion of survival Hart proceeds to unravel a skein of "simple truisms" observing that "in each case the facts mentioned afford a *reason* why, given survival as an aim, law and morals should include a specific content."[126] He heads his list with "rules forbidding the free use of violence and rules constituting the minimum form of property—with its rights and duties

[123] Hart, *The Concept of Law, op. cit.*, p. 187 f. See also Hart. "Positivism and the Separation of Law and Morals," (1958) 71 *Harvard L. Rev.* 593, 622.
[124] *The Concept of Law, op. cit.*, p. 187.
[125] *Ibid.*, p. 188.
[126] *Ibid.*, p. 189.

sufficient to enable food to grow and to be retained until eaten"[127] which have a "necessary nonarbitrary status . . . constituted as we are in a world like ours."[128] For "such rules are so fundamental that if a legal system did not have them there would be no point in having any other rules at all."[129]

The common ground between Hart and Aquinas should not be exaggerated; it is none the less striking when discussed on an empirical plane. Hart's use of "survival" as the irreducible minimum, his stress on the fact of human sociability ("the humble aim of survival in close proximity to our fellows,") his rational elaboration[130] of rules on the basis of the observed facts of man in society—all these parallel the items in Aquinas' elaboration of "natural inclinations" with one outstanding exception which we need not dwell on here.[131]

Hart does not back away from talk of "human nature,"[132] but he comments on it as "contingent fact"—

> . . . Though our bodies do change in shape, size, and other physical properties they do not do this so drastically . . . that we cannot identify each other as the same persistent individual over considerable spans of time.[133]

While mere "contingent fact," the consequences are monumental—

> Though this is but a contingent fact which may one day be different, on it at present rest huge structures of our thought and principles of action and social life.[134]

But, supposing, says Hart, all this changed, and "that men were to become invulnerable to attack by each other; were clad perhaps like giant land crabs with an impenetrable carapace, and could extract the food they needed from some internal chemical process." Would not "rules forbidding the free use of violence and rules constituting the minimum form of property" lose "the necessary nonarbitrary status which they have for us, constituted as we are in a world like ours."[135]

Hart's excursion here into the lobby of science fiction illuminates for us certain common misconceptions as to Aquinas' doctrines of

[127] "Positivism and the Separation of Law and Morals," *op. cit.*, p. 623; see also *The Concept of Law*, *op. cit.*, p. 190.

[128] *Ibid.*

[129] *Ibid.*

[130] ". . . the distinctively rational connection between natural facts and the content of legal and moral rules in this approach." *Ibid.* Hart here distinguishes the "*causality*" of physical, psychological or economic conditions.

[131] I.e. Aquinas' account of the "natural inclination" to mate and propagate as a basic indication of the content of a primary precept of natural law. I II, 94.2. Does Hart conceive Aquinas as suggesting that the physical or psychological "inclination" is a "causal" natural law? Or does he correctly understand St. Thomas' view, that these natural inclinations, above all the natural inclination of man to act reasonably, are "guides" to the content of the basic natural law precepts? See I II, 94.2.

[132] "Reflecting on some very obvious generalisations—indeed truisms—concerning human nature and the world in which men live, shows that as long as these hold good, there are certain rules of conduct which any social organisation must contain if it is to be viable." *The Concept of Law*, *op. cit.*, p. 188.

[133] "Positivism and the Separation of Law and Morals," *op. cit.*, p. 622.

[134] *Ibid.*

[135] *Ibid.*, p. 623.

natural law in general, and property in particular. Aquinas' discussion of moral laws of man's nature assumes in the theological sphere of revealed truth a God that has created a purposeful universe, capped by intelligent, free men. In a philosophical dimension, like Aristotle St. Thomas assumes a purposeful, basically fixed nature in man. Only on this assumption can objective moral laws be explained philosophically. In fact Aquinas takes here as aprioris certain basic prerational inclinations (later verified to some extent from their effects by our observation) as the guides to the basic precepts of natural law. So long as man needs to eat to survive, there is this irrevocable natural law regarding *some* form of property. But if a new type of human animality developed that made food unnecessary, the perspective of food-property as a necessity would obviously disappear.[136] If Hart wants to call man's nature a "contingent fact" in this sense, his preference, while eccentric, does not divide him and Aquinas (on a philosophical plane) as by a chasm.

On the other hand, there are rules and rights of natural law that Aquinas puts in a separate and secondary category, as we have seen. They reflect such observations about man as are not universally verified, but true for the most part. General change in them is perhaps unlikely, but not impossible to conceive. And in this category fits private ownership of property. If the practical premises upon which this doctrine is based utterly collapse, a development that is obviously not anticipated by either Aquinas or the papal doctrine, it would have to be acknowledged that private property would not longer qualify as a "natural right."[137] Meanwhile, as a general concept it is firm, as to content it is fluid. For Aquinas and the popes, as much as Professor Hart, teach the inadequacy of "the definition of the basic forms" of law and morals "without reference to any specific content or social needs . . .".[138]

[136] And if *species homo* ceased to be divided into male and female certain other interesting consequences would follow, etc., etc.

[137] For clear-cut statements to this effect see Maclaren, *op. cit.* Renard, "Propriété privée et propriété humaine," appendix to *La théorie de l'institution, op. cit.*, and O'Rahilly, "S. Thomas's Theory of Property," (1920) *Studies*, Vol. 9, pp. 337 *et seq.*

[138] *The Concept of Law, op. cit.*, p. 194.

The writer acknowledges with gratitude a Rockefeller Foundation grant in legal and political philosophy in 1962/3 which enabled him to study in France the Institutionalist jurists—Hauriou, Renard and Delos—whose works have been cited and views sometimes reflected in this study.

Part III
The New Classical Theory

[9]

THE FIRST PRINCIPLE OF PRACTICAL REASON:

A Commentary on the *Summa theologiae*, 1-2, Question 94, Article 2

Many proponents and critics of Thomas Aquinas's theory of natural law have understood it roughly as follows. The first principle of practical reason is a command: *Do good and avoid evil.* Man discovers this imperative in his conscience; it is like an inscription written there by the hand of God. Having become aware of this basic commandment, man consults his nature to see what is good and what is evil. He examines an action in comparison with his essence to see whether the action fits human nature or does not fit it. If the action fits, it is seen to be good; if it does not fit, it is seen to be bad. Once we know that a certain kind of action — for instance, stealing — is bad, we have two premises, "Avoid evil" and "Stealing is evil," from whose conjunction is deduced: "Avoid stealing." All specific commandments of natural law are derived in this way.[1]

I propose to show how far this interpretation misses Aquinas's real position. My main purpose is not to contribute to the history of natural law, but to clarify Aquinas's idea of it for current thinking. Instead of undertaking a general review of Aquinas's entire natural law theory, I shall focus on the first principle of practical reason, which also is the first precept of natural law. This principle, as Aquinas states it, is: *Good is to be done and pursued, and evil is to be avoided.*[2] Although verbally this formula is only slightly different from that of the command, *Do good and avoid evil,* I shall try to show that the two formulae differ considerably in meaning and that they belong in different theoretical contexts.

This paper has five parts. 1) Since I propose to show that the common interpretation is unsound, it will be necessary to explicate the text in which Aquinas states the first principle. 2) Since the mistaken interpretation restricts the meaning of "good" and "evil" in the first principle to the value of moral actions, the meaning of these key terms must be clarified in the light of Aquinas's theory of final causality. 3) Since the mistaken interpretation tends to oppose the commandments of natural law to positive action, it will help to notice the broad scope Aquinas attributes to the first principle, for he considers it to be a source, rather than a limit, of action. 4) Since according to the mistaken interpretation natural law is a set of imperatives, it is important to see why the first principle is not primarily an imperative, although it is a genuine precept. 5) Since the mistaken interpretation regards all specific precepts of natural law as

[1] This summary is not intended to reflect the position of any particular author. However, a full and accessible presentation along these general lines may be found in THOMAS J. HIGGINS, S.J., MAN AS MAN: THE SCIENCE AND ART OF ETHICS 49-69, 88-100, 120-126 (rev. ed., Milwaukee, 1958).

[2] "Bonum est faciendum et prosequendum, et malum vitandum." SUMMA THEOLOGIAE 1-2, q. 94, a. 2, c. (Leonine ed., Rome, 1882-1948). (SUMMA THEOLOGIAE will hereafter be referred to as S.T.)

conclusions drawn from the first principle, the significance of Aquinas's actual view — that there are many self-evident principles of natural law — must be considered.

I

Aquinas's statement of the first principle of practical reason occurs in *Summa theologiae,* 1-2, question 94, article 2. Question 90 is concerned with what law is, question 91 with the distinction among the various modes of law, and question 92 with the effects of law. Aquinas begins treating each mode of law in particular in question 93; in that question he treats eternal law. Thus he comes to the study of natural law in question 94. Questions 95 to 97 are concerned with man-made law. Questions 98 to 108 examine the divine law, Old and New.

Question 94 is divided into six articles, each of which presents a position on a single issue concerning the law of nature. The first article raises the issue: "Whether natural law is a habit." Aquinas holds that natural law consists of precepts of reason, which are analogous to propositions of theoretical knowledge. Hence he denies that it is a habit, although he grants that it can be possessed habitually, for one *has* these principles even when he is not thinking of them.

The second issue raised in question 94 logically follows. It is: "Does natural law contain many precepts, or only one?" Unlike the issue of the first article, which was a question considered by many previous authors, this second point was not a standard issue.[3] For this reason the arguments, which Aquinas sets out at the beginning of the article in order to construct the issue he wants to resolve, do not refer to authorities, as the opening arguments of his articles usually do. Three arguments are set out for the position that natural law contains only one precept, and a single opposing argument is given to show that it contains many precepts.

The first argument concludes that natural law must contain only a single precept on the grounds that law itself is a precept[4] and that natural law has unity. The second argument reaches the same conclusion by reasoning that since natural law is based upon human nature, it could have many precepts only if the many parts of human nature were represented in it; but in this case even the demands of man's lower nature would have to be reflected in natural law. The third argument for the position that natural law has only one precept is drawn from the premises that human reason is one and that law belongs to reason.[5] The single argument Aquinas offers for the opposite conclusion is

---

[3] Paul-M. van Overbeke, O.P., *La loi naturelle et le droit naturel selon S. Thomas,* 65 REVUE THOMISTE 73-75 (1957) puts q. 94, a. 1 into its proper perspective. ODON LOTTIN, O.S.B., LE DROIT NATUREL CHEZ SAINT THOMAS D'AQUIN ET SES PRÉDÉCESSEURS 79 (2nd ed., Bruges, 1931) mentions that the issue of the second article had been posed by Albert the Great (cf. p. 118), but the question was not a commonplace. Obviously no one could ask it who did not hold that natural law consists of precepts, and even those who took this position would not ask about the unity or multiplicity of precepts unless they saw some significance in responding one way or the other.

[4] A position Aquinas develops in q. 92, a. 2, and applies in rejecting the position that natural law is a habit in q. 94, a. 1.

[5] That law pertains to reason is a matter of definition for Aquinas; law is an *ordinance of reason,* according to the famous definition of q. 90, a. 4.

based on an analogy between the precepts of natural law and the axioms of demonstrations: as there is a multiplicity of indemonstrable principles of demonstrations, so there is a multiplicity of precepts of natural law. These four initial arguments serve only to clarify the issue to be resolved in the response which follows. Of themselves, they settle nothing. After the response Aquinas comments briefly on each of the first three arguments in the light of his resolution of the issue. The argument that there are many precepts of natural law Aquinas will not comment upon, since he takes this position himself.

Aquinas's response to the question is as follows:

> 1) As I said previously, the precepts of natural law are related to practical reason in the same way the basic principles of demonstrations are related to theoretical reason, since both are sets of self-evident principles.
> 2) But something is called "self-evident" in two senses: in one way, objectively; in the other way, relative to us. Any proposition may be called "objectively self-evident" if its predicate belongs to the intelligibility of its subject. Yet to someone who does not know the intelligibility of the subject, such a proposition will not be self-evident. For example, the proposition, *Man is rational,* taken just in itself, is self-evident, for to say *man* is to say *rational;* yet to someone who did not know what man is, this proposition would not be self-evident. Consequently, as Boethius says in his *De hebdomadibus,*[6] there are certain axioms or propositions which are generally self-evident to everyone. In this class are propositions whose terms everyone understands — for example: *Every whole is greater than its parts,* and: *Two things equal to a third are equal to one another.* But there are other propositions which are self-evident only to the educated, who understand what the terms of such propositions mean. For example, to one who understands that angels are incorporeal, it is self-evident that they are not in a place by filling it up, but this is not evident to the uneducated, who do not comprehend this point.
> 3) Now among those things which fall within the grasp of everyone there is a certain order of precedence. For that which primarily falls within one's grasp is being, and the understanding of being is included in absolutely everything that anyone grasps. Hence the primary indemonstrable principle is: *To affirm and simultaneously to deny is excluded.* This principle is based on the intelligibility of being (and nonbeing), and all other principles are based on this one, as Aristotle says in the *Metaphysics.*[7]
> 4) But just as being is the first thing to fall within the unrestricted grasp of the mind, so good is the first thing to fall within the grasp of practical reason — that is, reason directed to a work — for every active principle acts on account of an end, and end includes the intelligibility of good.
> 5) It follows that the first principle of practical reason is one founded on the intelligibility of good — that is: *Good is what each thing tends toward.* Therefore this is the primary precept of law: *Good is to be done and pursued, and evil is to be avoided.* All other precepts of the law of nature are based on this one, in this way that under precepts of the law of nature come all those things-to-be-done or things-to-be-avoided which practical reason naturally grasps as human goods or their opposites.
> 6) Because good has the intelligibility of end, and evil has the intelligibility of contrary to end, it follows that reason naturally grasps as goods — in consequence, as things-to-be-pursued by work, and their opposites as evils and

[6] PATROLOGIA LATINA vol. 64, col. 1311 (ed. J. Migne, Paris, 1844-1865).
[7] METAPHYSICA bk. iii, 1005^b29.

things-to-be-avoided — all the objects of man's natural inclinations. Hence the order of the precepts of the law of nature is according to the order of the natural inclinations.

7) First, there is in man an inclination based on the aspect of his nature which he has in common with all substances — that is, that everything tends according to its own nature to preserve its own being. In accordance with this inclination, those things by which human life is preserved and by which threats to life are met fall under natural law. Second, there is in man an inclination to certain more restricted goods based on the aspect of his nature which he has in common with other animals. In accordance with this inclination, those things are said to be of natural law "which nature teaches all animals," among which are the union of male and female, the raising of children, and the like. Third, there is in man an inclination to the good based on the rational aspect of his nature, which is peculiar to himself. For example, man has a natural inclination to this, that he might know the truth concerning God, and to this, that he might live in society. In accordance with this inclination, those things relating to an inclination of this sort fall under natural law. For instance, that man should avoid ignorance, that he should not offend those among whom he must live, and other points relevant to this inclination.[8]

Aquinas's solution to the question is that there are many precepts of the natural law, but that this multitude is not a disorganized aggregation but an orderly whole. The precepts are many because the different inclinations' objects, viewed by reason as ends for rationally guided efforts, lead to distinct norms of action. The natural law, nevertheless, is one because each object of inclination obtains its role in practical reason's legislation only insofar as it is subject to practical reason's way of determining action — by prescribing how ends are to be attained.[9]

Now we must examine this response more carefully.

In the first paragraph Aquinas restates the analogy between precepts of natural law and first principles of theoretical reason. The latter are principles of demon-

[8] S.T. 1-2, q. 94, a. 2, c. The translation is my own; the paragraphing is added. The two fullest commentaries on this article that I have found are J. B. Schuster, S.J., *Von den ethischen Prinzipien: Eine Thomasstudie zu S. Th.*, I-II, q. 94, a. 2, 57 ZEITSCHRIFT FÜR KATHOLISCHE THEOLOGIE 44-65 (1933) and MICHAEL V. MURRAY, S.J., PROBLEMS IN ETHICS 220-235 (New York, 1960). See also Van Overbeke, *op. cit. supra* note 3, at 450-58; Gregory Stevens, O.S.B., *The Relations of Law and Obligation*, 29 PROCEEDINGS OF THE AMERICAN CATHOLIC PHILOSOPHICAL ASSOCIATION 195-205 (1955). Many useful points have been derived from each of these sources for the interpretation developed below.

[9] After giving this response to the issue, Aquinas answers briefly each of the three introductory arguments. All of them tended to show that natural law has but one precept. To the first argument, based on the premises that law itself is a precept and that natural law is one, Aquinas answers that the many precepts of the natural law are unified *in relation to* the primary principle. To the second argument, that man's lower nature must be represented if the precepts of the law of nature are diversified by the parts of human nature, Aquinas unhesitatingly answers that all parts of human nature are represented in natural law, for the inclination of each part of man belongs to natural law insofar as it falls under a precept of reason; in this respect all the inclinations also fall under the one first principle. To the third argument, that law belongs to reason and that reason is one, Aquinas responds that reason indeed is one in itself, and yet that natural law contains many precepts because reason directs everything which concerns man, who is complex. Each of these three answers merely reiterates the response to the main question.

stration in systematic sciences such as geometry. From the outset, Aquinas speaks of "precepts" in the plural. The first paragraph implies that only self-evident principles of practical reason belong to natural law; Aquinas is using "natural law" here in its least extensive sense.[10] It is clear already at this point that Aquinas counts many self-evident principles among the precepts of the law of nature, and that there is a mistake in any interpretation of his theory which reduces all but one of the precepts to the status of conclusions.[11]

In the second paragraph of the response Aquinas clarifies the meaning of "self-evident." His purpose is not to postulate a peculiar meaning for "self-evident" in terms of which the basic precepts of natural law might be self-evident although no one in fact knew them.[12] That Aquinas did not have this in mind appears at the beginning of the third paragraph, where he begins to determine the priorities among those things "which fall within the grasp of everyone." No doubt there are some precepts not everyone knows although they are objectively self-evident — for instance, precepts concerning the relation of man to God: *God should be loved above all,* and: *God should be obeyed before all.* Man can be ignorant of these precepts because God does not fall within our grasp so that the grounds of his lovability and authority are evident to everybody.[13] However, basic principles of natural law on the whole, and particularly the precepts mentioned in this response, are self-evident to all men.

[10] In other texts he considers conclusions drawn from these principles also to be precepts of natural law — e.g., S.T. 1-2, q. 94, a. 4, ad 1. This point is merely lexicographical, yet it has caused some confusion — for instance, concerning the relationship between natural law and the law of nations, for sometimes Aquinas contradistinguishes the two while sometimes he includes the law of nations in natural law. See LOTTIN, *op. cit. supra* note 3, at 61-73.

[11] A careful reading of this paragraph also excludes another interpretation of Aquinas's theory of natural law — that proposed by Jacques Maritain. MAN AND THE STATE 84-94 (Chicago, 1951), is the most complete expression in English of Maritain's recent view. His position has undergone some development in its various presentations. Maritain suggests that natural law does not itself fall within the category of knowledge; he tries to give it a status independent of knowledge so that it can be the object of gradual discovery. He also claims that man's knowledge of natural law is not conceptual and rational, but instead is by inclination, connaturality, or congeniality. However, Aquinas does not present natural law as if it were an object known or to be known; rather, he considers the precepts of practical reason themselves to be natural law. Thus the principles of the law of nature cannot be *potential* objects of knowledge, unknown but waiting in hiding, fully formed and ready for discovery. Moreover, the fact that the precepts of natural law are viewed as self-evident principles of practical reason excludes Maritain's account of our knowledge of them. For Aquinas, there is no nonconceptual intellectual knowledge: DE VERITATE, q. 4, a. 2, ad 5. How misleading Maritain's account of the knowledge of natural law is, so far as Aquinas's position is concerned, can be seen by examining some studies based on Maritain: Kai Nielsen, *An Examination of the Thomistic Theory of Natural Moral Law,* 4 NATURAL LAW FORUM 47-50 (1959); PAUL RAMSEY, NINE MODERN MORALISTS 215-223 (Englewood Cliffs, N.J., 1962). Nielsen was not aware, as Ramsey was, that Maritain's theory of knowledge of natural law should not be ascribed to Aquinas.

[12] Nielsen, *op. cit. supra* note 11, at 50-52, apparently misled by Maritain, follows this interpretation. At any rate Nielsen's implicit supposition that the naural law for Aquinas must be formally identical with the eternal law is in conflict with Aquinas's notion of participation according to which the participation is *never* formally identical with that in which it participates.

[13] Thus Aquinas remarks (S. T. 1-2, q. 100, a. 3, ad 1) that the precept of charity is "self-evident to human reason, either by nature or by faith," since a knowledge of God

Why, then, has Aquinas introduced the distinction between objective self-evidence and self-evidence to us? I think he does so simply to clarify the meaning of "self-evident," for he wishes to deal with practical principles that are self-evident in the latter, and fuller, of the two possible senses.

Self-evidence in fact has two aspects. On the one hand, a principle is not self-evident if it can be derived from some prior principle, which provides a foundation for it. On the other hand, a principle is not useful as a starting point of inquiry and as a limit of proof unless its underivability is known. The objective aspect of self-evidence, underivability, depends upon the lack of a middle term which might connect the subject and predicate of the principle and supply the cause of its truth. In other words, the reason for the truth of the self-evident principle is what is directly signified by it, not any extrinsic cause. The subjective aspect of self-evidence, recognition of underivability, requires that one have such an adequate understanding of what is signified by the principle that no mistaken effort will be made to provide a derivation for it.

Aquinas expresses the objective aspect of self-evidence by saying that the predicate of a self-evident principle belongs to the intelligibility of the subject, and he expresses the subjective aspect of self-evidence in the requirement that this intelligibility not be unknown. These remarks may have misleading connotations for us, for we have been conditioned by several centuries of philosophy in which analytic truths (truths of reason) are opposed to synthetic truths (truths of fact). Only truths of reason are supposed to be necessary, but their necessity is attributed to meaning which is thought of as a quality inherent in ideas in the mind. Only truths of fact are supposed to have any reference to real things, but all truths of fact are thought to be contingent, because it is assumed that all necessity is rational in character. Thus the modern reader is likely to wonder: "Are Aquinas's self-evident principles analytic or synthetic?" Of course, there is no answer to this question in Aquinas's terms. He does not accept the dichotomy between mind and material reality that is implicit in the analytic-synthetic distinction. Nor does he merely insert another bin between the two, as Kant did when he invented the synthetic a priori. Rather, Aquinas proceeds on the supposition that meanings derive from things known and that experienced things themselves contain a certain degree of intelligible necessity.[14]

Thus, "the predicate belongs to the intelligibility of the subject" does not mean that one element of a complex meaning is to be found among others within the complex. But does not Aquinas imagine the subject as if it were a container full of units of meaning, each unit a predicate? No, he thinks of the subject and the predicate as complementary aspects of a unified knowledge of a single objective dimension of the reality known. An object of consideration ordinarily belongs to the world of experience, and all the aspects of our knowledge of that object are grounded in that experience. For example, both subject and predicate of the proposition, *Rust is an oxide,* are based on experience. We

sufficient to form the natural law precept of charity can come from either natural knowledge or divine revelation.

[14] A useful guide to Aquinas's theory of principles is PETER HOENEN, S.J., REALITY AND JUDGMENT ACCORDING TO ST. THOMAS (Chicago, 1952).

do not discover the truth of the principle by analyzing the meaning of "rust"; rather we discover that oxide belongs to the intelligibility of rust by coming to see that this proposition is a self-evident (underivable) truth.

But in this discussion I have been using the word "intelligibility" (*ratio*) which Aquinas uses both in this paragraph and later in the response. Here he says that in a self-evident principle the predicate belongs to the intelligibility of the subject; later he says that good belongs to the intelligibility of end and that end belongs to the intelligibility of good. I have just said that oxide belongs to the intelligibility of rust. Now what is an intelligibility?

It is not merely the meaning with which a word is used, for someone may use a word, such as "rust," and use it correctly, without understanding all that is included in its intelligibility. On the other hand, the intelligibility does not include all that belongs to things denoted by the word, since it belongs to one bit of rust to be on my car's left rear fender, but this is not included in the intelligibility of rust. One might translate *ratio* as "essence"; yet every word expresses some intelligibility, while not every word signifies essence. Thus "good" does not signify an essence, much less does "nonbeing," but both express intelligibilities.[15]

An intelligibility is all that would be included in the meaning of a word that is used correctly if the things referred to in that use were fully known in all ways relevant to the aspect then signified by the word in question. Thus the intelligibility includes the meaning with which a word is used, but it also includes whatever increment of meaning the same word would have in the same use if what is denoted by the word were more perfectly known. An intelligibility need not correspond to any part or principle of the object of knowledge, yet an intelligibility is an aspect of the partly known and still further knowable object. We may imagine an intelligibility as an intellect-sized bite of reality, a bite not necessarily completely digested by the mind. An intelligibility includes the meaning and potential meaning of a word uttered by intelligence about a world whose reality, although naturally suited to our minds, is not in itself cut into pieces — intelligibilities. These *we* distinguish and join in the processes of analysis and synthesis which constitute our rational knowing.

Hence part of an intelligibility may escape us without our missing all of it. The child who knows that rust is on metal has grasped one self-evident truth about rust, for metal does belong to the intelligibility of rust. The same child may not know that rust is an oxide, although oxide also belongs to the intelligibility of rust.

The important point to grasp from all this is that when Aquinas speaks of self-evident principles of natural law, he does not mean tautologies derived by mere conceptual analysis — for example: *Stealing is wrong,* where "stealing" means the *unjust* taking of another's property. Rather, he means the principles of practical inquiry which also are the limits of practical argument — a set of underivable principles for practical reason. To function as principles, their status as underivables must be recognized, and this recognition depends upon

[15] On "ratio" see ANDRÉ HAYEN, S.J., L'INTENTIONNEL SELON SAINT THOMAS 175-194 (2nd ed., Bruges, Bruxelles, Paris, 1954).

a sufficient understanding of their terms, i.e., of the intelligibilities signified by those terms.

In the third paragraph Aquinas begins to apply the analogy between the precepts of the natural law and the first principles of demonstrations. *Being* is the basic intelligibility; it represents our first discovery about anything we are to know — that it *is something* to be known. The first principle, expressed here in the formula, "To affirm and simultaneously to deny is excluded," is the one sometimes called "the principle of contradiction" and sometimes called "the principle of noncontradiction": *The same cannot both be and not be at the same time and in the same respect.* In this more familiar formulation it is clearer that the principle is based upon being and nonbeing, for it is obvious that what the principle excludes is the identification of being with nonbeing. The objective dimension of the reality of beings that we know in knowing this principle is simply the definiteness that is involved in their very objectivity, a definiteness that makes a demand on the intellect knowing them, the very least demand — to think consistently of them.[16]

To say that all other principles are based on this principle does not mean that all other principles are derived from it by deduction. In fact the principle of contradiction does not directly enter into arguments as a premise except in the case of arguments *ad absurdum.*[17] Rather, this principle is basic in that it is given to us by our most primitive understanding. All other knowledge of anything adds to this elementary appreciation of the definiteness involved in its very objectivity, for any further knowledge is a step toward giving some intelligible character to this definiteness, i.e., toward defining things and knowing them in their wholeness and their concrete interrelations. But the first principle all the while exercises its unobtrusive control, for it drives the mind on toward judgment, never permitting it to settle into inconsistent muddle.

In the fourth paragraph Aquinas states that *good* is the primary intelligibility to fall under practical reason, and he explains why this is so. On the analogy he is developing, he clearly means that nothing can be understood by practical reason without the intelligibility of *good* being included in it.

Now what is practical reason? Is it simply knowledge sought for practical purposes? No, Aquinas considers practical reason to be the mind playing a certain role, or functioning in a certain capacity, the capacity in which it is "directed to a work." Direction to work is intrinsic to the mind in this capacity; direction qualifies the very functioning of the mind. Practical reason is the mind working as a principle of action, not simply as a recipient of objective reality. It is the mind charting what is to be, not merely recording what already is.

It is easy to imagine that to know is to picture an object in one's mind, but this conception of knowledge is false. Even for purely theoretical knowledge, to know is a fulfillment reached by a development through which one comes to share in a spiritual way the characteristics and reality of the world which is

[16] In libros Metaphysicorum Aristotelis lib. 4, lect. 6.
[17] In libros Posteriorum analyticorum Aristotelis lib. 1, lect. 20.

known. Knowledge is a unity between man knowing and what he knows. In the case of theoretical knowledge, the known has the reality which is shared before the knower comes to share in it — in theory the mind must conform to facts and the world calls the turn. In practical knowledge, on the other hand, the knower arrives at the destination first; and what is known will be altered as a result of having been thought about, since the known must conform to the mind of the knower. The mind uses the power of the knower to see that the known will conform to it; the mind calls the turn.

Yet it would be a mistake to suppose that practical knowledge, because it is prior to its object, is independent of experience. Even in theoretical knowledge, actual understanding and truth are not discovered in experience and extracted from it by a simple process of separation. Experience *can be* understood and truth *can be* known about the things of experience, but understanding and truth attain a dimension of reality that is not actually contained within experience, although experience touches the surface of the same reality. In theoretical knowledge, the dimension of reality that is attained by understanding and truth is realized already in the object of thought, apart from our thought of it. Our minds use the data of experience as a bridge to cross into reality in order to grasp the more-than-given truth of things.

Practical knowledge also depends on experience, and of course the intelligibility of *good* and the truth attained by practical knowledge are not given in experience. But the practical mind is unlike the theoretical mind in this way, that the intelligibility and truth of practical knowledge do not attain a dimension of reality already lying beyond the data of experience ready to be grasped through them. No, practical knowledge refers to a quite different dimension of reality, one which is indeed a possibility through the given, but a possibility which must be realized, if it is to be actual at all, through the mind's own direction. The theoretical mind crosses the bridge of the given to raid the realm of being; there the mind can grasp everything, actual or possible, whose reality is not conditioned upon the thought and action of man. The practical mind also crosses the bridge of the given, but it bears gifts into the realm of being, for practical knowledge contributes that whose possibility, being opportunity, requires human action for its realization.

When I think that there should be more work done on the foundations of specific theories of natural law, such a judgment is practical knowledge, for the mind requires that the situation it is considering change to fit its demands rather than the other way about. Practical reason does not have its truth by conforming to what it knows, for what practical reason knows does not have the being and the definiteness it would need to be a standard for intelligence. Only after practical reason thinks does the object of its thought begin to be a reality. Practical reason has its truth by anticipating the point at which something that is possible through human action will come into conformity with reason, and by directing effort toward that point.[18]

[18] S. T. 1, q. 79, a. 11; 1-2, q. 57, aa. 4-5; 3, q. 78, a. 5, c.; IN LIBROS ETHICORUM ARISTOTELIS lib. 1, lect. 1. See JOHN E. NAUS, S.J., THE NATURE OF THE PRACTICAL INTELLECT ACCORDING TO SAINT THOMAS AQUINAS (Roma, 1959).

Now if practical reason is the mind functioning as a principle of action, it is subject to all the conditions necessary for every active principle. One of these is that every active principle acts on account of an end. An active principle is going to bring about something or other, or else it would not be an active principle at all. It is necessary for the active principle to be oriented toward that something or other, whatever it is, if it is going to be brought about. This orientation means that at the very beginning an action must have definite direction and that it must imply a definite limit.[19]

There are two ways of misunderstanding this principle that make nonsense of it. One is to suppose that it means anthropomorphism, a view at home both in the primitive mind and in idealistic metaphysics. If every active principle acts *on account of an end,* so the anthropomorphic argument goes, then it must act *for the sake of a goal,* just as men do when they act with a purpose in view. But the generalization is illicit, for acting with a purpose in view is only one way, the specifically human way, in which an active principle can have the orientation it needs in order to begin to act. The other misunderstanding is common to mathematically minded rationalists, who project the timelessness and changelessness of formal system onto reality, and to empiricists, who react to rationalism without criticizing its fundamental assumptions. The rationalist, convinced that reality is unchangeable, imagines that the orientation present in an active principle must not refer to real change, and so he reduces this necessary condition of change to the status of something which stably is at a static moment in time. What is at a single moment, the rationalist thinks, is stopped in its flight, so he tries to treat every relationship of existing beings to their futures as comparisons of one *state* of affairs to another. It is the rationalistic assumptions in the back of his mind that make the empiricist try to reduce dispositional properties to predictions about future states.

Let us imagine a teaspoonful of sugar held over a cup of hot coffee. It is nonsense to claim that the solubility of the sugar merely means that it will dissolve. Solubility is true of the sugar *now,* and yet this property is unlike those which characterize the sugar as to what it actually is already, for solubility characterizes it with reference to a process in which it is *suited to be* involved. The orientation of an active principle toward an end is like that — it is a real aspect of dynamic reality. In the case of practical reason, acting on account of an end is acting for the sake of a goal, for practical reason is an active principle that is conscious and self-determining. Purpose in view, then, is a real aspect of the dynamic reality of practical reason, and a necessary condition of reason's being practical.

But must every end involve good? In some senses of the word "good" it need not. Not all outcomes are ones we want or enjoy. But if "good" means that toward which each thing tends by its own intrinsic principle of orientation, then for each active principle the end on account of which it acts also is a good for it, since nothing can act with definite orientation except on account of something toward which, for its part, it tends. And, in fact, *tendency toward* is more basic than *action on account of,* for every active principle tends toward what its

[19] S. T. 1-2, q. 1, a. 2; Summa contra gentiles 3, c. 2.

action will bring about, but not every tending ability goes into action on account of the object of its tendency.

Practical reason, therefore, presupposes good. In its role as active principle the mind must think in terms of what can be an object of tendency. In other terms the mind can think, but then it will not set out to cause what it thinks. If the mind is to work toward unity with what it knows by conforming the known to itself rather than by conforming itself to the known, then the mind must think the known under the intelligibility of the good, for it is only as an object of tendency and as a possible object of action that what is to be through practical reason has any reality at all. Thus it is that good first falls within the grasp of practical reason just as being first falls within the unrestricted grasp of the mind.

In the fifth paragraph Aquinas enunciates the first principle of practical reason and indicates the way in which other evident precepts of the law of nature are founded on it.

He points out, to begin with, that the first principle of practical reason must be based on the intelligibility of good, by analogy with the primary theoretical principle which is based on the intelligibility of being. The intelligibility of good is: *what each thing tends toward.* This formula is a classic expression of what the word "good" means.[20] Of course, we often mean more than this by "good," but any other meaning at least includes this notion. "Good is what each thing tends toward" is not the formula of the first principle of practical reason, then, but merely a formula expressing the intelligibility of good.[21] "First principle of practical reason" and "first precept of the law" here are practically synonyms; their denotation is the same, but the former connotes derived practical knowledge while the latter connotes rationally guided action.

Until the object of practical reason is realized, it exists only in reason and in the action toward it that reason directs. Now since any object of practical reason first must be understood as an object of tendency, practical reason's first step in effecting conformity with itself is to direct the doing of works in pursuit of an end. Just as the principle of contradiction expresses the definiteness which is the first condition of the objectivity of things and the consistency which is the first condition of theoretical reason's conformity to reality, so the first principle of practical reason expresses the imposition of tendency, which is the first condition of reason's objectification of itself, and directedness or intentionality,

---

20 ETHICA NICOMACHEA bk. 1, 1094b3.

21 D. O'Donoghue, *The Thomist Conception of Natural Law,* 22 IRISH THEOLOGICAL QUARTERLY 101 (also, p. 107, n. 3) (1955), holds that Aquinas means that "Good is what all things tend toward" is the first principle of practical reason, and so Fr. O'Donoghue wishes to distinguish this from the first precept of natural law. However, Aquinas actually says: "Et ideo primum principium in ratione practica est quod fundatur supra rationem boni, quae est, *Bonum est quod omnia appetunt.*" S. T., 1-2, q. 94, a. 2, c. Fr. O'Donoghue must read "quae" as if it refers to "primum principium," whereas it can only refer to "rationem boni." The *primum principium* is identical with the first precept mentioned in the next line of text, while the *ratio boni* is not a principle of practical reason but a quasi definition of "good," and as such a principle of understanding. The principle of contradiction is likewise founded on the *ratio* of being, but no formula of this *ratio* is given here.

which is the first condition for conformity to mind on the part of works and ends. A sign that intentionality or directedness is the first condition for conformity to practical reason is the expression of imputation: "He acted on purpose, intentionally."

In forming this first precept practical reason performs its most basic task, for it simply determines that whatever it shall think about must at least be set on the way *to something* — as it must be if reason is to be able to think of it practically. Any other precept will add to this first one; other precepts determine precisely what the direction is and what the starting point must be if that direction is to be followed out. The first principle of practical reason thus gives us a way of interpreting experience; it provides an outlook in terms of which subsequent precepts will be formed, for it lays down the requirement that every precept must prescribe, just as the first principle of theoretical reason is an awareness that every assent posits. Awareness of the principle of contradiction demands consistency henceforth; one must posit in assenting, and thought cannot avoid the position assenting puts it in. Similarly, the establishment of the first precept of practical reason determines that there shall be direction henceforth. In prescribing we must direct, and we cannot reasonably avoid carrying out in reality the intelligibility which reason has conceived.

Practical reason, equipped with the primary principle it has formed, does not spin the whole of natural law out of itself. It is true that if "natural law" refers to all the general practical judgments reason can form, much of natural law can be derived by reasoning. But reason needs starting points. And it is with these starting points that Aquinas is concerned at the end of the fifth paragraph. The primary precepts of practical reason, he says, concern the things-to-be-done that practical reason naturally grasps as human goods, and the things-to-be-avoided that are opposed to those goods.

Of course, we can be conditioned to enjoy perverse forms of indulgence, but we could not be conditioned if we did not have, not only at the beginning but also as an underlying constant throughout the entire learning process, an inclination toward pleasure. We can be taught the joys of geometry, but that would be impossible if we did not have natural curiosity that makes us appreciate the point of asking a question and getting an answer. Our personalities are largely shaped by acculturation in our particular society, but society would never affect us if we had no basic aptitude for living with others. The infant learns to feel guilty when mother frowns, because he *wants* to please.

Practical reason's task is to direct its object toward the point at which it will attain the fullness of realization that is conceived by the mind before it is delivered into the world. But in directing its object, practical reason presides over a development, and so it must use available material. Hence the basic precepts of practical reason accept the possibilities suggested by experience and direct the objects of reason's consideration toward the fulfillments taking shape in the mind.

In the sixth paragraph Aquinas explains how practical reason forms the basic principles of its direction. The primary precept provides a point of view from which experience is considered. Within experience we have tendencies which make themselves felt; they point their way toward appropriate objects. These inclinations are part of ourselves, and so their objects are human goods. Before intelligence enters, man acts by sense spontaneity and learns by sense experience. Thus in experience we have a basis upon which reason can form patterns of action that will further or frustrate the inclinations we feel.

We can reflect upon and interpret our experience in a purely theoretical frame of mind. In that case we simply observe that we have certain tendencies that are more or less satisfied by what we do. However, when the question concerns what we shall do, the first principle of practical reason assumes control and immediately puts us in a nontheoretical frame of mind. This principle provides us with an instrument for making another kind of sense of our experience. The object of a tendency becomes an objective which is to be imposed by the mind as we try to make the best of what faces us by bringing it into conformity with practical truth. Practical reason is mind directed to direct and it directs as it can. But it can direct only toward that for which man can be brought to act, and that is either toward the objects of his natural inclinations or toward objectives that derive from these. If practical reason ignored what is given in experience, it would have no power to direct, for what-is-to-be cannot come from nothing. The direction of practical reason presupposes possibilities on which reason can get leverage, and such possibilities arise only in reflection upon experience. The leverage reason gets on these possibilities is expressed in the basic substantive principles of natural law.

At the beginning of paragraph six Aquinas seems to have come full circle, for the opening phrase here, "good has the intelligibility of end," simply reverses the last phrase of paragraph four: "end includes the intelligibility of good." There is a circle here, but it is not vicious; Aquinas is clarifying, not demonstrating. In the fourth paragraph he is pointing out that the need for practical reason, as an active principle, to think in terms of end implies that its first grasp on its objects will be of them as good, since any objective of action must first be an object of tendency. Now in the sixth paragraph he is indicating the basis on which reason primarily prescribes as our natural inclinations suggest. Is reason merely an instrument in the service of nature, accepting what nature indicates as good by moving us toward it? No, the derivation is not direct, and the position of reason in relation to inclination is not merely passive. Using the primary principle, reason reflects on experience in which the natural inclinations are found pointing to goods appropriate to themselves. But why does reason take these goods as its own? Not because they are given, but because reason's good, which is intelligible, contains the aspect of end, and the goods to which the inclinations point are prospective ends. Reason prescribes according to the order of natural inclinations because reason directs to possible actions, and the possible patterns of human action are determined by the natural inclinations, for man cannot act on account of that toward which he has no basis for affinity in his inclinations.

The seventh and last paragraph of Aquinas's response is very rich and interesting, but the details of its content are outside the scope of this paper. Here Aquinas indicates how the complexity of human nature gives rise to a multiplicity of inclinations, and these to a multiplicity of precepts. It is noteworthy that in each of the three ranks he distinguishes among an aspect of nature, the inclination based upon it, and the precepts that are in accordance with it. Nature is not natural law; nature is the given from which man develops and from which arise tendencies of ranks corresponding to its distinct strata. These tendencies are not natural law; the tendencies indicate possible actions, and hence they provide reason with the point of departure it requires in order to propose ends. The precepts of reason which clothe the objects of inclinations in the intelligibility of ends-to-be-pursued-by-work — these precepts *are* the natural law. Thus natural law has many precepts which are unified in this, that all of these precepts are ordered to practical reason's achievement of its own end, the direction of action toward end.

II

There is one obvious difference between the two formulae, "Do good and avoid evil," and "Good is to be done and pursued, and evil is to be avoided." That difference is the omission of *pursuit* from the one, the inclusion of it in the other. The mistaken interpretation of Aquinas's theory of natural law overlooks the place of final causality in his position and restricts the meaning of "good" and "evil" in the first principle to the quality of moral actions. In this section I wish to clarify this point, and the lack of "prosequendum" in the non-Thomistic formula is directly relevant.

We have seen how important the conception of end, or final causality, is to Aquinas's understanding of natural law. Practical reason understands its objects in terms of good because, as an active principle, it necessarily acts on account of an end. Practical reason prescribes precisely in view of ends. The first precept is that all subsequent direction must be in terms of intelligible goods, i.e., ends toward which reason can direct.

Nevertheless, a theory of natural law, such as I sketched at the beginning of this paper, which omits even to mention final causality, sometimes has been attributed to Aquinas. Thus to insure this fundamental point, it will be useful to examine the rest of the treatise on law in which the present issue arises.

In defining law, Aquinas first asks whether law is something belonging to reason. His response, justly famous for showing that his approach to law is intellectualistic rather than voluntaristic, may be summarized as follows. The end is the first principle in matters of action; reason orders to the end; therefore, reason is the principle of action. The principle in action is the rule of action; therefore, reason is the rule of action. The rule of action binds; therefore, reason binds. But binding is characteristic of law; therefore, law pertains to reason.[22] From this argument we see that the notion of end is fundamental to Aquinas's conception of law, and the priority of end among principles of action is the most basic reason why law belongs to reason.

In the next article, Aquinas adds another element to his definition by asking

[22] S. T. 1-2, q. 90, a. 1, c.

whether law always is ordained to the common good. His response is that law, as a rule and measure of human acts, belongs to their principle, reason. But in reason itself there is a basic principle, and the first principle of practical reason is the ultimate end. Since the ultimate end is a common good, law must be ordained to the common good.[23] What is noteworthy here is Aquinas's assumption that the first *principle* of practical reason is the last *end*. The good of which practical reason prescribes the pursuit and performance, then, primarily is the last end, for practical reason cannot direct the possible actions which are its objects without directing them to an end.

Thus we see that final causality underlies Aquinas's conception of what law is. But it is central throughout the whole treatise. In the treatise on the Old Law, for example, Aquinas takes up the question whether this law contains only a single precept. His response is that since precepts oblige, they are concerned with duties, and duties derive from the requirements of an end. Hence it belongs to the very intelligibility of precept that it direct to an end. Since the Old Law directs to a single end, it is one in this respect; but since many things are necessary or useful to this end, precepts are multiplied by the distinction of matters that require direction.[24] Again, what is to be noticed in this response is that Aquinas's whole understanding of law clearly depends on final causality. Obligation is a strictly derivative concept, with its origin in ends and the requirements set by ends.[25] If natural law imposes obligations that good acts are to be done, it is only because it primarily imposes with rational necessity that an end must be pursued.

In his youthful commentary on Lombard's *Books of Sentences*, Aquinas goes so far as to consider the principles of practical reason — which he already compares to the principles of demonstrations — to be so many innate natural ends.[26] He remarks that the habit of these ends is synderesis, which is the habit of the principles of the natural law.[27] Hence in this early work he is saying that the natural law is precisely the ends to which man is naturally inclined insofar as these ends are present in reason as principles for the rational direction of action.

Later in the same work Aquinas explicitly formulates the notion of the law of nature for the first time in his writings. Why are the principles of practical reason called "natural law"? Precisely because man knows the intelligibility of end and the proportion of his work to end. Suitability of action is not to a static nature, but to the ends toward which nature inclines. Evil is not explained ultimately by opposition to law, but opposition to law by unsuitability of action to end. This early treatment of natural law is saturated with the notion of end.[28]

So far as I have been able to discover, Aquinas was the first to formulate the primary precept of natural law as he did. Lottin informs us that already with

---

[23] S.T. 1-2, q. 90, a. 2, c.

[24] *Id.* at q. 99, a. 1, c.

[25] See Stevens, *op. cit. supra* note 8, at 202-205.

[26] SUPER LIBROS SENTENTIARUM PETRI LOMBARDI bk. 3, d. 33, q. 2, a. 4, q'la. 4, c. (ed. Mardonnet-Moos, Paris, 1929-1947).

[27] See LOTTIN, *op. cit. supra* note 3, at 68-73.

[28] SUPER LIBROS SENTENTIARUM PETRI LOMBARDI bk. 4, d. 33, q. 1, a. 1, c. (in ST. THOMAS, 7 OPERA, Purma ed., 1852-1873).

Stephen of Tournai, around 1160, there is a definition of natural law as an innate principle for doing good and avoiding evil.[29] While this is a definition rather than a formulation of the first principle, it is still interesting to notice that it does not include *pursuit*. In fact, several authors to whom Lottin refers seem to think of natural law as a principle of choice; and if the good and evil referred to in their definitions are properly objects of choice, then it is clear that their understanding of natural law is limited to its bearing upon moral good and evil — the value immanent in action — and that they simply have no idea of the relevance of good as end — a principle of action that transcends action.[30] William of Auxerre's position is particularly interesting. He not only omits any mention of end, but he excludes experience from the formation of natural law, so that the precepts of natural law seem to be for William pure intuitions of right and wrong.[31]

Thus it is clear that Aquinas emphasizes end as a principle of natural law. But it is also clear that the end in question cannot be identified with moral goodness itself.

To begin with, Aquinas specifically denies that the ultimate end of man could consist in morally good action. Moral action, and that upon which it immediately bears, can be directed to ulterior goods, and for this very reason moral action cannot be the absolutely ultimate end.[32] Moreover, Aquinas expressly identifies the principles of practical reason with the ends of the virtues preexisting in reason. Prudence is concerned with moral actions which are in fact means to ends, and prudence directs the work of all the moral virtues.[33] Hence the principles of natural law, in their expression of ends, transcend moral good and evil as the end transcends means and obstacles.

This transcendence of the goodness of the end over the goodness of moral action has its ultimate metaphysical foundation in this, that the end of each creature's action can be an end for it only by being a participation in divine goodness. The goodness of God is the absolutely ultimate final cause, just as the power of God is the absolutely ultimate efficient cause.[34] This end, of course, does not depend for realization on human action, much less can it be identified with human action. But moral good and evil are precisely the inner perfection or privation of human action. Hence the end transcends morality and provides an extrinsic foundation for it. This point is of the greatest importance in Aquinas's treatise on the end of man. Aristotle identifies the end of man with virtuous activity,[35] but Aquinas, despite his debt to Aristotle, sees the end of man as the *attainment* of a good. The good in question is God, who altogether transcends human activity. Hence an end for Aquinas has two inseparable aspects — what is attained and the attainment of it. But if these must be distinguished, the end is rather in what is attained than in its attainment.[36]

[29] Lottin, *op. cit. supra* note 3, at 16, n. 1.
[30] *Id.* at 17-18; cf. p. 108, lines 17-27.
[31] *Id.* at 35, n. 2.
[32] SUMMA CONTRA GENTILES 3, ch. 34 (ed. C. Pera, P. Murc, P. Caramello, Turin, 1961).
[33] S. T. 2-2, q. 47, a. 6, c.
[34] SUMMA CONTRA GENTILES 3, chs. 18-19.
[35] ETHICA NICOMACHEA bk. 1, 1098^{a}17.
[36] S. T. 1-2, qq. 1-5, esp. q. 2, a. 7.

Nor should it be supposed that the end's transcendence over moral virtue is a peculiarity of the supernatural end. Natural law does not direct man to his supernatural end; in fact, it is precisely because it is inadequate to do so that divine law is needed as a supplement.[37] Or, to put the same thing in another way, not everything contained in the Law and the Gospel pertains to natural law, because many of these points concern matters supernatural.[38] And yet, as we have seen, the principles of natural law are given the status of ends of the moral virtues.

An attentive reading of the last two paragraphs of the response examined above would be by itself sufficient for our present point. The goods in question are objects of man's natural inclinations. These goods are not primarily works that are to be done. Rather, the works are means to ulterior ends: reason grasps the objects of the natural inclinations as goods and so as things-to-be-pursued by work. The works obviously are means to the goods. And what are the objects of the natural inclinations? Not merely morally good acts, but such substantive goods as self-preservation, the life and education of children, and knowledge.

Some interpreters mistakenly ask whether the word "good" in the first principle has a transcendental or an ethical sense.[39] The issue is a false one, for there is no question of extending the meaning of "good" to the amplitude of the transcendentals convertible with "being." The very text clearly indicates that Aquinas is concerned with good as the object of practical reason; hence the goods signified by the "good" of the first principle will be *human* goods. It must be so, since the good pursued by practical reason is an objective of *human* action. But to grant this point is not at all to identify the good in question with moral value, for this particular category of value by no means exhausts human goods. The preservation of human life is certainly a human good. The act which preserves life is not the life preserved; in fact, they are so distinct that it is possible for the act that preserves life to be morally bad while the life preserved remains a human good.

The failure to keep this distinction in mind can lead to chaos in normative ethics. But more important for our present purpose is that this distinction indicates that the good which is to be done and pursued should not be thought of as exclusively the good of moral action. The pursuit of the good which is the end is primary; the doing of the good which is the means is subordinate. The good which is the end is the principle of moral value, and at least in some respects this principle transcends its consequence, just as *being* in a certain respect is a principle (of beings) that transcends even the most fundamental category of beings.[40]

---

37 S. T. 1-2, q. 91, a. 4.

38 *Id.* at q. 94, a. 4, ad 1.

39 E.g., Schuster, *op. cit. supra* note 8, at 54-55.

40 Although too long a task to be undertaken here, a full comparison of Aquinas's position to that of Suarez would help to clarify the present point. See WALTER FARRELL, O.P., THE NATURAL MORAL LAW ACCORDING TO ST. THOMAS AND SUAREZ 103-155 (Ditchling, 1930). We at least can indicate a few significant passages. Suarez offers a number of formulations of the first principle of the natural law. He manages to treat the issue of the unity or multiplicity of precepts without actually stating the primary precept. DE

Aquinas, of course, never takes a utilitarian view of the value of moral action. But his alternative is not the deontologism that assigns to moral value and the perfection of intention the status of absolutes. Utilitarianism is an inadequate ethical theory partly because it overly restricts natural inclination, for it assumes that man's sole determinate inclination is in regard to pleasure and pain. Aquinas recognizes a variety of natural inclinations, including one to act in a rational way.[41] Among the *ends* toward which the precepts of the natural law direct, then, moral value has a place. Hence good human action has intrinsic worth, not merely instrumental value as utilitarianism supposes. Moreover, because the end proposed by the utilitarians is only a psychic state and because utilitarians also hold a mechanistic theory of causality, utilitarianism denies that any kind of action is intrinsically good or bad. Thus actions are considered good or bad only by virtue of extrinsic consequences. Aquinas, on the contrary, understands human action not merely as a piece of behavior but as an object of choice. He considers a whole range of nonpsychic realities to be human goods. His theory of causality does not preclude an intrinsic relationship between acts and ends. Hence he holds that some species of acts are bad in themselves, so that they cannot become good under any circumstances.[42]

In sum, the mistaken interpretation of Aquinas's theory of natural law sup-

---

LEGIBUS II, 8, 2. Previously, however, he had given the principle in the formulation: "Good is to be done and evil avoided." *Id.* at II, 7, 2. But there and in a later passage, where he actually mentions *pursuit,* he seems to be repeating received formulae. The formula (*Id.* at II, 15, 2) referring to pursuit subordinates it to the avoidance of evil: *"Evil is to be avoided and good is to be pursued."* Perhaps Suarez's most personal and most characteristic formulation of the primary precept is given where he discusses the scope of natural law. There his formulation of the principle is specifically moralistic: *The upright is to be done and the wrong avoided.* (*Id.* at II, 7, 5: *"Honestum est faciendum, pravum vitandum."*) Here too Suarez suggests that this principle is just one among many first principles; he juxtaposes it with *Do unto others as you would have them do unto you.* As to the end, Suarez completely separates the notion of it from the notion of law. He considers the goodness and badness with which natural law is concerned to be the moral value of acts in comparison with human nature, and he thinks of the natural law itself as a divine precept that makes it possible for acts to have an *additional* value of conformity with the law. *Id.* at II, 6. In neither aspect is the end fundamental. For this reason, too, the natural inclinations are not emphasized by Suarez as they are by Aquinas. Although Suarez mentions the inclinations, he does so while referring to Aquinas. *Id.* at II, 5, 1-2. Before the end of the very same passage Suarez reveals what he really thinks to be the foundation of the precepts of natural law. It is not the inclinations but the quality of actions, a quality grounded on their own "intrinsic character and immutable essence, which in no way depend upon any extrinsic cause or will, any more than does the essence of other things which in themselves involve no contradiction." (We see at the beginning of paragraph 5 that Suarez accepts this position as to its doctrine of "the intrinsic goodness or turpitude of actions," and so as an account of the *foundation* of the natural law precepts, although he does not accept it as an account of natural law, which he considers to require an act of the divine will.) Later Suarez interprets the place of the inclinations in Aquinas's theory. As Suarez sees it, the inclinations are not principles in accordance with which reason forms the principles of natural law; they are only the matter with which the natural law is concerned. *Id.* at II, 8, 4. In other words, in Suarez's mind Aquinas only meant to say of the inclinations that they are subject to natural law. This interpretation simply ignores the important role we have seen Aquinas assign the inclinations in the formation of natural law.

[41] S. T. 1-2, q. 94, a. 3, c.

[42] *Id.* at q. 18, aa. 6-7; SUPER LIBROS SENTENTIARUM PETRI LOMBARDI bk. 2, d. 40, q. 1, aa. 1-2.

poses that the word "good" in the primary precept refers solely to moral good. In fact, it refers primarily to the end which is not limited to moral value. The mistaken interpretation inevitably falls into circularity; Aquinas's real position shows where moral reasoning can begin, for it works from transmoral principles of moral action. The mistaken interpretation offers as a principle: *Do good.* It subsumes actions under this imperative, which limits the meaning of "good" to the good of action. Aquinas suggests as a principle: *Work in pursuit of the end.* This principle enables the good that is an end not only to illuminate but also to enrich with value the action by which it is attained.

III

The mistaken interpretation of Aquinas's theory suggests that law is essentially a curb upon action. Law is imagined as a command set over against even those actions performed in obedience to it. And of course it is much more opposed to wrong actions. In this section, I propose three respects in which the primary principle of practical reason as Aquinas understands it is broader in scope than this false interpretation suggests. A clearer understanding of the scope of natural law will further unfold the implications of the point treated in the last section; at the same time, it will be a basis for the fourth section.

The mistaken interpretation suggests that natural law is a set of imperatives whose form leaves no room to discriminate among degrees of force to be attached to various precepts. All precepts seem equally absolute; violation of any one of them is equally a violation of the law.

For Aquinas, however, natural law includes counsels as well as precepts. In other words, the first principle refers not only to the good which must be done, but also to the nonobligatory good it would be well to do.

In the article next after the one commented upon above, Aquinas asks whether the acts of all the virtues are of the law of nature. In his response he does not exclude virtuous acts which are beyond the call of duty. He does make a distinction: all virtuous acts as such belong to the law of nature, but particular virtuous acts may not, for they may depend upon human inquiry.[43]

Later, in treating the Old Law, Aquinas maintains that all the moral precepts of the Old Law belong to the law of nature, and then he proceeds to distinguish those moral precepts which carry the obligation of strict precept from those which convey only the warning of counsel.[44] Indeed, in treating natural law in his commentary on the *Sentences,* Aquinas carefully distinguishes between actions fully prohibited because they totally obstruct the attainment of an end and actions restricted because they are obstacles to its attainment. Lottin notices this point. Today, he says, we restrict the notion of law to strict obligations. But Aquinas took a broader view of it, for he understood law as a principle of order which embraces the whole range of objects to which man has a natural inclination. Consequently, when Aquinas wishes to indicate strict

[43] S. T. 1-2, q. 94, a. 3, c.
[44] *Id.* at q. 100, aa. 1-2.

obligation he often uses a special mode of expression to make this idea explicit.[45]

Suarez refers to the passages where Aquinas discusses the scope of the natural law. Although aware that Aquinas includes counsels as well as precepts in natural law, Suarez prefers to limit his concern to matters of strict obligation: "But we properly inquire concerning precepts."[46] It never occurs to Suarez to wonder why he himself narrows the scope Aquinas attributed to law.

The difference between the two points of view is no mystery. Aquinas thinks in terms of the end, and obligation is merely one result of the influence of an intelligible end on reasonable action. "Good" in the first principle, since it refers primarily to the end, includes within its scope not only what is absolutely necessary but also what is helpful, and the opposed evil includes more than the perfect contrary of the good. Like most later interpreters, Suarez thinks that what is morally good or bad depends simply upon the agreement or disagreement of action with nature, and he holds that the obligation to do the one and to avoid the other arises from an imposition of the will of God.[47] Hence "evil" in the first principle of natural law denotes only the actions which definitely disagree with nature, the doing of which is forbidden, and "good" denotes only the actions whose omission definitely disagrees with nature, the doing of which is commanded. An act which falls in neither of these categories is simply of no interest to a legalistic moralist who does not see that moral value and obligation have their source in the end.

Perhaps even more surprising is another respect in which the first practical principle as Aquinas sees it has a broader scope than is usually realized. "Every judgment of practical reason proceeds from naturally known principles."[48] The derivative is from the underived, the underivable principles. In practical reason it is self-evident precepts that are underivable, *natural* law. Not only virtuous and self-restrained men, but also vicious men and backsliders make practical judgments. Indeed, if evildoers lacked practical judgment they could not engage in human action at all.[49] It follows that practical judgments made in evil action nevertheless fall under the scope of the first principle of the natural law, and the word "good" in this principle must refer somehow to deceptive and inadequate human goods as well as to adequate and genuine ones.

It is important, however, to see the precise manner in which the principle, *Good is to be done and pursued,* still rules practical reason when it goes astray. "Good" is not merely a generic expression for whatever anyone may happen to want,[50] for if this were the case there would not be a single first principle but as many first principles as there are basic commitments, and each first principle would provide the major premise for a different system of rules. Still, if "good" denoted only moral goods, either wrong practical judgments could in no way

---

[45] LOTTIN, *op. cit. supra* note 3, at 75, points out that Aquinas will add to the expression "law of nature" a further word — e.g., "precept" — to express strict obligation.

[46] DE LEGIBUS II, 7, 11.

[47] *Id.* at II, 7.

[48] S. T. 1-2, q. 100, a. 1, c.

[49] See DE MALO q. 3, a. 9, ad 7.

[50] A. G. SERTILLANGES, O.P., LA PHILOSOPHIE MORALE DE SAINT THOMAS D'AQUIN 109 (Paris, 1946), seems to fall into this mistaken interpretation.

issue from practical reason or the formula we are examining would not in reality express the first principle of practical reason.

Aquinas mentions this point in at least two places. In one he explains that for practical reason, as for theoretical reason, it is true that false judgments occur. Yet even though such judgments originate in first principles, their falsity is not due to the principles so much as to the bad use of the principles.[51] Similarly he explains in another place that the power of first principles is present in practical misjudgment, yet the defect of the judgment arises not from the principles but from the reasoning through which the judgment is formed.[52]

Just as the principle of contradiction is operative even in false judgments, so the first principle of practical reason is operative in wrong evaluations and decisions. First principles do not sanction error, but of themselves they set only limited requirements. As a disregard of the principle of contradiction makes discourse disintegrate into nonsense, so a disregard of the first principle of practical reason would make action dissolve into chaotic behavior. The insane sometimes commit violations of both principles within otherwise rational contexts, but erroneous judgment and wrong decision need not always conflict with first principles. Hence first principles must be supplemented by other principles and by a sound reasoning process if correct conclusions are to be reached. The first practical principle, as we have seen, requires only that what it directs have intentionality toward an intelligible purpose. The possible underived ends are indicated by the fundamental inclinations which ground appropriate precepts. "Good" in the first principle refers with priority to these underived ends, yet by itself the first principle cannot exclude ends presented in other practical judgments even if their derivation is unsound.

Assumption of a group of principles inadequate to a problem, failure to observe the facts, or error in reasoning can lead to results within the scope of first principles but not sanctioned by them. The first precept directs us to direct our action toward ends within human power, and even immoral action in part fulfills this precept, for even vicious men act for a human good while accepting the violation of more adequate human good. The good which is the object of pursuit can be the principle of the rational aspects of defective and inadequate efforts, but the good which characterizes morally right acts completely excludes wrong ones.

After observing these two respects in which the mistaken interpretation unduly restricts the scope of the first principle of practical reason, we may note also that this principle as Aquinas understands it is not merely a principle of imperative judgments. Rather, it is primarily a principle of actions. Aquinas thinks of law as a set of principles of practical reason related to *actions themselves* just as the principles of theoretical reason are related to *conclusions*.[53] Law is not a constraint upon actions which originate elsewhere and which would flourish better if they were not confined by reason. Law, rather, is a source of actions. Law makes human life possible. Animals behave without law, for they live by

---

[51] De veritate q. 16, a. 2, ad 6.
[52] Super Libros Sententiarum Petri Lombardi bk. 2, d. 39, q. 3, a. 1, ad 1.
[53] S. T. 1-2, q. 90, a. 1, ad 2.

instinct without thought and without freedom. Man cannot begin to act as man without law.

The first precept does not say what we *ought* to do in contradistinction to what we *will* do. Opposition between the direction of reason and the response of will can arise only subsequent to the orientation toward end expressed in the first principle. One whose practical premise is, "Pleasure is to be pursued," might reach the conclusion, "Adultery ought to be avoided," without this prohibition becoming a principle of his action. But the first principle of practical reason cannot be set aside in this manner, as we have seen, and so it cannot represent an imposition contrary to the judgment that actually informs our choice.[54] The first principles of practical reason are a source not only for judgments of conscience but even for judgments of prudence; while the former can remain merely speculative and ineffectual, the latter are the very structure of virtuous action.[55]

Throughout history man has been tempted to suppose that wrong action is wholly outside the field of rational control, that it has no principle in practical reason. Naturalism frequently has explained away evildoing, just as some psychological and sociological theories based on determinism now do. No less subversive of human responsibility, which is based on purposive — and, therefore, rational — agency, is the existentialist notion that morally good and morally bad action are equally reasonable, and that a choice of one or the other is equally a matter of arational arbitrariness. Aquinas's understanding of the first principle of practical reason avoids the dilemma of these contrary positions. The first principle of morally good action is the principle of all human action, but bad action fulfills the requirement of the first principle less perfectly than good action does. If the first principle of practical reason were *Do morally good acts,* then morally bad acts would fall outside the order of practical reason; if *Do morally good acts* nevertheless were the first precept of natural law, and morally bad acts fell within the order of practical reason, then there would be a domain of reason outside natural law. However, since the first principle is *Good is to be done and pursued,* morally bad acts fall within the order of practical reason, yet the principles of practical reason remain identically the principles of natural law. More than correct principles are required, however, if reason is to reach its appropriate conclusion in action toward the good.

The mistaken interpretation of Aquinas's theory of natural law, with its restrictive understanding of the scope of the first practical principle, suggests that before reason comes upon the scene, that whole broad field of action lies open before man, offering no obstacles to his enjoyment of an endlessly rich and satisfying life, but that cold reason with its abstract precepts successively marks section after section of the field out of bounds, progressively enclosing the submissive subject in an ever-shrinking pen, while those who act at the promptings of uninhibited spontaneity range freely over all the possibilities of life. The

[54] For the notion of judgment forming choice see *id.* at q. 13, a. 3.

[55] De veritate q. 17, a. 2; S. T. 2-2, q. 47, a. 6. For a comparison between judgments of prudence and those of conscience see my paper, *The Logic of Moral Judgment,* 26 Proceedings of the American Catholic Philosophical Association 67-76, esp. p. 70, n. 7 (1962).

true understanding of the first principle of practical reason suggests on the contrary that the alternative to moral goodness is an arbitrary restriction upon the human goods which can be attained by reasonable direction of life. The first principle of practical reason directs toward ends which make human action possible; by virtue of the first principle are formed precepts that represent every aspect of human nature. Together these principles open to man all the fields in which he can act; rational direction insures that action will be fruitful and that life will be as productive and satisfying as possible. Whatever man may achieve, his action requires at least a remote basis in the tendencies that arise from human nature. Similarly, actual being does not eliminate unrealized possibilities by demanding that they be not only self-consistent but also consistent with what already is; rather, it is partly by this demand that actual being grounds possibility.

IV

The mistaken interpretation of Aquinas's theory of natural law considers natural law precepts to be a set of imperatives. In this section I wish to show both that the first principle does not have primarily imperative force and that it is really prescriptive. The distinction between these two modes of practical discourse often is ignored, and so it may seem that to deny imperative force to the primary precept is to remove it from practical discourse altogether and to transform it into a merely theoretical principle. Hence I shall begin by emphasizing the practical character of the principle, and then I shall proceed to clarify its lack of imperative force.[56]

[56] Even those interpreters who usually can be trusted tend to fall into the mistake of considering the first principle of practical reason as if it were fundamentally theoretical. Lottin, for instance, suggests that the first assent to the primary principle is an act of theoretical reason. At first it appears, he says, simply as a truth, a translation into moral language of the principle of identity. A formula of the first judgment of practical reason might be "That which is good, is good — *i.e.*, desirable," or "The good is that which is to be done, the evil is that which is to be avoided." ODON LOTTIN, O.S.B., 1 PRINCIPES DE MORALE 22, 122 (Louvain, 1946).

Significant in these formulations are the "that which (ce qui)" and the double "is," for these expressions mark the removal of gerundive force from the principal verb of the sentence. Thus Lottin makes the precept appear as much as possible like a theoretical statement expressing a peculiar aspect of the good — namely, that it is the sort of thing that demands doing. Sertillanges also tries to understand the principle as if it were a theoretical truth equivalent to an identity statement. Among his formulations are: "That which is to be done is to be done," and: "The good is an end worth pursuing." SERTILLANGES, *op. cit. supra* note 50, at 102, 109.

Many other authors could be cited: e.g., Stevens, *op. cit. supra* note 8, at 199. They wish to show that the first principle really is a truth, that it really is self-evident. This desire leads them to forget that they are dealing with a precept, and so they try to treat the first principle of practical reason as if it were theoretical. They ignore the peculiar character of practical truth and they employ an inadequate notion of self-evidence. There is a constant tendency to reduce practical truth to the more familiar theoretical truth and to think of underivability as if it were simply a matter of conceptual identity. These same difficulties underlie Maritain's effort to treat the primary precept as a truth necessary by virtue of the predicate's inclusion of the intelligibility of the subject rather than the reverse. NEUF LEÇONS SUR LES NOTIONS PREMIÈRES DE LA PHILOSOPHIE MORALE 158-160 (Paris, 1951).

Maritain recognizes that "is to be" cannot be derived from the meaning of "good" by analysis. Thinking that the practical principle must be equivalent to a theoretical

The good which is the subject matter of practical reason is an objective possibility, and it could be contemplated. But in that case the principle that will govern the consideration will be that agents necessarily act for ends, not that good is to be done and pursued. For Aquinas, practical reason not only has a peculiar subject matter, but it is related to its subject matter in a peculiar way, for practical reason introduces the order it knows, while theoretical reason adopts the order it finds.[57] The object of the practical intellect is not merely the actions men perform, but the *good which can be directed to realization, precisely insofar as that is a mode of truth*.[58] Practical reason is related to the movement of action as a principle, not as a consequence.[59]

Laws are formed by practical reason as principles of the actions it guides just as definitions and premises are formed by theoretical reason as principles of the conclusions it reaches.[60] A law is an expression of reason just as truly as a statement is, but a statement is an expression of reason asserting, whereas a law is an expression of reason prescribing.[61] The primary principle of practical reason, as we have seen, eminently fulfills these characterizations of law. The principle is formed because the intellect, assuming the office of active principle, accepts the requirements of that role, and demands of itself that in directing action it must really direct. The precept that good is to be sought is genuinely a principle of action, not merely a point of departure for speculation about human life.

The principles of practical reason belong to a logical category quite different from that of theoretical statements: precepts do not inform us of requirements; they express requirements as directions for action. The point of saying that good is to be pursued is not that good is the sort of thing that has or is this peculiar property, obligatoriness — a subtle mistake with which G. E. Moore launched contemporary Anglo-American ethical theory. The point rather is to issue the fundamental directive of practical reason. "Is to be" is the copula of the first practical principle, not its predicate; the gerundive is the mode rather than the matter of law. To know the first principle of practical reason is not to reflect upon the way in which goodness affects action, but to know a good in such a way that in virtue of that very knowledge the known good is ordained toward realization.

But if it is significant that the first principle of practical reason is really a precept and not merely a theoretical statement, it is less clear but equally important that this principle is not an imperative, as the mistaken interpretation of Aquinas's theory considers it to be.

---

truth, he suggests that the opposite relationship obtains. The theoretical character of the principle for Maritain is emphasized by his first formulation of it as a metaphysical principle applicable to all good and all action. Only secondarily does he consider it a moral principle applicable to human good and free action. The difference between the two formulations is only in the content considered, not at all in the mode of discourse.

57 In libros Ethicorum ad Nichomachum, lib. 1, lect. 1.

58 S. T. 1, q. 79, a. 11, ad 2: *"Objectum intellectus practici est bonum ordinabile ad opus, sub ratione veri."*

59 *Id.* at ad 1.

60 S. T. 1-2, q. 90, a. 1, ad 2.

61 *Id.* at q. 92, a. 2, c.

Of course, so far as grammar alone is concerned, the gerundive form can be employed to express an imperative. However, Aquinas explicitly distinguishes between an imperative and a precept expressed in gerundive form. The imperative not only provides rational direction for action, but it also contains motive force derived from an antecedent act of the will bearing upon the object of the action. The prescription expressed in gerundive form, on the contrary, merely offers rational direction without promoting the execution of the work to which reason directs.[62]

To recognize this distinction is not to deny that law can be expressed in imperative form. At the beginning of his treatise on law, Aquinas refers to his previous discussion of the imperative.[63] Human and divine law are in fact not merely prescriptive but also imperative, and when precepts of the law of nature were incorporated into the divine law they became imperatives whose violation is contrary to the divine will as well as to right reason.

Nevertheless, the first principle of practical reason hardly can be understood in the first instance as an imperative. As we have seen, it is a self-evident principle in which reason prescribes the first condition of its own practical office. On the one hand, the causality of God is not a principle evident to us. On the other hand, the operation of our own will is not a condition for the prescription of practical reason; the opposite rather is the case.

Aquinas's theological approach to natural law primarily presents it as a participation in the eternal law. This fact has helped to mislead many into supposing that natural law must be understood as a divine imperative. Of course, Aquinas holds that God's will is prior to the natural law, since the natural law is an aspect of human existence and man is a free creation of God. But Aquinas does not describe natural law as eternal law passively received in man; he describes it rather as a participation in the eternal law. This participation is necessary precisely insofar as man shares the grand office of providence in directing his own life and that of his fellows.[64] Every participation is really distinct from that in which it participates — a principle evidently applicable in this case, for the eternal law *is* God while the law of nature is a set of precepts.

From man's point of view, the principles of natural law are neither received from without nor posited by his own choice; they are naturally and necessarily known, and a knowledge of God is by no means a condition for forming self-evident principles, unless those principles happen to be ones that especially

---

[62] *Id.* at q. 17, a. 1.

[63] *Id.* at q. 90, a. 1, *sed contra,* ad 3; q. 91, a. 2, ad 2. But these references should not be given too much weight, since they refer to the article previously cited in which the distinction is made explicitly. Although arguments based on what the text does not say are dangerous, it is worth noticing that Aquinas does not define law as *an imperative for the common good,* as he easily could have done if that were his notion, but as *an ordinance of reason for the common good etc. Id.* at q. 90, a. 4, c.

[64] O'Donoghue (*op. cit. supra* note 21) tries to clarify this point, and does in fact help considerably toward the removal of misinterpretations. Still, his work is marked by a misunderstanding of practical reason, so that precept is equated with imperative (p. 95) and will is introduced in the explanation of the transition from theory to practice. (p. 101) FARRELL (*op. cit. supra* note 40), by a full and careful comparison of Aquinas's and Suarez's theories of natural law, clarifies the essential point very well, without suggesting that natural law is human legislation, as O'Donoghue seems to think.

concern God.[65] Moreover, Aquinas simply does not understand the eternal law itself as if it were an imposition of the divine will upon creation;[66] and even if he did understand it in this way, no such imposition would count for human judgment except in virtue of a practical principle to the effect that the divine will deserves to be followed. Without such a foundation God might *compel behavior* but he could never *direct human action.*

Nor is any operation of our own will presupposed by the first principles of practical reason. Of course we do make judgments concerning means in accordance with the orientation of our intention toward the end. But our willing of ends requires knowledge of them, and the directive knowledge *prior to* the natural movements of our will is precisely the basic principles of practical reason. At any rate this is Aquinas's theory. He maintains that there is no willing without prior apprehension.[67] Moreover, the basic principle of desire, natural inclination in the appetitive part of the soul, is consequent upon prior apprehension, natural knowledge.[68] For the will, this natural knowledge is nothing else than the first principles of practical reason.[69] The precepts of natural law, at least the first principle of practical reason, must be antecedent to all acts of our will. There is nothing surprising about this conclusion so long as we understand law as intelligence ordering (directing) human action toward an end rather than as a superior ordering (commanding) a subject's performance.

The theory of law is permanently in danger of falling into the illusion that practical knowledge is merely theoretical knowledge plus force of will. This is exactly the mistake Suarez makes when he explains natural law as the natural goodness or badness of actions plus preceptive divine law.[70]

The way to avoid these difficulties is to understand that practical reason really does not know in the same way that theoretical reason knows. For practical

---

[65] The point has been much debated despite the clarity of Aquinas's position that natural law principles are self-evident; Stevens, *op. cit. supra* note 8, at 201, n. 23, provides some bibliography.

[66] Eternal law is "the exemplar of divine wisdom, as directing all actions and movements" of created things in their progress toward their end. S. T. 1-2, q. 93, a. 1, c. Those who misunderstand Aquinas's theory often seem to assume, as if it were obvious, that law is a transient action of an efficient cause physically moving passive objects; for Aquinas, law always belongs to reason, is never considered an efficient cause, and cannot possibly terminate in motion. By their motion and rest, moved objects participate in the perfection of agents, but a caused order participates in the exemplar of its perfection by form and the consequences of form — consequences such as inclination, reason, and the precepts of practical reason. See FARRELL, *op. cit. supra* note 40, at ch. 4, esp. pp. 98-103.

[67] S. T. 1, q. 82, a. 4, ad 3.

[68] SUPER LIBROS SENTENTIARUM PETRI LOMBARDI bk. 4, d. 33, q. 1, a. 1, ad 9.

[69] *Id.* at bk. 2, d. 39, q. 2, a. 2, ad 2.

[70] DE LEGIBUS, II, 7; FARRELL, *op. cit. supra* note 40, at 147-155. Even excellent recent interpreters of Aquinas tend to compensate for the speculative character they attribute to the first principle of practical reason by introducing an act of our will as a factor in our assent to it. Lottin, for example, balances his notion that we first assent to the primary principle as to a theoretical truth with the notion that we finally assent to it with a consent of the will. Only free acceptance makes the precept fully operative. (*Op. cit. supra* note 56, at 24.) Even so accurate a commentator as Stevens introduces the inclination of the will as a ground for the prescriptive force of the first principle. (*Op. cit. supra* note 8, at 202-203: "The intellect manifests this truth formally, and commands it as true, for its own goodness is seen to consist in a conformity to the natural object and inclination of the will.")

reason, to know is to prescribe. This is why I insisted so strongly that the first practical principle is not a theoretical truth. Once its real character as a precept is seen, there is less temptation to bolster the practical principle with will, and so to transform it into an imperative, in order to make it relevant to practice. Indeed, the addition of will to theoretical knowledge cannot make it practical. This point is precisely what Hume saw when he denied the possibility of deriving *ought* from *is*.

In an interesting passage in an article attacking what he mistakenly considered to be Aquinas's theory of natural law, Kai Nielsen discussed this point at some length.[71] He begins by arguing that normative statements cannot be derived from statements of fact, not even from a set of factual statements which comprise a true metaphysical theory of reality. He points out that from "God wills x," one cannot derive "x is obligatory," without assuming the non-factual statement: "What God wills is obligatory." He proceeds to criticize what he takes to be a confusion in Thomism between fact and value, a merging of disparate categories which Nielsen considers unintelligible. But over and above this objection, he insists that normative discourse, insofar as it is practical, simply cannot be derived from a mere consideration of facts. In this part of the argument, Nielsen clearly recognizes the distinction between theoretical and practical reason on which I have been insisting. He concludes his argument by maintaining that the factor which differentiates practical discourse is the presence of decision within it.

To such criticism it is no answer to argue that empiricism makes an unnatural cleavage between facts and values.[72] I have tried above to explain how Aquinas understands *tendency toward good* and *orientation toward end* as a dimension of all action. If every active principle acts on account of an end, then at a certain time in spring from the weather and our knowledge of nature we can conclude that the roses ought to be blooming soon. Similarly, from the truth of the premises and the validity of the reasoning we can say that the conclusion ought to be true. And from the unique properties of the material and the peculiar engineering requirements we can deduce that titanium ought to be useful in the construction of supersonic aircraft. But to get moral principles from metaphysics, it is not from the *is* of nature to the *ought* of nature that one must go. This illation is intelligible to anyone except a positivist, but it is of no help in explaining the origin of moral judgments. Moreover, it is no solution to argue that one can derive the "ought" of moral judgment from the "is" of ethical evaluation: "This act is virtuous; therefore, it ought to be done." Not even Hume could object to such a deduction. Precisely the point at issue is this, that from the agreement of actions with human nature or with a decree of the divine will, one cannot derive the prescriptive sentence: "They ought to be done."

71 *Op. cit. supra* note 11, at 63-68.

72 Vernon Bourke, *Natural Law, Thomism — and Professor Nielsen,* 5 NATURAL LAW FORUM 118-119 (1960), in part has recourse to this kind of argument in his response to Nielsen. Although Bourke is right in noticing that Nielsen's difficulties partly arise from his positivism, I think Bourke is mistaken in supposing that a more adequate metaphysics could bridge the gap between theory and practice.

Aquinas knew this, and his theory of natural law takes it for granted. *Good is to be done and pursued, and evil is to be avoided,* together with the other self-evident principles of natural law, are not derived from any statements of fact. They are principles. They are not derived from any statements at all. They are not derived from prior principles. They are underivable.

The intellect is not theoretical by nature and practical only by education. To be practical is natural to human reason. Reason is doing its own work when it prescribes just as when it affirms or denies. The basic precepts of natural law are no less part of the mind's original equipment than are the evident principles of theoretical knowledge. *Ought* requires no special act legitimatizing it; *ought* rules its own domain by its own authority, an authority legitimate as that of any *is*. Of course, one cannot form these principles if he has no grasp upon what is involved in them, and such understanding presupposes experience. However, one does not derive these principles from experience or from any previous understanding. Aquinas's position is not: we conclude that certain kinds of acts should be done because they would satisfy our inclinations or fulfill divine commands. His position is: we are capable of thinking for ourselves in the practical domain because we naturally form a set of principles that make possible all of our actions. Practical principles do not become practical, although they do become more significant for us, if we believe that God wills them. Nonprescriptive statements believed to express the divine will also gain added meaning for the believer but do not thereby become practical. For instance, that the universe is huge is given added meaning for one who believes in creation, but it does not on that account become a matter of obligation for him, since it remains a theoretical truth.

Of course, I must disagree with Nielsen's position that decision makes discourse practical. This view implies that human action ultimately is irrational, and it is at odds with the distinction between theoretical and practical reason. If practical reason were simply a conditional theoretical judgment together with verification of the antecedent by an act of appetite, then this position could be defended, but the first act of appetite would lack any rational principle.[73] However, the primary principle of practical reason is by no means hypothetical. It directs that good is to be done and pursued, and it allows no alternative within the field of action.[74] In fact, the practical acceptance of the antecedent of any conditional formulation directing toward action is itself an action that presupposes the direction of practical reason toward the good and the end. The prescription "Happiness should be pursued" is presupposed by the acceptance of the antecedent "If you wish to be happy," when this motive is proposed as a rational ground of moral action.

[73] Bourke does not call Nielsen to task on this point, and in fact (*id.* at 117) even seems to concur in considering practical reason hypothetical apart from an act of will, but Bourke places the will act in God rather than in our own decision as Nielsen does.

[74] The mere fact of decision, or the mere fact of feeling one of the sentiments invoked by Hume, is no more a basis for "ought" than is any other "is." Hume misses his own point — that "ought" *cannot* be derived — and Nielsen follows his master. If some practical principle is hypothetical because there is an alternative to it, only a practical principle (and ultimately a nonhypothetical practical principle) can foreclose the rational alternative.

But while I disagree with Nielsen's positive position on this point, I think that his essential criticism is altogether effective against the position he is attacking. If one supposes that principles of natural law are formed by examining kinds of action in comparison with human nature and noting their agreement or disagreement, then one must respond to the objection that it is impossible to derive normative judgments from metaphysical speculations. The invocation of a metaphysics of divine causality and providence at this point is no help, since such a metaphysics also consists exclusively of theoretical truths from which reason can derive no practical consequences. Of course, if man can know that God will punish him if he does not act in approved ways, then it does follow that an effective threat can be deduced from the facts. But no such threat, whether coming from God or society or nature, is prescriptive unless one applies to it the precept that horrible consequences should be avoided. I do not deny that the naked threat might become effective on behavior without reference to any practical principle. A threat can be effective by circumventing choice and moving to nonrational impulse. Such a derivation, however, is not at all concerned with the "ought"; it moves from beginning to end within the realm of "is."

V

The mistaken interpretation of Aquinas's theory of natural law considers the first principle to be a major premise from which all the particular precepts of practical reason are deduced. "Do good," together with "Such an action is good," leads deductively to "Do that action." If the first principle actually did function in this manner, all other precepts would be conclusions derived from it. As we have seen, however, Aquinas maintains that there are many self-evident principles included in natural law.

It would be easy to miss the significance of the nonderivability of the many basic precepts by denying altogether the place of deduction in the development of natural law. Aquinas holds that reason can derive more definite prescriptions from the basic general precepts.[75]

Consequently, that Aquinas does not consider the first principle of the natural law to be a premise from which the rest of it is deduced must have a special

---

75 S. T. 1-2, q. 91, a. 3, c.; q. 94, a. 4, c. However, a horror of deduction and a tendency to confuse the process of rational derivation with the whole method of geometry has led some Thomists — notably, Maritain — to deny that in the natural law there are rationally deduced conclusions. MAN AND THE STATE 91. Maritain points out that Aquinas uses the word "quasi" in referring to the prescriptive conclusions derived from common practical principles. He does not notice that Aquinas uses "quasi" in referring to the principles themselves; they are "in ratione naturali quasi per se nota." (S. T., 1-2, q. 100, a. 3, c. "Quasi" need not carry the connotation of *fiction* which it has in our usage; it is appropriate in the theory of natural law where a vocabulary primarily developed for the discussion of theoretical knowledge is being adapted to the knowledge of practical reason.) Maritain attributes our knowledge of definite prescriptions of natural law to a nonconceptual, nonrational knowledge by inclination or connaturality. (*Op. cit.* at 90-92. NAUS, *op. cit. supra* note 18, at 142-150, provides a compact and accurate treatment of the true sense of "knowledge by connaturality" in Aquinas; however, he unfortunately concludes his discussion by suggesting that the alternative to such knowledge is theoretical.) In fact, Aquinas does not mention inclinations in connection with the derived precepts, which are the ones Maritain wants to explain. Rather, Aquinas relates the

significance. Why, exactly, does Aquinas treat this principle as a *basis* for the law and yet maintain that there are many self-evident principles corresponding to the various aspects of man's complex nature? What difference would it make if these principles were viewed as so many conclusions derived from the conjunction of the premises "The human good is to be sought" and "Such and such an action will promote the human good" — premises not objectionable on the ground that they lead to the derivation of imperatives that was criticized above?

Lottin proposed a theory of the relationship between the primary principle and the self-evident principles founded on it. The basic principle is not related to the others as a premise, an efficient cause, but as a form which differentiates itself in its application to the different matters directed by practical reason. Reason transforms itself into this first principle, so that the first principle must be understood simply as the imposition of rational direction upon action.[76] Lottin's way of stating the matter is attractive, and he has been followed by others. Sertillanges, for example, apparently was influenced by Lottin when he remarked that the *good* in the formulations of the first principle is "a pure form, as Kant would say."[77] Stevens also seems to have come under the influence, as when he states, "The first judgment, it may be noted, is first not as a first, explicit psychologically perceived judgment, but as the basic form of all practical judgments."[78]

I think it would be a mistake, however, to suppose that the first principle is formal in a way that would separate it from and contrast it with the content of knowledge. Aquinas assumes no a priori forms of practical reason. The first principle of practical reason is itself formed through reflexive judgment; this precept is an object of the intellect's act. To hold otherwise is to deny the analogy Aquinas maintains between this principle and the first principle of theoretical reason, for the latter is clearly a content of knowledge.

It is difficult to think about principles. We tend to substitute the more familiar application for the less familiar principle in itself. Usually we do not need to think principles by themselves; we call them to mind only to put them to work. Principles that serve as premises are formed with some self-consciousness. Because such principles are not equally applicable to all contents of experience, even though they can be falsified by none, we can at least imagine them not to be true. Practical principles, other than the first one, always can be rejected in practice, although it is unreasonable to do so. We easily form the mistaken generalization that all explicit judgments actually formed by us must meet such conditions. Hence it is understandable that the denial of the status of premise to the first practical principle should lead to the supposition that it is a pure form — a denial to it of any status as an object of self-conscious knowledge. However, to deny the one status is not to suppose the other, for premises and

---

basic precepts to the inclinations and, as we have seen, he does this in a way which does not confuse inclination and knowledge or detract from the conceptual status or intelligible objectivity of the self-evident principles of practical reason.

[76] LOTTIN, *op. cit. supra* note 3, at 79.

[77] SERTILLANGES, *op. cit. supra* note 50, at 109.

[78] Stevens, *op. cit. supra* note 8, at 200.

a priori forms do not exhaust the modes of principles of rational knowledge. The first principle may not be known with genetic priority, as a premise, but it is still first known. It enters our practical knowledge explicitly if not distinctly, and it has the status of a self-evident principle of reason just as truly as do the precepts enjoining self-preservation and other natural goods. The fact that the mind cannot but form the primary precept and cannot think practically except in accordance with it does not mean that the precept exercises its control covertly. But it requires something extraordinary, such as philosophic reflection, to make us bring into the focus of distinct attention the principles of which we are conscious whenever we think.

It also is a mistake to suppose that the primary principle is equivalent to the precept, *Reason should be followed,* as Lottin seems to suggest. For Aquinas, right reason is reason judging in accordance with the whole of the natural law. Reason does not regulate action by itself, as if the mere ability to reason were a norm. Rather, it regulates action precisely by applying the principles of natural law.[79] Only one among the natural inclinations of man is that based on his rational nature to act according to rational direction. Like other inclinations, this one is represented by a specific self-evident precept of the natural law, a kind of methodological norm of human action.[80] As a particular norm, the injunction to follow reason has specific consequences for right action. One of these is that differences between practical judgments must have an intelligible basis — the requirement that provides the principle for the generalization argument and for Kantian ethics. However, the direction of action by reason, which this principle enjoins, is not the sole human good. It is not equivalent, for example, to self-preservation, and it is as much a mistake to identify one particular precept as another with the first principle of practical reason. In order to equate the requirement of rationality with the first principle of practical reason one would have to equate the value of moral action with human good absolutely. That is what Kant does, and he is only being consistent when he reduces the status of end in his system to a motive extrinsic to morality except insofar as it is identical with the motivation of duty or respect for the law.

As I explained above, the primary principle is imposed by reason simply because as an active principle reason must direct according to the essential condition for any active principle — it must direct toward an end. In issuing this basic prescription, reason assumes its practical function; and by this assumption reason gains a point of view for dealing with experience, a point of view that leads all its further acts in the same line to be preceptive rather than merely speculative. The first practical principle is like a basic tool which is inseparable from the job in which the tool is used; it is the implement for making all the other tools to be used on the job, but none of them is equivalent to it, and so the basic tool permeates all the work done in that job.[81]

---

[79] S. T. 1-2, q. 91, a. 3, ad 2; q. 95, a. 2, c.; SUPER LIBROS SENTENTIARUM PETRI LOMBARDI bk. 2, d. 42, q. 2, a. 5.

[80] S. T. 1-2, q. 94, a. 4, c.

[81] See QUAESTIO DISPUTATA DE ANIMA, a. 5, for the notion of first principles as instruments which the agent intellect employs in making what follows actually intelligible.

Because Aquinas explicitly compares the primary principle of practical reason with the principle of contradiction, it should help us to understand the significance of the relationship between the first principle and other evident principles in practical reason if we ask what importance attaches to the fact that theoretical knowledge is not deduced from the principle of contradiction, which is only the first among many self-evident principles of theoretical knowledge.

The principle of contradiction could serve as a common premise of theoretical knowledge only if being were the basic essential characteristic of beings, if being were *what* beings are — that is, if being were a definite kind of thing. Otherwise (and in truth), to know that something is a being, and so subsumable under being, presupposes the knowledge which that subsumption applies to it.[82] The principle of contradiction expresses the definiteness of things, but to be definite is not to be anything. To be definite is a condition of being anything, and this condition is fulfilled by whatever a thing happens to be. The principle of contradiction does not exclude from our thoughts interesting and otherwise intelligible things; it grounds the possibility of thinking in reference to anything at all. But the principle of contradiction can have its liberalizing effect on thought only if we do not mistakenly identify being with a certain kind of being — the move which would establish the first principle as a deductive premise.

Something similar holds with regard to the first practical principle. Of course, "good" in the primary precept is not a transcendental expression denoting all things. Nevertheless, it is like a transcendental in its reference to all human goods, for the pursuit of no one of them is the unique condition for human operation, just as no particular essence is the unique condition for being. The first practical principle does not limit the possibilities of human action; by determining that action will be for an end this principle makes it possible.

None of the inclinations which ground specific precepts of the natural law, not even the precept that action should be reasonable, is a necessary condition for all human action. If the "good" of the first principle denoted precisely the object of any single inclination, then the object of another inclination either would not be a human good at all or it would qualify as a human good only insofar as it was subordinate to the object of the one favored inclination. Philosophers have constructed their systems of ethics weighted in favor of one or another good precisely for this reason. Yet the first principle of practical reason does provide a basic requirement for action merely by prescribing that it be intentional, and it is in the light of this requirement that the objects of all the inclinations are understood as human goods and established as objectives for rational pursuit.

The gap between the first principle of practical reason and the other basic principles, indicated by the fact that they too are self-evident, also has significant consequences for the acts of the will which follow the basic principles of practical reason. The will necessarily tends to a single ultimate end, but it does not necessarily tend to any definite good as an ultimate end. We may say that the will

[82] GERARD SMITH, S.J., & LOTTIE H. KENDZIERSKI, 1 THE PHILOSOPHY OF BEING: METAPHYSICS 2-8 (New York, 1961), make the most of such dialectic in order to show the transcendence of being over essence.

naturally desires happiness, but this is simply to say that man cannot but desire the attainment of that good, whatever it may be, for which he is acting as an ultimate end.[83] The desire for happiness is simply the first principle of practical reason directing human action from within the will informed by reason.

Because the specific last end is not determined for him by nature, man is able to make the basic commitment which orients his entire life. The human will naturally is nondetermined precisely to the extent that the precept that good be pursued transcends reason's direction to any of the particular goods that are possible objectives of human action.[84] Yet man's ability to choose the ultimate concrete end for which he shall act does not arise from any absurdity in human nature and its situation. This ability has its immediate basis in the multiplicity of ends among various syntheses of which man can choose, together with the ability of human reason to think in terms of end as such. The latter ability is evidenced in the first principle of practical reason, and it is the same ability which grounds the ability to choose. Man's ability to choose his ultimate end has its metaphysical ground in the spiritual nature of man himself, on the one hand, and in the transcendent aspect that every end, as a participation in divine goodness, necessarily includes, on the other.

Hence the *good* of the primary principle has a certain transcendence, or at least the possibility of transcendence, in relation to the objects of all the inclinations, which are the goods whose pursuit is prescribed by the other self-evident principles. Only by virtue of this transcendence is it possible that the end proposed by Christian faith, heavenly beatitude, which is supernatural to man, should become an objective of genuine human action — that is, of action under the guidance of practical reason. If the first principle of practical reason restricted human good to the goods proportionate to nature, then a supernatural end for human action would be excluded. The relation of man to such an end could be established only by a leap into the transrational where human action would be impossible and where faith would replace natural law rather than supplement it. A first principle of practical reason that prescribes only the basic condition necessary for human action establishes an order of such flexibility that it can include not only the goods to which man is disposed by nature but even the good to which human nature is capable of being raised only by the aid of divine grace.

Thus the status Aquinas attributes to the first principle of practical reason is not without significance. This principle is not an imperative demanding morally good action, and imperatives — or even definite prescriptions — cannot be derived from it by deduction. Precisely because the first principle does not specify the direction of human action, it is not a premise in practical reasoning; other principles are required to determine direction. At the same time, the

[83] That the basic precepts of practical reason lead to the natural acts of the will is clear: SUPER LIBROS SENTENTIARUM PETRI LOMBARDI bk. 2, d. 39, q. 2, a. 2, ad 2. See also Van Overbeke, *loc. cit. supra* note 3. JOSEPH BUCKLEY, S.M., MAN'S LAST END 164-210 (St. Louis and London, 1950), shows that there is no natural determinate last end for man.

[84] G. P. Klubertanz, S.J., *The Root of Freedom in St. Thomas's Later Works,* 42 GREGORIANUM 709-716 (1961), examines how Aquinas relates reason and freedom. It is this "later" resolution that I am supposing here.

transcendence of the primary precept over all definite goods allows the conjunction of reason with freedom. On this open ground man can accept faith without surrendering his rationality. This situation reveals the lowliness and the grandeur of human nature. Man's lowliness is shown by the very weakness of reason's first principle; by itself this precept cannot guide action, and the instigation of natural inclination and the inspiration of faith are needed to develop an adequate law for human life. Man's grandeur is shown by the transcendence of this same principle; it evokes man's possibilities without restricting them, thus permitting man to determine by his own choice whether he shall live for the good itself or for some particular good.

GERMAIN G. GRISEZ

[10]

NATURAL LAW RECONSIDERED[1]

NEIL MACCORMICK*

I

'Natural Law' is a term so rich in ambiguities as to be rivalled only by 'Positivism'. So often have we had grand set piece encounters between natural law and positivism that we have misled ourselves into thinking that there is some single central issue at stake upon which only two views are on offer, one being right and the other one wrong—the only question being, *which?* My task in this paper is to review a book, John Finnis's *Natural Law and Natural Rights* (Clarendon Press, Oxford, 1980), whose merits include the high virtue of setting the record right upon that matter. There are at least as many ways of being a natural lawyer as there are of being a positivist, and it needs to be seen which is defensible, if any. There is accordingly no single 'positivism v natural law' question.

If we asked why we had ever thought there was, the answer would lead us back to the work of David Hume. Hume himself has a most attractive (to me) view of natural law. In the evolution of human societies, it is natural that certain conventions, laws, and institutions develop, covering such matters as restraints upon violence, restraints on sexual dealings, protection of possessions, and restraints upon various forms of deceit and breach of faith; it is natural that there develop agencies with the function of judging upon alleged breaches of such primary requirements of conduct. Considering the circumstances of human existence, and the fundamental traits of human beings, it seems justifiable to sustain and elaborate upon the laws and institutions we have thus naturally developed. We have reason to have and preserve these laws and institutions. In the common sense of the term 'reasonable', it is reasonable to have these.

Yet on the other hand, as Hume said, reasonable though such laws and institutions are, reasonable though it is to observe and sustain them, 'human reason' is not a faculty which reveals them or establishes their 'truth'. Our assent to such laws and institutions is in the last analysis rooted in 'the passions' as Hume called them, 'emotions' as Alf Ross's translators have called them. This last analysis is a complex and difficult analysis, according to Hume. Hume certainly would not have agreed with Ross's early assertion that to speak of justice is functionally equivalent to beating upon the table.

*Regius Professor of Public Law in the University of Edinburgh.

1 An earlier version of this paper was read to seminars in the Universities of Copenhagen, Aarhus and Lund. Its appearance enables me to record my gratitude to my hosts, Professors Blegvad, Jorgensen and Peczenik and Mr. Jes Bjarup, and to the Danish Social Science Research Council; also to Mr. M. J. Machan and Professor A. M. Honoré, for helpful criticisms.

Certainly, what Hume and Ross both wanted to deny was that 'rationalism' provides a theoretical answer to the way in which we argue about, and perhaps solve, moral questions. ''Tis not contrary to reason', said Hume 'to prefer the destruction of the world to the scratching of my little finger'. Putting his point in more modern terms, we might liken the reasoning faculty of the human mind to an extremely sophisticated and well programmed computer. When faced with a choice between two actions *a* or not-*a*, we can feed our data on these particular acts into the computer. The print-out informs us that doing *a* will result in the destruction of the whole human species, and that doing not-*a* will result in the scratching of the agent's little finger. So much for reasoning and computation, says Hume. We still have a choice to make and to justify. We cannot go back to the same computer and ask it the further question whether one should prefer *a* to not-*a*. Knowing what we know, we still must choose. The reasonable choice, of course, is not-*a* in this case. But it is not our ***reasoning*** faculty which tells us so. It is not a job for the computer.

If Hume was correct about that (and I think he was), he cut the ground from under the most influential and important school of thought of the preceding two centuries. The gloss put upon the traditional theories of natural law by writers such as Suarez, Grotius, Pufendorf and Locke said that basic principles of right action were deliverances of reason. The rationalists further claimed that more particular prescriptions could be derived by reasoning from the basic principles. In Locke's hands, this argument had the further consequence that one could derive by reasoning from basic rational principles a set of propositions about the natural rights of man. He summed these up as 'rights to life, liberty, and estate', all of them varieties of 'property' in the wide sense Locke gave that term.

The proper function of human laws and human governments according to Locke was to declare these rights in clear terms, and to give them effective protection. A necessary corollary was that no act of human legislation could be valid as law if it infringed natural rights. In such a case, the subjects whose rights were infringed had a right to revolt. What they revolted against was no valid law. It was an abuse of power, an *Unrecht* as our German friends would say. Such reasoning gave a new force and standing to the Augustinian maxim: *Injusta Lex, nulla lex*.

Hume's attack on this view has had many followers, not all of them perhaps conscious of the exact debt they owe to Hume. We may number among them in British thought Bentham, Austin, John Stuart Mill, A. V. Dicey and H. L. A. Hart; in Scandinavian writing, Hägerström, Lundstedt, Olivecrona and Ross; in Germanic, Kant in a qualified sense and Kelsen in a clearer one. The birth of modern legal positivism certainly owes a great deal to Hume's denial of the rationalist theory and its logical consequences. Thus in its simplest and most radical forms, legal positivism stems from a simple pair of simple negations: there is not a conceptual but a contingent connection between morality and positive law, and neither moral principles nor positive laws are deliverances of reason. To that is added an affirmation: human laws derive from, and are reflections of, human social practices, and they provide us with common social standards of conduct. As a corollary to the original negations: they are not derived from nor are they restricted by *a priori* rational requirements about human conduct.

So influential has been the stream of thought derived from Hume that we have come to think of 'natural law' as a theory based on two simple theorems, which many of us reject as fallacious. The two theorems are:

(i) Morality comprises observance of rationally demonstrable principles of conduct; and

(ii) Whatever be the other requirements of legal validity, no law which controverts these rationally demonstrable principles of conduct is valid or binding as law.

II

So much for the historical origins of one view of natural law theory. My main topic here, however, is a restatement of another view of natural law. It is a restatement which denies that the two stated theorems are central doctrines of the natural law tradition. It is a restatement which therefore denies that the positivist critique of these two propositions constitutes an effective denial of the true doctrine of natural law. It is a restatement which claims to incorporate and re-evaluate the general insights of modern so-called legal positivism, but to transcend them, and to reinstate them within a properly elaborated theory of natural law. It is the restatement made by John Finnis in his recent *Natural Law and Natural Rights*.

Finnis's basic exemplars are not the rationalist natural lawyers. They are Aristotle and St. Thomas Aquinas. From reflection on their work he sets up the proposition that there are certain basic goods for human beings. These are objective values in the sense that every reasonable human being must assent to their value as objects of human striving. He lists seven such basic objective values. His list comprises:

(1) *Life:* 'the first basic value, corresponding to the drive for self-preservation, is the value of life. The term "life" here signifies every aspect of vitality . . . which puts a human being in good shape for self-determination . . .
. . . we should include in this category the transmission of life by procreation of children . . .'

(2) *Knowledge:* a preference for true over false belief, corresponding to that basic drive which we call curiosity, a drive which leads us to reject any celebration of self-proclaimed ignorance or superstition. Finnis has in view here 'knowledge, considered as desirable for its own sake, not merely instrumentally'.

(3) *Play:* which Finnis claims to be 'a large and irreducible element in human culture': he adds that 'each one of us can see the point of engaging in performances which have no point beyond the performance itself, enjoyed for its own sake'.

(4) *Aesthetic experience:* the appreciation of sensible beauty, whether in human artefacts and performances, or in unadorned nature.

(5) *Sociability or Friendship:* implying minimally sociability in a human community; implying also collaboration between individual and individual in cases where each pursues an end of his/her own; but implying above all the fullest and most exalted forms of friendship. This last, 'involves acting for the sake of one's friend's purposes, one's friend's well being' because full friendship involves treating what is good for one's friend as being good for oneself. 'To be in a relationship of friendship with at least one other person is a fundamental form of good, is it not?' asks Finnis rhetorically.

(6) *Practical Reasonableness:* defined by Finnis as 'the basic good of being able to bring one's intelligence to bear effectively (in practical reasoning that issues in action) on the problems of choosing one's actions and life-style and shaping one's own character. Negatively, this involves that one has a measure of effective freedom; positively, it involves that one seeks to bring an intelligent . . . order into one's own actions and habits and practical attitudes'.

(7) 'What we summarily and lamely call "*Religion*"' (italics added). 'Is it reasonable', asks Finnis, 'to deny that it is, at any rate, peculiarly important to have thought reasonably (and, where possible, correctly) about [the] questions of the origins of cosmic order and of human freedom and reason—whatever the answer turns out to be . . .?'

To these seven basic values of life, knowledge, play, aesthetic experience, friendship (sociability, at least), practical reasonableness and religion, all other values and virtues are subordinate. They are *modes* of realizing or participating in basic goods. The basic goods are goods in themselves. Other values and virtues are forms of participation in basic goods. The character of each basic good is such that indefinitely many people can on indefinitely many occasions participate in it in an indefinite number of ways. Evil in the world is essentially negative. It comprises an attack upon or a total absence of or indifference to one or more of the basic goods.

How do we know that basic goods are good? Most men indeed have basic drives or inclinations towards them, but the factual existence of such basic drives does not prove their value, says Finnis. His view is that they are self-evident. Rather as the fundamental principles of theoretical reasoning—e.g. basic principles of logic—are not open to proof since they are presupposed in anything that counts as a proof, so, for example, the proposition that knowledge is a good is not open to strict proof. But, unprovable though that proposition is, anyone who sets out to deny this seriously cuts the ground from under his own feet. If I set out to demonstrate the falsity of a philosophical proposition, e.g. the proposition that knowledge is a form of good, I thereby evince a concern to discriminate between truth and falsehood. I set myself the objective of knowing whether p is or is not true. My aim is avoidance of false belief, and the persuasion of others to reject a belief which I have shown to be false.

Every activity of serious and systematic inquiry has as its end the understanding and explanation of the subject matter. Such activities need no further or ulterior end to justify them. No doubt the 'applied sciences'—

technology—take knowledge as a means to other ends. Whatever the other ends may be in particular cases (perhaps enhancement of the value of life, as in medical research), knowledge is at least instrumentally good, but since some finding out is finding out for its own sake, those who engage in that cannot but hold it for good in itself.

Some might reply that philosophy is just for fun. It is a stimulating intellectual game. At least some of the time some of us see it that way, though probably not all of us all of the time. Sometimes we argue just for argument's sake, and very diverting that can be. But Finnis is ready with an answer for us if we take that as a point against him. His reply will be that there is more than one form of basic good, and that 'Play' is one of the forms he listed. So argument is either good as a form of play, or good as a means to knowledge, which is sometimes an end in itself and sometimes a means to other ends. And there is no reason why an exciting and interesting piece of pure research with possibly useful applied outcomes may not be good in all three ways; if in turn it involves the friendly collaboration of a team of workers, those pursuing it participate also in friendship as a further form of the good.

It does seem to me that, at least as to knowledge, Finnis has fairly made his point. That knowledge is an end worth pursuing is not provable or demonstrable. But, setting playfulness apart, no one can argue that it is not worth pursuing without thereby defeating his own case. Why should he or anyone else care to *know* that knowledge is not worth having unless, after all, at least that knowledge *is* worth having?[2]

If this 'retorsive argument' satisfies us, in the case of knowledge, that there is at least one case of a *telos* or end, participation in which gives an ultimate and underived justification for some of the things we do, there is a case for believing that there can be other such ends. Manifestly, not all that we do is aimed at knowledge for its own sake. But, if not, it must be aimed at something for its own sake, some form of completeness or wholeness which needs no ulterior justification. So, at least, Finnis tells us, the Aristotelian grounding of his case being plain. And he claims to have given us a list of basic justifying goods as orientations of practical activity.

In a sense, of course, he concedes Hume's point; not surprisingly, since Hume too had read his Aristotle. There is not even in principle some grand computer or superbrain which can demonstrate what ends are worthy of pursuit. Yet on the other hand Finnis denies what Hume asserts, that these goods which he identifies are grounded only in human 'passions' as Hume called them. Even allowing for Hume's distinction between violent, transient passions such as anger or sexual lust and calm passions, such as benevolence or a desire for self-preservation, Finnis will not accept that psychology provides the basic explanation for why we hold that some states of being are good in themselves. No doubt there has to be

2 I have myself advanced an essentially similar argument in the concluding chapter of my recent book *Legal Reasoning and Legal Theory* (Oxford 1978).

some psychological explanation in terms of basic drives or urges which accounts for men's engagement with and attachment to basic practical goods. But that is not what makes them what they are, simply and underivedly good.

III

This, you may say, is deep philosophical water, far from the shallows in which legal theorists properly sport themselves. What has it all to do with law?

Finnis's answer is that his theory of the good has everything to do with law. Practical reasonableness is one of the basic goods. Any human being who has achieved any degree of maturity and wisdom has come to appreciate however dimly that while there are goods which sufficiently and underivedly justify and make sense of practical activity, there is no one single *summum bonum*. The good is multiform and diverse. Hence the wise man seeks to achieve an ordered—not regimented—plan of life. He seeks a way of living which permits a varied and spontaneous participation in some reasonably achievable range out of all that is of real and lasting value.

Among the principles of practical reasonableness which his reflections must disclose to him is the principle that one ought to take one's part in a communal life. Only within society may humans find the conditions for pursuit of knowledge, for sustaining and regenerating human life and its enhancements, for friendly intercourse with others, for the more rewarding forms of play, and for those exalted forms of aesthetic experience such as symphonic music available only in circumstances of highly complex social collaboration and the specialization of talents which these circumstances allow. More than a rudimentary mode of participating in basic goods would not be open to a solitary savage. The worst and most unreasonably or unjustly organized of human societies would still offer better conditions than a Hobbesian, or even a Lockean, state of nature.

All the better can a just and well-organized form of community further for each and all of its members the chance to realize the good in their own lives (and since friendship and parental love are themselves forms of good, each person's realizing of the good in his own life includes realizing it for others in theirs). What is a just and well organized society is a question itself of practical reasonableness. Only given a substantial degree of freedom from restraints and inhibitions on what one may do can one act as a spontaneous and self-regulating being. Only a spontaneously self-regulating person can *participate* in the good. Again, since what is good is equally and unconditionally good in all its manifestations no practically reasonable person can claim that *his* good is better than others' good as such. Each, no doubt, has a prior responsibility for his own flourishing and that of his friends and family. But that priority of responsibility implies no priority of right. Hence a good society enables humans universally a full and equal opportunity to realize whatever seems to them their best life plan consistently with others having that same opportunity. This leads to the elaboration of a theory of justice, both commutative and distributive. I shall not here say more of Finnis's interesting theory of justice, fascinating though I find it; though I must in passing commend particularly his discussion of bankruptcy law as a practical instance of a distributive justice problem which the legal system tries to solve.

Now, we may turn our attention to that central idea of Thomist political philosophy, the common good. A practically reasonable man recognizes that human goods are realizable only in human communities, the better so the more communities achieve reasonable freedom for all their members and the more they approximate to justice. He therefore recognizes it as an obligation upon him to participate in the communal life and to commit himself to playing his part in forwarding the common good of that community. That is not to say that it can ever be uncontroversial what exactly favours the common good. Controversial as it is, it is nevertheless clear, says Finnis, that the common good is not a meaningless phrase. That is in the common good which keeps a community in such a condition that its members can in their own lives and in the lives of their friends participate as fully as may be in the basic goods of human existence. Difficult practical questions here arise concerning adjustment of means to ends, and adopting and implementing political strategies. We inveterately disagree about such matters. But we recognize in at least some of our political opponents a like concern to our own with the fostering of a conception of the common good. We are oriented to the same general objective even though we disagree how to realize it.

One thing which any healthy community requires is some common authority. Unless we all in common accede to the authority of some common code of conduct we cannot live together in community at all. And the implementation of any common code of conduct requires the institutionalization of some agency or agencies which adjudicate upon breaches of the common code. The more complex a political society becomes, the more rich and varied are the opportunities it presents for diverse manifestations of the good. But the more that is so, the more we face problems of coordination each with another. Hence the more sophisticated are the common public agencies we need for adjudication, administration, enforcement and amendment or enrichment of our common and authoritative code of social conduct. One may notice here a parallel with Niklas Luhmann's 'system theory' in sociology of law.

What I have just sketched as a necessity of the common good is a legal order. Law, for Finnis, is a primary requirement of the common good and thus a requirement of practical reasonableness. We may have dreams of an ideal mode of anarchy. But the waking reality which faces us is of our inability to achieve practical goods save in legally and politically ordered societies, which acknowledge the authority of law and the subordinate and derivative authority of those who make and administer that law.

No doubt what is worst is the corruption of what is best. The very existence of legal and political authority makes possible the perversion and corruption of those very values which it is the proper end and purpose of law to serve. The legal order's internal criteria of validity can be manipulated to secure the validity of measures hostile to justice and the common good. In that case acute problems of obedience arise, as none of us alive in this century need doubt. On the one hand, no man ought even under coercion to join in an attack on any of the basic values; on the other hand, violence and revolution themselves involve just that, and even an imperfect legal order is a better vehicle for securing the common good than is mere disorder and anarchy. Should one seek to improve a bad order from within, or reject it and attack it from without?

Here, says Finnis, there is no room for simple-minded formulae like *injusta lex, nulla lex*. There is no room to suppose that the validity of laws, as distinct from their binding force on men's consciences, depends in every case on some external moral criterion as well as the internal criteria stipulated by basic laws.

But, says he, it is only a caricature version of natural law, a caricature set up by positivists the better to knock it down, which maintains any such simple doctrine about the conceptual link between law and morality.

The focal or central meaning of our concept of law is of an authoritative common ordering of a community, aimed at facilitating the realization of the common good. Much that we recognize as law is at best an imperfect or fringe instance of law in its focal meaning. Some is even a mere corruption of law in that focal sense. But it is the focal meaning which has to be grasped; and there we find a direct link with the moral order; the link between means and end.

IV

Even the brief thumbnail sketch which appears above by way of summarizing Finnis's main theses is enough to indicate the richness and subtlety of his arguments. By advancing a case for 'natural law' rather than merely playing the historian of ideas, Finnis brings to present life a set of powerful and historically influential ideas. There is here a case to answer, a case indeed which must either be answered or be accepted. As stated, it is a case which has certain particularly impressive features, of which I should like to mention three for special present attention.

First, though Finnis rightly makes no bones about the fact of his own Christian commitment and Roman Catholic faith, his argument does not start out from any Christian or even theistic assumptions. In his thirteenth and last chapter, Finnis shows why anyone who has found the preceding twelve chapters convincing has then strong reason to take the further step of embracing belief in an Uncaused Cause of the universe in which we find ourselves, and belief in that Uncaused Cause as an intelligent, benevolent, and personate being. In that case, one should (he suggests) see reason to seek to enter into a friendly and even playful (compare Plato) relationship with that being—with God, in fact. Finnis's argument does not start from any principles of moral theology as premises; it proceeds towards them as conclusions, or, rather, corollaries of the strictly juristic and secular-ethical conclusions.

To speak personally (as one must in such matters) I found this a powerful and even moving strategy of argumentation. For such as myself, who start from a standpoint of religious agnosticism, *Natural Law and Natural Rights* demands no undue initial suspension of non-belief. Rather, it ends by weighing the scale of doubt at least rather more heavily than before against that non-belief.

This is not to deny that Finnis sets up some premises which bluntly challenge a broader sort of agnosticism. The really tough point to accept is Finnis's bold claim for the existence of objective values. Some of what we think good *is* good. It is good independently of anyone's thinking it so. Those modes of being which are good are good for every human being as such, and they are *self-evidently* good.

Some people hold as valuable-in-themselves items absent from Finnis's list—a politician (though happily not *every* politician), power for its own sake; a miser, money for its own sake; a hedonist, sexual and other sensual gratification for its own sake. Such people, Finnis must suppose, have a corrupt or distorted sense of values. What they treat as valuable in itself is not in fact valuable in itself. They are mistaken.

The real difficulty here, however, is not so much about the particular items present in, or about any particular items absent from, Finnis's list of basic goods. Whether one agrees with it for one's own part (as I largely do) or rejects it, the question is whether *any* list of goods *could in principle be* a list of *objective* goods. Here lies a profound problem—the problem posed by what J. L. Mackie in his *Ethics: Inventing Right and Wrong* calls the 'Argument from Queerness'. The queerness in question is metaphysical and ontological. What have we to postulate and believe in as the real state of the universe in order to believe in some order of 'goods' or 'values' which truly constitute objective values independent of anyone's acts of valuation or attitudes of appreciation? Can we do so without postulating and trying to believe in an ontology too queer for actual credence? To this problem of 'queerness' raised by Mackie (as, in effect, by Hume) I do not find any compellingly convincing resolution in Finnis. The Scottish verdict of 'not proven' must be returned in relation to the claim about self-evidence. This verdict happily indicates that it is not much easier or more satisfying to be a subjectivist or relativist in the mode of a Mackie or a Hume than to be an objectivist in the mode of a Finnis or a Thomas. Here is the ultimate, and for me unresolved, question in the whole business.

Whatever be its proper resolution, to have entertained the question has led me to what I think the second salient virtue of Finnis's book. That I find in the way in which he treats of practical reasoning. For this, he says, the foundation lies in values rather than in norms (rules, principles, or whatever). Practical reasoning is reasoning towards the realization of that which is of value; the soundness of practical reasoning depends on its practicality to that end; soundness in that sense depends on the observance in practical life of certain principles of rationality in thought; whether we follow such principles or not depends upon whether or not we value the form of life which is, in that sense, rational.

One can accept (as I in fact do) or even advance (as I in a way have done elsewhere) such a thesis as this about practical reasoning, even while disagreeing with Finnis about the 'objective' standing of values; or, *a fortiori*, if only in doubt about that point. Hence even those who doubt or disagree with Finnis's premiss about the objectivity of values will find much of worth and interest in the analysis Finnis provides of the structure and form of practical reasoning (all the more so if they happen to adhere to a view of what is good akin to Finnis's, however doubtful about the objective rectitude, far less self-evidence, of such a view).

Thirdly and finally among the salient virtues of Finnis's work, I single out for special mention his argument concerning 'focal meaning'. Finnis adopts from Hart, Waissman and Wittgenstein among contemporary thinkers the idea that our fundamental conceptual terms do not have sharp edges—they have clear, core cases and penumbral applications, they are open-textured in their usage, they apply to families of related phenomena rather than to sharply definable categories. Hence the attempt to clarify a concept like that of 'law' must, says Finnis, aim to show forth what are the characteristics of central instances of legal systems, not simply fringe, penumbral, doubtful or otherwise sub-standard instances. In adopting and adapting this general strategy for conceptual elucidation, Finnis then uses it in effect to throw back at Hart a challenge to his purely formal elucidation of the concept of a legal system in terms of a union of primary and secondary rules. Why not further refine our conception of the central case of a legal system by building in a *moral* element—legal orders have indeed such formal properties as Hart identifies but have they not also some orientation to some conscientiously pursued conception of a common good of the community thus ordered?

In posing this challenge Finnis is, as usual, careful to relate his argument not only to contemporary philosophy and jurisprudence, but also to the classical tradition of natural law as he sees it. His theory of 'focal meaning' is, he argues, as much derived from Aquinas and Aristotle as from Hart or Waissman. He gives persuasive examples from the writings of the former to show that precisely such an approach to elucidation of concepts was used by his classical exemplars as well as his distinguished contemporaries.

In this way Finnis enables himself to draw into his natural law framework much in modern analytical jurisprudence which he sees as wholly compatible with it. So far from dismissing the analytical tradition, he sees it as complementary to, and essential for giving detailed substance to, a thoroughly elaborated theory of natural law. Again it appears that one who does not go along with his claims as to the objectivity and self-evidence of basic goods or with his particular account of those goods can nevertheless derive much instruction from the *rapprochement* he achieves as between analytical jurisprudence and natural law thinking.

Those of us who remain sceptical about Finnis's meta-ethical claims will, I think, remain resistant to his proposal to accept his characterization of the focal meaning of law as requiring an orientation to the common good. For we shall claim that 'law' is at least a *less* contested concept than 'the common good'. I can know what 'the law of the land' is, and can claim that it objectively *is* the law of the land even while I remain in doubt over what is in the common good or whether there is any objective truth of that matter. So, on the principle that one should not explain the obscure by reference to the more obscure, I hold back from accepting Finnis's proposal as to the focal meaning of law.

That said, I do for my part hold to a general moral position according to which the law of the land ought to be aimed at realizing justice and a conception of the common good not very far removed from Finnis's. Given that law is what it is, it can neither be operated nor fully understood without acceptance that it does and must serve some—doubtless both contestable and not wholly coherent—scheme of values. Thus the law is always and necessarily morally relevant. It is always and necessarily open to moral criticism. It is always and necessarily a topic for practical reasoning.

My final difference with Finnis then amounts only to a disagreement about writing elements of that moral position into a characterization of the focal meaning of 'law'. And that is, perhaps, not a very important difference.

Much more important is one's appreciation of this book as requiring us to abandon our caricature version of what a natural law theory is, and as requiring us to engage in argument with the real strengths of the classical theory in this modern and analytically sophisticated form.

[11]

Practical Principles, Moral Truth, and Ultimate Ends

I INTRODUCTION 99
A Please Note Well 99
B Framework for the Analysis: Free Choice 100

Part One: Practical Principles 102
II THE MOTIVES OF SPECIFICALLY HUMAN ACTS 102
A Purposes of Rationally Guided Actions 102
B Basic Goods as Reasons Underlying Purposes 103
C Benefit and Goal: Distinct Aspects of a Purpose 104
D First Principles of Practical Reasoning and Willing 105
III PRACTICAL PRINCIPLES AND THEIR GENESIS 106
A Which Are the Basic Goods 106
B Genesis of the First Practical Principles 108
C A Corollary: Two Theses about Incommensurability 110
IV DIALECTICAL DEFENSE OF FIRST PRACTICAL PRINCIPLES 111
A Dialectics: Theoretical Knowledge 111
B Dialectical Defense: Ineligible Candidates 111
C Dialectical Defense: Genuine Practical Principles 113
V PERSONS: WHY BASIC GOODS MOTIVATE 114
A Basic Goods and the Fulfillment of Persons 114
B Persons Themselves and the Basic Goods 115
VI PRACTICAL TRUTH 115
A Practical Truth's Adequation 115
B Human Fulfillment: Neither Found nor Made 117
C The First Principle of Practical Reasoning 119

Part Two: Moral Truth 121
VII FROM PRACTICAL PRINCIPLES TO THE MORAL OUGHT 121
A The First Principle of Morality 121
B How Possible Purposes Arise 122
C How to Make Immoral Choices 123
D The Emergence of the Moral *Ought* 125
VIII MORAL TRUTH: COMPARISONS AND CONTRASTS 125
A Practical Truth, Moral Truth, and Moral Falsity 125
B Practical Truths Which Are Not Moral Truths 126
C The Relationship between *Ought* and *Is* 127
D Formulations of the First Moral Principle 127
IX VIRTUES AND MORAL PRINCIPLES 129
A The Priority of Moral Principles 129
B Virtues and Moral Judgment 130
C How Virtues Can Be Acquired 131

Part Three: Ultimate Ends 131
X ENDS ULTIMATE IN THREE DIVERSE WAYS 131
A The Ultimate End Rectifying the Will 131
B Basic Goods: Ultimate Reasons for Choosing 133
C The Happiness for Which People Settle 135
XI HIERARCHIES AND ORDERS OF VALUES 137
A Natural Priorities among the Basic Goods 137
B No Hierarchy among the Basic Goods 139
C Purposes in Life, Commitments, and Life Plans 140
XII MORALITY, RELIGION, AND GOD 141
A Why a Religious Commitment Is Required 141
B God: Cooperator with Human Agents 143
C Religion and the Overarching Purpose of Life 145
D Christian Faith: "Seek First the Kingdom . . ." 146
Selected Bibliography 148

PRACTICAL PRINCIPLES, MORAL TRUTH, AND ULTIMATE ENDS

GERMAIN GRISEZ, JOSEPH BOYLE, AND JOHN FINNIS

The natural-law theory on which we have been working during the past twenty-five years has stimulated many critical responses. We have restated the theory in various works, not always calling attention to developments. This paper reformulates some parts of the theory, taking into account the criticisms of which we are aware. We append an annotated, select bibliography.

I. INTRODUCTION

A. PLEASE NOTE WELL

WHILE THIS PAPER PROPOSES PHILOSOPHICAL clarifications and arguments rather than textual interpretations, it uses some language common in the (broadly speaking, Thomistic) natural-law tradition from which we developed the theory. But what we say here differs in various ways from the theories articulated by Aristotle, Thomas Aquinas, and others.

In previous works covering more or less the same ground as this paper, we have expressed key concepts in various ways. Here, again, we use language in ways not in all cases the same as in our other works or in the tradition. But we try to be consistent throughout the present paper in using certain key terms which we put in small capitals in their first occurrences.

For simplicity, in this paper we generally use only the singular in speaking of actions, purposes, goods, and so on. For example, though an action often has more than one purpose, we usually talk about "the purpose" as if each action had but one. Likewise, one often chooses to do something with the hope of achieving diverse benefits for oneself and/or another (or others), but we usually talk about "the intended benefit" or "the good in which one is interested" as if an agent intended only a single benefit for a single person—himself or herself.

Similarly, very many actions are done (and some important ones can only be done) by groups of people. But, for simplicity, we almost always talk about "the acting person" or "the agent," as if all agents were individuals acting alone.

There is no adequate way in English to refer to the motivation, consequent upon sensory cognition, generically common to human beings and brute animals. Motivations of this sort *normally* are effective without one's being aware of them. So "feeling" and "emotion" have unwelcome connotations of conscious experience and intensity, but, for want of better words, we use these, and use them interchangeably.

The present paper reformulates only some parts of the theory of practical and moral knowledge on which we have been working. For example, we do not deal here with the distinction between an act's object and side effects. And we deal only incidentally with the important, intermediate moral principles which we call "modes of responsibility." Moreover, we treat no specific normative issue here, and articulate some practical and moral knowledge only as necessary for our theoretical purpose.

We deal here, mainly, with the following matters: the first principles of practical knowledge and of morality, their relationship to other cognition, their specific truth, their relationship to the ultimate ends of human persons (taking "end" in several different senses), and their relationship to religion.

As a theory of some of the principles of human action, what we offer here presupposes many theses of metaphysics and philosophical anthropology—for example, that human intelligence is irreducible to material realities, that doing and making are irreducible to one another, that human persons and their actions are caused by an uncaused cause, and so on. We defend many such presuppositions elsewhere.

B. Framework for the Analysis: Free Choice

Perhaps the most important presupposition from philosophical anthropology is that human persons can make free choices. Whether they assented to this proposition or not, most who have contributed to ethical theory, whether in ancient or more recent times, have denied, overlooked, or, at best, not fully appreciated the role of free choice in morality. Because of the importance of free choice, we have tried hard in other works to explain and defend the proposition that human persons can make free choices.

Since we hold that free choice is central (and choice presupposes both intellectual cognition and prior willing of goods), we frequently and sharply distinguish intelligible factors from factors contributed by sense and imagination, and volitions, including choices, from feelings. To those not accustomed to making these distinctions, our making them as sharply as we do may give the impression that we hold a dualistic view of human personality and action. But we do not. All the distinctions are made, for analytic purposes, among the dynamic aspects of one reality, the acting person, who alone is properly said to imagine, understand, feel, and will.

For some, the fundamental problem of ethical theory is how to escape egoism. They will wonder why we say so little about it. Our reason: The debate between egoism and its alternatives belongs to normative ethics—as one issue among many—not to the foundations of ethics. One can choose freely whether to be an egoist. But one has no choice whether harmony among persons is good, or whether harmony is fostered or blocked by egoism. And, in general, the practical principles which make choices possible—and which are not themselves chosen, egoistically or otherwise—must be presupposed in any inquiry about the merits of egoism. [We deal with egoism more fully in section V(A).]

Similarly, some wonder whether the theory we defend is teleological or deontological. The answer: Neither. Unlike teleological theories, this one shows why there are absolute moral norms. (We deal with this matter sufficiently in other works.) Moreover, unlike teleological and like deontological theories, the position we defend is that morally good free choices are intrinsic to the supreme good of human persons. But to assume that this theory must therefore be deontological is a mistake.

Deontological theories treat practical reason or will as a self-constituting source of morality. Excluding determination by naturally given desires as alien to morality, some theories of this sort—Kant's is the most famous—try to derive moral norms from freedom itself and its necessary conditions. On such an account, the fulfillment of natural human desires has no place in the definition of morally good will. Other theories considered deontological try to ground morality in God's free will, on the assumption that, being supreme, its only norm is itself. For such theories, rightness is determined by arbitrary divine law, not by divine wisdom directing humankind to its fulfillment.

Against deontological theories, we hold that moral truths direct free choices toward actions which tend to satisfy natural desires. Such actions help to fulfill persons as individuals and in communion. Against teleological theories, however, we hold that some of these desires are for fulfillments not only realized but constituted by morally good choices, including mutual commitments.

The centrality of free choice in moral theory explains not only why our account of practical and moral principles diverges from some contemporary views, but also why it departs in some respects from classical models to which it is in other respects indebted. As we show in this paper, the reality of free choice is incompatible with the supposition—for instance, of Aristotle—that there is a single natural end of human life [sections IV(B); X; XI(A).]

The theory we defned also departs from classical models—at least, as many have understood them—by taking full account of the fact that the moral *ought* cannot be derived from the *is* of theoretical truth—for example, of metaphysics and/or philosophical anthropology. Logically, of course, one can derive a moral *ought* from an *is*, whenever the *is* expresses a truth about a reality which embodies a moral norm. Thus, from "This is the act an honest person would do" one can deduce "This act ought to be done." But from a set of theoretical premises, one cannot logically derive any practical truth, since sound reasoning does not introduce what is not in the premises. And the relationship of principles to conclusions is a logical one among propositions. Therefore, the ultimate principles of morality cannot be theoretical truths of metaphysics and/or philosophical anthropology.

That this is not simply a logician's pedantry will be made clear by our account of practical truth and moral truth [sections IV(A-B); VII(D); VIII(A-C).]

Part One: Practical Principles

II. The Motives of Specifically Human Acts

A. Purposes of Rationally Guided Actions

Principles are uncovered by examining that of which they are the principles. The principles we are concerned with here are motives of human action. As principles, they will be basic motives, irreducible to any prior motives of the same sort.

Some things people do—instinctive behavior and intelligently planned performances whose only ultimate motives are feelings—are not specifically human in their motivation. For example, a three-year old child cleverly raids the cookie jar, or a traveler, spontaneously responding to nature's call, follows signs to a restroom. In some of our works, such behavior was said to be done by "spontaneous willing." It was a mistake to say "willing," for reasons which will become clear in section II(C). We here set aside such behavior, not specifically human in its motivation.

The actions we are concerned with in this paper are those initiated by *free choice*. Such actions are done for the sake of something; they are rationally guided (whether or not they are morally good and entirely reasonable in other respects). The first type of principle we treat is that for the sake of which such an action is done.

That for the sake of which one acts is one's PURPOSE in acting; one hopes that this purpose will be realized through and/or in one's action. A purpose in this sense is a state of affairs—something concrete which can exist or not exist in reality. For example, if one enters a contest, one's purpose is to win a prize; if one does not feel well and goes to the doctor, one's purpose is to get better.

People do not always have a purpose *distinct from* their action; sometimes doing the action is itself their purpose in acting. That is very often the case when one plays a game or reads a novel.

B. Basic Goods as Reasons Underlying Purposes

We distinguish between purposes and that about a purpose which makes one rationally interested in acting for it. We call the latter a GOOD. For example, among goods are winning and being healthy, considered insofar as they can be realized—protected, promoted, and so on—not only by one action but by many possible actions. In entering a contest or going to the doctor, one's purpose of winning or regaining health only PARTICIPATES in the goods of winning and health, in which one is interested more generally.

To explicate this participation relationship between a purpose and a good, we say: Achieving the purpose will INSTANTIATE the good which is the reason one is interested in acting for that purpose.

Even when one's purpose is not distinct from one's action, something about the action underlies one's rational interest in doing it. One's reasons for playing a particular game or reading a particular novel are goods which are only instantiated through actions chosen for these reasons. Thus, playing and knowing always have their basic appeal, insofar as they are goods, but like other goods they can be realized only in limited ways through particular actions.

Some goods are reasons for acting which need a further reason to explain the interest people take in them. We call such reasons for acting INSTRUMENTAL GOODS. For example, as a reason for acting, winning a prize needs a further reason which motivates one to win. The further reason will be the reason why one is interested in some further purpose, such as using the prize, showing that one has the necessary capabilities, and so on.

One does finish deliberating and begin acting, and there cannot be an infinite regress in the goods which are reasons for acting. Plainly, then, there are reaons for acting which need no further reason; these are goods, one or more of which underlie any purpose. We call these BASIC GOODS. Actions specifically human in their motivation are done for the sake of one or more of these goods; every such action is chosen in view of one or more BASIC PURPOSES. Basic purposes are those whose achievement will immediately instantiate basic goods.

C. Benefit and Goal: Distinct Aspects of a Purpose

This paper concerns rationally motivated actions. But people never do such actions without emotional motives as well [see section VII(B)]. Feelings bear not on the intelligible good as such but on the action's concrete purpose or on something linked by psychological association with that purpose. One perhaps has experienced and remembers a more or less similar state of affairs; in any case, one can more or less clearly imagine the purpose or something related to it. Something about it, as thus imagined, inclines one to do the action.

Because there are both rational and emotional motives, which bear upon the purpose of an action in different ways, one can distinguish between two aspects of a purpose. In one aspect a purpose is desired by reason of an intelligible good; in another aspect a purpose is desired as concrete and imaginable.

Insofar and only insofar as it is concrete and imaginable, a purpose is emotionally desired. As an object of feeling, a purpose is a particular objective. We call such an objective a GOAL. So a purpose is a goal insofar as envisaging the purpose arouses the feelings an agent needs to act for it.

Insofar as the purpose of one's action is proposed not by imagination but by intellectual knowledge, it is VOLITIONALLY desired. The purpose remains a concrete state of affairs. But when one deliberates about acting for it, propositional knowledge commends doing so by reason of an intelligible good, ultimately by reason of a basic good. If one chooses to act for the purpose, one hopes to share in the good and be more or less fulfilled (or to help another to share in it and be fulfilled). We use ANTICIPATE to signify the relationship between *practical knowledge* directing a rationally guided and chosen action toward fulfillment and the *fulfillment* for which one hopes.

We use BENEFIT to signify the intelligible aspect of a basic purpose. Like a goal, a benefit is particular, but unlike a goal as such, a benefit directly contributes to someone's fulfillment. And so, one who chooses to act for a purpose not only desires and expects to reach a certain goal but anticipates and hopes to realize and enjoy (or help another to realize and enjoy) some benefit through the action. Where the purpose is not basic but instrumental to some further purpose, it too has an intelligible aspect which may be called an EMPOWERMENT.

Since rationally guided and chosen actions always are done with emotional motivation as well, the purpose of every such action includes a goal. Rational motives motivate toward some fulfillment of the person as a whole; emotional motives motivate toward some fulfillment of the person's sentient part. But, although they are distinct from one another, emotional and rational motives are dynamically united.

Indeed, agents, by understanding and generalizing goals, can think of them as reasons for acting—that is, as intelligible goods. But they are only instrumental ones, since a fulfillment of sentient nature just as such is not yet a fulfillment of the person as a whole. Thus, eating a particular meal is a goal, and one understands eating in general as a good, in which one is interested. But eating can only be *deliberately chosen* insofar as it is instrumental to basic goods, such as life and fellowship. Or, to take the earlier example, winning is the goal of entering a particular contest; this goal generalized is the intelligible good of winning, for people who enter contests have a general interest in this sort of empowerment. The good of winning is an intelligible good, but not a basic one. Those interested in winning always are more interested in the benefits (in terms of one or more of the basic goods) which they hope to achieve from winning.

Even without the anticipation of any benefit or empowerment, feelings can incite behavior toward a goal. Understanding that goal—not as a reason for acting but as something to be brought about—an agent can pursue it by an intelligent causal process. A technical "means" (such as a tool, a manipulative process, a sign) is used to reach the "end." Such behavior often occurs even in small children. Being intelligently guided, it is easily confused with rationally motivated action. What is said in some of our works about "spontaneous willing" involves precisely that confusion.

D. First Principles of Practical Reasoning and Willing

In all rationally motivated actions, there is a guiding judgment and a choice. The judgment proposes and shapes the action as what is to be done or ought to be done. The choice is the will to do that action rather than not and rather than any other. This distinction in actions is rooted in a distinction in their principles. Thus, one can distinguish between the intellectual knowledge of the basic goods as *reasons for* choosing and the corresponding *volition toward* the goods.

The knowing which directly shapes action is neither mere insight nor a process of reasoning but a judging which proposes: This action is to be done or ought to be done. Such a judgment is reached by reasoning from one or more basic goods. The simplest case of such reasoning is: This is to be done because it probably will realize a certain benefit—that is, instantiate such and such a basic good. This reasoning process assumes: Such and such a good is to be realized (protected, promoted, and so on). Thus, one way the basic goods function as principles of actions is through being *known* as ultimate rational grounds (principles of practical reasoning) for proposing actions to be done for certain benefits (anticipated instantiations of those goods).

Correspondingly, the choice to do an action presupposes a volition toward the intelligible aspect of the purpose. This volition, in turn, presupposes a fundamental volition toward the relevant basic good. This fundamental volition corresponds to the principles of practical knowledge, which provide its object. Thus, the other way the basic goods function as principles of action is by being *willed* as the first objects of volition.

We use CHOICE to signify a volition bearing on an action to be done. We use INTEREST to signify a volition bearing on the intelligible aspect (whether benefit or empowerment) or some set of *potential* (or both potential and actual) purposes. We use INTENTION to signify a volition bearing on the intelligible aspect (whether benefit or empowerment) of a purpose for which an act *actually* is chosen. To signify the type of volition (presupposed by interest and intention) which bears on the basic goods, we speak of ALIVENESS to those goods or SIMPLE VOLITION of them—"simple" because basic and uncomplicated. Thus, specified by the first principles of practical knowledge, aliveness to the basic goods underlies one's various interests which, in turn, take specific form in the intentions with which one chooses to act for purposes.

The question naturally arises: If the principles of practical knowledge serve as ultimate rational grounds for proposing actions to be done, how can these principles themselves come to be known? As *first* principles, they cannot be derived from any theoretical knowledge [sections I(B); IV(A); VI(B); VIII(C)]. Thus, they cannot be verified by experience or deduced from any more basic truths through a middle term. They are self-evident.

Self-evident principles are *per se nota*—known just by knowing the meaning of their terms. This does not mean that they are mere linguistic clarifications, nor that they are intuitions—insights unrelated to data [see section III(B)]. Rather, it means that these truths are known (*nota*) without any middle term (*per se*), by understanding what is signified by their terms.

III. Practical Principles and Their Genesis

A. Which Are the Basic Goods

The most direct way to uncover the basic goods is by considering actions and asking, "Why are you doing that?" and "Why should we do that?" and so on. Persisting with such questions eventually uncovers a small number of basic purposes of diverse kinds. These purposes arouse interest because their intelligible aspects are instantiations of the diverse basic goods.

The diversity of the basic goods is neither a mere contingent fact about human psychology nor an accident of history [section IV(B-C)]. Rather, being aspects of the fulfillment of persons, these goods correspond to the inherent complexities of human nature, as it is manifested both in individuals and in various forms of community.

In other works we have provided somewhat different lists of the most general categories of basic goods. But the following seven categories now seem to us adequate.

(1) As *animate*, human persons are organic substances. Life itself—its maintenance and transmission—health, and safety are one category of basic good.

(2) As *rational*, human persons can know reality and appreciate beauty and whatever intensely engages their capacities to know and to feel. Knowledge and esthetic experience are another category of basic good.

(3) As *simultaneously rational and animal*, human persons can transform the natural world by using realities, beginning with their own bodily selves, to express meanings and serve purposes. Such meaning-giving and value-creation can be realized in diverse degrees. Their realization for its own sake is another category of basic good: some degree of excellence in work and play.

The preceding categories of goods we call SUBSTANTIVE. Although the substantive goods provide reasons for acting, their instantiations, even when caused by chosen actions, do not involve choices. Everyone shares in substantive goods even before deliberately pursuing them. They are first received as gifts of nature and parts of a cultural heritage. But children quickly come to see these substantive goods as fields in which they can care for, expand, and improve upon what they have received. Life, knowledge, and skilled performances are basic goods and principles of practical knowledge just insofar as they can be understood and, being understood, can be cherished, enhanced, and handed on to others.

Another dimension of human persons is that they are *agents through deliberation and choice*, who can strive to avoid or overcome various forms of personal and interpersonal conflict—or, to put the matter positively, who can strive to foster various forms of harmony. So, among the basic goods are certain forms of harmony. The instantiations of these goods include the choices by which one acts for them. So we call them REFLEXIVE goods.

For reasons which will become clear later [section XI(A-B)], not all instantiations of reflexive goods are morally good, although true and lasting fulfillment in them must be so.

(4) Most obvious among the reflexive goods are various forms of harmony between and among individuals and groups of persons—living at peace with others, neighborliness, friendship.

(5) Within individuals and their personal lives, similar goods can be realized. For feelings can conflict among themselves and also can be at odds with one's judgments and choices. The harmony opposed to such inner disturbance is inner peace.

(6) Moreover, one's choices can conflict with one's judgments and one's behavior can fail to express one's inner self. The corresponding good is harmony among one's judgments, choices, and performances—peace of conscience and consistency between one's self and its expression.

(7) Finally, most people experience tension with the wider reaches of reality. Attempts to gain or improve harmony with some more-than-human source of meaning and value take many forms, depending on people's world views. Thus, another category of reflexive good is peace with God, or the gods, or some nontheistic but more-than-human source of meaning and value.

Although actions through which one more or less directly participates in a basic good can be chosen by reason of that basic good, they also can be chosen for a purpose whose intelligible aspect is a benefit (or even an empowerment) which instantiates some other good. For example, although one can choose to play a game simply for play's sake, one can play for fellowship, to make money, and so on.

B. Genesis of the First Practical Principles

As we said [section II(D)], the first practical principles, although self-evident, are not intuitions—insights without data. What data are available?

Human persons have natural dispositions toward what will fulfill their potentialities. Some of these dispositions are natural appetites—that is, dispositions of a person's various parts and powers toward their own actualizations. Others are sensory appetites (including aversions)—that is, emotional responses. Both types of dispositions sometimes motivate behavior more elemental than intelligently guided actions, and one thus becomes aware of them. These natural dispositions, insofar as they are experienced, provide data for the insights in which one knows the first, self-evident principles of practical knowledge corresponding to the substantive goods.

Although the insights whose content is the self-evident principles of practical knowledge have for data one's natural inclinations, one's understanding of the substantive goods does not remain forever as limited as it is at first.

Knowing that health is a good to be preserved by appropriate actions, people study what health is. So, one acting to serve this interest today has the advantage of much theoretical study and a heritage of experience unavailable to early people.

Similarly, scientists who systematically pursue truth proceed from the same first practical principle as they did when as curious children they first chose to seek an answer to some question. But now they not only know better how to pursue truth, but have a deeper insight into the truth to be known, and can appreciate, in a way children cannot, how knowing is an aspect of integral human fulfillment.

In one's grasp of the practical principles directing toward reflexive goods, the data include volitions. Various forms of disharmony involving choices bearing upon substantive goods thwart one's interests. The will's frustrated intentions are natural inclinations which are data. And so, volitions specified by the substantive goods are part of the data for the insights whose content is the reflexive practical principles.

The volitions included in the data for understanding reflexive practical principles should not be confused with the volitions, specified by these principles, bearing upon the reflexive goods themselves. To be alive to any form of harmony, to be interested in it, and to choose for it, one must have practical knowledge of it as a good to be realized. The choices included in the instantiations of reflexive goods cannot be part of the data for understanding the principles of practical knowledge directing toward these goods. Thus, while some of the first principles of practical knowledge presuppose volitions, none of them presupposes the volitions whose objects it provides.

Just as theoretical knowledge, true opinion, and experience enhance the initial insight into the substantive goods, so they deepen understanding of the reflexive goods. For example, both sound metaphysics and experience in practicing authentic religious faith contribute to one's understanding of the good of religion. In doing so, they enhance the power of the practical principle underlying the religious quest [section XII(A)].

However, one's understanding of the reflexive goods also is affected by immoral choices [see section XI(A); XII(C)]. For instance, rather than understanding religion in terms of harmonizing human wills with God's will, people can understand it in terms of bringing a more-than-human source of meaning and value into accord with immoral human desires [see section XII(C)].

C. A Corollary: Two Theses about Incommensurability

Insofar as the basic goods are reasons with no further reasons, they are primary principles. Since they are primary principles, the goods of the diverse categories are incommensurrable with one another.

For, if they were commensurable, they would have to be homogeneous with one another or reducible to something prior by which they could be measured. If they were homogeneous with one another, they would not constitute diverse categories. If they were reducible to something prior, they would not be primary principles. Thus, they are incommensurable: No basic good considered precisely as such can be meaningfully said to be better than another. How even basic interests are naturally ordered to one another will be explained [in section XI(A)].

It follows from this incommensurability that all basic purposes are alike only in being desired for some reason. They differ in desirability because there is no single reason underlying every purpose for the sake of which one acts. Hence, the basic goods of diverse categories are called "good" only by analogy.

Sometimes we have intermingled and confused the preceding thesis with a thesis about a different incommensurability: that between instantiations of goods in the purposes for which one might choose to act. This incommensurability obtains even between instantiations of one and the same basic good. For instance, what makes vacationing at the beach appealing and what makes vacationing in the mountains appealing; what makes committing adultery appealing and what makes remaining faithful appealing—such alternatives are incommensurable in the sense that each possibility has some appeal not found in the purpose which makes the other appealing. When one has a choice, no option includes in the instantiation of the good it promises everything promised by its alternative—even when the alternative would instantiate the very same basic good.

Clearly, the incommensurability of the diverse categories of basic goods and that among prospective instantiations of goods are different. For the second incommensurability is present even where the same interest make both alternatives choiceworthy—for example, when someone who has only one set of reasons for taking a vacation chooses between mountains and beach. Here the incommensurability of the categories of goods is irrelevant, and so the relevant incommensurability is plain: The benefits anticipated somehow differ. Neither one's purpose in choosing to vacation in the mountains nor one's purpose in choosing to vacation at the beach offers in every respect a more adequate instantiation of those basic goods which are one's ultimate reasons to vacation.

GERMAIN GRISEZ, JOSEPH BOYLE, AND JOHN FINNIS 111

IV. Dialectical Defense of First Practical Principles

A. Dialectics: Theoretical Knowledge

The self-evidence of the principles of practical knowledge does not preclude their being rationally defended. One can argue for a proposition without using a middle term to prove it. Dialectical arguments relate a proposition to be defended to other knowledge, and show that denying it has unacceptable consequences.

The dialectical defense of the basic goods is a theoretical project. It presupposes natural, nontheoretical knowledge of the first practical principles, which are the subject matter of this theoretical reflection. Hence, the knowledge of these practical principles as practical in no way depends on these theoretical arguments. As we have said, the practical principles are self-evident truths, not conclusions from theoretical knowledge about human persons.

However, it is worth recalling that theoretical knowledge is relevant not only to the defense of the first practical principles, but to their function in guiding action. Theoretical reflection deepens understanding of the basic goods, and knowledge about facts bearing on their instantiation is necessary to pursue them effectively. For instance, one cannot effectively promote health without knowing biology, nor can one effectively pursue friendship with God without knowing (by reason and/or faith) at least some truth about God. Moreover, one needs theoretical knowledge about one's powers and actual situation to know what one might choose to do.

B. Dialectical Defense: Ineligible Candidates

Attempts to add candidates to the list of basic goods can be dealt with dialectically. However, there are many plausible candidates which are in different ways closely akin to basic goods. So the argument, fully developed, would be quite lengthy, and we only sketch it out.

There are intelligible goods which are not basic—for example, winning, being free to do as one pleases, being wealthy, and so on. These are *instrumental* [section II(B)].

There also are intelligible aspects of basic goods, which provide reasons adequate to motivate actions, but which are not themselves the complete reality of any fulfillment of persons—enjoyment, tension reduction, and so on. These are only *parts* of basic goods, and by themselves they fall as far short of being rationally desirable as the goods, of which they are parts, are wholes greater than these parts.

There are basic motives which are not intelligible goods—for example, pleasure and pain. Insofar as these are *not intelligible* goods, they provide *no reason* for acting. However, states of affairs which include them often instantiate a basic good or its contrary—the reflexive good of inner peace or its contrary, inner disturbance. Feeling pain usually is disturbing. But pain itself is naturally beneficial, inasmuch as it is a necessary signal, whose absence would impede every effort to maintain and promote health. Obviously, too, a state of affairs including pain often instantiates some basic good—for example, playing a strenuous game well.

One can imagine a state of affairs ("perfect happiness") such that if it were realized one enjoying it would have no further reason for doing anything except those actions which contributed to or constituted it. But, perfect happiness, being a state of affairs, would be a *purpose rather than a reason* for action, and so would not be one or all of the basic goods. Rather, if it were realizable, perfect happiness would promise the supreme benefit of action, and all the basic goods would be reasons for acting for it. (We shall argue [in section X(A)] that the nearest thing to what good people mean by "happiness" is the ideal of integral human fulfillment—a state of affairs which human actions cannot realize.)

There are personal qualities such as dignity and self-respect which *embrace globally* all or many aspects of personal fulfillment considered from the point of view of important relationships with other people or oneself. Such goods are *not basic* goods; they can provide reasons for acting only insofar as the goods which underlie them can do so. The point can be clarified by considering dignity and self-respect more carefully.

Dignity is primarily the worth of persons as persons, compared with everything subpersonal, and secondarily the worth of persons superior in various ways to others. Such personal worth or superiority cannot be directly realized or harmed through human action. However, the dignity of persons can suffer insofar as various aspects of personal fulfillment can be damaged or lost—for example, through the unfairness of others or through ill fortune. The various intelligible goods can then provide reasons for acting to protect or promote the person's fulfillment conceived of as dignity. For example, if a woman's dignity is damaged because she lacks the employment she needs to support her family, the only way to help her recover her dignity is by helping her find suitable work.

Similarly, self-respect is one's awareness of and satisfaction with one's fulfillment, judged by standards one accepts. In itself, it is an aspect of the goods which underlie it considered together. Thus, one acts for it by acting for those goods. So, if an alcoholic loses self-respect as he sinks into the gutter, the only way to regain it is by regaining the health and moral integrity which his alcohol abuse has damaged.

Self-respect also is an intelligible good insofar as it is instrumental to the pursuit of all other goods, since one lacking it is emotionally disabled from energetically pursuing them.

C. Dialectical Defense: Genuine Practical Principles

One way to argue for the first principles of practical knowledge is by considering actions and seeking their reasons. We identified this line of argument [section III(A)] as the proper method of locating the basic goods, to which the principles of practical knowledge direct actions. However, there are three other lines of dialectical argument which one can use to defend these principles.

First, theoretical studies of human persons, including empirical psychology and philosophical anthropology, uncover the natural inclinations. Some of these theories—for example, Freudian psychology, structuralist anthropology, behaviorism, dualistic philosophies of the person—are very inadequate. But the body of material taken as a whole testifies to natural inclinations to stay alive and healthy, to know, to do good work and to play, to get along with others, to be at peace with reality, and to get oneself together. Accepting the list of basic goods is supported by the data; rejecting it is *at odds with the data.*

Second, the very possibility that anthropological study can examine every culture points to underlying common starting points of cultural development. Anthropologists can look for and find the diverse ways in which peoples keep themselves alive, seek and hand on knowledge, attempt to maintain harmony among their own members, try to get right with the more-than-human source of meaning and value, and so on. Accepting the list of basic goods as first principles of action explains how the anthropological enterprise is possible, whereas claiming that all human values are culturally conditioned *renders the enterprise inexplicable.*

Third, attempts to remove some of the candidates from the list also can be dealt with dialectically. For example, some think that, while life is an intelligible good, it is only instrumental not basic. However, any attempt to establish this can be shown to involve a theoretically indefensible dualistic account of the person. Again, truth might be considered entirely instrumental, but any attempt to argue for such a theory can be shown to presuppose the basic goodness of knowing theoretical truth, and so to be self-defeating.

V. Persons: Why Basic Goods Motivate

A. Basic Goods and the Fulfillment of Persons

Why is it that the basic goods are the ultimate reasons for acting? Why do these goods have motivating power?

These are theoretical questions. In trying to answer them, we are not trying to *deduce* first practical principles; that cannot be done. Rather, we are continuing our dialectical defense of these principles, by explaining how basic goods are both one with and distinct from persons, who, therefore, in one respect are and in another are not the ultimate reason for every human action.

Any creature which acts is one whose reality is not fully given at the outset; it has possibilities which can be realized only through its acting. The basic goods are basic reasons for acting because they are aspects of the fulfillment of persons, whose action is rationally motivated by these reasons.

Does that mean that every rationally motivated action is done for the agent's individual self-fulfillment? No. As intelligible, the basic goods have no proper names attached to them. So they can be understood as goods and can provide reasons for acting whether, in a particular case, the agent or another will benefit.

Many actions are done by two or more persons acting together; the basic goods which motivate actions can be realized in all those acting, but need not—for example, a physician and patient may act together for the patient's health. Community in action also can embrace someone not at the moment a contributing member who is socially united with those who at present act for his or her benefit. For example, a couple can act for the coming to be and growing up of a child.

The objects of feelings, which are among the data of the principles of practical knowledge, do not have the universality of intelligible goods. Yet it does not follow that feelings are egoistic. Feeling motivates to action for sensible goods which will be realized in the agent and/or in individuals concretely related to the agent—for example, feeling motivates food gathering by animals for themselves, their mates, and offspring. However, animals' action does not involve the reflexivity needed to distinguish the agent's self from the selves of others benefited by an action. Thus, there is no "I" and "you" for animals and little babies.

So, the basic goods are motives for action in virtue of their being aspects of the full-being of persons without that entailing that human action is fundamentally egoistic. Living egoistically and living in communion with others are both possibilities, given the structure of human motivation. Therefore, it begs the question to assume that human motivation is fundamentally egoistic, and that a nonegoistic normative theory must show how to transcend this gratuitously presupposed fundamental egoism.

B. Persons Themselves and the Basic Goods

The basic goods of the diverse categories provide diverse reasons for choices which fulfill persons in diverse ways. Health, playing tennis, and marriage plainly fulfill different aspects of a healthy, tennis-playing, married couple.

Are we saying that the basic reasons for acting simply are persons—individually and in communion? Yes and no.

Yes, in the sense that in acting one primarily loves persons, oneself and others with whom one is somehow in community and who one hopes will benefit from one's actions. In acting *for the basic goods*, one's hope simply is to foster them *in and for persons*. In the fullest sense, one loves (and such love includes feeling) the whole person, including both the person's given reality (here love is not practical but is contentment or joy) and whatever still may be hoped for as that person's fulfillment.

But no, because the already existing reality of persons simply does not depend upon human action. So, the reasons for acting are more limited—the basic goods. These are not the whole reality of any individual or community, but those intelligible aspects of the fulfillment of persons (as individuals and in communion) to which human actions can contribute.

Thus, one loves in a secondary sense (1) the basic goods themselves and (2) their instantiations. For they are (1) what one is fundamentally alive to and (2) intends as benefits for persons.

VI. Practical Truth

A. Practical Truth's Adequation

The truth of theoretical knowledge is in the conformity of propositions to prior reality, actual and possible. This truth is signified by "is": So it *is*. The truth of practical knowledge, beginning with its self-evident principles, is not signified by "is" but by "is to be"—for example, Good *is to be* done and pursued.

The reason for this difference is that what is known by practical knowledge has its reality, not prior to that knowledge, but through it. In coming to know theoretically, one comes into accord with prior reality. But in coming to know practically, one becomes able to bring something into reality. It follows that practical knowledge cannot have its truth by conformity to what is known. Rather, a practical proposition is true by anticipating the realization of that which is possible through acting in conformity with that proposition, and by directing one's action toward that realization.

Some may reject this account of practical truth, on the assumption that "truth" can only mean conformity of knowledge to subject matter, adequation of mind to reality—in other words, that "truth" is used correctly of practical propositions only if it is used with the same meaning it has in speaking of theoretical propositions. One who takes this position tries to reduce practical to theoretical knowledge. However, "is to be" cannot be uniformly replaced by "is." (One cannot even try to reduce practical to theoretical knowledge without thinking—*practically*—that such a reduction *is to be* carried out.)

Others may concede that practical propositions concerning particular acts to be done find their truth in their anticipation of what is to be realized through action, but insist that the truth of the first principles of practical knowledge must be in their conformity to prior reality: the possibilities opened up by human nature. This position would leave practical propositions concerning particular acts to be done without any principles homogeneous with them. However, these propositions need such principles, for their directiveness, which plainly is derivative, logically cannot come from purely theoretical principles [section I(B)].

Thus, "truth" is said of practical propositions by analogy. Practical propositions, including first practical principles, are true by anticipating the fulfillment possible through action in conformity with them and directing action toward that realization; practical propositions are not true by conforming to anything. But, it will be objected, every possible human fulfillment plainly is grounded in human nature.

We agree that practical knowledge and freedom are not the only necessary conditions for fulfillment. The possibility of human fulfillment also presupposes both the given reality of human nature—with its capacities and natural inclinations—and people's actual abilities, skills, and resources, together with the challenges and opportunities offered by the real world in which humans live their lives. In general, what still can be presupposes what already is; in particular, what one naturally is grounds all that one is to be.

However, not only the realization but the specification and projection of one's possible human fulfillment depend on more than *given* human nature. For human nature also includes the capacities of practical knowledge and free choice, and these not only enable a person to realize possibilities which are defined independently of their exercise, but to define and project possibilities in and through their exercise. Thus, not only the actualization of the possibilities of human fulfillment but those very possibilities themselves partly depend upon human persons' practical knowledge, free choices, carrying out of these choices, and the results of carrying them out. For example, a person can be virtuous or, failing that, can become vicious, and the very possibility of being either—not merely the fact of being one or the other—presupposes practical knowledge, freedom, and action.

In sum. What human persons *can be* through their freedom and action depends on practical knowledge rather than vice versa, and so the adequation which is the truth of practical knowledge is not conformity to some already existing order. The adequation of practical knowing is not that of theoretical knowing, namely, conformity of knowledge to known. But neither is it a merely formal truth involving a "conformity to its own structures" or something of that sort. The *truth* (that is, the adequation) of practical knowledge is the *conformity of what is to be* through knowing *to* the *knowledge* which will help to bring it about.

Since "true" is said in radically diverse senses of theoretical and practical knowledge, someone might ask whether there is any basis whatsoever in reality for speaking of "truths" in both cases. There is. For although the relationships between the human mind and its objects are opposite in the two cases, truth in either case means that both the human mind and its objects conform to the mind of God, who makes many things true apart from human practical knowledge, free choice, and action, but makes some things become true only with and through this particular type of secondary causality.

B. Human Fulfillment: Neither Found nor Made

Against this account of practical truth, someone may argue: "There really are only two possibilities: Human persons must either (1) find and theoretically know in advance the possible fulfillment to which the is-to-be of practical knowledge points (and only realize this possibility through practical knowledge of it and action for it), or (2) somehow by their practical knowledge make (that is, invent and fashion) their own fulfillment's very possibility, not merely its realization. Plainly, the second is absurd, for human persons are not beings without an essence, who can be and flourish as anything whatever by some impossible process of self-creation. Therefore, one must accept the first alternative."

However, the dichotomy is false. Human persons do not *find* and theoretically know in advance the possible fulfillment to which the is-to-be of practical knowledge points. But neither do they *invent* and fashion their own fulfillment's very possibility—as if there were some sort of creative art or technology for living human life. The true alternative is: Beginning from first practical principles, which human persons neither select nor fashion, they *develop* their fulfillment's possibility. In this development, practical knowledge *anticipates* the possible fulfillment—which is to be—to whose realization it guides action.

Theoretical *knowledge* of this possible fulfillment begins and grows only as it is unfolded and actualized. Persons cannot know just what they can become *as persons* before they become—that is, act and know the fruit of acting. If the preceding theoretical statement seems strange, its strangeness is easily dispelled by going back to the relevant phenomena.

For example, by a first principle of practical knowledge, one knows that it is good to know, and one is therefore alive to knowing. This simple volition bears upon everything one can ever know. But one does not thereby find and know in advance the possibility of human fulfillment through knowing—to what knowing might extend and what it will be like as it gradually unfolds (perhaps for millions of years to come).

Yet because of one's anticipation of and interest in knowing certain sorts of things, one recognizes as choiceworthy many possible actions one might do for the sake of knowing. Available options, which depend on one's endowments and opportunities, are known in advance, and part of this advance knowledge is theoretical—for example, that we could proceed with our research in this way.

But the possibility of action and that of fulfillment through it are not identical. When one is interested in knowing, one is not primarily interested in what one can do by way of inquiry (or even in what one can be in carrying on the inquiry). Rather, one is interested in knowing what one will know, and in becoming what one will be, if one's inquiry succeeds. But precisely insofar as inquiry succeeds, one comes to know not only what one did not know beforehand, but also the fulfillment which practical knowledge anticipated in knowing that knowing is a good to be pursued. Once one goes beyond the knowing which occurs without deliberation and choice, one can only find out what one can know *and* what knowing really is by trying.

One might suppose that this example works only because it concerns knowledge. But there is a similar ignorance in all anticipations of any of the benefits one hopes for in acting through choice by reason of any of the basic goods.

Even in acting for health, although one knows what it is to feel well, one hopes for something more than that. One anticipates a certain smooth functioning, without knowing exactly what will constitute it. One has a choice whether and how to act—what regimen to adopt, what treatment to accept, and so on—because one cannot tell in advance exactly what benefit any particular action may yield.

Again, an engaged couple who are committed to building a happy marriage cannot predict what their marital friendship will turn out to be like as it unfolds. They will learn what the anticipated and intended benefits really are only by faithfully keeping their mutual commitment.

C. The First Principle of Practical Reasoning

The special character of practical truth can be further clarified by considering the first principle of practical reasoning, and seeing how it functions as a principle.

Every reasoning process which terminates in nonhypothetical truths presupposes self-evident first principles as its most basic premises. But every reasoning process also presupposes a self-evident first principle which does not serve as a premise—the principle of noncontradiction. No first principle which serves as a premise can be a principle of all reasoning, because the whole family of reality (about which one can reason) is not of one genus. But the principle of noncontradiction is a principle of all reasoning.

How does the principle of noncontradiction function as a principle of all reasoning? By prohibiting incoherence. Thinking can be incoherent, and the principle of noncontradiction cannot prevent that. But it does function as a norm of thinking by requiring that incoherence be eliminated when it is discovered. Incoherent thinking cannot contribute to genuine knowledge because reality, unlike thinking, cannot be inconsistent. Thus, by prohibiting incoherence, the principle of noncontradiction makes its proper and indispensable contribution to knowledge.

In demanding that incoherence when discovered be eliminated, the principle of noncontradiction exercises a certain priority over all self-evident first principles which are premises, for it puts them to work. It does this by demanding a reevaluation of any incoherent pair of propositions which one had considered true. Such a reevaluation of the contradictory pair of propositions will use as a standard something one thinks is, or is reducible to, some self-evident principle.

The principle of noncontradiction operates in practical as in all other reasoning. But another self-evident first principle, *Good is to be done and pursued*, operates in all practical reasoning. Unlike the first practical principles which serve as premises, it is like the principle of non-contradiction in not serving as a premise. For just as being is not a single genus, so the good is not a single genus [section III(C)]. That which arouses interest—goodness—can be instantiated through action only by the action's bringing about a benefit of one or another category.

How does the first principle of all practical reasoning function as a principle? By prohibiting pointlessness. The point of practical knowledge is the intelligent direction of action toward human fulfillment, and this point can be lost even though practical thinking goes on, just as thinking in general can go on despite its incoherence.

For example, people who have failed to do what in some sense they should have done often pointlessly deliberate about what they might have done, even though they do not think their reasoning can intelligently guide their action toward any benefit. Again, inasmuch as actions should embody practical knowledge, people often become aware of pointlessness when they continue to do something habitually after it no longer promises the benefit it once provided. Although the emotional motive is still effective, one can recognize the pointlessness of one's action: "It's silly to keep on doing this, but . . . ."

Thus, the first principle of practical reasoning does not *prevent* pointlessness. But it functions as a norm by directing that pointlessness *be eliminated* when it is discovered. In demanding that pointlessness be eliminated, the first, common principle of practical reasoning exercises its priority over the self-evident principles which are premises. It does this by requiring that every deliberate action be undertaken ultimately for the sake of some benefit—that is, something in which one is basically interested because one is directed to it by a practical principle which is a premise of one's practical knowledge.

Practical knowledge directs to the fulfillment possible through action, and benefits constitute this fulfillment. So pointless thinking, which cannot direct action toward realizing any benefit, adds nothing to the knowledge of practical truth. If pointless thinking is coherent, it does not fall short of truth and falsity in the way that incoherent thinking—whether theoretical or practical—does. However, since it does not direct action toward bringing something into conformity with a practical proposition, pointless thinking falls short of *practical* truth and falsity. Therefore, by prohibiting pointlessness, the first principle of practical reasoning makes its appropriate and indispensable contribution to practical knowledge.

GERMAIN GRISEZ, JOSEPH BOYLE, AND JOHN FINNIS 121

Part Two: Moral Truth

VII. From Practical Principles to the Moral Ought

A. The First Principle of Morality

Although the first principle of practical reasoning prohibits pointlessness, it does not in the same way prohibit every sort of unreasonableness in practical thinking.

Even morally bad actions have their point. One chooses to do what is morally wrong for some reason, and like any other deliberate action, the reason for which one acts immorally must ultimately be reduced to the basic goods. So far forth, even an immoral act responds to the first principle: Good is to be done and pursued.

However, morally wrong acts do not respond to this principle as perfectly as morally good acts do. To see why, one must consider the relationship between the principles of practical knowledge and those of morality.

In prohibiting pointlessness, the first principle of practical reasoning as it were demands: Take as a premise at least one of the principles corresponding to the basic goods and follow through to the point at which you somehow instantiate that good through action. This demand is minimal and leaves one free to do anything from which one can anticipate any benefit whatsoever.

One can imagine another principle making a far stronger demand: Insofar as it is in your power, allow nothing but the principles corresponding to the basic goods to shape your practical thinking as you find, develop, and use your opportunities to pursue human fulfillment through your chosen actions. This stronger demand is, not only that one be reasonable enough in one's practical thinking to avoid pointlessness, but that one be entirely reasonable in such thinking.

This stronger demand is inconsistent with many possible choices consistent with the weaker demand. The possible choices excluded by the stronger demand are those which are immoral, for the stronger demand is a way of expressing the first principle of morality. This expression of the first moral principle makes it clear that to be morally good is precisely to be completely reasonable. *Right reason* is nothing but *unfettered reason*, working throughout deliberation and receiving full attention.

Unfortunately, reason is not always unfettered. Basic goods are not the only source of motivation for rationally guided actions. Only emotionally appealing possibilities come up for deliberation, and feeling also is necessary to carry out any proposal one adopts by choice [section II(C)]. Since what is emotionally satisfying is not identical with but, at best, only part of what fulfills persons as such, feeling can and often does tend to motivate actions to goals more limited than the benefits for persons which practical knowledge proposes to be sought through action. The part can compete with the whole; satisfying the desires of the part can frustrate the interests of the whole.

B. How Possible Purposes Arise

It is worth looking closely at the process by which immoral choices come to be made. But first it is necessary to consider how possible purposes arise.

No choice ever is made unless one considers at least two incompatible possibilities: doing this or not doing it, doing this or doing that. For such deliberation to occur, one must have mixed feelings, which provide some motivation toward possible goals of action whose joint realization is inconsistent. One hesitates, looks for a way to dissolve the conflict, finds none, and becomes aware that a choice is needed.

The purposes of rationally directed actions are sometimes first urged by desire arising out of simple volition of basic goods and sometimes first urged by desire arising from feeling. For example, a physician interested in improving people's health may first think of the benefit promised by a particular project and only gradually become enthusiastic about pursuing it as a goal. But a patient seeking treatment may first have the goal of getting rid of unpleasant symptoms, and only with instruction appreciate the benefit of doing what is necessary to regain health.

Sometimes possible goals are fashioned by imagination under the direction of reason. Sometimes they are generated independently of reason. And sometimes each source contributes to an inconsistent set of possible goals.

Aside from those which presuppose a prior immoral choice, possible goals fashioned by imagination at the behest of reason cannot in themselves pose a challenge to reason. (Even so, as will be clear shortly, it can be wrong to choose to pursue them.) For the origin of such goals is in reason's own principles, by way of volitions, beginning with the simple volitions which the principles of practical reason specify. The purpose of the possible action proposed for choice includes a benefit whose prospect generated the goal; interest in that benefit preceded the emotional desire for the goal. Sometimes two purposes of this sort require one to make a choice, simply because one cannot act for both. Such choices are between morally good alternatives.

Sometimes a possible goal is generated independently of reason but is readily understood in terms of the principles of practical knowledge, so that the anticipated benefit could just as well have led reason to direct imagination to fashion that goal. For example, someone trying to finish some work in the garden on a winter day begins to think about going inside and leaving the work to be finished some other day. The goal of getting out of the cold, generated without reason's help, is readily understood as avoidance of dangerous overexposure—a purpose which could as well have been suggested by one's rational interest in staying alive and well. Thus, in such cases, too, the goal in itself poses no challenge to reason, and so one can choose to act for the purpose which includes the goal without fettering reason.

Sometimes, however, one chooses between an alternative generated in either of the ways just described and a possible action whose purpose will have been *synthesized* in a different way. The latter action, if chosen, will be rationally guided to its purpose; still, its goal will be gained at the expense of reason, part of whose directiveness will have been ignored by choice.

C. How to Make Immoral Choices

One can easily see how an immoral choice is made if the goal is set by some previous immoral choice. But it also occurs when a goal generated independently of reason leads one to synthesize a purpose of a peculiar sort. This sort of purpose is one for which a person cannot choose to act without that choice bearing upon other benefits and harms in a way different from that which unfettered reason would direct.

For example, hatred and anger suggest the goal of some harm to another.

The principles of practical knowledge of themselves *always direct* to the opposite—*to benefit persons*, both oneself and others. Moreover, these principles direct one to live at peace with others and to avoid hurting oneself, and everyone knows from experience that harming others is likely to have consequences contrary to these interests.

Still, in one or more of the basic goods one can find reasons which enable one to anticipate certain benefits from taking revenge—for example, that it will discourage future provocations and so make for more peaceful relations ("He'll never dare do that to me again!") or that failure to take revenge would be unjust ("It would be a crime to let her get away with that!").

One can know very well that such benefits are not reasonably anticipated here, and that, hostile feelings aside, one surely would not deliberately cause harm as one is tempted to do. Still, the unreasonableness of choosing to harm another can be ignored, for one never knows just what benefit can be achieved until one tries. And from the emotional point of view, there is no question that revenge would be sweet. This sweetness also can be understood as part of the potential benefit of vengeful action. For taking revenge will mollify hurt feelings and bring harmony between them and one's choice—since that *choice will be in accord with one's feelings!*

Thus, the vengeful person chooses, fettering reason by means of one of its own practical principles: that which directs toward the harmony of feelings with one another, and with judgments and choices.

Not all immoral choices come about in exactly the same way. Sometimes the action's purpose is morally sound: The goal poses no challenge to reason, the benefit is real, and similar acts can be chosen in other circumstances without any restriction of reason.

For example, in a public library, one sees a new novel one has been wanting to read, charges it out, and brings it home, having the goal of reading it and intending the benefit of esthetic experience. Thus far, no problem.

But one found the novel on a reserve shelf waiting to be claimed by another patron, and discarded a six-month waiting list, which had been attached to the book, before charging it out. The anticipated benefit, to be realized in oneself, is sought at the expense of others. And one knows that people cannot hope to live together in harmony if they treat one another as they themselves do not wish to be treated. Practical knowledge directs to fulfillment, which is reasonably anticipated only in community with others. Thus, feelings aside, one would not discard the waiting list and check the novel out.

Still, one is eager to read the novel, and so one can suppose that little harm need be anticipated to others if they must wait a while longer, that one has not used the library heavily of late and deserves a "fair share" of its resources, that the librarians are at fault for not providing extra copies of such a popular book and so on. A choice to take the book home satisfies one's eagerness to read it, and so brings *harmony between feelings and choice.*

The selfish person reasonably anticipates the same benefit as might have been derived from a similar act chosen without setting aside the interests of others. Nevertheless, like the vengeful person, the selfish person in choosing fetters reason by abusing one of its own practical principles.

In sum. If feelings simply determine action, then that action is not rationally guided, and so in itself is neither morally good nor evil. But feelings can impair the rational guidance of an action without determining it. They do this by proposing goals whose pursuit can be made into a purpose of rationally guided action, but only by a free choice which fetters reason and limits its directiveness.

D. The Emergence of the Moral *Ought*

Immoral choice fetters reason by adopting a proposal to act without adequate regard for some of the principles of practical reason, and so without a fully rational determination of action. And so, when an immoral choice is made, the principles of practical knowledge are embodied less perfectly than they would be if a morally acceptable proposal were adopted. This point deserves further consideration.

When practical knowledge is confronted with the tendency of feeling to restrict it by urging a possibility whose choice would fetter it, the is-to-be of practical knowledge becomes ought-to-be. The *directiveness* of practical knowledge *becomes normativity* because what is to be might not actually come to be and yet still rationally is to be. Of course, there is some reason in the basic goods for choosing the immoral possibility, and so it also is considered a purpose which is to be. But the ought-to-be which calls for morally right choice represents the full directiveness of the principles of practical knowledge, while the is-to-be which commends the morally wrong choice represents only a fragment of that directiveness operating in isolation from the whole.

Hence, it is clear in what sense morally wrong acts do not respond to the first principle of practical reasoning as well as good acts do. Since that principle underlies the directiveness of all the basic goods, it is embodied in morally wrong actions insofar as they are formed by that directiveness. But only morally right choices respond fully to all of the principles of practical knowledge. Thus, only morally right choices respond perfectly to the first principle of practical reasoning.

VIII. Moral Truth: Comparisons and Contrasts

A. Practical Truth, Moral Truth, and Moral Falsity

The truth of practical knowledge with respect to its first principles is their adequation to possible human fulfillment considered precisely insofar as that fulfillment can be realized through human action [section VI(A)].

Moral truth is a kind of practical truth.

Kinds within a genus often are differentiated by the addition of some further intelligibility. But moral truth as a kind of practical truth is not differentiated from moral falsity by the addition of any intelligibility other than the intelligibility proper to practical knowledge as such. Rather, *moral truth is differentiated by the integrity with which it directs to possible human fulfillment* insofar as that can be realized by carrying out choices. Thus, moral falsities—for example, "That so-and-so should be wiped out" and "One must look out for number one"—are specified by the incompleteness due to which they lack adequacy to possible human fulfillment insofar as that can be realized by carrying out choices.

Consequently, (1) moral truths and (2) moral falsities are differentiated by their opposed relationships to the whole set of practical principles, which can be brought to bear in practical judgment either (1) integrally or (2) only selectively.

Reality as a whole, which metaphysics studies, has some ontological conditions superior to human reason and some inferior to it, and so—Hegel to the contrary notwithstanding—the theory that truth is coherence is bad metaphysics. But the moral domain has no proper principle other than the principles of practical knowledge itself, although its ultimate principle is beyond human reason [section XII(A)]. Therefore, in the moral domain truth is the whole, and falsity is a part, abstracted from the whole and thereby made to rationally guide action in a misguided way, just as if the part were by itself the whole.

B. Practical Truths Which Are Not Moral Truths

Practical truths which are not moral truths are of two kinds. Of one kind are practical principles—for example: Knowledge is a good to be pursued—which fall short of integral adequacy to human fulfillment only because their proper directiveness is no more than an element of the directiveness of practical knowledge as a whole.

Practical truths of this sort are operative before moral issues arise. They are necessary conditions for the simple volition which gives rise to deliberation. So far forth, practical principles can be called "premoral."

But, as we have explained, the several practical principles are moral principles when the whole set of practical principles works together and constitutes the integral directiveness of practical knowledge. Thus, practical principles *never lack* the *moral relevance* which emerges when moral issues arise. So far forth, practical principles can be called "moral."

The other kind of practical truths which are not moral truths are moral falsities. Just insofar as moral falsities do give some rational direction to an action, they are practical truths. Action in their light is not pointless, but fruitful in realizing some benefit (though miserable), some fragment (though mutilated) of integral human fulfillment.

Practical truths of this sort operate by secession from moral consideration. So far forth, the practical truth of moral falsities can be called "amoral." But such partial truths can never escape their moral falsity. So far forth, their effectiveness in practical thinking is better called "immoral."

C. The Relationship between *Ought* and *Is*

In view of the preceding account of practical truth and moral truth, it should be clear why one cannot derive the moral *ought* from any theoretical *is*.

The moral *ought* cannot be reduced to the *is-to-be* of practical truth without eliminating the distinction between the directiveness of a practical judgment that something immoral is to be done and the normativity of the moral truth that it should not be done. The *is-to-be* of practical truth cannot be reduced to the *is* of human nature without eliminating the distinction between, on the one hand, action and fulfillment through it, and, on the other, what persons are by nature, prior to their exercise of free choice.

Still, this twofold irreducibility does not mean that morality is cut off from its roots in human nature. For the normativity of the moral *ought* is nothing but the integral directiveness of the is-to-be of practical knowledge. And any adequate theory of human persons will include among its true propositions: Everyone who does rationally guided actions naturally knows the first principles of practical knowledge and naturally wills (by simple volition) the goods to which they direct. In this sense, the is-to-be of the first principles of practical knowledge is itself an aspect of human nature.

D. Formulations of the First Moral Principle

As we have formulated and developed our basic normative theory over the years, we sometimes presented it without offering any explicit formulation of the first principle of morality.

On those occasions, we began with an account of the principles of practical knowledge corresponding to the basic goods and moved directly to moral principles such as those requirements of practical reasonableness which demand fairness, forbid revenge, exclude doing evil to achieve good, and so forth. These intermediate moral principles are the modes of responsibility. They do not refer to any specific kinds of acts, but they are more specific than the first principle of morality, because they specify, in several ways, how any action must be willed if it is to comply with the first principle of morality. Although modes of responsibility presuppose the first principle of morality, we have sometimes presented them as if they were direct implications of thoroughgoing practical reasonableness.

The preceding explanation [sections VII(A); VIII(A); VIII(C)] makes it clear why we sometimes failed to formulate the first moral principle. For that principle merely articulates the integral directiveness of the first principles of practical knowledge, when they are working together harmoniously in full concert.

Some of our attempts to formulate the first principle of morality also have been defective. For example, in several early works Grisez suggested that the basic moral requirement is to act for at least some good and to avoid violating any basic good. This formulation expresses two of the modes of responsibility but fails to express their common ground, which also is the ground of other modes, such as fairness.

Again, some of our works suggested that the basic moral requirement is to choose with an inclusivistic attitude—that is, an attitude which maintains respect for the values which are not chosen. This formulation points to the integrity which in fact is constitutive of moral truth, but fails to articulate the way in which the integral directiveness of practical knowledge constitutes moral truth.

Our current attempt to formulate the first principle of morality is: In voluntarily acting for human goods and avoiding what is opposed to them, one ought to choose and otherwise will those and only those possibilities whose willing is compatible with a will toward integral human fulfillment.

This formulation focuses on the principle of morality insofar as it is the principle of moral goodness which actualizes moral truth. We focused above on the principle of morality insofar as it is the integral directiveness of practical reason. [Sections VII(A-D); VIII(A)]. The relationship between these two aspects of the principle of morality is readily explained.

Moral truth is the integrity of the directiveness of practical knowledge. Ideally, free choices would consistently respond to this full directiveness. Since moral truth points to human fulfillment, ideally the freely chosen actions shaped by moral truth would bear fruit in the fulfillment of all persons in all the basic goods. This *ideal community* is what we mean by "integral human fulfillment." A good will is one fully responsive to thoroughgoing practical reason. Therefore, the morally good will is a will toward integral human fulfillment.

This ideal of good will implies intermediate moral principles—the modes of responsibility—from which specific moral norms can be deduced. Thus it enables one to bring the integral directiveness of practical reason to bear upon choices.

IX. Virtues and Moral Principles

A. The Priority of Moral Principles

Up to this point, we have not talked about virtue. As we have shown [sections VII(A-D); VIII(A)], the first principles of moral truth are the principles of practical knowledge, and so the virtues cannot be first principles of moral truth. But we do consider virtues to be essential to *moral life*, because they are aspects of a person who is (more or less) wholly integrated with moral truth, and only such a person can live a morally good life.

Apart from the theoretical inadequacy of attempting to reduce moral truth to the virtues, such an attempt also is unsatisfactory from the practical point of view. For ethical reflection really is helpful only if it can examine and criticize the assumptions underlying accepted virtues and vices. Reflection which takes a way of life for granted, as Aristotle, for example, did, fails to overcome the inadequacies in a society's political structure, religion, and so on which prevent its morally good members from attaining, or even accurately conceiving, the true happiness to which their hearts are open.

Virtues can be evaluated by moral principles. Virtues are character traits, which organize the various aspects of the complex human personality. The ordering of these aspects establishes some form of harmony among feeling, judgment, choice, performance, and so on. Such harmonies are themselves realizations of basic goods. But the *quality* of these realizations depends on the extent to which they *embody moral truth*. Hence, only those character traits are true virtues which realize harmonies within the personality acccording to the demands of moral truth.

Of course, these demands must be brought to bear. The very general theory of moral truth proposed above is not sufficient to do that. Nor can specific moral norms, even if assumed as certainly true, serve as an adequate standard for judging character traits, whose range will always extend beyond particular types of action. However, as we briefly indicated above [sections VII(C); VIII(D)], there are intermediate emoral principles—the modes of responsibility. These are specifications of the first principle of morality, and, in turn, provide premises for deducing specific moral norms. They also provide a standard by which one can evaluate character traits, to see which are genuine virtues.

For example, an element of character which too often affects the treatment of evildoers is the disposition to exact retribution out of anger and hatred. (Think of those arguments for capital punishment which have no principle but such passions.) In evaluating character traits to distinguish true justice from its counterfeits, one standard is the mode of responsibility that one should avoid taking revenge. By this standard, a character trait which involves the disposition to exact retribution out of hostile feelings clearly is not true justice.

Another of the modes of responsibility is fairness. So, in attempting to discern true justice, one also looks for that harmony between concerns for self and for others which disposes people to act according to the Golden Rule, rather than be satisfied with the conventional justice of their society, which allows them, if free Athenians to use others as slaves, if contemporary Americans to kill their unborn children, and so on.

Although virtues are not primary principles of moral truth, genuine virtues are starting points of morality in the sense that they are conditions for a morally good life. Virtues are aspects of the fully integrated personality of a good person. Such a personality concretely realizes the reflexive goods in accord with moral truth. Hence, such a person is not torn between a will toward integral human fulfillment and desires for mutilated fragments of it, which often have greater emotional appeal. Therefore, such a person can consistently choose what is morally right and fulfill the requirements of a truly happy life—one integrated by a morally good religious commitment [see section XII(C)].

B. Virtues and Moral Judgment

Without having virtues at the outset, people can proceed soundly from practical principles to judgments about what they ought to do. Yet there are two ways in which judgments reached by sound practical reasoning can fall short of full moral truth.

First, in their reflection, people often fail to take into account all available options and other relevant aspects of the situation in which they make a choice. For example, if someone whose interests are at stake is overlooked, a judgment otherwise soundly made is likely to be objectively unfair.

Second, a sound judgment often leaves open which of two or more morally acceptable options will comport best with those concrete aspects of the agent's personality and situation which, because they resist reflective analysis, can be evaluated only by a kind of moral taste or discernment. For example, a sound judgment that one should seek an education leaves open many options.

Such shortcomings in judgments about what one is to do or ought to do are possible despite sound practical reasoning, because parts of the personality other than the rational part contribute both to one's attention to what is relevant and to one's discernment in the area which resists reflective analysis. Therefore, these shortcomings cannot be overcome without virtues to dispose all aspects of the personality to function harmoniously in the light of moral truth.

C. How Virtues Can Be Acquired

It follows that virtues and judgments which attain full moral truth are mutually interdependent. Their interdependence raises the question: How can anyone acquire a virtue?

The answer is that a child whose character is not yet formed can freely choose in accord with a judgment reached by sound practical reasoning. Even if the child's *judgment falls short* of full moral truth, the child's *will*, both exercised and formed in such choices, in no way conflicts with moral truth and, indeed, *conforms* to it, insofar as the child is aware of it. Though character is still undeveloped, such good will is the budding forth of virtue.

Thus, insofar as people choose in accord with soundly reasoned practical judgments, especially in making major commitments, they have the core of the virtues. In carrying out such morally good choices, other aspects of the personality will gradually be drawn into line, errors in moral thinking corrected, and facility in carrying out right choices gained. In this way, virtues are acquired.

In this struggle, people can find some help in sound ethical theory. But they will be impeded by exhortations to embody the morally inadequate "virtues" of the model members of their society. So ethical theory must reduce moral judgments to first principles, rather than treat virtues as if they were irreducible starting points.

Part Three: Ultimate Ends

X. Ends Ultimate in Three Diverse Ways

A. The Ultimate End Rectifying the Will

Integral human fulfillment is not individualistic satisfaction of desires or preferences. The ideal of integral human fulfillment is that of the realization, so far as possible, of all the basic goods in all persons, living together in complete harmony [section VIII(D)]. Is not such a perfect community the ultimate natural end of all human persons and communities?

In a way it is. However, that community would include all persons, past, present, and future. And in the course of history, even in the course of each individual's life, new dimensions of goods unfold. Hence, "integral human fulfillment" cannot refer to a purpose to be pursued as a concrete objective of cooperative human effort. It cannot be anticipated as the outcome of some sort of human billion-year plan.

Moreover, integral human fulfillment is not a basic good alongside the others, nor some sort of supergood transcending all other categories of goodness. For integral human fulfillment is not a reason for acting, but an ideal whose attractiveness depends on all the reasons for acting which can appeal to morally good people.

One way in which integral human fulfillment is the ultimate natural end of persons and communities is that it is the ultimate object of good will. The ultimate object of good will is the ultimate end in the sense that what primarily rectifies the will orders to itself everything else one wills. But how can integral human fulfillment, which is neither a reason for all willing nor an ultimate benefit, rectify the will? How can it even be an object of will?

Integral human fulfillment is not an object of efficacious will. Morally good will, however, is specified (through the integral directiveness of practical knowledge) by the integral appetibility of all the basic goods [section VIII(A)]. Ideally, the fruit of such good will would be integral human fulfillment [see section VIII(D)]. Hence, a person of good will wishes (in accord with unfettered practical reason) for the realization of this ideal, and this wish rectifies the will in choosing.

Moreover, although only an ideal, integral human fulfillment is the nearest thing to what morally good people mean by happiness.

Happiness is usually taken to mean complete fulfillment—that is, having all one's desires satisfied. Everyone has some desires and wishes them to be satisfied. So, reflective persons who are morally good wish for all their morally acceptable actual and potential wishes to be fulfilled.

Such complete fulfillment of wishes, however, is impossible. The fulfilling of some wishes is incompatible with the fulfilling of others; people often must choose among morally acceptable alternatives. Therefore, although everyone wishes for perfect and fulfilling good—in which the will could rest—no one efficaciously wills such a good.

Rather, one at best settles for the happiness which can be achieved through efficacious willing of goods in accord with some specific ideal. For morally good persons, the ideal is integral human fulfillment. They settle for the happiness they have in benefiting themselves and others as they live a morally good life.

The happiness for which a morally good humankind would settle would be the most complete possible approximation to the ideal of integral human fulfillment. One can consider the happiness for which morally good persons settle their share in and contribution to this hypothetical approximation. So, although integral human fulfillment is an unrealizable ideal, there is a sense in which it can be considered the morally true ultimate natural end of persons, both as individuals and in community.

B. Basic Goods: Ultimate Reasons for Choosing

Nevertheless, integral human fulfillment cannot be the ultimate end in the sense of being the ultimate reason why one chooses or should choose whatever one chooses. In this sense, the basic goods are ultimate ends [section II(B)]. But they are aspects of human fulfillment—many, distinct, irreducible—which do not constitute a single ultimate reason why one chooses or should choose whatever one chooses. Is there no such thing?

There would be, if there were some one intelligible good unifying all the goodness of all the basic goods. But there is none. For there is no intelligible principle other than the basic goods to make choiceworthy the possibilities for which persons can act. And the basic goods correspond to the irreducibly diverse components of complex human nature.

But is not God the ultimate end of human persons? The remainder of this paper answers this question. To begin with, God is not the ultimate *reason* for acting.

The basic goods are reasons for actions [sections II(B-D); V(A)]. In choosing actions to instantiate the goods, one does not find the ultimate reason for one's choices in divine goodness. For, if divine goodness were the reason for one's actions, one's choices for its sake would lead to its instantiation as one's fulfillment, and that instantiation would be through one's actions. But, for two reasons, this cannot be. First, human fulfillment actualizes human possibility, and this possibility cannot be naturally actualized by any nonhuman sort of perfection, not even that of God. Second, human actions cannot lead to the instantiation of divine goodness.

Against the first reason, one might suppose that the human will's openness to anything good, together with its natural dynamism as appetite, somehow amount to a natural tendency toward divine goodness—as it were, amount to a habitual disposition underlying the will's aliveness to the various basic goods. On that supposition, one could naturally will everything else for the sake of divine goodness, which alone, being infinite, could exhaust the capacity of the will.

However, the truth is that one cannot naturally will everything else for the sake of divine goodness.

For: (1) Nothing is received except according to the capacity of what receives it. But the capacity for the full actualization of anything is determined by its nature. So, nothing receives its full actualization from goodness which does not fulfill its own nature. Now, divine goodness is the actuality of divine nature. Thus, it cannot be the actualization of human persons unless they either cease to be human or become simultaneously divine. Naturally they cannot be both human and divine. Hence, naturally human persons cannot be actualized by divine goodness without ceasing to be human.

But: (2) Human will is a human appetite. Every appetite tends toward the actualization of that of which it is an appetite. So, human will tends to human actualization. Now, nothing is actualized by ceasing to be. But whatever ceases to be what it is, ceases to be. Thus, nothing is actualized by ceasing to be what it is. Hence, human persons cannot be actualized by ceasing to be human.

Therefore: (3) Since human persons cannot naturally be actualized by divine goodness without ceasing to be human (from 1), and since they cannot be actualized by ceasing to he human (from 2), human persons cannot naturally be actualized by divine goodness.

And so the human will can have *no natural disposition to fulfillment in divine goodness*. In this sense, the hearts of human persons, considered precisely according to their human nature, are not made for God; rather they are made for human fulfillment. If human persons do not rest in human fulfillment, that is partly because they wrongly try to rest in mutilated fragments of it and partly because the human will (unlike the neoplatonic eros) is not for rest.

Furthermore, there can be no *natural* desire for what is *not the natural* end of human persons, namely, that vision, promised to those who "are God's children now," by which they "shall be like him" because they "shall see him as he is" (1 Jn 3:2). But Christian faith requires no such natural desire, for, according to it, that intimate vision of God is attained, not through human nature, but by a sharing in the divine nature, received as a gift by "water and the Spirit" (Jn 3:5) or by "adoption" (Rom 8:14-17, 23).

This Christian view that human persons can *be given* a share in the divine nature is perfectly consistent with the second reason why divine goodness cannot be the ultimate reason for one's actions: that human action cannot lead to the instantiation of divine goodness. For there is a difference between being given something as a gift and achieving it through one's action, and there also is a difference between divine goodness itself and its participations.

Human actions can and naturally do lead to the instantiation of certain *participations* in divine goodness.

The will's capacity is not limited to the basic goods, which mark out the finite boundaries of possible fulfillment. For any two options do have it in common that either can be chosen. The ground of their unity in this respect is not the different intelligible goods which make each choiceworthy, but their community in intelligible goodness, for which the will is the appetite. While each of the principles of practical knowledge directs that some good be done, all of them in common direct that good be done, and this common aspect of their directiveness corresponds to the will's natural openness to goodness.

For this reason, if one believes that unqualified goodness—goodness itself—is found in God, one will regard him as the source of the goodness of all the basic goods. In this perspective, every human fulfillment is a participation in divine goodness, and every human act is for the sake of divine goodness insofar as one can participate in it by the benefit for which one chooses to do the act. Hence, God can be considered the ultimate end of human persons and communities insofar as their fulfillment in their proper goods is a participation in his goodness.

One might ask whether God is not—or at least for some persons cannot be—the end of human life in a stronger sense than this. The answer is Yes. For among the goods which fulfill human persons and communities are knowledge of God and harmony with him. These ought to be the core of the ultimate end of human life in the sense considered next. [Also see section XII(C).]

C. The Happiness for Which People Settle

Not as an ultimate reason for their choices, but in a different sense, persons and communities find their ultimate ends in the fulfillment for which they settle as their approximation to happiness as they conceive it. If this fulfillment is unified, then everything they intend is either a part of it or a means to it. However, not all people have a single ultimate end in this sense.

One might suppose that immoral people necessarily pursue as their ultimate end some one good, such as riches, pleasure, or honor. But an immoral businessman can seek his fulfillment partly in his energetic acquisition of wealth and power, and partly in his exploitative relationships with women, without interrelating the two in any way except by assigning these diverse interests to different slots in his busy schedule.

Even morally good people can live nonintegrated lives. For example, a good ten-year old boy can find some fulfillment in his studies and some in playing Little League ball, without integrating these two areas of interest. Morally mature good people, whose lives are largely organized by morally good commitments, also can find fulfillment in some innocent activities which are not integrated with the rest of their lives—for example, a dedicated wife and mother may find some fulfillment by writing poetry in her occasional free moments, without integrating this activity with anything else in her life.

Still, while people *need not* live in view of anything unified which they settle for as happiness, people *should* pursue a single ultimate end in this sense [see section XII(C)].

And some people do. For example, Christians have in their commitment of faith a principle by which they can organize their entire lives. If they do so perfectly, their every thought, word, and deed carries out their commitment of faith; and so, always keeping the commandments, they love God with their whole mind, heart, soul, and strength, and love all their neighbors as themselves. Such a life fulfills, as perfectly as possible through their action, the wishes of those individuals and that community who live that life (insofar as they do). Therefore, such a life is a happy one, although it falls short of the unrealizable *ideal* of integral human fulfillment. For those who seek to live that life, the fulfillment it offers is the ultimate end *realizable* in this life through their human acts. (Christian faith also teaches that the life of faith both depends on God's grace and prepares for his reign, so that acts which make up the life of faith are cooperation toward human fulfillment in the heavenly kingdom [see section XII(D)].)

Yet the integration of one's life toward a single ultimate end is not guaranteed by making a commitment such as Christian faith which can organize one's entire life. For those who have made such a commitment nonetheless seek part of their fulfillment in activities which cannot be integrated by it. For example, Christians sometimes sin while maintaining their commitment of faith. But acts of sin and of faith cannot possibly have the same ultimate end.

The point is clearest in the case of a serious believer who is tempted to make a permanent commitment to a sinful friendship. Such a person may consider the alternatives of abandoning faith, giving up the friendship, or living in sin while trying to practice faith so far as possible. One who chooses the last of these, *in that single choice*, reaffirms faith for the sake of its ultimate end and adopts a sinful way of life for the sake of its ultimate end.

XI. Hierarchies and Orders of Values

A. Natural Priorities among the Basic Goods

The basic goods of the diverse categories are called "good" in irreducibly different senses, and none of the basic goods can be said meaningfully to be better than another [section III(C)]. It might seem to follow that these basic principles are an unordered crowd which offer no objective standard for setting moral priorities in life. But that is not so.

In three ways, the basic goods are involved in important hierarchies of values. Any basic good is an aspect of the fulfillment of persons, and so is superior to instrumental intelligible goods, which do not perfect persons as such. Any basic good is an aspect of the fulfillment of the person as such, and so is superior to sensible goods, each of which as sensible can fulfill only the sentient nature of a person. Any morally right action for any of the basic goods is superior to every morally wrong action for them, because morally right action contributes to the integral fulfillment of persons and communities while morally wrong action prevents that.

But none of these important hierarchies of values establishes priorities among the basic goods themselves. Thus, it might seem that their interrelationship depends entirely on individuals' free choices, which constitute diverse personal plans of life.

Some statements in some of our previous works may appear to suggest that view. But it is incorrect and incompatible with constant features of the theory developed in all of those works. For prior to anyone's free choice, unfettered practical reason establishes some priorities among one's interests in the different basic aspects of fulfillment.

One of the reflexive goods is harmony among judgment, choice, and performance. If one considers this harmony amorally, one can try to realize it by bringing one's judgments as well as one's performances into conformity with one's choices. However, if one considers this good morally—that is, with practical reason unfettered—one sees that the only way to realize it consistent with integral human fulfillment is by making sure that one's judgments are morally true, conforming one's choices to them, and striving to make one's performances carry out one's choices as perfectly as possible. Whenever one must choose between doing what is morally right and what is morally wrong, one must act according to one's conscience. In doing that, one rightly establishes the priority of one's interest in this form of harmony.

Another reflexive good is harmony among one's feelings and between them and one's choices. If one considers this harmony amorally, one can try to realize it by choosing in accord with one's feelings. However, if one considers this reflexive good morally, one sees that the only way to realize it consistent with integral human fulfillment is by bringing one's feelings into line with one's morally good choices: The fact that one option harmonizes feelings with one's reasonable choice requires one to prefer that alternative to another which simply harmonizes choice with feelings. In choosing the former option, one rightly gives reasonable choice priority over feelings.

The two preceding examples make it clear that interests in the reflexive goods understood from a moral point of view (that is, a completely reasonable point of view) take priority whenever these goods are at stake. But the moral point of view establishes priorities in other, less obvious ways.

No one can live a morally good life without living. The good of life can be pursued only in community with others; indeed, human persons come to be only in community with others who care for them. Morality demands that one play one's proper part in morally good cooperation with others, deal fairly with them, avoid taking revenge, and so on. Thus, without any choice on anyone's part, the good of harmony with others considered morally has as one of its specific forms the elementary community essential for survival. This form of harmony might be called "family solidarity." For children, one thing family solidarity means is obedience. So, for children, obedience to any morally legitimate command of their parents (and those who act on their parents' behalf) should take absolute priority over any other interest.

One could develop other examples to show how *unfettered practical reason* in various ways *establishes priorities among basic interests* in goods independently of anyone's situation or choice. Such priorities will hold always and everywhere; they are moral requirements for all human persons precisely as such.

Not all moral responsibilities are constituted by or derived from these natural moral priorities. Many duties arise from prior choices, either one's own or those of others, or from special conditions which do not affect every person. No one who has not wronged another has an obligation to make restitution. No one who has not made a marital commitment has an obligation to be faithful in marriage, and no one simply as a human person has an obligation to make such a commitment. No one who has not come to know truths important to others has an obligation to communicate truths to others.

In sum, while the basic goods, considered as principles of practical knowledge, are not ordered among themselves, it does not follow that these basic principles are an unordered crowd. Prior to anyone's choice, unfettered practical reason, together with the conditions which human nature inevitably sets for moral life, establish certain natural priorities among a good person's basic interests. It follows that these priorities set necessary conditions for any morally good life plan.

B. No Hierarchy among the Basic Goods

This order involving the basic goods, nevertheless, is not a hierarchy among them. It *does* establish a structure among the diverse aspects of human fulfillment, in the individual person and in community. But the principle of this order is moral truth—the integral directiveness of practical knowledge—not the primacy of any one of the basic goods. Thus, none of these is so absolutely prior that it prevails in every morally good choice.

One might suppose that the reflexive goods, morally considered, have such absolute priority. The most obvious example: The fact that a morally right alternative *is right* requires one to choose it. However, interest in this reflexive good prevails only in those situations of choice where it happens to be at stake. But in many cases, one chooses among morally acceptable alternatives. And in many other cases, a person can rightly prefer what is morally right, not because it is morally good, but for the sake of some substantive good. For example, a girl, hastening to the playground, chooses to stop to help an old man, who is confused and wandering in a busy street, simply because she intends his safety, not because she realizes her choice to be a moral obligation—a duty she has not yet grasped, although in the circumstances it would be objectively wrong for her to choose to go on to the playground.

It also is worth noting the implications of the fact that the initial understanding of the reflexive goods can be specified not only by moral truth but by moral falsity [section XI(A)]. Of course, the benefits people are interested in when they act for the reflexive goods cannot reasonably be anticipated unless the goods are morally specified and pursued accordingly. For instance, people cannot live together in peace without true justice. However, that is not self-evident nor can it be deduced from the relevant first principle of practical knowledge by itself. Thus, the first principles of practical knowledge which correspond to the reflexive goods are logically open to being specified immorally. When they are, interest in them may not have the priority which virtuous people give their interests in the reflexive goods.

Although it is difficult to conceptualize the reflexive goods without importing real or apparent moral values, a precise articulation of these basic goods would avoid describing them in moral terms. Generally, our previous writings did not avoid that. Rather, we called the harmony between judgments and choices "practical reasonableness," that between choices and performances "authenticity," that among persons "justice," that with God "holiness" or "the agreement of human free choices with God's will," and so on.

C. Purposes in Life, Commitments, and Life Plans

Morally good people do have definite purposes in life which extend far beyond anything they expect to realize through choices of particular actions. For example, a married couple with children have the purpose of raising their children. This purpose in obvious ways organizes a large part of their lives. And this structuring is morally required of them, not a matter about which they are free to do as they please.

Not every couple need have the purpose of raising children since not every couple has children. But for those who do, the requirements of basic goods to be realized in the children, together with the moral requirements of family solidarity, demand that the relationships of the woman and man to one another and to their children be chosen as a long-term ordering principle of their lives. This choice is a commitment. The object of the commitment includes all the benefits hoped for in raising the children. So, this purpose is a moral principle in the sense that it is a source of integration in the lives of parents.

Most people hope for benefits besides those which pertain to family life. Fulfillment in any of the basic goods can (at least under some conditions) require dependable cooperation for an indefinite period among two or more persons. The securing of such cooperation requires other commitments to act with others—for example, in work outside the family, in seeking knowledge and communicating it to others, and in maintaining social peace.

Each of the purposes in life established by a commitment organizes a significant part of a person's life. Indeed, as experience teaches, the parts of one's life organized in this way often overlap. Therefore, a good person, conscientious about fulfilling responsibilities, will try to work out a unified, rational plan of life so that anticipated benefits will be realized as fully as possible through actions which do not interfere with one another.

For such persons, living according to their plan of life and enjoying the benefits of doing so *is a significant part* of the happiness for which they are prepared to settle. A sign of the soundness of their attitude is that morally sensitive people regularly say of good people who have died, "So-and-so had a happy life," when they had a clear plan of life, held to it to the end, and within normal limits achieved their purposes.

Yet a happy life in this sense does *not comprise every benefit* which will be sought by a good person. Play often is the sole reason for choosing a morally acceptable action. The mother who writes poetry in her free moments, the pope who occasionally skis, are engaging in humanly fulfilling activities which they need not direct to any of the purposes set by their commitments and which they can undertake without making any additional commitment of the sorts considered thus far.

For this very reason, such activity and the benefits enjoyed in it often are considered of little moral significance, and the good of play often is considered a rather odd sort of basic good. Still, without being tightly integrated under one's life plan, play—and other goods as well, at times—can significantly contribute to the happiness of a good life.

XII. Morality, Religion, and God

A. Why a Religious Commitment Is Required

A morally good person's plan, as described thus far, will coordinate several purposes and leave room for activities done for still other benefits. But we said [section X(C)] and in this final part of the paper will try to show that the life of a virtuous person should be unified in view of a single purpose.

We think that such a purpose can be established by a religious commitment and cannot be established without it. Why do we think so?

Every human fulfillment can be considered a participation in divine goodness—goodness itself [section XI(B)]. Many morally good persons consider real this participating of their acts in the goodness of God, whom they regard as a transcendent source of meaning and value. So, such persons believe that the good of religion—that is, harmony with the source or sources of meaning and value—is morally exigent whenever it is at stake.

Clearly, this good is in fact realized whenever one must choose between what is right and what is wrong, and chooses what is right. The question, however, is: How does the good of religion come to be at stake in such a way that it becomes a distinct reason for acting? And why is a specific commitment to it morally necessary?

Contingent realities, including human persons and their lives, point to a transcendent reality: something which is, is not contingent, and is the source of everything contingent. Only such a source can account for the *is* of what *is but need not be*. Hence, there is a more-than-human source of the whole world, including human experience, feeling, thought, volition, action, and fulfillment. Moreover, because contingent reality *is but need not be*, its transcendent source is reasonably thought of as if it were causing through *free choice*. If so, it is like an acting human person, causing according to a plan, and so is the source of the meaning which human thought finds in reality.

The directiveness of practical knowledge is one contingent reality among others; like any other, it points to its transcendent source. But the directiveness of one's practical knowledge also points to a transcendent source in another and special way. For the is-to-be of the principles of practical knowledge not only is underived but is known to be underived—that is, to be a starting point which humankind does not give itself but naturally has as a precondition for all human self-direction and rationally guided action. Just as the *is* of any contingent reality as such points to its transcendent source, so the *is-to-be* of the directiveness of practical knowledge *points to its transcendent source.* But since, in this case, the transcendent source is of directiveness, that source can only be thought of as if it were a person anticipating human fulfillment and leading human persons toward it.

Aware of this more-than-human source of meaning and value, most human persons also are acutely aware that they are not in complete harmony with it. For everyone sometimes makes immoral choices. And everyone finds the natural environment, which so clearly points to its transcendent source, in some respects a hard and cruel world. The fish are not to be found; crops fail; fire destroys carefully built dwellings; everyone gets sick, is hurt, and eventually dies. Harmony with the more-than-human source of meaning and value plainly must be pursued.

But *how* to begin to pursue harmony with a more-than-human person is far from clear. It is not like pursuing harmony with the people next door. Thus, most men and women of most times and places have recognized that they should seek to know what they can about this transcendent source, learn how to get along with it, and put into practice what they learn. In other words, among the natural responsibilities of human persons is the duty to seek religious truth, embrace what appears to be that truth, and live according to it.

Those who sincerely try to fulfill this fundamental religious duty realize that they cannot do so as isolated individuals but only in their various communities. Different groups of people accept as true different views of God and his relationship to humankind, and so develop diverse practices in their efforts to live in harmony with God. Both because these practices aim to serve vitally important purposes and because these purposes are related to constant features of any community's life, dependable cooperation in them is morally required, and so morally good people make a communal religious commitment.

In a simple culture, people may not clearly ditsinguish this commitment from their commitment to live with one another at peace; religion is simply a vital and pervasive aspect of the people's whole way of life. But the religious commitment is distinguishable insofar as it structures cooperation not only among people themselves but also with God (or the gods). Prayer and sacrifice, for example, are parts of almost every people's effort to interact with the divine, using as a model the ways people living together in peace interact with one another: by conversation, sharing the necessities of life, and gift-giving.

B. God: Cooperator with Human Agents

To understand how only a religious commitment can integrate the whole of a morally good life, one must understand more exactly the inevitable and dynamic relationship between morality, immorality, and religion of various sorts. To understand this, one must consider two things: first, how the human will, although not naturally oriented toward divine goodness as its object [section X(B)], comes to will that goodness in the course of willing human fulfillments; and second, how this concomitant willing of divine goodness develops into selfish love in morally bad wills, but would develop into genuine mutuality in a morally good will.

The truth of practical knowledge anticipates that to which it is adequate [section VI(A-B)]. In every rationally guided and freely chosen action, one not only wills some basic good, emotionally desires to bring about an expected state of affairs as the goal of one's performance, and chooses to do something, but wills (intends) anticipated benefits, in which one is interested for oneself and/or another. So, every action is done in the hope that it will contribute to fulfillment.

Just insofar as a benefit is to be realized through the action whose intelligible purpose it is, this fulfillment is not known in advance. For one cannot know just what one can be before one lives (nor, for example, what one's children can be before one has children and brings them up).

Moreover, the fulfillment one hopes for is not in one's own power. In acting, one always hopes for the best. When action is fruitful as one hopes it will be, the fruit always depends on factors in addition to one's action. Thus, success in achieving the benefits one intends is anticipated but cannot be taken for granted.

And in hoping, even if one does not think about it clearly, one hopes in whomever or whatever will make one's effort fruitful. When success comes, one can say that fate smiled and thank one's lucky stars. Or one can receive the hoped for benefit as a gift—unexpected insofar as it is surprising—and thank God for it, thinking that his providence and benevolence made fruitful the work of one's hands.

Therefore, in intending an anticipated and hoped for benefit, every human person in every action wills, in more or less complete accord with practical knowledge, that the benefit come about both through the action and through whatever other causality is required, insofar as that fulfillment is beyond the agent's own knowledge and power.

Insofar as one hopes in persons rather than in mere things, the fruit of one's own action necessarily is seen as the fruit of the other's action as well. But, as we have explained, the transcendent source both of the is-to-be of practical knowledge and of the actuality of every hoped for fulfillment is naturally thought of as if it were a person. Therefore, for those who recognize the reality of a more-than-human personal source of meaning and value, *every human action is carried out in cooperation* with that unseen, more-than-human source, understood to be both directing human persons toward their fulfillment and helping them to bring it about.

In any cooperation, the other party, as a personal agent, also has intentions. Cooperation occurs because both parties hope to share in fulfillment. But common fulfillment is the set of benefits in which persons acting together are interested. So, in willing one's own fulfillment through action, one also wills what in fact will fulfill the other. Hence, in every action every human person naturally and *necessarily wills* (what cannot be thought of otherwise than as) a *fulfillment of the unseen source* of meaning and value.

(God's "fulfillment" is spoken of here and in what follows by relational predication; such predication posits in God only some perfection, in itself beyond human understanding, sufficient to sustain the relationship which some immanent reality has to him. Thus, propositions involving relational predication about God's "fulfillment" do not—though they may seem to—imply that he lacks anything. Indeed, they are not only consistent with, but are rightly understood only by bearing in mind, those propositions which exclude from God every conceivable kind of defect, lack, and imperfection.)

This willing is the fundamental human love of God, which is natural in the sense that nobody who recognizes the reality of a more-than-human, personal source of meaning and value ever acts without it. It might seem that this fundamental love of God necessarily makes him into a mere means of achieving human purposes. But that is not so. For a means is within one's power, while God emerges in the very exercise of human agency as one who directs human persons to act and brings about what is not within their power.

Moreover, as in other cooperative relationships, people can will what fulfills the other in this relationship not only insofar as it is necessary for their own fulfillment and in fact fulfills the other, but precisely insofar as it does fulfill the other. In other words, in their cooperation with God, people can will his fulfillment insofar as it fulfills him. If they do so will it, they truly love God as a person—someone distinct from themselves with whom they cooperate.

C. Religion and the Overarching Purpose of Life

Precisely here, morally good and bad wills differ. Insofar as a morally bad will intends benefits and wills what is necessary to obtain them, it also wills what is in fact the fulfillment of others, including God, just insofar as necessary to its own fulfillment. But the morally bad will does not, in its bad willing, will what fulfills God insofar as it fulfills him. Only a good will does so.

For in fettering practical reason, the bad will ignores part of the direction it receives. In rejecting morally good alternatives, therefore, it rejects the benefits which would accrue through those actions to others, including God—benefits to which unfettered practical reasons would guide action. Yet the morally bad will still hopes to benefit from the help of others, including God. Hence, the morally bad will subordinates the fulfillment of others to the benefit it seeks for itself. Rather than a relationship of mutuality, the morally bad will establishes an exploitative relationship.

Those who relate to others in this way try to coerce them, trick them, manipulate them, bargain with them, evade their claims for mutuality, and, ultimately, get along without them. Many entire religions and some forms of every religion are marked with these signs of morally bad will.

A commitment to such a religion cannot set any single, overarching purpose for one's whole life, for the purpose of such a religious commitment is strictly subordinated to one's other purposes. And such a set of purposes cannot be unified because immorality mutilates and disintegrates one's fulfillment.

But even in such cases, people's religious commitment can unify their entire plan of life as no other commitment can. For harmony with the divine, however misconceived, will be thought to condition one's hopes of achieving every other purpose in life.

A morally good will accepts all the direction it receives from practical knowledge and its transcendent source. Not rejecting any aspect of human fulfillment, it *need not subordinate* to itself *the interests of the other* with whom it cooperates. Enjoying the benefits of cooperation, the good will also can be grateful to God and rejoice in his fulfillment.

As in every cooperative relationship, in following God's direction—that is, unfettered practical reason—people sometimes find themselves unfulfilled: They do their best yet the anticipated benefit is not realized. In experiencing and accepting failure, morally good people submit to the intention of God, who could have granted them success, but did not, obviously for some reason of his own. In this submission, human persons will God's fulfillment insofar as it fulfills him—love him as a person.

For morally good persons, their religious commitment will provide at least one purpose to integrate all their other commitments. This is so because, as we explained above [section XII(A)], the good of religion is in fact realized whenever one must choose between what is right and wrong, and chooses what is right. And so, for one striving to live in harmony with the source of the moral *ought* and realizing that this harmony conditions all other hopes, this good's being at stake in every area of life sets one overarching purpose: always *to avoid immorality* as contrary to God's intention—that is, *as sin*—in order to avoid disharmony with this more-than-human source of meaning and value.

Therefore, a good person whose religious view includes nothing incompatible with moral truth will settle only for a happiness which consists in living according to a plan of life unified by the purpose of avoiding sin. Although this single, overarching purpose sets no specific affirmative requirement beyond that of moral truth itself, it does integrate the whole of life, because the religious good for the sake of which morally good persons intend this purpose becomes one reason why they do everything else they do.

D. Christian Faith: "Seek First the Kingdom . . ."

Some religious views specify commitments of faith with far richer purposes than the negative one of remaining blameless before God. Those who share the commitment of Christian faith and those who understand its moral significance, even if they do not share it, will easily see what such a positive purpose might be and how it could integrate the whole of people's lives.

For Christian faith teaches that a divine person, the Word, became a man, Jesus, and that Jesus set about to establish a universal community, the new covenant. In this community, all men and women can cooperate with God in completing his work of creating, redeeming, and sanctifying humankind. The purpose of this cooperation is the kingdom of heaven; life on this earth is no mere means to the kingdom but its embryonic stage. As Christian faith anticipates it, the kingdom will include every sort of benefit intended by morally good wills.

If one considers this teaching credible, one plainly ought to accept it, for it offers the hope of realizing the closest imaginable approximation to integral human fulfillment.

If one makes the commitment of Christian faith, one enters into human cooperation with Jesus: "Abide in me, and I in you. As the branch cannot bear fruit by itself, unless it abides in the vine, neither can you, unless you abide in me" (Jn 15:4). In bearing such fruit, one comes to love God in a new way. For, in willing one's own fulfillment in communion with Jesus, one wills the fulfillment of the divine person of the Word, according to his human nature. Jesus offers himself for those who cooperate with him: "Greater love has no man than this, that a man lay down his life for his friends. You are my friends if you do what I command you" (Jn 15:13-14). And precisely through this offering, Jesus attains his own fulfillment: He "for the joy that was set before him endured the cross . . ." (Heb 12:2).

Still, even this *human* love of God through *human* communion with Jesus in itself anticipates only *human* fulfillment: the overcoming of sin and death. However, Christian faith also teaches that as the Word became a man without ceasing to be God, so human persons without ceasing to be human can become sharers in the divine nature—can receive a second birth by water and the Spirit or a second nature by divine adoption. Sharing in the divine nature, human hearts are filled by the Spirit with divine love, so that they can enter into a communion whose purpose is fulfillment in divine goodness: "The glory which thou hast given me I have given to them, that they may be one even as we are one, I in them and thou in me, that they may become perfectly one . . ." (Jn 17:22-23).

Insofar as it is lived for the sake of the kingdom, Christian life has but one purpose. The happiness for which those who live such a life are prepared to settle embraces every human fulfillment for which they hope. Moreover, mediated by their human solidarity with Jesus but beyond the limits of merely human peace with God, they hope for intimate communion in divine joy. This gift they anticipate not insofar as they remain human but insofar as they also are somehow divine: "Beloved, we are God's children now; it does not yet appear what we shall be, but we know that when he appears we shall be like him, for we shall see him as he is" (1 Jn 3:2).

A Second Thought

Whenever one makes any choice, one's will, insofar as it is a rational appetite, must be specified by some intelligible good. Whenever one makes a morally good choice and in many cases when one makes a morally bad choice, that specifying good either is or is reducible to the instantiation of one or more of the basic human goods. Until after we completed the manuscript of this article, we assumed that what is true in many cases is true in all cases [see especially sections VII(A) and VII(C)].

However, as this article is about to appear, we are having a second thought on this point. It may be that the intelligibility which specifies the will in making certain immoral choices merely is to use effective means to satisfy desires, hostile feelings, or other emotions, whose precise objects are not reducible to any of the basic human goods. If so, the basic human goods are not reasons for such immoral choices, but only serve to rationalize them.

Even if some immoral choices can be made without in any way having their reason in any of the basic human goods, we do not think the account of practical truth and moral truth we offer here would require very much revision.

Selected Bibliography

Please note: This list includes only some of the authors' works in ethical theory; it omits other works, mainly concerned with aspects of their theory which are not treated in this article. The notations are intended primarily as guidance for those who wish to examine the theory critically.

Germain Grisez. "Man, Natural End of." *New Catholic Encyclopedia* (1967) 9:132-38. This article points out inconsistencies in Thomas Aquinas's teaching on the natural end of human persons, examines the efforts of various Thomists to make sense of that teaching, and stops just short of rejecting key aspects of it (and similar views of Aristotle and Augustine). None of Grisez's pre-1964 publications should be considered sources for the theory, which was first articulated in this and the next two items, written (in the order listed here) during 1963-64. Of works listed here, this and the next are Grisez's only attempts at Thomistic exegesis. Elsewhere, he tries to do philosophy or theology, not history, and freely parts company with Thomas, usually without saying so.

———. "The First Principle of Practical Reason: A Commentary on the *Summa Theologiae*, 1-2, Question 94, Article 2." *Natural Law Forum* 10 (1965): 168-201. (Abridged version in *Modern Studies in Philosophy: Aquinas: A Collection of Critical Essays*, ed. by Anthony Kenny, 340-82. Garden City, N.Y.: Doubleday, 1969. Because Kenny did some significant, unauthorized editing, this version should not be used by critics.) Insofar as this article goes beyond exegesis and begins articulating a free-standing theory, its treatment is superseded by recent works, not least the present article.

———. *Contraception and the Natural Law*. Milwaukee: Bruce, 1964. Chapter three is an early version of the theory; for understanding its mature form, only the critique of "conventional" natural-law approaches remains helpful, and that is supplemented in later works. The critique of consequentialism ("situationism") here, and up to "Choice and Consequentialism," mistakenly focuses on the noncommensurability of the *categories* of basic goods.

____. "Methods of Ethical Inquiry." *Proceedings of the American Catholic Philosophical Association* 41 (1967): 160-68. (Reprinted in *New Dynamics in Ethical Thinking*, ed. by George F. McLean, O.M.I., 99-107. Lancaster, Pa.: Concorde, 1974.) The statement of the theory here is superseded by later works. The brief critique of alternative theories also is superseded by later and more adequate exercises in dialectic, especially that in Finnis's *Fundamentals of Ethics*.

____. *Abortion: The Myths, the Realities, and the Arguments*. New York and Cleveland: Corpus Books, 1970. Chapter six is a restatement of the theory, with its application to abortion and other killing, including capital punishment and war. This statement of the theory is superseded by later works, including the present article. (However, the treatment of the issue of the personhood of the unborn and most of the factual content of this book remain useful.) Some find this statement of the theory attractive, perhaps partly because later and more adequate versions are more complicated.

Germain Grisez and Russell Shaw. *Beyond the New Morality: The Responsibilities of Freedom*. Notre Dame and London: University of Notre Dame Press, 1974; 2nd ed. rev., 1980; 3rd ed. rev., 1988. Intended for use with beginning students as part of an introduction to ethics, this is a simplified articulation of the theory by Shaw, a professional writer. Many important aspects of the theory and arguments for it are deliberately omitted, even from the newest edition. Those who wish to interpret and criticize Grisez's thought are warned in the introduction that he "has set forth his ethical theory at length and in the language of technical philosophy in other publications."

Joseph M. Boyle, Jr. "Aquinas and Prescriptive Ethics." *Proceedings of the American Catholic Philosophical Association* 49 (1975): 82-95. By clarifying the difference between Hare's prescriptivism and the theory's account of *is-to-be* and *ought*, this article shows that an evaluative conception of good need not entail noncognitivism.

Germain Grisez. *Beyond the New Theism: A Philosophy of Religion*. Notre Dame and London: University of Notre Dame Press, 1975. The metaphysical foundations of the ethical theory are explained and defended in this book, which had the benefit of many years of work with Boyle and Tollefsen, especially on the book listed next. The argument from the directiveness of practical reason for the existence of God is not developed in this book, and the implications of practical knowledge for knowledge of God are only hinted at (84-91). But relational predication concerning God is treated fully (256-72).

Joseph M. Boyle, Jr., Germain Grisez, and Olaf Tollefsen. *Free Choice: A Self-Referential Argument*. Notre Dame and London: University of Notre Dame Press, 1976. The most complete account of free choice and related elements of action theory, and a criticism of alternative views of these matters, which are so basic for sound ethical theory.

Germain Grisez. "Choice and Consequentialism." *Proceedings of the American Catholic Philosophical Association* 51 (1977): 144-52. The first presentation of the mature version (which corrects earlier ones) of the argument against consequentialism based on the noncommensurability of those anticipated benefits and harms which are the intelligible grounds for the options, one of which is freely chosen. This critique is superseded by the article listed next.

———. "Against Consequentialism." *American Journal of Jurisprudence* 23 (1978): 21-72. The most extensive critique of consequentialism, but completed in some respects by later treatments.

Germain Grisez and Joseph M. Boyle, Jr. *Life and Death with Liberty and Justice: A Contribution to the Euthanasia Debate*. Notre Dame and London: University of Notre Dame Press, 1979. Chapters eleven and twelve are still useful for their articulation of some aspects of action theory not treated in the present paper, and for application of the theory to life and death issues. Grisez and Boyle now recognize that the political and legal philosophy in this book needs some corrections. These made, their views in these areas would be closer to the positions developed by Finnis in the book listed next, yet some differences might remain.

John Finnis. *Natural Law and Natural Rights*. Oxford and New York: Oxford University Press, 1980. Chapters III-V deploy the ethical theory; chapter XI.8 gives an account of the relation between reason and will in choice; chapter XIII considers the divine cause and end of human existence. To understand this book aright, one should note that whenever Thomas Aquinas is quoted or cited, the author is to be taken (except in a few cases where he expresses a reservation) to mean to adopt Aquinas' view. The treatment of incommensurability fails to distinguish the two theses distinguished in the present paper. Partly because of considerations of audience and partly because the author did not then see the matter clearly, his exposition here of the ethical theory did not identify the role of integral human fulfillment.

———. "Natural Law and the 'Is'—'Ought' Question: An Invitation to Professor Veatch." *Catholic Lawyer* 26 (1981): 266-77. A defense of the theory's conception of practical knowledge against serious misreadings both of *Natural Law and Natural Rights* and (it is argued) of Thomas Aquinas.

John Finnis and German Grisez. "The Basic Principles of Natural Law: A Reply to Ralph McInerny." *American Journal of Jurisprudence* 26 (1981): 21-31. A defense against misunderstandings of the theory and (it is argued) of Thomas Aquinas; the authors point out, however, that the theory's adequacy is not its correspondence with the views of any previous thinker.

John Finnis. *Fundamentals of Ethics*. Oxford: Oxford University Press; Washington, D.C.: Georgetown University Press, 1983. A restatement of much of the theory by way of a dialectic with Aristotle, Kant, and contemporary English-language work in ethical theory.

Germain Grisez, with the help of Joseph M. Boyle, Jr., Basil Cole, O.P., John M. Finnis, John A. Geinzer, Jeannette Grisez, Robert G. Kennedy, Patrick Lee, William E. May, and Russell Shaw. *The Way of the Lord Jesus*, vol. one, *Christian Moral Principles*. Chicago: Franciscan Herald Press, 1983. (Boyle contributed more than six months of full-time work to this volume.) Chapters two through twelve offer the most mature statement of the theory as a whole. Chapters nineteen and thirty-four give a theological account of the ultimate end of human persons. The rethinking of the theory in a theological context and without reference to any particular issue (such as abortion or euthanasia) led to many important developments, and a considerable increase in the clarity and precision of the theory as a whole. Still, some aspects of this treatment are filled out in more recent works, including the present article, which also corrects some details.

John Finnis. "Practical Reasoning, Human Goods, and the End of Man." *Proceedings of the American Catholic Philosophical Association* 58, forthcoming. slightly revised: *New Blackfriars* 66 (1985): 438-51. A comparison of the ideal of integral human fulfillment with the ultimate end as Aquinas understands it. Finnis, whose view is closer than Grisez's to that of Aquinas, here emphasizes points of agreement.

Joseph M. Boyle, Jr. "Moral Reasoning and Moral Judgment." *Proceedings of the American Catholic Philosophical Association* 58 (1984): 37-49. An account of the extent to which nonrational factors necessarily and rightly enter into moral reasoning and moral judgment, and so require virtue for the perfect attainment of moral truth.

____. "Aquinas, Kant, and Donagan on Moral Principles." *New Scholasticism* 58 (1984): 391-408. An examination of various formulations of the first principle of morality, and criticism of the "respect persons" formulation, favored by Donagan over the theory in its previous formulations.

John Finnis, Joseph M. Boyle, Jr., and Germain Grisez. *Nuclear Deterrence, Morality and Realism*. Oxford and New York: Oxford University Press, 1987. A fresh, philosophical presentation of the theory, with a careful application to the morality of nuclear deterrence.

Germain Grisez. "The Structures of Practical Reason: Some Comments and Clarifications." *Thomist* 52, forthcoming. A reply to Brian V. Johnstone, C.Ss.R., defending the theory's conception of practical principles against the alternative views of them (which Johnstone tries to combine) as theoretical truths or as imperatives. The constructive presentation of the theory here is superseded by that in the present article.

____. "Natural Law and Natural Inclinations: Some Comments and Clarifications." *New Scholasticism* 61 (1987): 307-20. A reply to Douglas Flippen, both defending the theory against misunderstandings and criticizing misinterpretations of Aquinas. Here, too, the constructive presentation of the theory is superseded by that in the present article.

Part IV
For and Against the New Classical Theory

[12]

15

NATURAL LAW AND THE "IS"–"OUGHT" QUESTION: QUERIES TO FINNIS AND GRISEZ

John Finnis' achievement in his book, *Natural Law and Natural Rights*,[1] is nothing if not truly remarkable! Only yesterday it would have been no exaggeration to say that one would have had to beat the bushes to find even a single legal philosopher, or political philosopher, to say nothing of any ethicist or moral philosopher of note or standing, who would not have dismissed natural law doctrines out of hand as being utterly discredited philosophically and as entitled to survival only as historical curiosities. But not so today, especially since the publication of Finnis' book. And indeed, this sea-change in philosophical opinion is something that Finnis would appear to have wrought almost single-handedly.[2] To which one can only say, "Bravo!" and again "Bravo!"

Is it not, then, rather captious and in bad grace that I should now be taking it upon myself to come at Finnis with some rather sharp questions? Worse yet, my questions could seem almost irrelevant in that they are aimed largely at but a single section of what is otherwise a very substantial book, namely, section 4 of Chapter II, entitled "The illicit inference from facts to norms." Still, that section is rather fundamental, so far as the very theory and understanding of natural law is concerned; and what Finnis says there is so puzzling as to cause one almost to wonder whether he could have quite meant what he says, or

1. John Finnis, *Natural Law and Natural Rights* (Oxford: Clarendon Press, 1980). References in the text will be to pages of this edition.

2. No doubt, Finnis would be the first to deny that his achievement is in any way single-handed. For he most generously gives credit to Germain Grisez for practically all of the specific philosophical formulations of natural law doctrines, particularly with reference to the current philosophical situation, that Finnis himself has availed himself of. But although the formulations may be due to Grisez, I wonder if the actual turning of the tide of prejudice against natural law may not be due to Finnis himself and his excellent book.

said what he meant. Thus from the very title of the section one gets the impression that any inference from facts to norms must be illicit. And yet just how can the enterprise of a natural law ethics be anything other than an effort to find some sort of a basis for morals and ethics in nature itself, and thus in the facts of nature?

Still, let us hear Finnis out, and in his own very words:

(1) "It is simply not true that 'any form of a natural-law theory of morals entails the belief that propositions about man's duties and obligations can be inferred from propositions about his nature'" (p. 33).

(2) Speaking of the view of St. Thomas Aquinas in regard to natural law, Finnis notes that Aquinas "asserts as plainly as possible that the first principles of natural law, which specify the basic forms of good and evil . . . are not inferred from the speculative principles. They are not inferred from facts. They are not inferred from metaphysical propositions about human nature, or about the nature of good and evil, or about 'the function of a human being,' nor are they inferred from a teleological conception of nature or any other conception of nature" (pp. 34–35).

(3) Finally, in seeking to explain why it should ever have come to be so generally supposed that defenders of natural law do indeed fall into fallacies such as that of trying to make "an illicit inference from 'is' to 'ought'" (p. 34), Finnis suggests that one reason for so widespread a misapprehension is that "the very phrase 'natural law' can lead one to suppose that the norms referred to, in any theory of natural law, are based on judgments about nature (human and/or otherwise)."

What is one to make of assertions such as these? Were it not known that Finnis' whole book was devoted to a sustained and brilliant defense of natural law, one might suppose that anybody who insisted that "the norms referred to in any theory of natural law" must not be taken to be "based on judgments about nature (human and/or otherwise)"—that such a one must surely be an opponent of natural law doctrines in ethics, not their defender! Surely, though, our reaction must be over-hasty. For suppose that we put ourselves in Finnis' shoes for the moment. No one could have been more aware than he that so far as traditional defenders of natural law doctrines are concerned, they have ever been wont to affirm (1) that, in any natural law ethics, moral laws and moral norms have an existence right in nature itself; and (2) that it should be possible to discover such natural moral laws somehow from an examination of the facts of nature themselves. But remember, Finnis is an Oxford don; and in Oxford, no doubt, if anyone who would so much as dare to say that maybe moral norms do have a basis in fact, or that perhaps an "ought" can be derived from an "is"—of such a one, not just the Oxonians but doubtless the entire English philosophical establishment would exclaim, "Let him be anathema!" Clearly, then, if Finnis would wish to defend natural law in Oxford and at the same time avoid a total Oxbridge ostracism, he would have little choice but to do a Falstaff (Falstaff being never out of place in Oxford!) and acknowledge discretion to be the better part of valor.

All the same, while it is easy to understand why Finnis would not want to commit what is surely a capital philosophical offense in England today, namely, that of trying to extract norms from facts, or duties from nature, or an "ought" from an "is," still why would he continue to want to have himself regarded as a natural law philosopher? Could it be that the word "natural law" has an unsuspected aura of respectability about it, and that, unlike the proverbial rose, "natural law" is not a thing that by any other name would smell as sweet? And so the game would have to be one of seeking to enjoy all the sweet perfumes of the word "natural law" at the same time that one is careful to clear one's name of any possible taint that might come from putting it about that the thing itself was in any way a thing to be taken seriously!

Enough of such teasing, though. And why not instead come right out and unmask the battery from which I am choosing to bombard the position which Finnis has apparently taken up in that one section of his book? For I believe that in that section Finnis has somewhat inadvertently, and seemingly almost unwittingly, stumbled into a very curious dilemma. The dilemma is simply this: either figure out a way to get from facts to norms, or just give up trying to be a natural law philosopher altogether. But, of course, Finnis is quite insensitive to any such dilemma. Instead, he seems to see no reason why he should not simply disclaim all attempts at finding a basis for moral laws in nature, and at the same time insist that his ethics is nothing if not an ethics of natural law. Accordingly, I propose to mount my criticisms of Finnis on two fronts. First, let me try to give a brief and somewhat fanciful account of some of the major stages in the history of Western moral philosophy, just to show that the dilemma I have proposed is a real one and that, for that very reason, Finnis will have to make up his mind: either he is going to be a natural law philosopher and discard his Oxbridge superstitions about the wall of separation dividing "is" from "ought," and facts from values, etc.; or he will have to break with Oxbridge entirely (and, for that matter, with most of our latter-day establishment ethics) and then he can, in both good conscience and good grace, declare himself to be a natural law philosopher after the mind of St. Thomas Aquinas himself.

And what about my second front? Well, it will consist in a series of challenges that I would like to direct at the specific reasons Finnis gives by way of showing why he thinks it to be both bad logic and bad philosophy ever to make inferences from "is" to "ought," or ever to try to find a basis for morals and ethics directly in nature and in reality.

First, then, as to my somewhat off-the-cuff reading of the history of Western moral philosophy. Consider again Finnis' pronouncements to the effect that it is at once futile and illogical to suppose that propositions about man's duties and obligations can be derived from propositions about his nature, or that moral norms and moral standards can ever be based on considerations as to the nature of man, or the nature of things, either one. But must it not occur to one that for someone to take a line such as this in matters of morals and ethics is but to hark back to those ancient disputes between the Sophists on the one hand and Socrates on the other (and indirectly Plato and Aristotle as well)? For what was the position of a Sophist like Callicles in the *Gorgias,* if not that morals and ethics, as ordinarily understood,[3] are simply matters of νόμος, and not of φύσις? And in opposition to the Sophists, what was it that Socrates was contending for, if not that morals and ethics are not mere matters of human choice or convention, as rather that they are and ought to be grounded in nature—in the nature of man primarily, but also and more fundamentally in the nature of things generally?

Nor does such a line of argument in repudiation of natural law stop there. For coming down to the present day and to the contemporary scene in ethics, must not one say that contemporary moralists, be they utilitarians or deontologists, if the question were put to them directly, would find themselves to a man (or woman) having to agree with the Sophists, as opposed to Socrates, that there is just no way in which morals and ethics can be viewed as a matter of φύσις, rather than νόμος? True, the utilitarians would insist that in holding that morality is a matter of social convention, and not of nature, they do not want to think of themselves as being committed to the moral relativism and even scepticism of the ancient Sophists. Instead, present-day utilitarians think that they can combine a pure conventionalism in ethics with

3. This qualification is important, since, of course, the morals of might-makes-right that Callicles himself would advocate he would take to be a morals of φύσις and not of νόμος, whereas with the more standard views of right and justice it is just the other way around—at least so Callicles would say.

a nonrelativism, presumably by involving certain linguistic or logical considerations like that of universalizability. And for their part, even the deontologists, while they would doubtless not mean to say that morality is no more than a matter of νόμος, in the sense of mere social convention, would still deny that it could in any sense be considered an affair of nature or φύσις. No, our duties and obligations are recognized to be such, not in virtue of any investigation of nature, but rather in virtue either of a direct intuition of such obligations or else of a recognition of a supposed inevitable logical inconsistency that will manifest itself whenever one tries to deny such a thing as the categorical imperative.

Nor is it to be wondered at that contemporary moralists of whatever school would be so unanimous in repudiating anything like nature—the nature of man, the nature of things, or whatever—as a possible basis for morality. For given the almost unquestioned recognition in the modern world of modern natural science as being alone qualified to give an account of nature, be it either of the natures of things or of the nature of man, the evidence, in consequence, seems overwhelming: no so-called scientific study or investigation of nature is ever going to be able to turn up evidence of the existence of real norms or values right within the facts of nature. For the matter of that, was not Thomas Hobbes in the early days, alike of modern philosophy and of modern science, entirely correct in his insight that a scientific knowledge of the laws of nature can never give one instruction as to what is really right or wrong in terms of nature itself, but only of what is right and wrong in terms of the self-interest of human beings and of their need to preserve themselves in the face of what might be called man's natural situation, in which the life of man would be no better than "poor, nasty, brutish and short"?

Very well, if such a reading of the history of moral philosophy and of the contemporary lay of the land in establishment ethics be anything like a correct and accurate one, then anyone who would seek to rehabilitate a natural law ethics in the present day simply cannot hope to follow a course like that of John Finnis. To think that one could champion natural law, and yet at the same time insist that ethical principles can have no grounding in fact and in nature—no way! That would be like trying to run with the hare and ride with the hounds. No, for one to uphold natural law doctrines on the current philosophical scene must mean that one must be prepared to break not only with ancient sophistry, but with Hobbesian contractarianism, with Kantian deontologism, with the so-called naturalism of modern science, and, last but not least, with everything that is up to date in

Oxbridge philosophy! And who would dare to do this, save only a fool, and John Finnis is no fool. True enough; and yet the question I want to raise is not so much one as to whether John Finnis is, or meant to be, a fool; but rather whether, being so particular about not being a fool, he can any longer be a natural law philosopher, and if so, how!

And now to come to the second front on which I would mount my attack. For granting that I may have raised at least some doubts about whether John Finnis can very well claim to be a natural law moralist, if he is not willing to be written off as a fool by the majority of contemporary philosophers, still whatever his concerns may be not to be cast into outer darkness by his contemporary analytical philosophical colleagues in Oxford, Finnis is not behindhand in giving reasons to show just how and why it is impossible, alike in logic and in nature, ever to extract moral principles from considerations of reality and of the way things are. It's like trying to get blood out of a turnip, or possibly a rabbit out of a hat. Not only that, but in his arguments Finnis is ably seconded by the more than formidable Germain Grisez![4] Accordingly, my task now becomes one of trying to defuse these Finnis–Grisez arguments, which are designed to show that appeals to nature can never provide proper support for ethics and morality.

These arguments I shall classify under roughly three main headings, and the first such heading is that of the supposed logical "deducibility" or "inferrability" of a science such as ethics from either metaphysics or philosophical anthropology. Nor is it to be denied that the Finnis-Grisez position here is one that is exceedingly well-chosen. For certainly anyone will want to recognize that ethics has a characteristic autonomy of its own, with its own first principles; and hence there is no way in which ethical principles can be shown to be not so much principles at all as mere deductions from metaphysical principles, after the manner, say, of a Spinoza.

In response to this first argument, let me respond by conceding that of course there can be no *deduction* of ethics from metaphysics, or no simple *inference* of "propositions about man's duties and obligations" simply from "propositions about his nature." Yet is not the soundness of such contentions due to one's taking the terms "deduction" and "inference" in a somewhat straitened and overly technical sense? And

4. My references to Grisez will be confined simply to his brilliant and influential essay entitled "The First Principle of Practical Reason: A Commentary on the *Summa Theologiae*, 1–2, Qu. 94, Art. 2." This originally appeared in *Natural Law Forum*, Vol. 10, 1965; however, the references to this essay that I shall make will be to the abridged version that was published in the volume of essays on *Aquinas* edited by Anthony Kenny (Garden City, NY: Anchor Books, 1969), pp. 340–382.

can one legitimately extend such a point about the noninferrability of ethics from metaphysics to what might seem to be the somewhat overdrawn conclusion of Finnis that ethics may not be considered to be even based on metaphysics in any way, or that metaphysical considerations need be regarded as largely irrelevant even to rendering ethical principles intelligible?

It is true that we have all become accustomed to that sense of "deduction" that has sometimes been associated with modern logic, especially the older *P.M.* logic (*i.e.*, the logic of *Principia Mathematica*). And indeed, in that sense of deduction, we all know what it means to say that the principles of arithmetic are simply deducible from those of logic. Yes, it is not uncommon to hear the still further construction put upon this sense of deduction according to which any relation of premises to conclusions in a deductive argument never amounts to anything more than a mere tautology. Very well, let us say straightoff that, taking a natural law philosopher like St. Thomas Aquinas as our example, he would surely never say that ethics was simply deducible from metaphysics, or morals from anthropology, in this sense of deduction.

Of course, this is not the place for, nor do I have the competence to enter into any criticisms of the possible narrowness and even arbitrariness of this sense of deduction as it functions in modern logic. On the other hand, I don't see why I could not cite a perfectly plausible and familiar example of how one science or discipline might be said to be radically dependent upon another for the very intelligibility of its first principles, and yet without the one being considered to be in any sense merely "deducible" from that other in any *P.M.* sense of deduction. For take the case of Aristotelian physics in its dependence upon so-called metaphysics or first philosophy in Aristotle. Surely Aristotle would hold that physics has its own first principles, and that as first principles, the principles of physics are not simply inferrable from those of metaphysics, as if the former amounted to no more than a restatement of the latter, in the manner of mere tautologies. For instance, consider the famed three principles of change in Aristotelian physics—matter, form, and privation. Now these can of course be set out as if they comprised but a single first principle of change in the physical world: any change must be the change of something (the material principle) *from* something (the principle of privation) *to* something else (the formal principle). As a first principle, this could surely be considered as self-evident—at least in the traditional sense of that term, as signifying something *per se notum,* and therefore as something that may not be thought to be merely deduced or inferred from anything else. Yet for all of its self-evidence, is not such a principle regarding *ens mobile* entirely dependent for its proper intelligibility upon various prior principles of *ens*? For example, in his metaphysics, Aristotle would hold that to be a being, a being must be a substance (or at least ordered to substance). Likewise, to be a being, a being must be determinate—*i.e.* it must have an essence, or proper formal determination. And finally, if chapters 3–10 of Book A of the *Metaphysics* are properly a part of the Aristotelian metaphysics, then there is the further principle of metaphysics that for any being to come into being, it must be possessed of a principle of matter or of potentiality.

Very well, given such principles in metaphysics, may it not be said that the first principles of Aristotle's physics are indeed based upon, and even in a sense derived from, his metaphysics, and that while it certainly does not suffice for a knowledge of *ens mobile* to know only about *ens*, or about being *qua* being, it is no less true that there can never be a proper understanding of *ens mobile* for one who does not have a prior understanding of *ens*?

Very well, given such principles in metaphysics, there is certainly a sense in which the first principles of Aristotle's physics are based upon and even derived from his metaphysics. Yet this surely may not be taken to mean that one has only to know about *ens*, or the principles of being *qua* being, and these will tell you, at least by implication, all that you need to know or can know about *ens mobile*. Of course not! Accordingly, *mutatis mutandis*, why could not one say that for Aristotle—and certainly for Aquinas—while ethics is indeed an autonomous discipline with respect to metaphysics (or philosophical anthropology), and hence possessed of its own first principles, it by no means follows that the moral philosopher in his concern with *ens*, considered as *bonum*, need take no account whatever of the principles of *ens* just as such. And with this, have we not pretty well drawn the teeth of what we have labelled the first of the Finnis–Grisez arguments regarding the supposed absolute independence of ethics as over against metaphysics, or of morals with respect to a knowledge of nature? True, there is a sense in which our human moral obligations can scarcely be said to be simply "inferrable" from a knowledge of human nature. And yet Finnis is surely going too far when he would apparently conclude from this that "the norms referred to in any theory of natural law" are not to be regarded as being even "based upon judgments about nature (human and/or otherwise)" (p. 35).[5]

5. Be it noted that Finnis and Grisez would not argue that ethics is independent of metaphysics merely in the way in which, say, physics is independent of metaphysics. For

And now to come to the second line of argument which Finnis and Grisez would appear to use in order to show that even in a natural law ethics, the principles of morals and ethics are really not to be thought as being in any sense principles of being or of nature at all. This time, as it would seem to me, the Finnis-Grisez argument turns on a certain understanding, or perhaps misunderstanding, of what may be supposed to be meant by "nature" in expressions like "the nature of man" or "the nature of things." Moreover, the argument is presumably designed to show that any effort to derive one's morals or ethics from nature must inevitably involve the fallacy of trying to get from "is" to "ought." Nor is there any denying that the kind of example which Finnis and Grisez choose by way of fleshing out their argument is an eminently telling and well-chosen one. Let me, then, try to put this argument and this way of illustrating it first in my own words. In effect, what Finnis and Grisez would charge traditional, professed natural law moralists with doing is conceiving nature, and more specifically human nature, purely statically. In fact, though Finnis and Grisez do not say so in so many words, I would say that many of those natural law moralists, whom they are criticizing, doubtless have tended to conceive human nature and the nature of man largely on the model of the nature of purely geometrical figures. After all, recall that it was Aristotle who insisted that it is only proper to conceive of the natures of mathematical objects—squares, circles, triangles, etc.—as if they were purely static and allowed of no change or development of any kind. Thus the nature of a square or a circle is such that it neither comes into being nor passes away; it is not susceptible to any growth or development, or even to locomotion or change of quality: instead, it simply is what it is, and that's that! As a result, as Aristotle sees the matter, the so-called causes of being in the case of a triangle are reducible to the formal cause alone. Certainly, there can be no efficient cause or causes of a triangle just as such, since it neither comes into being nor passes away. And if no efficient cause, then no final cause or end or goal of any kind, in the case of a triangle. No, there is not even any material cause either, there being no potentiality for change in the case of a triangle.[6] And so it is that a triangle is, and can only be, just what it is, it having developed neither from nor out of anything else, nor is it the kind of being that may be considered to be aimed or directed toward becoming anything.

---

in addition, ethics is to be distinguished from metaphysics, they would say, in the way in which a practical science is different from, and hence independent of, any theoretical science. This further mode of differentiation, however, we shall consider later on.

6. True, there is so-called "intelligible matter" involved in Aristotle's account of mathematical objects; but that's a different story.

Very well, suppose now that we conceive of the nature of man, after the model of a triangle or a square. Clearly, so far as a square is concerned, we might say that it is contrary to the nature of a square that its size could ever be doubled by doubling the length of its sides. Correspondingly, then, if we were to conceive of the nature of man on such a model, one might say that it was contrary to the nature of a human being that he should not be characterized by upright posture, or that he not be either unequivocally male or unequivocally female, or that certain human organs should be put to a use other than their natural use. And so proceeding along these lines, one might be tempted to argue that, it being contrary to nature for a human being, say, to walk on all fours, it is therefore wrong for a human being to do so; or that certain sexual practices being deviant or perverse, when judged by the standard of a given, static human nature, such practices must therefore be wrong. Quite patently, though, inferences of this sort would be clear cases of an illicit process from "is" to "ought," or from the natural or the unnatural to the right or the wrong. Moreover, it I have understood them aright, this is just the criticism that both Grisez and Finnis would level against any number of natural law thinkers. Nor can it be denied that such criticism in such instances would seem to be entirely warranted and right on the mark: these are clear cases of illicit processes from "is" to "ought," or from facts of nature to alleged norms of nature.

Nevertheless, however justified Grisez and Finnis may be in leveling these criticisms at least at certain so-called natural law thinkers, it needs to be recognized that such criticisms are not necessarily warranted with respect to any and every seeming inference from nature to norms—and this for the very reason that there are other ways of understanding the natures of things than simply on the model of geometrical figures. Indeed, if it be human beings that one is concerned with, then it is nothing if not an errant mistake to try to conceive of their natures as if they were like the natures of squares or rectangles or circles. Moreover, the difference lies precisely in the fact that change is relevant to the nature of a being such as a human being, whereas it is not at all relevant to that of circle or a square. For what is a man, or a human being, if not a creature who, by his very nature and in his very nature, is a creature subject to development, a creature of potentialities, in other words, and therefore a creature who is not all that he might be or could be, and whose present or actual condition needs always to be compared with what, as such a person, he might be or could be? Nor may one stop there. For a human being is not merely a being who by nature is subject to change and development, but also a being of such a nature as to be in large part responsible for his either being or not being all that he or she might be or could be. In consequence, it needs to be added as a further characterization of human beings that they are seldom all that they should be or ought to be, and hence that they are usually not what they are morally responsible for being or what it is morally incumbent upon them that they be.

With this, then, is it not clear that an "ought" has been directly introduced into our very account of man and of human nature? Nor on this occasion can analytical philosophers—or Finnis and Grisez either—any longer say that the introduction has been made through a kind of illicit process from "is" to "ought. On the contrary, the very "is" of human nature has been shown to have an "ought" built right into it. That is to say, just as it is impossible to determine what a human being, just as a human being, really is in fact, without determining what he might be or could be—*i.e.* without taking account of a man's potentialities and the actualities toward which those potencies are oriented—so also it is no less impossible to determine, or really even adequately to state, what a human being is, without making reference to what he ought to be—*i.e.* without making reference to that natural end or fulfillment or good which it is incumbent upon any human being (by nature) to try to be or become. Here, clearly, there is no dubious inference from "is" to "ought"—as if somehow from out of an "is" that was exclusive of any "ought" one could somehow manage to conjure up an "ought," much as one might pull a rabbit out of a hat! No, for as our foregoing account should have now made clear, the very "is" of human nature already has its "ought" contained within it. Indeed, if it comes to a question of inference, it is now possible to say that the so-called inferences from "is" to "ought," or from nature to norms, are nothing if not inferences from an "is" that already involves an "ought" to the "ought" that is there already implicit in that "is." Or if one should prefer to use the language of "nature" and of "norms," one could say that the nature of man, when rightly understood, and not understood on any misleading geometrical model, is a nature that is inescapably ordered to certain norms or standards of its own perfection. Nor need we be fearful at this point of being open to any stern reprimands about how we need to go to school again to David Hume, and to listen once more to his complacent censures of supposed inferences from "is" to "ought." On the contrary, may we suggest instead that it is not the natural law moralist, but rather Hume, who now needs to be taught a lesson. For while there is no denying that there are ways of construing natures and the facts of nature such that inferences from what things are by nature to what they ought to be would be illicit, still those inferences which Hume thought he was confident of having disposed of as being fallacious were not so at all. Rather those were inferences that proceeded from a far richer and more versatile conception of the "is" of human nature than poor David "ever dreamed of in his philosophy"!

But where does all of this leave us with respect to Finnis and Grisez? Well, it leaves us at the point where we would readily concede to them that if human nature be conceived on what we have been designating as the geometrical model, then there can indeed be no proper inferences from "is" to "ought," or from natures to norms. Not only that, but we may also concede to Finnis and Grisez that no doubt many so-called natural law moralists, particularly in recent years, have, either consciously or unconsciously, fallen into the very bad habit of uncritically construing human nature simply on what we have called the false geometrical model; and to the extent to which these natural law thinkers did lapse into bad habits of construing human nature in this unfortunate way, then their would-be inferences from "is" to "ought," or from the natural to the normative, would need to be pronounced to be fallacious. Besides, come to think about it, it really is not so surprising that many such latter-day advocates of natural law should have thus carelessly come to construe "nature" in this misleading way, for it is, after all, the way in which nearly all modern philosophers from Descartes and Hobbes on have tended to understand a notion like that of the "natures" of things; and, of course, modern natural scientists have merely followed suit upon the philosophers in this regard.

But having made these concessions to Finnis and Grisez, we feel we must now round on them, and ask them how they would construe the notion of "nature" in those contexts in which, in a natural law ethic rightly conceived, one has occasion to use notions such as "human nature" or "the nature of man." Surely, they themselves would repudiate construing nature on what we have called the geometrical model. Instead, professing themselves to be Thomists of the true persuasion, one would imagine that they would be the first to acknowledge, with both Aristotle and Aquinas,[7] the geometrical model for

7. On the matter of Finnis' and Grisez's reliability in their interpretations of St. Thomas Aquinas on the subject of natural law, I have largely refrained from commenting in this paper—and with very good reason, considering my own limitations, when it comes to a knowledge of the texts of St. Thomas. Besides, a most illuminating article that is critical of many of Finnis' and Grisez's interpretations of St. Thomas has already been published by Ralph McInerney in *The American Journal of Jurisprudence,* 1980, Vol. 25, pp. 1–15.

natures is by no means to be carried over uncritically from the domain of mathematics to that of physics and metaphysics, and hence of anthropology and of ethics as well. No! But supposing that Finnis and Grisez would go along with us this far, our question then becomes one as to what all of the shouting is about, so far as either Finnis or Grisez is concerned. For the problem would now seem to be simply dissolved as to any possible illicit inferences from "is" to "ought," or from facts to norms. Not only that, but for all of Finnis' rather anguished formulations about how "the very phrase 'natural law' [must be so construed as never to] lead one to suppose that the norms referred to, in any theory of natural law, are based on judgments about nature (human and/or otherwise)," we may now calmly defuse and correct the greater number of the proposed Finnis–Grisez remedies and formulations. One has only to recognize the Aristotelian account of natures and essences and there is no longer any problem of how "the norms that are referred to in theories of natural law [can be] based on judgments about nature." On the contrary, that's what they are based on precisely. And what's wrong with that!

And now for a final line of argument which, as it would seem, Finnis and Grisez are inclined to resort to by way of maintaining their would-be wall of separation between nature and norms, or "is" and "ought," or ethics and metaphysics. This is an argument based on the old Aristotelian distinction between practical sciences and theoretical sciences. An entirely legitimate distinction surely! And not only is the distinction legitimate, but also the resulting relative autonomy and independence of a practical science such as ethics *vis-à-vis* a theoretical science like metaphysics. But still, it will be our contention that in exploiting this particular distinction, Finnis and Grisez would appear to push their argument rather too far.

Nevertheless, let us let Grisez articulate just how he would understand the distinction between practical and theoretical reason, and what he would make of the resulting autonomy of ethics with respect to metaphysics. First, he makes the entirely legitimate point that ethics being a practical science, it follows that our direct concern in ethics is with determining which actions we need to perform, and which we must not perform, if we are ever to attain our natural human end or goal—or, as Grisez might prefer to put it, the basic goods of human existence. And here Grisez adds, by way of a further specification, that "because good has the intelligibility of an end, and evil the intelligibility of contrary to end, it follows that reason naturally grasps as goods . . . all of the objects of man's natural inclinations" (p. 345).

And what, then, is practical reason for Grisez? He answers that it is just what it is for Aquinas. For according to Aquinas, Grisez states, practical reason is "the mind functioning in a certain capacity, the capacity in which it is 'directed to a work.' . . . Practical reason is [thus] the mind working as a principle of action, not simply as a recipient of objective reality. It is the mind declaring what is to be, not merely recording what already is. In theory, the world calls the turn, the mind must conform to the facts; in practice, the mind calls the turn . . ." (pp. 350–351).

And so Grisez continues: "Now if practical reason is the mind functioning as a principle of action, it is subject to all the conditions necessary for a very active principle. One of these is that every active principle acts on account of an end. An active principle is going to bring about something or other, or else it would not be an active principle at all. It is necessary for the active principle to be oriented toward that something or other, whatever it is, if it is going to be brought about" (p. 351). Moreover, against the background of statements like these it should be possible to understand the first principle of practical reason as enunciated by St. Thomas: *Bonum est faciendum et prosequendum, et malum vitandum,* which Grisez is careful to translate as "Good is to be done and pursued, and evil is to be avoided" (p. 341).

Directly at this point, however, it would seem not altogether out of place to ask the question as to just how this first principle of practical reason is to be understood. True, it is a first principle, and as such is self-evident, and in this sense indemonstrable. Nevertheless, we are not asking for a demonstration of the principle, "Good is to be done and pursued, and evil is to be avoided," but only for a clarification and explication of the principle. Remember, as St. Thomas was careful to point out, and Grisez repeats the point (p. 344), a principle may be evident in itself, and yet not be evident to us. And so I will particularize this lack of self-evidence with respect to myself, and say that I am in this case "the rustic" who doesn't quite see the self-evidence of this first principle of practical reason. Clearly, though, it being a self-evident principle, the only way it can be made evident to a rustic like me, or to anyone else for that matter, is through a further clarification of the subject term "good" (or "evil"). Just how is the notion of good to be understood here?

And by way of anticipation of my own answer to this question, I would suggest that the only way such a question in this context can be answered is by invoking certain principles from metaphysics. Moreover, this explication will turn out to be such that if I can really make good on it, then it should serve effectively to breach that wall of separation between ethics and metaphysics that Grisez would appear to think he has erected. But this is to anticipate. For the present let us just continue to follow Grisez's lead. In response to the question of how the notion of good needs to be understood in the first principle of practical reason, Grisez's move is to say that the notion of good is to be understood in terms of the notion of end. "Good," he says, "has the intelligibility of end" (p. 345), good being simply "what each thing tends towards."[8] Moreover, if one needs to have light shed on how such a notion of "tending towards" is here to be construed, Grisez invokes the notion of "inclination," and more specifically that of "man's natural inclinations" (p. 345). That is to say, to requote the already quoted passage from Grisez, "reason naturally grasps as goods . . . all of the objects of man's natural inclinations."

Nor can one possibly take exception to anything said thus far. No, for Grisez in large measure is simply following and paraphrasing Aquinas, and correctly so. Still, having got to the point of understanding good as being the object of inclination, Grisez cannot very well stop there. Nor does it seem to me that Aquinas stops there. Yet oddly enough, it is just there that Grisez would appear to insist on stopping, and to insist that Aquinas stops as well. And yet how so? For if good is to be construed simply as end, or as object of inclination or desire, a dangerous ambiguity immediately suggests itself—an ambiguity which I believe can be best brought out by what I like to call "the *Euthyphro* test." Thus it may be recalled how in the *Euthyphro* Socrates voices the question of whether a thing is said to be good (or an end) because it is beloved of the gods; or is it rather that it is beloved of the gods because it is good?

That the consequences for ethics can be of the utmost import, depending upon how one resolves this ambiguity, can be readily seen if we but try opting for the former, as opposed to the latter alternative: things are good for no other reason than that men happen to desire them, or go for them, or be inclined towards them. Immediately, the consequence follows that nothing is really good, but desiring (or interest, or inclination, or a tending toward) makes it so. And what does this do but completely shatter that first principle of practical reason that Grisez, following Aquinas, is so insistent upon? For if goodness and value be entirely relative to tastes and inclinations, then there is not the slightest ground for holding that good is anything *to be* done and or *to be* pursued (or evil *to be* avoided). No, for in the Latin of Aquinas' formula, *Bonum est faciendum et prosequendum*, the verbs have

8. This, of course, is a rendering of the opening sentence of the *Nicomachean Ethics*. See Grisez, *op. cit.*, p. 353.

a gerundive force, so that the force of the formula in English is that good is necessarily or self-evidently that which ought to be done and should be done. And yet clearly, if good be no more than "any object of any interest,"[9] then goodness will have not the slightest obligatory, or morally compelling, force at all. Nor, with respect to the supposed logically self-evident character of the first principle of practical reason, will it be in the least evident why that which we merely like or desire or are inclined towards should be the sort of thing that we ought to do, or to pursue, or to go for.

In fact, is not this last the nerve of the general Kantian line of criticism that is directed against all hedonistic theories, or interest theories, or supposedly teleological theories of ethics? Just because someone is naturally disposed or inclined toward something, or likes it, or wants it, or finds it a source of satisfaction, or even of happiness or contentment, all of this, Kant in effect says, has no bearing at all on the question of whether such a thing ought to be pursued or cherished or liked, or of whether it is right that it be pursued or done or sought after. To try to perpetrate such an inference would be to commit the "is"–"ought" fallacy surely—at least such would be the contention of any Kantian; and in this Kant would surely be right!

But what now of Grisez? Surely, he would be the last to want to opt for this first alternative, when called upon to apply the *Euthyphro* test. Instead, he has got to go beyond his own way of stating what is to be understood by a good or an end: goods in the proposed sense may well be said to be objects of inclinations; and yet this must immediately be construed to mean that they are objects of inclination in the sense of being things that we ought to be inclined towards, or should be inclined towards, whether we actually are or not. And this in turn means that goods in this sense are goods that are objectively so, or really so, or goods in themselves, and not merely goods relative to their being desired, or to how men happen to feel about them. What, though, does this mean but that goods must be understood as beings? Or to invoke Aquinas' formula, which he uses in order to contrast what might be called the ontological status of *bonum* as contrasted with that of *verum*: *Bonum enim est in rebus, ut Philosophus dicit in VI Metaphys.* (*De Veritate,* Qu. XXI, art. 1.)

Very well, having thus located good in being, Aquinas insists that good needs to be understood as being, and as a being. In other words, it is precisely metaphysics that here takes over, in order to clarify and

9. Those of us whose philosophical education dates back to ancient times will recall that this was the late R. B. Perry's key formulation of his so-called interest theory of value.

render intelligible that first principle of ethics or of practical reason, the principle, namely, that good is to be done and to be pursued. And indeed, it is precisely in his metaphysical treatment of the transcendentals, particularly in the *De Veritate,* Qu. I, art. 1, and Qu. XXI, art. 1 and 2,[10] that Aquinas addresses himself to the question of what *bonum,* or good, really is, as opposed to what some Tom, Dick or Harry may happen to think it is. *Bonum,* he there says, is nothing but *ens,* considered as an object of desire, or *appetitus.* Moreover, all of these terms—*bonum, ens,* and *appetitus*—need to be understood each in its fully analogous sense, as is proper to all notions in metaphysics. For as Aquinas here expounds *bonum* and *ens,* considered as so-called transcendentals,[11] he avails himself of the distinction between potency and act, which, taken as a metaphysical distinction, may be said to pervade the whole range of being or reality. How, then, is *bonum* to be understood in this fully analogous or transcendental sense, if not simply as *ens* or being, considered as just the actuality toward which a given potentiality is ordered, as to its proper fulfillment or completion or actuality? Or put a little differently, any potentiality is ordered to its proper actuality as being just that which such a potentiality may be said to lack and to need and to have an *appetitus*[12] with respect to. Or again, since the proper actuality of any potency is that to which the latter is objectively ordered as being what naturally fulfills or completes it, one may say that such an actuality, as the *bonum* of the relevant potency, is just that which such a potentiality "ought to" desire. In other words, with reference to the *Euthyphro* test, one may now say that good or *bonum* is defined[13] and determined by St. Thomas as nothing but being or *ens,* considered not as that which simply is desired, but rather as that which is *desirable,* or ought to be desired.

Moreover, if at this point one should feel inclined to protest that what we have just been discoursing about is what might be called the metaphysical good, whereas Grisez is concerned only with the ethical good, I am afraid that such an escape route is not here open to Grisez. For granted that he is concerned with the good, or the end, in ethics,

10. It is interesting that, so far as I know, Finnis, no less than Grisez, seems scarcely even to advert to these passages, much less weigh them carefully.

11. By a "transcendental" here, we mean, of course, that which is not classifiable under any one category alone, but rather which runs through them all, and thus transcends them all.

12. Again, be it noted that Aquinas is quite patently taking *appetitus* in a fully analogous sense, considering that he is maintaining that any and every potency may be said to be ordered its proper actuality in sense of having a "desire" for it, or being "inclined" towards it.

13. Need I add that *bonum* being a transcendental, it cannot be defined in any strict sense of *per genus et differentiam.*

and not in metaphysics, there just is no way in which the former can ever be determined without having recourse to the latter. For if it is Grisez's proposal simply to consider the human good as being such an end or ends as human beings have an inclination towards, then that ambiguity which, as we saw, the *Euthyphro* test is so aptly designed to expose, immediately comes to the fore. Nor can this ambiguity be successfully obviated without one's recognizing that the good or end that is here in question cannot be any mere good that is such only relative to the chance interests or desires of a human being, but rather a good that is so objectively, and in being, and in just the sense that it is something that ought to be desired, whether it actually is so or not. And to understand what good or the good is, considered simply as *ens* or being, it is necessary to have recourse to metaphysics, and to St. Thomas' "definition" of good as simply the actual as over against the potential.

Then retracing one's steps from metaphysics to ethics, one finds that to determine what the human good is, or the end or goal of a properly human existence, one needs but to specify the metaphysical good, or the good in general, in terms of the specifically[14] human good. Moreover, if good simply as *ens*, or the good in general, is but the actual as over against the potential, then obviously the human good specifically has to be understood as simply that full actuality or perfection, or flourishing or fulfillment, to which our specifically human potentialities are ordered, and without the attainment of which we human beings can scarcely be anything other than incompletely or imperfectly human.

Of course, it is not our place in this paper to spell out what our human good must thus consist in more concretely. After all, we are all familiar with how Aristotle attempts to spell this out in the *Ethics,* or Aquinas in the two *Summas,* or Grisez and Finnis themselves in the respective accounts which they give of what they call the basic goods of human life. But for present purposes, it is not what the end or the basic goods of human life are that is of concern, but rather how they are determined, and what the line of argument is by which one is able to show that such goods are truly human goods, and do not only seem to be so. This line of argument, we would insist, can only be in terms of what Grisez calls speculative or theoretical reason, and not practical reason. No, for even by Grisez's account, practical reason but serves to tell us how the good may best be attained once it has been deter-

14. In this rather loose use of terms like "in general" or "specifically," we trust that the qualification noted in note 13 above will not go unregarded.

Queries to Finnis and Grisez 311

mined. However, thus to determine what that good is can only be the work of theoretical reason, proceeding from the determination of what the good is metaphysically, and simply as being, to its determination in terms of the actuality or perfection of human life in its specificity as being human, rather than simply as being *qua* being. To paraphrase Grisez, but in a sense somewhat contrary to his, the mind is indeed in such a context concerned to declare "what is to be." But so far from this being in contrast to its "recording what already is," it is only in so far as it makes such a recording in metaphysics that it is ever able to make a properly warranted declaration of what is to be in ethics. Likewise, it is this same domain that is the domain of theory, where, as Grisez says, it is "the world that calls the turn," the mind having to "conform to the facts." In other words, it is definitely not the domain of what Grisez calls "practice," where in a formulation rather frighteningly suggestive of idealism, Grisez says "the mind calls the turn." And yet, clearly, there can be no such domain of practice or of practical reason, unless it be in terms of metaphysics and of theoretical reason, through which it gets its proper determinations.

With this, then, need one say more by way of breaching that wall of separation that both Grisez and Finnis would seem to want to maintain between practical reason and theoretical reason, between ethics and metaphysics, between nature and morals, between "is" and "ought"? Nor would it seem to be unimportant that we should have been able to effect such a breach, for without it, one wonders if both Finnis and Grisez would not have to be viewed as being on the slippery slope down into an ethics merely of νόμος rather than φύσις, which is everywhere so prevalent today, and which would seem radically irreconcilable with anything like an ethics of natural law. Instead, let me just conclude in the face of both Finnis' and Grisez's seeming equivocations, "Long live natural law!"

[13]

NATURAL LAW AND THE "IS"—"OUGHT" QUESTION: AN INVITATION TO PROFESSOR VEATCH

JOHN FINNIS*

Henry Veatch's "sharp questions" are directed to those who deny that morals and ethics have any basis in nature or the facts of nature; to those who believe in a "wall of separation dividing 'is' from 'ought' and facts from values"; to those who "insist that ethical principles can have no grounding in fact and in nature"; to those who suppose an "absolute independence of ethics as over against metaphysics, or of morals with respect to a knowledge of nature," so that "principles of morals and ethics are really not to be thought [of] as being in any sense principles of being or of nature at all"; and to those who "consider the human good as being such an end or ends as human beings have an inclination towards" rather than "the ends that truly perfect human beings."

Veatch's questions and objections, therefore, are not properly directed to either Germain Grisez or to myself. Neither Grisez nor I subscribe to any of the foregoing denials, affirmations, and suppositions; indeed, we reject them all. Neither of us has published anything which might reasonably be interpreted, in its context, as involving or entailing any such view. My invitation to Professor Veatch then, is twofold: first, to *read* what we have written, strictly and fully; second, and more importantly, to examine some of the *serious questions* which my book[1] addresses to those who interpret Aquinas and Aristotle in Veatch's manner.[2]

Who would guess, from Veatch's polemic, that I reached the same result in my book using the "Euthyphro test" as did Veatch. This was

---

* Reader in Law, Fellow and Praelector in Jurisprudence at the University College, Oxford.

[1] J. FINNIS, NATURAL LAW AND NATURAL RIGHTS (1980).

[2] *See* McInerny, *The Principles of Natural Law*, 25 AM. J. JURIS. 1, 1-15 (1980). *But see* Finnis, G. Grisez, *The Principles of Natural Law*, 26 AM. J. JURIS. 21 (1981).

done prominently in the text of chapter III,[3] a chapter devoted to a detailed examination of the nature of judgments concerning human good, by an exploration of our judgments regarding one particular basic human good, knowledge, or truth.

The chapter began by distinguishing "desire or inclination or felt want" from "grasp of value"—"value" signifying "the aspect under which a particular objective has its interest, attracts desire, choice and efforts and thus is (or is considered to be) a good thing."[4] Understanding of value was then shown to function as a principle of practical reasoning since "it formulates a want but makes the want more than a blind urge by referring its object . . . to the intelligible and general form of good which that object is one possible way of participating in or instantiating."[5]

I then turned to establish the "self-evidence of the good of knowledge."[6] In denying that the good in question can be demonstrated or inferred, I also *denied* that "there are no pre-conditions for recognizing that value."[7]

> On the contrary, the value of truth becomes obvious only to one who has experienced the urge to question, who has grasped the connection between question and answer, who understands that knowledge is constituted by correct answers to particular questions, and who is aware of the possibility of further questions and of other questioners who like himself could enjoy the advantage of attaining correct answers.[8]

To establish how I use the terms "infer" and "deduce," I added:

> But one who, thus knowing the possibility of attaining truth, is enabled thereby to grasp the value of that possible object and attainment is not *inferring* the value from the possibility. No such inference is possible. No value can be *deduced* or otherwise inferred from a fact or set of facts."[9]

Professor Veatch thinks that this usage of the terms "deduction" and "inference" is "somewhat straitened and overly technical." It seems to me a desirable precision, whereby one does justice to both Aquinas' insistence that basic principles of the form "X is a good to be pursued . . ." are *per se nota* and *indemonstrabilia*, and to our contemporaries' reasonable insistence on the *logically significant distinction* between propositions about what "is" and propositions about what "ought to be."[10] This logical

[3] Finnis, *supra* note 1, at 59-80.
[4] *Id.* at 60-61.
[5] *Id.* at 63.
[6] *Id.* at 64.
[7] *Id.* at 65.
[8] *Id.*
[9] *Id.* at 66.
[10] *E.g.*, H. Veatch, For an Ontology of Morals 119 (1971).

distinction is not at all a "wall of separation." To make this clear I added the following to the passage last quoted above: "Aquinas followed Aristotle's theory of the 'induction' of indemonstrable first principles by insight working on observation, memory, and experience, but extended the account to a parallel 'induction' of indemonstrable first principles of practical reason (i.e. of natural law) *by insight working on* felt inclinations and *a knowledge of possibilities*."[11] This induction from experience *could* of course be called a form of inference.[12] Like many philosophers, therefore, I prefer to restrict the term "inference" to reasoning that moves from one *proposition* or principle to another, so that my use of the term would correspond to Aquinas' notion of the *per se notum*.

In any event, I proceeded to deny that one could *infer* the basic values from the fact that they are universally affirmed or desired, from the fact that the corresponding desires manifest a deep structure of the mind, are ineradicable, are common to all animals or are peculiar to human beings,[13] or from the fact that one feels certitude about them.[14] Then I raised the "Euthyphro test."

> The principle that truth is worth pursuing . . . is thus an underived principle. Neither its intelligibility nor its force rests on any further principle. This may tempt us to say that knowledge is a good *because* we desire it, are interested in it, value it, pursue it. But the temptation has plausibility only if we abandon the effort to understand the value of knowledge. And we are tempted to abandon that effort only when, for bad philosophical reasons, we confuse a principle's lack of derivation with a lack of justification or lack of objectivity. . . . [F]or one who considers something like knowledge to be a good, the true expression of his opinion and attitude is *not* 'it is good because or in so far as I desire it' *but* 'I desire it because and in so far as it is good.'[15]

I then explained the potentially confusing Aristotelian tag " 'the good is what all things desire,' "[16] concluding:

> Those who used the tag were equally insistent that one's human desire is a pursuit of something in so far as it seems desirable, and that things seem desirable to one in so far as they (appear to) promise to make one better off. . . . [For] one who is judging something to be good and desirable, his desire and decision to pursue the object are consequential on his judgment: (i) that the object *is* good and (ii) that he will *really* be better off for getting

---

[11] J. FINNIS, *supra* note 1, at 77 (emphasis added).

[12] *See* H. VEATCH, ARISTOTLE 180 (1974).

[13] J. FINNIS, *supra* note 1, at 66.

[14] *Id.* at 69.

[15] *Id.* at 70.

[16] *Id.* at 69-70.

> or doing or effecting it."[17]

The whole argument of my chapter was summed up in a passage that says all Professor Veatch could reasonably want to hear about potentiality and actuality:

> It is obvious that a man who is well-informed, etc., simply *is* better-off (other things being equal) than a man who is muddled, deluded, and ignorant, that the state of the one is better than the state of the other, not just in this particular case or that, but in all cases, as such, universally, and *whether I like it or not*. . . . For the understanding affirmation of the practical principle [that truth is a good—and *mutatis mutandis* for all the other basic values] is neither a reference to nor an expression of any desire or urge or inclination of mine. Nor is it merely a reference to (or implied presupposition of) any desires that my fellows happen to have. It goes beyond the desires and inclinations which may first have aroused my interest in the possibility of knowledge and which may remain a necessary substratum of any interest in truth sufficient to *move* me to pursue it *for myself*. It is a rational judgment about a general form of human well-being, about the fulfilment of a human potentiality.[18]

In an appended note headed "Objects are desired as desirable, and considered desirable as making one better-off,"[19] I linked my idiomatic English "better-off" with the mature Thomistic texts such as *Summa Theologiae*.[20] I quoted from the texts in which Aquinas employs this analysis in relation to the good of knowledge. In later chapters, I settled for the terms "flourishing," "well-being," and even "full-being" to do duty for Aquinas' *perfectio*, Veatch's "actuality," and my own "better-off." Hence basic goods are "basic aspects of human flourishing" or "forms of well-being."[21]

At a crucial moment of the book's argument, when I set out to show how ethical or moral good is a participation in the basic good of practical reasonableness, I formally stated the relation between good and being and between ethics and human nature. I invite Henry Veatch to consider this passage concerning the requirements of practical reasonableness:

> Each of these requirements concerns what one *must* do, or think, or be if one is to participate in the basic value of practical reasonableness. Someone who lives up to these requirements is thus Aristotle's *phronimos*; he has Aquinas's *prudentia*; they are requirements of reasonableness or practical wisdom, and to fail to live up to them is irrational. But, secondly reasonableness both *is* a basic aspect of human well-being and *concerns* one's par-

---

[17] *Id.* at 70-71.
[18] *Id.* at 72.
[19] *Id.* at 78-79.
[20] *Id.*
[21] *See id.* at 23, 67, 87, 144.

ticipation in all the (other) basic aspects of human well-being. Hence its requirements concern fullness of well-being. . . . So someone who lives up to these requirements is also Aristotle's *spoudaios* (mature man), his life is *eu zen* (well-living) and, unless circumstances are quite against him, we can say that he has Aristotle's *eudaimonia* (the inclusive all-round flourishing or well-being—not safely translated as 'happiness'). But, thirdly, the basic forms of good are opportunities of *being*; the more fully a man participates in them the more fully he is what he can be. And for this state of being fully what one can be, Aristotle appropriated the word *physis*, which was translated into Latin as *natura*. . . . So Aquinas will say that these requirements are requirements not only of reason, and of goodness, but also (by entailment) of (human) nature. . . . Thus, speaking very summarily, we could say that the requirements to which we now turn express the 'natural law method' of working out the (moral) 'natural law' from the first (pre-moral) 'principles of natural law.' Using only the modern terminology (itself of uncertain import) of 'morality,' we can say that the following sections of this chapter concern the sorts of reasons why (and thus the ways in which) there are things that morally ought (not) to be done.[22]

III

Despite his assertions, it appears that Professor Veatch does not really believe that an "ought" can be inferred from a sheer "is." Veatch notes that "the so-called inferences from 'is' to 'ought' or from nature to norms, are nothing if not inferences from an 'is' *that already involves an 'ought'* . . . ." Veatch further adds, "the very 'is' of human nature has been shown to have an 'ought' built into it." Indeed, it is impossible to determine what a human being is, without making reference to what he ought to be—or to that natural end or fulfillment or good, which it is incumbent upon any human being (by nature) to try to be or become.

I quite agree. I invite Henry Veatch to consider this: does not his view that a *full* knowledge of human nature involves a knowledge of what is "incumbent upon" human beings suggest that, *epistemologically*, a knowledge of what is good for human beings, and thus incumbent upon them, is a condition precedent to any full knowledge of human nature. I invite him to consider the question I raised in the notes to the very pages on which he commented:

> It is true that the natural law theory of, say, Aristotle and Aquinas goes along with a teleological conception of nature and, in the case of Aquinas, with a theory of divine providence and eternal law. But what needs to be shown is that the conception of human good entertained by these theorists is *dependent* upon this wider framework.[23]

---

[22] *Id.* at 102-03.
[23] *Id.* at 52.

It cannot be said that Veatch's comments confront this challenge, despite my attempt to provoke such a confrontation in the next sentence:

> There is much to be said for the view that the order of dependence was precisely the opposite—that the teleological conception of nature was made plausible, indeed conceivable, by analogy with the *intro*spectively luminous, self-evident structure of human well-being, practical reasoning, and human purposive action. . . .[24]

My emphasized reference to the "*intro*spectively luminous" is an allusion to the section of text so singly omitted from Veatch's quotations of that particular page:

> The basic forms of [human good] grasped by practical understanding are what is good for human beings with the nature they have. Aquinas considers that practical reasoning begins not by understanding this nature from the outside, as it were, by way of psychological, anthropological, or metaphysical observations and judgments defining human nature, but by experiencing one's nature, so to speak, from the inside, in the form of one's inclinations.[25]

It is regrettable the way the last sentence ended. Readers might be left with the impression that the relevant understanding of one's nature is found in the experience of inclinations alone. Such an impression would be incorrect and non-Thomistic. My meaning is conveyed in the last of the three sentences which immediately followed:

> But again, there is no process of inference. One does not judge that 'I have [or everybody has] an inclination to find out about things' and then infer that therefore 'knowledge is a good to be pursued'. Rather, by *a simple act of non-inferential understanding* one grasps that the object of the inclination which one experiences is an instance of a general form of good, for oneself (and others like one).[26]

As stated at the beginning of the chapter on basic values other than the good of knowledge, to ask oneself whether there are indeed such other basic values "is, in a way, an attempt to understand one's own . . . nature."[27] Where, then, do I disagree with Veatch's thesis that adequate judgments concerning human nature "involve," "build right in," or "in-

---

[24] *Id.*

[25] *Id.* at 34 (footnote omitted).

[26] *Id.* (emphasis added).

[27] I added:

> The attempt thus parallels attempts made, in quite another way, by those anthropologists and psychologists who ask (in effect) whether there is a human nature and what are its characteristics. The anthropological and psychological studies ought to be regarded as an aid in answering our present question—not, indeed, by way of any 'inference' from universality or 'human nature' to values (an inference that would be merely fallacious), but by way of an assemblage of reminders of the range of possibly worthwhile activities and orientations open to one. *Id.*

corporate" judgments about man's "natural end or fulfillment or good," about "what he ought to be" and what "it is incumbent" upon any human being to be? The disagreement is this: I assert that judgments of the latter sort are primarily (though perhaps not exclusively) judgments of practical reason or practical science. Veatch asserts that they are all exclusively theoretical and *not* practical. Like so many interpreters of Aquinas and Aristotle, he believes that practical reason serves to tell us how the good may best be attained once it has been determined, . . . and that therefore to determine what the good is can only be the work of theoretical reason.

I have many objections to Veatch's claim that the basic aspects of human good are identified only by theoretical reason and that practical reason is limited to identifying means to the ends which theoretical reason has identified. I will indicate and illustrate my principal philosophical objection and will then briefly refer to some reasons for why Veatch's view is opposed by Aristotle and Aquinas.

In all that follows, I take as a given Aquinas' mature thesis that there is only one human reason, only one human intellectual potency or faculty, and that the differences between speculative and practical reason are differences between intellectual operations with differing objectives. Additionally, one should bear in mind that "speculative" (or "theoretical") and "practical" are analogous terms.[28] There are paradigm cases of purely speculative and purely practical intellectual activity but most actual reasoning is *both* speculative *and* practical.

It seems that one's primary understanding of human good and what is worthwhile for humans to have, do, and be is attained when one considers what it is good to be, have, and do and thus what it is (or would be) worthwhile to have, do, and be. Such consideration, however, is what is meant by "*practical* thinking"; *simpliciter*, when the consideration is of my own human predicament with a view towards undertaking my own commitments and actions here and now; *secundum quid* (but still primarily), when the consideration is more reflective, reviewing my present commitments and past actions, contemplating possible future commitments and actions, assessing the commitments, actions, and character of other persons. Hence, our primary grasp of human good, human fulfilment, and of what is "incumbent on" a human being to be is practical—which is not to deny that understanding can be integrated into a

---

[28] Unless this is borne in mind, Aquinas' use of the terms will be found merely self-contradictory. *Compare* AQUINAS I, q. 14, a. 16c: "Intellectus practicus ordinatur ad finem operatonis; finis autem intellectus speculativi est consideratio veritatis" *with* q. 79, a. 11 and 2: "*objectum intellectus practici est bonum ordinabile ad opus, sub ratione veri. Intellectus enim practicus veritatem cognoscit, sicut speculativus: sed veritatem cognitam ordinat ad opus.*"

metaphysical account of human nature as one nature amongst others.

My contention can conveniently be illustrated by a brief consideration of Henry Veatch's argument, advanced in his helpful book, *Aristotle*,[29] which identifies man's natural good, function, perfection, and full-development as living in accordance with reason. It must be remembered that in Veatch's view, this argument is exclusively speculative: practical thought takes off from but cannot constitute or even contribute to this prior theoretical determination of the end and good of human life. But let us examine Veatch's argument:

> (1) [M]an's function, or man's perfection or full-development, does indeed consist in . . . his living in the manner of someone with knowledge and understanding, and (2) . . . it is just this end that all men do strive for and that is consequently the source of their true happiness and satisfaction. For as regards (1), *would we not all acknowledge that* however healthy or fully developed a human being might be in a narrowly physical or biological sense, and however well he might be provided for in his ordinary needs and desires, if in general he acted and behaved in a way that was no better than a fool, we should hardly say that such a person's existence was quite what we would consider to be a full or proper existence for a human being. Similarly, as regards (2), *imagine yourself in a situation where you* would be offered all of the usual and perhaps unusual necessities and even goods of life . . . but at the price of not having any genuine knowledge or understanding either of yourself or of the nature of things generally—that is to say, at the price of your not asking any questions . . . and so of your not really knowing the what or the why of anything. Would you settle for this? Presumably not. But, then, is not Aristotle right in his insistence that the good or final cause of human life is precisely the intelligent life . . .?[30]

The structure and thrust of this argument makes it quite clear that knowledge of the human *telos* and good is attained not by asking what "all men do strive for," nor even by asking in a purely theoretical sense what is a "full and proper existence for a human being." Rather, the argument *works* as a determination of that full and proper existence, precisely by prompting one to "imagine yourself in a particular situation," and then asking the question, "Would you settle for this?" In other words, the argument compels one to acknowledge the metaphysical proposition concerning human nature through consideration of a question that is hypothetical, but *nonetheless practical*.[31] The argument would work *in just the same way* if the question were not hypothetical but required a choice here and now between the alternative lives. This shows that its hypothetical nature has no effect on its radically practical character.

---

[29] H. Veatch, Aristotle (1974).

[30] *Id.* at 106-07 (emphasis added).

[31] *See* J. Finnis, *supra* note 1, at 95-97.

Aristotle considers the end and good of man in his *Ethics*. Does not Aquinas repeatedly state that Aristotle's politics and ethics are expositions of *practical* science? Neither Aquinas nor Aristotle seem to hold the view of Veatch (and so many other neoscholastics) that the practical part of ethics and politics only begins after a theoretical determination of the human end and good. In their view, ethics and politics are practical—from their first principles to their specific recommendations for actions and motivations, and beyond that to the applications that you and I make in our choices here and now.

Aristotle is notoriously unclear with respect to the first principles of ethics and politics. Veatch recognizes that Aristotle's "theoretical" arguments for identifying the end and function of man are unconvincing. He reports Aristotle's argument that end is identified by identifying what is *peculiar* to man but rightly passes over that argument without comment and replaces it with the essentially practical and relatively convincing argument which I quoted above. That *practical* argumentation strategy corresponds more closely to Aristotle's usual procedure in his *ethics and politics*.[32]

Aquinas is much more explicit than Aristotle with respect to the first principles of practical reasoning, including ethics and politics. He forthrightly rejects the view of so many of his commentators (and of Veatch)[33] that practical reason and its particular virtue, *prudentia*, are concerned only with particulars (not universal truths) and means (not the identification of ends). These *principia* are comprehended by an intellectual disposition which he called *synderesis*.[34] Having identified this primary aspect of practical reason, he can use the term *prudentia* (which we have seen him use to signify practical reason in all its aspects) to specifically signify the application of principles to relatively particular problems of conduct.

The intellectual contents of *synderesis*—the first principles of practical reason—are expounded by Aquinas in his treatise on law, beginning with the article to which Germain Grisez and I so often return, and which will not now be expounded.[35] As Aquinas makes clear, practical reason's grasp *naturaliter apprehendit* of the human goods which correspond to the objects of natural human inclinations is a grasp of the ends of human existence. The first principles of natural law are an identification (indeed, the primary identification) of the ends of human life and thus of the *fines moralium virtutum quia finis se habet in operabilibus sicut principium*

---

[32] *See generally* J. MONAN, MORAL KNOWLEDGE AND ITS METHODOLOGY IN ARISTOTLE 60-143 (1968).

[33] *E.g.*, H. VEATCH, ARISTOTLE 111 (1974).

[34] THOMAS AQUINAS, SUMMA THEOLOGIAE I 79, 12 & II 47, 6, 1.

[35] *Id.* at I-II 94, 2.

in speculativis.[36] It cannot be denied that Aquinas' treatise on man's "last end" is not well integrated with his treatise on natural law and the first principles of practical reason. The former treatise is theology, not metaphysics but it is too easily read as a work of purely, or at least primarily, speculative reasoning. Appearances however, are deceptive. In my view, the argumentative strategy of Aquinas' long determination of what constitutes human *perfectio* or *beatitudo* is essentially the strategy of Henry Veatch's argument which I quoted and discussed at length above. At the outset an "objector" contends that "since *beatitudo* is man's *ultimus finis,* it exists in whatever is most dominating in human desire in *hominis affectu.*" Aquinas replies to this in a way which reveals his methodolgy: "It is to wise people, not to fools, that we should look for judgment about human goods (just as we should look to those with 'good taste' for judgment about flavours."[37] Aquinas and Aristotle, of course, frequently reserve the terms *sophia/sapientia/wisdom* for the purely speculative/theoretical knowledge of the ultimate explanation of things. The *sapientes,* however, to whose good judgment Aquinas appeals in identifying the human good, are surely those to whom he appeals in the very first words of his commentary on the *Ethics*: "sapientis est ordinare." The *ordo* considered in moral philosophy is the order of voluntary actions. So the *sapientia* in question is not *sapientia simpliciter* but that *sapientia in rebus humanis* which Aquinas calls *prudentia,* and which pertains "solely to practical reason."[38] In summary, we find the *consideratio* of the end of human existence in the philosophical treatise which Aquinas reckons is practical. So, too, in his own theological treatise on man's last end, Aquinas' methodological appeal to judgment of the wise is an invitation to the reader to ask himself: *What would I consider sensible and what silly in choices of whole lives?*[39]

Confronted by the embarrassing fact that Aquinas affirms that practical reason has its own basic principles which are simply *indemonstrabilia* and *per se* (not *per metaphysicam*) *nota,* Henry Veatch believes that we must invoke certain principles from metaphysics in order to clarify and explain what is meant by the term good as it appears in those basic practical principles.

I am in favor of metaphysics as part of (and in a sense the fundamental part of) the great search for clarification and explication. I devoted more than a chapter of my book on natural law to just such an explication. I frankly called it "not practical but theoretical or metaphysical,"[40]

---

[36] *Id.* at I-II 47, 6c.

[37] *Id.* at I-II 2, 1, 1.

[38] *Id.* at II-II 47, 2.

[39] *See* J. Finnis, *supra* note 1 at 66-67.

[40] *Id.* at 49, 371, 378.

and I claimed that answers to the theoretical or metaphysical questions there considered are *necessary* if there is to be any fully satisfactory answer to the deepest practical questions about the topic of human goods.[41] I also claimed—and this is what Veatch seems to object to—that just as "*a good explanation* of molecular motion can be provided"[42] without explaining the entire universe or the dependence of the universe and of molecular motion on the uncaused cause, "so too . . . natural law can be understood, assented to, applied, and reflectively analysed"[43] without exploring the metaphysical questions to which I have referred.

Veatch pretends he is a " 'rustic' who does not quite see the self-evident nature of [the] first principle of practical reason," since as St. Thomas was careful to point out, "a principle may be evident in itself, and yet not evident to us." Veatch's phrase is regrettably ambiguous: "the important thing about a self-evident proposition is that people (with the relevant experience, and understanding of terms) *assent* to it without needing the proof of argument; it matters not at all whether they further recognize it as belonging to the relatively sophisticated philosophical category, 'self-evident.' "[44] I assume Veatch's rustic is supposed to wonder not about the self-evidence of the basic practical principles but about the principles themselves: "What do they mean? Are they true?"

I do not believe in Veatch's rustic who does not understand what "good" means but who could be illuminated by being told some "principles from metaphysics"—that good is "being, considered as just the actuality toward which a given potentiality is ordered, as to its proper fulfillment or completion or actuality." That metaphysical "principle" is true, and thus relevant to the subject matter. It is not, however, "relevant to" the imagined rustic: it is *not necessary to an answer to his supposed question.*

The proposition I advanced in the passages quoted by Veatch was simply this: the basic principles of natural law can all be intelligently grasped without adverting to metaphysical principles concerning the universal relationship between being and good, or about human nature in its relation to divine and cosmic natures. I simply gave serious consideration to Aquinas' frequently repeated claim that *even rustics understand the natural law.*[45] Since, in postulating his rustic, Veatch appeals to the authority of Aquinas, I fail to understand why he makes no response whatever to the following challenge I have formulated:

> *Natural law, or morality, can be understood, assented to and applied with-*

---

[41] *Id.* at 371-73, 378, 405-10.
[42] *Id.* at 49.
[43] *Id.*
[44] *Id.* at 31.
[45] *Id.* at 30.

> *out knowledge of metaphysics or anthropology* . . . Aquinas, S.T. I-II, q. 58, a. 4c is very clear: no one can be morally upright without (a) an understanding of the first principles of practical reasoning and (b) the practical reasonableness (*prudentia*) which brings those principles to bear, reasonably, on particular commitments, projects, actions; but one can indeed be morally upright without speculative (i.e. theoretical, 'is' -knowledge) wisdom [*sapientia*, evidently *stricto sensu*], without the practical knowledge of a craftsman (art), and without speculative knowledge (*scientia*).[46]

If my work and that of Grisez is as influential as Veatch maintains it is, in reviving some philosophical respect for natural-law theory, it is simply because we have pressed our readers to acknowledge their own grasp of *principia naturaliter* (but not innately) *nota* which Aquinas says they have, even though they lack metaphysical or anthropological theories. Only *after* we have achieved that acknowledgment, and explored its moral implications do we endeavor to explain how the goods thus acknowledged are aspects of a being which participates in the four orders of created being. This pedagogical order of priorities seems to be more faithful to the content of Aristotle's and Aquinas' theories of ethical knowledge. It has the disadvantage, I acknowledge, of requiring the reader to attend to more than occasional sentences in fragments of our respective works.

---

[46] *Id.* at 52.

[14]

THE PRINCIPLES OF NATURAL LAW *

RALPH MCINERNY

The influential interpretation of Summa Theologiae, IaIIae, q. 94, a. 2, by Germain Grisez, has provided the structure of John Finnis's recent and important book, *Natural Law and Natural Rights*. After a summary of Thomas Aquinas's article, the Grisez/Finnis view is examined with an eye to showing why it has proved attractive to so many. The insistence that the Face/Value distinction is rigorously observed in the derivation of natural law precepts, that the first principles of practical reason are pre-moral and that the basic values are equally basic is examined and some critical remarks made.

WHEN I REFLECTED ON THE assignment that had been given me for this occasion—to tell you about the direction discussion of natural law among philosophers has taken over the past quarter of a century—I very swiftly came to the conclusion that I did not want to conduct you on a barefoot trek over the very uneven terrain that assignment suggests. Such a survey would be a very difficult thing to do, and I fear it would not be an unqualified treat for the mind. Confirmation in this thought came when I hit upon a more manageable and, I think, far more interesting approach.

Fifteen years ago Professor Germain Grisez published an article entitled "The First Principle of Practical Reason." It appeared in *The Natural Law Form*, since metamorphosed into *The American Journal of Jurisprudence*. On this occasion there is something especially fitting in concentrating on this essay of Grisez's; the fact that he has developed and expanded the views of his article in a number of subsequent volumes published by the University of Notre Dame Press adds to that fittingness. Not that I am motivated by a sense of loyalty to the *genius loci* alone. Grisez's article was reprinted in the anthology edited by Anthony Kenney devoted to Aquinas in the *Modern Studies in Philosophy* series. Moreover, it has been warmly commended by Alan Donegan and provides the basis for the approach John Finnis takes in his recently published *Natural Law and Natural Rights*.[1] I think it is safe to say that Germain Grisez's interpretation of the key text in Thomas Aquinas's Treatise on Law, IaIIae, q.94, a.

---

* This paper was read to the annual Natural Law Institute meeting held at Notre Dame, IN on April 9, 1980.

1. John Finnis, *Natural Law and Natural Rights* (Oxford University Press, 1980). G. Grisez, "The First Principle of Practical Reason," *The Natural Law Forum* (1965), pp. 168-96. I cite the reprint in A. Kenny (ed.), *Aquinas* (London, 1970).

2 has become for many the definitive and authoritative one. It is certainly true that some reflections on it, even if they served only to draw yet more attention to Grisez's work, would worthily, if modestly, fulfill my assignment today.

In what follows, I shall do three main things. First, I shall recall as rapidly and as accurately as I can the views of Thomas in the article in question. Second, I shall summarize Grisez's interpretation which is meant to supplant a traditional more or less Suarezian version of natural law and return to the more satisfying and, he feels, obscured if not forgotton Thomistic teaching on natural law. Finally, I shall offer a number of criticisms of Grisez and Finnis.

I. SUMMA THEOLOGIAE, IaIIae, Q. 94, a. 2.

Although Thomas Aquinas is rightly looked to as a major proponent of natural law—the view that there are a number of true directives of human action every person can easily formulate for himself—it is oddly true that there is only one place in the vast body of his writings where he engages in an extended and formal discussion of law and its various kinds. Any student of Thomas will realize how unusual this is. Given the nature and occasion of his writings, Thomas was destined to discuss the same issues again and again, so much so that, at the foot of any article in the *Summa Theologiae*, there is a list of *loca parallela* to which one can repair for discussions similar to the one in the *Summa*. There are references to parallel places in the *Treatise on Law* but these are due to the ingenuity of editors rather than to the fact that Thomas is here taking up anew matters he has discussed as such elsewhere. Most notably, there is no parallel discussion to the article which is the focus of this first portion of my remarks.

The article asks: *Utrum lex naturalis contineat plura praecepta vel tantum*: Is there one only precept of natural law or are there many? What does he mean by natural law? To this point we have in hand only the definition given in q. 91, a. 2: natural law is the peculiarly human way of participating in the eternal law whereby God governs creation. Every creature comes under the sway of God's governance but "Among the others the rational creature comes under Providence in a more excellent way, insofar as it shares in that Providence, providing for itself and others." The rational creature directs himself to his appropriate end and activity. Such direction is expressed in precepts[2] and the question thus comes down to: is one precept sufficient to express how we should achieve our appropriate end?

2. *Summa theologiae*. Thomas Aquinas. IaIIae. 92. 2c. "*. . . sicut enuntiatio est rationis dictamen per modum enuntiandi, ita etiam lex per modum praecipiendi.*"

RALPH McINERNY 3

Thomas begins by likening the precepts of natural law (his use of the plural indicates how the question will be answered) to the first principles which guide theoretical discourse: both are *per se nota*, known through themselves, not derived, self-evident. A proposition is *per se nota* when no middle term is required to explain the conjunction of predicate and subject. Rather, one who knows the meaning of its terms will immediately see that the proposition is true. In the theoretical use of our mind, there is a distinction between apprehension and judgment; we must grasp the meaning of the constitutive terms of a proposition before we can constitute a proposition from them. Being is something that no one can fail to know; *illud quod primo cadit in apprehensione, est ens, cujus intellectus includitur in omnibus, quaecumque quis apprehendit.* What is known is a being, whatever else it is. On this apprehension is grounded the first indemonstrable principle: you cannot simultaneously affirm and deny the same thing.[3]

Just as being is the first thing that without qualification the mind grasps, so the good is the first thing grasped by mind in its practical function of directing to some work. An agent acts for an end which has the note of goodness. So the first principle of practical reason is going to be grounded on the notion of goodness. What is the concept of the good? The good is that which all things seek. That is what "good" is taken to mean. Something is sought insofar as it is completive or perfective of the seeker. Thus "good" does not simply designate an object of pursuit, it suggests the formality under which the object is pursued: as completive, as perfective. The first precept, the parallel in practical thought to the first principle of reasoning without qualification, the principle of contradiction, is this: The good is to be done and pursued, and evil avoided.

> *Et super hoc fundantur omnia alia praecepta legis naturae, ut scilicet omnia illa facienda vel vitanda pertineant ad praecepta legis naturae, quae ratio practica naturaliter apprehendit esse bona humana.*[4]

---

3. One might ask why Thomas gives this expression to the first principle of all reasoning. He says it is grounded on the notion of being and not being, but then why not state the principle: it is impossible for a thing to be and not to be at the same time and in the same respect. The reason seems to be that the concept of natural law draws particular attention to the role of human reason in fashioning precepts directing action to man's end; given this, the mind's affirming and denying give rise to an expression of the first principle more obviously parallel to those of practical reason.

4. The "naturaliter" modifying practical reason's grasp of human goods refers to either or both (a) mind's apprehension of the goods in question, and (b) the immediacy of the judgment that such goods are to be pursued and their opposites avoided.

The precept is formed by human reason and it is meant to be directive of human action. The addressee is the human agent and the directive is: The perfection, the completion, the good in the sense of the ultimate end, is to be pursued and whatever is incompatible with that end is to be avoided.

Any other directive, any other precept which is a natural law precept, will be in effect a particularlization of this one. That is, we shall expect that there will be a multiplicity of apprehensions each expressive of some constitutive of man's end or good.

> *Quia vero bonum habet rationem finis, malum autem rationem contrarii, inde est quod omnia illa ad quae homo habet naturalem inclinationem, ratio naturaliter apprehendit ut bona, et per consequens ut opere prosequenda, et contraria eorum ut mala et vitanda.*

The good as end or completion is the object of inclination or appetite. Man is a complex whole comprising a number of inclinations, each of which will have an appropriate good or end. If we enumerate these inclinations and notice their hierarchy we will be able to glimpse the natural law precepts which take them into account.

What is meant by the order of inclinations? This: there are some goods which men share with all creatures, others they share with only some other creatures, and some which are peculiar to men. If the human good is taken to mean the good which is peculiar and proportionate to man, it would be that which is perfective of him as the special kind of agent he is. But man is a rational agent. Therefore the good or perfection of rational activity is man's end. But what of such inclinations as that to self-preservation, common to all creatures and thus to man, and that to reproduce and form a family and raise offspringing, common to all animals and thus to men: are the ends or goods aimed at by these inclinations to form no part of the human good? Of course they are parts of man's good, but only insofar as they are humanized, that is, are pursued not just instinctively, but as the aim or goal of conscious action. As human acts, the pursuit of these ends must be rational, deliberate, responsible. Natural law precepts relating to such goods must envisage them as human goods: the precept is a directive of reason as to how we should pursue such goods. Thus goods which are not peculiar to men come to be constituents of the human good insofar as they come under the sway of the distinctive mark of human agent, reason. Sex is a *human* good not just as such, but as engaged in consciously and purposively and responsibly. That is how it becomes a *human* evil too; there is no way in which humans can engage in sexual activity other than consciously which is why the "animal" part of our nature is always a layer and never autonomous.[5]

Natural law is a dictate of reason. Precepts of natural law are rational directives aiming at the good for man. The human good, man's ultimate end, is complex, but the unifying thread is the distinctive mark of the human, i.e., reason; so too law is a work of reason. Man does not simply have an instinct for self-preservation. He recognizes self-preservation as a good and devises ways and means to secure it in shifting circumstances. Man does not merely have a sexual instinct. Recognizing the desirability of sexual companionship, reproduction, offspring, he consciously directs himself to those goods as goods without which he would not be complete.

One familiar with the opening discussions of this part of the *Summa Theologiae*, discussions concerned with the human good and man's ultimate end, will see that the several precepts of natural law are directives aiming at constituents of the human good or ultimate end. The precepts are first: Pursue your good, your ultimate end, and avoid what is destructive of it. And then there are articulations of this in precepts which express constituents of that end: Rationally pursue self-preservation; rationally pursue the good of sex, reproduction, offspring; rationally pursue the good of reason itself, truth, in all its modes, and particularly truth about the most important things.

The natural law precepts other than the first do not express means whereby the good of the first most common precept can be attained, as if they were instrumental to it. Rather they express means only in the sense of constituents of the ultimate end. Thus, it seems that the precepts of natural law are general directives toward the ultimate end, either stated most generally (the good is to be done and pursued and evil avoided), or aimed at constituents of the ultimate end. We will see later, with reference to the distinction between *comunissima*, *communia*, and *propria*, that there may be need to modify this claim, but for now, by taking the obvious implication of the text, that all natural law precepts are general injunctions to pursue the ultimate end or the human good, and conjoining it with the truth that man's end is given, we can see how it can be claimed that natural law precepts are valid everywhere and at all times. That claim can seem controversial whenever a way of achieving or attaining the end is expressed, no matter how general the expression.

---

5. The dream of Kierkegaard's aesthete is to engage in sensuality in such a way as to be at once aware and unaware: to be at once a heedless innocent animal, and a conscious self-observing participant. This impossible dream is why the aesthete lives a life of despair.

II. GRISEZ ON THIS ARTICLE

The essay of Germain Grisez mentioned at the outset is polemical in the sense that he is out to correct what he takes to be a fundamental misunderstanding, or fundamental misunderstandings, of the teaching of St. Thomas with respect to the first principle of practical reason. It is Grisez's contention that a caricature of Thomistic natural law has been accepted as good money for a long time, that this caricature owes far more to Vasquez and Suarez than it does to Thomas, and that this caricature is open to a number of devastating criticisms which are ineffective against the view of Thomas Aquinas properly understood.

From the very first paragraph of his article, we would take it that one of the roots of the misunderstanding is connected with confusing commands and gerundive statements, that is, treating "Do good and avoid evil" as equivalent to "Good is to be done and pursued and evil avoided." "Although verbally this formula is only slightly different from that of the command . . . I shall try to show that the two formulae differ considerably in meaning and that they belong in different theoretical contexts."[6] Taking the first principle to be a command, the caricature of natural law is this:

> Man discovers this imperative in his conscience; it is like an inscription written there by the hand of God. Having become aware of this basic commandment, man consults his nature to see what is good and what is evil. He examines an action in comparison with his essence to see whether the action fits human nature or does not fit it. If the action fits, it is seen to be good; if it does not fit, it is seen to be bad. Once we know that a certain kind of action—for instance, stealing—is bad, we have two premises, "Avoid evil" and "Stealing is evil," from whose conjunction is deduced: "Avoid stealing." All specific commandments of natural law are derived in this way.[7]

I am interested in this caricature and Grisez's treatment of it only insofar as what he says of it fills out his own understanding of what Thomas really means to say. That such a caricature is or was current, I shall not contest; nor will I say anything about its alleged Suarezian roots. These are simple negations. I am not at all implying that an examination of these historical questions would lead to criticisms of Grisez's characterization.

When one gets into Grisez's article and begins to get a glimpse of his positive interpretation, reasons why it has commended itself to

---

6. "The First Principle of Practical Reason," as reprinted in Kenny, p. 341.
7. *Ibid.*, p. 340.

many are easy to find. Although he does not stress this just as such, Grisez gives no comfort at all to those who would see in the concept of ultimate end as highest superordinating good the implication that there is some one goal or course of action that all men should pursue. Many critics of the view of ultimate end that Thomas took over from Aristotle have seen in it the absurd claim that over and above birdwatching, carpentry, and practicing law there is some specifically human task that we should all perform and which is such that to perform it well makes one a good human being. Grisez and Finnis are refreshing in their gentle insistence that the natural law view is precisely the view that there is an all but numberless variety of ways in which men can attain their completeness or perfection as men.

So, too, Grisez's interpretation puts the emphasis on the positive rather than the negative precept. To see natural law as a series of shalt nots is truly a caricature of it, for natural law precepts point to that which is fulfilling and completive of man, not simply toward things to be avoided. The latter presupposes the former and however we stand in need of moral prohibitions, any discussion of the moral life which deals almost exclusively with prohibitions can give no sense of the liberating and expansive thing the moral ideal is. Certainly such an emphasis on the negative bears little or no relation to the writings of Thomas Aquinas.

But of course I am not here simply to praise Grisez and Finnís. I have long been puzzled by the reception Grisez's article received because it seems to me to be extremely obscure at just the points where it should be clearest. There are three general headings under which I can place most of my misgivings about the Grisez interpretation: (a) the somewhat excessive distinction between fact and value (where the understanding of practical reason becomes dubious); (b) the claim that the first principle of practical reason, and perhaps the whole set of basic values, are somehow pre-moral, not-yet-ethical matters; and (c) the denial of any objective hierarchy among the basic values. I shall first of all sketch Grisez's views on these matters and, in the next section of my paper, develop my misgivings.

THE FACT/VALUE DICHOTOMY

"If one supposes that principles of natural law are formed by examining kinds of action in comparison with human nature and noting their agreement or disagreement, then one must respond to the objection that it is impossible to derive normative judgments from metaphysical speculations."[8] Grisez is insistent on a distinction be-

8. *Ibid.*, p. 382.

tween the normative and factual, valuation and description, is and ought, and this insistence has, I think, a certain dated charm about it. The passage just quoted suggests that there is something illicit in the passage from such sentences as

Wheaties are good for you

to

You ought to eat Wheaties.

Finnis devotes a section of his second chapter to this matter. "Another of the three decisive issues formulated by Stone was this: 'Have the natural lawyers shown that they can derive ethical norms from facts?' And the answer can be brisk: They have not, nor do they need to, nor did classical exponents of the theory dream of attempting any such derivation."[9] Finnis feels this undercuts one of the most widespread misunderstandings of natural law. It is simply not true, he says, that "any form of a natural law theory of morals entails the belief that propositions about man's duties and obligations can be inferred from propositions about his nature."[10] The first principles of natural law are self-evident, underived; that is, for Finnis, the real basis for the denial that they are inferred or derived from any other propositions of whatever kind. "They are not inferred from speculative principles. They are not inferred from facts. They are not inferred from metaphysical propositions about human nature, or about the nature of good and evil, or about 'the function of a human being.' "[11] His denials become more and more sweeping.

> Principles of right and wrong, too, are derived from these first, pre-moral principles of practical reasonableness, and not from any facts, whether metaphyscial or otherwise. When discerning what is good, to be pursued (*prosequendum*), intelligence is operating in a different way, yielding a different logic, from when it is discerning what is the case . . . but there is no good reason for asserting that the latter operations of intelligence are more rational than the former.[12]

More positively, Finnis writes

> One does not judge that "I have (or everybody has) an inclination to find out about things" and then infer that therefore knowledge is a good to be pursued. Rather, by a simple act of non-inferential understanding one grasps that the object of the inclination which one experiences is an instance of a general form of good . . . .[13]

9. *Op. cit.*, Finnis, p. 33.
10. *Ibid.*, Finnis has in mind D.J.O. Conner, *Aquinas and Natural Law*.
11. *Ibid.*, p. 33.
12. *Ibid.*, p. 34.
13. *Ibid.*

The first underived principles of practical reasonableness, make no reference at all to human nature, but only to human good.[14] In Grisez, far more than in Finnis, this insistence leads to a somewhat unusual sense of practical reason. Grisez says that in theoretical thinking the world calls the turn, in practical thinking the mind calls the turn. Often he suggests that practical reason turns upon a malleable world which it can remake pretty much at will. One recognizes in this characterization what Aristotle and Thomas say of art far more than what they say of prudence, of the specifically moral.

THE PRE-MORAL CHARACTER OF FIRST PRINCIPLES

If Grisez *et sequaces ejus* are insistent that moral principles, the first principles of practical reasoning, are not derived from factual truths grasped by mind speculative, they nonetheless argue for an ethical heteronomy in the following sense. The first underived self-evident principles, the precepts of natural law, are pre-moral, not moral. Moral principles are nontheless derived from them. What this comes down to, in terms of the article in the *Summa* already cited, q. 94, a. 2, is the claim that the basic values, the goods pointed to or aimed at by the instincts, are not as such moral values. By this they do not mean, for example, that the instinctive desire for sexual congress is, when felt, neither good not bad, not yet a moral act; or that the surging up of an emotion, of anger or joy, is not as such moral or immoral. What they mean is that the comphrehensive good that is to be pursued is not a moral value. That comes down to saying that man's ultimate end is not a moral value. So too the basic values that Finnis lists, expanding a bit on Grisez, namely Life, Knowledge, Play, Aesthetic Experience, Sociability, Practical Reasonableness, and Religion are not moral values, singly, or cumulatively. "Neither this chapter nor the next [3 and 4, in which Finnis discusses basic values] makes or presupposes any moral judgments. Rather, these two chapters conern the evaluative substratum of all judgments. That is to say, they concern the acts of practical understanding in which we grasp the basic values of human existence and thus, too, the basic principles of all practical reasoning."[15]

What Finnis could mean is that the grasp of these basic values would be expressed in definitions rather than in precepts and in that sense no practical advice, moral or any other kind, is being given. Only when we judge that we should pursue the basic value or when

---

14. *Ibid.*, p. 36.
15. *Ibid.*, p. 59.

we judge that such-and-such would be a way of attaining or participating in the basic value, stating this in a prescriptive way, only then do we enter into the domain of the moral proper. Perhaps that is what he means,[16] and then it would be like saying concept formation is not yet an activity that is true or false; truth or falsehood enter in only when judgments, employing such concepts, are made.

But if that is what Finnis means, it does not seem to be what Grisez means by speaking of these self-evident principles of natural law as pre-moral. He seems more concerned to have principles that will govern the practical activity of all men, good or bad, and which thus must split the difference between moral and immoral. If the bad man as well as the good is guided by these first principles the one will not be called good nor the other bad simply because he is guided by them.

BASIC VALUE EGALITARIANISM

A moment ago I listed the Basic Values that are taken to emerge from the grasp of the goods aimed at by man's inclinations. One of the most distinctive marks of Grisez's interpretation is his claim that no one of these values is better than the others. There is no objective hierarchy among the basic values that one would have to be guided by in the formation of a life plan. Of course, in the nature of things, this man plans his life in such a way that the quest for knowledge, say, takes precedence over the other values; this man, a surgeon, puts life at the center of his life. In thus giving preference, so to say, to one basic value over others, one must not act directly against any basic value. Here we have, I think, the reason for the claim that the basic values are equally fundamental.

> More important than the precise number and description of these values is the sense in which each is basic. First, each is equally self-evidentally a form of good. Secondly, none can be analytically reduced to being merely an aspect of any of the others, or to being merely instrumental in the pursuit of any of the others. Thirdly, each one, when we focus on it, can reasonably be regarded as the most important. Hence there is no objective hierarchy among them.[17]

Finnis at any rate is aware that this tenet separates him from the text of Aquinas, to an analysis of which Grisez devoted his article. Thomas, we recall, wrote: *Secundum igitur ordinem inclinationum naturalium, est ordo praceptorum legis naturalis*. Finnis, taking note

16. *Ibid.*, p. 84.
17. *Ibid.*, p. 92

of this, and the way in which for Thomas the most basic inclination is one man shares with everything else, the next most basic one he shares with other animals, and so on, comments:

> But is it relevant to a meditation on the *value* of the various aspects of human well-being? Are not speculative considerations intruding into a reconstruction of principles that are practical and that, being primary, indemonstrable, and self-evident, are not derivable (nor sought by Aquinas to be derived) from any speculative considerations?[18]

Finnis concludes that Thomas here sets a questionable example and repeats that "in ethical reflection the threefold order should be set aside as an irrelevant schematization."[19] So we are back to an understanding of the speculative and practical, now so understood as to collide in important ways with Thomas's understanding.

III. REFLECTIONS ON THE GRISEZ INTERPRETATION

A view of practical reason that regards knowledge of the world to be irrelevant to it is clearly a view different from that which we encounter in Aristotle and Aquinas. The theory of practical reasoning developed by Aquinas is a good deal more complicated than either Grisez or Finnis seem to recognize. It is well known that Thomas provides not just one but three criteria for practical reasoning, suggesting that such reasoning is more practical to the degree that it satisfies more of these criteria.[20] One of these criteria is the nature of the object—is it something that can be made or done by us—and from this point of view a quite factual statement about a house will, since a house is precisely a product of human craft, count as a piece of practical discourse; minimally practical, it is true, but one sees that it is not going to be in terms of syntax that one is going to be able to set the practical off from the theoretical. Grisez tends to want to restrict practical discourse to gerundive precepts.

Allied with this is the insistence that no transition from *is* to *ought*, from *fact* to *value* is going on in natural law. The dichotomy involved, once thought to be sharp and distinct, has come to be seen as doing duty for a number of contrasts which cannot be reduced to absolute unity. Maritain in *Neuf Lecons sur la philosophie morale* made the point that all intellectual activity is concerned with value, truth value, for instance. Indeed this is now one of the basic values Grisez and

18. *Ibid.*, p. 94.
19. *Ibid.*, p. 95.
20. Cf. *Summa theologiae*, Ia, q. 14, a. 16.

Finnis recognize and thus comes specifically under the sway of the moral. The concern not to infer from *fact* to *value*, from *is* to *ought*, may be a sympton of over-fastidiousness.

Joe weighs two hundred and fifty pounds.
Joe ought to go on a diet.

That transition would be said to be justified by the understood premise "It is not healthy to be overweight." And that is a value-premise. It is action guiding. But is it? We may find it odd if someone says "Who wants to be healthy?" but would we want to say some fallacy has been committed? Grisez and Finnis are clearly concerned about avoiding fallacies. But one man's fallacy may be another's common sense. Does

Knowledge is good for man

entail

Men ought to pursue knowledge?

Grisez and Finnis often speak of the first proposition as a metaphysical truth having nothing to do with practical judgments. The fact is "Knowledge is good for man" is a special case of "Good is that which all men seek;" it is precisely the basic value which is the principle on which the precept "Knowledge ought to be pursued" is founded. Whatever fallacy there may be in passing from *is* to *ought*, Grisez's understanding of it threatens to undercut his own and Thomas' actual procedure.

> No philosopher, no matter what he may say, wants to regard facts about human beings as morally irrelevant. The sharp dichotomy between normative and non-normative discourse maintained by the empiricist does not obtain in fact: there are many propositions, such that tuberculosis is a disease, or that a human child ought to be able to talk before reaching the age of five years, which do not fit comfortably on either side of the dichotomy.[21]

The claim that the first principles of practical reasoning, the self-evident principles of natural law, are pre-moral rather than precisely the principles of morality, is, I find, a strange one. It certainly sounds Pickwickian as a characterization of what is going on in the *Summa Theologiae*, IaIIae, q. 94, a. 2. Once more Finnis is clearer on this than Grisez, that is, clearer as to what motivates him in saying it.

21. Philip Devine, *The Ethics of Homicide*, p. 43.

> The principles that express the general ends of human life do not acquire what would nowadays be called a "moral" force until they are brought to bear upon definite ranges of project, disposition, or action, or upon particular projects, dispositions or actions. How they are thus brought to bear *is* the problem for practical reasonableness. "Ethics" as classically conceived is simply a recollectively and/or prospectively reflective expression of this problem and of the general lines of solutions which have been thought reasonable.[22]

Finnis is being guided by what he takes to be the meaning of "moral" nowadays. The first prinicples of practical reasoning are not yet moral because they are too general, apparently, and Finnis thinks he finds this usage in Thomas.[23]

His reference is to the interesting text to be found at IaIIae, q. 100, a. 1 where Thomas asks if all the moral principles of the old law pertain to natural law. (Moral precepts are here distinguished from ceremonial and judicial precepts of the Old Law.) The text explicitly groups the first principles of natural law with moral precepts, so that there can be little doubt as to Thomas' own usage. But as a terminological matter it is of little importance. What Finnis wants to distinguish from what he calls moral or ethical are those precepts which direct us to pursue our ultimate end or the constituents of it.

> I reply that moral precepts, distinguished from ceremonial and judicial precepts, bear on things which of themselves pertain to good morals. Since then humans customs (*mores*) are said to be such by being ordered to reason, which is the distinctive principle of human acts, those customs are said to be good which agree with reason, those evil which are discordant with reason.
>
> Now just as every judgment of speculative reason proceeds from a natural knowledge of first principles, so every judgment of practical reason proceeds from certain naturally known principles.[24]

Here Thomas refers to q. 94, a. 2. These first precepts of natural law he now calls *comunissima*, most common, and since they are precisely most common *precepts*, they cannot be simply the grasp or

---

22. *Op. cit.*, Finnis, p. 101.

23. *Idid.* (See also p. 30. "Even when, later, Thomas Aquinas clearly distinguished a class of practical principles which he considered self-evident to anyone with enough experience and intelligence to understand the words by which they are formulated, he emphasized that moral principles such as those in the Ten Commandments are *conclusions from* the primary self-evident principles, that reasoning to such conclusions requires good judgment, and that there are many other more complex and particular moral norms to be followed and more judgments and decisions to be made . . . ."

24. IaIIae, q. 100, a. 1.

apprehension of basic values.[25] Nonetheless, it seems right to suggest that they are precepts which simply direct to the end, whether in general (The good is to be done and pursued, and evil avoided), or in articulating the constituents of man's good.

> From which it (reason) diversely proceeds in judging of diverse things. (a) There are some things in human acts so obvious (*explicita*) that with but a little consideration they can be approved or disapproved through the common and first principle. (b) Other things indeed are such that judgment of them requires lengthy consideration of diverse circumstances, the diligent inquiry into which is not possible for everyone, but only the wise . . .[26]

It is on the basis of these texts that I suggest that the first principles of natural law are absolute and changeless precisely because they direct to the end and do not express even at a level of high generality ways of achieving the end. The next level Thomas speaks of, a level of precepts deduced from the most common, could be thought of as directives expressing ways to achieve the end or ways to be avoided since they thwart the end. Here there could be absolutes whenever a certain mode of conduct would necessarily thwart the end, but clearly we are more likely to have precepts which are valid only for the most part. Furthermore, if "precept" in the proper sense of the word covers judgments which express means to the end and not simply end, and there is reason to think this is how Thomas understood it,[27] then one could say that the first precepts of natural law are less properly precepts, less properly moral precepts, than those expressive of means. And that would be a way of saying what Finnis and Grisez, perhaps for the same reason, want to say.

As for the denial of an objective hierarchy among basic values, one has to hold fast to the reasons for the denial—to wit, to guard against acting directly contrary to a basic value. Whether the acceptance of an objective hierarchy among basic values deprives one of a basis for forbidding acting directly against a basic value is not evident. Only if the hierarchy reduced a basic good to mere instrumental status would this follow. By the same token, recognition of an objective hierarchy among basic values in no way impedes that subjectively, that is from

---

25. *Op. cit.*, Aquinas, q. 99. a 2. ad 2m.

26. *Ibid.*, q. 100, a. 1.

27. Ibid., cf. q. 100, a. 9, ad 2m; see also q. 99, a. 1: "*praeceptum legis, cum sit obligation, est de aliquo quod fieri debet. Quod autem aliquid debeat fieri, hoc provenit ex necessitate alicuius finis. Unde manifestum est quod de ratione praecepti est quod importet ordinem ad finem, inquantum scilicet illud praecipitur quod est necessarium vel expediens ad finem.*"

subject to subject, a more personal hierarchy would obtain. In any case, what must be said is that Thomas himself, as Aristotle had before him, insists on the inequality of the basic values and recognizes a hierarchy among them. That a good might be end-like yet not an ultimate end, but, subordinable to a further end, does not make it merely instrumental. Both Thomas and Aristotle take that perfection of rational activity which they call contemplation to be objectively the highest. Neither man thinks that anyone could devote himself exclusively to contemplation; the human good remains complex, irreducible to a single kind of activity. And in this perspective, the moral virtues are taken to be dispositive toward, conditions of, the contemplative use of the mind.

IV. ENVOI

I hope these remarks about the interpretation of Grisez and Finnis will not seem churlish or petty or merely negative. If their interpretation did not have much to commend it, it would scarcely have become as influential as it is. I mentioned earlier some of its major merits, in my estimation, and I could add many more to those. Perhaps I will not be thought too docile a disciple of Aquinas if I say that I find Grisez and Finnis at their best when they are developing Thomas's thought along its own lines and weakest when they are consciously or unconsciously deviating from it. In any case, it seems to me that natural law has been largely a matter of footnotes to the *Treatise on Law* in the *Summa Theologiae*, and that it is likely to remain this insofar as it retains strength and persuasiveness. Quite apart from its independent merits, the view of Grisez and Finnis is seen as Thomistic. This is why I concentrated on it and I mean my humble observations to be tribute rather than carping criticism. My moral is simply that one should read Grisez and Finnis in conjunction with Aquinas. A major task before us, I think, is to draw out the relations between ultimate end and the *Treatise on Law*. When this is done the main emphasis of the work of Germain Grisez will have been brought to completion.

[15]

THE BASIC PRINCIPLES OF NATURAL LAW: A REPLY TO RALPH McINERNY

JOHN FINNIS AND GERMAIN GRISEZ

In the preceding volume of this journal, Prof. McInerny criticized certain theoretical positions of Finnis and Grisez as well as their interpretation of St. Thomas. In the present article Finnis and Grisez reply that McInerny's criticisms lack cogency, because he has misunderstood their theories, judged their exegesis by his own different interpretation assumed gratuitously to be correct, and mixed philosophical and historical criticism in a way which helps to clarify neither the problems of ethical theory nor those of Thomistic exegesis.

RALPH MCINERNY'S "THE PRINCIPLES OF NATURAL LAW"[1] is generous in its estimate of the significance of our work. But we think McInerny's criticism of Grisez's article, "The First Principle of Practical Reason,"[2] and Finnis' treatise, *Natural Law and Natural Rights*,[3] involves some serious misunderstandings of our views. We suspect that some of these misunderstandings are widely shared.

There is a methodological problem which makes a commentary on McInerny's article difficult. Grisez's article is a commentary on *Summa theologiae*, I-II, Question 94, Article 2, not a general treatment of Thomas' ethics, much less a summary of Grisez's own ethics. Finnis' treatise, by contrast, states and defends his own ethical theory. It points to texts of Thomas where "they can both illuminate and be illuminated by the theory presented in [the] book";[4] but it is not a commentary, and prescinds from the question whether it is *ad mentem Divi Thomae*. McInerny's article seems to take insufficient account of the restrictions of scope and purpose of the two works he has chosen to discuss.

McInerny says that his misgivings about "the Grisez interpretation [of the teaching of St. Thomas]" can mostly be grouped under three

---

1. 25 *American Journal of Jurisprudence*, pp. 1-15; hereinafter cited as *McI*.
2. "The First Principle of Practical Reason: A Commentary on the *Summa theologiae*, 1-2, Question 94, Article 2," 10 *Natural Law Forum*, pp. 168-201, hereinafter cited as *FPPR*. McInerny's references are to an abridged version in Anthony Kenny, ed., *Aquinas: A Collection of Critical Essays* (London: 1970), pp. 340-382. But the abridgement is not, as McInerny assumes (*McI*, p.1), a "reprint" of the original article.
3. (New York and Oxford: Oxford University Press, 1980), hereinafter cited as *NLNR*.
4. *NLNR*, p. v.

headings.[5] So our reply also is under three headings. Under each we take space for only a few main points.

I. "EXCESSIVE DISTINCTION BETWEEN FACT AND VALUE"[6]

At one point McInerny suggests that we share "a view of practical reason that regards knowledge of the world to be irrelevant to it."[7]

All the references McInerny offers in respect to Finnis to support this suggestion are to pages in chapter II.4 of his book. These pages are devoted to a necessary polemic against modern critics who claim that Thomas makes the logical error of trying to deduce normative propositions from theoretical propositions ("ought" from "is") and who therefore dismiss him out of hand. A Thomist must read these pages with care, particularly their statements of what Thomas' theory is *not*. To find Finnis' positive account of Thomas' theory of the relation of fact to value, the Thomist should look a bit further on in the book.[8] There Finnis explains:

> Aquinas followed Aristotle's theory of the "induction" of indemonstrable first principles by insight working on observation, memory, and experience, but extended the account to a parallel "induction" of indemonstrable first principles of practical reason (i.e., of natural law) by insight working on felt inclinations and a knowledge of possibilities: *S.T.*, I-II, q. 94, a.2. . .[9]

Having explained that for Thomas those first practical principles are of the form "X is a good to be pursued . . . ," Finnis gives his formal account of why such principles are principles of natural law:

> . . . thirdly, the basic forms of good are opportunities of *being;* the more fully a man participates in them the more he is what he can be. And for this state of being fully what one can be, Aristotle appropriated the word *physis*, which was translated into Latin as *natura* . . . So Aquinas will say that these requirements are requirements not only of reason, and of goodness, but also (by entailment) of (human) nature . . .[10]

Nor does Finnis himself think "knowledge of the world to be irrelevant" to practical reason, nor even to practical reason's grasp of its

5. *McI*, p. 7.
6. *McI*, p. 7.
7. *McI*, p. 11.
8. See especially *NLNR*, pp. 78-79, which should be read with p. 45, text at n. 60.
9. *NLNR*, p. 77.
10. *NLNR*, p. 103, concluding with a reference back to pp. 35-36, where relevant texts of Thomas are quoted and analyzed.

basic principles. Explaining what he means by "values cannot be derived from facts," he says: ". . . my contention is that, while *awareness of certain 'factual' possibilities is a necessary condition* for the reasonable judgment that truth is a value, still that judgment itself is derived from no other judgment whatsoever."[11]

McInerny makes two points in connection with the fact-value distinction with respect to Grisez.

First, he quotes Grisez's use of the objection "that it is impossible to derive normative judgments from metaphysical speculations."[12] McInerny thinks this "suggests that there is something illicit in the passage from such sentences as

Wheaties are good for you

to

You ought to eat Wheaties."[13]

Later, McInerny says[14] both of us consider it fallacious to pass from

Knowledge is good for man

to

Men ought to pursue knowledge.

"Grisez and Finnis," McInerny says, "often speak of the first proposition as a metaphysical truth having nothing to do with practical judgments."[15] For this claim about what we "often speak of" no citation is given. None can be given, for we nowhere say any such thing.

One of the principles of *practical* thinking is that knowledge is a good to be pursued; this principle entails that knowledge ought to be pursued. But in the *practical* principle that knowledge is a good to be pursued, "good" is understood *practically* in the light of the first *practical* principle: Good is to be done and pursued. If "Knowledge is a good for man" were understood theoretically, simply as a truth of metaphysical anthropology, then it would have no more normative implication than "Knowledge is good for angels" has practical implication for us.

Nothing in our accounts of practical reason in general or of ethics in particular belittles or excludes as irrelevant to ethics a nonpositivist, teleological understanding of nature and of human persons insofar as

11. *NLNR*, p. 73 (emphasis added). Finnis repeatedly discusses the relevance of knowledge of the world: pp. 17-19, 65-66, 71, and 77 (last note).
12. *McI*, p. 7, citing *FPPR*, p. 196.
13. *McI*, p. 8.
14. *McI*, p. 12.
15. *McI*, p. 12.

they are part of nature.[16] But if McInerny wishes to justify a conclusion such as

Joe ought to go on a diet

he had better not be content[17] with premises such as

Joe weighs two hundred and fifty pounds

and

It is not healthy to be overweight.

One must assume a more basic practical premise

Health is a good to be pursued and protected

which itself is a specification of the very first principle of practical reason. This very first principle is *not* the truth of metaphysics or psychology, "Good is that which all men seek," as McInerny seems to think,[18] but "Good is to be done and pursued and evil is to be avoided," as Thomas unequivocally says when he treats this matter in the famous passage on which Grisez commented.

Similarly, only with the practical principle, "Health is a good to be pursued and protected," and additional factual premises can one validly pass from "Wheaties are good for you" to "You ought to eat Wheaties." We have never said that one cannot pass from metaphysical and/or factual truths *together with principles of practical reasoning* to normative conclusions. Our point rather was that there can be no valid deduction of a normative conclusion without a normative principle, and thus that *first* practical principles cannot be derived from metaphysical speculations.[19]

The second point McInerny makes about Grisez with respect to fact and value is this:

> Grisez says that in theoretical thinking the world calls the turn, in practical thinking the mind calls the turn. Often he suggests that

---

16. See *FPPR*, pp. 177 and 194.
17. As he seems to be: *McI*, p. 12.
18. *McI*, p. 12.
19. See *FPPR*, pp. 193-196; *NLNR*, pp. 33-34. *McI*, p. 12, accuses us of "over-fastidiousness" in our concern not to derive *ought* from *is*, and he suggests that "one man's fallacy may be another's common sense." We think that bad arguments have bad consequences; the lack of fastidiousness in much current ethics and moral theology is exacting a terrible price. Also important, careful exercise of reason according to the highest standards is to be valued for its own sake; lack of fastidiousness shows a remiss love of the basic human good of truth. As for common sense, we consider its inarticulateness about basic principles perfectly acceptable for the plain man. The philosopher, however, has the duty to try to explicate the assumptions of common sense. In the present instance, one fails philosophically if one evades the underivability of first practical principles (which Thomas says are *per se nota*—and what can this mean to McInerny?—) by falling back on (formally invalid) common sense reasoning, which always is enthemymatic.

> practical reason turns upon a malleable world which it can remake pretty much at will.[20]

Again, no citation is given. Grisez nowhere says or "suggests" any such absurdity as that practical reason turns upon a malleable world which it can remake pretty much at will. In saying that "the mind calls the turn" in practical knowledge,[21] Grisez is making the same point as Thomas makes in the Prologue to his commentary on Aristotle's *Ethics:* that in contrast with the order of nature which reason finds and does not make, there are orders which reason itself makes—in the case of morally practical knowledge, in the acts of the will, and what is consequent upon them.

Grisez has taken pains elsewhere to show that there also necessarily is an order which reason does not make but only considers, an order of nature (including human nature), which is far from being "a malleable world which it [reason] can remake pretty much at will."[22] In the context of this exposition, Grisez sets out a thoroughly objectivist theory of value as *fulfillment of possibility,* in each order of reality, and emphasizes: "*What* the something is and to what order of entities it belongs must be taken for granted in distinguishing between the extent to which it already is, and the extent to which it is still short of its full possibility"[23] (and thus wanting in goodness). Thus for Grisez even in the moral world, where the mind calls the turn (reason makes, not finds, order), the subjectivism suggested by McInerny's unfortunate phrase, "can remake pretty much at will," is altogether excluded.

II. BASIC VALUES AS PREMORAL

In discussing the premoral character of the principles of natural law, McInerny seems to conclude that he agrees with what he thinks we perhaps also want to say on this question.[24] But McInerny's view

---

20. *McI*, p. 9.

21. *FPPR*, p. 176. McInerny possibly is misled by his reliance on the Kenny abridgement, which so reduces Grisez's exposition of this point as to leave "the mind calls the turn" standing as an enigmatic, provocative slogan.

22. On the four orders distinguished by Thomas in the Prologue to his commentary on Aristotle's *Ethics*, and on the irreducibility of nature, see Germain Grisez, *Beyond the New Theism: A Philosophy of Religion* (Notre Dame and London: University of Notre Dame Press, 1975), pp. 230-240, 353-356, and the treatment of metaphysical relativism, pp. 205-225; see also Finnis, *NLNR*, pp. 136-139, 380, 389-391.

23. Grisez, *Beyond the New Theism*, p. 291.

24. *McI*, p. 14. We do not here undertake to criticize McInerny's conception: end : means :: first principles of natural law: moral precepts deduced from the most common principles. But we do not concede the implicit theory, which seems to us to distort and greatly oversimplify the structure of moral reality and moral reasoning.

of this matter presupposes his assumption that in the absolutely first principle, *"Bonum est faciendum et prosequendum . . .,"* the word *"bonum"* refers to the *ultimate* end.[25]

Whether considered in itself or as an interpretation of Thomas, this presupposition seems to us quite untenable. Speaking of this absolutely first precept, McInerny comments:

> The addressee is the human agent and the directive is: The perfection, the completion, the good in the sense of the ultimate end, is to be pursued and whatever is incompatible with that end is to be avoided.
>
> Any other directive, any other precept which is a natural law precept, will be in effect a particularization of this one. That is, we shall expect that there will be a multiplicity of apprehensions each expressive of some constitutive of man's end or good.[26]

But note, first of all, that in Thomas' formula "Good is to be *done* and pursued," whereas in offering his interpretation, McInerny drops "to be done" and focuses on "to be pursued." This suppression of *faciendum* certainly facilitates the interpretation of *bonum* as *ultimus finis.* For either the last end is not done (though it may include doing), or, if the last end is done, it is done only when one rests in it and is no longer guiding action by reason toward it.

Second, it is by no means clear or even likely that Thomas considers all the goods to which man is naturally inclined (*omnia illa ad quae homo habet naturalem inclinationem*) to be constitutive of man's *ultimate* end. Indeed, what Aquinas does say about the ultimate end[27] seems quite unlike McInerny's view that basic human goods are "con-

---

McInerny is mistaken, too, in thinking that Finnis considers first principles to be "not yet moral because they are too general" (*McI*, p. 13). Moreover, in treating Thomas' effort to elaborate moral precepts from the first practical principles, Finnis refers (*NLNR*, pp. 30, 101, 128) to many passages other than the single text (*S.t.*, I-II, q. 100, a.1) McInerny cites (*McI*, p. 13). So far as we understand it, we do not accept McInerny's interpretation of *S.t.*, I-II, q. 100, a. 1; his translation of the passage he excerpts from the body of that article omits the word "immediately" (*statim*) which provides a pointer to the structure of Thomas' reply.

25. *McI*, pp. 3-5. On p. 13, McInerny says: "What Finnis wants to distinguish from what he calls moral or ethical are those precepts which direct us to pursue our ultimate end or the constituents of it." But what Finnis wants to distinguish from moral precepts are the precepts articulated in *S.t.*, I-II, q. 94, a. 2; and Finnis denies that these precepts are understood by Thomas (or should be understood by anyone) as directing us to our ultimate end. If Finnis thought that the first principles of practical reason direct us as McInerny thinks they do, then Finnis would have considered them to be moral precepts.

26. *McI*, p. 4.

27. *S.t.*, I-II, qq. 1-5, especially, q. 3, a. 8.

stitutive of" man's end. This view seems closer to Vatican II[28] and to some things Grisez has said[29] about the end of man than to the doctrine of Thomas.

Thirdly, Thomas holds that the absolutely first principle of practical reasoning is to its domain as the principle of noncontradiction is to the domain of thinking in general.[30] If this is so, the first principle must govern the practical reasoning of people who do evil. The Don Juan considers fornication a good to be pursued. This consideration is not simply irrational and it is action-guiding; thus, Don Juan's immoral reasoning is governed by the first principle of practical reason. But he is acting against, not towards, the ultimate end of man.

McInerny supposes that what Finnis means by saying that basic principles of natural law are premoral is different from what Grisez means, in that Grisez "seems more concerned to have principles that will govern the practical activity of all men, good or bad, and which thus must split the difference between moral and immoral."[31] But the fact is that—setting aside the last phrase, which neither of us would accept—Finnis is concerned to make the same point as Grisez, and both of us consider this to be the position of Thomas.[32] The basic principles of practical reasoning do underlie and make possible the reasoning of good people and bad people alike. The price for denying this is to say that the immoral are sheerly irrational, and thus free of moral responsibility.

However, neither of us has said that the immoral person responds to *all* the principles of practical reasoning and pursues goods consistently with all of them. The difference between moral good and moral evil arises just at this point. Practical principles do not "split the difference between moral and immoral"; rather, the less than upright conscience shapes action by some practical principles while ignoring others which also are relevant.

This important part of ethical theory (the problem of the first principle of *morality*) was not treated in the article of Grisez on which McInerny comments, for the simple reason that Thomas does not reach this problem in the passage on which Grisez was commenting.[33]

---

28. *Gaudium et spes*, sects. 38-39. Cf., e.g., Finnis, "Catholic Faith and World Order . . .," 64 *The Clergy Review* 309 (1979) at pp. 310, 317-318.

29. In "Man, the Natural End of," 9 *New Catholic Encyclopedia* (1967), pp. 137-138.

30. *S.t.*, I-II, q. 94, a. 2; cf. *FPPR*, pp. 170, 175-179.

31. *McI*, p. 10.

32. See *NLNR*, pp. 30, 51, with references to Thomas.

33. Finnis has argued that Thomas' account of the difference between moral thinking and merely prudential reasoning (in the modern sense of "prudential") is "at

When McInerny extended his critique to this problem, he ought to have attended to Grisez's treatment, in other works, of the first principle of morality.[34]

Since McInerny does not come to grips with our treatments of this problem, we say no more about them here. However, we do wish to stress that we would not call the basic human goods "premoral" in the same sense as do many contemporary moral thinkers and theologians who have adopted proportionalism.[35] Proportionalists think of the basic human goods as kinds of desirable states of affairs, measurable and commensurable, which are more or less instantiated in and by means of human acts. We think of the basic human goods as aspects of the full-being of human persons, aspects essentially immeasurable and incommensurable. For the proportionalist, the right choice is one which realizes as much premoral good and as little premoral evil as possible. For us, the right choice is one which is in accord with open-hearted love of all the basic human goods. Thus, for the proportionalist the goods are premoral in the sense that one might rightly choose to destroy, damage, or impede them. For us, the goods are premoral only in the sense that both morally good and morally bad choices are directed (although in different ways) toward one or more of them (or, at least, toward some partial aspects or appearances of one or more of them).

III. DENIAL OF OBJECTIVE HIERARCHY AMONG THE BASIC GOODS

We have agrued[36] that there is no objective hierarchy (i.e., none which would imply commensurability of value) among the basic forms of human good. McInerny says: "Finnis at any rate is aware that this tenet separates him from the text of Aquinas."[37] In fact,

---

best, highly elliptical, scattered, and difficult to grasp, and at worst, seriously underdeveloped; and that these deficiencies occasioned the unsatisfactory responses of those who professed to follow him in the later history of philosophical theology" (*NLNR*, p. 46). Finnis therefore gives his own account of the specific difference of the moral, and of moral virtue (*NLNR*, ch. V).

34. E.g., Germain Grisez and Joseph M. Boyle, Jr., *Life and Death with Liberty and Justice: A Contribution to the Euthanasia Debate* (Notre Dame and London: University of Notre Dame Press, 1979), pp. 361-368; Germain Grisez and Russell Shaw, *Beyond the New Morality: The Responsibilities of Freedom*, 2nd ed. (Notre Dame and London: University of Notre Dame Press, 1980), pp. 80-101.

35. For our criticisms of proportionalism, see *NLNR*, pp. 112-118; Germain Grisez, "Against Consequentialism," 23 *American Journal of Jurisprudence* (1978), pp. 21-72.

36. *NLNR*, pp. 92-95; *Beyond the New Morality*, pp. 74-78.

37. *McI*, p. 10. Grisez does not discuss the question of hierarchy of values in the article on which McInerny is commenting; he explicitly prescinds (*FPPR*, pp. 180-181) from the problems of this part of the article of Thomas on which he comments.

Finnis does not think that this tenet does separate him from the text of Thomas; Finnis says that Thomas' rationale for the "order" of the precepts of natural law "*all too easily* is interpreted as a ranking."[38] We deny what McInerny affirms, namely, that our position "collide[s] in important ways with Thomas' understanding."[39]

It is arbitrary to suppose that all order is hierarchy, and still more arbitrary to assume that the corresponding order of the precepts of natural law and of natural inclination identified by Thomas in *Summa theologiae*, I-II, q. 94, a. 2, is a hierarchy of *value*. The principle of the order identified there by Thomas is simply: what man "has in common with all substances," "has in common with all animals," and has "peculiar to himself." Why should this metaphysical principle of ordering be interpreted as a ranking of values? No doubt Aristotle has an argument that man's highest good is the good most proper to him.[40] But where does Thomas make this argument his own?[41] Would it not be disastrous for a Christian theologian, who thinks that man's supreme good is communion with God, to adopt Aristotle's line of argument, when communion with the divine persons is not proper to man, but is naturally proper only to the divine persons themselves, and is shared by their supernatural gift not only with men but also with angels?

We do not find in Thomas' text McInerny's theory that "if we enumerate [man's] inclinations and notice their hierarchy we will be able to glimpse the natural law precepts which take them into account."[42] What Thomas does say is that "all those things to which man has a natural inclination, reason naturally grasps as goods and, in consequence, as things-to-be-pursued by work, and their opposites as evils and things-to-be-avoided."[43] We do not find in Thomas what McInerny thinks he finds: that "goods which are not peculiar to men come to be constituents of the human good insofar as they come under the sway of the distinctive mark of human agent, reason."[44] Nor do

---

Nevertheless, McInerny criticizes what he takes to be Grisez's position without providing any reference to the places where Grisez states and defends it.

38. *NLNR*, p. 94.

39. *McI*, p.11.

40. *Eth. Nic.* X, 7 (1178a4-5); cf. I, 7 (1097b24-1098a7).

41. The argument in *S.t.*, I-II, qq. 2-3, is considerably more complex, precisely because Thomas does hold that communion with God is the ultimate fulfillment of man.

42. *McI*, p. 4.

43. *S.t.*, I-II, q. 94, a. 2, c.; the reply ad 2 is cryptic and must be interpreted in accord with the body of this article.

44. *McI*, p. 4. McInerny adds: "Sex is a *human* good not just as such, but as engaged in consciously and purposively and responsibly." By so saying he seems to

we think Thomas' text supports McInerny's further interpretation: "Precepts of natural law are rational directives aiming at the good for man. The human good, man's ultimate end, is complex but the unifying thread is the distinctive mark of the human, i.e., reason."[45] The first sentence undoubtedly expresses Thomas' position, but the second does not follow from the first, and will seem thomistic only to those who read into Thomas a degree and kind of Aristotelianism we do not find in him.

Thomas is clear enough that the primary precepts of the natural law identify the good*s* (in the plural) for man, and that *among* these goods is the good corresponding to the natural inclination to *act* according to reason.[46] But this inclination is only one among many, and all the inclinations are for goods naturally *understandable* by reason. Where does Thomas formulate the primary precepts of natural law in McInerny's mode: "Rationally pursue self-preservation," "Rationally pursue the good of sex, reproduction, offspring," and so on? What Thomas says more naturally suggests formulations in the mode: "Life is a good to be pursued and protected" and so on.

Even if Thomas' text supported an Aristotelian hierarchy of human goods, as McInerny believes, we would reject such a hierarchy. Our reason for doing so would be not only the noncommensurability of the basic goods, which blocks proportionalist rationalizations (which McInerny takes to be our sole concern), but also the transcendence of the *good* of the first principle of practical reason. As Grisez explains in a section of his article deleted in the Kenny abridgement:

> Only by virtue of this transcendence is it possible that the end proposed by Christian faith, heavenly beatitude, which is supernatural to man, should become an objective of genuine human action—that is, of action under the guidance of practical reason. If the first principle of practical reason restricted human good to the goods proportionate to nature, then a supernatural end for human action would be excluded. The relation of man to such an end could be established only by a leap into the transrational where human action would be impossible and where faith would replace natural law rather than supplement it.[47]

---

imply that the sexual capacity of human persons is per se infrahuman—an assumption which entails an indefensible dualism and which also is inconsistent with the use of *S.t.*, I-II, q. 94, a. 2, which Paul VI makes in *Humanae vitae*, sect. 10.

45. *McI*, p. 5.

46. *S.t.*, I-II, q. 94, a. 3, c.

47. *FPPR*, p. 200. That human nature grounds without limiting the possibilities open to humankind through freedom is an important truth of anthropology, unknown to Aristotle, articulated in the light of Christian faith in the supernatural vocation of humankind to fulfillment in Christ, and now universally accepted (although distorted) by contemporary, "postchristian" humanism of all sorts.

As Grisez argued in another article, contemporaneous with the one on which McInerny comments, Thomas' theory of the natural end of man remains incoherent just to the extent that he was more Aristotelian than the reality of human nature, open to divine life, allows.[48]

IV.

Because they rest on misunderstandings, McInerny's critical remarks on our work seem to us to lack cogency. These misunderstandings were compounded, we think, by McInerny's decision to criticize simultaneously our exegeses of Thomas' texts and our own independent theorizing.

We find nothing in McInerny's article which requires us to concede error in our reading of Thomas. To assume a different, "Aristotelian-Thomistic," reading of Thomas and to point out that we do not share that reading could be the point of departure for criticism of our reading. But until the alternative reading is established by arguments, its mere assertion against ours is question-begging.

McInerny's criticisms of our independent theorizing are all based upon the presupposed authority of what we have called Aristotelian-Thomism. Admirable as this philosophy is in some respects, we do not consider it as perfect as McInerny seems to think it is. Moreover, the fact that we sometimes purposely differ with Thomas himself clearly does not entail that we misinterpret him, unless one assumes that all of Thomas' positions are self-evident to those who correctly understand them.

McInerny ends his article by suggesting that a major task before us "is to draw out the relation between ultimate end and the *Treatise on Law.*" Grisez's work in ethics began precisely as an attempt to carry out this task. He became convinced that Thomas' account of the ultimate end is inconsistent with his account of natural law. This conviction led him to develop his own ethical theory, which is heavily indebted to Thomas but which is autonomously grounded. We think that all who are interested in natural law would do well to shoulder the responsibility of independent philosophical work, as we and many others have done, rather than to continue to be content with neoscholastic commingling of historical interpretation and philosophical construction.

48. "Man, the Natural End of," pp. 134-135.

[16]

REVIEWS

Recent Criticism of Natural Law Theory

Robert P. George†

Lloyd L. Weinreb. *Natural Law and Justice.* Harvard University Press, Cambridge, Mass. 1987. Pp ix, 320. $25.00.

Russell Hittinger. *A Critique of the New Natural Law Theory.* University of Notre Dame Press, Notre Dame, Ind. 1987. Pp vi, 232. $26.95.

A noteworthy feature of contemporary philosophy in the English-speaking world and beyond is a reawakening of interest in practical reason. The willingness to take reasons for action seriously in descriptive and prescriptive jurisprudence, as well as in political philosophy and ethics, has been a mark of many notable philosophical achievements over the past three decades. In jurisprudence, the works of H. L. A. Hart, Joseph Raz, and Ronald Dworkin certainly come to mind. In political philosophy, one immediately thinks of the competing theories of justice developed by John Rawls and Robert Nozick. In ethics, a long list of contributions would only begin with those of Alan Donagan, Alan Gewirth, Philippa Foot, David Wiggins, and John McDowell.

The revival of interest in practical reason has brought in its wake renewed philosophical attention to theories of natural law. Long relegated to merely historical interest (at least outside of Roman Catholic intellectual circles), natural law theory is once again a competitor in contemporary philosophical debates about law, politics, and morals. What this means, for one thing, is that the writings of St. Thomas Aquinas, Hugo Grotius, Francisco Suarez,

---

† Assistant Professor, Princeton University and Visiting Fellow, New College, Oxford. I thank Adam Sloane, Walter F. Murphy, and Germain Grisez for criticisms of early drafts.

and other leading scholastic natural law theorists have again found an audience in the secular academy. Moreover, a number of contemporary authors have developed modern theories of natural law. While certain of these theories remain more or less within the scholastic tradition, not all do. The natural law theory recently advanced by Michael S. Moore, for example, shares little more than a label with the theory of, say, Aquinas.

In the past year, two significant books on the subject of natural law theory have been published. The first, Lloyd Weinreb's *Natural Law and Justice*,[1] is a profoundly ambitious study. It not only charts the history of natural law theory through the ages, but also presents a sophisticated philosophical argument that, if valid, makes philosophy a largely meaningless exercise. He argues that all efforts to develop a credible theory of natural law are doomed and yet, that it is impossible to devise an alternative to conceiving of problems in moral and political philosophy as problems of natural law. The second book, Russell Hittinger's *A Critique of the New Natural Law Theory*,[2] presents a detailed case against a particularly influential modern theory. Hittinger's target is the theory of natural law originally developed by Germain Grisez, and widely publicized in John Finnis's influential book *Natural Law and Natural Rights*.[3] Weinreb also singles out this theory for detailed criticism, citing it as an especially significant example of contemporary "deontological" natural law theories.

In what follows, I shall largely, though not exclusively, focus on this recent criticism of what, following Hittinger's convention, I shall refer to as "the Grisez-Finnis natural law theory." My claims are that neither Weinreb nor Hittinger represents the theory accurately or presents compelling arguments against it. Before taking up criticisms of the Grisez-Finnis theory in particular, however, I shall describe Weinreb's general argument and criticize his treatment of Aquinas's theory of natural law.

I. Weinreb's *Natural Law and Justice*.

A. 'Ontological' Natural Law and the 'Normative Natural Order'

Among Lloyd Weinreb's goals in *Natural Law and Justice* is to "restore[] the original understanding of natural law as a theory

---

[1] Lloyd L. Weinreb, *Natural Law and Justice* (Harvard, 1987).

[2] Russell Hittinger, *A Critique of the New Natural Law Theory* (Notre Dame, 1987).

[3] John Finnis, *Natural Law and Natural Rights* (Oxford, 1980).

about the nature of being, the human condition in particular."[4] Weinreb claims that contemporary natural law theorists, among whom he counts not only Finnis, but Lon L. Fuller, David A. J. Richards, and Ronald M. Dworkin, have abandoned this understanding, which he labels "ontological." These theorists, as he reads them, seek to replace ontological understandings of natural law with "deontological" understandings. A natural law theory is deontological, as Weinreb uses the term, when it purports to identify principles of moral rectitude independently of inquiries into the nature of (human) being(s). Whereas yesterday's natural law theorists derived basic principles of natural law from knowledge of (human) nature, today's natural law theorists eschew the strategy of deriving the moral "ought" from the "is" of (human) nature.

According to Weinreb, the *questio vexata* of ancient and medieval natural law theory concerned human freedom in a causally determined universe. He asserts flatly that "[t]he question that Thomas Aquinas and others answered was, 'How can human beings be part of the natural order and still be free and morally responsible?' "[5] This is a problem, Weinreb supposes, because

> [f]ull moral responsibility seems to require that an act be *both free and determinate.* Unless a person's act is free, that is, self-determined, he is not morally responsible for it. But unless the circumstances of his act and the personal qualities that make him act as he does are determinate, the act seems to be the product of arbitrary occurrences as far as he is concerned and not something for which he individually is responsible. Yet if the circumstances and his personal qualities are determinate and determine his act, then once again the act is not self-determined and he is not morally responsible. In order for a person to act freely in the relevant moral sense, his act must be determined; but if it is determined, he is not free.[6]

Moral responsibility, as Weinreb understands it, both requires, and is inconsistent with, causal determinacy. We experience ourselves as self-determining choosers, and this experience of freedom grounds our very notion of moral responsibility. Yet, on reflection, we must acknowledge a causally determinate background order without which human acts would seem arbitrary (only a causally

---

[4] Weinreb, *Natural Law and Justice* at 7 (cited in note 1).

[5] Id at 3.

[6] Id at 6.

determinate background can provide *reasons* for action) and, thus, lacking in moral significance.

The great natural law theorists of the past, as Weinreb reads them, proposed to solve the problem by positing a "normative natural order."

> The contradiction in the idea of freedom is overcome by the supposition that the conditions and circumstances of a person's act compose a determinate background order that is itself normatively ordered: personal responsibility extends not only to what a person does but also to what he is and all the circumstances of his life.[7]

For Weinreb, "[t]hat solution . . . was the core of the old natural law."[8] But, if he understands Aquinas and his predecessors correctly, then Weinreb surely is right in saying that their solution, from our vantage point at least, "seems hopeless."[9] Belief in the sort of normative natural order he describes would apparently require us to conclude that natural evils such as deadly childhood illnesses "and all the other 'accidents' of our lives are not misfortunes but are deserved."[10] This, as Weinreb observes, "is not only incomprehensible but morally outrageous."[11] The modern insight is that laws of nature, which produce, among other things, deadly childhood illnesses, are not normative. Children stricken with meningitis, for example, do not "deserve" the disease.[12] What "is" is not necessarily what "ought to be." The ontological and moral orders can (and often enough apparently do) diverge.

Having rejected belief in a normative natural order as a solution to the problem squarely faced by their predecessors, modern natural law theorists, according to Weinreb, have attempted to change the subject. They simply ignore the problem of causal determinacy, and are thus able to present "natural law . . . as a response to the problem of freedom in a morally indeterminate . . . universe."[13] In short, they separate ontology from morality. While prescinding from the former, they reduce the latter to political theory and, ultimately, jurisprudence. "The question now is simply,

---

[7] Id at 6-7.

[8] Id at 7.

[9] Id.

[10] Id.

[11] Id.

[12] Id at 4-5.

[13] Id at 63.

'How can we be obligated to obey the law?' "[14] The dispute is no longer one with skeptics over the grand question of the nature of reality; it is with legal positivists over the comparatively mundane question of obligation. But, according to Weinreb, neither natural law theorists nor legal positivists can avoid the problem of freedom and cause. It lurks in the background, informing the terms of the debate over obligation, and rendering that controversy ultimately unresolvable. "Beneath the surface of an apparently inconsequential dispute," says Weinreb, "there lingers the central puzzle of the human situation."[15]

B. An Overview of Weinreb's Account of Natural Law and Justice

Weinreb's book is divided into two parts. In the first, entitled "Natural Law," he presents a largely historical account of what he views as the failures of traditional natural law theorists to come up with a satisfactory answer to the ontological question. He then provides a brisk review of what he sees as the unsuccessful strategy of early modern and Enlightenment thinkers, from Hobbes to Kant, to transfer the problem of "the normative basis of human existence"[16] from nature to the civil state. Finally, he offers a critical philosophical analysis of the efforts of modern natural law theorists to come up with a credible deontological alternative to the ontological question. His considered judgment is that the traditional authors failed because their question is unanswerable, and their successors fail because there is simply no avoiding that question.

> [T]he puzzle of human freedom in a determinate, causally ordered universe persists for ordinary persons and philosophers alike. The vocabulary and the conceptual context have changed; but we endorse answers to the problem in our daily lives and in our philosophizing, because we must. We could not carry on either otherwise.[17]

In the second part, entitled "Justice," Weinreb broadens his analysis by examining the attempts of certain contemporary thinkers to treat the problems of moral and political philosophy as problems about "the nature of justice" rather than about whether

[14] Id at 3.
[15] Id at 12.
[16] Id at 67.
[17] Id at 4.

nature is just.[18] In the thought of liberal political theorists such as John Rawls and Robert Nozick, and in the work of their communitarian critics, among whom Weinreb includes Alasdair MacIntyre, Michael Sandel, and Michael Walzer, the separation of ethics from ontology obscures the antinomy of freedom and cause. Yet, this antimony undercuts the efforts of deontological natural law theorists no less thoroughly than it did those of their ontological predecessors. To obscure the antinomy is not to eliminate it. It reemerges in the form of analogous antinomies of desert and entitlement (in respect of individual justice) and liberty and equality (in respect of justice in the social order) within the concept of justice. Such antinomies are ultimately rooted in the antinomy of freedom and cause (in respect of a putatively normative natural order).

Desert, Weinreb says, is an implication of moral responsibility, which in turn presupposes freedom. The upshot of this connection with moral responsibility and freedom is that desert is "insistently individual."[19] Entitlement, by contrast, "is based on the application of a rule according to its terms, without regard to individual qualities that the rule ignores."[20] The fulfillment of individual justice, as Weinreb understands it, would require a perfect harmony of desert and entitlement. Unfortunately, however, conflict between these elements of justice "is not an occasional, regrettable lapse but is inherent and unavoidable."[21]

The very concept of desert requires a background order of entitlement. For example, we regard persons as entitled to natural assets. When people successfully make use of their natural assets, we treat them as deserving (e.g., a prize in a footrace). However, the ground of that initial entitlement cannot itself be desert. As Weinreb puts it, "if every one of a person's qualities has itself to be deserved, the idea of a person as the *subject* of desert loses meaning."[22] But where the ultimate ground of desert is (undeserved) entitlement, in what serious sense can persons be understood as deserving? A way out of the dilemma could, of course, be a notion of free choice that would provide, at least in some respects, an ultimate ground of desert not reducible to sheer entitlement. But to appeal to such a notion, according to Weinreb, is precisely to confront the antinomy of freedom and cause that

---

[18] Id at 126.

[19] Id at 10.

[20] Id.

[21] Id.

[22] Id at 205 (emphasis in the original).

exercised the ancient and medieval natural law theorists. So, as Weinreb sees it, inquiry into the nature of justice ultimately reintroduces the "ontological" problem of the justice of nature.

Similarly, liberty and equality—the elements, for Weinreb, of a just social order—inherently contradict each other. Just as freedom requires a determinate causal background with which it is ultimately inconsistent, and just as desert requires a background order of entitlement with which it is ultimately inconsistent, liberty (the social analogue of desert and freedom) requires a background of equality with which it is ultimately inconsistent. According to Weinreb, "[l]iberty and inequality, equality and restriction of liberty, are the same, except that we ordinarily use the former member of each pair to indicate our approval and the latter to indicate disapproval."[23] Hence, every attempt to advance liberty comes at a cost in terms of equality. But to the extent that inequalities are tolerated, the conditions of liberty are erased. Inasmuch as one is "less" equal, one is unfree. Yet enforced equality would destroy liberty.

Weinreb maintains that attempts to overcome this antinomy by reference to a principle of "equality of opportunity" fail for reasons familiar to those acquainted with the current debate about justice. There seems to be no principled way to avoid either broadening the meaning of equality of opportunity to the point of requiring equality of results (thereby directly eliminating liberty) or narrowing it to a mere formalism (thereby sacrificing the substantive equality that serves as a condition of liberty). So, under Weinreb's analysis, Nozick rightly charges Rawls with throwing over liberty for the sake of equality. But, by the same token, Nozick must plead guilty to jilting equality for the sake of liberty. And since liberty presupposes a background order of equality—an order which the concept of equality of opportunity cannot provide—liberty itself cannot survive under Nozick's scheme. Unfortunately for egalitarian and libertarian theorists of justice alike, the very concept of justice is "antinomic."

If Weinreb's arguments are telling, moral and political philosophy are doomed to frustration. The antinomy of freedom and cause that, according to Weinreb, eventually undid ontological theories of natural law reemerges to undo every modern alternative, whether they be deontological natural law theories or theories of justice. Contrary to what the older natural law theorists supposed,

---

[23] Id at 225.

Weinreb insists, "[w]e cannot be part of nature and at the same time apart from it."[24] Yet it is ultimately untenable to hold that we are merely part of nature *or* that we are apart from it. We cannot hold that we have free will (which would set us apart from nature) because this would, he says, require us to deny the determinate background of causality upon which the concept of free will depends. We cannot hold that we are determined (which would make us merely a part of nature) because "whether we explain it or not, [our] experience of freedom remains."[25] And we cannot hold that we have free will and are at the same time determined (which would make us part of nature and at the same time apart from it) because "every compatibilist solution depends on a confusion of the manner in which we experience freedom and cause with the propositions that are necessary to sustain either."[26]

C. Weinreb on Aquinas's Natural Law Theory

For Weinreb, as for most commentators, Aquinas occupies a central place in the history of natural law theorizing.

> Aquinas stated the theory that has defined natural law as a school of thought. It is because they can be perceived as precursors or anticipations of his theory that earlier statements of Cicero and others . . . are regarded as part of the natural law tradition, even when they do not use that term. And it is their association with his theory, however abstract, that qualifies subsequent theories as within the tradition.[27]

Sympathetic interpreters of Aquinas differ on the question of whether he supposed that "nature is normative." Neo-scholastic natural law theorists understand Aquinas as saying that the standard of moral uprightness for human actions is conformity to (human) nature. In this sense, norms of human action, including moral norms, are implicit in the natural order. Ethics begins with a speculative inquiry: What is human nature like? This question concerns the human telos, viz., it intends knowledge of the natural ends constitutive of human fulfillment. Once we acquire such knowledge, we can judge proposed actions according to their conformity, or lack of conformity, to these ends.

It is at this point that what Aquinas, following Aristotle, calls

---

[24] Id at 263.
[25] Id at 126.
[26] Id at 201 n *.
[27] Id at 53-54.

the practical intellect takes over.[28] Aquinas formulates the first principle of practical reason as "good is to be done and pursued, and evil is to be avoided."[29] According to neo-scholastic interpreters, "good," in this formulation, simply refers to those actions that conform to properly human ends; "evil" refers to those actions that fail so to conform. Hence, the human intellect operating in its practical mode directs us according to its first principle to act in a morally upright fashion. But thus understood, the first principle of practical reason presupposes knowledge of what is morally upright and what is not. Such knowledge is acquired by the intellect operating in its speculative mode. The crucial point is that under this interpretation sound practical thinking depends upon a methodologically prior speculative (e.g., metaphysical—or "ontological"—and theological) inquiry. Such an inquiry yields the philosophy of (human) nature upon which moral philosophy rests. Inasmuch as we derive moral norms from speculative knowledge of (human) nature, nature is indeed normative.[30]

The neo-scholastic interpretation of Aquinas's moral philosophy has been challenged precisely on the question of the normativity of (human) nature. In an influential article published in 1965, Germain Grisez attacked the claim that Aquinas identified moral norms by reference to speculative knowledge of human nature.[31] Aquinas, Grisez argues, did not propose his first principle of practical reason as a moral imperative. Rather, Aquinas supposed that such a principle controls all coherent practical thinking—whether morally good or evil. "Good," as Grisez understands Aquinas's formulation, refers not only to what is morally good, but to whatever within human power can be understood as intelligibly worthwhile; "evil" refers to any privation of intelligible goods. Interpreted in this way, the principle neither presupposes a knowledge of right and wrong nor, a fortiori, enjoins us to choose the morally upright

---

[28] The distinction between the speculative (or what Aristotle called the "theoretical") intellect and the practical intellect does not imply two different intellectual faculties. For Aquinas, there is but one human reason. Speculative and practical reason use the same intellectual operations but aim at different objectives. While Aquinas allows for what might be called paradigm cases of purely speculative or purely practical reasoning, he understands most actual reasoning to be both speculative and practical.

[29] Thomas Aquinas, *Summa Theologiae* 1-2, q 94, a 2, in William P. Baumgarth and Richard J. Regan, eds, *Saint Thomas Aquinas on Law, Morality, and Politics* (Hackett, 1988).

[30] See, for example, Thomas J. Higgins, *Man as Man: The Science and Art of Ethics* 49-69, 88-100, 120-126 (Bruce, 1958).

[31] Germain Grisez, *The First Principle of Practical Reason: A Commentary on the* Summa Theologiae, *1-2, Question 94, Article 2*, 10 Natural Law Forum 168 (1965).

course of action. The work done by the first principle is more primitive. It states a condition of any coherent practical thinking, viz., that one's reasoning be directed toward some end that is pursuable by human action. Even morally wicked choices, to the extent that they are intelligible, meet this condition (although, as we shall see, not so well as morally upright choices). Consider, for example, a choice that treats another person unfairly. To the extent that such a choice has an intelligible point, it will be consistent with the first principle of practical reason, despite its immorality. Understood as a directive, the first principle is weak: It requires only coherence, not full moral rectitude.

Under Grisez's interpretation, Aquinas believed that ultimately any choice has its intelligibility by reference to the intelligible end(s) for the sake of which one terminates one's deliberation and acts. Our initial intelligent grasp of these ends requires no knowledge of metaphysical anthropology or any other speculative discipline, although various sorts of speculative knowledge (including sound metaphysics) can help one to pursue these ends more intelligently. The most basic knowledge of these ends is, rather, the fruit of practical insights. The practical intellect itself grasps certain ends as reasons for action that require no further reasons. They are intelligible as ends-in-themselves. As such, their intrinsic choiceworthiness is, as Aquinas says, *per se nota* (self-evident). It is by reference to such an end-in-itself, as the ultimate term in a more or less complex chain of practical reasoning culminating in a choice, that a non-baffling account of that choice can be given. Once one brings such an end into focus, no further questions relevant to the choice necessarily arise for someone seeking such an account.

For Aquinas, as Grisez reads him, the ends that the practical intellect grasps as ultimate reasons for action are properly understood as intrinsic human goods and, as such, aspects of human fulfillment. As goods "to be done and pursued" they are fundamental determinations of the first principle of practical reason, and, thus, basic precepts of natural law. They are not, however, singly and directly criteria of moral rectitude. Knowledge of human goods does not *by itself* resolve *moral* questions because it does not exclude some choices which, while intelligible, are morally wrongful. Rather, our intelligent grasp of human goods is what makes moral *questions* possible.

For example, is it morally wrongful for a scientist to kidnap a child and subject her to deadly experiments—not, let us suppose, out of any malice, but in a sincere quest to identify the causes and cure for a ravaging communicable disease? The question arises by virtue of our grasp of the genuine human goods at stake in a decision either way. Let us suppose that a moral norm does in fact forbid the kidnapping and experimentation. As Grisez understands Aquinas, the first principle of practical reason could not have generated this moral norm because a choice to go through with the kidnapping and experimentation would not be incoherent. The wrongfulness of such a choice would not consist in its being unintelligible. To the contrary, the goods of knowledge (here, scientific knowledge) and life and health (here, the lives and the health of victims and potential victims of the disease) provide the intelligible ends by reference to which even the morally wrongful choice would be intelligible.

But in view of the goods that the scientist could realize by carrying out the kidnapping and experimentation, it is worth asking whether a moral norm forbidding the decision to do so would itself come into conflict with the first principle of practical reason. The answer is that it does not; for the choice not to kidnap and experiment is also intelligible. The life and health of the child, among other goods, are the ends that provide the intelligibility of this alternate choice. The moral norm provides a decisive reason for choosing between two courses of action, both of which are consistent with Aquinas's first principle. It excludes as wrongful one of the intelligible choices. As a *moral* norm, it does not identify the "good[s] to be done and pursued"; rather, it guides and structures human choice and action respecting such goods.[32]

According to Grisez, Aquinas did not bequeath us a systematic account of moral norms. Nor did he establish the link between the specific moral rules he did articulate and the self-evident first principles (i.e., the determinations of the first principle of practical reason) specifying the goods "to be done and pursued." In his own natural law theory of morality, Grisez has sought to remedy these inadequacies. In so doing, he freely departs from Aquinas at a

---

[32] Of course, nothing changes if the correct moral norm requires a different result. Let us suppose not only that the scientist may kidnap the child and experiment on her but also that a moral norm commands this course of action. Either choice in the face of the putative moral norm in control of this situation would remain intelligible. The goods of life and health (here, the life and health of the child) would provide the intelligible determinants by reference to which the putatively immoral choice of not going through with the kidnapping and experimentation would be intelligible. Reference to these goods would provide a non-baffling answer to the question "why didn't you do it?" His choice not to do it, while, we are supposing, immoral, would be perfectly consistent with the first principle of practical reason.

number of points, while retaining Aquinas's fundamental theory of practical rationality as he understands it. Later, I shall discuss Grisez's revisions and development of Aquinas's moral theory. For the moment, however, I simply want to highlight the implications of Grisez's *interpretation* of Aquinas's theory of practical reason.

Grisez's Aquinas does not propose to judge the morality of acts by their conformity to human nature. The knowledge of human goods that sets practical inquiry in motion and ultimately accounts for the intelligibility of human choices is not the fruit of metaphysical anthropology or any other speculative discipline. Nor can speculative inquiry generate moral norms by reference to which human beings can uprightly guide and structure their choosing in respect of human goods. Such norms are needed, but they cannot be derived from (human) nature. Thus, under Grisez's interpretation of Aquinas, nature is "normative" neither in Weinreb's sense nor in the neo-scholastic sense.

While Weinreb cites Grisez's article in a footnote to his own discussion of Aquinas's first principle of practical reason, he makes no reference to the interpretive dispute in which it figures as a central text. Indeed, almost immediately after stating Aquinas's principle, he baldly asserts that "natural law thus directs us to fulfill our natural inclinations."[33] Weinreb does not even consider Grisez's alternative account. He states that natural law "is a reflection of human nature, the natural human inclinations toward appropriate human ends."[34] The role of reason, he says, is "to translate the natural inclinations into practical decisions and actions."[35]

If one accepts Grisez's interpretation of Aquinas's first principle of practical reason, then the idea of a normative natural order has no place in Aquinas's ethics. If one rejects Grisez's interpretation in favor of something like the neo-scholastic reading of Aquinas, an idea of what might be called a normative natural order is, indeed, required. But Weinreb's idea of such an order is nothing like what neo-scholastics (whose interpretation of Aquinas's first principle Weinreb seems to share) have in mind. When neo-scholastics claim that, for Aquinas, natural law theory hinges on matters of ontology (or metaphysics), they do not mean that the central problem that must be addressed is that of human freedom in the face of causal determinism. Rather, they mean that moral norms must be derived from speculative knowledge of (human)

[33] Weinreb, *Natural Law and Justice* at 58 (cited in note 1).
[34] Id at 59.
[35] Id.

nature.

According to the neo-scholastics, Aquinas's idea of a normative natural order does not purport to account for the putative responsibility of individuals for conditions and events in their lives over which they apparently exercise no control. As they interpret him, Aquinas saw no need for any such account because, contrary to what Weinreb says, he simply did not identify the problem of freedom and cause as one that natural law was meant to solve.

It is not that Aquinas failed to recognize that moral norms, if they exist, are norms for free choice. Nor is it that he was unaware that free choice was a philosophical problem. Indeed, he considered the matter of free choice directly in several of his works.[36] But having satisfied himself that *some* free choice exists in human affairs (i.e., that some events in the world are brought about by human choosing that, while conditioned in various ways by causes beyond the control of the chooser, remains in important respects free), Aquinas aimed in his moral philosophy, and thus in his theory of natural law, at clarifying the intelligibility (rather than the possibility) of human choices and identifying norms by reference to which reason could guide such choices reliably.

That the neo-scholastic reading of Aquinas is on this crucial point superior to Weinreb's is evident, I think, from the first sentence of the Prologue to the second main part of the *Summa Theologiae*—the part principally concerned with morals and containing Aquinas's fullest statement of his theory of natural law:

> [M]an is said to be made to God's image, in so far as the image implies *an intelligent being endowed with free-will and self-movement:* now that we have treated of the exemplar, *i.e.*, God, and of those things which come forth from the power of God in accordance with his will; it remains for us to treat of His image, *i.e.*, man, inasmuch as he too is the principle of his actions, as having free-will and control of his actions.[37]

Under the neo-scholastic reading of Aquinas, moral norms are, as I have noted, implicit in, and derivable from human nature. Knowledge of that nature—what is intended by the inquiring intellect in the (speculative) discipline of metaphysical anthropol-

[36] Thomas Aquinas, *Summa Contra Gentiles* Book II, ch 47 (Burns, Oates & Washbourne, 1923); Thomas Aquinas, *Summa Theologiae* I, q 82, a 2 (Christian Classics, 1981); id at I-2, q 10, a 2; Thomas Aquinas, *De Veritate* q 22, a 6 (Henry Regnery, 1954).

[37] Thomas Aquinas, *Summa Theologiae* I-2 Prologue (Benzinger, 1947) (emphasis in the original).

ogy—is, therefore, under this reading, the key to moral philosophy. But this sort of knowledge is not knowledge of some supposed "justice of nature." The "natural order" is normative precisely inasmuch as it provides moral norms for free human choosing. The normativity of that order has nothing to do with the ascription of moral responsibility "to what [a person] is and all the circumstances of his life."[38]

Weinreb seems to assume that Aquinas's theory of nature included something like the empiricist notion of causality that dominates modern understandings of the natural order. It is only in light of some such notion that the problem of freedom and cause, as Weinreb describes it, becomes an issue (in moral and political philosophy or anywhere else). But Aquinas's theory of nature was Aristotelian rather than modern. It allowed ample room for chance events. Aquinas understood the basic mode of causality to be the causality of the end—i.e, that for the sake of which the event happens. (This is commonly described as the "teleological" view of nature.) Under this understanding of the world, the belief that intelligent agents act freely for ends is not an anomaly, but rather a paradigm case of the way people behave. We correctly judge this to be defective physics. (We do not believe, for example, that love moves the sun and the other stars.) But, defective or not, it does not give rise to the problem of freedom and cause that Weinreb supposes Aquinas used natural law to solve.

Under Aquinas's theory, the whole of creation (everything other than God) can be divided into two parts: that which does not presuppose human thinking and free choice to be as it is, and that which does. It is the former that is "natural"; the latter is not. While both parts, inasmuch as they depend ultimately on God's free action, are suffused with meaning and value (by virtue of the contributions of human intelligence and free action), the meaning and value of nature is provided by divine intelligence and free choice *alone*.

Weinreb says of Aquinas that

> He started from the unquestioned propositions that the universe is the creation of a providential God and that it displays its Creator's purpose in all its aspects; hence, it is orderly throughout, and its order is normative.[39]

While Aquinas left very little "unquestioned," there is not much

---

[38] Weinreb, *Natural Law and Justice* at 6-7 (cited in note 1).

[39] Id at 63.

else to quibble about in this particular statement until the final clause, with which various sorts of Thomists would not only quibble but quarrel—at least if it is understood as Weinreb suggests we understand it. As I have observed, the *whole* of creation is, for Aquinas, suffused with meaning and value by divine intelligence and free choice. The universe is, indeed, ordered to the purposes of a providential Creator. But as Aquinas saw it, this does not rule out the proposition that some aspects of creation *also* are suffused with meaning and value by human intelligence and free choice. The natural (moral) law concerns meaning and value insofar as it is within the ambit of human intelligence and free choice. The natural law is a participation in the eternal law because even that part of creation subject to the norms of the natural law ultimately depends upon divine intelligence and free choice. Nothing that *is* lies outside of the divine plan. But, contrary to what Weinreb implies, personal responsibility, for Aquinas, extends only to a person's free choices. Such responsibility extends "to what [a person] is and all the circumstances of his life" *only* insofar as these depend on his prior free choices. Whatever does not depend on free choices is the responsibility of someone else—ultimately God.

Since Aquinas perfectly well understood that persons are often victims of evils for which they bear no responsibility, he recognized the need for a theodicy. But even here Aquinas made no appeal to a normative natural order under which "nature does justice." His theodicy was not designed to get God off the hook by showing that persons somehow deserve all they receive. As a Christian philosopher, Aquinas wanted to show that the evil to be found in the world is not chosen by God. God accepts the evil for the sake of the good, otherwise unattainable, that God will in His wisdom bring out of situations involving evil. As with any theodicy, there is ultimately a mystery about this, for the norms (if any) governing divine causality (if it exists) cannot be known by the human intellect. But this mystery has nothing to do with an alleged contradiction at the core of the idea of *human* freedom and responsibility. Weinreb misreads Aquinas's theory of natural law in supposing that that theory was proposed in an effort to overcome any such contradiction.

D. Weinreb on Finnis and "Deontological" Natural Law

Among those whom Weinreb classifies as contemporary "deontological" natural law theorists, John Finnis alone works self-consciously within the tradition of Aquinas. Weinreb singles out Finnis's work for special praise. "In his book *Natural Law and*

Natural Rights . . . , John Finnis has developed the most substantial and serious contemporary theory to which the label of natural law attaches."[40] As Finnis himself observes, however, there is "not . . . much that is original" in his arguments.[41] The natural law theory of morality Finnis proposes as a foundation for the political theory and jurisprudence he defends is, as he says, "squarely based" on the work of Germain Grisez.[42] And, as we have already seen, Grisez's approach to ethics builds upon his own understanding of Aquinas's theory of practical rationality. In the years since Finnis's book was published, Grisez and Finnis have collaborated on a number of projects (usually along with Joseph M. Boyle, Jr.), and have developed their ethical theory in important respects. I will deal with what is perhaps the most significant of these developments in the present section.

Weinreb's basic criticism of Finnis's natural law theory is that it is based on the mistaken "belief that, if one reflects carefully about the human condition, the principles of moral action are a self-evident basis for the determination of concrete obligations."[43] Weinreb supposes that Finnis "[r]eject[s] explicitly any proof for his claims except the self-evident truth of the claims themselves."[44] In one instance, Weinreb refers (dismissively) to "Finnis' apparent claim that his position on [the subject of abortion] is a self-evident truth."[45] More generally, Weinreb suggests that "even those who agree with [Finnis] on the merits may suppose that he has confused self-evidence with personal conviction."[46] And, while allowing that "[t]he conclusions that Finnis reaches may be correct," Weinreb flatly accuses Finnis of "repeatedly [suggesting that] arguments opposed to his own are . . . accepted only by persons who have not thought carefully or are blinded by bias or self-interest or convention."[47]

On this last point, Weinreb offers no citation to Finnis's writings, nor could he have done so. He has simply misunderstood the implications of Finnis's account of the reality of immoral choosing.[48] This account does not imply that arguments opposed to Fin-

[40] Id at 108.

[41] Finnis, *Natural Law and Natural Rights* at vi (cited in note 3).

[42] Id at vii.

[43] Weinreb, *Natural Law and Justice* at 115 (cited in note 1).

[44] Id at 109.

[45] Id at 296 n 32.

[46] Id at 113.

[47] Id at 112.

[48] Finnis offers this account as part of his reply to moral skeptics who cite the diversity

nis's own are only accepted by those who are thoughtless, biased, or self-interested. What Finnis, like most moralists, does suppose is that persons (and whole cultures) *can*, in their practical thinking, be led astray by factors such as bias, self-interest, convention, and emotion. It is hardly fantastic to think, for example, that such factors had something to do with the blindness of many Americans of another age to the immorality of slavery. But, while virtually no one today is unimpressed (or admits to being unimpressed) by arguments against slavery, it is worth noting that even certain arguments directly *in support* of slavery were accepted by some people who were *not* "careless in their thinking or blinded by bias, self-interest, or convention." Nothing in Finnis's account requires him to deny this in order to hold both that pro-slavery arguments were wrong, and that those who accepted them were wrong in so doing.

Weinreb's substantive objections to Finnis's theory have mainly to do with Finnis's appeals to self-evidence. Since putatively self-evident propositions do figure crucially in the moral theory Finnis defends and deploys, it is worth attending closely to these objections. I shall argue that Weinreb has seriously misunderstood the place of propositions claimed to be self-evident in the Grisez-Finnis theory of morality. Contrary to what Weinreb supposes, those subscribing to the theory do not hold *conclusions* in normative ethics to be self-evident. Once I have cleared away this interpretive mistake, I shall explain what sorts of principles they do suppose to be self-evident and offer a defense of the plausibility of such principles.

Weinreb makes a basic interpretive error in supposing that Finnis thinks that his *conclusions* (whether about abortion or any other issue in normative ethics or political theory) are self-evident. Specific moral norms (like a norm about abortion or its legal regulation) are, under the Grisez-Finnis theory, derived from more general moral norms that guide human choice and action in respect of intrinsic human goods. Any such derivation requires an *argument*. One must *argue* one's way to a conclusion. If, as Grisez and Finnis suppose, human life is an intrinsic good of persons, and if, as they further suppose, a general moral norm forbids direct attacks on such intrinsic goods, then abortion, if it destroys the human life of a person directly (i.e., either as an end or, what is more likely, as a means to another end, rather than as a foreseen and accepted side-effect of an otherwise morally acceptable choice) is immoral. But if

---

of moral opinion and, especially, cultural relativity, as part of their case against natural law. See Finnis, *Natural Law and Natural Rights* at 127 (cited in note 3).

a specific moral norm does forbid abortion, that norm is not, for Finnis and Grisez, self-evident.

As it happens, both Grisez and Finnis accept the argument that a specific moral norm forbids abortion. It will be still more illuminating for the present purpose, however, if we consider a question of the justifiability of killing on which they disagree. Their dispute has to do with whether a specific moral norm forbids the killing involved in capital punishment. Finnis takes the position that capital punishment does not (necessarily) involve direct killing. His argument is that the action of public authorities in executing someone guilty of a sufficiently grievous crime may immediately and in itself instantiate an intrinsic good, viz., the good of justice, thus enabling the killing accurately to be characterized as something other than the taking of life as a means to an ulterior end.[49] Capital punishment may, therefore, be morally permissible. Grisez disagrees. In his view, the intentional structure of any choice to kill as a punishment is such that executing even those guilty of the most heinous crimes cannot but be characterized as the choice of an evil means to a good end.[50] What is important to notice for our purposes about this dispute is that neither Finnis nor Grisez supposes that the other is failing to grasp a self-evident point. Each, to be sure, believes his own position to be correct and, therefore, by logical entailment, his interlocutor's position to be mistaken. But both understand the question as one to be resolved by *argument*, not by an appeal to self-evidence. The intentional structure of the choice to kill as a punishment—the decisive issue in the debate for Finnis and Grisez—requires, as they explicitly acknowledge, *analysis*.[51] It is not self-evident.

So, if specific moral norms are not supposed to be self-evident, what sorts of principles are supposed to be? The answer is: the first principle of practical reason, and its determinations; and what Grisez and Finnis call the first principle of morality. These are the (underived) foundational principles that provide the ultimate premises of moral arguments.[52] While they may be defended by

---

[49] See John Finnis, *Fundamentals of Ethics* 130 (Georgetown, 1983).

[50] See Germain Grisez and Joseph M. Boyle, Jr., *Life and Death With Liberty and Justice* 400 (Notre Dame, 1979). For what it is worth, I agree with Grisez.

[51] John Finnis, Joseph M. Boyle, Jr., and Germain Grisez, *Nuclear Deterrence, Morality and Realism* 317-18 (Oxford, 1987).

[52] The theory of morality Finnis defends and deploys in his book is foundationalist. And any foundationalist theory will rest ultimately upon principles that are themselves thought not to be deducible or derivable from still more fundamental premises. Various foundationalists argue that their first principles are basic intuitions, or necessary truths, or

dialectical arguments designed either to rebut arguments against them, or show up the defects or inadequacies of ethical theories that attempt to do without them, they cannot themselves be deduced or inferred or otherwise derived from more fundamental premises. One cannot argue one's way to them (the way one can, on the basis of more fundamental premises, argue one's way to a conclusion). The claim that they are self-evident does not imply that they are undeniable or, still less, that no one denies them. What it does imply is that the practical intellect may grasp them, and practical judgment can affirm them without the need for a derivation. (Which is not to say that they can be grasped without an understanding of the realities to which they refer.)

The reader will recall that the determinations of the first principle of practical reason refer to the intrinsic goods that render human choices intelligible, according to Grisez's interpretation of Aquinas, by providing ultimate reasons for action. These determinations thus serve as first practical principles—the most basic precepts of natural law. The goods to which they refer are, in the Grisez-Finnis parlance, "basic human goods." Included under this rubric is anything an instantiation of which can be intelligibly chosen as an end-in-itself. According to the Grisez-Finnis theory, the basic goods are not extrinsic to the persons by and in whom they are instantiated, but, are, rather, intrinsic aspects of human well-being and fulfillment.[53] While they are capable of being "participated in"[54] by limitless numbers of persons on limitless numbers of occasions in virtually limitless forms, they can be grouped, according to Grisez and Finnis, under a small number of categories.[55] In *Natural Law and Natural Rights*, Finnis categorizes them as: life (and health); knowledge; play; aesthetic experience; sociability (friendship); practical reasonableness; and 'religion.'[56]

Are these, as some (including Russell Hittinger) have charged, mere intuitions? Is the claim that they are "self-evident" nothing more than a piece of rhetoric masking naked conviction? Or, as Grisez and Finnis claim, does the practical intellect grasp the basic goods in non-inferential acts of understanding by picking out intelligibilities in the data that human experience presents? Well, let

---

self-evident precepts.

[53] Finnis, Boyle, and Grisez, *Nuclear Deterrence* at 277 (cited in note 51).

[54] On this locution, see Finnis, *Natural Law and Natural Rights* at 64 (cited in note 3).

[55] Grisez and Finnis, both individually and in their collaborative works, categorize the basic goods differently at different times. Not much turns on the differences.

[56] Finnis, *Natural Law and Natural Rights* at 85-90 (cited in note 3).

me tell a little story designed to demonstrate how Grisez and Finnis suppose we can grasp first practical principles that refer to basic human goods.

E. The Identification of a First Practical Principle

I regularly employ as a teaching assistant a graduate student named Adam. He has been remarkably successful as a teacher because he combines extraordinary intellectual curiosity and ability with genuine dedication to the education of his students. Indeed, he sometimes devotes himself so fully to his teaching that he is left with but little time for his own projects. Now, let us suppose that I discover that Adam has taken a part-time job on the late-night shift (9 p.m. - 3 a.m.) flipping hamburgers at the local Burger King. Naturally, my curiosity is aroused. I wonder why, in view of all the other demands on his time and energy, he has made a choice to spend time that he could, after all, devote to reading, writing, relaxing, being with friends, enjoying himself, getting some sleep, and the like, sweating over a hot grill in a noisy fast-food restaurant. I know that Adam is not irrational, so I assume, of course, that there must be some coherent explanation.

So, let us suppose that I ask him about it. Now, if he responds to my inquiry by saying that he took the job to earn some extra money, I would hardly find his explanation baffling. I am well aware of the utility of money. One can, after all, spend it on things one needs or wants. One can save it for a rainy day, enjoying the peace of mind that comes, I am told, with financial security. One can even collect and study money, in the form of bills or coins, as a hobby or amusement. Of course, I would suppose that if Adam took the job to earn money, he sought the extra income for some such reason. But if, contrary to my supposition, Adam should inform me that he wants the money *just for its own sake*, I would find his decision to take the job simply unintelligible.

Let us suppose I press him on the matter: "Surely, Adam, you want the extra money for a reason. Are there things you want to purchase with it?" "No, I already have enough money to buy anything I'll ever want." "Then, do you want it for the power or prestige available to those known to be wealthy?" "No, I am a Ghandian; I have no interest in such things." "Do you want it in order to give it away to a friend, or to a cause, or to the poor?" "No." "Then perhaps it is not the money you want, after all. Perhaps your reason for taking the job is that you enjoy that sort of work." "Are you kidding? Only a fool would work as a short order cook except to make money. As I said, the money is what I'm after. But

I'm not after it for *any* ulterior reason. It is an end-in-itself."

Well, this conversation *would* leave me baffled. The curiosity aroused in the first instance when I learned of Adam's decision to take the part-time job would remain unsatisfied. A question that the inquiring intellect cannot but consider relevant—why do you want the money?—would remain unanswered. The putative desirability of money for its own sake just "does not compute." So, Adam's account would leave me scratching my head in bewilderment. I would remain unable to make sense of his decision to take the job. It is not that I would view Adam's choice as somehow immoral or even imprudent. Questions of moral rectitude or prudence would simply not be reached. I would be stuck contemplating the (ir)rationality of the choice. Under Adam's account, his decision to take the job would seem utterly pointless, and therefore irrational. It would seem to violate Aquinas's first principle of practical reason (as Grisez interprets it).

The general lesson to be drawn from reflection on the matter thus far is that money can only have (important) instrumental value. It cannot serve as a reason for action that requires reference to no further reason in order to ground the action's intelligibility. If we trace a chain of practical reasoning culminating in a choice back to its ultimate term, and find that that term is money sought as an end-in-itself, the data provide no intelligibilities for the inquiring intellect to pick out.

But let us now suppose that Adam's account of his decision to take the job does not end with his desire to earn some additional money. In reply to my inquiry, he says that he wants the extra money for a reason—to buy an expensive medicine. Of course, I immediately suppose that he, or someone close to him, is ill. But, again, what if my supposition is incorrect? When I ask after his health, he says, "Oh no; it is kind of you to ask, but I'm not sick. No one I know is sick. I'm not buying the medicine to administer it to anyone. Medicine is worth having just for its own sake." "Have you become interested in pharmacology?" "Nope." "You haven't started a medicine collection, have you?" "Of course not." This conversation leaves me no less baffled than the one about money. Inasmuch as medicine, like money, is something of instrumental value rather than intrinsic value, it fares no better than money as an intelligible ultimate reason for action. It is not an "explanation stopper."

Of course, since Adam is a rational person, his account of his decision would not stop with the reference to medicine. He would give a reason for wanting the medicine. Let us suppose that his reason is that his sister has been afflicted with a serious illness that only a costly medicine can cure; so he has decided to take the job in order to earn the money to buy the medicine needed to restore his sister's health. If Adam's explanation stops here, has he left me baffled? Not at all. I now have the data I need to make sense of Adam's decision, and, thus, to understand it as, at least, rational. I can now see the point of his decision to take the part-time job. Acting for the sake of (his sister's) health as an end-in-itself is perfectly intelligible. The intelligibility of health as a reason for action need not be supplied, as in the case of money or medicine, by some more fundamental reason.

Of course, there is nothing to stop me from asking Adam why health is something he wants his sister to have. But there would be nothing baffling about the straightforward reply that, beyond any instrumental value health might have for his sister, health is one of those things worth having just for its own sake. Adam's decision, and the chain of practical reason culminating in that decision, are completely intelligible simply by reference to (his sister's) health as something intrinsically valuable. And this intelligibility is available to anyone inquiring into the matter—regardless of whether the inquirer himself would have acted as Adam did had a loved one of his own been ill.[57]

Grisez and Finnis notice that we do not grasp the intelligibility of health as something intrinsically valuable in the same way we come to understand the purely instrumental value of things like money or medicine. Instrumental values can (only) be established by way of deductions or inferences from still more fundamental premises. But intrinsic values, as *ultimate* reasons for action, cannot be deduced or inferred. We do not, for example, infer the intrinsic goodness of health from the fact, if it is a fact, that people everywhere seem to desire it. (Although this sort of anthropological information can figure usefully in dialectical arguments—especially those meant to rebut claims that our belief in the intrinsic goodness of health is merely culturally induced.) We see the point of acting for the sake of health, in ourselves or in others, just for its own sake, without the benefit of any such inference. Acts performed for the sake of health (even where we do not approve of them—e.g., when the scientist kidnaps the child in order to find a cure for the ravaging disease) do not strike us as utterly pointless. It is in this light that Grisez and Finnis claim that principles such

[57] Of course, affirming the intrinsic value of health does not preclude acknowledging that health, like other intrinsic goods, has tremendous instrumental value as well.

as "health is a good to be promoted and protected" are "self-evident."[58]

Once we have traced a chain of practical reasoning back to its ultimate term (e.g., health), if that term provides for its own intelligibility, it enables us to make sense of those terms in the chain of reasoning that do not supply their own intelligibility (e.g., medicine and money). The principle that we grasp in (at least implicitly) affirming the intrinsic value of the end indicated by the ultimate term is self-evident. Generalizing from our inquiry into Adam's practical reasoning, we can affirm, as a self-evident practical truth, the proposition that "health is a good to be done and pursued" (i.e., preserved protected, restored). Thus, we have identified a basic precept of natural law.

It must be emphasized that this is no more than a general prescription to act for the sake of health. As such, it is weak. It does not, for example, say anything about when, if ever, it is wrong not to act for the sake of health. Nor does it indicate whether it is ever right to sacrifice health ultimately for the sake of some other intelligible end.[59] While it grounds the intelligibility and, thus, our

---

[58] Adam or his sister might value her health, in part, because it enables her to participate in a sport which she enjoys and for which she has a special talent. They might be interested in restoring her health, in part, to enable her to finish her own studies, or find her own job, or care for an aged aunt. But besides all the respects in which they may value health instrumentally, Adam's acting to restore his sister's health—or a fortiori, his own—just for its own sake is perfectly intelligible.

[59] People make such sacrifices all the time, sometimes for profound reasons, other times for trivial ones. But if someone chooses to do something at a cost to his health, we shall only be able to understand *that* choice as rationally grounded (regardless of how we evaluate it morally) if it is made for the sake of some other ultimate end, the self-evident point of which we can grasp. Health is certainly not the only basic human good. Indeed, someone who, while enjoying perfect health, never had occasions to participate in other intrinsic goods—no opportunities for friendship, or recreation, or inquiry, or any other activity by which one participates in basic goods other than health—would hardly find his life satisfactory. The variety of basic goods reflects the range of respects in which human persons can flourish (and decline).

While I am on the subject of the diversity of ultimate reasons for choice and action, I should point out that reason is not the sole human attribute capable of projecting goals and motivating behavior. The fact that passion shares this capability with reason raises interesting questions for the Grisez-Finnis theory. Why, for example, do "emotional satisfaction" or "pleasure" not count as basic goods? They are after all, "explanation stoppers" in the sense that they often provide the ultimate term in accounts of human behavior. "Why did Joe have a drink?" "Because he was thirsty." Is any additional information needed to ground the intelligibility of Joe's action? No. It is perfectly understandable that someone would seek to quench his thirst for no other reason. But if this is so, are we not forced under the Grisez-Finnis theory to recognize the satisfaction of desire as a basic good? Weinreb does not raise this sort of skeptical challenge to Finnis's theory, so I will not respond to it here. A full defense of the Grisez-Finnis theory would, however, include such a response, which would work out in detail the relationships among emotion, motivation, and basic practical

judgment of the rationality of Adam's decision, it says nothing about whether that decision was morally required or even permissible.

F. From First Practical Principles to Moral Norms

Under the Grisez-Finnis theory, first practical principles and basic precepts of natural law (i.e., those concerning the basic goods) do not state moral propositions. As determinations of the first principle of practical reason, they are, in a sense, "pre-moral." They identify as self-evidently choiceworthy not only moral goods, but also non-moral goods (e.g., health, friendship, knowledge, and play). Taken together, they exclude as *un*choiceworthy only pointless activity. They are action-guiding in the sense that they are principles by which reason directs human choices toward intelligible ends. But if these were the only action-guiding principles, then there would never be a *reason* to choose (as distinct from an explanation for choosing—e.g., one's tastes, desires, sheer preferences) one intelligible course of action over another. For example, there may be an intelligible reason to play Russian roulette ("play") and an intelligible reason not to play it ("life" and the other goods attainable by the living). Are there reasons on the basis of which we can judge the choice to play, despite its intelligibility, less than fully reasonable? If there are such reasons, principles that are analytically distinct from the first practical principles must supply them. If these principles of full practical reasonableness could be identified, they would provide standards for distinguishing merely rational choices from morally upright ones. By prescribing some choices as morally required and proscribing others as immoral, such principles would accomplish what the determinations of the first principle of practical reason by themselves cannot do.

The Grisez-Finnis theory presents a set of general moral principles that, while analytically distinct from the basic practical principles and derived from a still more abstract foundational moral principle, in effect, put the ensemble of basic practical principles to work in concert. The role of these moral principles is to structure and guide human choosing between intelligible human goods. In *Natural Law and Natural Rights*, Finnis labelled these principles "requirements of practical reasonableness." In their collaborative work, however, Grisez and Finnis follow the former author's usual practice of referring to them as "modes of responsibility." I

principles.

shall do so here as well.

Insofar (but only insofar) as the Grisez-Finnis theory understands the intelligibility of human choices as grounded ultimately in human goods (understood as constitutive aspects of human fulfillment), it is "teleological."[60] Weinreb's labelling notwithstanding, Finnis's natural law theory is by no means purely deontological.[61] In its teleological dimension (but only in this dimension), it resembles consequentialist ethical theories as well as certain neo-Aristotelian and neo-scholastic natural law theories.

Any teleological theory of practical reasoning that identifies more than one human good will need, if it is to ground a theory of morality, a principle or set of principles capable of guiding human choice and action in respect of the various goods. For consequentialists, the master principle of ethics directs the chooser to act in the way most likely to produce the best net proportion of good to bad consequences, overall and in the long run. Grisez and Finnis reject this principle on the ground, among others, that it assumes what is false, viz., that the instantiations of human goods (and bads) are commensurable in such a way as to make possible the intelligent weighing or measuring of "value" necessary to consequentialist calculations. As *ultimate* reasons for action, the human goods, and their instantiations, must be irreducible to one another or to any more fundamental category. Thus, they are incommensurable.[62]

Grisez and Finnis maintain that the principle proposed by many neo-Aristotelian and neo-scholastic moralists as an alterna-

---

[60] The theory is not "teleological" in any sense that implies a commitment to a consequentialist principle of moral judgment, on the one hand, or a teleological view of nature, on the other.

[61] Under pure deontological theories, practical reason identifies moral norms without reference to human goods.

[62] On the damning implications of incommensurability for all forms of consequentialism, see Germain Grisez, Against Consequentialism, 23 Am J Juris 21 (1978); Finnis, *Fundamentals of Ethics* at 86-93 (cited in note 49); and Finnis, Boyle, and Grisez, *Nuclear Deterrence* at ch IX (cited in note 51). See also Joseph Raz, *Value Incommensurability: Some Preliminiaries, 86 Proceedings of the Aristotelian Society* 117-34 (1985-86); and Joseph Raz, *The Morality of Freedom* ch 13 (Oxford, 1986); Anselm W. Muller, *Radical Subjectivity: Morality Versus Utilitarianism*, 19 Ratio 115-32 (1977); Philippa Foot, *Utilitarianism and the Virtues*, 94 Mind 196-209 (1985); and Philippa Foot, *Morality, Action, and Outcome*, in Ted Honderich, ed, *Morality and Objectivity* 23-38 (Routledge & Kegan Paul, 1985); Alasdair MacIntyre, *After Virtue* 61-62, 67-68 (Notre Dame, 1981); Charles Taylor, *The Diversity of Goods*, in Amartya Sen and Bernard Williams, eds, *Utilitarianism and Beyond* 129-44 (Cambridge, 1982); and David Wiggins, *Weakness of Will Commensurability and the Objects of Deliberation and Desire*, in Amelie Oksenberg Rorty, ed, *Essays on Aristotle's Ethics* 241-65 (Cal-Berkeley, 1980).

tive to consequentialism is no more plausible. This principle supposes that speculative inquiry can identify an objective hierarchy among the goods. It directs the chooser, at least in certain conflict situations, to act for the sake of the superior good. Grisez and Finnis deny that anything in our grasp of fundamental practical principles warrants the conclusion that there is an objective hierarchy among the basic goods to which these principles refer—at least in any sense of "hierarchy" relevant to choice. Indeed, they suspect that any claim that such a hierarchy exists supposes the false thesis about commensurability that renders consequentialism untenable. It supposes, that is, that some goods have "more" good in them than others.

Having rejected consequentialist and neo-scholastic principles, Grisez and Finnis propose their "modes of responsibility." These are put forward as a set of general norms by reference to which various forms of unreasonableness in choosing in respect of human goods can be identified. But what do Grisez and Finnis take to be the standard of (un)reasonableness? The answer to this question remained obscure in Finnis's book and in Grisez's early work. As presented, the modes of responsibility, while intuitively appealing to many readers and defensible dialectically against various criticisms, appeared to pop out of nowhere. Especially perplexing to some readers was the mode that forbids acting directly against a basic good, i.e., "doing evil that good might come of it." Even some readers who found Grisez's and Finnis's criticisms of consequentialism and neo-scholasticism compelling felt uncomfortable with an apparently ungrounded moral norm capable of generating moral absolutes (e.g., no direct killing, no torture).

Perhaps the most important development in this theory since the publication of Finnis's book is what Grisez and Finnis call the "first principle of morality." As formulated in their most recent collaborative work, this principle enjoins persons to "choose and otherwise will those and only those possibilities whose willing is compatible with integral human fulfillment."[63] If sound, this principle provides an intelligible grounding for the various modes of responsibility. The modes themselves are, in effect, specifications of this first principle. They exclude as practically unreasonable (i.e., immoral) various types of willing inconsistent with a will that is well-disposed toward all of the human goods.

The concept of integral human fulfillment, as it figures in the

[63] Finnis, Boyle, and Grisez, *Nuclear Deterrence* at 283 (cited in note 51) (emphasis removed).

Grisez-Finnis statement of the first principle of morality, is easily misunderstood. It is not meant to indicate a supreme good above or apart from the basic goods. The basic human goods are reasons for action in a sense that integral fulfillment cannot be. But the fulfillments offered by basic goods, while genuine, are incorrigibly partial. No choice, or set of humanly possible choices, can bring about overall fulfillment. In none can one realize every humanly fulfilling possibility. The very open-endedness of the basic goods precludes this. The possibilities realized in and by human choices and actions are aspects, but only aspects, of complete human well-being. Inasmuch as no human choice, or set of choices, can realize anything more than aspects of complete human well-being, integral fulfillment cannot be a grand operational objective (whether of an individual, a community, or the whole human race). As Finnis and Grisez put it, "[e]thics cannot be an architectonic art in that way; there can be no plan to bring about integral human fulfilment."[64]

Thus, for Grisez and Finnis, the principle of integral human fulfillment is an ideal: not in the sense of a Platonic form of the good existing in a realm transcending this world, but in the sense of something that, while not a direct object of choices or attainable by and in them, can nevertheless be imagined (if imperfectly) and even wished for, and so can provide the standards by which choices may reasonably be guided.[65] The first principle of morality, in making reference to this ideal, does not direct us to choose in such a way as to bring about (or contribute to a project of bringing about) integral human fulfillment, for any such principle would be worse than utopian. It would direct us to do what in principle cannot be done. Any such principle would *itself* be an ideal—and a

---

[64] Id.

[65] The possibility of there being possibilities for choice the willing of which is compatible with integral human fulfillment depends on a particular (and controversial) theory of human action. Under this theory, the commonly accepted model of action—that under which an agent (i) wants to bring about a certain state of affairs; (ii) makes plans to bring it about by causal factors within his power; and (iii) carries out a set of performances to bring it about—must be rejected as inadequate. The theory proposes a more complex model under which persons choose not just for extrinsic purposes, but for ends which are intrinsic to themselves as persons—goods, in other words, in which they participate. A person's actions have moral significance as voluntary syntheses of the person with human goods in three ways: when one chooses something for its intrinsic value; when one chooses something as a means; and when one voluntarily accepts side-effects (good or bad) brought about incidentally to acting in the other two ways. All of this is rejected by consequentialists, for example, who deny that voluntarily accepted side-effects can be outside of the scope of an intelligent agent's intention in any morally significant way. Finnis, Boyle, and Grisez formally set out and defend their action theory (against consequentialist and other criticisms) in *Nuclear Deterrence* especially at 288-91 (cited in note 51).

useless one at that; it would be both too general to actually guide choices and incapable (in view of incommensurability and the lack of an objective hierarchy of basic goods) of rational specification. But the first principle of morality, though it makes reference to an ideal (which is not a principle), is itself not an ideal. It directs us to do something that can be done. It says that in choosing partial fulfillments, as we inevitably must, we should treat every possible human fulfillment for what it is; i.e., an essential aspect of integral human fulfillment.

This treatment has implications, for we often have incentives, and therefore confront temptations, to treat integral human fulfillment in some of its aspects (i.e., to treat some types of fulfillments or the fulfillments of some human beings) as expendable for the sake of others. When we act on these incentives, we opt for possibilities the willing of which is simply incompatible with the guiding ideal. We choose with a bad will, and hence, immorally.

Under the Grisez-Finnis theory, the modes of responsibility are derived from the first principle of morality.[66] They identify the various incentives to choose incompatibly with a will to integral human fulfillment, and they direct the chooser not to act on these incentives.[67] The modes thus provide premises for the often complex moral analysis by which persons can reason their way to specific moral norms. While our grasp of the modes gets moral argument off the ground, it does not always make such argument easy. Often, extremely careful and insightful analysis is required to determine whether a proposed act of, say, killing is direct and therefore impermissible; or, where an act of killing is clearly indirect, it sometimes takes equally subtle analysis to establish the fairness or

---

[66] Grisez and Finnis (both individually and in collaborative works) have formulated the modes in various ways. Finnis's list of the modes, as set out in chapter V of *Natural Law and Natural Rights* is reported in Weinreb, *Natural Law and Justice* at 110 (cited in note 1). Grisez's most detailed presentation of the modes is in his massive theological work, *The Way of the Lord Jesus, Volume I, Christian Moral Principles* ch 8 (Franciscan Herald, 1983).

[67] In addition to the mode that rules out doing evil for the sake of good, thus generating some absolute specific moral norms, Grisez and/or Finnis have identified modes forbidding, among other moral evils, unfairness, fanaticism, laxity, and dilettantism. The specific moral norms derived from these latter modes, unlike those derived from the one prohibiting the doing of evil for the sake of good, are, according to the Grisez-Finnis theory, rarely absolutes. For example, the specific norm requiring promise-keeping, derived ultimately from the mode forbidding unfairness, while ordinarily in force when one has made a promise, is non-absolute. This is because there are circumstances in which it is not unfair to break a promise. There are no circumstances, however, in which the norm against direct killing, e.g., of non-combatants (even as a means of winning a just war), is not in force. Inasmuch as this norm is derived from the mode against doing evil for the sake of good, it is absolute.

unfairness (forbidding unfairness is one of the modes) of the act.

Under the Grisez-Finnis theory, the identification of the modes is necessary because the first principle of morality, if left unspecified, is too general to make possible the derivation of specific moral norms. In the absence of modal specifications, one could not begin to derive norms about, say, abortion or capital punishment (not to mention economic justice or political participation) from an injunction to choose with a will toward integral human fulfillment. Such norms cannot be derived immediately from so abstract a principle. Thus, Grisez and Finnis sometimes describe the modes as "intermediate" moral principles; they occupy a place between the very abstract first principle and the most concrete and specific moral injunctions.[68] Inasmuch as the modal specifications of the first principle of morality are *derived* from that principle, they, unlike the determinations of the first principle of practical reason, are not self-evident.[69] But the first principle of morality itself, as an underived principle, *is* self-evident.

Is this a case in which Grisez and Finnis have, to recall Weinreb's charge, "confused self-evidence with personal conviction?" I think not. Of course, the charge cannot be rebutted by presenting a derivation of the first principle of morality; a successful derivation would prove that the principle is not self-evident, but rather dependent upon premises still more fundamental. So any defense of the claim that it (or any other principle) is self-evident will have to be a dialectical defense, rather than a derivation.[70]

The principal dialectical arguments for the first principle of morality demonstrate the failures or inadequacies of proposals that would deny the principle or leave it out of account. Especially powerful in this regard are arguments that reveal crucial flaws in the general moral principles put forward in theories that share with the Grisez-Finnis theory a concern for directing choice and action respecting human goods. If, for example, consequentialist principles go awry in treating basic human goods as commensurable,

---

[68] See, for example, Grisez, *Christian Moral Principles* at 189 (cited in note 66); Finnis, *Fundamentals of Ethics* at 70 (cited in note 49); and Finnis, Boyle, and Grisez, *Nuclear Deterrence* at 284 (cited in note 51).

[69] The status of the intermediate moral principles as *derived* principles was, in *Natural Law and Natural Rights*, unclear. Some critics interpreted Finnis as claiming that these norms were somehow derived from the first practical principles. Other read him as claiming that they were underived and, therefore, self-evident. Neither interpretation was wholly implausible. Clarification of the matter awaited the development of the theory to include an underived first principle of morality.

[70] See section II.A. for a general explanation of how dialectical arguments may be employed in defense of self-evident propositions.

then an adequate alternative will have to treat basic goods as incommensurable. But to do so, a general moral principle would have to direct choosing in a way respectful of each basic human good and each human individual as an ultimate locus of incommensurable values.[71] This, of course, is exactly what the first principle of morality, as formulated in the Grisez-Finnis theory, is designed to do.

In the absence of some understanding of human goods, knowledge of the first principle of morality would not be possible. Does this confute the alleged self-evidence of this principle? No. If anything, it establishes that our grasp of the principle is not, as some have charged, a mere intuition. Rather, it, like our grasp of first practical principles, is accomplished by intelligent reflection on data. Our practical intellects pick out intelligibilities in the data provided by our grasp of first practical principles, thus making possible additional practical—in this case moral—judgments.

Here, I think, it is worth spelling out briefly the relationship between the first principle of practical reason, its determinations, and the first principle of morality. We have already seen that, under the Grisez-Finnis theory, practical knowledge in its "premoral" aspect is directive (although not fully normative). It directs action toward intelligible ends and, thus, away from pointlessness. It identifies goods as "to be done and pursued." Thus, immoral choices are not irrational. (Indeed, purely irrational acts are not "chosen" in any morally significant sense.) One chooses immorally for a reason. The intelligibility of immoral choices, like that of all rational acts, is grounded ultimately in the goods for the sake of which they are made. These goods are, as we have seen, the subjects of first practical principles. Any immoral choice is, thus, consistent with at least one such principle. The immoral choice responds to the directiveness of that (or those) principle(s). The good available in such a choice can be sought as a genuine benefit. But it is a benefit that comes only at the cost of ignoring the directiveness of other practical principles.

The goods that are treated as something other than irreducible, incommensurable aspects of integral human fulfillment in an immoral choice are themselves, of course, the subjects of practical principles. Thus, the responsiveness of immoral choices to the first principles taken as a whole (i.e., to the first principle of practical reason) is imperfect. Indeed, they are imperfect in a sense in which

[71] In the next section I shall discuss the complex question of the relationship between human goods and the persons whom they fulfill.

morally upright choices cannot be judged imperfect. Let me explain.

In any morally upright choice, there will be "goods to be done and pursued" that are not done and pursued. No choice can bring about integral human fulfillment by perfectly realizing every possible human good. But the directiveness of first practical principles does more than identify goods as "to be done and pursued." It identifies the damaging of these goods as "to be avoided." A choice that is rational inasmuch as it responds to a practical principle, can still be less than fully reasonable in its failure to respect a different practical principle. To choose with a will toward realizing a certain good is to choose rationally. Both morally upright and immoral choices embody this sort of willing. But to choose with a will that another good be sacrificed or damaged is to seek a goal "at the expense of reason, part of whose directiveness will have been ignored by choice."[72] Such choosing is the mark of immorality—not because it contradicts the first principle of practical reason, but inasmuch as it responds to it imperfectly.

Does this imply that the first principle of morality is unnecessary because the determinations of the first principle of practical reason themselves are sufficient to forbid immoral choices? No. By making knowledge of the ideal of integral human fulfillment (and what is inconsistent with that ideal) possible, first practical principles provide the occasion (i.e., the data) for judging that a principle of complete reasonableness would direct action by reference to that ideal. Unless the judgment is made, and the principle formulated, however, there is no ultimate ground for full moral normativity, as distinguished from practical directiveness. Does this imply, then, that the first principle of morality is deduced or inferred from pre-moral practical principles? Again, the answer is no. The judgment is made in light of the data provided by the first practical principles, but it is not the fruit of a derivation from those principles. Such principles do not provide the grounds of the epistemic legitimacy of an affirmation of the first principle of morality. Those grounds are provided by the proposition stated in the principle itself. There is, for example, no relationship of entailment between the first principle of practical reason, and/or its determinations, and the first principle of morality.

---

[72] Germain Grisez, Joseph Boyle, & John Finnis, *Practical Principles, Moral Truth, and Ultimate Ends*, 32 Am J Juris 99, 123 (1987).

G. Free Choice, Causality, and Moral Responsibility

I presented the foregoing lengthy exposition and defense of the Grisez-Finnis theory to correct Weinreb's account of the role of self-evident principles in the Grisez-Finnis natural law theory and to answer his criticism of Finnis's appeals to such principles in *Natural Law and Natural Rights*. This, as I understand it, is the heart of Weinreb's case against "deontological" natural law theory of the Grisez-Finnis sort. Having assumed that Finnis's work confuses self-evidence with personal conviction, Weinreb does not develop a detailed case against the Grisez-Finnis theory for failing to solve what Weinreb himself takes to be the central puzzle of moral and political philosophy (and, indeed, human existence itself), namely, the "ontological" problem of human freedom in a causally determinate universe. I shall conclude my discussion of Weinreb by remarking on how the question of freedom and cause can be handled under the Grisez-Finnis theory.

Weinreb is correct to suppose that the problem of human freedom, i.e., self-determined action, is crucial in moral and political philosophy. In the absence of some free choice in human affairs, there could be no moral norms because such norms govern only free choices. Anyone who proposes a moral norm presupposes some free choice. But this presupposition does not establish that free choices are possible. It might be the case, after all, that no human actions are self-determined and, therefore, that there are no moral norms. If it is more reasonable to believe in complete determinism than in some free choice, then it is more reasonable to disbelieve than to believe in any moral norms. If, as Weinreb argues, the issue is inherently unresolvable, then no moral theory (and no moral norm) can be secure. Indeed, if Weinreb's argument goes through, there would appear to be no practical point to moral theorizing.

Recognizing the relevance of free choice to moral theory, Grisez, together with Joseph M. Boyle, Jr. and Olaf Tollefsen, took up the problem directly in a book published in 1976 entitled *Free Choice: A Self-Referential Argument*. Therein, the authors presented an argument for the proposition that someone can make a free choice. The argument is self-referential in the sense that it proposes to establish the falsity of the proposition that nobody can make a free choice by reference to the very act of asserting that proposition as true. Reducing a very lengthy and dense argument to its central propositions, here is a summary: The arguments made by those who deny free choice will, like any other arguments purporting to ground rational affirmations, presuppose both the existence of norms of rationality which prescribe unconditionally, *and* the physical and psychological possibility of one's refusing to adhere to such norms. Rational affirmation of the proposition that there are no free choices is possible only for one who chooses between the alternatives of, on the one hand, adhering to the prescriptions of the norms of rationality appealed to by those who argue against free choice, or, on the other hand, refusing to adhere to those prescriptions. But this choosing is itself an instance of free choice. So any argument that there cannot be free choices is ultimately self-refuting.

Retorsive arguments against complete determinism are familiar to contemporary philosophers. Determinists commonly defend themselves against such arguments by accusing their interlocutors of begging the question of whether reasons are anything other than causes (of behavior). The argument developed by Grisez and his co-authors is an especially compelling version of the retorsive argument for free choice inasmuch as its focus on the role of norms of rationality denies determinists this escape route. But Weinreb's case is not, the reader will recall, an argument for determinism as such. So, even if successful, the self-referential argument for free choice is not sufficient to meet Weinreb's challenge to theorists of natural law and justice. It is certainly the case, as Weinreb argues, that free choice is possible only against a background order of causality. Otherwise, the immediate consequences (if any) of self-determined human actions would be utterly random and unpredictable. Such actions would be merely arbitrary insofar as they would lack a rational ground. There would be no intelligible point to performing some action rather than another (or no action at all). Where there are no reasons for action, choice is pointless. In the absence of reasons, there could be no intelligent self-determined action, but merely arbitrary human behavior.

Determinists have long attempted to establish that unless human actions are caused, they are arbitrary. Defenders of free choice have countered with the proposal that free choice need only suppose the existence of reasons for action in order to avoid the implication of arbitrariness. Determinists reply that reasons, if they exist, are merely causes by another name. But among the problems with this reply is the fact that reasons differ from causes in that the former, unlike the latter, can exist without bringing about effects. One can have reasons to perform an act, yet not perform it. This is because one can, at the same time, have reasons not to perform the act. All questions of morality aside, either way one will act (or not act) on the basis of reasons. One's action (or inaction) will be rationally grounded and, thus, intelligible. Despite its being the fruit of choice, rather than causation, the rational grounding of one's action (or inaction) prevents it from being "arbitrary" in the strong sense alleged by determinists.

But Weinreb could argue, as critics of free choice have argued, that even if a choice between two live alternatives is "not arbitrary" in the sense that either alternative has an intelligible point, such a choice is in itself arbitrary in the sense that it lacks sufficient conditions apart from the person's choosing itself. There may be a "reason" grounding—and thus making intelligibly choiceworthy—each of the options, but in the absence of a reason to choose between them, the choice of one over the other is either determined (by desire, taste, etc.) or unintelligible—in other words, the intelligibility of an event depends upon its cause. But this is precisely what the proponent of (some) free choice denies in the first place: His whole point in claiming that someone can make a free choice is that the categories of "causally determined" and "random" do not exhaust the possibilities.

To assert that someone can make a free choice is precisely to claim that a class of actions (viz., free choices) have their own intelligibility without reference to something else (e.g., causes). If the critic of free choice (or one who holds free choice to be antinomic) responds by invoking a "principle of sufficient reason" (which, in Leibniz's famous formulation, holds that "there can be no fact real or existing, no statement true, unless there be a sufficient reason why it should be so and not otherwise"), he opens himself up to a different retorsive argument because there is no sufficient epistemic reason to accept the principle of sufficient reason itself.[73]

Moreover, one may admit a qualified principle of sufficient reason under the terms of which there must be a reason for everything *except* those things (e.g., free choices) by reference to which other things are ultimately explained. Adoption of a principle of sufficient reason qualified in this way comports with the view that there are boundaries of explanation (i.e., that explanation does not go on ad infinitum). At the boundaries, the intellect picks out intelligibilities in realities that are intelligible in themselves, and can therefore be understood without further explanation. Someone arguing on the basis of a principle of sufficient reason is hardly in a position to deny this supposition, for he himself implicitly relies on

[73] See Joseph M. Boyle, Jr., Germain Grisez, and Olaf Tollefsen, *Free Choice: A Self-Referential Argument* 86-87 (Notre Dame, 1976), citing Gottfried Wilhelm Von Leibniz, *Monadology* § 32 at 235 (Robert Latta translation 1898).

it in appealing to a principle of sufficient reason. Any such principle is either at the boundaries of explanation, and intelligible in itself, or else unintelligible. There is no sufficient reason for it (which is by no means to say that it is false).

Much earlier I quoted Weinreb's assertion that unless the circumstances of a person's act, together with the qualities that make him act as he does, are determinate, his act seems to be "the product of arbitrary occurrences as far as he is concerned and not something for which he individually is responsible."[74] This claim grounds the alleged antinomy of freedom and cause that Weinreb thinks is the central, unavoidable, yet unresolvable, question of moral and political philosophy. I think that his claim is confused. "Arbitrary" refers to human action, while "occurrence" refers to what happens apart from action. To the person choosing, the choice he is making seems "arbitrary" only in the trivial sense that he perceives nothing forcing him to make it. It does not seem "arbitrary" in the sense of irrational or non-rational, because whatever he opts for does not seem to him pointless. The choice does not, however, seem like an "occurrence." It seems like something he is doing, not like something that is happening to him. From his own point of view, at least, he is determining the outcome.

Of course, the particular options a person faces may have little or nothing to do with that person's (or, for that matter, anyone else's) free choices. The sheer givenness of a set of options does not mean that the choice between them is not free, nor does it mean that one cannot be responsible for choosing one way rather than another. Free choice does presuppose causality—otherwise there could be no determinate options for choice—but it does not presuppose a measure of causality with which it is incompatible. When we have a free choice to make, lots of things that are already determined, including everything that brings us to that point, provide the open alternatives among which we must choose and make our choosing possible. All that it means to say that this is a free choice is that nothing causes us to make the choice one way rather than another.

Implicit in many arguments that actions must either be caused or are random is the so-called phenomenalist conception of the self.[75] Under this conception, the self is a collection of discrete ex-

---

[74] Weinreb, *Natural Law and Justice* at 6 (cited in note 1).

[75] On the role of the phenomenalist conception of the self in many arguments against free choice, see Boyle, Grisez, and Tollefsen, *Free Choice* at 81 (cited in note 73).

periences bundled together only by various regularities. Any event, then, that is not integrated into these regularities by a cause, must be the product of mere chance. A "free choice" made by such a self would be a random event. And, as Alasdair MacIntyre argued many years ago, "[w]hat is random is no more free than what is caused."[76]

Were the phenomenalist conception of the self compelling, it would provide profound support for Weinreb's alleged antinomy. But a great many arguments can be marshalled against the phenomenalist conception, and Weinreb does not argue for it.

Implicit in the free choice position is an alternative conception of the self as substantially, but not completely, integrated. For a person to make a free choice that is not merely random but truly *his*, he must have a character and personality. Without these, there is no *self* capable of understanding the intelligible goods promised by the options, deliberating about them, and acting.[77] But, at the same time, his character and personality must be sufficiently open that these causal factors do not determine the choice. The conception of the self as substantially, but incompletely, integrated comports well with our common sense understanding of human agency. Under this conception, persons partially determine their characters and personalities by their own free choices. Heredity, environment, and free choice together account for a person's character.[78] Free choice accounts for the possibility of self-determined changes (for better or worse) in character, and hence for the possibility of, for example, repentance and reform.

The more or less determinate self that makes a free choice determines itself further in that choice. The choice, in a sense, then, "lasts" in the character and personality of the chooser—at least until the chooser makes another choice incompatible with it (thus re-orienting his character and personality by his own free choice).[79] The upshot of this self-constituting quality of choices is that subsequent acts performed in accord with a character established by one's free choices are acts for which one can reasonably be held (and hold oneself) morally responsible. Weinreb is correct to say that "[f]ull moral responsibility seems to require that an act be

[76] A.C. MacIntyre, *Determinism*, 66 Mind 28, 30 (1957).

[77] See Boyle, Grisez, and Tollefsen, *Free Choice* at 82 (cited in note 73).

[78] Id at 83.

[79] On the "lastingness" of choices, see Finnis, *Fundamentals of Ethics* at 139-44 (cited in note 49).

both free and determinate."[80] But he is wrong to suppose, if indeed he does suppose, that any self that is determinate enough to enable a person's act to be his own is completely determinate, and therefore incapable of doing anything other than whatever it does.

As we have seen, a central feature of the Grisez-Finnis moral theory is its account of ultimate reasons for action. The first principle of practical reason and its determinations guide action by reference to these reasons. Thus, they make free choice possible without implying "arbitrariness" in any sense that would undercut moral responsibility for one's actions. If these principles are sound, we need not account for every aspect of non-arbitrary human action by reference to causality. Causal factors will bear on human choice and action in a wide variety of ways, but some free choice can exist against the background causal order without contradiction. Moral norms, if they can be identified, provide the standards for fully reasonable (free) choosing where free choice exists. Moral and political philosophy are not, then, as Weinreb's arguments would lead us to conclude, doomed to frustration by an antinomy at their core. A theory of natural law, including a natural law theory of justice, need not adopt the implausible proposal that the causal natural order parcels out illness and health, plenty and privation according to the desert of the recipients in a desperate effort to dissolve the alleged antinomy.

II. Russell Hittinger's *A Critique of the New Natural Law Theory.*

Russell Hittinger's *A Critique of the New Natural Law Theory* is both narrower in its scope and less ambitious in its claims than Weinreb's book. Hittinger's work is a critical examination of the Grisez-Finnis natural theory—a theory Hittinger identifies as a product of the movement abroad in contemporary moral philosophy to recover a credible "pre-modern" tradition of ethics. This movement, which he labels "the recoverist project,"[81] is generated, in his view, by widespread disillusionment with what appears to be stalemate between utilitarianism and deontology in modern discourse about ethics. It was in reaction to this apparent stalemate, according to Hittinger, that Alasdair MacIntyre, perhaps the most prominent "recoverist," set about diagnosing what he called the "interminability" of contemporary moral debates in his influential

[80] Weinreb, *Natural Law and Justice* at 6 (emphasis in the original) (cited in note 1).
[81] Hittinger, *A Critique* at 2 (cited in note 2).

treatise *After Virtue*.[82] Other "recoverists," as Hittinger reads them, include Alan Donagan, Stanley Hauerwas, Elizabeth Anscombe, and, from a distinctively Marxist perspective, Ernst Bloch.

Hittinger justifies his focus on the Grisez-Finnis theory, which "[f]or lack of a better term" he labels "the new natural law theory,"[83] on three grounds: First, Grisez and Finnis claim to have recovered Aquinas's theory of natural law in a way that both avoids the standard Enlightenment and post-Enlightenment criticisms of Aquinas theory, and (according to Hittinger) "rescue[s] [that theory] from the problems inherent in the rest of Aquinas's work";[84] Second, "they contend to have retrieved the systematic core of natural law theory in a way that is congruent with the older tradition *and* in a way that is persuasive to contemporary ethicians";[85] Third, Grisez has recently undertaken to apply his natural law ethical theory to Roman Catholic moral theology in a massive project the first volume of which has now appeared.[86] The adequacy of the Grisez-Finnis theory for moral theology is an important focus of Hittinger's criticisms of the theory, but I will refrain from addressing these criticisms here. I shall concentrate instead upon Hittinger's critique of the Grisez-Finnis theory as a philosophical theory of morality.

Hittinger's thesis is that the Grisez-Finnis "project" fails, in the end, because it does not "interrelate systematically practical reason with a philosophy of nature."[87] The "reclamation of natural law," Hittinger declares, "obviously requires a commitment to law as in some way 'natural,' and nature as in some way normative."[88] This is a commitment which, as we have already seen, Grisez and Finnis steadfastly decline to make. They reject not only the rather perplexing idea of a normative natural order that Weinreb identifies as "the core of the old natural law," but also the neo-scholastic position that nature is normative in a way that enables us to derive moral norms from speculative knowledge of human nature acquired prior to the achievement of practical knowledge. Thus, they deny the rational basis of an identification of "the natural" with "the morally good" (and therefore deny the presupposition that the most basic moral norm is the imperative: "follow nature"). One

---

[82] MacIntyre, *After Virtue* at 6 (cited in note 62).

[83] Hittinger, *A Critique* at 5 (cited in note 61).

[84] Id.

[85] Id (emphasis in the original).

[86] Id.

[87] Id at 8.

[88] Id.

cannot derive the moral *ought*, according to Grisez and Finnis, from the *is* of human nature (or the human condition, or human *being*).

A. Practical Reason as Autonomous

Hittinger's book brings together a range of criticisms of the Grisez-Finnis theory marshalled over the years by neo-scholastic and neo-Aristotelian commentators, including Ralph McInerny, Vernon Bourke, and Henry Veatch. The chief criticism, perhaps, is the charge that relates to the proposition that practical reason operates autonomously. In other words, Grisez and Finnis contend that practical reason operates on its own first principles without dependence upon methodologically antecedent knowledge drawn from speculative disciplines like anthropology, metaphysics, or theology. Critics contend that this theory embraces Kantian deontologism and borrows all of its problems. As Veatch has put it, "though the hands are those of Germain Grisez, the voice is that of Immanuel Kant."[89] Hittinger, it seems, agrees.

The fundamental problem with Kantian moral theory, according to neo-scholastics (and others), is that, in refusing to ground morality in a concern for human well-being, it renders moral rules ultimately pointless. But if human well-being is identified as, in some sense, the ultimate ground of the intelligibility of moral norms, then some substantial knowledge of "the (human) good" becomes necessary if we are to discern "the (morally) right." Yet, the glaring teleological dimension of the Grisez-Finnis theory marks an obvious difference with Kantian ethics. As we have seen, the first practical principles and the basic precepts of natural law refer, under the Grisez-Finnis theory, to basic human goods. In this respect, at least, the theory is radically unlike Kantian deontology. So, we must ask, in what sense do neo-scholastic critics of the Grisez-Finnis theory suppose that theory to be Kantian?

Hittinger suggests the answer. In maintaining that the axiological knowledge needed to get moral theory off the ground comes as the product of purely practical reflection, rather than a speculative inquiry into human nature, Grisez and Finnis, in effect, accept Kant's supposition that ethics can dispense with the philosophy of nature. The Grisez-Finnis theory resembles Kantianism above all in its declaration of the methodological independence of ethics from metaphysics (or ontology). In Weinreb's pithy formulation, it

---

[89] Henry B. Veatch, *Human Rights: Fact or Fancy?* 98 (LSU, 1985).

represents a theory of "natural law without nature." Such an approach, in Hittinger's judgment, attempts "to recover natural law theory by way of shortcuts."[90] And, for him, no less than for Weinreb (although for a different reason), shortcuts will not do.

Hittinger's critique of the Grisez-Finnis theory begins with a set of arguments purporting to show that the attempt to identify human goods without appeal to a speculative philosophy of nature falls into a sort of intuitionism that leaves the basic goods vulnerable to skeptical attacks. Indeed, he implies that Grisez and Finnis themselves seem to perceive this inasmuch as they regularly marshal evidence acquired by various sorts of speculative inquiry (e.g., anthropological data) in support of the putatively self-evident basic goods. Arguments based on evidence of this sort ought to be unnecessary, Hittinger suggests, if the practical intellect can grasp the first principles that refer to basic goods without inferring anything from speculative knowledge of the goods as natural human ends.[91]

In criticizing Weinreb's account of Finnis's appeals to self-evidence, I discussed the familiar charge that the Grisez-Finnis theory of first practical principles is based on intuitions. Here I wish to say a word about the use of dialectical arguments in defense of propositions claimed to be self-evident. Dialectical argumentation focuses on the relationships between propositions (including putatively self-evident propositions) to be defended and other knowledge. The point of such argumentation is to highlight the unacceptable implications of denying the propositions to be defended, or the inappropriateness of relying on certain evidence (shown to be inapt or defective) to deny or cast doubt on those propositions.

Now, speculative arguments *can* be useful in casting doubt upon propositions alleged to be self-evident practical truths. For example, the presentation of anthropological evidence tending to show that no form of friendship existed in certain non-Western cultures prior to their contact with the West, while not itself a disproof of the self-evident value of friendship, would cast substantial doubt on the proposition that friendship is intrinsically valuable. It would provide an occasion for anyone who judged friendship to be objectively good to at least rethink the matter. One would be surprised to learn that a self-evidently worthwhile human end was unknown (or known but unvalued) by a substantial part of mankind.

In carefully rethinking the matter, perhaps one would discover

[90] Hittinger, *A Critique* at 198 (cited in note 2).

[91] Id at 44-45.

a mistake in one's practical judgment about friendship. Perhaps it would transpire that, while friendship is not intrinsically valuable, its historically contingent, but very close, links with certain more fundamental goods in one's own culture deflected one's understanding of the matter, leading one falsely to conclude that the value of friendship is intrinsic (rather than, say, merely instrumental). On the other hand, perhaps, even after a searching reconsideration, one's judgment of the intrinsic worth of friendship would not change. In this event, one would likely find the anthropological evidence perplexing in light of one's considered practical judgment. The phenomenon of a widespread failure to grasp what one judges to be a self-evident practical truth would itself demand an explanation; it would set a substantial question for further speculative inquiry.

Just as speculative arguments can cast doubt on propositions claimed to be self-evident practical truths, speculative arguments can be effective in rebuttal. An effective speculative argument of this sort does not estabish the self-evidence of a self-evident practical truth. It simply removes a particular doubt about that truth. For example, an argument that established that the apparent non-existence of friendships in certain non-Western cultures can be accounted for by the failure of Western anthropologists to appreciate the distinctive forms and expressions of friendship in such cultures, would itself remove the doubts raised by the disturbing anthropological evidence. But, one might ask, can there be doubts about *self-evident* truths? Yes—precisely because such truths are *not* mere intuitions or innate ideas. They are grasped by intelligent reflection on data presented by experience (e.g., one's own direct or indirect experiences of friendships). And any such grasp involves an act of understanding. Many factors capable of derailing understanding respecting non-self-evident propositions, whether practical or speculative, are equally capable of impeding sound judgment in respect of self-evident propositions. Thus, we would do well to follow Aquinas in distinguishing propositions that are self-evident to everyone, from propositions that are self-evident only to the wise.[92] It is possible for anyone to fail to grasp a self-evident truth; just as it is possible for anyone to mistakenly suppose that what is in reality a derived proposition (or even a false proposition) is a self-evident truth.

Dialectical arguments are, I think, especially powerful in re-

[92] Aquinas, *Summa Theologiae* at 1-2, q 94, a 2 (cited in note 29).

buttal. However, they may be employed affirmatively in support of a self-evident practical truth, often with persuasive force. For example, the considerable anthropological evidence tending to show that various forms of friendship, knowledge, and religion are to be found in virtually all cultures, while not evidence of the self-evidence of the value of these realities (for there can be no "evidence" of "self-evidence"), does show that a practical judgment of their intrinsic worth comports well with the data. It places something of a burden on anyone who would deny the proposition stating this practical judgment to account for the universality of phenomena such as friendship, intellectual inquiry, and worship. Any theory that proffers an explanation proposing a sociologically deterministic or psychologically reductionistic account will be subject to the increasingly familiar criticisms of all forms of determinism and reductionism. Perhaps someone skeptical about basic goods could meet these criticisms. But here the skeptic would, in any event, be the party attempting to rebut dialectical arguments supporting self-evident practical truths (but not, of course, establishing their self-evidence).

In view of the foregoing analysis, I see no warrant for Hittinger's suspicion of Grisez's or Finnis's use of evidence procured by way of speculative inquiry in support of propositions they hold to be self-evident practical truths. But Hittinger has another, more substantial, argument against the proposal that first practical principles are not derived from speculative knowledge. He argues that there are respects in which at least a certain minimum amount of speculative knowledge is indispensable to our practical judgments. For example, a basic understanding of the integral organic functioning of the human body (i.e., of being alive) is a condition of any judgment, including any practical judgment, about the status of life and health as basic goods. Grisez himself has implicitly acknowledged this, as Hittinger points out, especially in his early work on contraception.[93] There, as Hittinger reports, Grisez argued, for example,

> that the good of life must be judged as a whole rather than in relation to the end of each faculty or physiological power. Accordingly, respiration and nutrition cannot be said to be basic human goods. However, from a biological point of view, the "work of reproduction is the fullest organic realization of the living substance." [Citation omitted] In other words, it differs

[93] Germain Grisez, *Contraception and the Natural Law* (Bruce, 1964).

from respiration in the sense that it bestows the good of life as a whole, and therefore ought to be included within the basic good of life.[94]

Hittinger assumes that Grisez's use of this sort of argument shows that he "does in fact directly rely upon anthropological, if not metaphysical, evidence for including procreation in the list of basic goods."[95] Grisez indeed judges that the generation of a new human life is not merely an instrumental end, but is intelligibly worthwhile just for the sake of the new life generated. Hittinger's claim is that the above-quoted passage shows that Grisez himself relies "upon a theoretical [i.e., speculative] argument concerning what is essential or accidental to human organicity"[96] in reaching this judgment. As Hittinger sees it, then, Grisez's own analysis of at least one basic human good is "not consistent with his understanding of the inferential and deductive underivability of the basic practical principles."[97]

Is Hittinger's allegation of inconsistency telling? No. His argument rests on a misunderstanding of what Grisez expects to get out of arguments like the one Hittinger cites. Grisez need not, and, in fact, does not, deny that a certain minimum amount of speculative knowledge is needed as a condition of practical judgment. (Nor does he deny that additional speculative knowledge has any place in moral reasoning.) While practical knowledge is not *derived* from propositions about the realities judged to be intelligibly choiceworthy, practical judgments (i.e., that something is a "good to be done and pursued") are not, according to Grisez, made in the complete absence of data for reflection. Without a basic understanding of the realities one is supposed to be making practical judgements about (e.g., life, friendship, religion), one simply could not judge. In the complete absence of speculative knowledge of what Hittinger calls human organicity, for example, no practical judgment of the intelligibility of life or health as an ultimate reason for action would be possible. Can we make sense of someone's choice to act just for the sake of preserving, or protecting, or transmitting human life? It will be impossible to answer that question unless we first have some basic idea of what "human life" is; thus, some speculative (i.e., biological) knowledge is a condition of our practical knowledge of the goods of life and health. But to ac-

---

[94] Hittinger, *A Critique* at 62 (cited in note 2).

[95] Id.

[96] Id at 63.

[97] Id.

knowledge the need for a minimum of biological knowledge as a condition for reaching axiological judgments of this sort is not to imply that such judgments are inferred, deduced, or otherwise derived from the biological knowledge.

Even perfect knowledge of human organicity, including perfect knowledge of what is essential and what is merely accidental to it, could not provide a warrant for judgments about the intelligibility of choosing life or health as ends in themselves (although such knowledge would profoundly enhance our capacity to preserve and promote these goods). The intelligibility of such choices, to the extent that they are intelligible, will be picked out of the data by insights that, while not unconditioned by speculative knowledge, are not logically entailed by it. Any such insight will therefore be not only fundamental, but fundamentally practical.

In arguing that Grisez smuggles speculative knowledge illicitly (on his own terms) into judgments about basic goods, Hittinger claims (without citation) that among the terms Grisez variously employs "for the 'goods'. . . [are] 'tendencies' [and] 'basic inclinations.' "[98] This report comes after, and seems to support, Hittinger's claim that "[a]ll of Grisez's goods have content derived from inclination."[99] Now, the fact that something is a "tendency" or "basic inclination" is straightforwardly an item of speculative knowledge. To treat the fact that humans "tend" or are "basically inclined" toward something as a logical warrant for a judgment of the intrinsic value of whatever the tendency or inclination is toward, is to suppose that knowledge of basic practical principles *can* be derived from speculative knowledge. Were Hittinger's report accurate, Grisez *would* be guilty of an inconsistency in his treatment of first practical principles. But Grisez *never* implies, much less says, that basic goods are "tendencies" or "basic inclinations." Hittinger's claim that Grisez "employs" these terms for the goods has no basis in anything Grisez has written.

Hittinger's misunderstanding of Grisez's theory of basic goods is further evident in his assertion (again without citation) that, for Grisez, "goods are defined as actions which are attractive to the agent."[100] Not only does Grisez carefully distinguish goods from the actions by which persons may participate in goods, he never defines the goods by reference to their attractiveness to the persons who participate in them. Any value theory that does define

[98] Id at 40.
[99] Id at 28.
[100] Id at 55.

"good" as what is "attractive to the agent" flirts (at a minimum) with subjectivism. But Hittinger does the Grisez-Finnis theory an injustice by implying that a derivation of value from a speculative philosophy of nature is necessary to rescue that theory from subjectivism. Nowhere in the theory is the intelligibility of first practical principles made to depend upon the attractiveness of the basic goods to the acting person (which is to deny neither that basic goods can be attractive nor that their attractiveness can motivate action).

At one point, Hittinger accuses Grisez of holding an axiology in which the basic goods "are curiously Platonic-like forms."[101] The charge is untenable. Repeatedly, and in virtually all of their works on ethics, Grisez and Finnis make the point that goods do not exist in some transcendent realm, but are constitutive aspects of persons. To cite perhaps the most forceful statement, Finnis says in *Natural Law and Natural Rights* that

> the basic aspects of human well-being are . . . not abstract forms, they are analytically distinguishable aspects of the well-being, actual or possible, of you and me—of flesh-and-blood individuals.[102]

Hittinger seems to assume that the Grisez-Finnis theory *must* rely on some mysterious Platonic notion of the good *because* it does not propose to derive basic goods from speculative knowledge of human nature. But, as a critique of the Grisez-Finnis theory of practical knowledge, this assumption simply begs the question. Grisez and Finnis claim that first practical principles are self-evident truths grasped in non-inferential acts of understanding. It is this claim that Hittinger set out to prove false. But this proof cannot be accomplished by a gratuitous assertion—directly contrary to what Grisez and Finnis actually say—that basic goods are "curiously Platonic-like forms."

Does the Grisez-Finnis axiology imply a wall of separation between knowledge of human nature and knowledge of human good? Indeed, does the Grisez-Finnis theory implicitly deny that humans have a (knowable) nature? Neo-scholastic critics of the Grisez-Finnis natural law theory frequently raise these questions, and they are suggested at various junctures in Hittinger's analysis.[103] The

---

[101] Id at 187.

[102] Finnis, *Natural Law and Natural Rights* at 371-72 (cited in note 3).

[103] Hittinger frequently implies an affirmative answer to the first question and, at least once in his book, implies an affirmative answer to the latter. See Hittinger, *A Critique* at

answer to both questions is "no." To see why, it will be useful to distinguish the epistemological mode of inquiry from the ontological mode in respect of basic goods. Grisez and Finnis maintain not only that human beings have a nature, but also that human nature is a worthwhile object of speculative inquiry. They follow Aquinas, however, in maintaining that we come to know human nature by knowing human potentialities; and that we come to know these by knowing their actuations; and that we come to know these, in turn, by knowing their objects.[104] And how do we come to know the objects of human acts? Not by reflection on human nature, for it was the question of human nature that prompted our inquiry in the first place. Rather, we come to know the objects of the actuations of human potentialities by grasping self-evident first practical principles. The objects of human acts are the intelligible ends of such acts, i.e., the basic human goods to which first practical principles refer.

Knowledge that comes as the fruit of practical reflection becomes available to (i.e., provides data for) speculative inquiry (e.g., in metaphysics or theology). On the basis of one's practical grasp of the intelligible ends of human acts, one may derive propositions about the nature of human beings. The point is that in the epistemological mode of inquiry, our (practical) knowledge of human good(s) is methodologically prior to our (speculative) knowledge of human nature. The latter knowledge presupposes the former: It is not, as neo-scholastics suppose, the other way around.

Let us shift for a moment to the ontological mode. Here, if we reflect on Aquinas's methodological principle, it is clear that the human goods *are* goods for (i.e., fulfillments of) human beings precisely because human beings have the nature they do. As Finnis says, "[t]he basic forms of good grasped by practical understanding are what is good for human beings with the nature they have."[105] Were human nature otherwise, human goods would be correspondingly different. In this sense, the basic human goods depend, ontologically, upon human nature. So, in the ontological mode of inquiry, an account of the human goods will refer back to human nature: "Why are these the ends fulfulling of human beings?" "Be-

---

195-96 (cited in note 2).

[104] For a clear and concise statement, see John Finnis, *Natural Inclinations and Natural Rights: Deriving "Ought" from "Is" According to Aquinas*, in L.J. Elders, S.V.D. and K. Hedwig, eds, *Lex et Libertas*, 30 Studi Tomistici 43 (Libreria Editrice Vaticana, 1987) (NB: The title of Finnis's article is misleading.).

[105] Finnis, *Natural Law and Natural Rights* at 34 (cited in note 3).

cause human nature is constituted as it is." But this answer in no way entails that our knowledge of the ends *as* human fulfillments is derived from prior speculative knowledge of human nature.

B. Goods and Persons

Near the end of a discussion of Grisez's stated opinion that "Kant's view of moral principles is not so much false as grossly inadequate,"[106] Hittinger raises some questions about "the meaning and implications of shifting one's focus from persons to goods."[107] Hittinger asks:

> Does this not assume, or suggest, that goods and persons are strictly co-extensive both ontologically and in terms of actions which bear upon them? Is moral agency, for instance, something more than the sum of the parts of the goods with which practical reason is interested? In other words, is there something of value in personhood that needs to be affirmed in terms quite different from merely our concern for goods which fulfill persons?[108]

Alan Donagan shares Grisez's interpretation of Aquinas's theory of practical reasoning and has, in his own Kantian "respect for persons" ethics, defended many of the specific moral norms defended by Grisez and Finnis.[109] Still, Donagan has long criticized the Grisez-Finnis theory along the lines Hittinger's questions imply. Here it must be recalled that, under this theory, basic human goods, while analytically distinguishable from the persons whom they fulfill, are not extrinsic purposes of human action, but rather intrinsic aspects of persons. In the earliest statement of the theory, Grisez held that persons "actualize and receive the human goods into personal existence."[110] But, from the point of view of action in respect of a person, the person is not a value standing alongside the values that are constitutive aspects of the person. To act for the sake of a person, for example, is to favor some constitutive aspect(s) of that person's well-being—i.e., to promote or preserve or

---

106 Grisez, *Christian Moral Principles* at 108 (cited in note 66), reported in Hittinger, *A Critique* at 27 (cited in note 2).

107 Hittinger, *A Critique* at 29.

108 Id at 29-30. It is worth noting that the criticism implicit in the last of these questions will seem especially compelling to anyone who supposes—wrongly—that "our concern for the goods which fulfill persons" can be judged a "mere" concern inasmuch as these goods are mere tendencies, inclinations, attractions, or are in some other sense subjective.

109 See Alan Donagan, *The Theory of Morality* (Chicago, 1977).

110 Grisez, *Contraception* at 78 (cited in note 93).

protect basic goods as instantiated in that person.

Of course, one respects or loves the person for the sake of whom one acts as a unity, not as an amalgam of distinct parts.[111] But the good that is sought in a choice made for the sake of the person is, in the end, only that which one supposes can be attained in the choice. There can be no act for the sake of the person considered apart from the various aspects of his well-being and fulfillment. Specific actions undertaken for the sake of a person are directed toward these aspects. But it is, as I have said, regard for the person as a unity that motivates specific actions. In view of the complex relationship between goods and persons, Hittinger's questions are far from trivial; but they are hardly embarrassing ones for the Grisez-Finnis theory.[112]

Elsewhere, in accusing Grisez of an equivocation on the question of whether "the emphasis or focus of morality [is] given to the goods, or to my own fulfillment,"[113] Hittinger ignores an important feature of the Grisez-Finnis account of the relationship between basic goods and the persons whom they fulfill. The problem of whose flourishing, or whose good, is the ultimate point of moral norms is a perennial issue in discussions of eudaimonistic ethical theories. Is the rational basis of one's obligation to choose in a morally upright fashion ultimately a concern for one's own flourishing (which would be somehow profoundly damaged by one's own immoral choice)? Or, is it a concern for the flourishing of others, one's own well-being aside? In the Grisez-Finnis theory, it is, as we have seen, a regard for the ideal of integral human fulfillment, which would include, in principle, one's own flourishing as well as everyone else's. Thus, the theory excludes, again in principle, an essentially egoistic account of moral obligation.

Hittinger generates this alleged equivocation by interpreting in a strictly individualistic sense a reference to "human self-limitation" in Grisez's formulation of what one avoids in morally good choices. Not only is there no warrant for such a reading in Grisez's work, but specific passages in Grisez's writings specifically exclude

[111] Grisez made this point early on as well. See, for example, id.

[112] See Grisez, Boyle and Finnis, 32 Am J Juris at 115 (cited in note 72), where they formally treat the problem of the relationship between goods and persons, identifying certain respects in which basic goods "simply are persons—individually and in communion," and certain other respects in which they are distinguishable from the persons whom they fulfill. For a detailed critique of Donagan's claim that a "respect persons" approach to ethics is preferable to a "respect the goods of persons" approach, see Joseph M. Boyle, Jr., *Aquinas, Kant, and Donagan on Moral Principles*, 58 The New Scholasticism 391 (1984).

[113] Hittinger, *A Critique* at 53 (cited in note 2).

this sort of individualism. For example, Grisez says that "[basic human] goods do not have anyone's proper name attached to them."[114] And in his formal discussion of the ideal of integral human fulfillment, Grisez states that the ideal "is that of a single system in which all the goods of human persons would contribute to the fulfillment of the whole community of persons."[115] This is a point that Grisez and Finnis have repeated many times.[116]

I have identified a variety of respects in which Hittinger has misunderstood (or misrepresented) the Grisez-Finnis theory at the level of first practical principles. His misinterpretations lend apparent plausibility to his basic claim that the Grisez-Finnis theory cannot succeed without drawing on a speculative philosophy of nature from which knowledge of fundamental goods is derived. Once these misinterpretations are brought to light, the credibility of this claim vanishes. I shall now turn to Hittinger's critique of the Grisez-Finnis theory of moral principles. Again, basic interpretive errors ground Hittinger's most powerful criticisms.

C. Moral Norms and the Ideal of Integral Human Fulfillment

The reader will recall that, under the Grisez-Finnis theory, the first principle of morality refers to the ideal of integral human fulfillment. Our knowledge of this ideal comes from our understanding of the complete set of first practical principles—the self-evident determinations of the first principle of practical reason. While specific moral norms cannot be directly derived from the first principle of morality, they can be derived from intermediate moral norms—the modes of responsibility—that are themselves directly

---

[114] Grisez, *Christian Moral Principles* at 576 (cited in note 66). See also Grisez, Boyle, and Finnis, 32 Am J Juris at 114 (cited in note 72) ("As intelligible, the basic goods have no proper names attached to them. So they can be understood as goods and provide reasons for acting whether, in a particular case, the agent or another will benefit.").

[115] Grisez, *Christian Moral Principles* at 185 (cited in note 66).

[116] Grisez and Finnis are careful not to imply that integral human fulfillment is the fulfillment of communities considered as distinct from the individual persons who comprise them. The "common good," under the Grisez-Finnis theory, "is fundamentally the good of individuals (an aspect of whose good is friendship in community)." Finnis, *Natural Law and Natural Rights* at 168 (cited in note 3). It is "the well-being of you and me, considered as individuals with shared opportunites and vulnerabilities, and the concrete conditions under which that well-being of particular individuals may be favoured, advanced, and preserved." Id at 372. Nor does the ideal of integral human fulfillment imply that *self*-preference in choosing is never consistent with a will to integral human fulfillment. Grisez and Finnis recognize that one's own well-being (and that of those for whom one is in some special way responsible) has a reasonable first claim on one's interest, but they deny that the rational ground of this claim is any judgment that one's own well-being is more valuable simply because it is one's own. See, e.g., id at 107.

derived from the first principle of morality. These norms identify and forbid various forms of unreasonableness in human willing.

Hittinger erroneously interprets Grisez in particular as maintaining that the first principle of morality is an ideal. This misinterpretation is important for Hittinger's analysis of the adequacy of the Grisez-Finnis theory for moral theology:

> In his transition from moral principles to moral theology, Grisez regards Jesus as the concrete good that annuls the ideality of the Fpm [first principle of morality]. Its ideality, therefore, makes room for (even requires) a move into moral theology.[117]

But the implications of this misinterpretation for the Grisez-Finnis theory when it is considered solely as philosophical ethics are profound. As I noted in the previous section, if the first principle of morality were itself merely an ideal, then it would be both too general to guide concrete human choices, and incapable of rational specification. Although our grasp of first practical principles gives us some knowledge of integral human fulfillment, it is nevertheless an ideal in the sense that it cannot be realized in human choices.[118] But the first principle of morality is anything but an ideal. It *is* capable of specification, and the norms thereby derived direct us to do things that *can be done*.

The point is critical: We cannot choose to bring about integral human fulfillment, but we can choose compatibly with a will to integral human fulfillment. The standard of practical reasonableness is not how close we come to bringing about integral fulfillment in our choices (nor is it how "much" fulfillment, in some aggregative sense, we bring about); rather, it is whether our choices are compatible with a will to integral fulfillment. Hittinger seems to miss this point altogether. Indeed, in the course of his theological discussion, he accuses Grisez of "taking away with one hand what was just given with the other" because Grisez, as Hittinger understands him, holds that "[t]he achievement of the state of integral human fulfillment (*the goal of the moral life for ethics and moral theology*) is not a human act."[119] Hittinger judges this to be "a

---

[117] Hittinger, *A Critique* at 51 (cited in note 2).

[118] The "ideality" of integral human fulfillment does indeed have theological implications. Although we can *wish* for integral fulfillment, it can only be *hoped* for in the light of religious faith. If it is to be realized—if *its* ideality is to be annulled—divine action is required. In Christian terms, grace is needed to perfect nature.

[119] Hittinger, *A Critique* at 135 (emphasis added) (cited in note 2).

contradiction in terms, or at least a paradox of some sort,"[120] and he is correct. But the contradiction or paradox is generated not by Grisez's first principle of morality, but by Hittinger's own fundamental misunderstanding of it; Grisez never proposes integral human fulfillment as a "state" (or state of affairs); nor does he imagine that it can serve as a "goal" to be sought in human choosing.

D. The Question of a Hierarchy of Basic Goods

The centerpiece of Hittinger's case against the Grisez-Finnis theory of moral principles features the claim that unless an objective hierarchical ordering of the goods is built into ethics at the axiological level, moral problems raised by the plurality of goods and opportunities for their instantiation will render many moral problems unresolvable. His proposal is, of course, that a speculative philosophy of human nature is needed to provide the hierarchical ordering.

As discussed earlier, the Grisez-Finnis theory relies not on a principle of hierarchy to govern choice and action in respect of basic goods, but, rather, on the modes of responsibility. Hittinger does not allege that the modes are incapable of resolving any moral problems, but only that there are many important moral problems that they cannot resolve. He does not suppose, as do some critics of the Grisez-Finnis theory, that the modes cannot rule out any rational choices as practically unreasonable inasmuch as any choice, qua rational, will ultimately have its intelligibility by reference to some intelligible good(s) sought in the choice. (These critics, overlooking the force of the modes altogether, argue, for example, that, inasmuch as aesthetic appreciation is as much a fundamental good as life is, a healthy adult may reasonably (i.e., morally) stand by the side of a wading pool appreciating the beauty of the sunshine and not raise a finger to help a drowning infant easily within reach. Indeed, some might argue that nothing in the Grisez-Finnis theory forbids the adult from tossing the infant into the pool in order to appreciate the beautiful nobility of its struggling.) But Hittinger does claim that reliance on the modes to rule out immoral actions done for the sake of intelligible goods is rather odd. I shall present Hittinger's argument in his own words:

> Grisez has reserved moral grounds for objecting to[, for example, Aztec religious practices involving human sacrifice]. For

[120] Id.

instance, he might argue that these practices violate some other human good, such as life; but this moral judgment does not disqualify the rituals as the good of religion; it only indicates that this particular religious observance violates the good of morality by failing to respect other basic goods. In other words, the Aztecs, according to nature, participate in the good of religion, for they find their religious practices attractive and gratifying; yet the practices, according to natural moral norms, violate [the mode of responsibility that forbids doing evil for the sake of good]. Nature appears to speak with a forked tongue.[121]

My first task here is to clear away some, by now familiar, interpretive mistakes. First, religious rituals, practices, and observances are not, under the Grisez-Finnis theory, the good of religion. Hittinger's statement to the contrary reflects his failure to notice Grisez's distinction between goods and the actions by which persons may realize and participate in goods. Second, what rationally excludes the Aztec rituals, under the Grisez-Finnis theory, is not "the good of morality," but a specific moral norm forbidding direct killing (which is itself derived from the mode of responsibility Hittinger cites). Third, the fact that the Aztecs find their religious practices "attractive and gratifying" is not, for Grizez (or Finnis), a ground of the goodness of the practices. Here again Hittinger imports into Grisez's axiology a conception of the basic goods as mere subjective motives. Such a conception has no foundation in Grisez's writings.

The Grisez-Finnis theory of natural law recognizes (and gives an account of the fact) that the Aztec rituals were not unintelligible acts. To the extent that they were sincerely performed (and so far as I know there is no reason to doubt the sincerity of those who performed them), the intelligible point of the rituals was harmony with the divine, or "religion." That someone would choose ultimately for the sake of such an end is hardly baffling. Even if one's own considered judgment is that there is nothing beyond the material world—no divine realities with whom to seek harmony—one may still understand the religious acts of those who have reached different conclusions. Inasmuch as the Grisez-Finnis theory understands "good" as that which provides an ultimate reason for action, it is hardly an occasion for puzzlement that the murderous Aztec rituals can be said to have been performed for

---

[121] Id at 111-12.

the sake of a good. This understanding in no way implies that such rituals were *morally* good—not even "a little bit." In truth, they were evil—not because they were pointless (for they were not) but because they violated moral norms (e.g., those derived from the modes forbidding the moral evils of direct killing and injustice). They were, then, objectively immoral (although this need imply no subjective guilt on the parts of those individuals who performed the murderous rituals). But notice this: Any theory of basic practical principles that excluded an understanding of the rituals as acts performed for the sake of the good of religion would undercut the possibility of judging the murderous acts by standards of morality. Lacking an intelligible point, the acts would have to be judged irrational and, as such, not susceptible to moral evaluation.

But let us get back to the issue of hierarchy. What if one finds oneself in a situation in which the modes of responsibility do not narrow one's morally acceptable alternatives down to one? Don't we need to know which good is the superior in order to choose correctly? It is here that the Grisez-Finnis theory is bound to disappoint absolutists. The theory seems incapable of providing norms that would generate a single, uniquely correct answer to every practical dilemma. It will not, for example, provide an answer for a gifted, morally serious undergraduate facing a choice of careers between law and medicine, who would like to know whether life and health are, in the great scheme of things, objectively more or less important than justice. Both options offer fulfillments (for the student and others), but no mode of responsibility will in principle rule out one or the other. The choice of either option, then, can be made compatibly with a will to integral human fulfillment. And the choice of neither option can bring it about (or somehow bring mankind nearer to bringing it about).

Of course, one's moral obligations can, sometimes, be affected by choices one has already made. For example, if I promise to do something, certain modes of responsibility ordinarily require me to do it, even where, but for my promise, no mode would generate such a requirement. Even aside from promises, prior commitments can give rise to moral obligations where, but for those commitments, none would exist. And the modes do forbid choosing in dilettantish, uncommitted ways. Self-integration is itself an intelligible good. Anyone who chooses with an utter disregard for it chooses some possibilities incompatible with a will to integral human fulfillment. So a morally serious and upright person will, inter alia, take care in his choosing to integrate his choices and harmonize them with one another.

In *Natural Law and Natural Rights*, Finnis analyzed this mode under the rubric of "a coherent plan of life." Quoting John Rawls, Finnis said that

> we should 'see our life as one whole, the activities of one rational subject spread out in time. Mere temporal position, or distance from the present, is not a reason for favouring one moment over another.' But since human life is in fact subject to all manner of unforeseeable contingencies, this effort to 'see' our life as one whole is a rational effort only if it remains on the level of general commitments, and the harmonizing of them. Still, generality is not emptiness . . . .[122]

Despite Finnis's explicit warning not to "confuse the adoption of a set of basic personal or social commitments with the process, imagined by some contemporary philosophers, of 'choosing basic values,' " his references to "life-plans" (and his citation of Rawls) confirmed the worst fears of certain neo-scholastics. They perceived Finnis here as implicitly endorsing value (and therefore moral) relativism. After all, they reasoned, does not the idea that one can choose—free of the constraints of moral norms—"basic personal and social commitments," reek of the modernist conception of human liberty against which the natural law tradition has long held out?

There are, certainly, modern ideas of moral liberty that are radically inconsistent with anything that can plausibly be claimed to be within the tradition of natural law theorizing. But the Grisez-Finnis theory of natural law allows no place for any such ideas. It emphatically rejects subjectivist conceptions of value (which make the value of an end *depend* on someone's choosing it or, at least, desiring it). And the modes of responsibility provide abundant guidance (many critics say that they provide far too much "guidance") in choosing respectable human goods—including choices of basic personal or social commitments. Although a great many options remain, the modes rule out more than a few live options for individuals and societies. Still, Henry Veatch, in a slightly different context, has warned Grisez and Finnis about supping with the devil: In the words of the old saw, "one needs a very long spoon."[123] But, recognizing that fundamentally important choices are often choices among morally acceptable options hardly places

[122] Finnis, *Natural Law and Natural Rights* at 104 (cited in note 3), quoting John Rawls, *A Theory of Justice* 420 (Belknap/Harvard, 1971).

[123] Quoted in Veatch, *Human Rights* at 98 (cited in note 89).

one at the dinner table with the devil—even if the devil is a moral relativist (which I doubt).

Hittinger seems to share the suspicions of some neo-scholastics. In an article published just before his book, he tries to win the point and establish the need for a hierarchical ordering of basic goods by seizing on a hypothetical case Grisez once employed to illustrate the implications of his view on the question of hierarchy:

> [I]n *Beyond the New Morality* Grisez states that on Sunday morning one can either participate in the basic good of play (a round of golf perhaps), read the Sunday paper (the good of knowledge), or attend church. Since there is no objective hierarchy prior to choice, one can do any of these, so long as one chooses "inclusively"—that is, so long as one remains open to the goods which are not chosen.[124]

The lesson Hittinger invites us to draw from this is that religion and other ends cannot be judged to be good "without an antecedent justification of their rationality."[125] This justification, of course, must be the fruit of a speculative inquiries: "Whether God exists, or in any event, whether human desires which are identifiably 'religious' are good, are," he declares, "crucial questions."[126]

Now, whether God exists is a very important question. (I am not quite sure what Hittinger means by identifiably "religious" human desires.) If one judges that God exists (a speculative judgment), one will base one's understanding of the good of religion (i.e., that end by reference to which human religious acts have their intelligibility) on one's (further speculative) judgments about God and what He reveals and commands. But nothing in these judgments need alter one's grasp of foundational practical and moral principles, nor one's basic understanding of how to employ these principles in one's practical thinking. Let us suppose that one believes that God has authorized certain human authorities to establish rituals and set rules for worship. Among the rules, there is a requirement that one attend a certain ritual on Sunday. In view of these (speculative) religious judgments, one would, as far as one's own understanding of the good of religion is concerned, be acting directly contrary to that good in failing in what one judges to be one's obligation to attend church. The genuine goods to be

[124] Russell Hittinger, *The Recovery of Natural Law and the "Common Morality"*, 18 This World 62, 69 (1987).

[125] Id.

[126] Id.

realized by reading the paper or playing golf would not excuse one from one's responsibilities under the moral norm.

The subject in Grisez's hypothetical will not be able to reach the judgment that he is under a moral obligation to choose to go to church on Sunday over reading the paper or playing golf, without some speculative knowledge (here, religious knowledge). But the knowledge that he needs is not knowledge of the hierarchical ordering of religion in relation to the other possible goods. Rather, it is the sort of speculative knowledge (whether of religion, or health, or any other good) whose relevance to morally upright choosing the Grisez-Finnis theory never denies. Indeed, in the most recent statement of the theory, Grisez, Finnis, and Boyle explicitly acknowledge the bearing of speculative knowledge on particular moral judgments:

> Just as [speculative] knowledge, true opinion, and experience enhance the initial insight into the substantive goods [e.g., life and health, knowledge, and aesthetic appreciation], so they deepen understanding of the reflexive goods [e.g., friendship, self-integration, authenticity, and religion]. For example, both sound metaphysics and experience in practicing authentic religious faith contribute to one's understanding of the good of religion. In doing so, they enhance the power of the principle underlying the religious quest.[127]

Attending to Grisez's hypothetical shows that speculative knowledge can enrich one's understanding of human goods, and even affect thereby one's judgments about moral responsibilities. This is by no means uniquely true for the good of religion. Speculative knowledge of various types can also, as Grisez and Finnis observe, enrich one's understanding of the goods of health, friendship, aesthetic appreciation, and, certainly, knowledge itself. But the hypothetical does not show that a hierarchy of basic goods must be posited if the religious believer is to judge himself to be under a moral obligation to observe his sabbatarian requirements. Nor does it show that speculative knowledge is needed (or able) to ground an inference that religion, health, friendship, aesthetic appreciation, or knowledge is "a good to be done and pursued." It leaves the Grisez-Finnis claim that any such judgment must be a non-inferential practical judgment untouched.

In other words, speculative knowledge of this sort cannot be a substitute for foundational practical knowledge (e.g., knowledge of

---

[127] Grisez, Boyle, and Finnis, 32 Am J Juris at 109 (cited in note 72).

the basic practical principle that harmony with the divine—if there is a divine—is a "good to be done and pursued," and the intermediate moral principle that one ought never to act directly against a basic human good). It can only supplement it (albeit in ways that can make critical differences for one's judgment in specific situations of choice).

Here again it is evident that the Grisez-Finnis theory erects no wall of separation between practical and speculative knowledge. But it does try to sort out the specific contributions of practical and speculative knowledge in understanding specific moral norms. And it eschews what I now hope to show is the ultimately hopeless strategy of trying to make decisions by reference to an alleged objective hierarchy of basic values.

Let us suppose, for a moment, that such a hierarchy does exist, and let us further suppose that religion ranks higher than knowledge or play. We are, to be sure, likely to conclude that Grisez's newspaper-reading golfer ought to go to church on Sunday. (As we have seen, the Grisez-Finnis theory can reach the same conclusion on the basis of different principles.) But we are likely to have trouble figuring out what he ought to do on Monday morning when he faces the option of going to a morning church service or getting to work on time. Does the supposed hierarchical priority of religion release him from the moral obligation (to be at work promptly) entailed by his prior commitment to his employer? Perhaps the principle of hierarchy does not control this particular choice; perhaps we can conclude that, despite the priority of religion, our subject ought to go to work in this case rather than to church. But what if he can manage to attend the service and still make it to work on time, thus avoiding any violations of moral norms? Does the priority of religion entail that he behaves immorally if he opts instead to spend his time before work reading the paper, or listening to some jazz recordings, or playing with his children? Suppose he does forgo all these possibilities in favor of the morning church service. Is he also morally required to forgo a pleasant walk in the park after lunch in order to attend a noontime religious observance? Does the priority of religion over the other human goods mean that in every situation of choice in which one is under no moral obligation to do something else, one must, if possible, act specifically for the sake of religion? If not, then when must one so act? The hierarchical ordering does not seem to indicate.[128]

Under the Grisez-Finnis theory, to fail to meet what one understands to be one's religious obligations, where one could meet them, is to violate a moral norm. But it is not the case that every choice not made for the sake of religion, even where a choice for religion could uprightly be made, implicates one in such a violation. Speculative knowledge will be required in order to judge what one's religious obligations in fact are, but, as we have seen, the Grisez-Finnis theory freely admits the relevance of such knowledge to one's practical judgments. The attempt to resolve choices involving religion (or anything else) by reference to an alleged principle of objective hierarchy, by contrast, seems hopeless inasmuch as it either requires us virtually always to choose for the sake of religion, or fails to provide a principle on the basis of which to decide when choices for religion are required and when they are not.

Hittinger's argument that a principle of hierarchy is necessary for morally upright choosing is no more successful than his other arguments purporting to establish that the Grisez-Finnis theory of natural law fails. Once we dispense with his interpretive mistakes, and his misguided criticisms of the proposition that knowledge of the foundational principles of natural law is the fruit of practical insights, all that remains of Hittinger's case is the gratuitous assertion that a speculative philosophy of nature is "obviously" required to ground axiological and moral first principles. Hittinger's critique, for all its pugnacity, leaves the Grisez-Finnis natural law theory unscarred.

III. Concluding Remarks

Whether or not Aquinas himself supposed that sound practical philosophy necessarily depends upon a methodologically antecedent speculative philosophy of nature, this supposition has long prevailed among those who have understood themselves to be working within the Thomistic tradition of natural law theorizing. It is hardly surprising therefore that the Grisez-Finnis theory, inasmuch as it dispenses with this supposition, strikes many thinkers who are sympathetic to natural law theory as woefully inadequate.

---

[128] Have I merely drawn a caricature of the neo-scholastic idea of choosing by reference to an objective hierarchy of values? If so, I would welcome correction. The problem is that neither Hittinger nor the (other?) neo-scholastic critics of the Grisez-Finnis theory seem willing to present a detailed account of how choosing in accordance with a principle of hierarchy is supposed to work across a set of cases. Until they present such an account, one can only speculate.

It seems "obvious" to them that natural law theory *must* be about deriving norms of conduct from nature. To deny that moral norms can be so derived is to embrace Kantian formalism, at best, and moral relativism or even skepticism at worst.

The attacks on the Grisez-Finnis theory that Weinreb and Hittinger mount represent attempts to identify with precision the inadequacies that they and others suppose must attend any theory of natural law that appeals other than to the normativity of nature in identifying fundamental moral principles. Both authors take the Grisez-Finnis theory seriously; but, unfortunately, neither manages to understand it adequately. Each proposes a set of criticisms based on fundamental misunderstandings of important claims and arguments Grisez and Finnis make in their elaborations and defenses of the theory. Perhaps the theory is vulnerable to damning criticisms. If so, the basic flaws in the theory are unlikely to be brought to light by critics who have not first achieved an accurate grasp of what is and is not being claimed by those advancing it.

That authors as competent as Lloyd Weinreb and Russell Hittinger *have* misunderstood the theory in such significant respects should, I believe, give Grisez, Finnis, and their collaborators pause. Misinterpretations are not always exclusively the fault of interpreters. Some texts invite misinterpretation. Whether or not the writings of Grisez, Finnis, et al., are culpable in this regard, it is evident that special care will be needed in the presentation of "the new natural law theory" if it is to get a fair hearing even among the philosophically most sophisticated of those to whom it is proposed.

Name Index

Anderson, John 114
Anscombe, G.E.M. 390
Anselm of Canterbury 151
Antigone 97
Aquinas, St Thomas *xiii*, *xvi–xix*, 61–5, 67–8, 70, 72, 79–95, 97–8, 100–1, 103–13, 122, 124, 138, 145–9, 155–63, 165–6, 168–78, 191–8, 201–24, 227, 233–4, 237, 294, 296, 299–300, 304–10, 313–17, 319, 321, 322–27, 330–31, 333–9, 341–2, 344–51, 353–54, 356, 360–7, 393, 398–9, 410
Aristotle *xii*, *xiii*, *xviii*, *xix*, 20, 56, 99, 102, 113, 130–9, 141–6, 161, 171–2, 175–6, 178, 180, 184, 187, 206, 227, 229, 234, 237, 296, 299–301, 304, 310, 319, 320–22, 331, 333, 335, 339, 342, 345, 349, 360
Augustine, St 146–7, 150, 180
Austin, John 226
Ayer, A.J. 119, 123, 124

Baier, Kurt 123
Barker, Ernest 175
Barth, Karl 104
Bentham, Jeremy 226
Bergson, Henri 184
Berkeley, George 113
Bloch, Ernst 390
Bourke, Vernon 391
Boyle, Joseph M. Jr 368, 384, 408
Bréhier, E. 113
Broad, C.D. 114
Broderick, Albert *xvi–xvii*
Brugger, Walter 131
Butterfield, Herbert 55

Cairns 160–1
Carlyle, Thomas 161
Cathrein, Viktor *xix*, 152–3
Chrysippos 150
Cicero 150
Cohen, M.R. 55
Copleston, F.C. 98, 99, 100, 108–9

Davitt, Thomas, *xvi–xvii*
Delos, J.T. 179, 180, 183, 187
Dennes, William 116
Descartes 113, 304
Dewey, John 5, 55, 123
Dicey, A.V. 226
Donagan, Alan 325, 353, 390, 399
Duguit, Leon 183
Dworkin, Ronald *xiii*, 353, 355

Edwards, Paul 114

Falk, W.D. 124
Finnis, John *xiii*, 225, 227–35, 293–305, 310–11, 325, 326, 331–9, 341–3, 347–9, 354, 367–72, 374–82, 384, 389–92, 394, 397–406, 408–11
Foot, Philippa 353
Friedman, Wolfgang 156, 178
Fromm, Erich 112, 123
Fuller, Lon L. *xiii*, *xiv–xvi*, 13–18, 23, 41–8, 50–8, 355

Galileo 113
George, Robert P. *xix–xx*
Gewirth, Alan 353
Gilson, Etienne 181
Grisez, Germain *xiv*, *xviii–xx*, 298–311, 313, 321, 325–6, 330–31, 333–36, 338–9, 341, 343–45, 347–8, 350–1, 354, 361–64, 368–82, 384–5, 389–92, 394–411
Grotius, Hugo 99, 151, 178, 226, 353

Hägerström, Axel 226
Hall, Jerome 114
Hare, R.M. 123
Hart, H.L.A. *xiii*, 185, 186, 187, 226, 234, 353
Hauerwas, Stanley 390
Hauriou, Maurice 179, 180, 183, 187
Heidegger, Martin 184
Hepburn, Ronald 114
Heraclitus 150
Hitler, Adolf 44–6
Hittinger, Russell *xxiii*, 354, 371, 389–410, 411
Hobbes, Thomas 178, 185, 297, 304, 357
Holmes, Oliver Wendell 178
Hume, David *xiii*, 103, 104, 107, 111–12, 114–15, 123–4, 181, 184–5, 217, 225–7, 229, 303–4

Husserl, Edmund 184

Jaspers, Karl 184
John XXIII, Pope 156, 162, 169–70, 181
Joyce, James 97

Kant, Immanuel 55, 83, 114–15, 148–50, 196, 220–1, 226, 308, 357, 391, 399
Kelsen, Hans *xviii–xix*, 39, 178–9, 226
Kenny, Anthony 325, 350
Kierkegaard, Sören 104, 119
Kleanthes 150
Koyré, A. 113

Laski, Harold 183
Lawrence, D.H. 123
Leibnitz, Gottfried 386
Leo XIII, Pope 156, 161, 162–70, 172, 181
Linton, Ralph 111
Lippman, Walter 97
Locke, John 87, 161, 172, 178, 226
Lombard, Peter 205
Lottin, Odon 205, 220–1
Luhmann, Niklas 231
Lundstedt, A.V. 226
Luther, Martin 104

McDowell, John 353
McInerny, Ralph 341–51, 391
MacIntyre, Alasdair 358, 388–9
Mackie, J.L. *xx*, 233
Marcel, Gabriel 184
Maritain, Jacques *xvi–xvii*, 98–104, 106–7, 109, 111, 121, 124, 180, 335
Marx, Karl 162, 172
Merleau-Ponty, Maurice 184
Mill, John Stuart 55, 226
Moore, G.E. 101, 122, 123, 214
Moore, Michael S. 354

Nagel, Ernest *xi, xiii, xiv–xvi*, 19–26, 28–32, 34–5, 37–40, 114
Nakhnikian, George 36
Newton, Isaac 113
Nielsen, Kai *xvi, xvii, xviii*, 217, 219
Nietzsche, Friedrich 123
Nowell-Smith, P.H. 123
Nozick, Robert 353, 358–9

Ockham, William 103
O'Connor, D.J. 114
Olivecrona, Karl 226

Paine, Thomas 99
Peirce, Charles 100
Pius XI, Pope 156, 162, 166–8, 169–70
Pius XII, Pope 156, 162, 168–9, 177–8
Plato *xii*, 108, 133, 171, 180, 232, 296
Pufendorf, Samuel 226

Rawls, John 353, 358–9, 406
Raz, Joseph 353
Renard, Georges 180, 183, 187
Richards, David A.J. 355
Ross, Alf 225–6
Russell, Bertrand 103, 104, 107, 111, 123, 124
Ryle, Gilbert 102

Sandel, Michael 358
Santayana, George 55
Sartre, Jean-Paul 123, 184
Sauter, Johann 150
Scotus, Duns 103
Selden, John 178
Sertillanges, A.D. 220
Smart, J.J.C. 114
Socrates 296, 307
Spinoza, Benedict de 55
Stephen of Tournai 206
Stone, Julius 328
Suarez, Francisco 210, 216, 330, 353

Thucydides 118
Tollefsen, Olaf 384
Toulmin, Stephen 113, 123

Ulpian 176

Veatch, Henry 313–24, 391, 406

Waissman, F. 234
Walzer, Michael 358
Watts, G.S. 114
Weber, Max *xiii*
Weinreb, Lloyd 354–72, 377, 381, 384–9, 391, 411
Wiggins, David 353
William of Auxerre 206
Wittgenstein, Ludwig 6, 9, 32, 102, 234